BEFORE NOVELS

BEFORE NOVELS

The Cultural Contexts
of Eighteenth-Century
English Fiction

J. PAUL HUNTER

W·W·NORTON & COMPANY   New York London

Printed in the United States of America.

The text of this book is composed in 11/13 Goudy Old Style,

with display type set in Nicolas Cochin.

Composition and

manufacturing by the Maple-Vail Book Manufacturing Group.

Book design by Margaret M. Wagner.

Library of Congress Cataloging-in-Publication Data

Hunter, J. Paul, 1934–

Before novels: the cultural contexts of eighteenth-century

English fiction / J. Paul Hunter.

p.   cm.

Includes bibliographical references.

1. English fiction—18th century—History and criticism.

2. Literature and society—England—History—18th century.   3. Books

and reading—England—History—18th century.   4. England—Popular

culture—History—18th century.   5. Literacy—England—History—18th

century.   I. Title.

PR858.S615H8   1990

820.9'005—dc20   89-29478

ISBN 0-393-30861-8

W. W. Norton & Company, Inc., 500 Fifth Avenue, New York, N.Y. 10110
W. W. Norton & Company Ltd., 10 Coptic Street, London WC1A 1PU

3 4 5 6 7 8 9 0

Contents

■

Journalistic
works

Journalistic
Subspecies

*Personal Lit:
autobio, bio, diaries*

*Literature of Perspective:
travel books, memoirs,
histories*

Preface

■

NO BOOK comes into the world altogether naked, new, or alone. Every text has a past and a history of its own, and its friendships with people and other books identify the place it seeks in the world and establish its relationship with potential readers. Some of what clothes a text or comes along as baggage is authorially chosen, but some is not: larger cultural contexts impose more, in fact, than style and accessories, influencing shape and direction and often determining as fully as the author's individual consciousness the text's character, identity, and aim, as well as its situation and force. The independence of an individual text, so much treasured in traditional literary history, is compromised in other ways as well, for unless readers leave a text altogether unread and untouched they too impinge, bringing a context of reception and response that determines not only the social place that the text comes to occupy but what it means and ultimately can do. For all the would-be autonomy of texts, their originality and liberty of spirit, they exist like human beings in a world of assumption, interaction, and implication. Texts without contexts are both meaningless and impossible; the power of texts is in relationship, their ability to reach outward and their nature in reaching backward to their own origins. Just as surely as the people who make them, texts are a part of all they have met, a complex product of a cultural moment in which a past is receding and a future developing.

This cultural claim about reading, particularized for English novels in the eighteenth century, is the burden of this book. I argue that, to understand the origins of the novel as a species and to read individual novels well, we must know several pasts and traditions—even non-fictional and non-narrative traditions, even non-"artistic" and non-written pasts—that at first might seem far removed from the pleasures readers find in modern novels. What writers wish to offer, what readers want, what cultural contexts make available, what reading requires, what texts provide, and what readers actually get—all these intentions, desires, and givens inter- acting tell us how novels came to "work" in a particular way and (to some extent) suggest how they came to be. All texts—at least all texts that find or create readers—construct a field in which desires and provi- sions compete, and the history of texts (both literary history and a larger cultural history that involves texts beyond "literary" ones) involves a continuous sorting out of needs, demands, insistences, and outcomes.

Preparing readers to read the text at hand is always the first task of any textual beginning, and in the late seventeenth century in England—at a moment in the history of reading when audiences were broadening and readers were learning to read for new purposes, and when generic cate- gories were loosening and new species were becoming visible—texts con- stituted themselves self-consciously from other texts for readers newly discovering how their needs and desires interacted. Readers read, as writ- ers write, in a context of the continuity of their own experiences and desires; they bring to their reading human desires to know and to shape and to interpret, and they take from texts things sometimes quite other from what writers believe they are offering. Any text we address takes us at once outward and backward, and to grapple with its power is to con- front its location, its readership, its past, and its friendships, as well as its form and its own record of desire. To understand the nature of any text or group of texts that share common properties means sorting among the conditions and events that created the climate of desire and finding the places where readerly and writerly interests merge and create for themselves a cultural moment that leaves a record of itself. Whatever else they may be, texts are cultural events that represent a moment in time and a historical consciousness.

What is true about the eighteenth-century texts I discuss here is also true about the book I have written. The territory that I traverse and the claims I make about it are conditioned by my own procedures in research- ing and writing the book, by the way others have formulated the problem before me, and by the way readers—varieties of readers well beyond aca- demic ones who specialize in novels and eighteenth-century culture— have already thought about how texts relate to contexts. My intentions, no doubt less decisive than I have assumed them to be but also more determinative than pure formalists or structuralists would admit, have steered this book from the beginning toward historical and cultural questions. Such aims have always driven my professional interests in literary texts, and, even earlier, they governed the etiological reading habits I formed young. Those aims have, in turn, been influenced by the directions of study of literature in the academy—sometimes formed in opposition to prevailing trends, sometimes riding with them—and then (quite beyond my wish or control) my own interests have had to set themselves alongside what other literary students were willing—or determined—to think about.

I

I HAVE written this book for readers who are interested in the novel, in the history and theory of literary forms and species, and in eighteenth-century literature and culture. But I have not written with only professional critics, historians, and theorists in mind. Although highly "specialized" in the sense that it unearths many texts that time and habit have long buried and tries to map territory in the past that is largely *terra incognita* even for specialists, this book is meant also for readers who read novels for pleasure and who care about the past out of intellectual curiosity rather than for professional reasons. Literary and cultural history is not the business only of academics, and the issues about how different kinds of writing relate to each other and about how writing relates to various forms of cultural desire involve questions of enough general intellectual importance that I have tried to make what I have to say here available, without too much technical jargon or obtrusive documentation, to any intelligent reader of fiction or history. The story of how cultures express their desires and impose their ideals, and of how different kinds of writing interrelate in their expressions and ministrations of cultural value, is not just a story for professional historians or for academics. It is the kind of story that tells us who we are, by telling us what kind of past we come from and how the various parts of a culture work together to forge a newness from continuity.

The academic study of literature has tended to underrate general or "common" readers—that is, readers who read for pleasure rather than because their livelihood depends on it—and academic criticism has paid a high price for its priestly snootiness. Much of that price has involved, rather than an emphasis on specialized knowledge, a kind of professional "know-nothingism" that tried to negate what readers might bring to any text from other texts, insisting instead that all truths were somehow within. Such privileging of the text itself—apart from its past, its author, the power of its cultural consciousness, its referentiality to some larger world of thing and event, and its interaction with readers who know and care about some of these extratextual matters—marked academic teaching and writing from the New Criticism until quite recently. Attacks on intention, accounts of the death of the author, anxieties about textual stability and its power to represent anything beyond itself, hostility toward any attempt to historicize a text or even admit its own cultural basis, and elevation of the critical over the creative faculty—all these conventions of mid- to late twentieth-century criticism (some formalist, some structuralist, some post-structuralist) have a common tendency. They try to elevate the text itself and to give the critic special proprietary (priestly) power that ordinary readers (the laity) cannot achieve without going through rites of passage that involve dextrous intraverbal acts and monuments determined by those who own the texts and determine how they are to be used. This privatizing strategy for texts now seems, fortunately, to be on the wane, but whatever its present status it has done major damage to any sense of a reading community, making "professional" readers arrogant and amateur ones defensive. Looked at in one way, the new historical consciousness in the academy involves professional readers catching up with the amateurs, for "common" readers remained curious about issues of biography, history, and temporal consciousness during all the years that such interests were unfashionable in universities.

I I

ONE relevant context for this book is its past, its own origins and its private record of evolution, something I will trace below. Another context involves the climate of opinion now—what readers are prepared to think about the eighteenth century, about novels as individual phenomena and the novel as a species, about the way texts of all kinds represent a culture. In that context I am especially fortunate, for the winds of change in scholarship have blown my way; the kinds of questions I engage here—about historical definitions of literary species, about origins, about what causes texts to be formulated in particular ways—are now on the minds of many, and the turn of the eighteenth century seems in the process of becoming the most productive venue for thinking about them. And novels in particular have begun to seem the most promising texts for investigating all kinds of cultural issues involving the textual shapes that ideas and issues most readily take in the developing world of modernity.

It was not always thus. Until quite recently, study of the novel suffered

from the kind of inferiority complex that large and baggy forms are apt
to experience in times when formalisms prevail, and eighteenth-century
studies more generally were a critical and theoretical backwater. During
the years when academic literary study made its most dramatic critical
strides—the 1950s, 1960s, and early 1970s—there was, for many theorists, critics, and even literary historians—no "literature" in the eighteenth century, only failed texts and deserts of vast background. For reasons
that have never been fully explored, the most influential mid-twentieth-
century literary history—usually masquerading as criticism or theory—
all but ignored, as some kind of textual eddy, everything written between
the "Glorious" Revolution in England and the American and French
Revolutions, finding it too trivial, or precious, or narrow, or contentious,
or particular, or time-bound. The triumph of rhetoric, ideology, and utility meant, for a whole generation of thinkers about literature, the failure
of art. The literary "line"—and there was a line, not just in extremists
like F. R. Leavis but in standard anthologies and syllabi—jumped from
Milton directly to Blake, and courses made barely a pause—for Pope as
wordsmith, Swift as ahistorical wonder, and Johnson or the prose "thinkers" as watchword or fossils—to explain the missing hundred years. Thus,
Harold Bloom in his influential and powerful *The Anxiety of Influence*
(New York, 1973) could develop a sophisticated theory of creativity on
the basis of a presumed literary history that omits a full quarter of the
English tradition, and in many of the most powerful thinkers about lit-
erature—Northrop Frye, Frank Kermode, M. H. Abrams, and Stanley
Fish, for example—there is room between 1667 and 1787 only for
Renaissance leftovers and anticipations of the High Romantics.

The eighteenth century was then the embarrassment in the English
curriculum, the black sheep no one would talk about. Anthologies consistently gave it the least space and the most defensive apologies, and
introductory textbooks—those powerful makers of taste aimed at bright
and retentive freshmen who, it turns out, grow up to be graduates and
academics—regularly excluded eighteenth-century examples completely.
Who older than thirty can remember reading as a university freshman
even a single Pope poem, Congreve play, Swift or Johnson essay, or any
novel at all before Austen? Departments of English divided their graduate wares into "periods," defining those before and after the Restoration
and Eighteenth Century into forty- or fifty-year chunks while leaving
almost a century and a half to be covered by anyone so benighted as to
wish to read the literature of utility and morality. Curricula were designed
to underrate—and educations calculated to underappreciate—this long
and crucial cultural moment in which the old passed away and almost all
became modern and new. Even the Marxists of this generation could find

only an occasional novel to show that anything between the revolutions
was not simply a mirage in a history of misguided or mishandled ideas
about what literature could be or do.

Those attitudes are well past now (though the curriculum in some
places lingers on), and it would be hard to find anyone willing to express
what was so oft thought a generation ago. But there is a legacy to such
omissions, and present literary study bears the brunt of it. Much of that
"brunt" is of course positive; study of the eighteenth century is flourishing in universities, graduate students are flocking to topics and texts long
ignored, and everywhere there is sophisticated theoretical and historical
curiosity about the lost years and issues long set aside. The eighteenth
century is, in fact, becoming the locus for many of the feminist, new
historicist, and cultural studies. It has become the logical center for cultural historicism as taste has broadened to include popular and para-
literary texts and as curiosities about ordinary life and deep cultural
desire have become primary even to students of literature. The forgotten
in literary history has thus begun to be replaced by healthy curiosity about
the reasons for forgetting, and a new literary history—less belletristic,
less positivist, less elitist, more inclusive, and more determined to read
the cultural texts that priestly literary theories were anxious to ignore—
is on the horizon. Eighteenth-century studies, finally touched by contemporary theory and then hit broadside by various historical and cultural
analyses, are flourishing in interdisciplinarity. The forgotten century turns
out to involve, after all, a rich cultural moment, and literary scholars
and theorists have joined historians, anthropologists, and philosophers
in trying to recover a suggestive sense of what those neglected texts and
forgotten groups of people may represent. Not all is sweetness and light
here—bees and spiders and mirrors and lamps still battle unceremoniously for turf, and scholars with single interests often seem to write past
each other rather than putting their observations together—but what
once threatened to become more than a hundred years of blank page in
literary history, with a little footnote recording battles of the books fought
by harmless drudges in archival anterooms, now promises a full and resonant account of one of the richest moments of change in the history of
developing modernism.

Literally hundreds of crucial texts are now being rethought, and (even
more fundamentally) questions about generic relationships, the assumptions of authorship and readership, and the interactions between cultural
texts and everyday life are now open, no longer dependent on elitist
notions of what life was like in the eighteenth century and what "literature" ought to be like. Literary history now seems, as it has not seemed
since formalism designed a geography of texts, part of a larger cultural

history that can introduce us, in some basic sense, to ourselves and our own pasts, for rather than seeing modernity springing more or less full blown from some Romantic rebellion and resistance of history, we begin to see continuities in the post-Restoration moment that causally gave us the identity we still bear in our post-modernist state. No longer can "Augustan" literature (or the popular literature it tried to suppress) seem an irrelevance, and no longer can the canonical texts seem the only—in many cases not even the major—ones crucial to knowing the culture from which we developed.

No one can now say where the rethinking will end or what sort of redrawn sense of eighteenth-century culture or of "literature" more generally will result. What is already clear, though, is that many different texts will become the locus of crucial questions, and that even basic "old-fashioned" questions about cause, self-consciousness, and definition will have to be asked in different ways across different categories of inquiry. Novels—never "secure" texts in the eighteenth-century literary canon because they seemed too much at odds with official notions of what "literature" and "art" should be—have quickly become the "literary" texts in which basic issues are being examined, and many of the novelistic texts that seem most deeply implicative are ones dismissed by earlier generations of literary historians. To move toward questions of cultural definition, it is now necessary to think about the texts of Charles Gildon and Delariviere Manley as well as Daniel Defoe and to consider the career directions of Eliza Haywood and Sarah Fielding alongside those of Tobias Smollett and Henry Fielding.

The "when," "what," and "how" questions of old literary history—when did the novel "really" begin? was Richardson "first," or Defoe or Behn? at what point did the romance break off and the novel start? who taught whom exactly what about how novels were to be written? was "realism" what defined novels or was it "individualism" or "subjectivity" or some essence yet unfound?—have started to become "why" questions. Why novels at all? Why these particular novels, with these particular cultural interests and concerns? Why, when this "new species" lacked even a name or agreed-upon definition, did it develop so intense a readership and so concentrated a set of features? Why so radical a move away from traditional forms and principles even while assertion and allusion sought to make traditional claims?

Ultimately, of course, novels represent only one phase of the historical and cultural investigation now moving into prominence in eighteenth-century studies, but—because they represent a broad social range among writers and readers and because in sheer magnitude they demand to be dealt with—they offer the most readily accessible route to some basic cultural questions, and they have quickly (just in the past four or five years) become the site for the most provocative thinking. Books by Nancy Armstrong, John Bender, Terry Castle, Cathy Davidson, and Michael McKeon (and studies in progress by Homer Brown, Margaret Doody, and John Richetti) not only challenge received opinion about early novels but offer serious reconstitutions of history based on different ways of thinking about culture and cultural texts.[1] There is more than simple revisionism here. No single "new" eighteenth century seems likely to emerge from the present ferment and no single, easy view of the novel; but there is a powerful sense of commonalty in confronting cultural and historical issues—about politics, gender, economics, class, national and regional identity, and shared ambition and desire—and in insisting that such issues are important rather than peripheral to formal or aesthetic or other "timeless" issues.

I I I

THIS is not the same river into which I stepped when I began thinking about this book in 1975. Then, formal issues dominated, and the most challenging critical tasks involved mapping the literary terrain; I wanted to sort out the forms and varieties of eighteenth-century fiction, hoping to account historically for why some narratives took confessional and personal directions while others concentrated on wider social interactions, group behavior, and the definition of regional or national character. I wondered why even so new a phenomenon as the novel already found itself tending to break into subkinds—novels of character, panoramas of society, satirical novels, novels of ideas, or politics, or sentiment, or terror. Though decidedly untrendy in its engagement with historical contexts and anxiety to find cultural causes for literary events, the project was somewhat in harmony with then prevailing concerns about formal questions and societal guideposts, for I imagined that my primary task was to develop a typology of the forms of fiction being written in England in the eighteenth century. In a matter of months, however, I had reconceived the study contextually and turned my main attention from definition to matters of origins and cultural desire. More and more of my reading, I found, was not in novels as such or in romances or other early fictions but in the materials that readers read before there were novels to read—materials that were often non-narrative, non-fictional, and non-literary in the accepted modern sense. I decided that novels had to be read against a far broader context of cultural texts and materials in order to have any notion of how they seemed to early read-

ers. Novels, I came to be more and more persuaded as I followed the
tracks of late seventeenth- and early eighteenth-century readers who used
books for devotional and utilitarian purposes as well as for pleasure, had
their relevant contexts—ultimately even their origins—in a culture that
was partly oral and partly written, where functions traditionally performed in communal and family rituals and by oral tradition more and
more fell to the impersonal processes of print. In 1977 I published "The
Loneliness of the Long-Distance Reader," the first of a series of essays
that predicted the thesis I argue here and that dealt with various pieces
of literary and cultural history I thought needed to be addressed sepa-
rately before I was ready to present a full and coherent argument.[2] I
continued to read heavily in journalistic, didactic, polemical, private,
and other "para-literary" materials, and by 1981 I had completed a draft
of what became this book. The argument—in its basic shape as a thesis
about the satisfaction of fundamental cultural needs, the relationship
between high and low culture, written and oral texts, and the quasi-
conscious making of a major literary species from generally unidentified
subkinds of popular literature—was largely complete, or so I thought at
the time.

But if I had published this book then, it would have been a very different book. It might well have seemed more radical or revolutionary in
that context, for little was known about "subliterature" or "oral texts,"
and there was very little curiosity about questions of origins or about
historicity more generally. There was, in other words, a more narrow
and spare cultural and intellectual world into which such ideas would
have been introduced. The readers it might have attracted would have
been far less knowledgeable—and less sophisticated both theoretically
and historically—than are large numbers of readers now, and less friendly
to the kinds of issues—and arguments—I am interested in. The past decade
has brought new directions to literary study—interdisciplinarity, curiosity about generic issues, interest in theory for its typological potential
and for its ability to sort among the strands of intention and outcome in
texts, belief in history as a serious interpretive dimension for texts and
in historiography as a means to analyze and recover cultures as wholes,
pursuit of the dimensions of desire in both readers and writers and concern with its communal and cultural forms as well as its individual and
psychoanalytical ones, distrust of canonical categories and the disinter-
ment of "minor" and "utilitarian" texts, replacement of strictly literary
categories by cultural ones. These directions mean not only that wide
interest has developed in the kinds of questions behind this study but
that much important thinking about historical matters has come forward.
The kind of historical and theoretical curiosity that now exists offers this

study a far wider context for discussion and debate than would have seemed possible a decade ago, and, whatever the fate of this book or the thesis behind it, I am grateful for an intellectual context curious about the issues and receptive to the methods of cultural analysis. The river—no longer serene, steady, and calm—now swirls with excitement and disagreement.

And of course I am not the same person who, fifteen years ago, stepped in the river, nor is this, in crucial ways, the book I then planned. The many changes in literary study and in the several disciplines that impinge on it—especially anthropology, philosophy, and social and cultural history—have very much affected the way I have come to understand my project. My way of describing the novel as a cultural phenomenon is different, I have a different sense of definition within variety, and I conceive rather differently the interactions among texts and literary species. Now, too, I write unabashedly as a "literary historian," a term I would once have been ashamed to own even though it was what I in fact was—though it is true that what I now think of as proper literary history comprises a variety of texts and issues that traditional literary historians would have avoided (or worse), and it is also true that the literary history I here produce will not sit comfortably alongside the standard traditional histories and handbooks of literature. My concerns and biases are, however, at home in the present discourse about culture, group consciousness, and causality, and even though my emphases are somewhat different from those in other recent studies of the novel's origins, I celebrate the fact that we are engaged in a common mission of reconceiving literary history along new philosophical and ideological lines.

I V

READERS steeped in the present contexts of criticism, theory, and literary history will readily see how my argument differs, methodologically and in its conclusions, from that of other recent students of novels, origins, and cultural consciousnesses. I have not spelled out those differences in detail here. Those most interested in sorting out such differences will find it easy to do for themselves, and I prefer to tell my version of the story of the early novel and its contexts without pausing often to argue about disputable details. Besides, given the still powerful opposition to historicism of any kind in literary study, it seems to me important to emphasize the common agreement of those of us engaged in developing a new literary and cultural history. I have no taste for minor skirmishes when major issues are at stake in defining the entire nature of literary study.

Still, though I am unwilling to quarrel with allies about particulars, I do want to make as clear as possible just what my own assumptions and aims are. I want, therefore, to be open about the most prominent beliefs that inform this study and explicit about some of the more controversial stands I take. The cultural historicism that I here practice and defend can, I think, be extremely useful in creating a new literary history if its principles and procedures are understood, practiced carefully, and refined to reflect developing knowledge. I am anxious that it not be quickly reduced to some easy ism and shunted into a ghetto so that the world can again be safe for aestheticism, universalism, or some new kind of formalism. Here, then, straightforwardly and without extended comment, are some of the most important things that I have hoped to do:

—provide a working description of the novel, though not a single-term essentialist definition, so that we know what it is whose origins we are looking for;
—offer an inclusive sense of novels that comprehends titles that are untypical, unsuccessful, non-canonical, and admittedly minor, as well as the best known work by the best known writers;
—demonstrate the independence of the novel from previous narrative models because of its popular, non-"literary" status at its beginning, and detach its fortunes especially from the history of the romance, which it has sometimes been said to "displace";
—show the danger of models of literary definition that depend upon the designation of some one particular example as a historical first, rather than belief in the gradual "formation" of new structures that cannot always be dated with precision or shown to exist in a single instance;
—particularize the causal interaction between so-called high and low culture, and show how influence can move "up" as well as "down" between reigning cultural models and competing popular ones;
—suggest that intellectual history can comprehend ideas at all levels of culture, and not necessarily just offer an elitist record of such concepts as meet standard philosophical standards;
—show how readers gain the power to create texts by communicating, though not necessarily consciously or directly, their needs and desires to those in a position to make books;
—provide an account of human "desire" as a cultural and communal phenomenon, not just as an aspect of individual psychology, supporting the kind of insights into cultural directions provided by the so-called *Histoire des Mentalités;*
—suggest the importance of oral culture in setting human expectations of verbal patterns and therefore in creating desires that may eventuate in written structures;
—demonstrate the importance of the "minor" and the "ordinary," not only in assessing the directions of everyday life but in deciding the total shape of culture and its characteristic institutions;
—document the power of a "cultural" consciousness to influence individual

consciousness, with or without the awareness or permission of the individual;
—illustrate the significance of anthropological models for literary study, and
support the directional influence of such figures as Clifford Geertz, Robert
Darnton, and Roger Chartier;
—argue the historical distinctiveness, in given times and places, of particular
patterns that people, behavior, attitudes, and events assume, and show the
crippling effects of presentism in coming to grips with historical difference;
—acknowledge the need to read non-verbal texts as significant documents in
defining the character of a culture;
—demonstrate the possibility of a significant new literary history that is
responsive to theoretical questions, self-conscious in its philosophical
assumptions, and based in informed cultural historicism.

Readers of lingering debates on eighteenth-century fiction will recognize that my position owes a lot to the pioneering work of Ian Watt even
as it disagrees on some major issues.[3] But I want to record explicitly my
high regard for the courageous position Watt took in 1957 about the
"sociological" basis of the English novel. Watt's then defiant act of
attributing creative power to readers is his most important and, I think,
enduring contribution, and the nature of his study has often been misunderstood by admirers and detractors alike. Much of the resistance to
Watt seems to me to derive ultimately from a fear of the implications of
his fundamental premise about readers, though it is often disguised as
disagreements about lesser matters; and although I have a number of
reservations about Watt's assumptions and procedures—his teleology, for
example, and his reading of individual books and authors—I admire both
his academic courage and his prescient cultural insight. He is the proxi-
mate cause of my obsession with the issues discussed here. I once would
have said that his book provoked this one; now I would say it inspired it,
for, deep as my disagreements with Watt are, they derive from what I
now understand to be a basic sharing and assumptions about literature
and culture. A late colleague used to interview faculty job candidates by
asking two questions: What critical or scholarly book would you most
like to have written? And, what book would you most like to rewrite? It
has taken me a long time to discover that the two questions are one.
Everyone in the past thirty years who has written about the beginnings
of the English novel has been engaged in rewriting Watt and, in so doing,
renewing him.

V

I SHOULD also say frankly what I have done about two classic dilemmas
that have particular force at this moment in literary history and admit to

(and defend) one highly eccentric choice. The first dilemma involves how to decide, in defining and illustrating what the novel is, between using canonical texts upon which old definitions have been constructed and texts less familiar to most readers. My sense of the character of the novel—embodied in the description of novelistic features in Chapters One and Two—in fact derives from as wide a reading among novels as I have been able to do. The canonical texts are, I admit, the ones I came to know first, and who can say in just what ways my judgment and expectations may have been conditioned or narrowed by those first acquaintances? But then I have gone on to range, read, and sample widely, looking at long novels and short ones; those by familiar names and those by obscure or unspecified authors; those aimed at a broad spectrum of readers and those that try to create specific effects for a specific audience; books that are clear in their fictional claims and novelistic aims and those that obscure or deny their nature and their intentions, books that are quasi-novels or near-novels or refusals-to-be-novels as well as those that plainly are near the center of the novelistic spectrum; successful novels, failures, and those of limited accomplishment. No single description can, of course, do justice to all the texts that might reasonably be called novels; the term "novel," even when it is used carefully to describe a limited number of books with features in common, cuts a wide swath, and not every book that can appropriately be called a novel in a non-essentialist definition will contain all the characteristic features of novels. And it is of course true that, at the beginning, any species unsure of itself and its identity is continually testing itself and experimenting, so that the margins of the novel in the eighteenth century are even more uneven and uncertain than in other times. Still, even though the description of novels that I offer may be imperfect and may apply with different force to different examples, the characterization I give is based broadly on novelistic practice, not on a few "canonical" instances selected by contemporary or subsequent taste.

But providing effective examples for my reader is another and more complicated matter rhetorically, and here I have frankly compromised. Largely I illustrate points about characteristics by citing novels readers are likely to know, and even though many more readers now will know, say, *David Simple* or *The Female Quixote* or *Betsy Thoughtless* than did five years ago, the really familiar texts to most readers are still the titles that have been available a while in paperback and taught to generations of students. I have, therefore, taken the majority of my examples from the best known texts, especially when I needed to allude to something already in a reader's memory, but I have pointed to less familiar books whenever I could do so without requiring a reader's detailed recall. The sense of novels that emerges here will, therefore, be richer for those who have read most fully, but I hope that some reasonable sense of the territory will emerge even for those who know only the few books that have traditionally defined the field.

On the second difficult matter, I did not compromise but instead felt I had to make a clean, hard choice. The choice was between an emphasis on the way the novel reflects a particular culture and the way it participates in another kind of context, the commonalty of other novels, especially preceding ones. It seems to me impossible, at this point in critical history, to do justice at the same time to the cultural aspects of origins and to structural questions—those matters that cross national and linguistic boundaries—and I have firmly chosen to anchor my account of the nature of the novel in cultural specificity. There is, ultimately, much to be said about how the novel—a cross-cultural phenomenon that is, after all, almost international in scope by the early nineteenth century—develops out of the interaction of Spanish, French, and English traditions (and then of several others), but it seems to me important to have a detailed sense of the distinctive cultural influences within each national tradition before proceeding to these questions of interaction, though I understand that others will have different priorities and different versions of what is possible. For me, at least, to have tried to fold in the developing influence of the French on English novels would not have been possible in a study of this kind; much less would it have been possible for me, at this juncture, to talk about "the novel" fully across cultural definitions. Plainly, the novel as we have it by the nineteenth century had folded in more than I describe here because various "modern" cultures had come to interact significantly and each brought its own distinctive biases into novels: that is why nineteenth-century novels are somewhat different from eighteenth-century novels and why, for some, "the novel" really means the nineteenth and twentieth centuries and nothing before. But for me the crucial *formative* influences on the species are historical, cultural, and particular, and I think these need to be sorted out in detail for each national strand before moving too quickly to the intertwinings. In the best of possible worlds, I would like to go further, saying for example something useful about the Spanish tradition, especially Cervantes, for the English novel (let alone the larger novel species) could hardly be what it became without him. But interested as I am in what happens when Cervantic imitation and reaction comes into the novel in England, this is the only place that I mention *Don Quixote*—partly because others have interpreted Cervantes's influence extensively already, but mostly because I feel unqualified in the present context of knowledge about different cultural traditions to speak comprehensively and authoritatively. The grander task of reconciling cultural accounts of literary species with structural ones remains, I think, for later students who may know more and see more sophisticated ways to merge structural and contextual studies.

The eccentricity involves the extensive presence here of a figure little known in literary history, John Dunton. I confess to a certain fascination with the way Dunton's mind works, but my primary intention in using him so obtrusively is to suggest how cultural desire works beyond the power of individual intention and accomplishment. Whether he is the best figure to use to make the point is certainly debatable, but his status as a bookseller, writer of all sorts of popular materials, and champion of novelty (and the fact that so much of his thinking is available in undigested form) makes him a dramatic example of how readers and writers, low and high culture, cultural desire and authorial intention divide the field at the time the novel is beginning to define itself in England.

Any book with as long a prehistory as this one accumulates obligations more extensive than can readily be specified, and I have been more than usually fortunate in the generosities of friends, colleagues, students, and institutional resources. A fellowship from the John Simon Guggenheim Foundation in 1976–77 enabled me to begin this book, and fellowships from the National Endowment for the Humanities and the National Humanities Center in 1986 gave me time to revive, revise, rethink, and move the book toward completion after five slow years when my primary energies were used in administration. Equally important have been the many institutional libraries that have made their resources available and often provided aid and counsel. I am especially grateful to the British Library, the Bodleian Library, the National Library of Scotland, the Dr. Williams Library, the Congregational Library, the William Andrews Clark Library of UCLA, the Houghton Library of Harvard University, the Beinecke Library of Yale University, the Newberry Library, the Boston Public Library, the New York Public Library, and the libraries of Emory University, the University of Rochester, the University of North Carolina, Duke University, and the University of Chicago. Special thanks for special efforts are due to Marella Walker of Emory, the late Robert Rosenthal of Chicago, Susan Green of the Clark, David Paisey and Michael Crump of the British Library, and Alan Tuttle of the National Humanities Center.

A host of friends and colleagues answered queries, read portions of early drafts of the book, or offered criticisms and suggestions, and I am grateful to them all: Paul Alkon, Paula Backscheider, Jerome Beaty, Lewis · White Beck, Wayne Booth, Martine Brownley, James Bunn, J. Douglas Canfield, Gay Clifford, Ralph Cohen, Robert Darnton, Natalie Zemon

Davis, the late Richard Ellmann, Carol Flynn, John Miles Foley, Bertrand Goldgar, Lila Graves, Dustin Griffin, Elizabeth Helsinger, Christine Heyrman, Myra Jehlen, Donald Kelley, Gwin Kolb, Joseph Levine, Roger Lonsdale, Janel Mueller, Ronald Paulson, Ruth Perry, John V. Price, Claude Rawson, Bruce Redford, John Richetti, Stuart Sherman, Joan Stewart, Philip Stewart, Richard Strier, James Thompson, Dennis Todd, and Aubrey Williams. Participants in three seminars at the University of Chicago—on the beginnings of the English novel, canonical and non-canonical eighteenth-century texts, and the novels of the 1750s—helped enormously in shaping, honing, and extending my argument. I wish especially to thank Vincent Bertolini, Timothy Dykstal, Kevin Gilmartin, Nancy Henry, Amy Kessel, Candler S. Rogers, Deborah Stevenson, Douglas Sun, Cynthia Wall, and Tracy Weiner. For detailed and perceptive commentary on long sections of later drafts, I am deeply indebted to James K. Chandler, Kathryn Montgomery Hunter, Lisa Hunter, and Kristina Straub: their generous and compassionate suggestions and demands resulted in crucial revisions of thought and direction. And for exceeding all obligations of friendship and collegiality in reading closely the entire manuscript, I am extremely grateful to Jackson I. Cope, Patricia Meyer Spacks, and William Beatty Warner. Whatever mistakes in judgment or fact I stubbornly retained, they saved me from more inaccuracies and inelegancies than I care to count. In the days before I learned to compute for myself, Trudy Kretchman, the late Katie Leone, and Dana Rittenhouse meticulously typed or processed draft after draft, smiling through my atrocities and cajoling me toward clarity: their grace was only half their art. Finally, I thank all the wonderfully supportive, efficient, and demanding people at W. W. Norton, especially Barry Wade, a better editor than any author deserves—or even expects.

My parents, Paul Wesley and Florence Walmer Hunter, set me on the reading road that led to this book, and to their memory it is lovingly dedicated.

Chicago and London
September 1989.

A Note on Texts

■

WHEN I have quoted extensively from a text, footnotes usually specify edition and location, with the following exceptions. For *Joseph Andrews* and *Tom Jones*, I have used Martin Battestin's Wesleyan Edition (Middletown, Conn., 1967 and 1975) and indicated book, chapter, and page number in parentheses in the text. Similarly for *Tristram Shandy*, I have used Melvyn New's Florida edition (Gainesville, Fla., 1978) and followed the same citation procedure. For short quotations of a phrase or a few lines from well-known works such as *The Rape of the Lock* or *MacFlecknoe*, I have provided only line numbers from standard editions, assuming that a detailed bibliographical reference would be both cumbersome and unnecessary. For lesser known "para-literary" works, I have worked when possible from the first edition, but have quoted from the edition most relevant temporally to the historical point I was making. The place of publication is London unless otherwise specified.

I

TEXTS

CHAPTER ONE

What Was New About the Novel?

■

NEITHER time nor texts now have the stability that literary history once seemed to pledge. To many, the present critical context threatens all the sacred certainties and casts into doubt revered assumptions about why individual texts are written, what values they represent, and how kinds of texts—modes, forms, genres, species—come to exist. And it is true that the old literary history—with its formal texts, firm judgments of quality, and neat generic clarity—is, if not gone, forgotten by all but the most habitual. Is this the time to write a new literary history? Many questions about how history is to be conceived and written are, it is true, up for grabs, and before anything like "authority" can again obtain, a mountain of work needs to be done on texts and contexts that the old history (and the new criticism) ignored. But suddenly there is real interest in matters historical and a substantial commitment to thinking about the process of cultural change, and the fact that some old assumptions have been cleared away means unusual opportunity. Crucial issues about causality, for example—between texts and from context to text—now seem open in ways inconceivable a generation ago, and it seems plausible to think of redrawing lines and lineages to indicate relationships between polite and popular culture. A lot of issues, granted, must be settled before big conclusions can be drawn, but there are advantages as well as disadvantages in trying to write history in the midst of ferment. Waiting for the dust to settle is a more attractive metaphor in road racing than in

3

archival research, and in any case positivist literary history may never again be either possible or desirable.

Questions about the novel and its origins are especially enticing just now—because of the rising curiosity about generic origins more generally, because of a burgeoning interest in early English novels that have remained largely unread, because novels have a special relationship to popular culture and to texts that traditional literary history altogether passed by, and because there has recently been a flurry of very good work on novelistic beginnings. As canons have been opened, as readers have been empowered along with writers as makers of taste and desire, as theories have matured and mated and multiplied, as the Smithfield Muses have begun to seem fit subjects for serious discourse rather than figures of derision, and as historical questions have again come to be compelling in literary studies, issues of beginnings and origins have taken on new dimensions, and a lot of matters that once seemed settled now seem not only capable of being rethought but worth it. Writers no longer seem so authoritatively in control of their texts, literary species are not seen to be so simply defined or so readily found at a specifiable moment of beginning, and neither the ideas nor the arts of post-Restoration English culture (or any culture) now seem like such a top-down affair. "Literature" now seems to comprise a much larger, and ultimately more significant, part of the culture than just the certified texts of a chosen few, and far broader contexts of writing (and telling) may be applied to issues of form and origin. If culture does not dictate literary species by determining their formal inheritance from intellectual aspiration, the question of where innovation comes from—philosophers or journalists, artists or ministers of the marketplace, writers or readers, moralists or unself-conscious responders to stimulus or impulse—is then wide open, with no easy assumption that literary direction comes from great thinkers and competing programs of leadership rather than from popular culture and the tastes and values among ordinary people in everyday life.

There are, of course, dangers in an intellectual moment as volatile as ours, for if some new orthodoxy should step in too quickly to displace the old and discredited literary history, the next generation of literary students could have a yet rougher time undoing structures of a new literary history built thoughtlessly on the rubble of the old. With a rash of "reference tools" now again being written, with desire for authority running high, and with some issues in such a muddle that any proposed simplification is bound to seem attractive, the risk of bad new truisms replacing bad old ones is not trivial. But instability is opportunity, and the collocation of theory and history now at work has already led to lively exchange between students of literature and those in related disciplines,

*Sermons
prose romance
polemics*

especially cultural anthropology and social history. In the work of Arm-strong, Bender, Castle, Davidson, and McKeon, implications for the novel have already begun to be thought out.

I join the debate here by arguing that the emerging novel must be placed in a broader context of cultural history, insisting that popular thought and materials of everyday print—journalism, didactic materials with all kinds of religious and ideological directions, and private papers and histories—need to be seen as contributors to the social and intellec-tual world in which the novel emerged. I urge greater awareness of pat-terns of literacy, social aspiration and demographic trends, available reading materials, reading habits, and the interrelationship of oral and written, popular and polite forms of culture. I will argue that readers, publishers, and other bit players in traditional literary history played a powerful role in creating a new textual species responsive to human concerns about the structuring of everyday life as well as about the feelings that flow from—and inspire—ordinary actions. And I will argue that the energies of popular culture—what the Augustans worried most about—wrested the literary tradition from its conservative guardians. My differences with other students of origins (as well as with older historicists) are thus sub-stantial, and the story I tell involves more people from a greater variety of walks of life than literary history usually entertains. The rather differ-ent implications of our different emphases will become clear in due course, but I turn first to the grounds of our agreement against ahistoricists of various kinds.

In spite of the popularity of New Historicism, widespread interest gen-erally in all kinds of cultural issues, and the present lively debates about origins, ahistoricism remains a powerful force in literary studies. Ulti-mately it is a threat to the very idea of literary history, and its premises are directly contrary to the aims, assumptions, and methods that I engage here. Sometimes disguised as "theory" and often flying under the flags of formalism, structuralism, post-structuralism, narratology, myth criticism, or even reader response criticism, ahistoricism finds friendly cover wher-ever it can and boldly blurs distinctions rather than sharpening them. It wants both issues and texts to seem the same yesterday, today, and for-ever, with no need for beginnings, referents, or contexts. Universalism and essentialism have wondrously seductive appeals, especially to those who miss deeply the certitude of former generations, but they are deeply subversive of any literary history. Before detailing the grounds for think-ing that the novel emerges out of cultural particulars in late seventeenth-century England, I turn to the ways ahistoricism has undermined, obscured, and perverted the issues that involve the novel's cultural basis.

I

EVER since the serious study of English literary history began, the early eighteenth century has seemed the time when a distinct new form of prose fiction emerged, and the only questions have been why and exactly when. But given historical ferment and contemporary efforts at redefinition, it may be time to reexamine the grounds for thinking that the "novel" was indeed a new and distinct phenomenon, to resurrect other popular literary novelties in order to describe more fully the meanings and contexts of innovation, to reopen the question of what constitutes a literary species, and to assess the interactions between literary species and the cultures that develop them. If the when and why questions are still the crucial ones, they now seem dependent on issues more basic, issues of definition, differentiation, and interaction, as well as on questions about the character of a culture that chose the novel as its major means of expression. To describe the novel's "rise" or "emergence" at a particular cultural moment and to account for its "origins" involves matters historical and theoretical, formal and contextual. And so, in suggesting why the novel became the characteristic expression of English culture and then of Western modernity more generally, I want first to think about what was distinctive and new about the novel—questions of formal definition in a historical context—before proceeding to the more vexed questions of why.

Some of the doubts about the novel's newness are trivial, involving just formal quibbles, special pleading for particular writers or traditions, and fashions of asking questions or proposing categories and terminology. Quarrels about terms and disputes about temporal boundaries are often, consciously or not, distractions from central questions; small minds problematize the unproblematic. But some doubts are serious and many are bold. Definitions of literary modes and forms—both genres and species— are no longer so easy to agree on, and the relationship between literary phenomena and other cultural artifacts now seems far more complex than old accounts of intention and causality allowed. As formal issues and historical ones have come to seem more interdependent, questions of origin have become more intellectually rich and less easily decidable. As questions of context, history, and culture have come to seem more interesting, more complex, and more unsettled, formal questions—what is the novel? how exactly is the new prose fiction to be differentiated from all the old prose fictions?—have themselves begun to unravel or seem at least open to challenges. Doubts about the newness of the novel raise, or seem to raise, questions about both form and history. The ultimate questions about the novel's beginnings *are* when and why, but it is important to ask first what issues are at stake in claiming that a new species emerged in England in the eighteenth century when a Protestant, capitalistic, imperial, insecure, restless, bold, and self-conscious culture found itself confronting a constrictive, authoritarian, hierarchical, and too-neatly-sorted past. So I turn first to the doubts—both serious and merely sophistic—about the newness of the novel, before trying to clarify the muddy waters of definition and then (from Chapter Three on) addressing temporal and spatial questions of contexts and origins.

I I

SOME of the doubts have arisen out of resistance to particular theses about the beginnings of the novel. The desire to discredit Ian Watt's thesis about formal realism has, for instance, led to extravagant claims for earlier realistic examples, ones supposed to contradict Watt's evidence that the "rise" of the novel results from a particular concatenation of social circumstances. Those doubts, whatever their impact on the specifics of Watt's thesis and whatever implications they may have for the relationship between English and other national traditions, do not confront the question of why there are suddenly so many novelistic texts compared to earlier widely spaced examples, and they rely too simply on a single characteristic—realism—as their defining mark. They do not really challenge the dating of the novel's emergence. It is easy enough to push back the date for any artistic or cultural phenomenon by fiddling with definitions and by being selective about particular features. "Realism" or any other single feature of the novel can easily be shown to exist, in some form or other, in almost any age or any genre, and arguments marshalled against the newness of the novel or against attempts more generally to make historical distinctions about form, mode, and attitude amount mostly to footnotes and discriminations honed too fine. Other attempts to broaden or diffuse the definition of the novel—to include a variety of early Continental traditions, classical prose of several kinds, and narratives of China, India, and Japan—muddle the cultural and formal issues in similar ways, however useful they are in extending knowledge of narrative generally. The question of beginnings is a real one, with significant implications for generic definition and ideas of temporality and continuity, but it is easily blurred into pedantry, triviality, and the stalking of game that has been chosen for the chase. Making all prose fiction, from all ages and places, into the novel is not a serious way of dealing with either formal or historical issues.[1]

A more formidable challenge arises, however, out of what I take to be a resistance to the whole idea of literary history. This resistance, a perennial outgrowth of formalism in one of its shapes, has most powerfully been carried on during the past three decades under the banner of Northrop Frye, although not always with either his personal or his philosophical blessing. That challenge tries to neutralize temporality by transforming the historical landscape into spatial maps so that all forms seem to coexist eternally. Newness is thus reduced to illusion, displacement, or, at best, metamorphosis. Ernest Vinaver claims that it is improper to speak of origins for literary forms,[2] and his reasons derive from a Platonic bias and a faith in forms beyond history, not despair that origins are too complex to disentangle. His metaphor in *The Rise of Romance* is fundamentally different from Watt's in *The Rise of the Novel*, for he sees romance manifesting itself into a dimmer world, becoming flesh, rising through the floor of human history from some eternal cellar of forms. Watt, on the other hand (although I distrust, too, the teleological overtones of his "rise"), fully engages issues of time, change, and causality.

Frye's own attempt to revive an interest in romance as a genre is, in many ways, an admirable and welcome one, for (as Scholes and Kellogg said in 1966), criticism of prose fiction has traditionally tended to be "almost hopelessly novel-centered."[3] But it is no favor to literary taxonomy, let alone to literary history, to blur formal distinctions and deny the philosophical possibility of the innovation implied by the name that the "novel" finally claimed. Keeping a sense of the enduring and changeless alongside the changing and ephemeral may be valuable, but there is no need to deny temporality in order to appreciate continuity and recurrence. In the very idea of literary modes, forms, and genres lies temptation to excessive neatness, a passion for order that may readily falsify the foul rag-and-bone shop in which real people produce texts for other real people, often driven by motives more prosaic than the desire to found a new branch of aesthetics. Frye himself often seems to me too engaged with Platonic models and too rigidly dependent on a Christian sense of cyclical history and of fulfillment in event and circumstance, and some of his spiritual heirs lack Frye's own subtlety and tact in their anxiety to find in literature a working out of cosmic destiny. The attempt, for example, to claim *Tom Jones* for romance seems almost to deny any history at all, for it tries to blend all literary and cultural study into an examination of eternal themes and variations.[4] And the grander claims of Frank Kermode about all kinds of modes, texts, and features infer a world more static, predictable, and determined than the most staid neoclassical critic would have dared posit.

More subtly, some versions of structuralism have given dignity (though the fashion now seems almost past) to the avoidance of temporality, preferring to see texts as interdependent across time. Such approaches deny the possibility of innovation as fundamental change or find it unaccountable in the Foucaldian way. Even the best narratology seems to derive from an assumption that texts have no essential cultural grounding, in either place or time.[5] Like Frye's spatial world of forms, this Platonism too appeals to the need for security and authority, the desire for a universe in no danger of erosion, meteorite, or sudden weather. Ultimately, the question of change and innovation is fundamental to the idea of literary history, for if all meaningful questions are synchronic ones, the tasks of the literary theorist and critic are all philosophical ones, and history can be left to describers and annotators. Whatever its taxonomic design or however rooted in personal religious belief, the tendency to deny innovation or to treat all texts as mere variations on some ur-text not only reduces the importance of contextual issues but makes all distinctions arbitrary and irrelevant. I do not wish to underrate the value of comparative mythology, and there are important insights to be found by studying the common structures of narrative, myth, fiction, and prose discourse, but I do want to insist on other contextual issues that can only be seen through the lenses of time and circumstance. My aim is to recover the contexts of creativity and innovation in the early eighteenth century and to restate the case for the novel as a distinct and definable literary form that exists in time, that emerges and develops in a particular context (although not, shazam, full-blown at a certain moment), and that has a particular place in the history of cultural phenomena.

A closely related question about historicism and beginnings involves a reluctance to categorize at all. In this equally anti-historical view, all fictions are novels, ever have been and ever shall be, and all narratives, within tolerable variations, are fundamentally alike as well, so much so that they can be described irrespective of aim, author, language, place, or time. Questions of definition are thus irrelevant except for some broad starting assumption. If there are only modal tendencies corresponding to universal human processes of cognition, there is no need to ask questions about the beginnings of species, the waxing and waning of literary kinds, or the relation of writing to other cultural particulars, for categories come not from history and circumstance but from some universal human trait. Such views often stress (as I do from quite different assumptions) the power of the reader, but ultimately the reader in these systems restricts and polices what can happen rather than opening it up in the fullnesses of time.

Still more serious ultimately is the issue of what beginnings mean in one culture or linguistic system when similar "beginnings" can be found at different times, earlier or later, in other systems. Is it proper to speak of "origins" for the *English* novel when novels, similar in many formal features although quite different in some culture-specific leanings, already exist in other places? The answer to such a question is both no and yes—no, because the novel as we know it is not properly described in any single national or linguistic dress so that the study of origin and development must finally pursue more than a single point in time or space; yes, because a crucial part of that story took place in England at a particular time, and ultimately the history of the beginnings of the novel (because it took different features and emphases from various traditions in various places) must encompass several converging stories. What I want to do here is tell one of those stories in some detail and suggest its place in a larger narrative. To do so involves putting aside for the time being the virtues of perspective and retrospection and listening attentively to those who were there at the time the change was taking place.

I I I

THE question of whether something new happened in English fiction in the early eighteenth century ultimately must be decided on textual evidence, but it may be well to begin by recording the perception of literary change by those who were involved as writers or readers. Any analysis of the culture itself must begin from the nearly universal perception in England by midcentury that a literary revolution was taking place. The observation was similar regardless of the evaluation or the stakes: conservative observers worried about the change, rebels celebrated it. Those who feared change and put their careers on the line in defense of the status quo ultimately agreed in their analysis with those who desired a new literary world and sought to design it. New readers, new modes of literary production, changing tastes, and a growing belief that traditional forms and conventions were too constricted and rigid to represent modern reality or to reach modern readers collaborated to mean—in the eyes of both proponents and critics—that much modern writing was taking radical new directions. From the point of view of traditionalists—men like Alexander Pope who believed in the continuing vitality of the Christian humanist heritage—the new, modern way of writing meant slipped standards and debased values, the destruction of all that was honorable and fine in the tradition. From the point of view of innovators—those who rejoiced in changing social values and who sought new varieties of expression and communication because they distrusted what they saw as the exhaustion or corruption of the tradition—the new world of writing, although still uncharted and uncertain, represented fresh opportunities and a challenge to creativity. The amount of experimentation and the energies of novelty were enormous. For all its satiric exaggeration, *A Tale of a Tub* in its slam-bang exuberance suggests both the wildness and the excitement of the new style. Novelty was, of course, about much more than just novels, and at first the innovations had little to do with either fiction or narrative. But by the time the careers of Swift and Pope came to an end—in the middle of the fifth decade of the century— the literature of novelty had established itself and chosen a clear direction that focused the energies of innovation and stored them in a form destined to become emblematic of the new modernity.

Whether there was a new literature or not, most observers thought that there was. Retroactive observers, as the evidence accumulated for two centuries, came to take a change—substantial, even radical—for granted. Where the novel fits into the change—where its philosophical loyalties lie—is the central issue.

Claims for novelty in the literary world—claims that a significant interruption of tradition had occurred and that new forms and directions had taken over—actually came in two waves two generations apart. The second wave involved specific claims for a "new species" or "new province" of narrative fiction in the 1740s, and it followed a far more general claim for novelty at the turn of the century. The most articulate spokesmen in the forties were Richardson and Fielding, although they received support from lesser novelists as well as from reviewers, critics, and a generality of readers. The responses of imitators made clear that something approaching a movement—with leaders, disciples, and debates about orthodoxies—was quickly on foot. The earlier claim dates from the 1690s. It had less literary respectability and in fact was taken by the reigning literati to represent a hostile reaction to "literature" itself as then understood—that is, as a republic of letters with a distinct history, a given variety of forms, and a specific burden of truths to impart.

Not much of enduring merit came from the turn-of-the-century claim, although most of the celebrated literary works of the early eighteenth century were written in reaction to it. Pope claimed that to respond to it was to break a butterfly on a wheel, but then went on to make something far more elaborate than a simple machine. The response generally, in fact, was to get out the heavy artillery and try to discourage the rebellion before it gained followers or took territory. The claims of novelty in the half century between the 1690s and the deaths of Pope and Swift represent tastes that at first seem simply aberrant, transitory, and trivial. But by the mid-1720s most of the Augustan effort to preserve a humanist heritage and keep literature on its established course was directed against moderns who championed novelty as a major tenet in their program to discover an originality and literary innovation that would appropriately represent "modern" experience. The fact that the first wave of novelty left so little mark had something to do with the powerful Augustan counterattack, but equally important was the fact that the innovators had little sense of what a vital new literature might look like. There was little form, no firm sense of direction. Still, there were indicators.

One of the literary history's most bizarre moments illustrates both the disorder and the ultimate power of the early claims for literary novelty. On March 17, 1691, an enterprising bookseller named John Dunton founded a weekly periodical that soon became known as *The Athenian Mercury* and began to be published twice weekly.[6] Its unique feature involved participatory journalism, an early instance of a phenomenon that in various forms has become a staple of periodicals ever since: it entertained questions from readers and answered them in print. Any kind of question—as long as it seemed serious—was welcome, Dunton promised in the first number,[7] and he hinted that behind the publication were editors with vast funds of learning. Writing anonymously himself, Dunton promised anonymity to those who submitted questions—"to remove those Difficulties and Dissatisfactions, that shame or fear of appearing ridiculous"—and encouraged a wide range of curiosity: "The Design is . . . to satisfie all *ingenious and curious Enquirers* into *Speculations*, Divine, Moral and Natural, &c." The project was an instant and sustained success. After only two issues, Dunton saw that he had material and interest enough to publish twice a week, and *"curious Inquirers"* were quickly asked to hold new questions until "we are got clear of those already on our hands,"[8] a request that had to be repeated on a number of later occasions because of an epidemic of interest. The questions were of all sorts, but there was a strong bent toward casuistical questions that inquired into the ethics of unusual situations—forerunners of those addressed by the likes of Dear Abby and Dr. Ruth. A single number of *The Athenian Mercury* usually tackled a dozen or so questions, although occasionally a whole number (or a series of numbers) was devoted to one subject.

The Athenian Mercury lasted nearly six years, and the numbers were regularly gathered into volumes which, early on, often included additional material to lure regular readers into further purchases. And there were supplements and other spinoffs (such as Charles Gildon's *History of the Athenian Society*, 1692) which netted substantial profits and brought increased attention to the Athenian "movement"—not to mention a host of imitators who similarly curried public favor for instant profit.[9] Like late twentieth-century "two-way" radio programs that are networked, syndicated, and rebroadcast, *The Athenian Mercury* found a free source of material and a public that would pay to hear itself puzzle aloud. It also managed, in print, to assert an authority over individual cases and circumstances that did not precisely conform to set rules and principles, a subtle challenge to traditional literature but (as it turned out) a prophetic one.

The popularity and reputation of *The Athenian Mercury* constitute an amazing chapter in the history of publishing. Public figures of note and learned men in a variety of fields were unaccountably impressed by the knowledge and sagacity displayed in the "answers" supplied by *The Athenian Mercury*, and Dunton collected letters and testimonials from an impressive list of people, including George Savile, Marquis of Halifax; James, Duke of Ormond; Sir Thomas Pope Blount; and Sir William Temple.[10] The taking in of Swift by Dunton's project is well known, and, if indeed his "Ode to the Athenian Society" was a genuine tribute instead of an elaborate spoof, the irony of Swift's being gulled is startling—not only because of Swift's lifelong battle against false learning and upstart pretensions to authority but because the Ode (Swift's first published poem) was published by Dunton on All Fools' Day, an occasion Swift himself often employed for his own jests and hoaxes.[11] Swift got revenge in an elaborate attack on Dunton in *A Tale of a Tub*, but I shall not here trouble the reader with an account of the matter.[12]

Dunton was not the only mind behind *The Athenian Mercury*, although his was the innovation, audacity, and profit. Less than two months into the periodical, Dunton began to hint that a formal group was involved in his project, and a year later he announced that a society of the learned, "The Athenian Society," was responsible for its contents. Actually, the society consisted of three people, and it is debatable whether any of them would have seemed authorities if their identity had become known. The other two were brothers-in-law of Dunton, Richard Sault and Samuel Wesley. Sault was a mathematician and a man of some small talent (*"our Algebraick Brother,"* Dunton called him [*Athenianism*, fol. A2]); he is now chiefly remembered as author of a fraudulent pamphlet, *The Second Spira*, published by the perhaps unsuspecting Dunton.[13] Wesley later became the father of John and Charles Wesley and the author of a versified Old Testament, but his credentials then were quite modest. He had been ordained in the Church but was still without place and in need of money; he had, however, already made his literary debut with a volume of sophomoric poems published by Dunton and entitled *Maggots* (1685): it contained such titles as "*A Tame Snake left in a Box of Bran*," "*A Pindaricque, On the Grunting of a Hog*," "*An Anacreontique on a Pair of Breeches*," "*On a Cow's Tail*," "*On a Hat broke At Cudgels*," and "*On a Supper of a Stinking Ducks*" (sic).[14]

The young Wesley was only good-natured, facetious, and immature—

hoping for a quick reputation as a humorist and wit—but his volume quickly became and remained a symbol of false wit and downright silliness. References to "maggoty" writing abound in the early century, and Pope's allusion to him in *The Dunciad,* although muted,[15] suggests what a comic figure Wesley's poem still cut more than forty years later. Wesley had quickly given his age a word for novelty and singularity of a particularly ridiculous sort. Its connotations were comic and unfortunate, but it stood for a whole climate of receptivity to innovation for its own sake, and Dunton repeatedly insisted that his own originality, while creative and eccentric, was not really "maggoty." Later, in trying to renew the "Society" and repeat the success of *The Athenian Mercury,* Dunton tried still harder for respectability and authority by claiming that nine new experts, *"all Masters in their several Faculties,"* had been elected to membership.[16] But it mattered less whether his answers were from a recognized authority, or even if they were true, than that they responded to a need in the reading public to have its curiosity satisfied about a variety of practical and abstruse matters. Whether or not Dunton's ideas were "maggoty," his timing in the 1690s was very good.

Dunton himself gave the age another, more expressive, more comprehensive, and more lasting term in his choice of the word "Athenian" for his periodical and his "Society." Beyond Wesley, Sault, and Dunton there was actually no society and only a trumped-up historical meaning behind the word. Dr. John Norris, the Cambridge Platonist, contributed some help to Dunton (although prudently refusing "to become a stated Member of *Athens*"),[17] and some others, including Defoe,[18] may have provided information or occasional written material, but there is no evidence that membership in the Athenian Society ever exceeded the number of its three "founders." Still, Dunton had found a label that stood for much more than an imaginary learned society and his own fevered imagination.[19]

The Athenian Mercury may have contributed to the beginnings of the English novel in a variety of ways,[20] but I mention it here to suggest the extraordinary attention to novelty and innovation that Dunton and many others articulated around the turn of the century. For Dunton, the word "Athenian" implied a taste for novelty and restless curiosity, and he used the term in publication after publication over a period of nearly thirty-five years in hopes of capitalizing on the public preoccupation with what was new. The last decade of the seventeenth century and the first decade of the eighteenth were especially "Athenian" in their interests, and Dunton offered a variety of Athenian titles. In different versions, *The Athenian Oracle* collected the casuistical materials from *The Athenian Mercury,* and a bewildering range of other volumes—*Athenae Redivivae: or The*

New Athenian Oracle (1704), *The Athenian Catechism* (1704), *The Athenian Spy* (1704, 1709, and 1720), *Athenian Sport* (1707), *Athenianism* (1710), and *Athenian News: or, Dunton's Oracle* (1710)—stressed the newness of what they said and how they said it in an effort to capture the interests of the restless and trendy. Repeatedly, Dunton defined "Athenians," whether members of the supposed society or their readers and sympathizers, as "lovers of Novelty,"[21] calling Athenianism "a search after Novelties"[22] and characterizing curiosity as "the Athenian Itch." On several title pages he repeated his trademark couplet (actually written by Robert Wilde):

> We are all tainted with the *Athenian Itch*
> News, and new Things do the whole World bewitch.[23]

And he assured readers of *Athenian Sport* that ". . . if the Novelty you find here, don't cure the *Athenian Itch*, there is nothing will" (p. vii). Charles Gildon, in his *History of the Athenian Society*—of which Dunton first denied any knowledge but later admitted to having had another printer issue for him—cites Acts 17:21 as the source of Dunton's term "Athenian": ". . . all the Athenians and strangers which were there spent their time in nothing else, but either to tell, or to hear some new thing." In work after work, Dunton sought to gratify public taste for "News, and new Things," and he continually promises more. "[H]aving printed Seven Hundred Books written by Other Persons," he exaggerated in the dedication to *Athenianism*, "I was willing to add Six (or perhaps Twelve) Hundred of my own writing, to convince the Lovers of Novelty how much I have labour'd to gratifie their Curiosity" (p. x). He calls his collected projects "Athenianism," he says, because of "the *Newness* of their Garb and Habit" (p. viii), and his aim is "to present you with what is new, strange and surprizing" (p. vi).

In entitling his first major work of prose fiction *The Life and Strange Surprizing Adventures of Robinson Crusoe*, Defoe (or his publisher)[24] is capitalizing on the whole sprawling context of attention to the new, strange, and surprising, a context for which Dunton is a spokesman and symbol but not (as in the Athenian Society) a lonely figure pretending to be legion. When the Augustans poked fun at those who sought originality, eccentricity, and novelty, their targets were the many writers on the side of the moderns against the ancients. Few of the moderns were as outspoken as Dunton or as extravagant and colorful in their advocacy of novelty, but enough rising writers were at one in their distrust of tradition to make humanists and conservative men of letters feel beleaguered and defensive. Whether it is Swift in *A Tale of a Tub* parodying modernists who protest that what they say is literally true this minute that they are writing or Pope in *The Dunciad* isolating the phenomenon of novelty-worship, the analysis is very much the same: the one thing that held the Augustans, with their very different temperaments, together was their shared analysis of contemporary writing.[25] From a perspective of Christian humanism, taste for the strange and surprising meant an undue confidence in one's own talents as well as a lack of reverence for tradition, an insensitivity to the humanist heritage and code, and a refusal to honor crucial categories and make fine distinctions. The dunces and hacks of the new print world earn their cautionary place in amber for a variety of reasons, but the preoccupation with newness and originality is one of the main ones. The presence of Ned Ward, Charles Gildon, Eustace Budgell, Thomas Woolston, Orator Henley, Colley Cibber, Wesley, Dunton, and Defoe in the annals of Modern Dulness is largely due to what the Augustan keepers of tradition perceived as their rebellion against established tradition and their devotion to the cult of novelty.

Journalistic phenomena such as *The Athenian Mercury* are only the most obvious and obtrusive examples of the published novelties at the turn of the century. In poems, plays, pamphlets, narratives of many kinds, anthologies and collections, even in religious treatises, innovation and experimentation often ran wild. The prefatory materials that stand between a reader and the main body of *A Tale of a Tub* and the insistent intertextuality of the machinery in *The Dunciad Variorum* are, despite their parodic intentions, in many ways the logical outcome of the early phase of novelty in the eighteenth century. In their grudging acceptance and domestication of devices of novelty, such strategies represent the best art that immediately emerges from the new consciousness Athenianism represents (one of the ironies of Augustan literary history), but the more lasting harvests of novelty come a generation later, in a garb more subdued, more subtly designed, and ultimately more lasting. In the journalism of Ned Ward and Abel Boyer, the histories of John Oldmixon and Gilbert Burnet, the poems of Thomas Tickell and Ambrose Philips, the narratives of Charles Gildon and Delariviere Manley, and the jumbled mix of writings that come from everywhere and everyone, one can see which way the wind was blowing, but the time was not yet.

I V

IF the early wave of novelty was unfocused, sprawling across genres and modes more or less indiscriminately, it also lacked official recognition except for the negative reaction orchestrated by the reigning literary establishment. There were, however, some small attempts to attain or claim literary respectability, and Dunton's words again represent in heightened form the ambitions of the tribe in general. The term "Athenian" represents to Dunton intellectual pretensions as well as devotion to novelty. One of Dunton's Athenian volumes has as its frontispiece an emblem showing Athens, Rome, Oxford, and Cambridge at its four corners as the world's centers of learning where curiosity is to be satisfied; the emblem pictures several dozen learned scribes and scientists in the center, presumably members of the society who draw upon all four traditions.[26] Dunton's boast that the society included "*several* Cambridge and Oxford *Scholars*"—although, as Gilbert McEwen wryly notes, by the phrase Dunton means only the redoubtable Samuel Wesley[27]—represents the desire for recognition and respectability that dunce upon dunce hoped to achieve in spite of their attacks on tradition and authority. Perhaps more than most hacks, Dunton is conscious that his work may be full of flaws because he believes himself to be charting new territory. "Gentlemen," he writes in *Athenianism*, "—as to any other ERRORS you may meet with in this Book, I hope your good Nature will be as ready to forgive 'em, as your Wit is able to find 'em, for my Projects are NEW, and as I venture to embark for *Terra Incognita*, I hope the Hazard I run to oblige the CURIOUS will be accepted, were my Errors in Sailing never so many" (p. xvi). Dunton is as convinced of the necessity of novelty as Pope is of the test of tradition and authority. "[U]nless a Man can either *think or perform something out of the old beaten Road*," he writes in his *Life and Errors* (1705), "he'll find nothing but what his Forefathers have found before him" (p. 247). But he still wants to defend himself from the charge of being "magotty" and wishes to distinguish between true originality and pure nonsense, although in talking about his own writing he is choosing a rather poor example:

As this *Idea* . . . is an Original Project, perhaps some will call it one of *Dunton's Maggots*; For having printed . . . W——'s writing, it wou'd be strange if I shou'd not, by Immitation, become one my self. But how little I deserve to be so accounted, is sufficiently shewn in the following Sheets. I confess, Six Years ago, I printed my LIVING ELEGY (*or represented* John Dunton, "*as Dead and bury'd, in an Essay upon my own Funeral*") and perhaps some may think it a little MAGOTTY, that I shou'd come again from the Dead to write *The History of my own Life*, but (Gentlemen), cease to wonder at this, for I have (almost) finish'd *The Funeral of Mankind, or an Essay, proving we are all dead and bury'd, with an Elegy upon the Whole Race: To which is added, a Paradox, shewing what we call Life is Death, and that we all live and discourse in the Grave*," &c.

Now this Subject is New and Surprising, but is far from being *Magotty;* for if a Man must be call'd a *Magot* for starting Thoughts that are WHOLLY NEW, than Farwell Invention.[28]

Listing Dunton's titles often sounds like caricature, and the "forthcoming" titles projected by Swift's Hack in A *Tale of a Tub* do not improve very much on Dunton's originals.[29] To quote Dunton is to illustrate what Swift had in mind in attacking his contemporaries for being so attached to innovation and novelty—and also to illustrate why he was concerned. Dunton's obsessive writing to the moment, his fickle and unfocused oratory, and his often bizarre self-consciousness represent values, habits of mind, and cultural attitudes feared by traditionalists, and, if much of the writing that emerged from this sort of mind-set deserved the abuse heaped upon it by the Augustans, that writing also indicated the way the culture was moving. A sense of deep dissatisfaction with what the European literary tradition offered modernity began to be matched with the sense that new native veins were ready to be tapped. The wild wandering among forms and modes that characterized Dunton's own writing accurately suggests how little notion he or his contemporaries had of what shape novelty might take, and only the fiction of Defoe, Rowe, Manley, Barker, and Davys gives much of an indication in the early years of the century that any real creative innovation is afoot. But Swift's isolation of the modern mentality in A *Tale of a Tub* and *The Battle of the Books* is essentially accurate in its characterization of what the new consciousness consists in, what its values are, and where it tends. He was only a little early in his observations—and wholly unable (or unwilling) to see that any good could come out of new ways that emphasized the strange and surprising. It was not really clear, in the first wave of novelty, what the new directions of literature would be, but it was clear that there would be new directions and that the only question was what creative form they would take.

V

TWO generations after the first wave of novelty, Henry Fielding's attempt to provide a pedigree for the new species he claimed to be founding tries to defuse the worries of traditional literary critics by de-emphasizing the new and unusual aspects of the species. His "history" represents a significant step in the cultural conception of what we have come to call the novel, but the cultural guardians and moral doubters did not immediately run for cover. It took, in fact, nearly a hundred years for the novel to achieve the respectability Fielding sought for it,[30] although the forces that produced that respectability were set in motion by Fielding and the rival Richardson. In quite different ways those two novelists addressed directly the strong cultural resistance to any new form of fiction, and, even if the resistance did not immediately fall away, their impact was substantial on both a general readership and the moral and literary establishment. Richardson's accomplishment was primarily in suggesting, to sophisticated and unsophisticated readers alike, the moral, ideological, and ideational possibilities of the novel and in creating an intense and cogent whole which was informed by a consistent sponsoring idea. Even the parodic attacks that lash out against his values in effect underscore how deeply he had incorporated his sense of morality into his artistic framework. The contemporary recognition of this achievement provided perhaps the firmest sense in the 1740s that something new had happened in Richardsonian fiction. Many contemporaries, including Samuel Johnson, doubted on the other hand the values imbedded in Fielding's fiction (although others, including Fielding himself, defended them vigorously), and his accomplishment then tended to get defined more in terms of literary and traditional, rather than moral and ethical, categories. In effect, Richardson and Fielding considered together became a kind of double-barreled answer to the literary and moral objections raised by the Augustans against innovation and novelty a generation earlier, but of course the effectiveness of their answer lay as much in their talents and in a readied cultural context as it did in the fact that they met classic objections to fiction and novelty head-on.[31]

Fielding's claim that he was the founder of a new kind of writing resides in a framework of familiarity, and traditionally educated readers—those used to poetic conventions and the rhetorical legerdemain of high-minded prose—could feel right at home in his new form from the beginning. However disconcerting and radical some of his strategies were, his art seemed designed for initiates. In the opening pages of *Tom Jones*, for example, the Judicious Reader is treated to a clever exercise in self-compliment when Fielding quotes from Pope's *Essay on Criticism:*

> [T]rue Nature is as difficult to be met with in Authors, as the *Bayonne* Ham or *Bologna* Sausage is to be found in the Shops.
>
> But the whole, to continue the same Metaphor, consists in the Cookery of the Author; for, as Mr. *Pope* tells us,
>
> > True Wit is Nature to Advantage drest,
> > What oft' was thought, but ne'er so well exprest.
> >
> > (I, 1, 32–33)

One need not stop to enumerate the meanings of "drest" here to note Fielding's sleight-of-hand, and a good bit of the comedy lies in the pace of the passage so that a reader can slide quickly past before quite realizing that Pope's couplet is as comfortable in Fielding's cooking metaphor as a formal dancer would be in a pile of sausages. Ignorant and superficial readers (Fielding directly and categorically addresses many kinds of readers, from the best to the worst) can pass over Fielding's deliberate misreading unperturbed and go on to excitements more within their ken, but experienced traditional readers—those taught to read poetry slowly for implication and the precision of metaphors—are quickly bonded to the facetious irony of the sophisticated Fielding by such devices as this, often repeated in other literary allusions and quotations, especially when Latin or Greek is "rendered" into English. Traditional, even Augustan, modes of expectation are set up and drawn upon just as they are in the implicit contrasts between writer and reader in the established literary genres, and it is not difficult even for a conservative reader to swallow Fielding's claims (largely nonsense, even when they are not based on faked literary history) that he can trace his precedents to antiquity. There really is much that is old in the novel (though crucially modified by the new), and Fielding uses traditional clothing to obscure the fact that he is subverting the tradition as then understood. Fielding seems always to have had one foot on old ground and one foot on new. Pope, as a leader of the older generation of Augustanism, probably would have resisted *Tom Jones* at least as vigorously as did Johnson and for many of the same reasons. He lived only to witness the earliest of Fielding's ventures into the new species, and it may have been just as well, for Pope had spotted his apostasy in earlier and still traditional literary forms, and it is hard to imagine him more satisfied with the novels of the 1740s than with earlier novelties in verse and drama, although the talent and formal grace that informed them were clearly superior. Fielding's style and grace would, from the point of view of someone like Pope, only make his work more dangerous than that of, say, Dunton or Defoe, and it is easy to imagine him flapping this bug with gilded wings, rejecting the whole direction of his work regardless of his "neoclassical" attempt to give it a heritage, history, and respectability.

Critics who emphasize Fielding's traditional loyalties at the expense of his innovation fall into the literalist trap set for the classical reader of the 1740s without quite realizing that they have become his victim instead of his collaborator. Fielding and his first readers were emphatic about his "newness." Fielding does not wish to be only the modern Homer but the Aristotle as well, and as describer and lawgiver he assumes the validity of the claims he makes as artist. But we do not have to regard his definitions and rules as absolute to recognize that his claims to originality are mostly legitimate. As William Park has pointed out, contemporaries of Fielding and Richardson tended to think of the two as having jointly made the claim for "what was new about 'the new species of writing,' "[32] and even though each had strong partisans among readers, as well as direct imitators who tended to minimize the claims of the rival master, the surrounding critical context offers a kind of overview of what the newness consisted in. Followers of Richardson tended to emphasize certain features and those of Fielding rather different ones, but, except for patently specious claims by each separate master that no rival could possibly be taken seriously, there was no noticeable tendency to regard their accomplishments as two separate species or forms, despite what could have been easy formal, modal, or tonal definitions.

In his "Preface" to *Joseph Andrews* (1742), Fielding equivocates in his claims of founding a new "species of writing." "[I]t may not be improper," he says at the beginning, "to premise a few Words concerning this kind of Writing, which I do not remember to have seen hitherto attempted in our Language." At the end he again phrases his claim ambiguously— is he claiming to be founding a new English species or to be the first in English to describe it critically?—although he prescribes rules as if he were writing with the authority of a founding father. In *Tom Jones*, though, there is no equivocation, and he proclaims, "I am, in reality, the Founder of a new Province of Writing . . . [and] am at liberty to make what Laws I please therein" (II, i, 77). Richardson's claims are less brazen, public, and self-ironic, but his correspondents and minions kept reassuring him of his place, a reassurance he clearly wanted very badly. With rival claims of novelty volleying back and forth between camps, the public seems to have accepted that something was indeed new and important, whatever it might be called, no matter what its ultimate direction was, or whoever created it. Some simply assume the novelty; others try to specify it. The anonymous *Essay on the New Species of Writing founded by Mr. Fielding* (1751) assumes Fielding's claim (although uncertain whether the species is a subset of biography or of history). Its opening warning testifies to the success of the innovation: "The new Sect of Biographers (founded by Mr. *Fielding*) is already grown . . . very numerous from the Success of the Original," and it worries about ". . . the unbounded Liberties the Historians of this comic Stamp might . . . indulge."[33]

A swarm of imitators there were, and the number of works of fiction showed a dramatic increase in the 1740s and 1750s in the wake of the success of Richardson and Fielding. In 1750, Johnson notes the popularity of the new fiction and carefully distinguishes it from the older "heroic romance" dominated by "giants . . . knights . . . desarts . . . [and] imaginary castles": "The works of fiction, with which the present generation seems more particularly delighted, are such as exhibit life in its true state, diversified only by accidents that daily happen in the world. . . ."[34] At midcentury, the new form—innovative, rebellious, surprising, and full of novelty but not yet named "the novel"—was still searching for a clear identity, terminology, and definition; it took almost another half century for a name and a lasting description to stick. But the species was securely enough established that a young and ambitious writer like Tobias Smollett could cast his lot with it as his major direction in his quest for literary immortality, a choice that would have been unthinkable for a serious young man of letters a decade earlier, and serious, moral young women like Charlotte Lennox, Sarah Scott, Sarah Fielding, and Frances Burney dared venture into public under its auspices with the approval of figures as venerable as Johnson. A generation before, writers as diverse as Defoe and Haywood, Manley and Aubin had already constructed significant works of fiction of the emerging kind, taking early advantage of the first wave of the taste for novelty and offering readers some of the features and most of the values articulated by Richardson and Henry Fielding. What these two did was to codify and extend the bold novelty of their predecessors, creating a broad consciousness among readers and potential writers that a significant and lasting form had been created and that whole careers—genuinely *literary* careers, not just hack existences—could be built upon their sound foundations. Narrative and fiction had begun to define—had begun to be—the modes of the future. Interiority and scope had plainly become necessary to their effectiveness, and an appeal both to familiar tones and to new ones—an acceptance of an old world dying as well as of one just being born—had begun to be put together for an audience hungry for mixed fare. The contents, directions, and magnitude of the species were determined, even if there were still major issues of definition.

V I

THAT definition did not come all at once, but if one looks back from the perspective of, say, Clara Reeve in 1785 one can readily see that the new species had established, in spite of disagreements among individual novelists, a distinctive character earlier—at least by the 1750s in the wake of Fielding and Richardson. But no single word or phrase distinguishes the novel from romance or from anything else, and to settle for "realism" or "individualism" or "character" as the defining characteristic diminishes the very idea of the novel and trivializes the conception of a literary species. Had the novel "developed" from romance—or were it simply a "transformation" or "displacement" of romance—a single distinguishing feature might indeed be sufficient to describe it, but there is no reason at all but custom and habit to think of the novel as growing out of romance. There are, however, several features that, in combination, characterize the species, and I list them briefly here before turning, in the next chapter, to some other features that are less agreed upon or at least less talked about.

1. *Contemporaneity.* Unlike literary forms that feature an appeal to the exotic and the far-away in place and time, novels are fundamentally stories of now, or stories about events in a relevant past, one that has culminated in a now, a moment poised in instability and change.

2. *Credibility and probability.* The people who exist and the things that transpire in novels are recognizable as behaving and occurring in believable human ways, and readers are given the sense that things happen in the fictional world according to laws that are essentially like those governing the everyday world they themselves experience. Credibility seems the essential quality for readers to experience in entering a novel and probability the essential quality once they are inside the fictional world.

3. *Familiarity. Everyday existence and common personages.* In offering her famous distinction between romance and novel, Clara Reeve in 1785 speaks of the "picture of real life and manners" provided by the latter, and by "real" she seems to emphasize the lower social rank of characters just as much as a philosophical loyalty to personal observation rather than traditional artifice. Reeve also notes that "The Novel gives a familiar relation of such things, as pass every day before our eyes."[35]

4. *Rejection of traditional plots.* Novels differ from earlier, more communal and more aristocratic forms of narrative fiction in their relative freedom from stereotypes in plot, character, and naming. Traditional literary formulas obtain less often and less fully until the species becomes so established and predictable that it develops its own new formulas. The refusal to follow set patterns in plot and character represents a defiant turn in narrative and a determination to be independent of traditional notions of the "universality" of human nature and human rituals.

5. *Tradition-free language.* Just as novels differ from romances by avoiding traditional plots and stylized conceptions of character, they also choose consciously to be "unliterary," making few claims of a privileged or even formal style, as if writers were deliberately rejecting in their language any sense of a fictional tradition or of continuity with earlier writers and forms.

6. *Individualism, subjectivity.* The difference between the individual in romance and the individual in the novel derives from the different moments in the rise of individualism that the two literary forms take hold of and memorialize. The crucial difference between individuals in romances and novels involves the degree and quality of self-consciousness in novels, a strikingly

different awareness of the processes of thought and feeling that affect individuals in relation to their world and their experiences in it. The subjectivity of the novel involves not just a raised status for the individual self but an intensified consciousness, individual by individual, of what selfhood means.

7. *Empathy and vicariousness.* Perhaps because novels probe so deeply and sensitively (at their best) the subjectivity of one individual, novels typically give readers a sense of what it would be like to be someone else, of how another identity would feel. Readers of novels, especially "ordinary" readers of novels who read for pleasure and not for professional enhancement, regularly report that they "identify" or "empathize" with the heroes and heroines of novels (and have anxieties about their conflicts) in ways that suggest a greater closeness between readers and novel characters than between readers and characters in other fictional forms.

8. *Coherence and unity of design.* Modern readers nourished on the "well-made" novel of the nineteenth century are not always impressed with the coherence of eighteenth-century novels, but the novel does seek to gather its multiple parts under the auspices of some single guiding design, to be one continuous action. And novels seriously engage ideas, at their best allowing some theme or governing idea to pull together every thread of narrative and connect every digressive loose end. Novels tend to be more explicitly ideological than most literary species, testimony both to their representational quality and their subjectivity, and even when their ideological loyalties are uncertain or obscure, their ideational heritage is almost always clear.

9. *Inclusivity, digressiveness, fragmentation: The ability to parenthesize.* If their is a peculiar unity in the novel, there is also a peculiar looseness and apparent shapelessness, summed up best in Fielding's insistence in the second chapter of *Tom Jones* that "I intend to digress, through this whole History, as often as I see Occasion: Of which I am myself a better Judge than any pitiful Critic whatever" (I, ii, 37). The freedom to digress in novels (freedom within the given of a single imaginative conception), what I will call their parenthetical tendency, differs from a similar freedom in romances in a way analogous to how oral narrative differs from written. Romances and oral narratives of other kinds often contain loops or tangents (in the technical sense) which are structural, formulaic, and predictable. They depend upon functions of memory and the ability of hearers to hear in sequences and parallel patterns. The digressions in novels may relate in more indirect and complex ways to the narrative centers in their respective books, and they have greater freedom of size and movement because they can depend upon the habits of readers in reading print.

10. *Self-consciousness about innovation and novelty.* Although they are often anxious, like Fielding, to claim a literary pedigree and a place in literary tradition, the tribe of novelists is adamant about the originality of their enterprise. The reputation for oddity that *Tristram Shandy* quickly developed is barely an exaggeration of the kind of reputation that almost every novelist since the beginning has coveted. The repeated claims of novelty and inno-

vation, whether about the specifics of a single book or about new variations for the species itself, taken together are a strong reminder of how odd the novel looks among traditional literary forms.

V I I

THE term "novel" is ultimately the right one for the form of prose fiction that emerged as dominant in the eighteenth century in England, but its rightness was not immediately recognized.[36] Until quite late in the eighteenth century, the term "novel" was used very loosely and imprecisely (not that more recent use has been all that precise either), often implying little more than opprobrium or contempt. Sometimes it designated tales shorter than traditional romances, sometimes it claimed a plot of love and intrigue, sometimes it implied native heritage rather than Continental loyalties. In the late seventeenth century and early eighteenth, "novel" was often applied to narratives not substantially different from romances; sometimes the terms "romance" and "novel" were used interchangeably, and the generic term in other linguistic traditions often does not make the distinctions that have come to seem crucial to the English tradition of lengthy fiction, *roman* in French or *novelle* in Italian encompassing, in each case, both novels and romances.[37] More often, however, early on the terms "novel" and "romance" appear cozily together, not to imply a distinction but rather to catch, between them, all known fiction and some long narratives whose factitiousness was uncertain.[38] Eighteenth-century commentators on fictional narratives— especially moralists who worried about the promotion of idleness, the wasting of time, or some other human degradation that reading them might promote—often paired the terms to engage the whole tradition of old, conventional (and by then quite trivial) fiction, much as Fielding does when he distinguishes the character of his new province ("history") from the "Swarm of foolish Novels, and monstrous Romances" (*Tom Jones*, IX, i, 487) of his contemporaries. When a distinction was made, it usually involved length, novels being relatively short compared to romances (much as we now distinguish novellas from novels), a usage that seems to have developed from the French *nouvelle* or the Italian *novelle*—"a diminutive story whose material is fresh, untraditional, and whose resolution is extraordinarily surprising."[39] But short English "novels" did not necessarily follow their French and Italian models in rejecting traditional plots or other established features, and the works labeled "novels" in late seventeenth-century or early eighteenth-century England most often looked backward—in spite of their name—rather than forward.[40]

Some early writers did use the term "novel" in a way that, in a quite general sense, points to our modern idea. Congreve, for instance, in 1692, distinguishes novels from romances as "of a more familiar nature . . . [with incidents] not such as are wholly unusual or unpresidented [unprecedented], such which not being so distant from our Belief bring also the pleasure nearer us."[41] But even so hesitating and imprecise an attempt to set a distinction is rare, and one cannot find common agreement about the meaning of the term until the kind of retrospective view that Clara Reeve began to codify in 1785.[42] And so, despite some of her own ambivalences, it was Reeve who has set the tone for most subsequent discussion of what the novel is because it was she who separated the novel definitively from romance. Her distinction was incomplete and ultimately insufficient, and the critical tradition has not substantially enough extended her observation to perfect the task, but it is to her that modern criticism of the species owes its primary definitional debt, despite a good deal of grudging and even hostile recognition among latter-day historians who tend to dislike her moralism, eclecticism, and the fact that a woman novelist aspired not just to narrative but to critical and even theoretical tasks. Literary history has always been kinder to women poets and novelists than to women critics, evidently fearing judgment more than "mere" imagination.

However slow to gain precision and acceptance, the term "novel" is a particularly apt one historically because of the central conflict in the eighteenth century over the whole question of ancients and moderns, tradition and the past versus originality and innovation. The Augustan moment in English culture—a moment I would describe as existing between the composition of A Tale of a Tub and the final publication of The Dunciad, but taking its most intense form in the late 1720s when Swift, Pope, and Gay all published their most distinguished credos—articulates the issue in a way that modernity had to answer if in fact a modern literature was to develop.[43] The novel—or rather the various traditions of prose and poetry, some fictional, some not; some narrative, some not; some long and comprehensive, some not, that ultimately came to fruition in long prose fictional narratives that we have come to call novels—represents the central thrust of that answer, even though the early answerers were, most of them, far less articulate than Defoe, far less clear about their art or craft than Fielding, and far less effective in their ability to allure and to manipulate readers than Richardson, Burney, and Sterne.[44]

The fact that a good suggestive, descriptive term came to exist for the new prose fiction has been, in the long run, fortunate for English literary history, even if its acceptance is more fortuitous than designed. Simply *having* a terminological distinction that does not exist in some other languages in the literatures of which, in fact, a similar historical phenomenon occurred, has made it a little easier to be clear about historical change, the reason perhaps why Anglo-American criticism had almost a corner on novelistic theory until, past midcentury, Continental structuralism began to make claims for a different narratological territory.[45] But in fact, the changes in France—and similar ones earlier in Spain and later in Italy and Germany—seem closely related to changes in England, the Continent at first nudging England toward novelty, and England later pushing prose fiction in Romance languages much further toward the full implications of the new species.[46] But regardless of the historicity of the term, it is the one we live with now, even with its imperfections and varieties of outright misuse. Neologisms have no chance in competing with the word "novel," a linguistic irony but a historical truth about the way languages work.

It is not, however, the power of the term "novel" as a totalizing—or even organizing—force in criticism and literary history that focuses our attention on the early eighteenth century in England as the time when the species became defined and self-conscious. Whatever names they went under (and there were many), the lengthy fictions that harvested the popular heritage, claimed literary status, and gathered together the features I have described here began to be a self-conscious body of work by midcentury. The reason that, to some critics, the term seems "totalizing" rather than the phenomenon seeming real is that they have learned their formal distinctions from a Tory literary history that privileges intention in established literary genres. Such a literary history recognizes only what neatly fits carefully labeled boxes because its interest is in boxes. The writers of novels at midcentury did not always know they were writing in a "genre" or "species" (though some, like Richardson and both Fieldings, did): they were simply writing the kinds of books that had become the latest lasting novelty, writing to a public hungry for the combination of delight, instruction, information, and cultural satisfaction provided by such books.

By the 1750s, when scores of new examples appeared (many of them called histories, but some with other labels, too), it was clear that a wide variety of people were writing consciously in the wake of *Clarissa* and *Tom Jones* and shaping their wares to innovate noticeably from, or between, these models. The phenomenon was real, its characteristic features were (if not often articulated) abundantly clear, and its authors and readers knew they were participating in a cultural event of major proportions even if they didn't know what to call it. One measure of the establishment of the species is the number of innovative or rebellious texts that worked variations on it, and in the fifties the public was deluged with experiments involving self-conscious departures—*Amelia, Betsy Thoughtless, The Female Quixote, The Cry,* the first two volumes of *Tristram Shandy.* Here was a species restlessly casting about for varied directions, forms, stances, focuses, magnitudes, themes, and relationships with its audience, but hardly a phenomenon without definition or distinction.

V I I I

ANOTHER result of Reeve's distinction is less fortunate, although she is not really responsible for it. Because the novel traces its terminological existence from a distinction from romance, literary history and theoretical criticism have generally assumed some kind of parent-child relationship between the two, a misleading historical state of affairs born of the inappropriateness or inadequacy of metaphors. If the novel needs to be distinguished from romance, and if the novel came to provide, in effect, an alternative to romance, it does not necessarily follow that the novel descended from romance, or that we must look for its roots there, or that the lineage of the novel lies altogether in fiction or narrative at all. The novel may have replaced romance as the central narrative structure in Western tradition without necessarily being a "displacement" of it in any but a purely functional sense. To assume that the novel is a version of romance is to buy into a whole philosophical outlook, and there is an altogether different way to consider the issue, one less neat perhaps and less absolute, but more tied to historical and cultural particulars and to time as a dimension in reality. I turn now to certain features of the early novel—some of them features that distinguish the novel from other fictional forms, some of them shared with other prose fictions, narratives, and other literary kinds—which imply that we should look beyond romance, and in fact beyond fiction itself, in order to grapple with the complex origins of the English novel.

CHAPTER TWO

Novels and "the Novel": The Critical Tyranny of Formal Definition

■

NOT everything in novels—even in good novels—goes the way critics and critical theorists think it should, and some of the "failures" are characteristic of the species, even definitive. Novels, especially early novels, often bear features that do not "fit" later conceptions of what the novel is or ought to be, and even the most sophisticated later novels often have features that embarrass readers who bring to them rigid formal expectations. Novels remain, for example, too loose and digressive in structure to seem focused and well made, and their directions and tones are often too rich and complex for those who want their aesthetic structures tight and systematic and their ideologies implicit or subdued. Traditional novelistic theory, based as it is on analogies with more traditional and more conservative literary forms and the structures that support them, does not like to hear the multiple discourses in novels or recognize the presence of competing modes within individual works. Recent narrative theory has been more receptive to odd, lumpy, and unexpected features, but most criticism of novels retains its *arriviste* snootiness, remaining intolerant of features that do not meet preconceived standards. Definitions remain high-minded, novels recalcitrant.[1]

Some of the difficulty stems from the novel's inferiority complex. Because of its obscure beginnings and insecure place in the hierarchy of literary forms and kinds, the novel historically has asserted itself by comparison to more established forms. Fielding set the terms for that defense early on by inventing an ancestry and claiming the legitimacy of certain features because they were to be found in literature which had passed the test and had already entered the tradition.[2] As an upstart species, the novel was at first reluctant to stray far from established aesthetic standards, and critics ever since have been loath to emphasize, or even admit to seeing, features—digressiveness, for example, or didacticism, or sensationalism—that might threaten the novel's formal claims. But the difficulty also results from an opposite cause—the desire to make clear that the novel was new and different, needing to be defined carefully to show its distinctiveness from other forms of fictional narrative, especially romance.

Making a clear case for the novel as a new kind with characteristic features of its own became, and has remained, a critical mandate with enormous implications for literary history. The novel has thus become subjective, individualistic, realistic—an account of contemporary life peopled with ordinary characters in everyday situations using the informal language of everyday life to describe, for ordinary readers, the directions and values that inform a series of particular, connected actions and events. Such a description does suggest crucial features of the new fictions that became popular in the early to mid-eighteenth century, and such a definition is important to literary history and often necessary to understanding the features of individual books. The trouble is, attention to distinctive novelistic features tends to obscure characteristics that novels share with romances or other fictional kinds and thus to present a distorted sense of the species. Together the urge to define and the desire to be respectable, while they have produced enormous good, have also produced some harm. That harm is the subject of this chapter; I want to describe nine prominent novelistic features that criticism tends to ignore or underemphasize because their presence in novels upsets formal generic notions. In eighteenth-century English novels, the features I am going to describe are blatant and ubiquitous, but they also exist, although sometimes disguised or metamorphosed, in novels of other times and cultures. I turn first to three features involving forbidden subject matters, then to three others that result from assumptions about audiences, and finally to two structural features and one involving tone. My purpose in doing so is to describe the species in a way consonant with the character of real novels—to reject Platonic notions in favor of what actual novelists write and real readers read.

I

THE "marvellous," according to Henry Fielding, has a tenuous place in the new species of writing for which he wishes to set the rules, but his concern as a theorist is not matched by his practice as a novelist, not even in his definition-setting example, *Tom Jones.*[3] The brilliance of Fielding's plotting can make us forget from page to page how unlikely it is that, say, all roads lead to Upton or that the only peddler in the world who knows Joseph's secret just happens to choose the Boobys' gate in his aimless wanderings around England. Marvelous? Not technically, perhaps, for no natural laws are expressly violated, but the fine line of likelihood is drawn precariously, and no reader would wish to have to depend, in life, on coincidence so shaky or fortune so slippery. Finally we marvel not only at Fielding's ingenuity but at the events themselves and a conception of probability that allows us to believe them. This is not because Fielding indulges the world of romance, but because Fielding has it both ways: he is a faithful historian of a world of everyday reality governed by predictable laws, but he also loves the sense that life is made lively and significant by unexpected events that are surprising and wonderful. *Tom Jones* seems odd in Ian Watt's chapters on formal realism not because it does not belong, but because it so obviously challenges Watt's relentless thesis, becoming a test case of just what the new realism consists in.[4] If the "new species" cannot be said to exist in its first self-conscious example, how can it exist at all?

And yet there are surprises on page after page which, while they do not involve the literal suspension of any law of nature, certainly startle the reader's ordinary sense of probability and sometimes seem to challenge Fielding's insistence that "it may very reasonably be required of Every Writer, that he keeps within the Bounds of Possibility" (VIII, i, 396–97). Tom's rescue (and more) of Mrs. Waters, Sophia's chance meeting with Mrs. Fitzpatrick, the finding of Tom's £500 by Black George, the intricacies of overhearing in the London labyrinth—scores of things happen in *Tom Jones* that involve astonishing luck, that hint at the miraculous, and that border on the impossible. Fielding rightly distinguishes what he does in his province from what happens in the fantastic world of romance, for the "magic" he insists on is of a different order from romantic magic. There are no supernatural agents in Fielding (if we except Fielding himself), no actual violations of nature's steady and discoverable laws. And yet we do his art (and the art of the novel in general) a disservice if we fail to observe the emphasis upon the unusual, the unpredictable, and the uncertain—strange and surprising events calculated to inspire, in readers, open-mouthed wonder without transporting them to a world involving different laws of probability. Fielding's defense of his practice, a version of the providential explanation of how unlikely events may be made to seem probable within a system that orders even the miscellaneous, offers a logic for the intricacies of his plot without diminishing our sense of surprise at how full of unforeseen happenings and of unperceived wonders life is.

The critical reluctance to examine the strange and surprising aspects of novels stems, in part, from insecurities among students of eighteenth-century fiction and, among students of the novel more generally, from anxieties about "realism." Realism is a relative matter, but in discussions of the novel, the term has tended to become normative, so that novels tend to be judged qualitatively on the degree or amount of realism to be found in each, as if more is better. Students of traditional novels seem to worry that students of the post-modern novel will be able to outclaim them, students of Victorian novels worry that they will be outclaimed by students of the naturalist school, and students of the eighteenth century are sure that students of all later cultures will find more realism in their periods and therefore expel eighteenth-century fiction into some anteroom, barely attached to the only respectable house of fiction. If Scholes and Kellogg are correct that the criticism of fiction is too narrowly centered on novels,[5] it is even more true that modern criticism of all kinds, criticism of fiction in particular but also criticism of drama and poetry and autobiography, tends to be realism-centered, with individual works achieving a place on the scale directly proportional to the amount of "reality" that can be certified and tallied up in each.

In this normative context, it is no wonder that instances in novels of the supernatural or para-natural, the miraculous or the magical, the inexplicable or the uncertain, the improbable or the coincidental—varieties all of the strange and surprising—tend to be seen as flaws, or explained away, or overlooked.[6] But the novel as a species, in spite of its strong commitment to credibility and probability, is full of incidents that do not admit of a quick and easy rational explanation. Not many novelists flaunt their ability to include unlikely events as boldly as Fielding does (especially while writing in the same breath about the advisability of avoiding the marvelous), but most novelists are concerned to take us beyond the narrow bounds of expectation within which our rational sense of the world confines us. What are the odds that in the middle of an island one solitary footprint will suddenly be visible, with no others anywhere nearby? What are the odds that a man living on that small island, only a few square miles in size, will bypass all evidence, for more than twenty years, of cannibal rites regularly held there, and then suddenly see the terrible leftovers for the first time? What are the odds that Tom and Sophia (and Mrs. Waters and Squire Western, and Mrs. Fitzpatrick and Mr. Fitzpatrick) will stay at the same small remote inn on the same night? That Clarissa will get letter after letter delivered in spite of all the impediments a repressive, watchful, and intelligent set of family keepers can muster? That Joseph Andrews will go to sleep at the precise moment when staying awake would reveal the secret of his birth, or that he will turn out to be the long-lost son of the "parents" of his one true love or that she, in turn, will still be available to him because she also has been displaced from her actual family? In some of these cases the odds are surely several million to one; when several are strung into a single plot, the odds become infinite. But my point is not that unlikelihood leads to lack of realism: far from it. Many everyday events are, taken in the abstract, wholly unlikely, yet novels dare to feature them. Things that may be statistically possible, even statistically probable when enough cases are considered, seem astonishing when they happen to a particular individual, like the winning of the Irish sweepstakes by some one real person, or the reuniting of a child, separated from the time of birth, with its real parents. But such things do in fact happen against great personal odds, and novels dare to feature a limited number of them in worlds that are essentially familiar, rational, and realistic. Such events respond to a widespread taste for surprise and wonder, a modern substitute for an older lore that admitted metamorphoses and transformations, fairy godmothers and houses made of cake.[7]

Both credibility and probability—but of a global rather than local kind—are crucial to the novel. They represent a conceptual difference from romance: things that cannot happen in our world do not happen in novels. People do not turn into trees, walk on water, materialize from a cloud, or stand up intact after being run over by a train because novels are loyal to a modern, "scientific" conception of the world in which immutable physical laws operate. But modern readers—readers from the eighteenth century to our own time—seem to take rational pleasure in having things happen against individual odds if the global odds are satisfactory; if something surprising can happen to someone in the world, it might just as well happen to someone singled out in a novel. Within the loyalty to credibility, there is room for some uncertainty and cosmic ambiguity; even a law-ridden universe leaves some things open to doubt. Some phenomena are not fully explained by our orderly and scientific view of reality; some things seem to challenge or contradict law but do not actually (or too pointedly) do so. Perhaps we treasure these modern moments because there are so few of them, because it is lovely to think of laws being stretched or rules momentarily relaxed, or because the lingering human taste for awe and wonder has so few outlets in a "rational" world or in a realistic and probable literary species. Novelists are always exploring the border country, and often they try to push back the line just a few more yards.

The strange and surprising events in eighteenth-century novels—the overlapping at Upton, for instance, or the revelation of Joseph's true parentage at the Boobys'—test the limits of probability and sometimes the limits of knowledge of natural laws. They are beyond our normal sense of expectation and may not be explainable by known laws; sometimes they hint at patterns beyond our ken. It is as if the scientific explanation thrust upon early eighteenth-century readers threatened to make their world too predictable, and in their fiction they sought some evidence that it would not be so. The rational, probable, and credible world of the eighteenth century thus licenses surprises that range from unusual coincidences (like those in *Joseph Andrews* and *Tom Jones*) to events that seem destined but cannot be proved to be so—the misnaming of Tristram Shandy and his misadventure with the window sash, or the unexplainable arrival of Friday in Crusoe's domicile, or the apparent voice "communication" of Moll Flanders with her Lancashire husband over a distance of twelve miles. "I then began to be amaz'd and surpriz'd, and indeed frighted," Moll reports after hearing Jemy repeat exactly the words she had uttered in wishing him to return.[8] Later novels feature similar surprises within a trustable framework of rationality and firm order: Rochester's discovery of Jane Eyre's voice after calling, "Jane, Jane, Jane . . ." in her absence is a prominent nineteenth-century example, and the not quite explainable but never quite hieratic underground in *The Crying of Lot 49* a suggestive twentieth-century one. Such vestiges continue to show the longing for magic and wonder in times devoted to, and insistent upon, rational explanation.[9]

When Fielding distinguishes himself from the writers of romance who regularly trade in the marvelous, his vocabulary is significant. He is willing to share the "strange and surprizing" with those writers, as well as that which will "raise the Wonder and Surprize of [the] Reader," but he insists that those who follow his lead in the new species must, to achieve these effects, use a mode different from the writers of romance, a mode that eschews the supernatural entirely. He thus sets himself a more difficult task than that of his predecessors and insists that his disciples will have to follow suit, but he claims a wider expanse of possibility for his effects than it may at first seem in his disclaimer about the marvelous. He perceives clearly the cultural needs of the audience he writes for, and, in distinguishing his species from species of earlier times, he is careful to observe the demands of the modern world, demands based upon orderly and rational assumptions, without cutting his art off from effects important to readers.

The taste for surprise in a world seen scientifically—the desire to wonder in a world increasingly explored, understood, and (it seemed) conquered—led to many cultural and literary phenomena in the late seventeenth and early eighteenth centuries, from voyages to exotic or unknown places to imaginary voyages in the mind, from Grand Tours to minute analyses of the antiquities of England, from Royal Society experiments to freak shows at fairs and festivals, from the founding of museums for curiosities and rarities to a domestic taste for orientalism and gothicism in gardens, houses, and storytelling, from the reading of wild but "true" collections of wonders and curiosities and miraculous events to fictions that probed the unusual and bizarre in the world of everyday. Novelists both before and after Fielding turn aside the wilder wish to make readers gape at any cost, channeling reader desires into a wonder about human events that—if not really marvelous, miraculous, or magic—still provides a sophisticated outlet for that human curiosity. We do the novel—and not only the early novel—a disservice if we fail to notice, once we have defined the different world from romance that novels represent, how fully it engages the unusual, the uncertain, and the unexplainable. When we admit such concerns as part of the novel's territory, it also allows us to see more clearly where the novel came from, for the novel is only the most successful of a series of attempts to satisfy, in a context of scientific order, the itch for news and new things that are strange and surprising.

A closely related feature involves the novel's engagement with taboos. Operating from a position of semi-respectability from the start, the novel has always been self-conscious about appearing to be pornographic, erotic, or obscene. The fuss raised in this century over *Lady Chatterley's Lover* or Henry Miller's *Tropics* volumes—rather mild matter in the full perspective of human history—may remind us just how careful mainstream novelists have been to avoid even the appearance of pandering to salacious tastes. And yet there has been a quiet boldness from the start in exploring alleys of human privacy and dark corners of human behavior. In its eagerness to engage the range of ecstasies and pains that grip the human heart, the novel has found itself repeatedly concerned not only with sexuality and eroticism but with events of physical violence and emotional brutality, murder, incest, and rape. Only quite recently has there been the kind of preoccupation with physical detail that has meant graphic representation, and often microscopic amplification, of acts of love or violence themselves, but from the beginning the novel involved itself with forbidden, repressed, or secret arenas of human activity, as well as those private recesses of the human mind, will, and appetite that produce them. Relatively seldom have novels themselves been as salacious as a plot summary of them would suggest—novels are usually too concerned with perspective and the varieties of human responses that taboos dramatically elicit—but there has always been a taunting, teasing quality about the way novels promise to tell secrets and open up hidden rooms.

Much of what happens in the novel for two hundred years is suggested by what happens in *Moll Flanders*. The title page sounds daring, and its enticements are bold and almost leering: *The Fortunes and Misfortunes Of the Famous Moll Flanders, &c. Who was Born in Newgate, and during a Life of continu'd Variety for Threescore Years, besides her Childhood, was Twelve Years a Whore, five times a Wife (whereof once to her own Brother), Twelve Year a Thief, Eight year a Transported Felon in Virginia, at last grew Rich, liv'd Honest, and died a Penitent.* The book is not, however, inflaming and lurid. It is not that the title page lies (except for a few numerical details and the fact that the report of Moll's death is greatly exaggerated), but that pickpocketing, robbery, adultery, bigamy, and incest—things that are categorically clear when they are bared in an outline—tend to lose their labels and most of their shock in the context of day-to-day narrative. Part of Defoe's accomplishment—an accomplishment repeated in kind in novels ever since—is in making Moll's life seem ordinary even though it violates community standards in ways unthinkable to most readers. The novel is aimed at readers very different (at least in circumstances) from its narrator: that is part of its strategy of demonstrating the commonality of repressed desires and disapproved behavior in a human history controlled by intrusive circumstance.

Few eighteenth-century novels—and almost as few nineteenth- or even twentieth-century ones until after midcentury—are racy or incendiary in any way, but their stories contain a lot of aberrant, impolite-to-talk-about, forbidden conduct. The worlds of Defoe and Smollett are (not surprisingly, given the courses of life they choose to depict) full of physical violence and brutality; their characters do what their readers only worry or fantasize about. In Richardson, the major events are rape and attempted rape in two of his three novels; his elongated, tantalizing prose—which, even to his moral champions, seems teasing and suggestive, and to some readers downright prurient—lingers over events, threats, and thoughts that belong to a world of taboo-ridden nightmare. In Sterne, the central subjects are the wounds of war and love, and the hint of illegitimate birth or even incest casts a broad shadow across the whole narrative and the consciousness that both reports the story and is its subject. For Henry Fielding, the possibility of incest spices the single most worrisome moment in his first two novels, and in Burney and a host of other novelists—whatever their surface calm or pretended avoidance of the lurid—the hint of incest, molestation, or some other hideous fear hovers over episode after episode, plot after plot.[10] For a long time, criticism of the novel cast aside as inferior the lively narratives of writers like Behn, Manley, and Haywood because of their "scandalous" plots and themes while pointedly ignoring similar episodes and anxieties in the canonical novels, a way of at once keeping the canon closed and defining the novel in narrow and partial terms.[11] But for eighteenth-century novelists generally—and for many more recent ones—the idea of the horrible and the forbidden exists side by side with everyday reality, sometimes offering a coloration of sensationalism and frenzy that threatens to associate novels with low tastes, disordered conduct, and inferior characters, and always heightening the contemporary sense of ordinariness.

The extraordinary thing about the violations of taboo in novels is, finally, how ordinary they all seem. The novel tames violence and sexual aberration within a structure of everyday existence very much as it domesticates the surprising, the unexplained, and the wonderful. The novel implicitly claims that we do not have to move beyond the annals of ordinary existence to discover events that are strange and conduct that is "irrational," unlikely, or weird. In the familiar world of ordinary people, the novel claims, there is plenty. Taking advantage of its commitment to novelty means for the novel not a flight into enchantment or romance, but rather an admission that human nature involves more variety than classical and neoclassical theorists had admitted. The individual, the eccentric, the bizarre, and even the unique all have a place in novels almost by definition, yet the early novel concentrates not on true extremes (the unique or near unique) but rather on people who slip beyond the norm and test the social fabric. Here are murderers, thieves, rapists, those who commit incest, and those who father bastards or malidentified offspring; and here are victims who receive the violence or are drawn into disruptive or confused behavior of their own. But even when acts are horrible or characters heinous, the novel finds ways to comprehend them without violating our sense that we are reading about recognizable people in a world we know.

Perhaps because we tend to think of the novel as a social form, we are also prone to neglect a third feature, the novel's tendency toward the confessional and the exhibitionistic. The willingness of novels to portray aberrant behavior or engage events that show human beings in violation of traditional taboos is closely related to the novel's tendency to be, in itself, exhibitionistic: both features result from the fundamental desire to explore recesses formerly neglected or suppressed by fiction and, to a large extent, by literature generally. The novel's willingness—indeed, incessant need—to invade traditional areas of privacy (the bedroom, the bathroom, the private closet) and explore matters traditionally considered too personal to be shared leads to an entirely new understanding of the relationship between public and private, a moving beyond, even, the ordinary reaches of personal conversation and private discourse. No longer can the individual cordon off whole areas of existence—either actions or thoughts—as inappropriate for examination and discussion. In the novel, readers can peek into traditionally secret spaces—physical, mental, or emotional—and if readers are made to feel voyeurs and violators of traditional mores in doing so, they still are allowed to peep and encouraged to think that their curiosity is natural and appropriate to art. But the other side of voyeurism is exhibitionism, and readers would never get their view if novelists were not determined that they should have it. The insistency of writers in the early eighteenth century matches the curiosity of readers in a way that allows something quite new.

The process of lowering the traditional barrier between public and private is a complex one, and it happens culturally over a period of years, not in a momentous instant when one individual makes it happen. Part of the story of the public sharing of the intimate involves the close relationship between autobiography and the novel, for the novel's regular adoption of the features of autobiography—not just the first-person point of view but also such features from spiritual autobiography as the obsessive enumeration of minute trivia and the careful reexamination of them in quest of possible patterns of meaning—leads to confessional possibilities that easily become, with only minor changes in the conception of one's audience, exhibitionistic.[12] The line from Bunyan to Cleland and Boswell is probably inevitable; that to Sade, Harris, Mailer, and Jong is not very surprising.

The willingness of Moll Flanders to share the secrets of her lusts and larcenies with us differs from Tristram Shandy's willingness to tell the intimacies of his conception and crucial injury only in the depth of commitment to probing the traditionally private and in devotion to pictorial detail. Manley, Haywood, Richardson, the Fieldings, and Smollett are just as stricken with the urge to spill all, and their novels differ primarily in the definition of what "all" might mean. Manley and the early Haywood are anxious to expose the private sides of public figures and dramatize the hypocrisy of the rituals and claims of modern life while exploring the ruthless insensitivity to categorical victims cast by the roadside. For Richardson, no secrets of the mind dare remain secret, and when his epistolary method fails to give him enough room to display the intricacy of the secrets, he resorts to footnotes, glosses by other personae, cross references, and other direct authorial intrusions to be sure that real motives are bared and the ultimate ends of confessional (as he understands them) achieved. Henry Fielding's obsession involves the nuances of temptation and behavioral departures from principles and norms. He is dedicated to showing how observers can discover the innermost thoughts, feelings, and commitments by watching carefully a person's actions, a dedication that derives from his sense that basic to human nature is a need ultimately to exhibit one's true self and make one's *actions* a confession of the soul, almost the inverse of Manley's philosophical reason for what is finally a similar attraction to exposure. Sarah Fielding, anxious to "unfold the labyrinths of the human mind," explores both conduct and motives extensively, sometimes ruthlessly.[13] Smollett has more of the satirist's interests in confessional and exhibitionism—he likes to do it for others and keep a certain distant guard over himself—but here too are clear instances of the novel's tendency to try to get all of life by poking into the crevices and letting the nooks and crannies pop open to view. Or at least appear to. Actually, the novel is still more hesitant and squeamish than its confessional commitments might suggest, but its reluctancies, especially at the beginning, are primarily about details of behavior and not a matter of hiding the fact of actions, thoughts, or feelings.

I I

ANOTHER cluster of ignored or underrated features involves the novel's unusual relationship to its audience. Unlike older literary forms, the novel does not depend upon an established community of readers, and several of its most insistent features—not just the undervalued ones I am discussing here—derive from its conscious sense of novelty and interrupted communality. Its rejection of familiar plots, conventional mythic settings, and recognizable character types represents a recognition that its future lies in developing a new kind of relationship with new combinations of readers.[14] Eighteenth-century observers—Charles Gildon, for example[15]—quickly observed that actual readers of novels were an unknown breed. But the broad observations about readership—"the young, the ignorant and the idle," Samuel Johnson called them, suggesting distinctions of class and predictability as well as literal experience—have more often led to discomfort and humor than serious analysis.[16] "Middleclass" and "bourgeois" have become the code words, a sign to both traditionalist and radical critics that it is all right to be dismissive, and historical readers have been maligned by innuendo rather than analyzed for their precise role in the texts.

One audience-related feature involves the novel's tendency both to probe and promote loneliness and solitariness, rather ironic in view of the novel's expressed design to portray people in their societal context. If the tendency to expose secrets of personal life points one way, the tendency to enclose the self, to treat the self as somehow inviolable and insistently separate in spite of the publication of secrets once thought too personal to articulate, points the other. This feature is more than an extension of the novel's characteristic emphasis on subjectivity, although it is from a concern with subjectivity that this feature begins. Somehow the novel has always communicated a terrible sense of isolation and artic-ulated dramatically the breakdown of the relationships between individ-uals. The sense of isolation is just as strong when the novel's protagonist is surely and comfortably situated in a family or proto-family group, as in *Tristram Shandy*, *Emma*, *Portrait of the Artist*, or *Absalom, Absalom!* as it is in novels of loneliness like *Robinson Crusoe* or *Oliver Twist* or *Tess*. Perhaps because of its commitment to showing individuals fully in all of their several social relationships, novels are better positioned to see the void that remains. And perhaps because the novel emerged when it did, just as the urban consciousness began to focus the overwhelming sense of solitariness among the many, it developed early a generic ability (nearly instinctive among its authors) to record poignantly the modern percep-tion that, however close to another consciousness one came, whatever the relationship between people, there is always a sense of incomplete-ness, isolation, and frustration that approaches despair.

The novel's addictive engagement with solitariness may be seen most clearly not in the lonely heroes of novels but in their lonely readers. Partly because of social and architectural changes and partly because of the dynamics of print, readers of novels from the beginning tended to read in solitude, and novels from the beginning presumed to be dealing with one reader at a time rather than with a communal audience. Moral distrust of works of imagination and other books that might "turn the heads" of the young helped to drive readers of novels into solitude and keep them on their guard against intrusion. Plays, autobiographies, and moral treatises that issue warnings of the evils of such "idle reading" are full of anecdotes and allusions that cumulatively suggest a vivid picture of just how closeted readers of novels tended to be, especially young readers and women readers who were the primary targets of moral watch-dogs. It was not just novels, of course, that posed such threats, and often moralists lump together plays, romances, and tales from the oral tradition as excessive stimulants of fancy and desire. Nor was it just novels that were read in privacy. Many of the standard devotional and didactic trea-tises were designed for closet reading, and in fact any lengthy volume— an uncharted outcome of the print revolution—required individual, usu-ally solitary, contemplation. But novels were increasingly associated with forbidden reading in lonely secrecy because their popularity in the mid-eighteenth century was increasingly seen as a moral and cultural threat. And the official sanctions placed on their perusal by the young meant that the phenomenology of solitariness was intensified by the cultural disapproval.[17]

Private space of the sort so dear (and crucial) to Pamela and Clarissa had begun to be more readily available to individuals at about the time of the novel's emergence, too. Country houses increasingly provided closets or cabinets where individuals could be entirely alone, and even the crowded space of urban housing was divided so that individuals (even servants) could have secluded, if cramped, places of their own.[18] The movement toward urbanization, in fact, intensified the need; the greater density of people and greater proximity of individuals crowded into restricted space created an ever-increasing psychological need for both physical and psychic distance. In short, readers—even readers in groups that a century before would not have been expected to have any private space of their own (women, young people, servants)—had private spaces to use as retreats when they needed or wanted to be alone, or when they were reading something not publicly approved by the moral or political or family establishment.

From the beginning, moreover, novels were artifacts of the world of print. They had been conceived that way, and they lent themselves readily to the physical, social, and psychological circumstances that affected potential readers of printed books. Print had, of course, been around for centuries by the time the novel began to emerge, and many literary kinds had already exploited some of its distinct possibilities, but (as A Tale of a Tub and The Dunciad Variorum and The Tragedy of Tragedies suggest) the awareness of print as a special phenomenon that offered specific possibilities became very much heightened for writers at the beginning of the eighteenth century. Even though earlier fiction occasionally showed itself aware that readers were reading printed books and not listening to a storyteller, their conventions—that of the reliable and unironic narrator, for example, or that of repetitive and predictable verbal patterns— are recognizably tied to oral conventions and ways of organizing.[19] It is the emerging novel that systematically begins to use a full range of print possibilities in developing and holding its relationships with readers. Print technology allows not only the visual devices in a novel like Tristram Shandy but the psychological assumptions made about epistolary voyeurism in Clarissa and Evelina, and one-on-one strategies that permit the ironies of the narrator to work in Tom Jones, and the presumption in Moll Flanders that readers can be sympathetic to the heroine because they are each responding alone as individuals seeing the difficulties of a particular case, rather than responding as a group with some sort of communal expectation agreed upon as a result of common social and moral assumptions.

Readers alone perhaps find it easier to empathize with the single individual who is usually the subject of a particular novel, and probably, too,

the concern with subjectivity finds a readier context among solitary readers than it would among a communal audience in a theater or a group
reading of the sort that became popular in Victorian times. Very likely
the phenomenology of reading novels has something to do, as well, with
the way novels capture the sense of loneliness and isolation that has
seemed to many cultural observers to be characteristic of modern life, for
the reading process and the central subject of attention seem to have a
common meeting ground in their attention to isolation as a phenomenon. There is a deep irony—rather like that at the center of *Tristram
Shandy*—in the way a communication process cuts us off from communion with other consciousnesses, but the act of reading a novel is, like
the act of contemplating one's own consciousness, an anti-social (or at
least asocial) act—very different from the sociality involved in hearing a
story or attending the performance of a play. The novel may be, in spite
of its famous societal concerns, an essentially individualistic and isola-
tionistic form. Certainly it impels its readers toward solitariness and
intensifies urban awareness of what it means to feel lonely and self-enclosed
even when hundreds of people are almost close enough to touch yet
beyond communal reach. The novel does represent humankind in society but it typically represents a single individual—alone—perceiving and
reflecting upon his or her place in that society.

The audience for novels has been often misunderstood in another way
as well, a way that has diverted attention from a second audience-con-
scious feature of early novels: its tendency to categorize and differentiate
readers and try to mediate among their conflicting habits and interests.
Just because it engages one reader at a time, the novel does not presume
either that all readers are hopelessly unique and subjective or that its
whole readership is ultimately similar. *Tristram Shandy*, which struggles
with one theoretical problem after another involving the novel, wrestles
the former issue rather fully in its concern to ask how novels can communicate at all when every individual in the world seems to have his or
her own hobbyhorse. Sterne ultimately suggests that common grounds of
awareness are possible when writers and readers are sufficiently self-conscious about their own eccentricities and capabilities of sharing. The
latter issue is, however, a prior one, for earlier forms of fiction had tended
to work in terms of an assumed community of response. Such an assumption was not, in fact, reasonable when some sort of communal ritual was
involved in the reception of the work, and in the early eighteenth century one can still see that assumption working in poetry, satire, and the
drama, although one can also see in the "scholarly" machinery of such
works as *The Dunciad Variorum* an awareness that communal response
was disintegrating and that some radical new address to the problem of

print readership was required. But writers of novels know that they are writing for readers alienated (at least in part) from that older world, and the early writers of novels consciously address the many and various readers they hope to attract.[20] Often writers struggle consciously with what they assume to be a new and critical problem of rhetoric, hoping to make all kinds of people feel at home in their texts. From the earliest stirrings of novelistic sensibility to the present, writers have shown an exceptional eagerness to appeal to wide and varied audiences, trying to make their work at once available to novice readers newly and barely literate at one extreme, and, at the other, writing for experienced, traditional, and demanding readers. The range of actual readers of novels—and the range of presumed readers—is extraordinary in literary history, and the novelistic consciousness of this range suggests that curiosity about the novel, or about its "emergence" or "rise," leads inevitably beyond "literature" to popular and ephemeral writings and to the remnants of the oral tradition that moral, urban, and enlightened observers were busy trying to destroy.

One other word about the novel's conception of audience. Those contemporaries who worried about the sociology of fiction in the early eighteenth century placed special emphasis upon the reading of novels by young people, those embarking upon a career, beginning marital relationships, or making other decisions involving their transition into the adult world. Adults of all kinds, whether or not they were themselves parents, public guardians of traditional institutions, or otherwise outgoing about their social and moral views, seem to have taken a proprietary interest in youth and produced a steady flow of conservative advice, most of which ran toward warnings that novels could corrupt young people in their turn toward adulthood. The novelists themselves had very different ideas, but novelists and moralists concurred in their notion that young people were an important segment in terms of both size and effect. One novelist after another clearly wrote with that expectation in mind. Almost all eighteenth-century novels, from those of Davys, Defoe, and Barker to those of Burney, Godwin, and Radcliffe, concentrated on character and situation with which the young could readily identify, and novelists ever since have continued to be preoccupied with the crises of the decisive moments in adolescence and early adulthood. Even those characters who are allowed to grow old in the course of their novels—and there are not many of them in early novels unless one considers figures like Tom and Sophia whose later life is briefly summarized at the end—primarily appear in early, formative stages of their lives when youthful readers would find them useful as potential models, cautionary figures, or simply as people in whose lives one could take a personal and vital interest.

A third neglected feature deriving from the novel's consciousness of audience is epistemological. One question that novels repeatedly ask is: How do you know? Most novels seem to begin in epistemology; certainly most address epistemological issues in ways that suggest urgent engagement. How do you know when someone loves you? How do you know when you are fit (or destined) for a certain course of life? How do you know whether, in a time of plague, you should stay in the city or flee to the country? How do you know when to trust your own instincts and desires rather than those of family and friends that you have been taught to respect? How do you know how to judge the motives behind people's actions, getting beyond the fogs of gossip, community opinion, and conventional conclusions that tend to limit our perceptions of humanity and neatly confine our responses into categorical approval or disapproval? Novels are not of course the only texts with these concerns, but they make the concerns readily available to readers who can comfortably "live" within their texts.

Novels like *Tom Jones* or *The Ordeal of Richard Feverel* or *David Copperfield* or *Point Counter Point* are sometimes called novels of education, and others (*The Plague,* for example, or *The Counterfeiters*) are sometimes called philosophical novels because in different ways they forcefully address epistemological questions of enduring interest. Direct impact on readers is usually hard to measure, and (especially in later novels) the pragmatic aims of novels are often difficult to unravel. Even the several kinds of criticism that concentrate on readers offer little real practical help in sorting out epistemological issues, for (following the basic trends of earlier criticisms) reader response criticisms seem ultimately after larger game, preferring aesthetic, or sometimes political, concerns to issues involving basic and simple human needs to know about the world and to pursue that need in the reading of novels. But novels do minister to such simple, low-brow needs, often openly. The guidance provided by the narrator in *Tom Jones,* often in ironic or otherwise indirect ways but nevertheless always firmly controlled toward a systematic examination of how the faculty of judgment works, offers the reader practical experience in epistemology. In the words of John Preston, "the book is *about* judgment. . . . Fielding is quite aware that his fiction has the same aims as Locke's *Essay*."[21]

Omniscient novels, when they are not too busy showing off the *author's* extraordinary ability to sift and sort, sometimes offer practice in discrimination and interpretation of one or another difficult aspect of the world they describe. The fact that they provide the illusion of "giving" us the world—providing a key that unlocks the secrets of principles unknown to the novice—has a lot to do with the authority that novels often possess for the young. The process by which we come to know is sometimes clarified by the way shrouds of uncertainty fall away in novels. The relentless sense of sorting—finding the "rules" that govern a particular social or cultural or political ritual or round—is characteristic of novels as we experience them. It has sometimes been less easy for modern readers to see how thoroughly first-person novels, especially eighteenth-century first-person novels, are involved in epistemological concerns, although at the time the novel emerged as a significant reading phenomenon it must have actually been easier to see Defoe's and Richardson's concern with epistemology rather than Henry Fielding's more complex, experimental, and openly intellectualized engagement. The easier access of eighteenth-century readers to Defoe's or Richardson's epistemological concerns involves their deeper and clearer engagement with the purposes of diary and spiritual autobiography, purposes which the novel took over more or less intact simply by imitating first-person narration and pretending that its lives were actual rather than fictional. Because a major function of autobiography (or more precisely of the journal keeping which preceded autobiography and upon which the finished form of early English autobiography ultimately depended) was to clarify for the autobiographer the patterns and meanings that could presumably be discovered by the close observation of the details of a life, the epistemological function of first-person narrative was deeply imbedded in the form. Even the most naive readers knew how to see it.

Non-readers, in fact, participated as well in that particular kind of knowledge because of the prominence of oral versions of personal narration in confessionals, autobiographical anecdotes, and the distinctive Puritan phenomena of public "testimonies," so that first-person narrative, suspect in its biases and conclusions, had become for eighteenth-century readers a form of discourse readily available because of widespread prior knowledge of its purposes and expectations. The expectations were, in fact, quite sophisticated, for built into them was the implicit need to evaluate the observation—not just take it at face value—and to distinguish between an immediate observation and the context it ultimately is placed in as time passes and related observations stack up. The extraordinary implications of this expectation become clear if one remembers that in traditional oral tales the reliability of the narrator had never been an issue. Such easy authority is, however, never available to written narrative in the eighteenth century, for the prevalence of diary keeping—and the epistemological practices it harbored and promoted—created a climate of incessant questioning and second-guessing. Instead of authority and certitude, therefore, first-person perspective offered a field for speculation and sorting; to recount events as personal experience was to raise the questions of meaning and significance that a diarist faced in reviewing his or her own life. "Face value" was not a viable option for a

diarist, spiritual autobiographer, or a first-person narrator of any kind at
the beginning of the eighteenth century. Questions of reliability of fact
and interpreter were always open and always urgent.

Novelists as early as Defoe used this sense of uncertainty and questing
as an essential aspect of their narrative. Robinson Crusoe, once he becomes
self-conscious and curious about the direction of his life, keeps a journal
as long as he has ink, and part of his "finished" narrative—a revision,
retelling, and summary from a perspective later in life—involves comparing his initial chronicle of events on the island with two distinct later
perspectives. The narrative of Moll Flanders constantly raises, simply
through its choice of point of view, questions about her intentions and
the reliability of her judgment about herself. *Journal of the Plague Year*,
written in the same year as *Moll*, makes the question of the narrator's
knowledge the metaphor for that book's central issue. What *is* the evidence of providential intention in the plague? Should the healthy flee to
safer climes or remain behind in the city and trust in the divine power
to protect? Defoe finally does not say, but the preoccupation of the narrator with how to read the signs and decide what he should do is an
epistemological paradigm for the age. In the many epistolary novels (e.g.,
Pamela and *Evelina*) that harvest the first-person heritage of diaries, the
perspective of the protagonist is repeatedly tested against that of other
participants in the narrative, and the effect often depends on gaining a
comparative view on facts and potential meanings. Epistemology is not
all there is, but often (even in so sophisticated a novel as *Clarissa*) the
wrestling with contradictory perspectives is more important to the reading process than following the action.

Learning how to read events is an essential aspect of discovering character—for readers of someone's narrative and for narrators about themselves—and the meaning of the narrative often is almost coincident with
the meaning that emerges about the pattern of the protagonist's life. It
is central to the narrative workings of many, perhaps most, eighteenth-
century novels for an epistemological tension to exist between an "I"
perspective and another larger perspective struggling to emerge through
the I or through comparative perspectives. The "flawed omniscience" of
Tom Jones aspires to the same effect, presenting as it does an authoritative voice and view that often turn out to be facetious or misleading so
that readers, as a crucial step in their reading experience, have to sort
matters for themselves, being sure not to fall too quickly for what appears
to be true. Such epistemology is central to almost all eighteenth-century
fiction, however it chooses to present the choices of meaning to the
reader. No later reader, no matter how well schooled in rhetorical method
or critical skills, has ever been as well equipped to probe uncertainties of

perspective and to question how things appear—on the way to deciding how to construe personal events in some larger sense of cosmic meaning. A significant possibility of point of view is thus open to written narrative at the beginning of the eighteenth century even before any literary "creators" (in the usual sense) have begun to experiment with it, and the ability of the novel to cope with epistemological issues is, first, built into the most "natural" form of narration, and then projected into more indirect and complex forms.

I I I

"YOUR story, if you please," says Parson Adams to Mr. Wilson a few moments after they first meet in the middle of *Joseph Andrews*, and for the next three chapters Mr. Wilson obliges with the story of his life. Mr. Wilson's autobiography is one of three insets, or stories-within, in *Joseph Andrews*. *Tom Jones* includes even more stories-within and achieves a greater variety in them: the Man of the Hill recites his life story much as Mr. Wilson does; the King of the Gypsies provides an historical account of his people; there are inset performances of *Hamlet* and of a traveling puppet show; and Mrs. Fitzpatrick, Sophia, and Tom all have a turn telling their version of their own life story up to the moment. Similar stories-within occur in Defoe, Haywood, Sarah Fielding, Smollett, and other eighteenth-century novelists, and in fact, both the novel and older kinds of narrative often incorporate into themselves complete stories that are not, strictly speaking, related very closely to the main thrust of their own plot. Such stories-within have never seemed troublesome in either romance or epic where they have always been more or less expected, but modern criticism has found them embarrassing and difficult to bear in novels, probably because they violate formal preconceptions of how novels are supposed to be organized. When they are being polite, critics often call stories-within "interpolations," as if they were a foreign substance adulterating an otherwise pure text, and less politely they are often called "excrescences" or "blots" that ruin or at least mar the unity of the whole that contains them. The recent fashion has been to explain them in some way—usually painfully—as part of some larger and hitherto unperceived holistic conception of form. But whether or not they can be pardoned or justified formally, stories-within plainly are a feature of eighteenth-century novels, a feature that was at the time common and readily accepted and that was subtly adapted into later novels as inset, flashback, anecdote, or pretended exposition. Stories-within are one of several digressive and interruptive features that novels regularly possess, and for-

malist criticism has been especially embarrassed by these features because
they seem to threaten the simplistic notions of unity and organicism that
sponsor most discussions of structure.

The presence in *Peregrine Pickle* of "The Memoirs of a Lady of Quality"—a story-within of more than 50,000 words—is perhaps the most
extreme single instance in an eighteenth-century novel, and Smollett's
decision to put it there in a 1751 novel, just in the wake of *Tom Jones*,
suggests how clear Smollett as a fledgling novelist was about novelistic
expectation of this feature even that early in the novel's history. A second story-within, involving the famous contemporary episode known as
the Annesley case, confirms Smollett's willingness to incorporate stories
altogether complete in themselves; one can account for Smollett's two
"interpolations" (which together encompass more than a fifth of the novel)
on the grounds of their contemporary interest, their thematic relevance,
or his desire to parody competing forms of narrative; but the most interesting thing about them is that they are, like Fielding's and Sterne's
stories-within, incorporated and not just simply interpolated. That is,
their presence in the novel involves an ongoing interaction with the
characters involved in the main narrative action, and (although the main
plot may for all practical purposes stand still) the fact of the telling of
the story-within is somehow taken account of.

Stories-within exist in romance and epic, too, but there they have
neat and tidy borders that divide them from previous and subsequent
action. Hearers may applaud or otherwise show their approbation or disapproval of the story and the storyteller, but seldom do they interact with
the telling. In novels, however, there tends to be emphasis on the telling
itself—the tone of voice, facial expressions, body movement—and on
the varieties of response that are elicited. Instead of a communal response
or one in which one hearer speaks for all in a kind of synecdoche of
consensus gentium, the several responses may vary considerably, and the
story-within becomes part of the process of action, even though events
there may not necessarily have later implications for the main plot. The
tendency of novels to involve the story-within integrally into the larger
whole, to take something already whole in itself and treat it as part of
another whole-in-the-making, is strong enough to infect most eighteenth-century novels and novelists and powerful enough in its organi-
zational effects and implications to affect as well the practice of later
novelists. The "whole-as-observed-part" strategy allows novels to take
into themselves ready-made, already organized chunks of material and
domesticate that material to quite other uses.[22]

The Man of the Hill episode in *Tom Jones* is perhaps the most famous
story-within in any novel, and in many ways it is typical, although no

one instance adequately suggests what novelists are able to do with the feature. By comparing it, however, with other stories-within, we can gain some idea of the varieties of artistic possibility and also begin to notice how some of the novel's roots reach outward from traditional narrative, entangling neighbors and colonizing as they go. Anyone coming to Tom Jones for the first time is apt to notice immediately how stylistically distinctive the Man's story is in the context of Fielding's novel. The Man is solemn, dogmatic, self-righteous, and withdrawn from all social caring, in sharp contrast to the narrator of the novel who wants to seem the precise opposite of each of those things, and the Man's style is heavy and grave, asking for an audience response almost opposite to that demanded by Fielding's larger, friendlier, and more expansive narrative style. As a whole, the Man's story may remind us of a certain sort of autobiographical novel (Defoe's perhaps) or of the kind of spiritual autobiography that lies behind so much eighteenth-century fiction; its rhetorical force in the text is partly parodic, and some hint of what Fielding thinks of its tone and style is provided by the kinds of responses the man gets from his audience. Tom tries to be respectful and polite, but ends up unimpressed, and he has to spend most of his energy keeping order because Partridge, the other hearer, is so busy responding enthusiastically—but with no understanding or appreciation of the Man's didactic aims. Tom, on his way to becoming sensible and mature, is the type of the Judicious Reader, and Partridge of the Credulous one, and the two sets of responses together, which absorb a lot of our attention throughout the Man's story, make the story-within a performance and episode in the novel, rather than an inset of the type included impersonally in romance. We continue to learn about Tom's character and Partridge's, about the whole process of responding to the actions and words of others, and about the nature of education by example (learning in fact the reverse of what the Man had apparently hoped to teach), and although the main plot of the novel stands still (unless perhaps the Man's example serves as a cautionary factor for Tom), the story-within is still incorporated into the basic fabric of the novel.

The Man's story operates in another way, too—or rather, it appears to operate in another way but does not, thereby exhibiting a contrast to the way other stories-within do operate. The episode of the Man of the Hill is strategically placed in Tom Jones near the center, at a parallel point to the episode at Mr. Wilson's house in Joseph Andrews, and the Man's life story is in many ways like that of Mr. Wilson, although he has become a bitter recluse rather than the disengaged, retired benevolist that Mr. Wilson had become. Mr. Wilson had, of course, proved at last to be a central figure in Joseph Andrews, emerging from the story-within to take a place among the main characters and to participate crucially in the plot, and the parallel situation in a novel seven years later by the same novelist sets up rhetorical significance to the plot, making the Learned Reader or Experienced one suspect that the Man will turn out to be someone significant to the plot and to Tom. That expectation is, of course, frustrated in *Tom Jones*—the better the reader, the more easy the rug-pulling victimization in Fielding's use of expectation—but its very rhetorical possibility of self-allusion is a reminder of one other way the novel can involve and incorporate stories-within instead of just surrounding and interpolating them. However rambling and digressive novels may be, they tend to connect the loose ends, giving some sense of movement forward in time and human evolution rather than simply gathering miscellanea into a basket.

Another variation occurs in the "Memoirs of a Lady of Quality" in *Peregrine Pickle*. The Lady's narration there is quite straightforward and proceeds without interruption (and perhaps therefore is less functional than the typical stories-within of Fielding or Sterne), but at the end her veracity seems to be challenged when "one of the gentlemen present, roundly taxed her with want of candour, in suppressing some circumstances of her life, which he thought essential in the consideration of her character," a taxing that made her "redden . . . at this peremptory charge."[23] Actually, the challenger only wants to compliment the Lady and increase the audience's sense of her basic decency, and she has already been more than frank about her weaknesses. But Smollett here toys with novelistic expectation—again one explored by Fielding—that first-person narration may not be altogether reliable, reminding us that tellers of autobiography are not necessarily their own best judges or the most accurate reporters, nor do they necessarily have the most detailed and precise memories of crucial facts.

Both Mr. Wilson and the Man of the Hill apparently do their best to tell their stories accurately and without any attempt to whitewash their motives or actions, and if we disagree with their views it is because we may think that they have overreacted to their experiences or drawn the wrong conclusion rather than having been "unreliable" in the usual sense. But Mrs. Fitzpatrick is a more complex case. When Sophia and Tom have opportunities to tell their stories, we are dramatically reminded that even the best characters may not tell the whole truth however committed they may be to wisdom and virtue. Tom tells Mrs. Miller "his whole History, without once mentioning the Name of *Sophia*" (XIV, v, 760), and Sophia likewise gives her history without mentioning Tom. And Mrs. Fitzpatrick, although capable of repeating a long letter word for word, conveniently omits several matters material to her own character and destiny; her worry that "I shall tire you with a Detail of so many minute Circumstances" (XI, iv, 585) camouflages her reluctance to be candid about other matters, and what she omits to tell has a darker side than the lacunae of Sophia and Tom. The novel's allegiance to the written mode, in which the reliability of the narrator is an issue, as distinguished from oral literature where the narrator's reliability is unquestioned, is thus clear in the way even "oral" stories-within function. It happens in novel after novel at a time in literary history when recognizing formal and historical allegiances was always helpful, sometimes crucial.

The wholes that Sterne ingests—sermons, ecclesiastical and legal documents, tales like that of Slawkenbergius or the quite different one of Maria—are also incorporated, rather than simply included, and Sterne is eager to prove to his readers, often flamboyantly, that he can absorb *anything* into his fabric and make it seem part of the larger whole. No anecdote or verbal formula or tale or life story or even visual device can escape his sense of interrelationship or contamination: those parts may be in fact set pieces or in some way excerptible as wholes in themselves, but they cannot be pulled out of *Tristram Shandy* without leaving the traces of their incorporation. Even after completing the reading of the novel, readers cannot see or hear about a long nose again or encounter a whisker or a piece of bridgework—let alone read the tale of Slawkenbergius or the story of Toby's wound—without remembering exactly how Sterne has made it irretrievably his own, part of some larger whole, in the process of ingesting it and letting his own words and plots entangle and interact with it. One of the novel's most exquisite ironies is that Walter Shandy's great rival work, the *Tristra-paedia,* had no effect on Tristram's life or on his book, in effect self-destructing in its own creation—"every day a page or two became of no consequence" (V, xvi, 448)—even while works which have no earthly connection became entangled hopelessly with Tristram's fate and art. *Tristram Shandy* "proves" that novels can alter reality, as works of education and philosophy cannot.

Richardson is a little different, and I have avoided citing examples from him because, although he does use stories-within, the wholes he incorporates are largely of a non-narrative kind that point forward in the history of narrative and backward in the history of literary forms more generally, and I turn now to another structural feature that is clearly related, one involving a larger kind of inclusivity that, although practiced by almost all novelists, Richardson among early novelists represents best.

Stories-within are not the only "interruptive" feature that contributes to the digressiveness of the novel that Fielding and Sterne celebrate.

However comfortably or uncomfortably stories-within fit into novels, they are still *narrative* in their basic organization, and, even when they advance the main plot not an inch or even when their tone is in sharp contrast to the prevailing tone of the whole, they still operate in the same causal and temporal fashion as does the main narrative. They may digress from the main narrative at a variety of angles and only return to the point of departure after some singular moves and contortions (like Tristram's diagram of his digressions [VI, x1]), but as long as some story is being told, a basic narrativity is still involved, and the human desire for narrative is still in some form being addressed, even if in a piecemeal kind of way. But there is more to any novel than narrative, and the way novels acquire or annex other forms of discourse is one of their most important features. In two and a half centuries, few critics have felt at home with the promiscuous inclusivity of the novel, perhaps because it is so hard to talk about within a conventional formalist aesthetic. Even tolerant narratologists fall silent in the face of discourse that seems not to further the story. But readers seldom seem disturbed by it unless it goes absurdly out of control. Despite its critical awkwardness, it is a feature that any theory of the novel has to account for and any history of the novel should study, for it has implications both for how novels work and for any account of how they came historically to take the odd shape they did.

For long stretches at a time, Richardson's novels do not read like narrative at all, and they are only more blatantly discursive, not more fundamentally so, than those of Fielding or Thackeray or Melville or Lawrence or James or Barth. Reading one of the many abridgments of *Clarissa* easily demonstrates the point: an abridger can cut the bulk of the novel by half or more without necessarily diminishing the plot.[24] In the novel as Richardson wrote it, Clarissa endlessly elaborates and so do all her correspondents, not only filling in details but also explaining thoughts, diagramming reasons, laying out plans, providing context and elaborating assumptions and metaphors, reflecting, expanding, arguing, dickering, qualifying. It is easy to steer around this "texture," skipping whole pages without losing one thread-end of action or even noticeably affecting our basic loyalties. Readers of an abridged *Clarissa* might easily not know that they were missing anything at all, but an experienced reader of *Clarissa* comes away from even the best abridgment feeling frustrated and cheated, as if it were an altogether different novel, faster, less complex, less convoluted and suggestive. We have no way to measure the texture of novels as we have for action and plot; I could assert, much like an eighteenth-century commentator, that the soul of *Clarissa* lies in its sentiments rather than its plot, and I would be right, but we still have no way to chart what verbal texture is to the whole of the novel. But any detailed examination of the several directions of the prose—in Richardson or almost any other nov-elist except those like Hemingway who have been consciously spare in their exposition—will suggest how much of most novels has nothing to do with narrative movement or indeed with any action or story or plot at all.

Sometimes there are set pieces of discourse in novels, such as the ones in the first chapters of almost every book of Tom Jones or the ones Mel-ville places strategically in Moby Dick. Such mini-essays (or even maxi-ones) may deal with anything—literature, philosophy, education, ethics, whaling, hats, cats, gnats, knots, the nature of madness. But although such pieces are important to notice as continuing features in novels of age after age and culture after culture, they are by no means the most frequent and pervasive kind of discourse contained in novels. We are in the realm of that discourse when Joseph and Parson Adams argue about public schools and private education, when Adams and Barnabas discuss Methodism or Adams and Trulliber charity, when Lovelace speculates about libertinism or Clarissa waxes nostalgic for old family values, when Walter Shandy discourses on names or rhetoric or educational philoso-phy, or my Uncle Toby wanders onto bridges and hornworks, or Crusoe or Moll hold forth on the virtues of the middle station in life or the joys of a new world of colonization and trade or the horrors of restlessness and confinement, or Evelina speaks of preparations for a ball. These inclusions sometimes involve formal compositions, essays, or disserta-tions, sometimes they exist as conversation, controversy, or debate, sometimes as description, "fine writing," or undigested chunks that writ-ers cannot bear to "prune."

It may be that there is no such thing as "pure" narrativity, and cer-tainly it is true that any story is likely to point a "moral," imply some larger "truth," or engage one or more ideas in some way that seems at least momentarily persuasive. Romance and epic are no more free of elements of such discourse than novels, and it is not that the presence of discursive wholes, fragments, and degradable parts is a feature of novels that distinguishes them from other forms of fiction. Rather, novels carry to a greater extreme what any narrative kind necessarily engages to some degree. Romances contain discursive passages, but novels take the fea-ture and run with it, sometimes in extended ways that illustrate and stretch their ideological and ideational commitments. The fact that nov-els are conceived within the expectations and possibilities of the print medium is once again crucial here because any discourse can more readily expand in a printed version, move in more directions, stay longer, go on less predictable tangents, and become a focus of attention for long periods of time without endangering the narrative center. When the excursion is ended, the book is still there and the story goes on, and readers who have become distracted or forgetful can look back if they need to, while an oral teller is not subject to devices of instant replay or individualized review.

Because novels use discursive elements so liberally and do such varied things with them, they look to models beyond those available in romances whose tendency to discourse is relatively subdued and suppressed because of the form's oral origins. The penchant of critics to treat novels almost altogether in narrative terms, ignoring the non-narrative parts, obscures the discursive resonances that novels achieve, a resonance that is greatly enhanced by the size and magnitude of eighteenth- and nineteenth-century novels, which typically take advantage of the fact of print, the phenomenology of solitary reading, and a conviction that readers have plenty of time to invest. Novelists can write long and inclusive books that touch many bases and work many styles and modes. Neglecting the inclusiveness of novels also has helped obscure some important roots of the novel in non-narrative forms, forms that released some of their hold on readers when the novel took over functions that a generation before had been performed—in response to reader needs—by a variety of discursive writings.

Much of the novel's appeal has always been in its ability to do so many things, to meet at once so many needs of readers, and one reason for that capability is its incredible capacity to include—to absorb other things whole, to take over strategies and teaching devices perfected in other forms, to move easily among different modes and styles in the process of telling a story and at the same time doing some thinking out loud, some propagandizing, and some wandering. No single novel is all things to all people, but it may be a great many of them, and as a literary species the novel is distinctive for its eclecticism and imperialism, almost as if writers in the early eighteenth century surveyed the field of things in print, made a list of needs being addressed in literature and para-literature, and set out to create an inclusive form that would take over and put the smaller, more simple, operators out of business. John Steinbeck described one of his novels as a box into which he could put whatever he had.[25] It is an apt metaphor except that few novels, even well-made ones, are as shapely as a box. But what novelists put in has many shapes and sizes, not all of which fit neatly or comfortably into the containing whole.

I V

OF all the prominent features of the novel, the one that has most often embarrassed critics is a tonal and rhetorical one: its didacticism. In eigh-

teenth-century novels and many nineteenth-century ones, the didacticism is open and intense, and modern readers often balk at being addressed
so directly and insistently, especially when (as is frequent in eighteenth-
century examples) what is being taught goes against the grain of modern
sensibility. The world behind the early novel is quite a different world
from our own even if the buds of modernism were beginning to open
noticeably then, and a good many ethical and religious concerns that
were of great importance to eighteenth-century writers now seem to us
dated, provincial, and unbearably trivial. When criticism has had to deal
with didacticism in the eighteenth century, in the novel and elsewhere,
it has almost always become hesitant and apologetic, and the tendency
has been to minimize or deny the presence of didactic elements as much
as possible and to pronounce the residue an unfortunate flaw. But finally
it is no favor to the novel as a literary species to ignore or explain away
so prominent an early feature—especially since the feature is retained in
somewhat more disguised form in novels up to the present time—and in
any case it seems important to try to understand why eighteenth-century
writers and readers collaborated in allowing it, even insisting on it.
Didacticism is a standard feature of the novel, early and late, and the
rhetoric associated with didactic aims remains crucial to its tone, pace,
and effects. Besides, its aggressive attitude toward readers and its critical
view of contemporary social mores—both products of didacticism—played
a vital role in the emergence of the species.

Almost any eighteenth-century novel, even *Fanny Hill,* shows how
central didacticism was to a conception of the novel in the beginning.
All of Defoe's major characters preach to us, and so does Defoe himself
in his own voice, sometimes in counterpoint. The prefaces to the novels,
as well as many passages put in the mouth of the first-person narrator or
of some other character, are mostly at one with Defoe's didacticism elsewhere in his moral treatises, political and economic pamphlets, periodical essays, biographies, and miscellaneous acts of journalism in which he
reviews his culture and proceeds unabashedly to instruct the times. There
are in Defoe (as we might well expect in a writer who wrote so much and
who sought so many different perspectives on his world) inconsistencies
and contradictions, but in almost everything he wrote he has a palpable
design on the reader, and he speaks to us for our own good. His tone is
insistently didactic; he wants to affect his society, even straighten it out,
and his method is essentially a homiletic one: point out what is wrong,
tell your audience what is right, cite an authority or provide a reason,
and exhort, exhort, exhort. Defoe exhorts very well, and when his subject is economics or politics or social reforms likely to be supported by
later generations, few readers are bothered by his bias and his fire. On
subjects on which we have different biases, however, such as religion

and ethics, we are much more likely to bristle regardless of the subtlety or power of his rhetoric. Rhetoric, in modern criticism, remains a good word when those who employ it do so in support of aesthetic ideas or cultural notions that we continue to treasure; but its odor offends us when it rises from issues that are for us tainted or suspect, especially issues in theology or moral philosophy where our emotions attach quite differently from those of Defoe's contemporaries.

We can't help it that we are twentieth-century readers, of course, any more than Defoe can help it that he is a figure dyed in Restoration, Puritan, and London wool, but we are better off noting our own presentist limits and admitting the historical prominence of the feature. The didacticism of Aubin, Davys, Richardson, both Fieldings, Rowe, Lennox, MacKenzie, Burney, and even Sterne poses essentially the same problem for us as does that of Defoe. Attempts to rescue writers by making them more urbane, "modern," or "universal"—Richardson for his clinical interest in feminine consciousness, female sensibility, and the psychopathology of rape and other coercions; Sterne for his wit, humor, and bawdry—seem ultimately a dooming strategy. Their texts are still going to show where they stand, and their heavy hands on our shoulders are not going to go away. To read Sterne or Richardson without the didacticism is to read a deformed novelist, one missing crucial parts. It is easy enough to read any eighteenth-century novelist for something else and find the text palatable in spite of the unfortunate didacticism, but such selective reading is perverse and destines writers to a short life of fashion. Many early novelists traditionally left out of the canon—Jane Barker, for example, or Sarah Scott—would find their rightful place in literary history if critics could suspend their disbelief long enough to embrace the didactic rhetoric in their books and see their accomplishments both as units of discourse and as novelistic wholes.

Ultimately it is more promising to admit the prominent and lengthy didacticism in eighteenth-century novelists and inquire why it is there. Did it serve a useful function for readers? Did it meet a specific cultural need? Did writers find satisfaction in engaging it? Smug presentism does not grapple with the issue, for although it is true that most writers do more than they know when they write, it is also true that conscious intention is worth something (if not everything) in art as in life. By engaging didactic impulses so directly and openly, eighteenth-century novelists sent their books on their way in a definite, specific, and usually irreversible direction. It will not finally do to "explain" Defoe's didacticism by saying that he only mouthed moral platitudes about Moll Flanders and that his real interest was to explore the sociology of eighteenth-century criminals or to produce irony for its own sake. It will not do because such explanations are too simple in rejecting the obvious to look at some chosen obliquity. It will not do even though the explanation is party right: mouthing platitudes *is* something that Defoe does, but it is not *all* he does. The snide and dismissive approach to Defoe—and the same could be said for almost any eighteenth-century writer who participates in the social and ethical issues of the day—confuses convention, adaptation, rhetoric, and complexity of mind with insincerity and then with inauthenticity. It does not help us understand the novel because it does not lead us to its actual, describable features.

Recognizing didacticism as a prominent novelistic feature suggests, yet again, that in seeking the origins of the novel we ought to cast our net widely, recognizing that the greedy maw of the novel takes what it wants where it can find it. But the importance of recognizing this feature points not only backward but forward as well. Later novelists—Twain, Lawrence, Joyce, Woolf, Bellow, Lessing, Mailer, and Coover, for example—have found ways more acceptable to our culture (because their culture is more like ours) to convey their didactic aims, but they are clearly in the line of writers who have a palpable design on us.

V

NOT all of the features I have named are attractive or pleasing features to a modern or even an early eighteenth-century sensibility, but they are in fact features that must be admitted and understood if one is to have a proper notion of what not only novels are but what the novel is and can do. One question that literary criticism must ask about any literary form is: What does it do for its readers, not just on an aesthetic level and not just immediately—but what does it do for the total reader who leaves the book and reenters life beyond its covers? What functions—educational, recreative, psychological, aesthetic, philosophical, social, or emotional—does it perform? For literary history that seeks to explore a species at a particular moment in history, the adaptation of the question is: What did it do for its original readers? Why did they seek it out? What did they see in it for them? And when one seeks the origins of a species whose beginnings can be traced to a more or less specific period of time, a variety of questions are corollaries: What needs did the species meet? Were these needs new to the culture or were they previously met by some other literary form or cultural ritual? If I am right that the novel emerged from a context rather than flashing out of the blue, materializing from some preexistent form, or updating some older form, then there ought to be a historical continuity from species to species or form to form as needs modify and writers discover how to adapt to those needs.

The novel's imperialism—its ability to take over features from other species and assimilate them into a new form—is well known, but we have to be clearer about what those features are and where they come from. The features that I have described here and at the end of the previous chapter—especially those resisted by traditional criticism and literary history—need to be accounted for in any theory of origins, and I turn in the rest of the book to two kinds of tasks. In Chapters three through six I describe the social history of the late seventeenth and early eighteenth century as a way of suggesting things on the minds of potential readers; my task here is to recreate the cultural consciousness, or rather, the piece of it most relevant to readers of novels. Then I turn to writings—few of them narrative, even few of them fictional, most of them materials of popular print that had little or no "literary" status—that contain some of the crucial features I have been describing.

II

CONTEXTS

CHAPTER THREE

Readers Reading

■

FOR literary historians, everything ultimately comes down to what people read. But culturally there are more basic issues and prior ones. What people read depends upon several things, not all of them traditional concerns of the literary historian: what reading material is available, how open the avenues of access are to it, what strictures, biases, and expectations the culture imposes on reading choices, and what readers want and expect from their reading. All these are in a sense extra-literary issues, but the last one especially involves broad questions about human psychology and about experiences and desires far from the world of books and print. Because what readers want may not be altogether the same as what they say they want or think they want, and because writers, publishers, and booksellers have tried to impose agendas of their own, three centuries of bookshelves have been lined with season after season of remainders—"Martyrs of Pies," Dryden called them unceremoniously, and (reminding us that paper can be put to other purposes than print) "Reliques of the Bum."[1] Still, the failed programs and bad guesses of commercial publishers should not be allowed to obscure the fundamentally shrewd analysis of human desire that made the publishing industry, for three centuries, the central vehicle for broad-scale human communication. It is not that publishers and writers have always provided the right answers to readers' questions and satisfied their desires, but they have been very good—much better than critics and historians using hindsight—at sensing areas of interest and concern. Desire is by nature too subtle and

6 1

complex to be readily addressed or translated by words or those who employ them, and seldom do historical records of dazzling success suggest precise readings of cultural taste or need, but in the record of patterns of publication are reliable indicators of issues and concerns on the minds of readers at specific cultural moments.

Reading—even in bookish times like the nineteenth century—is, of course, only one of the possible ways to acquire knowledge, stimulate fancy, gain pleasure, and otherwise minister to human needs, and in Chapters Four through Six I will put the literary experience of the early novel into a larger historical and cultural perspective by suggesting prevailing social and psychological patterns that influenced readers at the time the novel emerged. But first I want to sort out what we know about the identity of readers and about their habits in the years immediately before the emergence of the novel, for (to some extent at least) the history of the novel is the history of readers—their needs, their desires, their concerns, and their potential.

However similar or dissimilar in other ways, readers of eighteenth-century English novels all had one thing in common: they had the ability to read, an ability that was far from universal then and that a century before had been a very scarce skill indeed.[2] The question of who was literate in early eighteenth-century Britain is a complex one, muddied by unreliable statistics, uncertain definitions, and considerably different incentives to read among different social and religious groups and from one part of the country to another. That question is tangled with the question of what portion of the reading public became readers of novels, and because these two questions are crucial to any account of the novel's origins and there has been widespread misinformation and misunderstanding on both questions, I want to set out here what we know historically about readers and reading in the seventeenth and eighteenth centuries and then suggest what we can reasonably conclude about the audience that early English novels tried to address. It is still to some extent true that "information [about the reading public] is scanty and difficult to interpret," as Ian Watt said thirty years ago,[3] but some crucial facts are now available, and we are in a better position to infer the desires of readers who turned to the novel when they found their needs recognized there.

I

IN 1790, Edmund Burke is said to have estimated that there were 80,000 readers in all of England.[4] It is the only contemporary estimate of English

literacy before the nineteenth century, and, except for retrospective estimates—based on signatures in documents, on what modern demographers call "back projection," or on analogy and intuition—it is the only
numerical "figure" we have for eighteenth-century literacy in England,
Wales, or Scotland.[5] That number, although disputed from the beginning, has always haunted the study of literacy, in part because it is a
clean number and carries with it the tyranny of apparent "fact" and in
part because it is so shockingly low. If Burke is right, only about 1.3
percent of the approximately six million people in England at the time
of the American Revolution could read and write. The figure may of
course have been wrong, wildly wrong. It is only a guess in the first place,
and we do not know whether it is based on any meaningful calculation:
it may have been a figure in whole cloth, a stab in the dark like police
or newspaper estimates of crowds at picnics and parades, and (since it
was published after Burke's death) it could even have been invented for
Burke by someone else in a later generation.[6] But because of its "eyewitness" status and because it has about it the aura of authenticity that any
number (however generated or invented) tends to command among even
the most skeptical scholars, the guess of Burke has always had to be
reckoned with, and it still casts shadows today, in spite of projects to put
such issues on a factual basis. There is a powerful tendency to interpret
scattered data either to correct Burke dramatically (as nineteenth- and
early twentieth-century social historians tended to do) or to correct his
correctors and return to his pessimistic conclusion.

Beyond guesses like Burke's and contemporary anecdotes about individual habits and circumstances, what we actually know about seven-
teenth- and eighteenth-century literacy comes primarily from the
observations of social historians and, more recently, from minutely detailed
but still fragmentary studies of local records, where signatures on documents can be counted and an approximation of reading ability estimated
from the ability to sign. The results of the latter effort, systematically
engaged in recent years by the Cambridge Group for the History of Population and Social Structure, are scattered and far from definitive. But
even with their substantial limitations, the figures and statistical estimates generated by recent historical studies of literacy provide for the
first time a fairly accurate sense of what proportion of people in the seventeenth and eighteenth centuries were literate, who those people were
and where they lived, and how and when their habits changed.

A few years ago, literacy study was the glamour stock among historians, and there was widespread confidence that we would soon be able to
talk with great precision not only about exactly who was literate but what
literacy meant for societies as wholes; correlations could be established,

it was widely believed, between literacy rates and economic growth, for example, and the historical model could help to address poignant con-temporary issues, especially in the Third World. High hopes have now given way to disappointment about historical data and disillusionment with modern applications. Information coming from different sources has sometimes been contradictory and interpretations incompatible, and def-initions of terms and measurement of data are often so problematic that it has become fashionable in some intellectual circles to distrust literacy experts and treat them as cliometric quacks. But if confidence was once too great and expectation too high, the disappointment is now too easy as well, and the best scholarship—properly sorted, collated, and inter-preted—gives us crucial information about eighteenth-century readers, information that is useful in surveying the contexts of the early English novel and suggesting why it emerged and took some of the directions it did.

Studies of historical literacy cannot, of course, tell us exactly who early readers of novels were, one by one, or give us detailed individual portraits, nor can they describe in profound detail the full character and deep psychological profile of readers more generally. Still the information they offer, qualified appropriately, can suggest how the reading of novels was related to other kinds of reading, provide clues about the emergence of the novel at a particular cultural moment, and help us understand what kinds of intellectual and emotional needs early readers had and how they expected novels to minister to those needs.

A word of caution at the beginning. All the numbers and percentages I will quote about literacy—although arrived at by good scholars using the best methods available—must individually be taken with several grains of salt. I use these numbers at all with some trepidation because of the rhetorical tyranny of numbers that I have spoken of, but they do provide a reliable comparative measure of changes taking place in the culture. For the most part they are superior as evidence to the anecdotes of earlier social history because they gauge, as stories cannot, differences from place to place and time to time. Their value lies not in the certainty of any individual statistic but rather in their comparativity, for the statistics have been produced by consistent methods used to examine different times and places. Whether, for example, 20 percent or 70 percent of male Londoners in 1740 had enough reading ability actually to read nov-els is less important for my immediate purposes than that some consistent measure of literacy can be used to assign a figure that can be compared confidently to earlier and later dates and to rural localities. We need to know when literacy was rising and approximately how sharply; we need to know among what particular groups and in what locations literacy was rising (or falling) at particular times; but we do not necessarily discover much from knowing, in isolation, that a certain number of people in a particular place at a particular time could read. Fewer always do than can, and having raw "factual" information about total literacy is usually less important than knowing the comparative likelihood that someone in one time, place, and socioeconomic status could be considered a potential reader. Ultimately, we need to know as much as possible about grades of reading ability and about motivation. Definitions of literacy— does literacy mean the ability to read, or to write, or both?—are ultimately very important too; students of historical literacy make some broad assumptions that we shall have to question and interpret. But I postpone a detailed consideration of those issues until we have before us the broad outlines of what we know about patterns of literacy from 1600 to 1800.

I I

WE can now say with confidence what intuition and nineteenth-century social history only guessed: that literacy in the English-speaking world grew rapidly between 1600 and 1800 so that by the latter date a vast majority of adult males could read and write, whereas two centuries earlier only a select minority could do so. The evidence is strong, and, even though one might have concerns about the amount and quality of data available and sometimes about the way those data are used and interpreted, there can be little doubt that broad cultural campaigns to spread literacy, begun in the late sixteenth century for religious reasons and continued for reasons that were economic, political, and even psychological, had borne substantial fruit by the time of Wordsworth and Scott. The scope of literacy had broadened socially and economically, and the daily habits of a modern, print-centered culture were well on their way to being established.

By 1800, the expectation that a child, whatever its gender, parentage, economic aspirations, or social pretensions, would learn to read and write was firmly set; not all children did yet learn to read, and illiteracy was still a national concern, but reading was a regular feature of English life. Burke was wrong. Whatever he meant by his figure of 80,000 readers— whether he meant to include all readers or only those who could, and did, read frequently and deeply and write readable prose—his figure is far too conservative. Perhaps no more than 80,000 Englishmen and Englishwomen could read Edmund Burke with attention and profit (one of his works did sell 30,000 copies),[7] and certainly many fewer still could write with the elegance of Burke himself, but a great many of Burke's country-men could, and did, read the Bible and the newspaper, account books and novels with regularity and ease. The correct number is closer to a million and a half, perhaps two million. Estimates based on quantitative evidence vary somewhat, but probably between 60 and 70 percent of adult males in England and Wales were, on a conservative test, able to read by 1800. In 1600, the comparable figure had been around 25 percent, so that it is safe to say that male literacy was at least twice—perhaps nearly three times—as common at the beginning of the nineteenth century as it had been two centuries earlier. And in Scotland the gain was even more dramatic. One informed estimate sets Scotland's literacy gain among males at nearly sixfold, from 15 to an astonishing 88 percent.[8] Only New England boasted a more literate population than Scotland,[9] and together the English-speaking world had become the most literate culture, all things considered, in the world.[10] Even if we allow for generosity, uneven data, and interpretive error, the gain in two centuries was indisputably enormous, confirming in general outline the more approximate correctors of Burke among social historians of a century ago. By 1800, England had developed a substantial reading public, broadly based among socially, economically, occupationally, and geographically diverse segments of the population, and the reading habit was part of the national profile.

At first blush, the new quantitative evidence seems to confirm the old "triple rise" thesis popularized by Ian Watt—that the rise of the middle class led to the rise of the reading public, which in turn led to the rise of the novel—for the new readers added over those two centuries were indeed from social strata in which literacy had been, in 1600, unusual. Nearly all gentlemen and professional men could read by 1600; the increase comes almost completely in the classes of artisans, shopkeepers, yeomen, husbandmen, laborers, and servants. The "new" readers available to a world of print were, then, "middle" class at least in the sense that most of them were not in the highest social strata and, at least at first, more of them were from "middle" occupational groups than from the servant classes. Their values, habits, tastes, and aspirations I will consider at greater length later, for simply thinking of them as middle class is not conceptually very helpful and runs some interpretive risks because that term has become so inclusive, so loaded, and (lately) so distrusted. But for now it is sufficient to confirm that there were, in fact, during the seventeenth and eighteenth centuries, many readers newly introduced to the world of writing.

Yet there is serious difficulty for the triple-rise thesis in the matter of timing: the quantitative information we now have suggests that the steepest acceleration in literacy occurred early on in the seventeenth century, at least three generations before the novel began in any meaningful sense to emerge. The evidence suggests that most—probably two thirds to three quarters—of the two-century gain I have indicated in England, Wales, and Scotland had already taken place before 1675. According to Law-rence Stone, the male literacy rate in England and Wales had nearly doubled between 1600 and 1675, from 25 percent to 45 percent of adult males.[11] The rate of increase late in the seventeenth century and through most of the eighteenth was, all scholars agree, very minimal indeed. There may even have been declines during some decades (although high mortality rates among the urban young may skew the numbers),[12] and it is not at all certain that a child in 1775 was more likely to learn to read than a child in 1675. The evidence then is that, after a literacy boom in the first three quarters of the seventeenth century, few new readers (in terms of percentages) were added to the literacy rolls during the genera-tions just before the emergence of the novel and during its early decades of popularity.[13] Readers of novels in, say, 1750 may well have been "new" readers in the sense that they came from groups who, in 1600, had little or no access to print, but most of them were, by the time of Richardson, the Fieldings, and Lennox, at least third-generation readers, many of them sixth- or seventh-. It was their great-grandfathers and great-great-grandfathers who had crossed the linguistic divide in the brawling but heady years between James I and Charles II. (The question of great-grandmothers I shall take up in just a minute.) The most fundamental issue has to do with what three generations (and more) of readers did while they were waiting for the novel to rise. Was their literacy "on hold," or did they read only the Bible, the catechism, and their account books? Or did they find, at first, other kinds of reading materials that ministered to the same needs novels later came to address?

In times that regarded literature more "purely," as a formal phenome-non unrelated to cultural and social contexts, it may have been possible to believe that changes in literacy and the social makeup of the reading classes had no causal effect at all on literary forms. Some literary histo-rians, like many literary critics, have always resisted social or cultural explanations of artistic change, and in the light of the evidence about literacy it may be tempting for some to return to formalist definitions and to biological metaphors for the birth of the novel, as if at some specifiable moment some identifiable parent brought forth something brand new out of her- or himself rather than having it emerge and develop, helped by many minds and hands, from a resonant social, intellectual, and cultural context. The metaphors of origins are indeed complicated, and some-times they channel or limit thought more than they should. The ques-tion of how social contexts, whether of readership or of other matters, affect the emergence (or rise, or founding, or discovery, or invention) of new literary forms or species is a vexed one, imperfectly understood even in cases where contexts and results are the clearest. Ultimately, however, no formalist explanation is any longer sufficient for most late twentieth-century theorists, literary historians, or students of the novel. It is not just that the novel, as a species structurally committed to social issues and deeply set in the bedrock of the culture, seems especially to need a social context and a range of readers even to exist as an idea, but that literature more generally, even in its more "pure," esoteric, formal, and sophisticated kinds, now seems so fundamentally connected to larger human contexts, to history in its largest sense. It is not just literary species that show clear ideological commitments, have behavioral designs on readers, or grow out of a social context and cultural lineage.[14]

Watt's fundamental cultural assumptions about literary origins, although thirty years ago they may have seemed the most questionable part of this thesis, are not at issue here. Just because the novel did not blossom forth and abundantly flower immediately after the reading public expanded and created new opportunities does not mean that the reading public was not a crucial factor for the novel. The "new" readers were a necessary but not sufficient condition for the emergence of the English novel, and the lengthy gap between the expansion of literacy and the stirrings of a novelistic consciousness suggests that the newly literate took their needs and desires to other reading materials before there were novels to address them. If I am right in my assumption that novels, like other artistic and cultural phenomena, owe their existence ultimately to their ability to address specific and identifiable human needs, there are two historic possibilities: (1) that sometime between about 1719 and 1750, the English reading public developed specific new needs that the novel quickly identified and immediately came to address; or (2) that in the years before the novel emerged, the new readers read texts other than narrative or fictional ones.

The first of these alternatives, at least in its pure form, seems unlikely. England was changing deeply as a culture in those crucial years, but everything we know about that change suggests that it was gradual, that human needs may have evolved importantly (as I shall in fact argue in the next two chapters) during the seventeenth and eighteenth centuries as the culture moved from feudal, land-driven models to modern, market-driven ones, but that no sudden and radical shift took place in group psychology. It also seems clear that the most radical changes in the culture had their major impact before 1700, not after. Without foreclosing the possibility that some new conditions did in fact dictate some revised needs and desires, I want to ask what needs the new reading public would already have had by 1675. Some of these needs can be inferred from a detailed knowledge of what in fact was printed (a matter I shall pursue in Chapters Seven through Fourteen), but much can be decided as well from more detailed analysis of who was in that newly literate group; before speculating further about the missing three generations of readers, I turn to other implications of recent scholarship on literacy.

I I I

BEYOND the implications of broad diachronic patterns of literacy, some of the details we now know about who read when suggest specific characteristics and concerns of novel readers and point to particular concentrations of desire and need among earlier readers. The major social and demographic question that literacy students have always had trouble with involves the place of women in the reading public. Evidence about female literacy in the eighteenth century is scarce and hard to interpret, and wildly contradictory claims have been made: that women dominated the taste for certain kinds of reading materials (not only novels, but plays, *chroniques scandaleuses*, and other frothy accounts of contemporary life) or, on the contrary, that female literacy was in sharp decline during the seventeenth and eighteenth centuries so that women were less and less a factor in the world of print. Both claims demean female capacity and taste in the service of a larger cultural or historical thesis: one insists that women misuse the skills they are generously given, the other justifies the refusal to offer such skills. Even the quantitative evidence of the past few years has not led to a consensus or to sophisticated discussion of the complex evidentiary issues. Still, there is important evidence, of a variety of kinds, and I want to review what we know or can reasonably infer about the reading abilities and habits of women.

The national literacy pattern that I have been describing rests on information about the ability of males to sign legal documents. Comparable evidence about female literacy is hard to come by until the second half of the eighteenth century. Records that indicate male signings have no legitimate counterpart for females, for until after Lord Hardwicke's Marriage Act of 1753 no significant records required female signatures across a meaningful range of situations and places: tax rolls, wills, marriage applications, and parish registers offered only scattered opportunities for females to sign, and the absence of requirement renders what little evidence we do have unreliable. Social historians are thus thrown back on other means of determining female literacy, none of them involving evidence comparable to that available for males. The most careful demographers, Cressy and Schofield, for example, make few guesses for earlier years; bolder historians attempt rather grand generalizations, some of them careless and, I think, misleading. One persistent position (more or less espoused by Lawrence Stone) is that female literacy decreased during the seventeenth and eighteenth centuries, and that position has been adopted by some unlikely followers.[15] It is an extraordinary assertion, counterintuitive, and based on no evidence at all except the uncritical acceptance of random anecdotes and the opinions of rhetorical posturers.

Such impressions derive from two kinds of written sources, and it seems astonishing to me that social historians have been so apparently uncritical in accepting their authority. One source is the writings of women in the late eighteenth or early nineteenth century who are part of a new female consciousness. Figures like Mary Wollstonecraft legitimately announce a new present in which the rights and needs of women take on a different cultural importance. But moments of progress often make the immediate past seem bleaker than it was, and there is a tendency to regard that past as a deterioration of a once more golden age—progress seen as glory restored. This statement about the early eighteenth century by Lady Louisa Stuart in the 1820s, quoted by Stone as evidence of the supposed trend, suggests a predictable stance: "the education of women had then [in the eighteenth century] reached its lowest ebb, and if not coquettes or gossips or diligent card-players, their best praise was to be diligent housewives."[16] As careful as Stone is in his *Past and Present* summary of male literacy to evaluate reliability and to separate reasonable surmise from irresponsible conjecture, his account of female literacy and education in *The Family, Sex and Marriage in England 1500–1800* stands in stark contrast: it is anecdotal and uncritical, full of conjecture, careless argument, and flimsy evidence, and why those who are normally critical of Stone's methods should trust him here is not clear. There is a good reason—lack of firm fact—why Stone and social historians resort to rumor, received opinion, and vague generalizations when speaking of female literacy while sounding methodical and precise on male literacy. The absence of data is frustrating, but there is no need to abandon good sense or critical examination of the data we do have; it is silly to treat the social history of women as simply a subject of gossip, while being rigorous and quantitative about men.[17]

The second kind of written source is suggested by the social details Lady Louisa mentions. Her opinion itself probably has no identifiable referent, but her evidence sounds as if it came from satirists, and if so she is at one with many later social historians who base their estimates of female literacy—and female conduct more generally—on eighteenth-century satirists. Addison and Steele were keen social observers, and portraitists like Pope may have worked from historical originals, but no satirist ought to be taken too literally as a recorder of wholes—only as a portrayer of foibles and extremes, or sometimes as an observer of fads or trends. As comparative historians, satirists can be worse than inaccurate; it is their job to be misleading (just like reformers) about the difference between past and present. If reformers make the past seem worse, satirists make it seem better than the present, and when the two sources are used consecutively, as they have been on female literacy and the social history of women more generally, we are apt to get a distorted view of what women actually were like in the days of Milton or Swift.[18] One might admit the poignancy of Pope's insight about Belinda or the realistic basis of Swift's portrait of painted and patched-over women without thinking that all fashionable young ladies in the early eighteenth century were vacuous, flirtatious, narcissistic, and illiterate—and certainly without concluding that Pope's or Swift's contemporaries were substantially more trivial than those of earlier or later times in which women were assigned equally degraded roles and expected to be silly, stupid, or silent. The point is that satiric images—like winning anecdotes or made-up numbers—can take very powerful holds on the imagination and historically burst beyond the bounds of even their own distorting intentions. By definition, satire involves radical exaggerations.

Besides, Belinda (whatever her other limitations) evidently could read, as Pope portrayed her, for *The Rape of the Lock* is addressed to her original for edification, and Pope's patronizing introductory epistle to Arabella Fermor, for all its insults to her taste and understanding, does not imply that someone else will have to read the poem to her. Belinda's female contemporaries apparently could and did read too, without raising male eyebrows or great cultural consternation. Reformers early in the century repeatedly complain (as do earlier and later ones) that not enough women read (and that they read the wrong things), but contemporary commentators do not report a female slide down Literacy Hill: they want more progress but do not report regress. Defoe feels no need to prove that Moll Flanders or Roxana is a plausible author of her own story, and Fielding (riding herd on Richardson's social inversions) attacks the quality of Pamela's prose and spelling, not the fact that her creator makes her a letter writer and author. Defoe in fact makes Moll, despite her social status and obvious lack of formal schooling, rather easily and comfortably literate, having her engage in wit battles by scratching rhymes on a glass in flirtatious competition with her lover. And early eighteenth-century writers like Trotter, Manley, Barker, Rowe, Aubin, Davys, and Haywood—evidently writing primarily for women readers—never seem obliged to prove that a narrator (that is, putative writer) can readily, even pre-dictably, be female. The state of female education was nothing to brag about, and literacy was certainly lower than reformers desired, but to claim that it was worse than in previous ages involves reliance on shaky, prejudicial evidence, usually in the service of a specific social thesis that ultimately is unhistorical. Evidence from literature or the contemporary social commentators I have cited may, of course, also be over—or under—read or seen inappropriately as representative. Ultimately it is the coales-cence of different kinds of evidence that must decide the issue. But when we weigh anecdotes, opinions, or scenes and situations from literature, the crucial interpretative question involves the context of the story or remark, and the would-be historian has to sort out the assumptions and expectations behind particular opinions.[19]

Female literacy almost certainly was lower than male literacy through-out the seventeenth and eighteenth centuries, in almost all regions, classes, and categories, but the real question is how much below. By the time we have quasi-reliable figures to go on, after midcentury, the differential was substantial but not as large as gentlemanly generalizations tend to sug-gest. In the late eighteenth century, female literacy is typically about two thirds of male literacy; in the 1750s, for example, when male literacy was around 60 percent, female literacy was about 40 percent.[20] Unless we are prepared to believe that 40 percent of adult females were literate in 1600—when the male literacy rate was around 25 percent and much lower in areas outside London and the major commercial centers—we must deduce that female literacy, like male literacy, climbed substan-tially in that 150-year period. It may be, as Cressy assumes but does not really argue, that female literacy rose faster early in the eighteenth cen-tury than did male literacy and that the periods of increase and decline for women were not the same as were those for men, but unless there was a stratospheric leap in the first half of the eighteenth century—and there is no evidence of such a leap, whereas it is precisely in this period that most of the anecdotes and complaints about female stupidity and ill education arise—female literacy must have increased substantially by the late seventeenth century, much as it did among males. Tradition and anecdote are no help in sorting out when. The old canard that female literacy actually declined[21] makes no temporal distinctions over a two hundred–year period and seems to involve, for whatever reason, serious misuse of evidence.

We can be reasonably sure that women became increasingly literate, just as men did although not necessarily at the same rate, during the literacy boom in the first three quarters of the seventeenth century. If 45 percent of adult males were literate in 1675, back projection suggests that about 30 percent of adult females were probably literate, up from perhaps 15 to 20 percent seventy-five years earlier. Like those for male literacy, the numbers themselves may be uncertain, but the comparative figures are probable. When there were novels to be read in the middle of the eighteenth century, we can be sure—as were novelists themselves—that large numbers of female readers were ready for them. And three genera-tions earlier, the great-grandmothers of those readers were, in about the same proportion, finding something else to read instead—and not just romances, or the printing figures on romances would have been enor-mous.

I do have one major caveat about the definitions of literacy assumed in recent studies, and it affects female literacy especially. R. S. Schofield has argued persuasively that the most important thing in determining literacy rates is to have a common criterion so that students are not measuring one thing at one place and time and using different standards elsewhere,[22] and the wild discrepancies of claims about comparative European literacy—where in different countries varieties of definition and technique have led to conclusions impossible to compare reliably— make one appreciate the reliability of the studies of the Cambridge pop-ulation group, even in their rigid adherence to the test of signing one's name. Schofield has gone on to assert, with some plausibility, that the ability to sign one's name, all things considered, reliably represents the ability to read: "a measure based on the ability to sign probably overesti-mates the number able to write, underestimates the number able to read at an elementary level, and gives a fair indication of the number able to read fluently."[23] But given the nature of female education, the social and economic expectations of women, and differences between the ways men and women used their time in the seventeenth and eighteenth centuries, what is true for men about equivalences in writing and reading skills may not be true for women. Such a supposed difference is not, of course, easy to measure, but if there is a difference, the likelihood is that more women than men unable to sign would be able to read. Evidence is scanty but suggestive.[24] Men were more likely to be engaged in occupations and tasks that put a premium on the ability to sign; some occupations, espe-cially among the increasing number of positions in trade and commerce, required the ability to write and keep records, and even those whose work did not require writing were sometimes called upon to sign legal documents—property records, parish rolls, wills, and so on. Those who could not sign were legally permitted, of course, to make only their mark, but the legal requirement itself exerted a certain pressure toward signing, a pressure more likely to fall on males than females because of the greater variety of circumstances in which the issue would come up for them.

Women, because of their inferior legal status, because they were less involved in commerce and in public exchange, and because they owned so little property, were much less likely to face situations in which they had such an obligation or choice; the fact that women were not asked even to sign marriage applications until Lord Hardwicke's Marriage Act accurately suggests the lesser number of occasions.

The pressure or desire to read, however, might have been just as great; certainly it would have been different. Some household tasks would be made easier by the ability to consult printed information, and servant girls like Pamela had obvious advantages for households in which the householders themselves were not fully literate. Reading to children— about godly and useful matters, of course—was also considered desirable in mothers. Fathers, it is true, were the presumed family readers at devotional exercises and family prayers in most of the courtesy books aimed at gentlefolk in the seventeenth century, and to some extent the later conduct books and family guides intended for broader distribution—to servants, to young people, and to parents in lower-class households— carried on that assumption. But as the seventeenth century moved on, there was increasing attention to what mothers and older sisters could do for the young in intellectual ways as well as nurturing ones. Patriarchal households were in no danger of foundering on the rocks of sexual equality (despite what some disgruntled observers of "modern" women thought),[25] yet a larger place was being assumed for female readers. The ability to write might well have been helpful too, both for keeping household accounts and for teaching children, but reading ability was more important—more valued, and more useful day to day.

We also have some evidence that, especially among the leisure classes, there were women who read extensively who could not write at all, not even sign their names. Signing is clearly a more relevant test of reading ability in some cultures and circumstances than in others. In Sweden, for example, we know that although more than 80 percent of the population could read, fewer than 30 percent could write,[26] and in France, at least, some women who could not sign had extensive library holdings.[27] Whether this phenomenon would be as pronounced in a Protestant country—especially in Tudor and Stuart England, Scotland, or Wales where so much emphasis was placed on diary keeping—is difficult to say. But diary keeping, extensive as it was among women in the British Isles, was apparently less common—judging from those documents that have survived (not a sure test incidentally, because it implies the values of later generations)—among women than among men, and it is possible that, rather than offering evidence that women were less "literate" generally, fewer simply had the ability to write.

We just don't know how accurate the "signing" test was for women (however persuasive Schofield's point may be for men), but if a distinction is to be made, *pace* modern demographers and literacy students, between signing and the ability to read, the distinction is more likely to be important for women. At least a modest number of women readers, beyond those accounted for in analogy to male signing statistics, should be added to the rolls of potential readers for the novel and for its lesser ancestors. If even one out of ten women who could not sign was able to read at the level of males who could sign, the number of female readers to be added to the "reading public" would be well over a hundred thousand in the late seventeenth century. Even a more modest number of women who read but could not write would close the gap considerably between male and female literacy in the seventeenth century.

I V

RECENT literacy studies also tell us several other things about readers that are, finally, relevant to features in the early novel or to aspects of the literary context that fostered and helped to shape the novel. Literacy was not the same thing for all those who could sign a legal document, and there are a variety of distinctions to be made about the kinds of reading most likely to be undertaken by particular readers and about varied rates of literacy within different geographical, occupational, and social categories. Not all readers in 1675 (or 1750) were potential readers of novels, and some readers were far more likely than others to expect certain topics or features in their reading and certain results from it. Out of the new social history, and especially out of the historical study of literacy, a new historical phenomenology of reading[28] should ultimately emerge to clarify not just the early directions of the novel but also the proliferation of other literary manifestations of modernity made possible by new readership, new print technology, and authorial sensitivity and experimentation. But for now I want simply to point to four characteristics of the "new" readers in the late seventeenth century that made them, among other things, potential consumers of novels.

When literacy was rising, it rose very unevenly indeed. In the North, for example, the increases seem generally stronger and steadier than in other parts of the nation, but there was further to go. Most areas, however (on the basis of the figures we have) show rather unpredictable ups and downs from decade to decade, the result often of local conditions, emphases, and incentives, or sometimes perhaps simply of records that are too fragmentary and unreliable. Scotland and several parts of the

North seem to have placed heavy (and profitable) emphasis on literacy in the early seventeenth century and made up much of the lag behind the Southeast. Regional differences in literacy suggest that, at different points between 1600 and 1800, attempts to move the whole land forward to modernity often bore notable fruit so that, although there were still very backward-looking areas, regional unevenness had begun to be smoothed out. The main geographical distinctions, though, continued to be between country and city; as towns and cities—and particularly London—increased in size relative to the total population, larger percentages of readers (as well as greater total numbers) tended to be concentrated there. Even at the beginning of the seventeenth century, the literacy rate in London was far higher than anywhere else in the kingdom (this despite its concentration of the poor), and as the century progressed London vastly outstripped the national growth rate in literacy and widened the gap further and further. To a lesser extent, the same pattern obtained in the smaller cities and towns, where literacy also grew more rapidly than in small villages and the countryside. Readers were more likely to be urban than rural in 1600, even more likely to be so in 1675 or 1750. Those with the ability to read—irrespective of what they might choose to read—were concentrated in the more highly populous areas, especially London, and were more likely to have urban concerns, attitudes, and tastes than the average Englander. Those who sought the attention of new readers ignored the growing urban bias at their own peril, and every passing year there were more of these urban readers, for increasing numbers of people each year were living in towns and cities, and thus, even when the national literacy rate remained relatively stable, the proportion of readers who came from the rising urban class was growing.

A second characteristic of the "new" class of readers involves ambition. Some people were then, and are now, more likely to learn to read than others. A variety of factors is always involved: parentage, social contexts, community attitudes, opportunities, potential teachers, need, desire, motivation. While community factors were always important, individual ones were crucial. Whatever the prime cultural causes for the national campaign to move literacy forward, individuals were pulled along or not because of their own desires and values. And those most likely to learn to read were those most likely to wish to change their circumstances, to be dissatisfied with their lots, to have ambition above the station they were born into. Moralists anxious that reading skills be encouraged and extended are full of ambivalences and sometimes anger about some of the results of their labors in behalf of literacy. Samuel Johnson described readers of novels as "the young, the ignorant and the idle": he was certainly right in his first adjective, a matter I shall discuss presently, and knew what he meant by the second, that the people he had in mind ignored classical truths and traditional values, trusting modernity, innovation, and subjectivity over received formulas and conclusions. But in using the third adjective, Johnson simply mouthed the cliché of his contemporaries; there is no evidence that readers of novels were more idle than non-readers, except perhaps at the moment of their "passive" contact with print,[29] and there may be in Johnson, as in many of his moralist contemporaries, some deep suspicion of the contemplative life and some distrust of time invested strictly in curiosity, the basic Judeo-Christian intellectual dilemma. The evidence is, in fact, that novel readers, like most other readers and like Johnson himself in spite of his self-flagellation about his perceived indolence, were less idle in their aspirations, less passive about themselves and their prospects than non-readers. Ambition was, in fact, what moralists worried about. Novels and other works of fiction and imagination were widely believed to stimulate too warmly a reader's sense of what might be.

Those in the rising classes most likely to be ambitious enough to learn to read were also most likely to be willing to be mobile—a third characteristic of new readers—and their mobility was most likely to take them from their native rural pasts to a present in the growing towns and cities. Motivation to read, ambition to rise in the world, and desire to migrate to places associated with progress all coalesce in an increased taste for commerce with a larger world (whether of trade or ideas) and a commitment to modern life more generally. The primary place likely to attract those appetites—and for many young Englishmen and Englishwomen the *only* place that fully realized such possibilities—was London. London was the symbolic gateway to the rest of the world, no longer just Europe but America and India and increasingly the Far East as well, and for the small but now-again-growing number whose ambitions began to transcend English traditions and the English language, London was a first crucial step—toward the Grand Tour and its hint of possibilities quite beyond a quick veneer of European culture, toward international trade, or toward broader (or at least different) traditions of learning and habits of education and reading. But London (and to a lesser extent other cities and regional centers in England) represented as well something in itself, the desire to define and distill the national character and translate it to a new time, the kind of attitude represented in Pope's image of the trees of Windsor turned into navies so that the rest of the world was touched by England, reached, and then brought home, retrieved, "civilized," domesticated—Englished as well. Defoe's attempt to domesticate the Grand Tour, providing a sense that within England itself, when properly visited and analyzed, lay an education adequate to send youths into the larger world, derives ultimately from the same sense that maturity was to be gained and knowledge acquired by movement through space. The willingness of people (especially the young) to be mobile, to explore, to try new places at least for visits but increasingly also for new abodes and careers became, for many, a kind of test of ambition and desire to cope successfully with a modern world and its problems and challenges. Travel was not of course easy, and pulling up roots was painful even when it seemed exciting or necessary; relocation involved all sorts of risks beyond the cutting of family ties and tradition. But those who aspired greatly, or who felt the appeal of a modern future, or who distrusted the past or rebelled against family, community, or habit, found their mobility rewarded (in a sense) by new challenges and a sense of frontiers (of whatever kind) rolling back. Whether from countryside to village, from village to town, from town to city, or from Norwich and Bristol to London and beyond, the migration represented basically the same force, and it was those caught up with this force who were the most likely to learn to read and who, in turn, were the most likely to be voracious and omnivorous practitioners of the skill once learned.

Mobility, especially among those just beginning their careers or ambitious to raise their place in the world, involved special incentives to be literate, not just because writing and reading were skills valuable to a variety of professions but also because the act of leaving familiar surroundings for lesser known places involves, in itself, a necessity to provide cultural substitutes for home, family, and community. Books are not, of course, brothers or sisters, but printed materials had already begun to seem comparable to intimate friends, and they did provide a kind of companionship that was, however inadequately, often a substitute for human contact.[30] Those who brought literacy skills to their adopted homes probably spent more time (because individually they had more time to spend) in reading activities than did equally bright and skilled counterparts who stayed at home in rural England. The volume of reading one might expect among the mobile was thus greater than the volume to be expected from equally literate people who were not on the move, and this in spite of more active lives and crowded schedules. The ability to read, the incentive to read, and the amount of time spent reading were all apparently greater among migrating Englishwomen and Englishmen than among more stable (and probably less personally ambitious) rural counterparts. No doubt some of the difference between urban and rural literacy I have mentioned involves greater opportunities for formal education and more intense pressures—both practically because of professional needs and socially because of the interaction of more people, many of them already literate—but urban literacy is also high because the already literate were simply more likely to move and (when they did) to move to more populous areas. It would be too simple to say that curiosity was ultimately the same motivating force, whether it involved personal experience, professional advancement, or the ability to read, but there is a certain redundancy in the phrase when Henry Fielding (or Swift or Dampier) addresses the "curious reader." Those who wanted, wanted greatly: reading was part of the fare.

A fourth group, the largest and most comprehensive, among the newly literate was the young. Novels have traditionally captured a disproportionate readership among the young, perhaps because youths seek knowledge the novel contains, perhaps because new readers are perpetually seeking promising new outlets as alternatives to what their elders recommend. Moralists and cultural guardians in every age regularly train their fire on imaginative literature thought to corrupt the young—they think it heightens expectations or fires desires—and the attacks on novels in the mid- to late eighteenth century (like the warnings half a century earlier about plays, romances, and other books thought to be incendiary or head-turning) presume that the imminence and depth of the danger involves the fact that most readers are at a stage of life when they are impressionable, ready to make crucial choices of their own about life and career.

Whatever their intentions about regulating conduct or influencing life choices, novelists seem regularly to make similar assumptions, repeatedly choosing plots, characters, and situations that feature choices of life and the consequences of such choices. Choices of career and marriage partner and their outcomes dominate the action of most novels in most ages but particularly in England in the eighteenth century. Novelists either began with private concerns about such matters and drew an audience along, or (consciously or unconsciously) they recognized, as cultural and moral critics did, that their potential readers were those facing imminent life choices of their own. Literary critics habitually, in their pursuit of artistic and aesthetic concerns, tend to underrate the "real-life" issues that draw readers to novels or condition their choices of reading material more generally—questions about how the world works and how other people make the structural decisions that face us all[31]—and the evidence from novels themselves, from what novelists and social observers say about readers and from what readers report about their own reading experiences, all suggests that the young (males and females under the age of twenty-five) were highly motivated toward novel reading and that they constituted the single largest age group of novel readers. Others, especially those in age or occupation groups that had more time than the young, consumed novels frequently too—to see what they had missed, to find out how others had solved or not solved the crucial life questions, or to pursue more abstract pleasures; but at least until the electronic age, the plot-determining novel readers were the young.

Such an age concentration of readership for the novel is not surprising, given what we know about readership more generally, for (at least indirectly) the statistics on readers suggest that it was the young who would have been most likely to have the skill, as well as the motivation. During the years after 1675 when the sharp rise in literacy tapered off, the sheer number of readers continued to grow because the population kept rising, and there was significant population growth among the young. Mortality rates remained high throughout the eighteenth century, in fact increasing rapidly during part of the century, and life expectancy actually declined somewhat.[32] Even if the proportion of those attaining literacy each year had been altogether frozen, the number of children coming to that choice increased measurably. Here are the Wrigley and Schofield raw population estimates for some key years, together with an approximation, based on their calculations of age distribution, of the numbers of people in the age groups 5–14 and 15–24:

	1601	1651	1701	1751	1801
Total population	4,109,981	5,228,481	5,057,790	5,772,415	8,664,490
Ages 5–14	847,889	1,058,245	1,001,948	1,171,800	1,999,764
Ages 15–24	795,281	944,264	826,949	1,008,441	1,536,214

Because population grew faster in the towns and cities—especially London—than it did in the countryside, because much of that increase came in migration from rural areas, and because literacy among the young increased more rapidly in urban areas, the number of young people achieving literacy each year increased more rapidly than either the gross population or the nationwide literacy rate. Even though the rush to literacy of the early seventeenth century had slowed and the sharpest increase in literacy had already occurred, large numbers of the young entered the ranks of readers every new year, more than replacing those who moved into an older group or who died, so that novelists and writers more generally had an ever larger potential audience to draw upon. If we assume—as I think we must from the social commentary, the content of novels, and what little demographic data we have about actual readers—that novels got more than their proportional share of young readers because of motivational factors and the content of novels, the readership, among the young, of novels was very great indeed.

The four groups that I have described do not show up under these labels in the tables of modern demographers of literacy, nor are they described there in the terms I have used here, for these studies seek, as far as possible, to be value-free, and my terms and my concerns are openly and functionally value-laden. But the segments of the population most likely to be literate in the late seventeenth century and early eighteenth—just after the literacy boom—may be logically inferred from the figures that scholars like Schofield, Cressy, and Moran have arrived at and from the estimates and interpretations of cultural commentators such as Stone, Laqueur, Lockridge, and Hall. Ultimately someone qualified in mathematical modeling will need to calculate exactly what we can know with certainty about the numbers of potential readers in each group at various points during the seventeenth and eighteenth centuries so that we can gain a firmer notion of how audience tastes may have shifted. But the broad outlines of the demography are clear enough to suggest a composite picture of those most likely to pick up a novel in 1750 or, in 1675, to look for a piece of reading material that addressed similar needs and desires. The groups I have described overlap dramatically, and it is where they most overlap that we find the most intense, and the most needy, readers. Novels attracted, of course, a great variety of readers—among the old and the learned, among country gentlemen and Tory poets, among the infirm, retiring, and isolated as well as the lively, the rising, and the overcommitted—but we go far toward comprehending the content, concerns, and directions of the early novel if we imagine ambitious, aspiring, mobile, and increasingly urban young people, both men and women, as among the most ready patrons of novels, those who were already able to read by the later seventeenth century and poised for reading materials that would address who they were.

V

BECAUSE the quantitative studies of literacy are so recent, tentative in their conclusions about absolute numbers, controversial about definitions, and uneven in their applications to various cultures and subcultures, one cannot be sure how the rapid rise in literacy in England and Scotland in the early seventeenth century compares with that in other developed nations. But the data we have suggests that, from a position of relative weakness as readers in the late sixteenth century, the inhabitants of the British Isles moved to one of strength. It looks, in fact (although one must be cautious still), as if by the late seventeenth century the literacy rate in England, Scotland, and Wales taken together may have been higher than any European country, although some other Protestant nations (notably the Netherlands and perhaps Sweden) may have been important challengers.[33] Certainly the pressure had been put on, and, within limits, it had worked. The pressure had come both from those trying to preserve what they took to be "traditional" and "conservative" values and from those determined to construct a new and modern nation. What is surprising is how widespread the pressure was and how steadily it was kept up, largely by exhortation it is true, but to some extent structurally and institutionally in the systematic modification of national habits and patterns and in the recurrent emphasis on the founding of schools. And the insistence that girls be able to read was as strong, or nearly as strong, as that boys should. The pressures to teach young women to read— and to educate them more generally, although only up to a certain point— intensified through the first three quarters of the seventeenth century, and the rhetoric held steady throughout the eighteenth.

One looks almost in vain for those who had doubts about such an intellectual, cultural, and social agenda. The desire for literacy was apparently based deep in the national consciousness, rooted in Protestant imperatives. It seems not to have been the product of a particular partisan initiative. There must have been doubters and those who refused to comply, as well as those whose commitment was weak or whose energy flagged; the nation did not rise up as one individual and expel illiteracy. But the fact that literacy moved forward so forcibly and dramatically— in London especially and in towns and urban areas more generally, as well as in parts of the nation and segments of the populace that communed most frequently with urban life and values—suggests that only remoteness or isolation allowed illiteracy to go unchallenged. Commitment seems as close to universal as any social aim can reasonably be expected to be. The famous worries expressed by Mandeville about the socially disruptive implications of literacy[34] must have been shared by some contemporaries, and, earlier and later, there must have been those who, when they experienced first hand the fruits of heightened expectation, wished the agenda could be unset. But educational theorists remained adamant and enthusiastic, and the shrillness of those who fumed against uppity females and servants seems to have fallen mostly on deaf or unsympathetic ears. For reasons that began to be practical, commercial, and political, as well as religious, the nation was listening to pleas for expanded literacy, piety, and improvement, not to misogynists and hierarchists. The novelist, hymn-writer, and teacher Isaac Watts pretty well spoke for the culture in insisting that reading was necessary for everyone, of whatever class, and that "The *Art of Writing* also is so exceeding useful, and it is now grown so very common, that the greatest Part of Children may attain it at an easy Rate." And, he added, "*Reading* is as needful for one Sex as the other."[35]

The explicit reasons usually involve religious benefits, both individual and communal, to be derived from universal literacy—a powerful argument in a Protestant culture devoted to the biblical text, insistent on the power of individual believers to interpret for themselves, and bent on kicking over the traces of dependence on both oral tradition and the orality of daily community life."[36] Some envisioned a world where everyone could (and would) read the Bible daily, perhaps almost continually, and there is often a utopian, as well as visionary, quality in their analysis. But the piety was serious and furthered by practical everyday needs and desires. Moralists and religionists were sincere in their devotion, anxious to extend and intensify the commitments of their own constituencies, and concerned about papist competition for both political and religious reasons. A number of other factors—political, social, and economic—in fact supported the argument from piety. But piety was the most acceptable, most persuasive, and perhaps most fundamental basis for literacy.

Some of the factors that helped piety along were less high-minded. Historical literacy studies show, not surprisingly, a high correlation between literacy and occupation, a correlation that suggests that function and need may be more important than birth, peer expectations, or pressures of social class, although such matters are notoriously hard to separate in a traditional society where the fabric of family and occupational life seems all of a piece.[37] Those in jobs that required reading learned to read, even when conditions were difficult or when formal education was not readily available. A major reason for higher literacy in cities and towns involves occupations that required record keeping and knowledge of comparative information. It is true of course that some prominent tradesmen were not literate and that even new entrants could get by surprisingly well in some positions without literacy; but the commercial march to modernity increasingly required (or at least encouraged) those, even in relatively menial jobs, who could read and write. The ability to rise economically—and to some extent socially—was more firmly tied to literate skills in a trade economy than in an agricultural environment, and increasingly there was pressure, even when formal requirements were missing, for literacy especially among the young and ambitious. It is surprising how few exhortations and warnings there are about the declining market for those who lacked modern skills—a notable contrast to the high-tech rhetoric of our own time—but the relative silence probably means three things: that voices urging economic change were not yet being heard as a communal chorus; that the societal message was carried sufficiently by an oral tradition among the young; and that the literacy was correlated closely with the desire and need to move away from villages and the rural countryside into towns and cities, especially London, for motion was already something that social observers (and especially old-fashioned moralists) were concerned about. The pragmatic pressure to literacy, then, was caught up in one of the fundamental paradoxes of the transitional society, a paradox faced repeatedly by both traditional moralists and Enlightenment reformers—that the doctrine of progress and the retreat from oral and folk tradition collided with the doctrine equating the countryside with salt-of-the-earth human values.[38]

The version of the pragmatic argument that was most often seen in print involved character development rather than economic improvement and thus was presented as a subset of the religious argument. Aimed largely at the would-be gentleman (with a version for upwardly mobile women as well, a version that Pamela both alludes to and represents), the appeal was jointly to vanity and a sense of self-fulfillment. David Brown, for example, in 1638 claims that he can teach "those that cannot write at all, or not well or not true English, neither can read written hand, write without rule nor keep accounts . . . to attain all these better in one month, an hour only in a day."[39] The rewards associated with literacy were thus regarded as instrumental, although within a context of piety and individual and social improvement—instrumental to salvation, character development, and economic amelioration—and pleasure seldom comes into it in any explicit way. Like my Uncle Toby, readers believe they do it for the sake of some higher good. No one argues that people should learn to read just for the sheer joy of the skill or in order to read works of entertainment or imagination. And probably few readers did actually learn for hedonistic reasons, no matter to what use they put their reading skills later.

Utilitarian reading may, in practice, have often given way quickly to the pursuit of romances or poems, but the sequence was from serious reasons—religious, economic, or social—to personal pleasures that came as a bonus. There was, as well, a cultural and patriotic equivalent to the argument of filling up or suiting out the individual: the nation stood to gain, in dignity and prestige as well as economic power, just as individual readers did. The argument is a subtle one and usually lies just beneath the surface of the rhetoric, but one can hear, in the chorus of exhortations to read, a growing spirit of national pride and a sense of competition with other nations and with more backward domestic traditions.[40] Intensifying arguments for literacy coincide more than incidentally with the growing imperialist aggressiveness about trade and with the developing consciousness of the need to develop a nationalistic literary tradition.[41]

Literacy was a part of the agenda for modernity, the city, and the Enlightenment, as well as for religious leaders and social reformers. Whatever their differences they united in their desire to leave behind

the rural culture of primitivism, paganism, and superstition, a past associated with narrowness, darkness, and terror.[42] No one could imagine
the rolling back of the darkness without the aid of better education,
which largely meant improved literacy and increased amounts of reading,
done by a broader range of people; it seemed especially important to
capture the eyes of the young before they restlessly strayed to something
worse. Reading seemed such a good thing to so many people for so many
reasons that a note of alarm begins to sound, a warning mostly about the
misuses and misapplications of reading but sometimes becoming an attack
as well on the industry that arose in response to the successful drive for
increased literacy.

V I

IN spite of warnings, readers did read for pleasure and sometimes read
works of pure entertainment. But the pleasures of reading were usually
introduced more guardedly and subtly. Changes had been taking place
since midcentury, and by the early 1680s the quantity and variety of
printed materials had begun to suggest some of the things that modern
readers sought in their "leisure" reading. Novelty and experimentation—
not always conscious and seldom programmatic—created a different climate of expectation for those who were by now, many of them, second-
and third-generation readers. Such readers were both carrying on and
modifying the practices of parents or ambitious role models: they were
rural rebels, gentlefolk stymied by village life, urban émigrés, aspiring
tradesmen, restless footmen, waiting maids hoping to better themselves—readers all, raising their expectations of both art and life, and
they included Marjorie Pinchwifes as well as Industrious Apprentices,
those bored with their limited lot as well as those driven by ambition or
vision. The pattern of restlessness was less than a constant one; high
mortality rates throughout England (but highest in towns and cities,
especially London) meant that many aspirations were of short duration
as upwardly mobile youths were cut off in mid-flight, and other hopes
ended in frustration, failure, and return to the countryside; but family
after family, and generation after generation, replicated the direction of
change. It was a time when new needs were being defined and others
were developing, perhaps the first time in Western history when a distinctive youth culture was beginning to have an effect on the marketplace, including the intellectual marketplace and the world of booksellers
and print.[43]
   The pressures for literacy were not necessarily coincident with the

desire to read, and ultimately the question of what people did read has to do with needs and tastes as well as with what was available. But if desire played a significant part in producing the tendency toward novelty in the new fiction, older reading materials—the locus of the pressure to know and to discipline—were tied to the "traditional" and "conventional" aspects of the novel. What did "new" readers read while they were waiting for the novel to rise? Later (in Chapters Seven through Fourteen) I will survey relevant print materials after considering how old and new desires interdepend, but here I want just to sketch the range of materials in bookstalls in the first generations of expanded literacy. For there were plenteous materials and a reasonable variety. Even though relatively few long fictions were available (compared to the middle of the eighteenth century when novels had begun to dominate the publishing industry) and despite the relative scarcity of longer narratives of any kind, readers had substantial choice among other materials that may have, indirectly at least, addressed the same needs.

The dominant character of most practical materials was religious and Christian in a quite specific, insistent, and zealous way. Some of these works of piety were theological and many involved specific interpretations of biblical texts, but by far the majority of religious texts were in "practical divinity"—that is, works that addressed ethical issues of behavior in daily life. Insistent practicality asserted itself in a variety of other materials as well. By the late seventeenth century, print had taken on functions formerly left to oral tradition, and the increasing complexity of ordinary life—especially in the city, especially for rising generations—put new demands upon the press. "Manuals" of all kinds addressed particular problems, and more complex and comprehensive works incorporated various kinds of pragmatic advice. Mixing and additiveness characterized available materials as well, and a modern reader is apt to be struck by the choppy, fragmented character of even the shortest and least complicated pamphlets. Haste of composition, uncertainties of aim, the newness of the publishing industry, and lack of respect for popular tastes contributed to this sense of disorganization and imcompletion, but a larger generic uncertainty and anxiety about textual direction gave even the most ambitious and formal texts a seeming randomness and lack of governing certainty. Plenty, variety, piety, practicality, and fragmentation—these characteristics of the print marketplace and the texts offered there meant that readers were "prepared" for the novel in a distinctive reading context. That context produced four kinds of texts that ultimately were influential on particulars of the novel: journalistic texts, in which current events, practical concerns, and items of "newsworthy" interest were confronted (discussed in Chapters Seven and Eight); didactic texts and rhetorics of advice (Chapters Nine through Eleven); private and personal writings, in which writers confronted subjective desires and struggles to establish the integrity of individual lives (Chapters Twelve and Thirteen); and perspective narratives in which some larger philosophical or ideological sense was used to comprehend details and events and rescue them from fragmentation and randomness (Chapter Fourteen).

There were, of course, "works of imagination" available, too—romances on the Continental model, plays, poems in a variety of modes and kinds— the sorts of materials that worried the moral guardians of youth. Whether those who took pleasure in reading these works moved readily to novels when there were novels to read is a matter of some doubt. The appeal of works of imagination in the traditional kinds differed substantially in its design from that in novels, and romances—for all the moral suspicion they generated from the establishment—were quite traditional, conventional, and communal in their nature, with an appeal that looked backward for its values rather than forward as did the novel. Readers of poetry— pastorals, poetic epistles, social and political verses, philosophical poems, georgics—probably did often go on to read novels, but not as a replacement for poetry. Poetry, even when it was luxurious, lascivious, or occasional, was thought to be "serious" and demanding in a way that new novels were not, and the movement from one to the other was not a natural one, for both the needs addressed and the pleasures afforded were thought to be quite different in the two modes. Only readers of plays seem to have moved easily and naturally to the new narrative fiction from motives that suggest continuity of desire, need, and pleasure.

"Works of imagination" count for relatively little in the total world of print in generations of readers just before the novel. Readers of novels came to regard pleasure, entertainment, and delight among their chief attractions, but it does not follow that readers necessarily translated their desires from one kind of "works of imagination" to another; pleasure comes in many forms and works itself out in mysterious ways. A little later, I shall argue that the fundamental "preparation" for novels came not from other fictional or imaginative works but from works that seem to have had forms and rationales that were superficially quite different. But first I want to describe in more detail the fundamental directions of feeling and value in the groups most likely to find novels satisfying—and thereby describe what concerns readers took to their reading whatever its content, tone, or form—in the generations just before the novel.

Beyond what people were told to read or actually did read lies a series of other, prior issues about attitude, interest, and desire. The ability to read—and thus to bring a particular acquisitive skill to a great variety of human problems, practical as well ss theoretical and artistic—lies after all near the surface of human characteristics; it is "superficial" not in terms of what it can do for the individual but in terms of determining the human needs to which it can minister. Reading may respond to an aesthetic longing, a desire to reason out a philosophical or theological question, or a need to acquire a specific piece of information—the price of wheat, the way to get to Upton, or how to act in a particular set of human circumstances—and it may even create, or enable, specific desires or needs that did not exist for individuals before they became literate, for it raises horizons and expands the sense of epistemological possibility. But prior to literacy are most of the basic human concerns, intellectual as well as emotional and pragmatic, that may or may not be articulated. Many of those concerns are specific to individuals and individual circumstances and thus are, if not beyond the reach of psychological study, beyond the range of consideration for cultural studies of a particular time or set of circumstances. But many are shared concerns peculiar to cultural movements and social conditions, and I turn now to questions of social pattern and cultural consciousness that suggest why readers of the later seventeenth century were ready for fictional narratives of a new kind.

CHAPTER FOUR

Looking Forward: Time

■

READERS reading—whether novels or newspapers, in London or Boston, during the eighteenth century or the twentieth—are impelled by a variety of forces personal, cultural, and temporal. They come to a particular text both because they are attracted and because they are driven. Many attractions are, of course, specific to a particular text and constitute what a large proportion of literary criticism (both as a discipline and as conversation or gossip) is still about. And many drives are equally specific to individual readers—why criticism even when it is reader-centered often seems rigid, insensitive, and irrelevant to real readers. But there are generic considerations on both sides of the reading act as well, characteristics of novels that tend to attract one group of readers rather than another, and characteristics of readers in a given time and place that lead them to seek books that readers from other contexts might ignore.

Each is hard to be precise about, and the two are delicate to bring together, although (in a sense) that is what every author tries to do in writing a book and every publisher in marketing one. Nothing I can say here about the attractions of novels will be true of all novels, nor can I provide a cultural characterization of readers that will do justice to all, but I can isolate some patterns that suggest why readers and books come together in such a distinctive way in the early eighteenth century—in the novel and to some extent in lesser texts that point readers and writers to features that become characteristic of the novel. In Chapters One and

Two, I discussed a number of features of eighteenth-century English novels that suggest, implicitly, why certain readers would be attracted to
them. Here I want, first, to draw out those implications, focus, and amplify
them, then to look again to readers—to the other, human side of the
reading act. My aim in both procedures is to suggest what was on the
minds of potential readers, either when they picked up a novel or, before
there were novels to pick up, when they rummaged the bookstalls for
other reading materials that might answer similar questions or fulfill similar needs.

I

PROFESSIONAL readers—critics, historians, and others who read books
for a living or for academic credit—have a bad reputation with ordinary
readers, those who read for pleasure or for any other reason or whim that
suits them. In some measure we deserve it. In our anxiety to tell the
complex truths of literature we often neglect or deny the simple ones,
and, while it is true that books do for readers many complicated things
that go beyond conscious desire, they also perform straightforward and
mundane tasks—providing a pastime, giving information and worldly
guidance, telling stories, offering companionship and conversation as a
kind of human substitute, amusing or distracting us, insulating us not
only from other activity but also from introspection, boredom, and nothingness. Some of these functions bother critics more than others. Ideas
we tolerate more readily than feelings, though feelings can be forgiven,
too, as long as they are general enough or in the service of some higher
good and not too personal or pragmatic. Going to novels to learn about
human nature seems to be acceptable, but not going to them for simple
information. The more abstract the reason for reading, the better; the
functions of reading that come closest to the practical seem the most
threatening to our enterprise. Or such at least is the position we most
often espouse, leaving quietly aside all the half-known, accidental, and
downright selfish reasons that bring tens of thousands of readers every
year to novels for reasons that neither authors nor critics are flattered by.

I have no desire to diminish the sense of how involved an intellectual,
emotional, and aesthetic experience reading can be, but I do want to
emphasize here some quite elemental things about reading, things that
may be easier to see among new readers or casual and unsophisticated
ones, although they are not necessarily any less important even to the
most experienced or professionalized ones. The eighteenth-century novel
has no corner on these attractions: nineteenth- and twentieth-century
readers, as well as moviegoers, museum visitors, and concertgoers, seek

them as well. But, because the novel was new in the eighteenth century and just finding its sea-legs, novels like *Robinson Crusoe, Pamela,* and *Evelina* suggest in a plainer and less displaced way some of the features that promote such attractions. And defining those attractions, or even simply admitting that they exist, suggests a creative kinship between the novel and some of the less sophisticated, less "literary" forms that precede it.

The early novel's insistent attention to daily life in contemporary circumstances among more-or-less ordinary human beings who communicate in informal language signals a whole range of powerful attractions for eighteenth-century readers. In spite of a lot of attention to such matters in varieties of rhetorical, psychoanalytic, and reader response criticism, our sense of exactly how readers relate to imaginary worlds is not much advanced over Coleridge's view or even Aristotle's. Whatever vicariousness toward characters is ultimately all about, eighteenth-century readers could see a lot of themselves in English novels, more than they could locate in earlier fiction that described more extraordinary circumstances and was set in more remote places. Readers of novels often found fictional events occurring in streets they themselves actually walked every day, confronted conflicts or choices they might (or did) themselves face, met characters with backgrounds exactly like their own or those of people they associated with in their regular lives, or read words they might themselves have said or written if they were to describe their own existence or tell their own story. Readers did not necessarily have to "identify" with a hero or heroine, fantasize themselves into particular circumstances, or even consciously compare their own situations with those in novels to find fictional worlds that were in a broad sense educational, satisfying intellectually and informationally as well as emotionally and aesthetically.

How systematic, or even how conscious, readers were in their quest for information may be impossible to sort out. But even when they moved to remote or exotic places (as in *Robinson Crusoe*) or traced circumstances unlikely to find parallels in a reader's own life (as in *Moll Flanders* or *Tristram Shandy*), the ordinary and everyday character of novels meant not only that recognizable reality lent probability but also that it provided practical facts. Readers, especially young readers, have always found novels a ready source of information about worlds they have not yet quite entered or circumstances still unmet. Just as young readers in the mid-twentieth century openly went to novels for the practical secrets of courtship, sex, and contraception (often only to be disappointed or misled), so have readers in many ages turned to novels to discover how the world "really" works in matters of love, marriage, money, career, conversation, negotiation—virtually everything that we wish to feel more comfortable and sophisticated about than we ordinarily do. Novels are an easy place—impersonal, unthreatening, and (if they truly *represent* contemporary manners) reliable—to sort out the ways of the world, to see how experienced people react in a variety of circumstances, to crack the code of adulthood and social expectation. For many, novels have always been parent substitutes or even parent antidotes, a place to go when peer information fails, or when advisers are unavailable, unsympathetic, or untrustworthy, or when other printed sources—advice columns, manuals, or reference books—seem old-fashioned, corrupted, fainthearted, quaint, restrained, or boring. What Johnson says in *Rambler* 4—in a context that essentially belittles the novel—is, like so much of Johnson, basic, forthright, a digest of what his contemporaries would oft have said had they been intelligent or articulate enough: readers get from novels, says Johnson, "lectures of conduct, and introductions into life."[1]

Readers who covet no imaginary substitute for life may well need, nearly all the time, a guide for it. In books like *The Practise of Pietie*, *The Whole Duty of Man*, and *A Serious Call to a Devout and Holy Life*—or *The Seaman's Monitor*, *The Husbandmans Calling*, *The Young Man's Guide*, and *The Ladies Library*—readers were supposed to be able to find, according to their cultural guardians, useful advice about manners and customs. When the Bible was not particular or accessible enough, Guides like these were widely expected to fill specific needs, and probably they did for many readers, especially in the generations before the novel emerged and began to cover, in narrative and fictional form, some of the same ground.[2] The casuistical tradition, especially in its Puritan forms, in which specific cases of conscience were examined in detail in relation to general ethical principles, carried didacticism to more and more particular lengths in sermons, pamphlets, and periodicals designed especially to the purpose.[3] Here, too, readers might find thoughtful consideration of practical questions about behavior in the real world, with firm advice about how to survive. When novels began to present extended fictionalized versions of such situations, in effect fleshing out "cases" and making them part of some larger whole, they came to provide for readers a carefully distanced, "safe" version of life information. Because the novel purports to offer a large picture of life in several dimensions and because it shows us outcomes and presents a sense of causality while always pretending to be about someone else, it offers ready advice, easy to translate unasked into our personal experience. Its clues are subtle and unthreatening because it pretends to show us what happens without forcing on us any shoulds, or musts, or shalt nots. Such information was especially valuable at the beginning of the eighteenth century to potential readers not only because of their youth but because of the particular mix of changing social circumstances that obtained in the culture then.

The questions that novels answer may not always be ones that a reader asks or knows to ask, and they may be formed in ways that require translation and adaptation. Usually they are quite specific to a particular person and set of circumstances: how does a woman who is a veteran of a variety of marital and sexual relationships cope with the discovery that she is now married to her own brother? How does a servant girl deal with sexual advances from her master? How does a spirited, open, and guileless young man protect himself from a conniving and mean-spirited half brother? But they engage human situations and anxieties faced by people who are quite different. Sometimes novels seem to have originated in an abstract question answered in terms of a particular character and specific situation. Defoe claimed, clearly exaggerating but not necessarily lying, that the fable is always created for the moral, and not vice versa.[4] Novelists' minds work in notoriously convoluted, mysterious, and varied ways, and they become involved in their stories and situations in different ways and in different waves of intensity. But their success ultimately lies in an appeal to things on the minds of readers who, while individuals all, share recognizable concerns. Novelists, no matter what their commitment to specificity, work hard to give the impression that a grid of abstract patterns underlies the constellations of particulars. Whatever the interest in individual plots and characters for individual novelists, novels characteristically address certain broad human questions—some timely, some enduring, some both—and develop human paradigms that, however unconsciously or uncalculatedly, can readily become referential and didactic for readers.

The need for help with the ways of the world may be the most immediate motivation for many readers when they turn to novels, possibly outranking—or at least challenging—entertainment and the sheer joy of disappearing into an alternative world. How does the world work? What are the rules? How do others manage the difficult pressures and choices that the world offers? How do they cope with competing demands of love and honor, of reason and passion, of personal life and professional responsibility? How do people talk in particular circumstances? What do they think about? How do they act? How do they feel? We may never know how much of modern human history has gone the way it has because people at crucial moments have said or done a certain thing in imitation of some character in a novel who had acted that way, on the assumption that that was the way it was to be done.

Life *does* imitate art, often quite self-consciously, and sometimes to ill ends because novelists do not always wish or intend to offer models. None of us would rationally decide to turn our personal decisions over to novelists, but the desire for instruction (usually a little disguised) still remains one of the most powerful motives for reading a novel, or autobiography, or history, or for seeing a film. Wiser novelists usually understand that they have taken on this responsibility, whether they had intended to or not. The instruction we seek usually involves not so much specific situational advice as a larger sense of the way things are, a knowledge of human habits, rituals, and expectations, a cracking of the code. But specifics often linger into life, too, if only because vivid novels join our memory, and what they offer—phrases, actions, postures, paradigms—is ready at hand even to the unwitting imitator.[5]

The well-known story of how Samuel Richardson came to write *Pamela* is suggestive of how novelists may merge different aims and meet more than one need at a time. Busy compiling a practical guide on how to write letters for various circumstances (a volume to be called *Familiar Letters*), Richardson found himself writing letters that began to tell a story as well, thus addressing a different set of practical questions about modes of action in certain circumstances. How is an innocent servant girl to act when her wicked master decides it is his right to seduce her? How can she preserve her virtue and keep her position, or (better yet) improve herself as a result? The situations and themes of early novels suggest how often novelists saw their function partly in terms of addressing readers' needs to know about the ways of the world—how others handled particular difficulties or responded to habits and rituals larger than themselves. Novels sometimes seem founded in an abstract question answered in terms of a particular character and specific situation. What is a beautiful and sensible young woman to do when she finds herself in love with a man she disapproves of? What is one to do about love, integrity, and the marriage market when caught in the middle of family greed for prestige, money, and power? How does one conduct oneself when thrown into the arms of a libertine as the only seeming alternative to a toadlike suitor approved by one's parents? How can someone retain integrity and self-respect when opposing inappropriate parental wishes? At what point does parental authority cease? How does one live with having been raped by a suitor? Or . . . what is it like to be born an orphan girl and have to live by your wits, your dextrous hands, and your attractive body? What is it like to be thrust back upon the primitive circumstances of society and have to make do with only the resources of nature for food, shelter, and company? How does one cope with being utterly—totally—alone?

The questions that novels try to answer for the curious and the innocent easily slide from intellectual ones (about the ways and means of the world) to emotional ones, and much of what the novel does in answering questions about ordinary grown-up life involves the needs of readers to fantasize and wonder about the quality and particularity of experience as well as just know the fact of it. When the question becomes "What would it be like to be a thief and a prostitute like Moll Flanders?" instead of "What does one do when faced with a choice between poverty and prostitution?" we have subtly shifted to readers' needs to transcend themselves, to participate imaginatively in another existence. Unlike conduct books and treatises on contemporary manners, novels offer vicarious pleasure in the information they provide and thus "transcend" their context as they transform advice to story or fantasy, but they often begin from prosaic premises and openly court the practical curiosity of the young and inexperienced. *Evelina's* title page, for example, promises to recount "a Young Lady's Entrance into the world," indicating precisely the kind of information some readers need.

I I

MOST, in fact nearly all, protagonists of eighteenth-century novels are young men and women, and plots typically explore the central life choices of those about to embark on a career or marriage. Characters usually come before us at their most formative stage of life, and the main interest lies in how choices are made, the obstacles to human fulfillment, and the results of the choices. Most novels—*Clarissa, Tom Jones, Evelina, Tristram Shandy, The Female Quixote,* or *Roderick Random,* for example— dwell at length on a relatively short amount of time in which choices are made and patterns are set, although others explore over a longer haul the consequences of youthful determination or lack of it. Robinson Crusoe, after refusing to learn from the several warnings provided him in his early adventures at sea, spends half a lifetime trying, in a far-away miniature, to recreate his life and build a culture from seeds and scraps. Moll Flanders moves from degradation to degradation—from petty deceit to thievery, adultery, whoredom, incest, almost to murder—after lapsing into a life of lust, crime, and will-lessness. Amelia lives out a difficult marriage with an errant husband, reproducing the years and complications of *Pamela II,* although in a radically different tone. *Sir Charles Grandison* offers us the adult, family implications of good marital choices, and *Ferdinand, Count Fathom* recounts the sad results of early depravation. *Tristram Shandy,* having it both ways, stretches out the strands of time across years and miles to deal with outcomes and implications, always outcomes and implications in spite of its apparent preoccupation with the epiphanies of sperm, slips of forceps, dropped window sashes, and other moments trying to be momentous in themselves.

The eighteenth-century novel is full of long looks and often painful examinations of how things come out in the long run; many of the novels were, after all, written by older men who thought of themselves as having seen it all. But most often the thrust has to do with how things got that way, what choices got made, and what the variables were in those decisions. The long run may be the ultimate emphasis, but youthful choices are the focus—not a contradiction, because those novelists with the most pressing concerns about youth (concerns pressing enough to write about) are not those worried about tomorrow, but about tomorrow and tomorrow and tomorrow. Youthful readers may be more concerned about the short run, one of the central tensions in novels, but they get their insights from bursts, sprints, and dashes rather than from long distances and the challenge of endurance.

It is the young, unformed heroes and heroines who are generally the liveliest in eighteenth-century fiction. They are the ones who have lasted best in the historical memory and public imagination, and it is they who made the greatest impact when they first appeared, if one is to judge by the reception expressed by insistent individuals or recorded in the public press. *Tom Jones*, for example, was received far more enthusiastically than *Amelia*.[6] In later ages and other cultures, novels similarly pay an inordinate amount of attention to youthful years and the factors that form character and set the habits and outcomes of life. Not all readers of novels, then or now, were young, of course, and reading about youth at the crossroads carries pleasures and insights for those well beyond, or not yet ready for, the central moments of choice. But modern readers in challenging situations of their own tend to like to read about themselves (or about some version of a self they might become); that is one reason novels with their everyday, ordinary, subjective qualities become, in an age of urban mobility, the fiction of choice over remote and romantic narratives. Young readers tend to choose books with young protagonists in the midst of things, while older ones lean toward novels in which protagonists linger into implication and live out in triumph or (more likely) pain and sorrow their early choices. It is a point that every teacher making out a syllabus knows or comes to regret not knowing, for twenty-year-olds may ultimately appreciate *Antony and Cleopatra*, *King Lear*, *The Return of the Native*, and *Madame Bovary*, but these are not the texts they would choose if left to their own tastes and instincts, and such stories about older protagonists seldom make a quick initial impact. The pleasures of extreme vicariousness—imagining oneself to be a totally different kind of person in wholly different places and circumstances—are major reading pleasures, but they are seldom the ones that attract readers at first or that get them started on a particular book.

If young readers saw themselves and their immediate choices addressed forcefully and directly in most eighteenth-century novels, they brought to their reading a somewhat different set of concerns, contexts, and attitudes than did those facing the same choices a century earlier. What was distinctive about their needs and expectations gave their reading an urgency that was not present in earlier generations when social change was more slow, when family and community were more stable, and when choices were not so likely to be radical or far reaching. The fact that England had changed so substantially during the seventeenth century from a rural culture to an urban one—or rather, from a culture that took its values from a rural past into one that looked toward modernity with eagerness and anticipation—meant that those approaching crucial choices of life brought with them an unprecedented relationship with their cultural base, and it was precisely those in the new reading class and those most likely to have major choices to make—because they were young, ambitious, and mobile—who were the legitimate heirs of the changing attitudes. Whatever young readers found when they picked up a novel—whether *Pamela, Betsy Thoughtless,* or *Peregrine Pickle*—they brought with them drives, needs, compulsions, and biases given them by their historical present, a present that needs to be understood in some emotional and psychological as well as intellectual detail.

I I I

THE polite literature of the early eighteenth century, in spite of its increasingly urban settings and insistent London locations where it was conceived and created by writers who had consciously sought the city, provides an inadequate idea of how powerful the forces of modernity really were. Even the urgency of the great conservative manifestos— Swift's *Battle of the Books,* for example, or Pope's *New Dunciad*—fails to suggest how the lines were drawn or how the culture perceived the change, and subsequent generations have largely depended on that one side. Because those who speak for the old values are so articulate, so rhetorically effective, and have stood so well the test of time and literary criticism, it is (ironically) hard to see how the future looked to those who welcomed rather than dreaded it. Dryden, poised as he was on the border of two centuries and even more delicately balanced between old and new values, gives a much fairer sense of what contemporaries saw when they looked forward than does Swift or Pope. And the typical consumer of novels—or those who a generation in the future would consume novels when there were novels to consume—represents the view of the future that Swift and Pope refused and that Dryden only tentatively and ambivalently represented. Those who would read novels—and those who earlier needed most what novels would come to offer—were those who were least likely to espouse the Augustan view but who, instead, saw change as inevitable and (more important) as a personal opportunity to join the future and make their home there. The underclasses in the old culture, including women, could take little comfort from the Augustan desire to preserve traditional values, and the espousal of new values, however frightening or uncertain they might be, for them meant at least the possibility of altered opportunity.

The equivocation and vacillation of Dryden about past and present perhaps typifies the complicated plight and determined compromise of literary figures in the Restoration. Because of his ambivalence, Dryden is sometimes patron saint and sometimes scapegoat for each side when the sharp division comes. Mostly he deserves his reputation as a double agent: often he is Neander, articulating the loyalties and possibilities of new directions, but sometimes he is almost Crites in his backward-looking, dogmatic, and unflinching wars against Shadwell and the whole scribbling race of competitors. As long as he could be, clean and clear, chief spokesman for the moderns, Dryden wore that mantle comfortably and becomingly, but when he felt the hot breath of competitors he often donned livery that, as Swift pointed out, fit him loosely if at all. Swift's comic portrait of Dryden trying to wear Virgil's helmet and finding it swimmingly loose around his head suggests the way many of his younger contemporaries regarded his uncertain allegiances. But he is also (and as justly) the spiritual father of English Augustanism, and Pope and Swift are his heirs even when some aspects of his fatherhood disappoint or embarrass them. There he is, Janus-like, looking forward in one of his aspects and backward in the other, standing for the difficulties of honest choice when a culture comes to a sharp division of direction.

Dryden's ambivalences may represent a more perceptive and reasoned view of modernity than do the more categorical stances of Pope and Swift—certainly they represent a more balanced one—and there is conviction and a clear-eyed sense of temporal change in the mellowed, resigned pronouncement, in *The Secular Masque* of 1700, that " 'Tis well an Old Age is out, And time to begin a New." Still, Dryden's engagement with the old age was strong, and he would have disliked what the new brought as much as the younger Augustans did. But he often felt the freight of the past heavily on his shoulders, and he saw clearly, sometimes resignedly, that the new world would have its day whether he liked it or not. Few of the early ushers of that new world—Defoe as well as Locke, Lennox as well as Dunton—had Dryden's resonant sense of the past or his reasoned perspective on how old values could be transformed and reborn. In differing ways they all felt that the seventeenth century was well behind them, and many of them meant to start the new world from nothing, without reference to existing institutions, or structures, or patterns, or even ashes. New was what they desired, not renewal or transformation; they wanted innovation, not renovation or restoration: the only time that mattered was now. They were modern, they were young, they were ready. They were the new breed in a new world that valued the moment and the momentary more than all the mountains of past time and accumulated tradition, and they perceived the needs and desires of the public to be all shiny and new with hardly a trace of the past relevant to any of them—or so it seemed in their celebration of the new and their willingness to scuttle anything old. Theirs was a one-sided view, of course, more shortsighted and less experienced even than the dogmatic dismissal by orthodox Augustanism of all its enemies in the modern world; but it led to new ways of seeing, thinking, and writing, and ultimately it prepared readers for a whole new literature and a far broader cultural base. Not all the young saw things this way, of course (these were not the views of Pope even at age twelve when Dryden pointed to a new age and then died), nor were even the most vociferous advocates of modernity always so clear and convinced. But loyalties to past and present did divide the world dramatically.

After Dryden, the turn-of-the-century writers largely felt that they had to choose a loyalty, as philosophers and scientists had already had to do. Either they looked back to a past with authority, dignity, and a clear set of guidelines for subsequent ages, or they looked toward a future that might be unlimited but certainly was unknown. It may have been party factionalism and personal spite that determined the lines as often as cultural assumptions or philosophical loyalties, but the result was still the same. It is not difficult to pin badges of "ancient" or "modern" on almost anyone at the beginning of the eighteenth century, and—as if there could be doubts—Pope's catalogue of the damned in *The Dunciad* provides a permanent, nearly infallible record. Dunces espoused the present and sought the values of the future. Heroes looked backward.

I V

IF John Dryden was Neander for many intellectuals and traditionalists at the end of the seventeenth century, John Dunton was a more nearly representative type of the new man who, despite an ingrained respect for authority and a conservative religious temperament, championed modernism and worshiped the dawn of every day as a pointer to an improved future.[7] Dunton was one of the journalistic pioneers who articulated unabashedly a doctrine of progress and called attention daily, as the term "journalism" implies, to the immediacy of time's import. Dunton's beloved Athenianism is as close to the exact opposite of Swift's Augustanism, both in its philosophical presuppositions and in its practical implications, as any dichotomy in the real world is likely to be, and if Dunton was not ultimately the most successful of the age's dunces, either as author or bookseller, his fleeting moments of success and fame and his lifelong battle against poverty and neglect suggest that it was like to be devoted to new tastes and temperaments. Such a figure was dependent on a fickle public for whom the latest novelty became quickly outdated, a public who (paradoxically) retained a residual respect for the world and times that they had lost and felt only passing attachments to the fads and trends they patronized and practiced. The frustrations and failures that the very term "Grub Street" represents underscore the public reluctance to accept new values and new ways of writing, but any clear-sighted observer could see by 1700 that the culture's energies now resisted the past and sought new directions yet to be defined.

The first generation of modern London hacks—the generation of Dunton, Gildon, Manley, and Ward[8]—was a sorry lot not so much because its members lacked talent as because they lacked focus and a clear sense of where, besides winding back alleys and steep-staired garrets, novelty and innovation might lead. Often they were as sloppy, ignorant, mercurial, and uncertain of their aims as their detractors said, but they also glimpsed a different world ahead, and the first generation of novelists— as well as later Romantic rebels—owed them more than literary history has traditionally admitted. To make any sense of the novel, and of the directions of mid-eighteenth-century writing generally, one has to hear the new accents entering the literary world as well as the familiar tones of Congreve, Swift, Pope, and Gay. These new voices did not yet have much to say, and the way they said it often showed appalling taste and worse judgment, but the reality they were striving to reflect was a reality moving fast to take over the public press and try to dominate a popular readership that was not so much growing as settling and defining itself. One doesn't get pretty literary history by including wilderness warbles, squawls in the night, and hesitant verbal pauses, but one doesn't get accurate literary history by considering only the books and humankind that dwell in elegant drawing rooms or among the calf-lined shelves of the libraries of the great.

Less natively brilliant and more psychologically confused than some contemporary writers, and less shrewd and more eclectic than some contemporary booksellers, John Dunton typifies the restless, ambitious, and often feckless turn-of-the century Londoner. No single individual is, of course, typical of all the moves of that unstable moment. But Dunton's stable family past, firm roots in the countryside, and anxiety to make a new life and living in a world of public information accurately represent the shift in altered balance and values. His was the swirling confusion and the determined new thrust of a tidal change, and he is at once a response to a new sensibility and contributing cause of it. Dunton was born in Grafham, Huntingdonshire, in 1659, a rural son of a family with deep, if undistinguished, roots in country soil. He was the son, grandson, and great-grandson of Anglican clergymen. His great-grandfather and grandfather were both vicars of Little Missenden (Bucks), and his father was successively rector at Bedford, Grafham, and Aston Clinton; he ended his career less than a dozen miles from the vicarage of his father and grandfather.

The young Dunton grew up in Aston Clinton, thirty miles from London, and when he left home in 1674 at the age of fifteen to be apprenticed to a London bookseller, the rift in family tradition reflected altered circumstances typical of the time. Dunton's father had been born in Little Missenden, where generations of his family had lived before him, and his Cambridge B.A. and successive preferments represent a professional advance over previous generations as well as a geographical mobility of a few miles. But it was the young John Dunton as a London apprentice who disrupted the family pattern and who represents the cultural shift. His father had intended him for the clergy—the family tradition for eldest sons—but the young John by his own admission was not an apt pupil, and the decision to apprentice him to Thomas Parkhurst ultimately was a practical one. The choice of Parkhurst represents, however, another break with tradition, for Parkhurst was the nation's most prominent Presbyterian bookseller and a Londoner. No doubt the elder Dunton chose Parkhurst because of his character and reputation as a firm master rather than because of his religion or politics—a judgment that was ultimately rewarded, although not before the son had once run away, led his fellow apprentices in a hapless political demonstration, engaged in several pranks that he later admitted with some disdain, and married into a dissenting family. Dunton completed his apprenticeship and was admitted to the Stationers' Company in 1681 at the age of twenty-two. In his autobiography he described his youth in Adamic terms as a "whole world before me" (*Life and Errors*, p. 63), but it was a far different world from Milton's or his father's.

Dunton early considered himself a figure whose interests lay out of the common road, and it is no wonder that his father decided, or agreed, that Dunton's calling was not to the clergy which had sustained and defined the family in previous generations. In his own several accounts of his childhood, Dunton repeatedly emphasizes his "rambling humor" and his recurrent desire to be in physical motion, investigating new things in new places. The steady and secure life of the village clearly did not satisfy his taste for adventure and novelty, and if Defoe had needed a model for the restlessness and "rambling thoughts" of the young Robinson Crusoe he could have located one in this son-in-law of his friend and pastor, the Dissenter Samuel Annesley. In an early allegorized account of his adolescence, Dunton insists that his entire "Life is a continued Ramble" (*A Voyage Round the World,* p. 25) and describes himself as "a Citizen of *London,* and all the World" (p. 24), and later in a more straightforward (if just as eccentric) autobiography, he describes his whole life as determined by his "Humour of *Rambling"* (*Life and Errors,* p. 215). When he finished his apprenticeship and had his own bookshop, Dunton remained restless, footloose, and somewhat aimless, and on several occasions he made long voyages, ostensibly in an attempt to expand his book trade but actually more to gratify his rambling humor than to further his business. He made a lengthy voyage to New England in 1685–86, leaving his new wife behind to mind the shop, and shortly after his return left again for Holland.

There were always legal or commercial reasons for his wanderings, but he admitted that he preferred rambling (which he equated with writing) to business. Writing and bookselling together addressed Dunton's continuing desire to explore the length and breadth of his world and to seek his fortune in modern, experimental ways. He sometimes spoke of his fast-paced and chaotic writing style in the same tone—and in similar terms—as his itinerant wanderings. Both were "rambles," and his writing and traveling both reflected his impatience with the world as he found it and his restless desire to discover and describe something new, strange, and surprising. Dunton insisted that "unless a Man can either *think or perform something out of the old beaten Road,* he'll find nothing but what his Forefathers have found before him" (*Life and Errors,* p. 247), and he meant to find something very different from what his father saw at Aston Clinton. Dunton's native restlessness and dissatisfaction with things as they were are accurate gauges of his generation, and his Crusoe-like unwillingness to settle for the fortunes of his father represent, well beyond Adamic errantry, the movement of the age visible in new locations, ways of life, vocations, and cautionary anecdotes—and growingly in new books.

Even Dunton's eccentricities are, in a sense, typical of an age proud of its reluctance to be too predictable, but Dunton increasingly carried his oddness to extremes, ultimately to a point beyond the reaches of reason. "Eccentric" is not a strong enough word to describe Dunton in his later years, when a combination of bad luck and his own naive and disorganized refusal to stay on top of his business interests led him into serious debt, legal tangles, political turmoil, spells of dubious sanity, and perpetual clashes with competitors, customers, and his wife and mother-in-law. His attempts to capture the public's attention became increasingly shrill and wild after the turn of the century, indicating not only his own increasingly fragile grasp on reality, but also a context in which audiences became progressively more difficult to surprise and impress. If some of his writing projects now seem hilarious and born only of a novelty-for-novelty's-sake mentality, they also imply a readership increasingly jaded by claims by originality and innovation yet insistent on knowing the latest modes and fashions. Dunton's several Athenian projects—from *The Athenian Mercury* of 1691 to *The Athenian Library* of 1725—are only slightly more emphatic and exaggerated in their claims for novelty than the scores of similar examples of hackwork that streamed from the London press at the turn of the century. Behind all of them—digests of popular accounts of scientific discoveries and hypotheses, narratives of strange and surprising events and of wonderful phenomena to be seen when traveling or to be discovered by some unique means at closer hand, essays that broached some hitherto unexplored topic or that employed a method altogether new, exposés of private behavior and behind-the-scenes events or of secret negotiations and clandestine agreements—were the needs of the audience to feel "in," up-to-date, aware of the latest facts, and current in the intellectual, cultural, and social trends of the moment.[9]

These are the needs of an expanding and changing society which prized knowledge, valued competition, and rewarded those who were the first to know or do anything. Such needs come to exist when a large enough portion of the society is gathered together closely enough to make the personal sharing of information an issue. The population of England considered in absolute raw terms was still overwhelmingly rural, but the audience for the rapidly expanding publishing trade was decidedly and evangelically urban, marked by special concerns and needs that allowed and encouraged every individual reader or news sharer to take a determined pride in his or her self-consciousness at being near the forefront of rapidly changing times, of worlds repeatedly and forever new.

In his fulsome autobiography *The Life and Errors of John Dunton Late Citizen of London; Written by Himself in Solitude* (1705)—probably the first autobiography in England to be at once I-centered and concerned primarily with events more secular than spiritual, and still of its kind the perhaps unique example—Dunton claims that he conceived his casuistical *Athenian Mercury* in a flash as he was walking in London with two companions. "[O]n a suddain I made a Stop, and said, Well Sirs, I have a Thought I'll not exchange for Fifty Guineas" (p. 249). The idea was in fact worth far more to Dunton. Most of his bookselling successes traded on it, and later, when others borrowed the notion and set up competitors to his "Athenian Society," Dunton complained bitterly that he had been pirated, forgetting perhaps that much of his own career (like that of most London booksellers) had been based upon adapting, imitating, or outright stealing some competitor's brainstorm of the moment. Dunton's Athenianism finally ran thin, and his later works in the Athenian manner did not do well in the London marketplace, but his original project represented the canniest reading of London taste in his career as writer and bookseller. In a London hungry for novelties, even the most successful innovations had a short life, for the fickle public devoured its pleasures and swiftly moved on, and bookstalls always teemed with new temptations. For all his own restless searching for novelty, Dunton could never quite accept the fact that the public gradually tired of his single best idea, and perhaps he secretly hoped (like projectors before and since) that this one-time novelty would defeat time and last forever.

Often Dunton seems to be trying too hard, and at other times he retreats toward conventionality in the face of shifting waves of taste he could neither control nor ride. His later Athenian projects often include miscellaneous essays that wander hopelessly from surmise to wild surmise. Little can be said for the structure or even the local craft of many of these essays, although Dunton wrote with a passion and energy that seems part of some larger historical force as if he were hurried along by prevailing cultural winds. But often Dunton, like his competitors for the eyes of quixotic London readers, is hardly trying, depending on a catchy phrase or odd construction to carry him through flimsy structures, scanty syntax, and thin ideas. Some of the writing was plainly done at top speed, and it often reads as if the words were tossed helter-skelter in hopes that some few would catch hold. And the sponsoring ideas behind the essays are often suspect or downright fraudulent: what passes for novelty and imagination sometimes sounds like an idea more than actually being one. Swift's parody of hackwork titles in A Tale of a Tub is no advance on Dunton: Swift's tubthumper claims to have written such gems as

A Panegyrical Essay upon the number THREE;

An Analytical Discourse upon Zeal, histori-theo-physi-logically considered;

A Critical Essay upon the Art of Canting, Philosophically, Physically, and Musically Considered;

A general History of Ears; and

A Panegyrick upon the World.

Dunton is his match, claiming to have written books or essays with the following titles:

A Compendious History in Folio, of the lives, and Deaths of all the most eminent Persons, from the Crucifixion . . . to this time;

"The Double Life: Or, a new Project to redeem the Time by living over to Morrow before it comes";

"The Funeral of Mankind: A Paradox, proving we are all dead and bury'd";

"Philanthropia Divina—or a General History of the remarkable Conversions which have happened to great Sinners, from the Thief upon the Cross, down to the present Year";

"Non Entity: Or, a grave Essay upon Nothing";

"The Spiritual Hedgehog, *a Project (or Thought) wholly new and surprizing,*"; and

"Of every Thing."

"I'll endeavour," Dunton promises at the beginning of *The Art of Living Incognito* (1700), "to Treat of Subjects that are most Surprizing" (p. 2). Dunton's determination to be innovative—or at least to *sound* new at any cost—leads him to extraordinary claims and rational leaps, but there is no real threat to the Gates of Horn. In a 1709 work, he claims to "have been Six Years preparing this *Nice Work* for the Press, that nothing might be wanting in this PACQUET to gratifie a curious Palate" (*Christian's Gazette*, p. x), but his testimony is to the human desire for novelty rather than his own ability, or that of other writers, to deliver on their promise to satiate it. For forty years Dunton seldom flinched in his effort to scratch the Athenian itch that he thought infected all his contemporaries, but repeatedly he suffered the ultimate humiliation for anyone who craved public attention so badly. By 1710 he was virtually a forgotten man in London, although he lived for twenty years more, dying within a few months and a few blocks of Defoe. There is a certain justice in his claim that, for all his public activity, he lived "incognito." He spent his final years in the second most populous city in the West altogether alone.

Dunton did not have unmixed feelings about his perpetual quest for the new and the strange, and his rhetoric on Athenianism often shows him conscious of Judeo-Christian warnings about intellectual overreaching. Sometimes—often while luring Athenians on with his promises—Dunton dissociates himself from common lovers of novelty, claiming that his loyalties are to a more respectable version of curiosity. In a 1700 essay entitled "Of the Athenian Itch," he claims that, although he had the itch for five years, he is now "quite cur'd." "I need say little to prove I'm cur'd of this *Itch*; my forsaking *London,* and all Company, plainly shews it. . . . I now Itch after Nothing. . . ." (*Incognito*, p. 26). In a later work dedicated "to the Lovers of Novelty," he admits that the itch is back and celebrates the love of novelty: "Having been an ATHENIAN (or *Lover of Novelty*) almost from my Infancy . . . I hope to present you with something NEW (I wish I cou'd say with something CURIOUS)" (*The Christian's Gazette*, p. i). A few pages later, he claims that the work "is not design'd to promote *the Athenian Itch,* but to cure it" (p. x), although his account of his devotion to this new and approved "Christian" curiosity sounds very much like his Athenian quest in other works, even if he claims religious authority: "tho' I insert nothing here but what is *new* (or very uncommon) yet I venture on no Subject . . . but what is founded on Scripture and Reason" (p. x).

Dunton did sometimes acknowledge that the sin of intellectual pride might be involved in the desire to know: "And as to the *Art of flying*, I have no reason to be against it, if discoverable by human industry. . . . Yet I doubt it may have somewhat of the Babylonish presumption in the eyes of God; and that such high curiosities are so far from being *useful*, that they may be dangerous" (*Incognito*, p. 37). "There's nothing," he says earlier in the same treatise, "the Nature of Man is more desirous of, than Knowledge; he pursues it to a Fault, and will fly even to Hell it self to advance it" (*Incognito*, p. 29).[10] However often he repented his new-fangledness, however, Dunton never strayed far from his commitment to Athenian values. "I so little like the *Way of the World* (i.e., am so great a Lover of Novelty)" he wrote in *Stinking Fish* (an exposé of his enemies) in 1708, "that I had rather err by my self in *a New Discovery*, than travel the Common Road" (p. iv). Dunton's own departures from the "Common Road" include only one novelistic venture, the unfocused and bizarre but suggestive *A Voyage Round the World* (3 vols., 1691), but his life and career illustrate the values and trends that lead to the novel; more important, his journalistic and publishing ventures become enabling devices for the working out of experiments in writing devoted to new directions based on new thoughts and untraditional assumptions.

V

WHATEVER his own attraction to the energies of modernity, Swift acknowledged no such ambivalences, and when he set out to scourge the likes of Dunton and the whole scribbling race who loved novelty, he took aim at the central values emerging in the culture. Swift's attack is nicely differentiated, articulating three separate but related preoccupations with newness. The first involves the new discoveries and new theories that apologists for modern writers derived, or thought they derived, from scientists, theologians, and philosophers. Many of these ideas impinged, as did the central religious fiction of the *Tale* itself, upon the authority of religion or of classical tradition. Audiences receptive to what they had not heard before might give credence to anything bold and brash that flew in the face of authority and received opinion, but Swift saw in such appeals only repeated assertions, flash, and an illogical use of analogy to principles that were already suspect. The idea that there could be new paradigms for thought or action sharply divided the contemporaries of Dunton and Swift; it was the most serious and threatening sense of novelty, and Swift gave it the most structural attention in *A Tale of a Tub* as well as making it the center of debate in *Battle of the Books*.

The second involved the desire to know the latest news, to have a gossip's sense of which present-day events everyone wants to talk about. It meant seeming *au courant* on happenings at court, social intrigue, military movements, and Continental rumors. Swift's attack on the mentality that prized gossip, scandal, up-to-the-minute awareness, and the desire to be thought the first to know is traditional, in the mainstream of satirists who regard such preoccupations as a national disease.[11] Still, his criticisms seem more pointed than those of Ben Jonson before him and Henry Fielding after, more firmly tied to historic particulars. The journalistic explosion in the late seventeenth century highlighted current events in an unprecedented way; London talk placed a high premium on "knowing" for even the most casual and unconnected observer, suggesting that everyone was crucially affected, even in the routines of daily life, by all public matters.[12] Such concern with news led to the third preoccupation isolated by Swift, a savoring of present time without regard to its antecedents, causes, or place in history. For many of Swift's contemporaries, the present moment seemed quite enough to be concerned with, and such a celebration of the present at the expense of the past— without any notion of causality or continuity—meant to Swift distortion of perspective and skewed values. Swift was prejudiced but clear. All three preoccupations suggest directions of contemporary writing that culminate in the novel, and Swift is good on all of them, but on the first and third he is especially acute. The second amuses him as a foible and superficiality of manners, but the other two imply deeper debasement.

"I profess . . . in the Integrity of my Heart, that what I am going to say is literally true this minute I am writing . . . ," wrote the putative Tale-teller in his dedication, anchoring truth altogether to timeliness. Swift's consciousness of mutability and transience focuses in the *Tale* on the modern preoccupation with freezing a moment as if understanding lies in intensity rather than in extensity or perspective, and Swift is at some pains to point out the fallacy of writing based upon such fleeting "realistic" observation.

> If I should venture in a windy Day, to affirm to *Your Highness*, that there is a large Cloud near the *Horizon* in the Form of a *Bear*, another in the *Zenith* with the head of an *Ass*, a third to the Westward with Claws like a *Dragon*, and *Your Highness* should in a few Minutes think fit to examine the Truth, 'tis certain, they would all be changed in Figure and Position, new ones would arise, and all we could agree upon would be, that Clouds there were, but that I was grossly mistaken in the *Zoography* and *Topography* of them.
>
> ("Dedication to Prince Posterity," p. 35)

Swift takes such transparent pleasure in the goofy intensity of passages like this that readers often suspect he finds his joy by indulging himself in attitudes he dare represent only parodically. But whatever private temptation Swift may have felt to absorb the modernist tendencies he isolates so ruthlessly (and however much he actually did so), he was suspicious of the self-indulgence in any writing-to-the-moment strategy. His attack upon its fragmentariness and lack of perspective is a vigorous intellectual one. He does not, in fact, speak directly about the emotional appeal of concentration upon the moment, choosing instead to view it as a part of the larger subjectivity which he sees as characteristic of modernism and of the new writing that celebrates modernity. Throughout the *Tale*, Swift brilliantly isolates one quality after another of the modern sensibility and temperament. To isolate the attitudes and features of contemporary writing that Swift attacks as reprehensible involves making a comprehensive list of features that found their labyrinthine way into the novel as it emerged in the half century after the *Tale*—subjectivity, novelty, contemporaneity, interest in individual lives, digressiveness, circumstantiality, the eccentric, and the bizarre. A *Tale of a Tub* is not exactly a parody of the novel—it is hard to parody something that has as yet no concrete form, tradition, or definitive example—but it is an exposure of the cast of mind and set of values that ultimately produced novels, and its attack upon the tastes and desires of contemporary audiences suggests that Swift understood modern readers early and well. Even if Swift thought that the directions of literature should be set by higher loyalties, he saw the causal relationship in a commercial world of print between the desires, however inarticulate, of potential readers and the responsive practice of writers.

Like other novelistic features that derive from specific, demonstrable cultural changes, writing-to-the-moment has a cousin's relationship to many other phenomena in eighteenth-century England. The concern with the simple instant of present time has outcomes in politics, theology, psychology, and educational theory as well as in the novel. In a time when the Christian religion was still the lens through which most people viewed their lives and adventures, the earliest and strongest signs occurred in theology, and one might argue (in the way that Christopher Hill argues the formative influence of Puritanism on scientific inquiry and a host of other aspects of English life) that religious belief and practice started the ripple that took in one realm after another of English culture.[13] But whatever the cause and wherever the starting point, the isolated moment is central to new ways of thinking about plot and temporal continuity. If the momentary experience of "conversion" can reverse a whole pattern of life and character, or an epiphanic moment of religious or psychological truth can provide an altogether new context of explanation, narrative can be based on notions of probability and character consistency quite different from traditional ones. Such conceptions open the possibility that the briefest moment may carry enormous interpretive or narrative weight, and they justify the kind of literary form in which a single instant of time can be the subject (or crux) of a very long book. If tradition and continuity could be interrupted or even reversed in the emotion of a moment, the implications of time and duration and permanence were now very different. Rather than the long shadow of the past, the quick flash of the present moment was to be the new focus of experience and the center that would control modes of thought, systems of value, and the content and form of literature. Swift's analysis of the emerging significance of the moment probably had little direct impact on the focusing of this cultural feature in the novel, but he pushed forward the growing cultural recognition of what an age of moment-centered consciousness could mean.

Swift's analysis of the intellectual pretensions of novelty—the first objection I mentioned—depends on terms established in the Ancients / Moderns controversy. What Swift has to say may well come directly from William Temple's sincere but flat-footed position about modern methodologies; in any case, there is little original in what he has to say, and his position is not only simplistic but anti-intellectual. Still, his understanding of what is at stake in the epistemology of modernism and his sense of what modern methodology means for the literary tradition is perceptive and accurate. The humanistic tradition, old elitist literary values, and the security of established authority all were, in fact, threatened by philosophical optimism, the new trust in human reason, and (especially) by belief in empiricism and the validity of individual observation. Swift's analysis of modern "progressive" thought is more detailed in *Gulliver's Travels* (especially in Book III), and the implications are there more fully drawn out, especially for science and technology. But the epistemological premises of modernism influenced not only science, philosophy, and theology but (among other things) the directions of writing and popular thought as well, and Swift's analysis, simplistic and prejudiced as it is, has the virtue of taking a clear view of contrasting premises. The novel was not the only beneficiary of the new thinking, but it was the most visible and influential one to manifest the new cultural spirit. The novel's dependence on an epistemology that privileges personal observation and empirical evidence more generally has crucial effects on its shape and ideological commitments, a matter I will put into a formal perspective in Chapter Eight. But all three branches of novelty isolated by Swift at the turn of the century are part of a larger mentality that quite beyond the novel—and long before it—involved place as well as time.

CHAPTER FIVE

Looking Forward: Place

■

NOT everyone in early eighteenth-century England lived in London or regarded London as the center of English experience, but to read the texts of the time, one might well think that they did. Even writings that reject urban values and champion the countryside or those that minutely chronicle rural life—Gay's *Rural Sports*, for example, or Thomson's *Seasons* or Cowper's *Task*—operate from implicit and often explicit nostalgia, their authors consciously aware that the city has become the operable norm in society and that love of the country, while it may be genuine and resonant, is quaint if not necessarily reactionary. From a position a century earlier as an odd and rather unpleasant outgrowth of English life—a place where the extremes of wealth and poverty, international power and individual insignificance, high art and ugly filth dramatically met—London had become by the eighteenth century the symbolic center of English life, perhaps already more important to the daily lives of the typical Englishman or Englishwoman than Paris would ever become to the average Frenchman or Frenchwoman. The centrality of Paris to French life may be more fabled, but London was more central to its nation's economy, and it touched personally the lives of a greater number of its nation's citizens.[1] It had taken on a symbolic significance to the nation that would have been inconceivable a century earlier and had become, in published writing, the assumed center of English life and values.[2]

I

PRECISELY when London came to symbolize England is hard to say, but by the time the novel emerged it was clearly so.[3] The Restoration itself was a major impetus. That single event established an English equivalent of Parisian habits and values. When the Caroline court returned, it brought urban manners and tastes and a predilection for urban institutions, such as the theater, that depended on a heavy concentration of people with similar desires. The Restoration introduced into English life the kind of imported cultural customs that a government in exile in the Continent's most sophisticated city had been able to annex. London just after 1660 could not yet claim the urbanity of Paris or the tradition of Rome, but what had already been established was a national taste for things more cosmopolitan, things associated with the great European cities, things that had always been regarded with suspicion and provincial contempt in a nation that prided itself on simplicity of heart, honesty of mind, and plainness of taste. Opera, for example, soon became a London rage, although many social observers, including some of the most articulate and civilized writers and cultural guardians, openly made fun of the fashion, not just because it was trendy and often theatrical at the expense of the verbal but also because it represented an invasion of foreign customs and challenged the integrity of native cultural institutions. The change did not come in a moment—it was full of developments like the growing concentration of commerce and finance, the acceptance of public entertainments for the select as well as for the masses, the establishment of coffeehouses, the coming of newspapers—and the resistance was often passionate, articulate, and chauvinistic. England had begun to have a sense of its relation to Europe, and if it never quite felt connected to the Continent—and never quite wanted to be—its older sense of unbridgeable distances was never again to be quite so sure. The basis for the bridge was, of course, economic, and England's maritime power, military strength, diplomatic finesse, instinct for trade, and financial acumen had long ago put the English in a way to assert their connection to the Continent whenever their sense of native tradition became sufficiently defined and strong to allow a confident positioning.

If 1660 seems a convenient date to mark the beginning of a substantial change, the tide of events over the next half century repeatedly swept forward urbanization and the prominence of London in particular. The wars with Holland and France and the increasingly complicated pattern of alliances among European nations, the increasing colonization of the Americas and the rapid expansion of world trade, the sheer physical growth of London as a geographical area and as a population center, and the disproportionately rapid development of London as an industrial, business, commercial, and financial hub cooperated to enhance the sense of London's importance to the Continent and reinforced its position at the center of English life. Besides, the growth of London meant both that the rest of the nation became more and more dependent on things produced in London (including books and other artifacts for the expanding publishing industry) and that an increasing proportion of the agricultural output of the nation was consumed in London, thereby binding at both ends the economic ties between London and the "country."[4]

Because reliable population statistics are hard to come by and because a lot of speculation by literary historians in earlier generations has been based on false or misleading information, it may be well to recall the facts of London's size and its proportion to the rest of the nation. London's population reached 900,000 just after the end of the eighteenth century (the census of 1801 provides a quite reliable figure), but earlier figures are more speculative. Because there were no official counts, the estimates now generally agreed upon have been cumulatively arrived at by studying historical documents in detail and by using modern statistical methods. Here are population figures now regarded, largely on the strength of the researches of the Cambridge population group, as the best we are likely to have for some time:

Year	Population of London	Population of England	% in London
1600	200,000	4,100,000	4.9
1650	400,000	4,900,000	8.2
1700	575,000	5,000,000	11.5
1750	675,000	5,800,000	11.6
1801	900,000	8,300,000	10.8[5]

In the rate of increase three things seem worthy of comment. First, rapid growth in the early seventeenth century meant that London doubled within fifty years. Second, the raw increase in London population was almost as great during the second half of the century in spite of the Plague of 1665 and the Great Fire of 1666—which might have been expected, quite beyond the numerical ravages the former took directly, and the indirect deterrent to growth that both represented, to have dulled urban attractiveness and discouraged emigration.[6] Third, the first half of the eighteenth century represents a relatively modest and stable period of growth (or, if one accepts Dorothy George's population estimate of 1700 [674,350], a period of no growth at all). It was then that the character of urban life became somewhat more defined, identifiable, and self-conscious—perhaps because the shockingly high mortality rates in London meant that a larger-than-ordinary proportion of the population was young and relatively new to the city. All the old urban malefactors and some new ones—crime, filth, disease, solitude, depression, an inept and corrupt medical practice, and cheap gin—conspired to deprive of pleasure and then life itself the aged, the infirm, the lonely, and the weak of body or spirit. To survive in those years in London, one had to be lucky as well as hardy, and it is no wonder that children and youth became—relatively suddenly—the object of advertising and merchandising for all sorts of goods, including pamphlets, newspapers, and books. If that period was, looked at in one way, one of the most squalid, dangerous, and depressing ages in urban history, looked at in another it was a time of great vitality and youth, a time when the survivors were vigorous and strong if not necessarily cheerful about their daily existence and difficult lot. There was little human continuity in those years. Disease felled many, and damages physical and psychic drove others into inaction, retirement, or back to their rural past, but a new supply of ambitious and vigorous youths moved into their place. For all the human fears, London continued to be the place to be.

A case could of course be made for the significance of London to English culture before 1660. The classic tension between country and city had meant, in some sense, London versus the rest of the nation for centuries before 1660. But if London had always been England's urban symbol and exercised disproportionate influence, the period from the Restoration through the early eighteenth century was especially crucial because the perception of London changed so substantially then. In the early seventeenth century, "typical" Englanders were still rural, tuned to the seasons, dependent on the soil; they looked to old traditions and familiar beliefs, even if they moved to London and made careers there. Despite Shakespeare's tenure in London theater, for example, he was always from Stratford, the bard of Avon. But less than a century later perception had changed radically. Dryden was a Londoner; only scholars remember that he was born in the rectory of Aldwincle All Saints and had a childhood in the Northamptonshire countryside. London was his life, and he came to depend on it for social and spiritual sustenance as much as for recognition and economic well-being. And Johnson not only thought that a man who is tired of London is tired of life but could scarcely think of traveling elsewhere or returning "home": we remember that he is from Lichfield for the opposite reason from Shakespeare, for we are conscious of all that he deliberately left behind, aware that he chose not to keep his emotional anchor there or to return for inspiration, sustenance, and support. He was from Lichfield, of London. Even as a struggling young poet and dramatist new to London, he was not the bard of Lichfield.

For the three generations of "Roman" writers that began with Dryden, London was home, no matter where they came from. Drawing upon the public and urban traditions of classical Latin literature, the generations of Dryden (b. 1631), Swift (b. 1667), and Pope (b. 1688) assumed the literary stances and moral rhetoric of a Christianized Roman tradition, and they took for granted that their residence in London, their friendships, and their social and professional converse were part and parcel of their decision to make a career in letters and to be part of the public social conscience that, for them, was requisite to a literary career. For writers the century before, London had sometimes been home too. Some (Spenser, Donne, Jonson, Herrick) were born there, and others lived there for convenience, but the powerful attraction that gathered virtually all writers to London by the end of the seventeenth century had only begun to develop. For most of Shakespeare's contemporaries and for most of the next two generations of writers (until the generation of Dryden), the resonance that sponsored and supported their work had developed in the countryside of their birth: for Sidney in Kent; for Shakespeare and Drayton in Warwickshire; for Daniel in Somerset; for Herbert in Wales; for Burton in Leicestershire; for Waller in Hertfordshire; for D'Avenant in Oxfordshire; for Marvell in Yorkshire. London was a familiar fact for most writers in Elizabethan, Jacobean, and Caroline times. For Restoration writers and later, it was a choice—but a choice they felt obliged to make. Urban values became the norm as country and village ones had been to earlier ages.

And in the late eighteenth century and early nineteenth, the turn back to the country—a kind of rural rebellion against the idea of Roman and urban literary assumptions—took even writers who were from London to the country and to an imaginary country of the mind. Except in a few distinctive verses, urbanness has little to do with the writings of Blake or Keats, despite their lifelong residence in London, for the world they imagined was full of village and country things—birds, trees, fields at harvest, chapels, village greens—and only fever, fret, and coercive institutions posed the threat of encroachment from the urban world. For the Wordsworths and Coleridge, the road to letters wound through London but led quickly to Somerset and ultimately to the Lake District; for Byron and the Shelleys, London was barely a way station on the way to rural—in their cases rather artificially rural—life in France and Switzerland, Italy and Greece.

But for Dryden and his contemporaries and followers, becoming a writer meant coming to London and making a physical and spiritual home there.

Dryden moved to school in London at age thirteen and returned in his mid-twenties to stay. Most of his distinguished younger contemporaries made their lasting move to London a little younger, just as they began to seek fortune or fame: Rochester at seventeen, Southerne at eighteen, Otway at nineteen, Wycherley at twenty, Behn probably a little older.[7] The Restoration's literary energies came altogether from London, and writers clearly thought of their literary careers as invested only there, wherever they were. Congreve is one kind of example. Born near Leeds and educated in Ireland, he moved to London at twenty-one to enter the law, then turned to literature and wrote his major works there before becoming a gentleman of ease, luxuriating in the attention given him by sophisticated London for many years after his early retirement. For Swift, London was both the center of his literary life and a road he was not able to take. Dublin became his London,[8] but even its urban setting was only a painful substitute for a consciousness that was spiritually at home only in London. As in many other aspects of Swift's career, things he did not choose impinged on things that he did, and that his career was at St. Patrick's instead of St. Paul's is an irony as great as any he himself imagined. Defoe, Aubin, and Richardson were to the urban manner born, the manor a forgotten world away; without London their work is unimaginable. Haywood was also born in London, and although her life and surroundings were not especially visible in her early writing, London later emerges as significant. Addison, Steele, and probably Manley[9] have in common with lesser journalists and scribblers like Dunton, Gildon, Oldmixon, and Ward an obliged emigration to the city, and their lives as well as their careers came to belong there.

Pope, Gay, Thomson, Young, Parnell, and scores of lesser figures all fit the basic pattern of those who early sought their fortune in London and remained there almost as if no other choice occurred to them, and even when they depict the countryside, their sensibilities have about them an urban planner's sense of chartered orderliness and an indoor sense of outdoors. Not that their engagements with gardens or even with the wilds were not sincere: it was simply that more important to them were the cultivation and love of those who were habituated to close human commerce, urban habits, and limited space. By midcentury one can readily see that for some writers, a rebellion had begun, and in Collins (b. 1721) and Cowper (b. 1731) there begins to be a major, prophetic shift in urban/rural loyalties. But the generation of Samuel Johnson (b. 1709), Henry Fielding (b.1707), and Laurence Sterne (b. 1713) is still best characterized by the sense of urban necessity that surrounds the whole idea of The Club, the daily routine of urban sociality chronicled by Boswell, and the sense that a writer's reward—wherever the writing itself was done—was located only in London. A new world rebellious and attracted to rural isolation was on its way, but London was still the place to focus a writing career or a full and resonant life. When the country surfaces for this generation, it is a matter of alternatives, flight, or nostalgia, a green place of the mind, memory, or imagination.

Aspiring figures in other fields than literature turned to London as well. The old image of the retired philosopher or scientist or statesman in a rural setting of retrospective contemplations became more and more a stylized fictional figure, or a conscious, carefully crafted role played by someone who had spent a majority of life in London and now chosen retreat, usually temporary, often in a newly built grand house or an old one purchased with new money made in or from the city as was Sir Robert Walpole's Houghton or Timon's villa. Considering the overwhelming dominance of London as a center of transportation and commerce, it is no wonder that leading figures either lived in London or maintained a second residence there, but the significant thing is that London came more and more to be considered the logical center of area after area of English life. The story is not entirely the same across lines of class and gender, but the tendency is similar, and when mobility is an issue at all the flow is toward London for nearly everyone. The most powerful migration seems to have been among rising classes—those who had the most to gain by going to the center of economic and social action and who had the most to lose by staying put. But even those who were secure and satisfied socially and economically found themselves increasingly caught up in London's orbit, whether or not they uprooted themselves from their past. Women seem to have been more hesitant to go to London than men, for there were fewer opportunities for them to change the directions of their lives anywhere, but those with specific ambitions almost always focused them in the city. Once writers, for example, became "professionalized"—that is, once writing as a vocation became somewhat detached from patronage and older "man of letters" notions—women who sought employment in the profession found London as necessary as men. Behn, Manley, and Haywood, for example, made careers there, not necessarily going specifically to write, but certainly finding that, once economic necessity took over their lives, London was the only possible place.[10]

In the years between the Restoration and the middle of the eighteenth century, literature came to be about London, too, as it had not been before. Restoration comedies made the first major move, transforming the nature of drama. The simple legend "The Setting: London" signals the change.[11] But the sharpest turn for writing seems to come right at the end of the century, when works like Ward's *The London Spy* (with the cumulative portrayal of the city as a new and vital organism) begin to appear with regularity. London assumes in the new century an increasing importance as a setting that reflects the concerns of an urban writing community and that also suggests what daily life is like for a variety of Londoners well beyond writers themselves. Swift's "Description of the Morning" and "Description of a City Shower," Gay's *Trivia; or the Art of Walking the Streets of London* and *Beggar's Opera,* Pope's *Rape of the Lock,* the *Dunciads,* and many of the later satires, Defoe's *Moll Flanders, Journal of the Plague Year,* and *Roxana* represent a literary concentration upon London unmatched in earlier generations, despite occasional London settings in polite literature and a minor preoccupation in the popular literature of the Elizabethans.[12] Until 1700, only stage comedies were regularly set in London in anything close to the present time;[13] after 1700, works of many kinds were, whether or not Londonness was really crucial to the story. Yet more often than not Londonness was crucial; it became not only setting but an essential part of most works, what in many cases they were about. London was not just place but time. Swift was right. In the modern sensibility, the moment was everything: London stood for the concern with contemporaneity itself.

The way that London enhanced its symbolic significance both in what writers wrote about and in the way they lived their lives partially reflects an altered symbolic conception among the people more generally, and the fact that literature increasingly treated London as typical of contemporary England—not an excrescence or blot upon it—clearly had an accelerating effect upon public opinion as well. There is no such thing as an average Englander in the eighteenth century, someone who combines and sums up the many contradictions and disparities of social class, economic status, occupation, and religious or philosophical assumptions. But if one were to construct a type of the Englishman or Englishwoman in, say, 1720, 1730, or 1740—a figure who would in a measure stand for the society and its preoccupations and directions, and especially one who would illustrate societal changes over the past century—that type would have to live in London, just as a type for a century earlier would have to live in the country or a village. By the late eighteenth century, poets had to create rural figures—as in Goldsmith's *Deserted Village* or Gray's *Elegy Written in a Country Churchyard*—out of whole nostalgic cloth. In the mid-seventeenth century, no one had had to make country symbols, only to harvest them, as Herrick, Herbert, Donne, Traherne, Waller, Milton, and many others did quite unself-consciously. The late Restoration and eighteenth century made sparks, cits, roués, coffeehouse habitués, apprentices, thieves, politicians, hacks, and merchants into the characteristic fictional figures of their times. The exceptions—Sir Roger de Coverly, for example, or Old Bellair—largely achieve their standing as figures against the current or as leftovers of a bygone world.

The importance of London is, of course, temporally relative. It did not happen in a single moment, and size itself is not really as important as the cultural perception of influence and currency of taste. Literally speaking, almost nine tenths of the nation in 1700 or 1750 still lived somewhere besides London, and the percentage of Englanders who lived in London did not change much after the late seventeenth century, until much later. But as E. A. Wrigley has argued, the impingement of London on non-Londoners substantially intensified after the middle of the seventeenth century, and Squire Western and his sister in *Tom Jones* stand for many another English family of the later seventeenth or early eighteenth century in their polar feelings about the city and their recurring acquaintances with it. For all his hatred of everything associated with London—from formal manners and urban filth to political compromise and the Hanoverian rats—Western ultimately finds himself having to go there on urgent business, for the city had impinged on his life and family without his permission. And for Mrs. Western, London is the only measure of life even when she seems hopelessly detached in time and space in a Somerset that yearns for old time and a life of total stasis. To say that London had become the symbolic center of England and that Londoners were typical representatives of the culture is not to reduce the issue to abstraction, but rather to suggest that in the minds of people then living—in the living consciousness of the time—looking backward and countryward involved conscious nostalgia and not a little fantasy, mistaken memory, and fictionalization. Just as the Act of Settlement of 1702 cast only an acknowledging glance at the past while dealing head-on with a contemporary world driving furiously into a new time, so the common consciousness in England at the turn of the century regarded the streets of London as the current route of time's winged chariot in its pursuit of the practical and the real.

I I

DAILY life in eighteenth-century London was not the same for Brick Dust Moll and Ned Ward as it was for Mirabell and Lady Mary. Social standing and economic circumstances made huge differences in comfort and regimen. But many facets of life were widely shared regardless of personal circumstances.[14] The "quality" of life for the eighteenth-century Londoner was often obtrusive and striking because of its difference from other contemporary ways of living. Many of these city people had recently been country people, and for most coming to London was a deliberate choice, often wrenching and traumatic even if adventuresome and exciting. Then, too, many citizens of London (an increasing number almost every year) had been born there, and some could date their London heritage back a few generations. A distinct urban identity—something akin to the old attachment to land and place—had begun to develop, and a London way of life was by 1700 fully enough established that newcomers were rapidly absorbed into it, perhaps modifying it as they came, but certainly being themselves changed by set expectations of what London was and by the kind of life Londoners conceived. The insistent contrast between Londoners and country types in Restoration comedy suggests a conscious—even zealous—attempt to establish awareness of a distinctive urban character, but by the turn of the century texts seem to assume it. When, for example, *The London Spy* presents details of the city to the uninitiated, it does so from the confident posture that even the greenest bumpkin already knows what London character is.

Like any city, London collected a wide sampling of those on the fringes of society: the poor, the helpless, the dispossessed, drifters, hangers on, those who worked unsteadily or not at all, beggars sturdy and otherwise, those who stole for a livelihood or on principle. But it also collected the ambitious and successful, those who aspired beyond their inherited reach. London gathered—almost, it seemed, consciously—those in flight as well as those on a mission. In coming to London, fear was as likely a motive as hope. A better life could mean money or power, freedom from family or expectation, an open road or a narrow alley to a new preoccupation. Some sought anonymity, others connection. Londoners lived their lives of desire and demand in a context of psychic opportunity constrained by physical circumstance, and readers read for release as well as for pleasure and knowledge.

The feelings and attitudes that readers brought to their reading were conditioned by the structures of everyday life,[15] and I want to isolate three clusters of perceptions that highlight differences between London and rural life and that suggest changing conditions and values. Perceptions of what urban life is like—and what it is about—involve not only expectations about the representations of daily life but the personal conditions of reading itself. Because of some of the intensities of London life, readers came to the solitude and quiet of reading with feelings different from those of previous generations or their contemporaries in the countryside.

The first set of perceptions has to do with pace. In all ages, visitors from the countryside remark on how busy life in the city seems to be, and if there is ultimately a greater difference in the tempo of life between,

say, Norwich and London than between Norwich and the farm villages
that surround it, the feelings associated with urban pace have something
in common everywhere. Pace is of course always relative. By modern
standards, London in the early eighteenth century does not seem especially bustling even in contemporary accounts of the crowdings and street
jostlings along the walls and kennels. But observers then—even foreign
observers used to Continental cities—were struck by London's bustle,
and their continual sense of being thrust into a hurly-burly in which
more was going on than they could comprehend is a reliable index to
contemporary perceptions and feelings. A lingering disorientation, a sense
that things were moving too rapidly to be altogether gathered in, was a
part of everyday life for experienced Londoners as well as for visitors,
although of course in very different proportions. The other side of the
excitement and challenge of surroundings bursting with a sense of expansion, complexity, and mystery is uncertainty of one's own place in a
drama whose range had no precedent and whose distribution of parts was
often incomprehensible. In its pace and constant surprise, even among
the most mundane routines, London not only offered complication and
bewilderment but insisted on it.

Exactly how pace affects human perception of time and possibility is
not clear, but expectations, especially expectations about one's own
appetites and capabilities, plainly increase as pace intensifies. Increased
speed of living may not contribute to thoughtfulness or contemplation—
and in fact probably impedes it—but being caught up in the flow actually
does seem to provoke more reading, or at last more sampling, of printed
materials. The pace of urban living and the appetite for information or
fantasy seem to be reciprocal. Fantasy in the context of a busy life might
well be of slow time and effortless ease, but the alternative—the one that
seems most often to attract the young in urban settings they themselves
have chosen for reasons of desire—involves success and purposefulness
in real-life situations. Hectic pace may be a stimulus to self-assertion and
ambition, and in the London of the early eighteenth century some of
that ambitious energy seems to have gone into increased reading, especially about people in like circumstances or with like desires. How much
reading actually got done in the midst of such busy lives is impossible to
calculate, but those in the busiest situations seem to have read the most
ambitiously, finding serenity in the act of reading though not necessarily
in the fictive lives of those they read about. The urban young in the early
eighteenth century certainly give the impression of wide reading, and
the pace of their lives (together with their motives for choosing it over
other possible paces) seems to have contributed to the emergence of a
new species of writing rather than, as intuition might suggest, deterred

it. Crowded time was what early readers brought to novels and to their proto-novelistic reading in the generations just preceding, and the phenomenology of reading followed from that condition. The fabled Victorian leisure that encouraged three-deckers and lengthy reading-aloud sessions in families and community groups was a long way from the reading-on-the-run typical of early eighteenth-century encounters with books, and the books that emerge from this phenomenology show the effects in breathless style, plots that tangle as they go, and the kind of repetition that recalls oral habits but is designed for readers skimming backward to catch what they missed.

All the encouragements to thoughtful reading that moralists could muster justified readers (young readers especially) in their investment of precious time.[16] *What* they read may not have pleased very much the moralists who were ultimately responsible for the literacy that made such behavior possible, but the constant pressure to read things that were practical and devout—and warnings to avoid romantic stories that might unrealistically heighten expectations—plainly had their effect not only in the prosaic, pragmatic emphases in didactic and journalistic materials prior to novels but in novels themselves. The task for the writer responding to a market of hardworking and overcommitted but eager youths was to provide fantasies that did not seem to be fantasies, to offer some alternative sense of ordinary life within the parameters of everyday expectation. The daily circumstances of readers—including their overcrowded hours—were a crucial part of the desire that the early novelists, working from the notes of their prosaic predecessors, learned to fulfill.

A second set of feelings has to do with the assault upon the physical senses, especially the senses of hearing and smell, that even the most experienced and jaded Londoners faced every day. One of the extraordinary features of Augustan satire—one often picked up in eighteenth-century novelists, particularly Defoe and Smollett—is its acute consciousness of the power of sense impressions. Emphasis on how physical sensations overwhelm more subtle and more important human issues in fact characterizes writing of all kinds, often creating spectacular and inconsistent effects, as in Swift's observation of the uncleansing effects of city rain:

> Now in contiguous drops the flood comes down,
> Threatening with deluge this devoted town
> . . . .
> Now from all parts the swelling kennels flow,
> And bear their trophies with them as they go:
> Filth of all hues and odours, seem to tell
> What street they sailed from, by the sight and smell.

They, as each torrent drives with rapid force
From Smithfield, or St. Pulchre's shape their course;
And in huge confluent join at Snow Hill ridge,
Fall from the conduit prone to Holborn Bridge.
Sweepings from butchers' stalls, dung, guts, and blood,
Drowned puppies, stinking sprats, all drenched in mud,
Dead cats and turnip-tops come tumbling down the flood.
("Description of a City Shower,"
ll. 31–32, 53–63)

Here are the miscellaneity, clutter, indiscriminateness, and accumulation that urban pace and energy produce, and the effects go beyond the visual. The "excremental vision" that Swift shared with other Restoration and Augustan satirists, the particularity of which depends upon the synesthetic responses of readers who experienced open sewage every day, derives from (among other things) the pervasive insistence of smell in an urban environment almost devoid of sanitary facilities. In an age and culture when personal hygiene was hardly fastidious, it might seem that Londoners would become inured to odors of vomit, human waste, and rot, but the evidence is that they did not. Complaints are legion; consciousness of olfactory assault permeates the age, from the dung, guts, and blood flowing through ordinary streets to Gulliver's excessive sensitivity to all human smell once he returns to civilization so that he feels he has to stop his nose with lavender, tobacco, and rue. Pope's portraits of Curll slipping in Corinna's "lake"—"Fal'n in the plash his wickedness had lay'd"—because of hers and the city's habits,

(Such was her wont, at early dawn to drop
Her evening cates before his neighbour's shop)
(1728 Dunciad, II, 72, 67–68)

or his description of Cloacina's nether powers (II, 79–100), depend as much upon the reader's recognition of urban civilization's inability to cope with elemental physical functions as with ritual revulsion and disgust.[17] Hogarth in the cluttered detail of print after print gives us the sense of space filled beyond plenitude that Gay's verse or Smollett's prose also offer as an account of crowding and eyes filled to overflowing.

The glut of sound gets similar attention from the satirists and again seems to echo daily London reality. Pope makes the most of couplet sound effects to record the aural clutter he insists is pleasing to dunces because of its familiar tones:

Now thousand tongues are heard in one loud din:
The Monkey-mimics rush discordant in;

'Twas chatt'ring, grinning, mouthing, jabb'ring all,
And Noise and Norton, Brangling and Breval,
Dennis and Dissonance, and captious Art,
And Snip-snap short, and Interruption smart,
And Demonstration thin, and Theses thick,
And Major, Minor, and Conclusion quick.
"Hold (cry'd the Queen) a Cat-call each shall win;
Equal your merits! equal is your din!
But that this well-disputed game may end,
Sound forth my Brayers, and the welkin rend."
                    (1743 Dunciad, II, 235–46)

The sense of aural invasion remarked by London observers suggests shock at rising decibel levels, but the comparative context is again the relative quietude and simplicity of rural life, what still seemed the sound norm. Similarly the other two senses, though more difficult to read historically, seem to have been more "concentrated" in a London being modernized. Consider what a sense of touch amounted to in Hogarthian clutter or the descriptions in Moll Flanders or A Journal of the Plague Year of people jostling each other in the streets. Or think of the heavy new sauces, new-found spices, and exotic foreign foodstuffs in relation to the plain roasted fare of Old England. Heightened sense impressions, even if they made the world seem more tight and concentrated and raised the premium on space and privacy, must have provided a powerful impression of presence and energy, a sense of always (whether one wanted it or not) being in the center of action.[18] Sense gluttony was part of the larger perception of moment-centered consciousness (about which I shall have more to say in Chapter Seven) that valued present time and emphasized urgent, practical, immediate physical needs, and mitigated against abstraction and theoretical thinking.

The many accounts of eighteenth-century sense experience—whether by satirists intent on provoking disgust or realists celebrating the savoring and recall of particular moments—all bear a consistent record of personal invasion. The walls of the self are clearly insufficient to protect sojourners who are not in some way cut off from or desensitized to sense perceptions, and if the eighteenth century is in its aspirations characterized by its powers of observation and accrual of experience and perception, it is also figured by the many human gestures (in prints, verbal descriptions, and later in illustrations in novels) of sense stoppage—the held nose, the hand over the eye, the regurgitation of food and drink, the hand withdrawn or stopped short of touch. It would have been difficult for the stoutest hearted of observers not to feel vulnerable to invasion and contagion. The invasive sights, smells, and noises—not to mention jostling and physical crowding—hint at the violence and brutality that were regularly the lot of one passing through the streets. Metaphorical seizure was not the worst fate that one might reasonably expect. Sense invasion might well mean, as the narrator H.F. fears in A *Journal of the Plague Year* (1722), pollution and disease as well as the simple glutting of the senses.

> Once in a publick Day, whether a Sabbath Day or not I do not remember, in *Aldgate* Church in a Pew full of People, on a sudden, one fancy'd she smelt an ill smell, immediately she fancies the Plague was in the Pew, whispers her Notion or Suspicion to the next, then rises and goes out of the Pew, it immediately took with the next, and so to them all; and every one of them, and of the two or three adjoining Pews, got up and went out of the Church, no Body knowing what it was offended them or from whom.
>
> (Oxford English Novels ed., pp. 207–208)

When Defoe describes responses to the physical tokens of the Plague of 1665–66 but writes in the context of the 1720s, he captures very well the sense that the ugly world beyond one's person is an active agent of terror and a threat to life as well as spirit. And he suggests its present insistence though ostensibly in historic garb:

> I heard of one infected Creature who, running out of his Bed in his Shirt, in the anguish and agony of his Swellings, of which he had three upon him, got his Shoes on and went to put on his Coat, but the Nurse resisting and snatching the Coat from him, he threw her down, run over her, ran down Stairs and into the Street directly to the *Thames* in his Shirt, the Nurse running after him, and calling to the Watch to stop him; but the Watchman, frighted at the Man, and afraid to touch him, let him go on.
>
> (Ibid., p. 162)

If the overwhelming of the senses and the threats of disease and violence symbolically suggest the invasion of personal space and the fear of bodily harm, the smallness and physical closeness of alleys, streets, public buildings, and the homes of all but the wealthiest city dwellers meant that urbanites were literally crowded into cramped spaces at nearly every moment and that feelings of confinement, impingement, and crowding were common. Hogarth's prints, like the works of many another urban satirist visual or verbal, record the clutter and the sense of things tumbling indiscriminately together that mirror a psychological state as much as a physical situation. In the opening lines of the *Epistle to Arbuthnot*, Pope portrays his own sense of modern infringement as personal invasion, and although he is self-comic about it all, his observation is pointed and his perception almost paranoid. It may be, as Alvin B. Kernan has argued, that a sense of clutter and the glutting of physical space is a standard feature of satire, but the reasons seem to involve temporality, not form.[19] They have to do with particulars of a satirist's predicament and with historical moments, for it is when satirists find themselves in the confines of the city that they feel surrounded and encroached upon, their options limited by the presence of other people or bulky things in the spaces next to them. It is, in fact, in the city that most writers or artists discover themselves to be satirists. Often they come from less complex and crowded places and situations and bring with them an idealistic vision that had once hoped to manifest itself in panegyrical forms or some other kind of art less angry, critical, and claustrophobic than satire. And it is not only satire that contains the satiric clutter that Kernan isolates. The illustrations of early eighteenth-century books, even when their attempt is to amuse or only to portray, are just as full and crowded as satiric engravings. The verbal descriptions in Tom Brown's *Amusements* (of "The City Circle," say) present the same urban landscape as Hogarth or Rowlandson.[20] It is urban clutter that we spy in satire as much as satiric clutter that we find in urban art. It may even be that urbanness itself is more crucial to the development of an age of satire than particular social conditions or literary tendencies. One could argue that the satiric sensibility depends more on the psychology of urban life— its own artificial attempts at community governed by a sense of communality lost—than upon artistic bent or cultural crisis. In any case, the great distinctive literary forms of the English eighteenth century—satire and the novel—both have something crucial to do with urbanness, and both are characterized by an addiction to representing human space filled beyond comfortable capacity.

Most satire is urban in subject and origin, and if its response to urbanness is fundamentally quite different from that in the novel, it is no accident that satire dominated the literary climate in England just before the emergence, and then domination, of the novel. In their contexts, the novel and satire have much in common; certainly the central foci of satire, as my discussion of A Tale of a Tub may suggest, was the world that the novel came to occupy as its own. Satire does not, I think, lead directly to the novel in some progressive or even Hegelian sense,[21] but the novel was able to occupy the ground it did in part because the programs of Augustan satire failed. When modernity overwhelmed the world of Swift, Pope, and Gay—outflanking and outlasting it more than outwitting it, relying on cultural inertia more than individual initiative— the novel with its sense of the acceptance and celebration of contemporary time and space addressed the triumphant sensibility and took over some of the most pointed devices, metaphors, and topoi. Satire, in the forms it took in the Restoration and eighteenth century, was a last-gasp attempt to incorporate the new sensibility and its habits into the old assumptions, the final cry of a dying world, and that is the quality that critics often pay homage to, especially in Swift and Gay but sometimes in Pope as well, when they describe the author as getting too involved in the subjectivity under attack. Pope's sense of invaded privacy in the *Epistle to Arbuthnot* (with its indulgence in subjectivity and its representation of everyday life) belongs, in a sense, to the novel, except that there the crowding would be accepted and in some of its aspects seen as positive, for it points to a new kind of connection. City dwellers felt every day the kind of invasiveness that Pope rhetorically exaggerated; by portraying the physical laws as nearly suspended so that mobs can encroach upon time and space, he captures almost perfectly the claustrophobic sense that was daily urban life in his time. The novel would soon show the impinged upon, the crowded, the trampled that a sensibility could be made available to them out of themselves, and that the solution was not to reject modernity in all of its forms and implications.

Much of what older social historians have had to say about growing urbanness in the nineteenth and early twentieth centuries, during the times of increasing industrialization and a migration that was almost exclusively one way into the city and its ever-expanding circles of influence, is true of London in the early eighteenth century.[22] The difference between responses then and now is largely a matter of familiarity and expectation; in 1700, London was *the* English urban experience, and the contrasts between life there and life in the country were much more stark and dramatic. The second and third largest cities in the land, Norwich and Bristol, were tiny compared to London, and when city was contrasted with country it meant London versus tiny villages and hamlets or open landscapes.[23] The chief difference, one that repeatedly stuck in the minds of observers, involved space, the amount available, and its uses. It is true that the poor everywhere lived in extremely cramped quarters, had little privacy, and must have felt altogether minimized in their concept of self by the enforced restraint in domestic space, although their feelings, if not their plights, have been sparingly recorded. But in rural areas and small towns and villages, the spaces beyond one's immediate home were ordinarily fairly open. Physical access to lands owned by the wealthy had been restricted, but one could always see openness and moving horizons. People were perhaps more likely to feel agoraphobia than claustrophobia on the farm, and that is one reason London expanded so fast. It is no wonder that mountains and wilds chiefly affected the literary imagination well into the eighteenth century as seats of terror and despair, and Marjorie Hope Nicolson's findings about the gloom that infected the challenges of open spaces and unconquered heights or unmapped exotica are not really surprising if we merely keep in mind how close, in time and space, were seventeenth-century folk to the human struggle to conquer natural environment or keep its ravages at bay.[24] It took a thoroughly urbanized generation of writers and artists—a group for whom London had become a cultural norm—to appreciate a Mont Blanc, a Skiddaw, or a Yorkshire moor, and to notice what they had given up for urban life.

For the wealthy, or even for those whose quality of indoor living was minimally comfortable, the problem was almost exactly the opposite as for the poor. If in their lodgings they had generous space, the gentlefolk and the aristocracy swiftly entered a world of clutter and cramping as soon as they left their houses or alighted from their coaches. Townhouses, although built on a smaller scale than country houses, retained the same sense of spaciousness in their general dimensions, high ceilings, and multiplicity of rooms, and those who dwelt in such surroundings repeatedly express displeasure and shock when they venture into the smaller scale of the streets and ways of the city itself. They quite literally did risk their lives when they walked in the park (as Johnson said)[25] or when they jostled with crowds in streets and shops. But the sense of enclosure, of being hemmed in, of having one's liberty of physical movement severely curtailed and one's vision repeatedly shut off was as important psychologically as was the threat of crime, filth, and pestilence.

In this tight atmosphere of everyday life, reading was an escape of a peculiarly spatial kind. The sense of open possibility that narrative can represent, even when it is circumscribed by the claims of actuality and human limit, offered a relief that might sometimes have seemed physical to readers—an almost literal outlet from ordinary physical expectation and especially from the cramped spaces in which much private reading took place.[26] Some of the features of early novels—the digressiveness, for example, and the refusal to settle for structures that were too predictable or confining—owe something to the sense of place from which readers begin, not because novelists imitated some concrete strategy or feature that they discovered in popular writing or because they set out consciously to answer human cravings but because they "knew" the daily world of reading at first hand and offered basic relief, some would say escape. The conditions of reading are responsible for all kinds of effects in literature—surely many more than literary critics anxious to talk about aesthetic considerations will admit—and novels are not the only beneficiaries of reader desires and needs that derive from physical conditions. But the phenomenology of crowding is one causal factor in literature that produced specifiable effects in narratives about ordinary life.[27]

A third characteristic urban feeling was especially intense in an early eighteenth-century world still conscious of the historical community that it perceived to be near the center of English culture. Whether or not Londoners alive in 1700 were right in thinking that generations before them enjoyed a vast and easy social familiarity among themselves and felt deep personal ties with those near whom they lived and with whom they conversed daily, their perception of such a past meant that early eighteenth-century London seemed especially impersonal and even inhuman. Institutions characteristic of cities—clubs, political groups, occupational organizations, professional societies, and other clusterings based on common interests and affiliations rather than mere physical proximity—had begun to develop. Much of the history of eighteenth-century London involves what happened in these new and "artificial" gatherings of people, but emigrants to London from Kent, Hants, or Devon found themselves in an awesome, intimidating, and alien place—just as much so as did later Jamaicans and Pakistanis. In that mass of people shoehorned into narrow streets, tiny garrets, and cramped shops, newcomers found in each other a stony refusal to recognize that in all their multiplicity of backgrounds there was a common desire to connect and belong. It is an old tale now, beginning just then to be told with regularity. The sense of rootlessness was especially strong, too, for those who left behind in their native shires something they cherished or an unbroken string of ancestors who were all born, christened, and laid to rest within a few miles of each other and who felt (perhaps inherited) a strong sense of land, place, and family. Even if they came to London with family intact— not the commonest of migrations since it was usually the young in search of new employments and horizons who made the urban move—they experienced a severing from the sustenance of extended family that had long characterized the land. Besides, other traditional communal institutions had begun to decline. The Church, for example, quickly lost some of its force as the population clustered, not just because theology got into intellectual trouble but because urban people changed their habits: they lost faith, or became busy with other commitments, or just drifted. The cultural shift that in our time has meant neglected, abandoned, or rented-out historic churches throughout London had already then begun. Eighty-seven churches were burned in the Great Fire, and they were replaced by a mere fifty-two even though the population had grown substantially. Most emigrants ultimately developed a place for themselves in their new urban world, and older residents had begun to feel a kinship with neighborhoods, districts, various kinds of groups or institutions, and the city itself. But the strong sense of displacement, of rootlessness, of having a past that existed somewhere else lay at the base of many personal feelings one finds in the consciousness of the age.[28]

London meant loneliness, too, that specific kind of loneliness that twentieth-century sociologists describe as characteristic of the past two or three hundred years of Western civilization.[29] Closely related to impersonality, rootlessness, and estrangement from one's immediate past, this kind of loneliness expresses the profound feelings of emptiness and desire for connection that result from physical, emotional, or spiritual isolation but not necessarily from literal solitude. It is the feeling that results primarily from being in collections of people in which one is not personally relevant.

The modern lonely crowd described by urban sociologists may be larger than that in the eighteenth century in London, but it is no more lonely and it feels no more intensely the impersonality of urban contact. In the early years of great urban expansion, before the impact of mass industrialization, the kinds of jobs done by the great masses of workers were ad hoc and occasional, and little of the heavy labor involved in London's early expansion as a port city, commercial center, and distribution point for imports involved sociality or human contact of any significant kind. Even the minimal kind of contact with one's fellow workers that assembly lines and complex administration involved was missing from the lives of many workers in early eighteenth-century London, and most of their waking hours were involved in producing a livelihood. Greater sociality may have been available to those who had more leisure, but even for the middle and upper levels of society the sense of urban impersonality severely restricted human contact, especially among people who did not already know one another socially. Accounts by Londoners of their lives are strikingly free of anecdotes about meetings and conversings with strangers—all of England's rural and village heritage mitigated against easy acquaintance—and among newcomers especially, circles of acquaintance were small. London life offered few opportunities for ready expansion outside one's occupational group (where contacts were in most cases minimal anyway) and religious groups (where interest was on the decline and where, oddly, newcomers seem to have led the ranks of non-attenders, as if their emigrant status gave them license to cut themselves off from the tradition of their fathers and mothers rather than prompting a need to connect).

If newcomers were initially restricted by their lack of acquaintance, shyness, and fear, longer-time residents developed a kind of pride in the impersonality and anonymity offered by the city. Emigrants who became committed urbanites in fact often sought the kind of isolation in a crowd that London offered as an alternative to the ready visibility that was quickly thrust upon one anywhere else in an England that was, after all, still largely agricultural and, for a vast majority, still tied to the customs and rituals of agricultural life. Those new to London who expected or longed for the communal lives they had left behind must have quickly learned that the expectations of a Londoner were very different, involving a pride in separation, impersonality, and privateness. How the generality of people *felt* about that assumed personality, as distinguished from what they said or did about it, is not easy to prove at this distance in time, but there are significant signs in two phenomena that involve quite different pursuits of self-isolation. These two phenomena are, in a sense, both "alternatives" to novel reading, ways of "coping" with a pervasive loneliness that took its victims one by one.

I I I

ONE of these phenomena is the prodigious increase in gin drinking in London, often considered the greatest scandal of national life in the early eighteenth century. Gin drinking (and the drinking of spirits more generally) was, of course, more than a simple response to feeling out of place, invisible, or unloved, and it has economic, political, and social meanings as well as psychological ones. But all the valid interpretations depend, near their center, on a pervasive sense of human despair, personal desperation, and flight in the wake of lost or clouded identity. The cheapness of gin—"Drunk for a penny, dead drunk for tuppence, straw free," as a sign was supposed to have said[30]—contributed to the quantitative consumption, and contemporary surveys showed that in some parishes every fifth house sold spirits.[31] Sharply increased taxes and repressive laws at first had little effect. Social historians who claim that gin drinking accounts for the mortality rate in London in the first half of the century may exaggerate, but they are not wrong about the widespread devastation. Hogarth captured the essence of contemporary perception in his companion prints of Gin Lane and Beer Street, emphasizing that eighteenth-century drinkers of beer were prosperous, friendly, convivial, and communal, the right stuff for a thriving community, but that gin drinkers were solitary, selfish, hostile, and unconcerned about the rest of the human race, even family, perhaps even themselves. Hogarth's gin drinkers, and apparently London's during the second quarter of the century, were a sad lot, without much sense of human connection. They seem to operate from a poverty within, to search for quick oblivion and even early death. They are dramatically solitary and noticeably lonely, and they seem to have chosen to be so. Grim economic opportunities, oppressive social conditions, and bad lives may have fired their thirst, but an abiding loneliness seems to have contributed substantially to making London lives even more nasty, brutish, and short. Reading was not the simple alter-native to drinking, but the two activities were both direct responses to one of the culture's most pervasive urban feelings.

The other phenomenon is, in its broadest reach, the rise of Method-ism. As a cultural event, it is very complex, with both causes and effects that range widely, but one way of seeing it is as a response to the same human bankruptcy, the same sense of disappointment and loss, the same isolation of the self. As a total phenomenon in English history, it is still badly understood, perhaps because few observers feel neutral about it even now or are willing to contemplate what it means about cultural desire. Some have been too eager to see in its independence the wave of a larger political futurity that bursts beyond England and culminates, for better or worse, in the French and American revolutions.[32] Burke, for example, saw it that way, and so do (often) more liberal historians friendly to the results. Others have been just as eager to notice the ridiculous extremes to which events often fell in Methodist meetings and have found the combination of enthusiasm, excessive solemnity, and preoccupation with the inner self both repulsive and, somewhat contradictorily, mean-ingless. No doubt Methodism does represent a forceful reaction to passiv-ity and complacency in the established Church, another rebellion against ecclesiastical hierarchy, and an obliviousness to tradition and to classic religious doctrine. But it also represents a vital response to human needs that must have been very widespread for it to have taken root and spread the way it did.

Once it became a national movement, as it did by the mid-1740s, Methodism took on a variety of social dimensions that, fascinating in themselves, go well beyond my interests here. What I want to isolate is the desire at the heart of Methodism to find meaning, significance, and value in the individual human life by giving prominence to a single moment of experience—the instant of "conversion" or "holiness"—which can exist without any cause in the past and apart from any prior history. Such an emphasis was peculiarly suited, in the contexts of developing urbaniza-tion, to those whose cultural roots had been severed and who therefore needed a sense of personal significance and a way of dealing with a hol-lowness within. It is not surprising that Methodism flourished as indus-trialization intensified and as work became increasingly divorced from any sense of the cultural past and especially from any sense of play that had a traditional basis. In the years just before the rise of Methodism proper into a genuine movement, William Law was a kind of forerunner (although there are other, equally legitimate ways to think of him in intellectual history as well), and his thinking suggests the grounds of what became a very widespread appeal.[33]

Law's *Serious Call* (1728) was one of the most popular books of the first half of the eighteenth century, and his treatise on *Christian Perfection* (1726) may be one of the most underrated books of the century, for it articulates a strain of absolutist thought which, although explored in its political implication, has hardly been considered at all by intellectual or literary historians. Law's friendship with John Wesley and his early influence on him is well known; what Law addresses involves feelings of spiritual isolation and despair, and what he provides involves an acceptance of isolation and feelings of spiritual well-being based upon the ability of an individual to exist spiritually apart from any organized community of believers.

Law himself lived in retirement from the world in King's Cliffe, Northamptonshire. He was no misanthrope or hermit in the spirit of Fielding's Man of the Hill, but his model of isolation for human possibility was a relevant one for the years that lay just ahead, and his analysis of the spiritual deprivations of his culture is a shrewd and sometimes profound one. Although himself a faithful Anglican who (like Wesley) never separated himself from the established Church, Law comes out of the Puritan intellectual tradition, and one repeatedly sees the asceticism, determined introspection, and concern for the individual's private relationship with God that are characteristic of Puritan thought both inside and outside the Church in the seventeenth century. As intellectual historians often observe, Puritanism pushed to its logical conclusion the individualistic emphasis latent in Protestantism from the beginning, and seventeenth-century theologians (drawing at least implicitly on Calvin) often dramatized the essentially solitary plight of mankind in this world. Bunyan, for example, typically represents human life as an individual and lonely struggle—largely unaided by companions and often actually impeded by social obligations—to attain salvation and spiritual equanimity. *Pilgrim's Progress* first, in Part I (the most popular and most poignant part), has Christian leave his wife and family behind in his search for fulfillment—and wend his way to the Holy City alone. Only when his own attainment is secure is he allowed, in Part II (published six years later), to return home and help them along the difficult way.

The broad connection between the Methodism of the eighteenth century and the Puritanism of the seventeenth is often seen in their common criticism of the complacency of the established Church and its reluctance to recognize changing perceptions of human needs, but more specific parallels are crucial to contexts that encouraged the novel. Like Puritanism in most of its strands, Methodism was based on a rigorous intellectual system that worked out Protestant theology in logical detail; but the fundamental appeal of both Puritanism and Methodism was emotional, keyed to a perception of individual drives, based on an analysis of deep human needs for a spirit and vitality that got beyond ritual and form. And both perceived the human experience as crucially, definably, and inevitably lonely.

Much of the difference between the two movements involves Methodism's updated analysis of cultural deprivation and desire. Puritanism responded to what it perceived to be a corruption of human community based upon the continuity of oral traditions, and it offered instead an emphasis on the sufficiency of the self. Methodism, with roots in London life and assumptions, found human beings feeling isolated and lonely in spite of their dense social surroundings. It approved and reinforced that isolation and tried to provide a justifying support for the sense of individuation and uniqueness. The distinctive genius of Methodism was in discounting temporal continuity and emphasizing the possibility of an epiphanic moment that involved experience wholly new and without a basis in the individual's past—a moment that could, paradoxically, be shared with others in a community of believers so that individual, even ecstatic, experience could become the basis for a new kind of spiritual communality very different from the old communality of rural and traditional England. Founded in London and experientially based in urban experience wherever it traveled, Methodism prized a sense of group identity based on a collection of thoroughly individual experiences that, individually as well as collectively, were discontinuous. Having an epiphany was the crucial thing that characterized the saints and separated them from others, never mind finding the source or cause of the supreme moment. And never mind the results ("works"): the moment was all. History and futurity were both irrelevant, at least theoretically.

Methodism was one response to the lonely crowd phenomenon that evolved in eighteenth-century London, and it was successful in other parts of England as well as London because what I have been calling a London experience very quickly pervaded other parts of England too. As Cowper was to put it in 1785,

> The town has ting'd the country; and the stain
> Appears a spot upon a vestal's robe,
> The worse for what it soils. The fashion runs
> Down into scenes still rural, but alas!
> Scenes rarely grac'd with rural manners now!
> Time was . . .
> (The Task, IV, 553–58)

The mentality of urbanness and its sense of what human life—and spirituality—was like was specifically and surely based in London early in the century, but its outreach was wide as towns and even villages more and more imitated the city. And if Methodism was one response to that mentality, the novel was another, related one, for it grew out of the same perception of human needs and the same reading of the daily realities of modern life.

Methodism and the novel ultimately, though, housed very different responses to urbanness, and if the two were repeatedly competitive for human attention, they offered quite different conclusions about the proper response to loneliness. Early on, the novel repeatedly attacked Methodism and in fact achieved some of its acceptance in the broader social community by its intemperate tirades against Methodist faith. Henry Fielding's attacks on Whitefield, and his resolution of Blifil's future by turning him into a hypocritical Methodist—whose disbelief in works and implications continued to betray him in spite of his verbal protestations about faith—typify the species' basic allegiances. Often this pervasive distrust of Methodism has puzzled critics of the novel. There are, after all, important senses in which Methodism and the novel serve similar clienteles, and each embraces, in important senses, a new world against an old one.

But the novel has some commitments that Methodism refuses, and the question of epiphanic moments is crucial to the distinction. Superficially, both prize a celebration of the moment, privileging it as worthy of extensive attention and analysis. But the novel depends, as Methodism does not, on a sense of successive moments with accumulating value and, crucially, on a sense that every moment has a meaningful past. The novel's sense of time seems to be, in this sense, "old-fashioned": that is, it believes in sequence and causality and refuses to honor any present moment as altogether original or unique. Finally, though, this commitment is not old-fashioned at all—though it often appeals to nostalgic commitments, as I shall discuss in the next chapter—but instead owes its loyalty to an emerging sense of history in which human choices cause events and give meaning to successive events, rather than their ultimately being contained in some timeless purpose held in the mind of God. Not that the novel was always clear about its loyalties or the basis of them: Defoe and Richardson are classic examples of writers who often got old and new loyalties powerfully mixed up and who therefore send quite mixed signals in their plots as well as their appeals.

Novels then, looked at phenomenologically, are an alternative to Methodism growing out of a pervasive perception of cultural experience. I have triangulated gin, Methodism, and the novel because all three of them are products of a temporal perception about the individual and social circumstance. Gin and Methodism are opposites in the sense that gin drinkers succumb to their lonely feelings and celebrate them to oblivion, while Methodism "converts" these feelings into the basis for a group.

The novel—or rather, the reading of novels—is, however, a different kind of alternative to both considered together. It uses loneliness as a basis for a fully historicized exploration of self. If gin drinking is fatalistic and Methodism similarly evasive (though in a way that puts a more cheerful face on things, seeming to retrieve sociality under a new guise), the novel offers individuals an alternative activity—even an alternative consciousness—for solitude, providing intellectual and spiritual companionship, though only for a limited time.[34] Because the content of novels is everyday, ordinary, and often practical, it offers an interpretive bridge from the self in isolation to a self in society. Fantasy is its means but not its end; its early practitioners were in fact not lying about its didactic potential, for reflection in solitary tranquility could have outcomes in life.

Novel reading, a solitary activity, is thus active in a significant intellectual and emotional sense as the other two phenomena of loneliness I have described here are not. Gin drinking and Methodism both prize passivity; they represent surrenders to urbanness rather than attempts to transform it. That Methodism does a better job of presenting itself as solutional may account for its relative—at the time, sensational—success, and it may partly account as well for the novel's hostility, a hostility that, incidentally, Methodism returned in kind by mounting some of the most vocal opposition to the novel's "morality."[35] Such deep competitiveness for urban souls glosses the sibling discomfort that Methodism and novels jointly articulate.

I V

WHEN Defoe tried to defend his veracity to life in *Robinson Crusoe,* he claimed (among other things) that Crusoe's long years of solitude were based on historical fact: "[T]he story, though allegorical, is also historical. . . . [T]here is a man alive, and well known too, the actions of whose life are the just subject of these volumes" ("Robinson Crusoe's Preface," *Serious Reflections,* in Maynadier, III, ix). A few critics over the years have taken Defoe literally and assumed that his "allegory" represented his own lonely and often fugitive existence in London. One notorious essay of a half century ago even imagined in considerable detail what his solitary life in London for twenty-eight years must have been like.[36] In making his allegorical claim, Defoe could have had someone else specifically in mind, too, perhaps one Henry Welby who, according to John Dunton, lived near Defoe in London for many years and remained altogether unknown to any of the thousands of people who lived and moved within a few yards of him in Cripplegate parish.[37] Dunton claimed in fact that his own solitary life emulated Welby's, and his account of "living incognito" revels in the joys of solitude:

> The design . . . is to teach (or rather recommend) the Art of living *incognito;* for (Reader) as others squander away their Time in Publick Hurries, and in rambling from one Vanity to another, I chuse rather to retire to a solitary village, (bless'd with a Neighbouring Grove, a purling Stream, two Cuckoos and one Nightingale) and here, under the Covert of a spreading Tree, I intend to devote the remaining Part of my Time to study my self. . . .
>
> (*Christian's Gazette,* 1709, p. 54;
> most of the passage appeared earlier in *Incognito,* p. 1)

Defoe's explanation of the origins of *Crusoe* was probably only a quick and easy defense, the first to come to mind, at most a metaphor for the way he felt about his lonely and unappreciated existence. But it suggests how in touch his contemporaries were with a sense of separateness and isolation, how easy it was to believe that someone could exist in such isolation, a point that Defoe's novel makes plausibly, whatever real-life situation it may or may not have been based on. Swift made considerable fun, in the conclusion of *Gulliver's Travels,* of the idea that a person could remain sane or readjust to human society so quickly after extended isolation, and nothing illustrates more simply and poignantly the different assumptions about human nature and human behavioral possibility than the respective endings of *Crusoe* and *Gulliver.* For Swift the hard Anglican, humans are social animals, for better and worse, and isolation is a sign of bewildered otherness. For Defoe, isolation is a metaphor of earthly existence, and the state (while deplorable) is not only tolerable but productive of healthy reinstatement into a social context.[38]

Urban pastoral in the eighteenth century turned out to be made of things quite different from what Dunton imagined for himself or Henry Welby, although both Dunton and Defoe had the kind of isolating personal experiences (in the midst of London) that might have enabled them to write that version as well. What they did write, however, is in each case a long episodic record of an urban loneliness that partook relatively little of pastoral detachment or nostalgia. They both record an existence anxious about the pressing demands of crowded rooms and fast time, and if they both glory in the excitement and vitality of being in London and being alive at a rising urban moment, they both also record the plaintive cry of modern urban man. Dunton's ludicrous representation of his ideal solitary life with cuckoos and nightingales derives from a London sense of what solitude is like. The furtive Defoe, in debt and in trouble as often and usually more dramatically than the hapless Dunton, understood just as well the sense of loneliness and impersonality in the city, and the most poignant moments in his greatest work are those in which he captures a sense of isolation and despair based on internal states rather than physical solitude. His account, for example, of how Crusoe's sense of isolation in Brazil was transformed into actuality on his island, ultimately is a description of solitariness in the mind:

> I used to look upon my Condition with the utmost Regret. I had no body to converse with but now and then this Neighbour; no Work to be done but by the Labour of my Hands; and I used to say I liv'd just like a Man cast away upon some desolate Island, that had no body there but himself. But how just has it been, and how should all Men reflect, that when they compare their present Conditions with others that are worse, Heaven may oblige them to make the Exchange.[39]

And Crusoe's reaction to the single footprint he finds, perhaps the most moving passage Defoe ever wrote, suggests the utter terror in confronting, within one's own accustomed isolation, the other:

> I stood like one Thunder-struck, or as if I had seen an Apparition; I listen'd, I look'd round me, I could hear nothing, nor see any Thing, I went up to a rising Ground to look farther, I went up the Shore and down the Shore, but it was all one, I could see no other Impression but that one, I went to it again to see if there were any more, and to observe if it might not be my Fancy; but there was no Room for that, for there was exactly the very Print of a Foot, Toes, Heel, and every Part of a Foot; how it came thither, I knew not, nor could in the least imagine. But after innumerable fluttering Thoughts, like a Man perfectly confus'd and out of my self, I came Home to my Fortification, not feeling, as we say, the Ground I went on, but terrify'd to the last Degree, looking behind me at every two or three Steps, mistaking every Bush and Tree, and fancying every Stump at a Distance to be a Man; nor is it possible to describe how many various Shapes affrighted Imagination represented Things to me in, how many wild Ideas were found every Moment in my Fancy, and what strange unaccountable Whimsies came into my Thoughts by the Way.
>
> When I came to my Castle, for so I think I call'd it ever after this, I fled into it like one pursued. . . . (p. 154)

Defoe turned his own feelings and perceptions into print in ways that Dunton only projected, writing for an audience just then beginning to perceive their own condition and the possibilities that print provided them for understanding (and learning to cope with) that condition.

Still, there was nostalgia, and I turn in the next chapter to some of its manifestations as well as to the narrative realities behind rural feelings, for the old oral traditions once honored in villages and towns had their effect too on the habits and desires of early generations of readers.

CHAPTER SIX

Looking Backward:
A World Well Lost?

■

EIGHTEENTH-CENTURY poems often ask readers to think explicitly about the past—carefully, reverently, and repeatedly—but novels seldom do. "Augustanism" and "Athenianism" tended to look in opposite temporal directions, the former finding models in Eden, Golden Ages, or civilizations past, while the latter looked to an ideal in some future version of now, and poems and novels reflect those opposed worlds of value. Still, readers of novels—if they are attentive—often find much that has been carefully harvested from the past: novelists are deeper than they sometimes try to seem. The harvest in eighteenth-century novels was not, however, mainly from the enclosed literary gardens in which approved literary kinds were planted and carefully nurtured, but from wild growths that sprang up everywhere, even on unpromising plots of ground. The story of how novelists moved among these growths and found what they needed for their new art is a complex one, but before looking at that process in detail (beginning in the next chapter) I want to describe cultural attitudes that made the past accessible, though often in a rather surprising way. For novels do look to the past, too. Novelists learned their craft in a world vibrant with a sense of loss, and they wrote for readers who, however restless about the present and ambitious about the future, needed to feel firmly grounded against uncertainty and flux.

Attitudes toward the past—all pasts—were unstable at the end of the seventeenth century in the wake of eroding authority, fascination with novelty, and desire for progress. But if in the cultural consciousness the past was no longer what it used to be, it still carried for many a primitive power. Science and other attitudinal forces in the party of the "moderns" had dimmed the glow of antiquity, and the reverence for the past that traditional writers still counted on was now felt by a diminishing few. Yet fascination with the past and curiosity about it—and about its causal relationship to the new present—is visible in many modernist texts, including novels. Impatience with old notions of the past is especially prominent (and noisy) among younger writers, but the past, in particular the recent past, always haunts the celebrations of modern values, even in effusions about innovation and novelty. This is because the moderns did not have a know-nothing attitude toward the past, as the "ancients" charged, but felt it as a burden. At the turn of the century, traditional writers seldom felt the burden of the past in either Bate's or Bloom's sense,[1] but champions of novelty did, for they were painfully conscious of a past—usually an immediate, personal one—that had got them to a present anxious to declare its independence. Novelty escapes the past, but the past is always in pursuit, always threatening to overtake it. Beyond insisting that modernity must be honored and its enemies discredited, texts friendly to the new world show a surprising respect for heritage and often honor the historical process even more than supporters of the ancients do. For one thing, the "progressive" philosophy of moderns assumes that amelioration grows out of particular contexts of difficulty and depression, so that their texts have to care about the recent past—and know its virtues as well as its liabilities—in a way that the texts of the ancients dare not reciprocate. No "ancient" feels compelled to honor modernity at all: within the assumptions of chronological primitivism, it is possible to live entirely within the values of the past. Basic to the conservative position is a disbelief in change except as deterioration or slippage; time does not mean revision, only loss.

The gap between past and present, then, tends to seem greater in the texts of the ancients than in those of the moderns, and if the past is less obvious and insistent in modern texts, it is more pervasive and more deeply intrusive. Celebrants of the modern were anxious to distinguish themselves from tradition and the past (though sometimes they trumpeted novelty so loudly that audiences could not hear themselves think of any past), but often their feelings for days gone by—nostalgia, loyalty, residual filial piety, longing for green worlds anywhere—and their curiosity about the causes and dynamics of change mean that issues become confused. In modernist writings of all kinds, the past sometimes shows itself oddly, even anachronistically, in a cozy borrowing—or plagiarism—that blurs distinctions between present and past by presenting the old as new, or vice versa. An elemental example: early in Dunton's publishing career he published several books that purported to be by his father—sermons and devotional writings that often do have an older world flavor—but it is not clear where the father's work stops and the son's new prose begins to spin away. The blur reflects Dunton's youthful effort to ride the coattails of the past even while pushing forward a modern agenda.[2] Defoe's method of setting his novels about contemporaneity two generations into the past involves the same hedge, based on like ambivalence. By pretending that Crusoe, Moll, and Roxana are figures from an earlier age, Defoe reaches for the past's authority while featuring events and issues of the moment and espousing present values.[3] Both Defoe and Dunton (and many others) perceived this confusion as filial piety and respect for tradition. They liked to think there was no conflict in their commitment to a new world.

Like other modernist texts, novels quickly participated in the bashing of the past—they had reason to distrust much that the past represented in the culture—but they also were willing to draw on its authority when it was convenient to do so. The novel as a species, indeed, draws on that confusion of loyalty, for while it points forward in style, form, subjectivity, and its validation of the ordinary and everyday, it also longs for what is gone: its consciousness is borne back into a past where it searches for its origins and identity. It hovers in delicate balance, distrusting the past yet finding it indispensable—one reason why critics sometimes think it subversive and sometimes a new outpost of conservatism. Some of the fascination is simply with the past's strangeness (once modernity had won the day, the past was as exotic as far-away places), but there is also curiosity about causality and simple wonder that something as alien as bygone days and country values could have created urban modernity. And there is nostalgia: the excitement of new reaches does not altogether make up for the loss of the warm, familiar, and predictable.

The confusion of past and present values, something novels later tried (almost as hard as histories) to sort out, permeates not only texts but other cultural institutions, especially those keyed to the city. The confusion (and the cultural energy it generated) was tied in two ways to basic changes taking place in English life, both of them involving the shift toward urbanness. One has to do with causality, the other with nostalgia. Curiosity about the forces that had allowed daily life to change so quickly and thoroughly generated a variety of analyses, from Defoe's economic determinism and the philosophical claims of Locke or Hume to the behaviorist musings of Mandeville and ethical lucubrations of Josiah Woodward or James Janeway. What matters about these analyses, for my purposes, has less to do with their cogency or accuracy than with the fact that many observers, from many perspectives, felt obliged to account for change by addressing one feature or another in the immediate past. The nostalgia was seldom intellectual and almost never analytical: the heart often made the past seem appealing even when the head said otherwise. Personal consciousness of new lives—a mixture of excitement and frustration—led to longing for old ways as easily as to thrusts forward into the now, and analysis and nostalgia often mixed indiscriminately. What is important about the mixture is that mind and emotion interacted in an attempt to see what the new world meant for those who remained committed to their locus in the future even when they looked to the past for comfort, explanation, or excuse.[4]

What novels are about—where they are set, what values they embrace, what people they present, and what stories they tell—reflects the cultural ambivalence about past and present, and readers often found in novels versions of themselves in more than just categorical senses. It is not just that narrators and protagonists are young, mobile, vulnerable, and ambitious; they act and yearn in characteristic cultural ways as well and invite vicariousness. But not only in representations do novels honor and renovate the past. In the act of narration itself, novels reenact past life even as they point to new worlds of love and work. Their narrational past involves formal paradigms and precedents less than a question of where narrative has been in the culture and what it has been used for. In considering how the novel ministered to and furthered the culture's desire to look backward, I want first to consider the functions narrative had performed before there were novels to perform them. Again, my focus will be less on the way the high culture formalized human desire than on structures available to larger audiences. Continental-style romances and other stories of the written culture did their part in describing human aspiration, but stories in the oral world represented cultural desire as well. In an important sense the novel took up where old oral tales left off, for the communality novels seek has more in common with stories shaded across social and economic lines than it does with romances that had formulated an ideology of privilege.

I

I BEGIN with a mystery story, often told but written down only in part. The story is not about literature, as defined by traditional literary history, but it is about narrative and its relationship to culture, and the missing objects created a cultural vacuum into which the novel moved. The missing objects are not, however, books or manuscripts, but something much more difficult to miss—and more difficult to imagine at all—in conventional literary history.

The mystery involves what happened to fairy tales during the seventeenth century, for they disappeared from the English public consciousness, their household familiarity in Shakespeare's day having dwindled to nothing by the time of Henry and Sarah Fielding. In England, as on the Continent, fairy tales had been prominent in the oral culture when the seventeenth century began. Frequent allusions to fairy tales suggest how wide and deep the Elizabethan engagement was with familiar stories of initiation and enchantment. Robin Goodfellow, Tom Tit Tot, and Jack the Giant-Killer just as surely as grand heroes of myth occupied the popular imagination. The childhoods of Drayton and Herrick were peopled with magical creatures and mysterious rituals, and sons and daughters of tinkers or princes, as well as those of poets, enjoyed early years of easy intercourse with a rich folk heritage of narrative. Children heard tales from parents or trusted servants; the oral culture bridged age and class, offering pleasures of familiarity and repetition. Fancy had an honored place in the nursery and around firesides or when villagers gathered to tell stories or celebrate the seasons. There was, of course, far more to early seventeenth-century country life—privation, disease, brutality, and hard work—than such a description of festive communality suggests, but late-century retrospect, in the wake of the retreat of tales, tended to see old times as idyllic, and it is true that the world of imagination and the narratives it sponsored were more liberally shared then across social and intellectual barriers.[5]

On the Continent (and in Ireland and the Scottish Highlands) the tradition of fairy tales remained intact into the nineteenth century when the writing down of such materials began to be systematic. But in England the tradition was interrupted between the early seventeenth century and the mid-eighteenth; for some reason the tales were no longer passed down from generation to generation, and the joy once associated with their telling turned to fear and distrust. Some historians of English folklore claim that *no* fairy tales survived into the mid-eighteenth century, and all agree that the native tradition atrophied severely in the face of disuse and active suppression.[6] When the treasuring of folk materials began to surface in the late eighteenth century and when collectors began systematically to record the oral tradition, the findings were few and disappointing. The scarcity of such stories relative to other western cultures means that something—probably something very particular, very Protestant, and very modern—happened in English culture, and both its causes and effects were significant to the future of written narrative.

The leading candidate for villain in this story (as in so many other stories of England and America) has long been Puritanism. A century ago, the pioneering folklorist who first noticed the demise of fairy tales assigned the blame to Puritan distrust of festivity and fun.[7] Disapproval of oral tradition, distrust of a folk heritage that mixed pagan and Christian practices indiscriminately, fear of time wasting and play, moral objections to fictions as forms of false representation, and general suspicion of communal activities in which levity could become infectious added up to a formidable resistance to the form and substance of fairy tales. Conduct books in which parents are instructed on the rearing of the young are full of cautions and threats. Even if there had been room in the tight daily regimen, fairy tales were unwelcome reminders to devout Puritan households of the looser standards of an unreformed age, their plain absence of religiosity and uncertain moral meanings marking them as dangerous intruders on piety. The Puritans were no friends of stories like these.

But there were also other enemies to the whole folk heritage, and it may be too easy to find in Puritanism the single answer to what happened: Scapegoat Theory usually is too easy. Equally suspicious of the old world of popular tradition and superstition were several groups of strange bedfellows, intellectuals and moralists of many progressive stripes, prophets of modernity like Hobbes, Tillotson, and Locke who did not necessarily share Puritan values, approve their ways, or agree with each other about most things. Their ideas of an improved world also precluded allegiance to discredited beliefs and old inefficient rural habits, and they had little time for warm feelings about simple folk. Their agenda, insofar as one can speak of a single shared vision among them, involved a tough-minded sorting of facts in the service of truth; tolerance of tradition was not one of their generosities, and their view of folk habits and popular culture was in some ways more restrictive than that of narrow Puritan moralists.

Exactly what happened to the old oral culture of the English country-side we may never know in detail, for the history of the word when it is not written down is hard to trace. But we do know that when fairy tales are later collected in England, the survivors show unmistakable evidence of having been reintroduced from the written versions of other cultures. For whatever reason, fairy tales had retreated from their central place in the culture, and (whether old prejudices were responsible or new ones) the net result was that the power of traditional tales had seriously dissipated. An important part of the oral tradition had ceased to be a tradition with clear and living channels. The disappearance of familiar stories meant changes in habits of sharing the culture, perhaps even changes in the cultural consciousness itself. The question of why fairy tales disappeared from English culture, even though it may not be answerable in absolute terms, is a crucial one in defining the contexts for narrative in the years immediately preceding the novel's emergence, for the fate of fairy tales tells us important things about cultural attitudes in the face of religious and political change.

I I

THE disappearance of fairy tales is part of a larger picture of distrust and suppression of oral culture in the seventeenth century. Puritanism, in rejecting any traces of pagan tradition and anything even vaguely associated with Merry Old England, may have been heavily responsible for the interruption of tradition, but the suspicions that led to suppression were widespread in English culture, casting their net far more widely than any single Puritan, or all Puritans together, could manage. Even if nursery rhymes, legends, sagas, and other kinds of folk tales managed to maintain a continuous tradition, they were under heavy suspicion too, and the fear of their power spread as the Enlightenment sought to destroy old pockets of darkness.[8] When Pope alludes, in The Rape of the Lock, to "all the Nurse and all the Priest have taught" (I, 30), his tone is warm and a bit nostalgic about the parallel passing down of oral tradition through religion and folk channels, but many of his Protestant contemporaries were less charitable, and in fact the culture at large was hostile enough to have prevented such stories from being available to Pope for his poem. Nurses, in fact (as the principal carriers of traditional stories), had an especially bad reputation by the late seventeenth century, and no one seems to have very much trusted their influence on children: "It is from . . . Ignorance of Nurses," according to An Essay on Modern Education (1747), "that almost all our ill Habits proceed" (p. 42), summing up rather crudely what progressive educational theorists had been saying for more than half a century. Writer after writer pauses in the midst of almost any kind of discussion to denounce the incorrigibility and bad influence of servants allowed to rear children. Anyone, says The Ladies Library (1714), who has seen "how very little Sense is to be met with, or can be infus'd into Nurses and Nurse-Maids . . . will soon be perswaded how little fit it is to trust Children, any more than is necessary, in such hands" (II, 210–11). The difficulty lies in the way they corrupt children by the stories they tell. "Nothing is more common," says The Young Gentlemen and Lady Instructed (1747), "than for servants and nurses to amuse and terrify their young masters and misses with stories of spirits and apparitions, of ghosts as pale as ashes, that stand at the feet of a bed . . . with many other old woman's fables of the like nature" (I, 99).

Nurses probably did sometimes use their stories to intimidate children, keep them dependent, and simplify problems of discipline. But they seem also to have valued the stories themselves and taken pleasure in repeating them. Their critics evidently regarded their practice of storytelling as incorrigible both because it involved a deeply ingrained habit and because servants could not be made to understand the harm they were causing. Those who attack the tales of the nursery often write in a tone that mixes exasperation with cool social superiority, implying that parents of respectable families simply have to do the best they can with the servants one could get thenadays. Throughout the seventeenth century, the warnings are frequent and often shrill in the standard Guide books for parents and families, but by the beginning of the eighteenth century the urgency (if not the distrust) had abated. Educational reformers—Locke, for example—had by then taken up the cause, and mere parents and observers no longer had to rail against the night. The discussion became more theoretical, as if the dangers were by now no longer quite so wide-spread and all reasonable cultural guardians could surely agree on the right social values.

The question of social class comes into the issue because those who criticize nurses and servants seem sure that no one of their own social background and educational concern could possibly be involved in simi-lar storytelling practices. No doubt their assumption was too haughty and easy, for many members of sturdy and respectable families must have been corrupted in their own nurseries and retained at least an awareness of oral traditions, even if they shared a reluctance to pass it on. And not all did resent their heritage. "The telling of stories is a great help to life and conversation," a mid-eighteenth century Guide book for Youth insists; "we should therefore always encourage them, if they are pertinent and innocent."[9] There is evidence that communal storytelling events contin-ued throughout the eighteenth century to include people of divergent social groups, especially in small villages and towns. Still, the cleanness of the assumption suggests that rigidifying lines were trying to divide England into two cultures. One—poor, uneducated, superstitious, and illiterate—depended on oral traditions for its history, information, and sense of how the world worked: the other—respectable, pious, at least minimally educated, ambitious to know systematically what one could learn from the print culture—prided itself on its divorce from native lore and the old oral culture. The division never was complete, and it did not follow neat lines of literacy and illiteracy in any case, but the basis for deep social division was brooding, and literature—including popular lit-erature—helped to create it.

One might call this division the triumph of middle-class culture, and it does resemble bourgeois revolutions elsewhere, but the point has more to do with the breakdown of communal heritage and the pitting of social groups against one another than with any new social agreement.[10] Although the distrust I have described seems largely to divide along lines of class, other factors were involved too, especially geographical ones. In the country, in villages and towns, and even in the provincial cities, the retention of attitudes and habits from a rural culture was significant, and the continued interaction of people of all social, educational, and religious backgrounds—a practice that dated back to feudal culture—lasted well into, and in some cases beyond, the eighteenth century. The division articulated by the suspicion of nursery tales is roughly—but only roughly—parallel to political divisions that came to be Whig and Tory. The suspicions also tended to be from the kinds of occupations that were upwardly mobile and from people who held reformist and progressive religious ideas, and certainly they were guided by an allegiance to values associated with new and modern ways of doing things rather than looking to the past for values. Actually, of course, the lines were never so clear as these tendencies one by one seem to claim, but one might characterize those who were critical of the oral tradition as primarily urban, whig, middle-class, Puritan, "modern," enlightened, and anxious to be free of a dark, primitive, rural past: they are the people who would be most offended by Squire Western. But however suspicions of the oral tradition are described geographically, politically, socially, or religiously, their distinct commitment is to "progress"and change, a reformist urge that views old ways as superstitious, primitive, and simplistic. "The World is grown more refin'd, and polite, since your youthful days," a speaker in a pamphlet of 1691 says to someone of an older generation; "Women are not mew'd up in the Nursery, as in Queen Elizabeths Time, but have Liberty of Conversation. [W]e are more . . . wean'd from the Winter-tales of the Chimney corners."[11] There is as much modishness as analysis in such a description of the 1690s, but the "modern"—novelty in language, new ways of thinking, reformist notions of conduct, trendiness in fashion— was thus defining itself against the rural and folk past.

The suspicion of the tales themselves focuses primarily on the psychological damage they may do—another issue that seems class-related because it tends to be put in terms of what "they" may do to "our" children— although sometimes the worry is expressed in terms of the loss of religious authority or intellectual standards. The first Marquis of Halifax phrases his worries this way:

Religion doth not consist in believing the Legend of the Nursery where Children with their Milk are fed with the Tales of Witches, Hobgoblins, Prophesies, and Miracles. We suck in so greedily these early Mistakes, that our riper *Understanding* hath much ado to cleanse our *Minds* from this kind of *Trash*; The Stories are so entertaining, that we do not only believe them but relate them; which makes the discovery of the *Truth* somewhat grievous, when it makes us lose such a Field of Impertinence, where we might have diverted our selves, besides the throwing some shame upon us for having ever received them. This is making the *World* a *Jest* and imparting to God Almighty, That the Province he assigneth to the Devil, is to play at Blind-mans buff, and shew Tricks with Mankind; and is so far from being Religion that it is not *Sense*.

(*The Lady's New-Year's Gift:*
or Advice to a Daughter, 6th ed., 1699, pp. 7–8)

The emphasis here on "Sense" is characteristic of the widespread concern that children learn to cope with the "real" world, a world rationally and scientifically describable. *The Young Gentleman and Lady Instructed* worries that the "horrors and imaginations, raised by such Stories" cannot be shaken off when children "are grown up to years of discretion" (I, 99), and Isaac Watts frets that bad discourse drives out good:

Let not nurses or servants be suffered to fill their Minds with *Silly tales and with senseless rhimes,* many of which are so absurd and ridiculous that they will not bear to be represented in a grave discourse. The imagination of young creatures is hereby flattered and deceived: Their Reason is grossly abused and imposed upon: And by this Means they are trained up to be amused with follies and nonsense rather than to exercise their understanding, which is the glory of human nature.

("A Discourse on the Education of Children and Youth,"
in 1753 *Works*, V, 383)

John Locke cites his own traumatic experiences in the nursery as evidence of the evil wrought by such stories,[12] and he became an example in the writings of others. According to a frequently retailed anecdote, the "Prattle" of his childhood nurse had so infused him with the "Fear of Spirits and Hobgoblings" that he remained all of his life unable to "enter the Dark without Trembling and Horror" (*An Essay on Modern Education*, pp. 41–42). The idea of the leading English philosopher of the Enlightenment being afraid of the dark obviously startled his contemporaries and dramatized the conflict between a new world now becoming and an older oral world that hung on tenaciously. Nothing could much more poignantly illustrate the harmful and lasting effects of early impressions upon a human *tabula rasa,* and the necessity of lighting up the dark corners of ignorance and error in a single mind suggested the larger necessity to enlighten the residual darkness in the whole world of superstitions and folkways represented by traditional stories. "Let not any persons that are near [children] terrify their tender minds with dismal *stories of witches and ghosts, of devils and evil spirits, of fairies and bugbears in the dark,*" Isaac Watts sums up, perhaps with Locke's own experience in mind. "This hath had a most mischievous effect on some children, and hath fixed in their constitutions such a rooted slavery and fear, that they have scarce dared to be left alone all their lives, especially in the night" ("Discourse," p. 383). Writer after writer, from whatever social or religious persuasion, associates servants with stories, stories with the past, the past with a darkness that was determined to resist the light, and good emotional health with dissociation from the whole oral heritage.[13]

The social reforms undertaken at the end of the seventeenth century, largely under the guidance of King William, represent the logical culmination of the movement to repudiate the more relaxed ways of the past. The rise of the Societies for the Reformation of Manners is, in effect, a third stage of the Protestant Reformation. The first had been Continental and represented a theological and philosophical break with the past; the second had detached England from the Continent and represented a political and geographical break. The third represents a social and ethical break with the past. Its focus was unalterably urban. The societies sprang up in cities throughout the nation but their main thrust was always in London, and the kinds of vices they attacked were those primarily associated with (if hardly restricted to) urban life: drunkenness, swearing, gambling, sabbath breaking. They were serious about manners.[14] It is easy to patronize the societies now, pointing to the relative superficiality of their attack while more profound things were happening to the fabric of English society; surely such attention to drinking, swearing, and "lewdness" barely scratched the surface of problems deeply built into the new modes of urban life. But the significance of reform historically lies neither in the accomplishment (or lack of it) nor in the profundity of their social analysis: the fact that they addressed issues of distinctly urban significance, whether or not they addressed them meaningfully, is a profound manifestation of deep social change. It is probably true that the enormous efforts expended by the societies—and by their sister societies born of the same anti-parochial spirit, the Society for the Promotion of Christian Knowledge (SPCK) and the Society for the Propagation of the Gospel (SPG), and the Charity School movement[15]—had little discernible effect on English society measured by any of the traditional indicators of ethical change, and the elaborate statistics published by the defenders of the societies are, in that sense, rather comic and pathetic. But the significance of the societies lies in the visions they represented for millions of Englanders who found themselves in a new world which they only partially understood and only partially liked. Sometimes in their urban upward mobility they yearned for another time, perhaps another place. And yet they did not altogether want out of the present, certainly not out of the city. They thought to refine it, improve it, re-form it in an image that was not a return to a past but rather was a design for a new kind of simplified world. They did not, like those who had gone to America, expect to establish a New Canaan, nor could they imagine anywhere in this world a New Jerusalem or a City of God. But neither did they want all the trimmings they had got with the modern urban world, and the program they tried to establish for the city was a version of the purification an earlier generation had sought to impose on the country and its traditions. Squire Western has almost all the manners to have made him a target for the societies, but he was in the wrong place. The societies are, in one sense, not so much aimed at city vices per se as at traditional vices that had persisted into cities and become more sophisticated there, more established and more accepted as ordinary social behavior.

If the 1690s represent the cultural moment when England admitted that its cultural allegiance had shifted from the country village to urban sprawl, there was as well a powerful conservative, reactionary, and nostalgic force operating in the city, even among those thoroughly committed to urbanness and modernity. It involved a widespread feeling of displacement, regret, a sense of being detached from one's past. Disinheritance was widely felt in the land, for the English consciousness had experienced a literal disenchantment. And it is this attitude in those most likely to be readers of novels—because they were young, uncertain, ambitious, and newly placed in unfamiliar urban solitude—which helped guarantee that new literary forms born in modernity would honor some sense of regret for the lost (but only partially forgotten) world of enchanted magic.

Between the reign of Queen Elizabeth and that of Queen Anne— between A *Midsummer Night Dream* (c. 1595) and The *Rape of the Lock* (1714)—relationships between "literature" and popular belief changed profoundly. From a cultural moment when fairyland, the world of everyday work, and aristocratic leisure could interact peaceably and in fanciful ease across regional, social, and intellectual lines, England moved to a time when audiences expected a clear line between fact and fancy and when class distinctions were nearly as rigid. A poet who needed supernatural forces could not call them up from the world of folk belief; they had to be invented or culled from some learned world of artifice.[16] Pope's esoteric reach for another layer of life and imagination, however successful artistically, reflects a time when the oral world had severely receded—

or been pushed—from the public consciousness and when popular culture was no longer trusted to contain allusive power, let alone mythological truth. The world of belief in Pope's London no longer included the rich sense of mischief and play that could be called up to measure the pretensions of human aspiration, and when sylphs and gnomes invaded the boudoir and toilet they were obviously imported there by an artful stage manager from a different world of allusion, one that involved learned research, not a popular heritage shared by priests and nursemaids.[17]

Not only did the prominent animistic sense of mysterious forces disappear from daily life and conversation at places like Hampton Court, but the whole sense of the relationship between the supernatural and the everyday seems to have changed so radically in the culture that belief and practice in even the most remote rural huts was also altered forever. What had once been trust in the old ways came to seem dangerous.[18] Religion and learning took turns at destroying this kind of past, for from quite different motives they both feared old ways that threatened their authority. "I write of Groves, and Twilights," Robert Herrick had written at the beginning of Hesperides (published in 1648 but written a generation earlier), "and I sing / The Court of Mab and of the Fairie-King." Early in the eighteenth century, Thomas Tickell tried hard to keep such lore alive for his contemporaries, writing in Kensington Gardens a touching account of simplicity that deserves to be better known. But the world had changed. Poems involving fairy tales and magic greens simply wouldn't take, not only because audiences had turned to other things but because poets no longer belonged either in that old world of easy belief. No doubt hundreds of thousands still believed in spirits and witches and magic. For many, ideas of the supernatural were still a wild mixture of Judeo-Christian tradition and pagan superstition; but in Kensington Gardens in 1722, one was more likely to find botanists than fairies, and London liked to think of itself as a million years from a rusticity that looked for fairy rings and chimney sprites. Tickell was a university man writing for Londoners; at most he could expect the ironic nostalgia that courtiers felt for sophisticated Elizabethan pastoral, also written in the city for urban hearers who might never again see a live sheep.[19] But Tickell's attempt, consciously old-fashioned and, like Gay's Rural Sports, more reminder of olden times than a serious attempt to preserve them in a modern world, vividly suggests who readers had by now become and what was required. In prose the situation was more dramatic still, prosaic reality having moved even further away from Herculean stables and giant beanstalks and into cramped urban garrets that despite their steep stair-climb did not rise high enough to escape the stench of sewage in the streets.

I I I

LOGICALLY prior to the question of why fairy tales disappeared from England is the equally speculative one of why they enjoyed such widespread popularity in the first place. Almost universally in European cultures, fairy tales somehow gained a powerful and lasting place, and their role in the culture has recently commanded a lot of attention. When "history" only involved kings and queens, dominant social groups, and "great" books and ideas, and when "literature" meant texts written by authors with conscious and clear intentions, fairy tales were not taken very seriously in intellectual circles except as a backwater annoyance. But in the past two decades they have achieved a prominence that may even exaggerate their importance. They have become the spoiled child of narratological circles, and they can do no wrong among literary theorists. In the 1970s especially, when an enormous wave of child-is-father-to-the-man nostalgia swept through academic (especially male academic) circles, the significance of fairy tales came to be so frequent a subject of discourse that to discover a fairy-taleless era was to find a moonscape, the end of life as we know it. But since the romanticizers of fairy tales tend to pursue universals and seldom know history, the fairy-tale deprivation of England during the eighteenth century went largely unnoticed then and has been little discussed since as attention has turned from formalist issues to questions of effect and audience response. Just as questions about the causes of unusual historical patterns have seemed only local to fairy-tale experts, so have questions about effects been confined to psychological rather than cultural questions. Contexts are not interesting to those who believe in a key to all mythologies. Still, speculations about what fairy tales can accomplish psychologically do have cultural application, and just because the study of tales has traditionally been ahistorical does not mean that there are no cultural issues to be explored.

When Vladimir Propp first elevated the consideration of fairy tales to sophisticated discourse sixty years ago, the emphasis fell primarily on structural elements that allowed the tales status as art.[20] After that "arrival," a lot of rather patronizing comments—about simplicity, elegance, profundity, universality, and human perfectability—dropped from lesser formalists, and for several decades the study of fairy tales (unlike folklore more generally) made the kind of grand claims that usually signal puzzlement about how to justify newly attained status.[21] But the maturing of folklore and popular culture as disciplines brought imitations of literary criticism, and if fairy-tale students have not always read criticism and theory wisely, they have studied its reaches well. From explanations that cited the pure, uncomplicated, and mindless pleasures of storytelling,[22] attention turned insistently toward psychoanalytic interpretation. For fairy tales, though, that interest has taken a narrow form, and the psychoanalytic tendency to translate individual empirical observations into universal truths has given the impression that the tales have little historical or cultural resonance. The best work has almost all been done by behaviorists and social optimists who regard the tales with a reverence befitting a primitive force, and sometimes their claims are grandly inflated.

For Bruno Bettelheim, fairy tales satisfy deep human needs, certainly for children now and presumably (since their status as children's stories is quite recent) for adults in earlier times:

> Fairy tales, unlike any other form of literature, direct the child to discover his identity and calling, and they also suggest what experiences are needed to develop his character further. Fairy tales intimate that a rewarding, good life is within one's reach despite adversity—but only if one does not shy away from the hazardous struggles without which one can never achieve true identity. These stories promise that if a child dares to engage in this fearsome and taxing search, benevolent powers will come to his aid, and he will succeed. The stories also warn that those who are too timorous and narrow-minded to risk themselves in finding themselves must settle down to a humdrum existence—if an even worse fate does not befall them. . . . Through most of man's history, a child's intellectual life . . . depended on mythical and religious stories and on fairy tales.[23]

Bettelheim offers extensive analyses of individual tales to prove that "fairy tales deal imaginatively with the most important issues in all our lives" (*The Uses of Enchantment*, p. 194), and his views, largely derived from the studies of others in the psychoanalytic community, are widely shared. Often individual analyses depend on questionable readings, but the patterns of relationship between plot structures and the anxieties of childhood and adolescence are generally persuasive. No listener, then or now, would consciously have said, "I must now deal with my fear of sex or my excessive love for my mother and therefore must hear a fairy tale, specifically *Sleeping Beauty*." But appeals to unconscious need may not be, even if psychoanalysts are right, the full answer. Conscious needs for guidance in critical decisions may have created narrative desires as well, and the popularity of the tales across cultures—from China to Peru— may in part derive from effects that are emotionally specifiable and that have an impact on cultures as well as individuals. Even though children deprived of this heritage have managed to grow up successfully, the broad cultural power of these tales, spread through country and city across all social strata, seems impossible to deny. Folk knowledge inherent in the tales and imparted subtly through narrative devices must have filtered on even to non-readers in societies steeped in the tales, and presumably the wisdom of the ages contained in the tales found a place in other forms that helped them to permeate the culture as well. Presumably, too, the tales were told not because a teller consciously sought to impart philosophical truths or because listeners wanted to take in some keen psychological insight, but because both teller and listener liked the stories themselves. Unlike "literary" forms such as fables, a fairy tale seldom has an explicit moral to justify the narrative, and most tales are straightforward stories of adventure and enchantment on a conscious level. Tellers and hearers alike have traditionally regarded them—as children do now— as good, "bad" stories that have all the right elements: excitement, terror, interesting "others," safe workings out of basic conflicts, and ultimately an assurance that rightness will triumph. [24]

If present-day analysis sometimes seems too ingenious in explicating individual tales, it is persuasive about the dynamics of fairy tales as a body of narrative. [25] The traditional beginning of fairy tales ("Once upon a time . . . ") remembers a human moment when things were at once thrilling and secure, and the confident ending (" . . . and they lived happily ever after") promises an ultimate narrative control that can surmount any difficulty even though it may take magic to do it. What fairy tales seem to offer is a compact confidence that even the worst circumstances and most threatening happenings will eventuate, after a tough struggle, in a satisfying solution, a structure therapists and theorists like Bettelheim understandably find appealing. I mention such explanations of efficacy, speculative though they are, to suggest two points: (1) Even if the efficacists are not right about the precise functions that fairy tales perform, they may be right that tales perform tasks of some human or cultural kind, giving individuals information, confidence, and emotional satisfactions and providing the culture an effective communication system for knowledge and values; and (2) any historical interruption of functions raises questions about displacement. Whatever oral stories (especially fairy tales) may have done for English hearers in the early seventeenth century, the mechanisms had changed by the time the novel emerged, and it is worth speculating about the possible relationship between the atrophying of some narrative traditions and the emergence of others.

In what ways are fairy tales like novels and in what ways unlike? Such questions may seem a little perverse, for fairy tales have so many elements that seem to ally them to romance and other older forms of fantasy narrative that their resemblance to a species that "realistically" treats ordinary life may not be obvious. The world of fairy tales does resemble the world of romance—in its exotic settings, extraordinary people, and magic transformations—but the terrors and difficulties are too particular, too circumstantial, too "realistic" for the comparison to hold very far. Fairy tales not only contract the scope of romance; they also domesticate its problems and intensify its psychological reach—in some ways very much as the novel would go on to do. To the fantasy elements of exoticism and successful closure in the world of romance, fairy tales admit invasions from dream and nightmare, the macabre, the surreal, and the grotesque.[26] Fairy tales address the real world even if they do not altogether grapple with it; they are not among the species of escape literature, in spite of the elements of miracle, magic, and happy ending. As an insistently oral form existing in a literate world, fairy tales do not neatly fit any of the standard categories of genre or species, but they differ from romance without including many novelistic features.

They do, however, seem to minister to some of the same narrative needs as novels do a little later on: they present ordinary people (Cinderella, Jack, Little Red Riding Hood) with real human problems (wicked stepsisters, poverty, distrust, long odds, invasion, breakdown of family relationships, homelessness), and they draw in their hearers to an intensive empathy with the people and situations they present before providing psychological release at the end. Besides a form of social and psychological realism, fairy tales share with the novel an extraordinary concern with individual characterization and the subjectivity of hero or heroine (as much of the latter as the former, actually, since they represent an oral world where hearers are likely to be quite evenly divided). And, like the novel, they tend to find accommodation for the individual within a larger social framework; it is always "they" (and not just a "he" or a "she") who live happily ever after. This is not to say that fairy tales lead to novels or provide a missing link. I see no direct line of descent and little conscious borrowing until novelists like Richardson decide, in rhetorical calculation, to take over fairy-tale motifs, and I do not wish to minimize the significant differences—stock plots, for example, or stereotypical character traits, names, and situations—involving fundamentally different conceptuality.[27] But the historic role of fairy tales in the oral culture meant that something quite specific was missing when they lost their place, and the fact that fairy tales drop away helps to define some of the functions that written literature would need to take on when oral tales were not available. With the demise of fairy tales in England, other species of oral narrative—legends, sagas, and etiological tales, for example—may have picked up some of the slack, but the broader distrust of orality meant that traditional channels for cultural meaning and individual adjustment were not easily available and not sanctioned when they were.

We still know little about the nature of the human need for narration, despite a dramatically growing awareness among students of literature that such a need seems to manifest itself in vastly different cultures, perhaps almost universally. A quarter century ago, Scholes and Kellogg considered the question "of how and why stories play a part in the life of man" as "largely unexplored territory,"[28] and despite many explorations since, no comprehensive theory of why narrative is humanly necessary has been persuasive enough to gain wide acceptance. All human cultures seem to have narratives, even a definable narrative tradition, whether or not there has been a conscious attempt to write it down or otherwise fix it or extend it beyond the society itself. As early as 1785, Clara Reeve was convinced that "the passion for tales and stories is common to all times, and all countries, and varies only according to the customs and manners of different people" (*Progress of Romance*, II, 64). Whether or not universal, the widespread need for stories means that in narrative human beings seem to find clues to understanding themselves in relation to their culture, perhaps because the ethos of a narrative provides cultural guidance about what individuals must do to adapt and succeed. Narratives in primitive cultures share with those in more sophisticated ones the tendency to explain mysteries, address recurrent curiosities, and articulate values—besides providing entertainment and pleasure. Narrative offers comfort and even "answers" to readers or hearers, sometimes giving information and often psychological satisfaction or at least relief from some persistent anxiety. Whatever individual pleasures narrative offers, it does something deeper and broader in the culture—passing on vital codes, satisfying desire for ritual, play, and resolution of conflict, providing a "safe" sense of continuousness and causality by showing implications and outcomes for others. Narratives may address many needs beyond the ones particularized by the individualized story. In any case, disruption of a developed narrative tradition is no small matter, and with the disappearance of fairy tales and the thinning of the oral tradition more generally, English culture experienced a narrative deprivation that opened possibilities for alternatives.

It was no foregone conclusion that novels would move into the vacuum. But it does seem likely that some practice or system of information—narrative or otherwise—would try to address some of the needs that had been met by the lost tradition. If there was to be new narrative, it would be likely to have certain interests and features. Given the interests that lost oral narrative had had, one might expect in any new narrative a significant psychological dimension, alertness to crucial life choices, curiosity about how the human mind works, awareness of the individual's need to cope with cultural expectations, consciousness of locality and human individuality, affirmation of a social world in which individual needs are accommodated, willingness to portray major problems and (at least sometimes) allow satisfying solutions, and an interest in events that are strange, surprising, and sometimes inexplicable. And, because of the distrust of the old traditions, one might also expect a sensitivity to changing values and shifting modes of communication and an engagement with a new world of aspiration which, when it looked back, looked down on habits and facts that seemed (however appealing) not good enough for the ambitious present. Whatever interests and features any new narrative offered, however, they would almost certainly take quite different forms if they were written rather than told.

Novels do not so much imitate the features of oral narratives as pick up where they leave off, offering to meet some of the same emotional and intellectual needs by alternative means. The answers to cultural questions in novels are not the same as those in oral tales, but the questions they address are closely related. Novels tell young people about a world beyond their own personal experience, but in doing so they use fantasy differently, pretending in fact only to give unvarnished accounts of reality and not to tolerate fantasy at all.[29] And, before novels, a host of other written materials—journalistic accounts, collections of anecdotes, political and religious pamphlets, conduct books—performed many of the same functions, often without apparently using fiction of any kind.

I V

READING is a far different kind of activity from listening. Writers are absentee tellers, and there is no necessary relationship between reader and writer, only the amount of intimacy or closeness each chooses to allow. A society that passes along its wisdom orally in ritualized events controls the communication relationship in a way that modern, post-literate society cannot, for it has far better measures of response and instant corrective abilities. Writers cannot go back and revise a passage when readers disapprove or quit reading—even if writers were to be aware that such a response had taken place—whereas tellers can observe, adjust, almost guarantee a response because they can actually know (and read) their audience.

As McLuhan, Ong, and others have insisted, differences between written and oral modes are in part determined by the medium of print itself,[30] but it is too easy now to say that the phenomenon of print causes everything and make that the beginning and end of the matter. Equally significant at this historical moment are other, and prior, structural changes in the information system of the culture produced by pre-print factors, and a major part of the story in the seventeenth century involves the way writers—the messengers behind the medium—responded to the challenge. It is not that print outbid talk or overwhelmed it, so much as that oral culture lost its occasion and its cultural sanctions. Many who wrote books—not "literature" as such but popular materials read more for profit than fun—tried to step into the vacuum, often haltingly, sometimes blunderingly, and (until much later) usually without much success. The situations and audience they faced involved not only individuals cut off from their past and its familiar institutions but also individuals who, when they read for solace, largely did it in solitude.

Sometimes during the seventeenth century, a describable world of privacy and secret sharing began to develop among the young, men and women alike. A kind of "closet culture" came to exist throughout England, most noticeable perhaps in London and the towns but present also in country houses and increasingly in villages and even in country huts where architecture and family government would allow it. Fundamentally, it involved habits of privacy and solitude, a natural outgrowth of Protestantism's respect for the individual. It was probably a direct result of emphasis on private devotions and closet prayers which, even at the height of praise of family worship, never lost their place in Protestant homes as the central expression of piety. The "religion of the closet" marked the place and time when an individual communed directly, without the intervention of priests, friends, family members, or even of texts, with his or her God.[31] "Closets" for the more affluent (and even for servants among the affluent) meant private cabinets which might or might not be an extension of the individual bedchamber. For those in poorer circumstances the private space might be a nook or loft or barely a kneeling or reading place, but however small or inauspicious, it was "owned" by an individual, a space apart where the self was externalized, recognized, and certified. The grottos and garrets of early eighteenth-century writers—with all of life apparently centered in confined mental workspace—are logical extentions of such space, and the closets of Pamela and Clarissa (although to some extent merely part of the enabling architecture for fiction) testify to the uses to which closets were increasingly put.[32] Ultimately the most significant aspect of this admission of individual privacy was temporal, even beyond its spatial representation, and the insistent socialization of group reading and family devotions in Victorian times was probably an attempt to reclaim individual time for communal needs. But well into the eighteenth century the closet was the primary locus for secret contemplation and private reading, a kind of imitation of the gentleman's library for the poor, the young, and the female.

Moralists of the time record plentiful worries about the uses private space and time were put to, especially by the young. Most of these worries come down to anxiety about idleness or, worse, stimulation of the mind and imagination toward improper longings, but there was also concern that privacy itself might be carried too far or that its outer manifestations might be abused. Clarissa's ability to hide her letters represents a liberty feared by the adult world, and illicit traffic between colluding individuals (Anna Howe and Clarissa, for example, but the examples might also include men and women contriving together) meant not only that secret papers and books could be stored there but that such private space was the external symbol of a secret world youths could protect from adult scrutiny. Whatever form the warnings took—whether about romantic love or sexual stimulation, marriage above one's station, ambition, wanderlust, or religious or political unorthodoxy—the basic concern was about change, a perception that the old values, as represented by old locations and familiar ways of life, were slipping away under the threat of newfangledness. What is surprising is not that such suspicion and conflict existed—it is present in every generation in every culture and always intense in any period of rapid change—but that older generations tolerated so easily the structures of the change while inveighing against particulars. Encouragement of literacy at whatever risk and acceptance of private time and space even in the face of serious misuses are important marks of a culture committed to evolving, however fearful it may have been about it.

By the mid-eighteenth century, we can see novelists bidding to be a substitute for communality. Sometimes they pretend they are tellers going over the story with readers in the process of reading; sometimes, when they use the pretense of autobiography or letters, they claim presence as editor or discoverer, there to gather textual fragments of people whose loss of human context has driven them to letters as a personal substitute, a frozen version of presence-in-absence. But long before the novel tried to deal with a phenomenology built deep into its structures, writers of other kinds tried to make it up to readers that they were not there personally to deal with prevailing feelings of absence and loss.

Swift—as part of his program of noticing what is happening, giving it a low mark, and predicting new disasters—parodies ruthlessly one of the most important strategies to provide a sense of presence, the prefatory addresses to the reader that introduce nearly all seventeenth-century texts. As the seemingly endless prefaces, prologues, dedications, and epistles in front of A Tale of a Tub suggest, texts did not come naked into the world.[33] Whether they were thought to be too stark, too forbidding, too much a stranger, or too unknown an entity, it is hard to say; few are the books or authors who comment on, much less analyze, the practice that, by late century, is a fully established (and often extended) convention. A few prefaces are self-conscious enough to explain—or apologize for—their necessity; some others comment on their function as buffer between reader and text, almost (but never quite) suggesting their role as intermediary between solitary silence and solitary interaction. The assumption that a text cannot come forth alone, without a proper introduction, is almost universal; a text, no more than a person, can enter a company unintroduced.

Most prefaces are simply headed "To the Reader," but many are called "An Epistle to the Reader"—a letter of introduction, a credentialing, a personal-impersonal passport to the private closet. In either case, the reader—you—is addressed directly, as if the text itself is constructed for a readership, but the preface is for just one person, whoever you are. This is the language of print, but it self-consciously tries to carry over the habits of conversation and personal interaction. Books were trying to be what letters then were, a presence-in-absence, a communication (even a connection) not too intimate and yet thoroughly personal. They could be read by someone for whom they weren't intended without endangering the privacy of the writer or the intimacy between writer and intended reader, but still there is a sense of a slightly improper intrusion, a sense of being overheard, snooped upon, invaded in one's own confined private space. Yet all without the loss of secrets, without any threat to either relevant self, the giver or the receiver.[34]

Another quite mechanical strategy by which writers, especially writers late in the seventeenth century, faced the issue of lost community was by direct address of the reader within the text itself. There are "gentle readers" and "learned readers" and "candid readers" in books long before the novel, and they are addressed directly, often to make some specific point about varieties of personality and experience involved in the reception of the text: it is the written equivalent of an oral aside to a particular subgroup in the audience, an explanatory parenthesis for those not in the innermost of circles. It invites readers to feel recognized, trusted, admitted, even initiated into some sort of undefined community.

Another appeal to nostalgia for community involves attempts—of many different kinds—to create subgroups of the committed, a kind of diaspora of those who share a passionate common interest but who, for some unavoidable reason, are now prevented from sharing each other's company and personal interaction. In one sense, this address to common interest—and the implied bond that goes with it—is no more than the idea of genre applied to kinds of writing ordinarily not given the dignity of an awareness of kinds. It also represents a major reason that most seventeenth-century writing has an intense focus either in a religious or a political position. Organizing ideologists in these two categories skip across time and space to unite their adherents, and writers claim community—and in fact extend the sense of it—just by identifying common interest: commitment to millennialism, for example, or the abolishment of church music, the distrust of the French, or unification with Scotland. Many conventions of the seventeenth century's elaborate title pages have to do with this address—the identification of the author or occasion, the presentation of context in terms of the support of a particular position or as a response to a certain other book, the careful definition of the variety of exhortation.

The incredible popularity of some few titles—Lewis Bayly's *Practise of Pietie*, for example, in early century, *Pilgrim's Progress* in late—suggests how a substitute for physical community developed among readers who "joined" each other as sharers in a particular text. Controversy is often emphasized when speaking of the variety of publication in the seventeenth century, but it seems to me that, although many—perhaps most—books participated in some dispute or other (usually theological or political), very little persuasion, or even attempt at persuasion, took place. The changing of minds was not one of the major results of bookmaking; instead, side-choosing and careful delineation of factionalism served to bind more closely people who already agreed with each other, although they might be physically separated. Books came to be badges, the livery of a party on a particular issue; they were both a symbol and a means to an end, although an artificial one. No quantity of books of whatever quality could altogether reestablish the sense of lost unity, just as no voyage could rediscover the lost Atlantis. But the activity of reading—an act to establish human contact in absence—became, as alienation and literacy both grew, a more and more significant substitute for a primary sense of community. And more and more writers—some quite consciously, others with no idea they did any such thing, still others with quite different primary aims—labored to produce whatever sense they could of human contact against the developing sense of an insularity of self.

Yet another strategy was to bring identifiable oral materials directly into the text of a printed work so as to suggest that pages operated just as voices did to spread rumor, belief, or news. Not many of the prenovelistic works I will be discussing in the second half of this book are primarily narrative in mode, but many of them use anecdotes, openly borrowed from the oral culture, as support for whatever point they are making. Often these stories are presented offhandedly and informally, imitating the rhythms of ordinary life while elevating the authority of orality and anecdote to "evidence." The simple repeating in books of stories from "life" addresses, in one sense, the diminution of narrative, for they seem to respond to the culture's cry for narrativity. They tell anecdotes with recognizable people, poignant episodes, and clear out-comes that often "prove" a larger point. Such anecdotes are the pub-lished equivalent of stories people tell at firesides; many of them are not only derived from stories circulated orally but are recirculated to the oral culture through their book appearance. They become, that is, an exten-sion of oral tradition rather than, strictly speaking, a substitute for it. But they modify traditional oral materials in at least three major ways: the narratives are purported to be literally true, having happened to a person actually named in the account; they eschew relying on magical forces or beings (such as fairies or goblins), even though they may present outcomes quite wonderful or marvelous; and people in the narratives were knowable as ordinary human beings, often still alive and at a par-ticular address, or from the recent past and in a nearby part of the world. The anecdotes also show that narrative needs could be addressed in materials that were not, in themselves, fundamentally narrative in nature or structure.[35]

V

IT would be too much to say that books became the substitute or the solace for everything lost in English culture during the seventeenth cen-tury, but cultural guardians put an extraordinary emphasis on the possi-bilities of print, and authors often give the impression—because they felt their vocation to be crucial—that they regard their task as recuperative. In Chapters Seven through Fourteen, I will describe varieties of reading materials that tried to address directly the needs of the culture in the years before the novel. But before looking at those materials in detail, I want to consider how writers felt about audiences and readerly needs at this crucial moment of cultural change. Two distinct attitudes, almost diametrically opposite, are visible at the turn of the century.

One attitude, held largely by conservative writers who saw themselves inheriting a classical past that they felt obliged to keep intact and pass on, was pessimistic and almost desperate in its clinging to old traditions and old habits of addressing an audience that it perceived to be in need of its accreted wisdom. These "ancients," whose attitudes toward the past I described at the beginning of the chapter, often find themselves exas-perated with readers who are either not the right ones or not grateful enough for the rescue effort writers are trying to perform. These writers saw in the present such a slippage of values that communication was almost impossible; present readers, because of present conditions, simply could not understand. The writers see the continuity of tradition as the constant and find modernity to be insensitive to the true values they try to pass on. They lament the contexts of literacy, finding "new" readers less adequate than old and distrusting the larger ignorance they bring to reading, yet such writers fear their loss of audience. When they are not worried about present readership, they fret about the future and the ingratitude of prince posterity. In the evolution of language, they see another threat to their authority: linguistic change will mean that texts like theirs will no longer be available. The form of this worry is important, for it is never phrased in terms of authorship or text being inflexible and thus unable to adapt to changing conditions or desires, but rather in terms of the "problem" of change itself. Audience "needs," particularized by time and place, are not for them an issue. The problem is that audiences do not recognize the greater needs that the tradition addresses. Needs, like human nature, are universal.

The other attitude, espoused by "moderns" of many stripes, is equally anxious about the present, but regards the contemporary needs of readers as the determining factor in what is to be written. The moderns can sometimes sound cynical about these needs, but their firm sense of practicality—usually they see writing as functional and only an aspect of some larger social agenda—and devotion to contemporary issues mean that they try to be students of desire. They try to remain in close touch with readers' tastes; they read readers assiduously. Most of them have close (although not necessarily friendly) relationships with their publishers, and some are themselves booksellers primarily and only writers in a second role. At its worst, this attitude leads to trendy, fickle, uncertain, and commercial stances; at its best, it is responsive to real needs of real readers.

Both groups see a kind of crisis in writing (a reflection of a larger crisis in the culture), but they propose radically different solutions to it, and in their opposite thrusts lie the two primary directions of literature in the eighteenth century. The moderns, willing to use any innovation or novelty to reach readers loosened from their moorings by revolution, emigration, urbanization, and economic change, look to a potential readership that includes many whose great-grandfathers and great-grandmothers were illiterate, and they offer a cautious optimism about what writing—hardheaded, practical, and problem-centered—can provide. These moderns, often sad about the lost oral past of immediately preceding generations, try consciously to write in the wake of a lost oral community. The ancients, thinking of a more remote past and regarding the cultural forgetting of this past as a threat to the sacred functions of "literature," are more personally afflicted by their sense of loss and worry about whether they still have any audience at all—fit, few, or otherwise.

Literary history has traditionally been more just to the attitudes of the ancients, for while they did not ultimately prevail, they did dominate the best writing in the early years of the eighteenth century, and it is "their" literary history that we have largely inherited. Without gainsaying their accomplishment or doubting their sincerity, however, a newer literary history needs to see how their attitudes resisted cultural opportunity and failed to take advantage of either the enlarged readership that their times offered or the vacuum produced by the retreat of the oral tradition. The fears of the Augustans—genuine, poignant, and often brilliantly verbalized—ultimately opened the gates for novels because traditional literature rejected a ripe potential, deciding instead to attack virulently both popular directions and populist desire. For all the warmth Pope feels for folk traditions and the attraction he has to modernist values (energies suppressed but still visible in poems from *The Rape of the Lock* to the final *Dunciad*), he refuses the Smithfield muses and rejects at every turn the tastes that allow them sway, and Swift is, even if more divided temperamentally, even more ruthless.[36]

The "sorting" tendency in all the Augustans—a desire to separate sheep from goats and provide a roster so that all readers would know who was on which side—produced some of the best literature we have from the late seventeenth and early eighteenth century, but it refused a crucial cultural possibility too. Rather than comprehending new readership and admitting the legitimacy of modern writing that responded to contemporary desires, works like *MacFlecknoe*, *A Tale of a Tub*, and the *Dunciads* systematically abandoned—even expelled—writers and readers who failed the taste test. The sorting is brilliant in all three of these works (and *Gulliver's Travels*, insofar as it represents an anthology and review of contemporary writing, is similar in its thrust), but the writers who are cast into outer darkness here (however personally deficient artistically or morally) represent the literary future. It is among these outcasts that a new outlook, conducive to new forms, can develop. It is not always easy to defend the accomplishment of the likes of Flecknoe, Wotton, or Theobald (although a pretty good representation of modern novelty might be assembled from Shadwell, Dunton, Defoe, Haywood, and Cibber), but they were helping to define directions that meant a new sensibility for the new age and that ultimately meant a place for novels.

In traditionalists, steeped as they are in a deep sense of the past and its modes, there is often receptivity toward orality; one of the strengths of the verse of Pope, Gay, and Swift is the consciousness of conversational rhythms and the sense of a tight, cozy world of friendly listeners held together by common bonds of friendship and agreed-upon values. But the orality here, like the lawns, barges, grottos, and drawing rooms in constant danger of being invaded, depends on exclusivity. It participates in the fear that outsiders—as bad really as new and uninformed readers—may come in and not appreciate the true value of all this bonding. Needs identified by the oral attritions I have discussed in this chapter had to find a different kind of written substitute, and it was the attitudes toward audience of the "moderns" that provided the kind of receptive context which ultimately made a place for the novel.

V I

THE presence of features like these do not prove that writers or book-sellers were about to invent the novel, but they do suggest what some of the needs of seventeenth-century readers were like, and they suggest that books existed—or came to exist—which, one by one, or sometimes in combination, tried to address those human needs, sometimes with conscious intent, sometimes in the process of trying to do something else. Many of the needs relate to basic human patterns, and versions of the needs may exist in a variety of times and places. But particular circumstances dictated that these needs took specific forms in England during the seventeenth century. Yet besides the changes from old culture, there were new forces arising, too, that stimulated new needs in readers. In turning now to the printed materials that readers found in the generations before the novel was there to be read, I turn first to journalistic modes that represented the materials of everyday life.

III
■

PRE-TEXTS

CHAPTER SEVEN

Journalism: The Commitment to Contemporaneity

■

LONG before Samuel Richardson showed readers and writers of fiction how to savor a single human instant a thousand ways, the world of print had begun its long liaison with the up to date, the latest news, and the present moment, trying to provide a sense that the printing press offered a technology for nearly instant replay of human experience. Such a sense was crucial to many kinds of art and cultural experience in England in the late seventeenth century because the culture had developed a fixa-tion on contemporaneity, part of its larger interest in discovery, enlight-enment, and novelty. When the journalist, publisher, and would-be narrative writer John Dunton insisted (repeatedly) that "News, and new Things do the whole World bewitch,"[1] he was characteristically blurring a distinction, this time between intellectual curiosity and the desire to be *au courant*, the fundamental motivations, respectively, for readers of science and journalism. But the blur represents a shrewd perception of connection—between acute awareness of the latest events and a desire for innovation and originality. Both features of contemporary conscious-ness contribute to the emergence of the peculiar, present-centered form of narrative that we now call (appropriately enough) the novel, and in fact the fusion of the two helps create the cultural mind that makes novels possible.

The preoccupation with novelty, often motivated by a simple desire to be thought trendy and in-the-know, developed in one of its aspects into pure ephemeral silliness. Publishing ventures, including most of

Dunton's, often tried to read fickle public taste in the simplest ways, producing a proliferation of anonymous ballads, broadsides and broadsheets, narratives of public or private intrigue, prophecies, criminal confessions, and other ephemera that took events and rumors of the street and returned them to the street in printed form. But in other aspects, the attraction to novelty represents the legitimate line—from Bacon through Newton, a line that later moved through Darwin and Einstein to Heisenberg and McClintock—that denied Aristotle his old authority and that opened new directions of thought and human behavior. And the desire for "news," although it, too, often ends in byways, trivia, and solipsism, also represents higher reaches of communicative possibility, the side of the Enlightenment that leads away from elitism and toward political as well as literary radicalism.[2]

The sense that the moment (any isolated moment potentially, but some species of moment in particular) was in itself a kind of art object— to be adored, meditated upon, savored, and contemplated again and again—had far-reaching, long-term implications for literature. Three major intellectual thrusts—philosophical explorations of time; psychological interests in memory, continuity of consciousness, and the nature of personal identity; and the new theological concerns with conversion, the individual epiphany, and the enlightened inner instant—all relate to (and grow out of) the developing concern with contemporaneity, a wish to recognize the momentous in the momentary and to feel the power of all time in its most fleeting moment. When the novel began to emerge, the English culture had already given tacit approval to a widespread devotion to radical contemporaneity, an urgent sense of now.

The celebrations of literary novelty that I described in Chapter One represent a formal attempt to incorporate innovation and originality and to accept the limitations of tradition. They reflect a larger cultural embracing of the present moment as a legitimate subject not only for passing conversation but for serious discourse. For a half century before the novel emerged, the world of print had experimented in assuming, absorbing, and exploiting the new cultural consciousness based on human curiosity—on the one hand "preparing" readers for novels and on the other offering later writers of novels some sense of potential subject matter and potential form, a sense of how the present could be won over to serious literature. The process was an odd and unstructured one, and in its early manifestations it did not seem destined to lead to a significant new literary form. Even in retrospect, the print novelties of the turn of the century hardly seem a teleology of form or thought, yet the broad ferment that authenticated the new, together with the apparent permanence that print seemed to bestow on accounts of the temporary and passing, ultimately led to a mind and art that transcended occasions and individuals. Still, it engaged them first of all—energetically, enthusiast-ically, evangelically. The first fruits of the modern moment-centered consciousness were not very promising, but the emergence of that con-sciousness enabled, when other cultural contexts were right, a new aes-thetic and a different relation between life and literature.

I

IT is hard to say exactly when the present time became such an urgent issue in the English cultural consciousness. In one sense, of course, con-temporaneity always has been important to every culture, the immediacy of human needs and fears overshadowing all more abstract concerns; but long before the advent of print, or even of any means of written com-munication, art had taken as one of its essential functions the need to steer the human mind away from immediate gratification and to some longer and larger view—toward distancing, abstraction, perspective, an historical view that saw the present as a result, and largely a reiteration, of a past that stretched amiably across a canvas as large as the mind of humankind itself. Literature (like painting, music, and told tales) had always celebrated or encompassed occasions and events, many of them urgently contemporary. But in traditional literature—oral creations that aspire to answer cultural questions and be formally satisfying—the demands of the moment are subordinated to a concern with a larger story of the culture that includes but quickly transcends individuals and individual times,[3] putting them into a perspective of history and slow time.[3] And print technology, whatever its own attraction to the quick and the new, extended the assumption that human beings needed to be pried away from the immediate and the momentary to consider greater matters. It saw its function mainly in the need to educate people rather than just inform them, to delight with lasting joys rather than repeat the passing effects of conversation or oral discourse, to extend and expand human considerations rather than narrow, intensify, and gratify the immediate. And so printed books early on consisted primarily of works that offered, or aspired to, perspective: classics from the past, attempts to describe the universals of human experience, works of theology, philosophy, or his-tory, narratives of long ago and far away.

The seeds of dissension are, of course, early visible in the world of print, especially at moments when "art" is not a secure notion or when traditional forms and audiences are under close scrutiny. Certainly in Elizabethan times one can spot tares prospering outside the traditional enclosed garden. The urban para-literature in the time of Nashe, Dek-ker, Gosson, and Jonson instantly suggests that print had uses that could extend well beyond the traditional and invade unaccustomed social groups. It is in this sense (rather than in the existence of particular novel-resembling books) that the novel—with its distinctively modern and anti-aristocratic tendency to encompass the daily, the trivial, the common, and the immediate—has roots that reach back into older times and domestic traditions.[4] But the relationship to that curious para-literary past is a complicated one because definitions of "literature" hardened during the seventeenth century, and the gap between "art" and popular culture increased enormously before the novel narrowed it again later.

The formal programs for serious literature in the Restoration and early eighteenth century betray a divided heart about present events. Certainly the poets wanted to feel themselves an integral part of their own culture and its public faces, and they sought, as in few ages before or since, to affect the direction of politics and social history in their own time. They often seem obsessed with even the most minor happenings around them, and their accounts of public affairs, their concern with the current health of the state, and their anxieties about social change are seldom far from the surface in what they write, even when they address the eternal issues of a *Religio Laici*, a *Solomon*, or an *Essay on Man*. And when they set themselves, as they often do, the task of evaluating critically the directions of modern life—in poems like *Absalom and Achitophel* or *The Dispensary* or *The Rape of the Lock*—they treat contemporary matters in great, often painful, detail, regarding themselves as legitimate heirs of the Roman tradition of public commentary and responsibility. Still, public poets and aspiring men of letters retain always a decorum. It is not so much that they hold back in detail or restrain themselves in tone as that they try to restrict their subjects—the persons, events, *and* ideas they treat of—to ones generally thought appropriate to public consideration. Among themselves they play and take holidays in verse or prose, and the range of banter and facetiousness in personal letters and light verse is sometimes astonishing. But until their exasperation is heightened and their anger turned to righteous indignation, they avoid the contexts of common debate and street life—unless trying to locate it in a larger context (as in "A Description of the Morning" or *Trivia: or, The Art of Walking the Streets of London*) or undermining its values in some sort of mock-heroic contrast (as in *MacFlecknoe*). When, in desperation, they turn to full programs of satire that engage the present as the nearly full burden of their content, they have been largely driven to it by the energies of what has begun to happen in the popular mind.

Certainly it is accurate to think of Augustan literature as aggressively public and heatedly anti-innovative, so that prose attacks on novelty like *A Tale of a Tub* or poetic ones like *The Dunciad* contain as much energy and vitality as the newly funded creativities they opposed. But writers

modern vs ancient
Tale of Tub
Dunciad

like Swift and Pope come to their position and achieve much of the force that drives their writing from a basic change in the culture. The best taste and the best brains in literature in the early years of the century fought the change every step of the way; while getting mileage out of its weaknesses and silliness, they never came to terms with its virtues or its implications for future writing except as blind, often indiscriminate, hatred. The justification for public poetry and occasional literature that Augustans took from their Roman models, while always the putative sponsor of High Art about contemporaneity, does not fully account for the best of Augustan addresses to the present time, and (much as a Pope or a Swift would have dreaded to think it) popular culture not only provided grist for the Augustan mill but also the energy for doing the grinding.[5]

The quality of innovation among the "moderns" was not at first very high, and it is no wonder that the talented and the thoughtful had great fun at the expense of novelty for its own sake. What was most significant about early innovations had less to do with specific literary accomplishments than with the very idea that experimentation could be defended plausibly and that modern occasional writing seemed to fit the mood, tone, and needs of the culture even when it was not very good. The defenses of the moderns against the ancients—whether by Dryden or Dunton, Robert Boyle or Richard Bentley—ring with a surprising energy, even when they argue or illustrate foolishly. In retrospect it seems astonishing that a traditionalist like Temple or Swift took the new movement seriously enough to answer in such detail. The recognition that such works as *A Tale of a Tub* and *The Dunciad* bestowed on literary modernism legitimized the issue, and the "popular culture" aspects of novelty and journalism come to exist, ironically, in a canonical literature because the most traditional rivals put them there.

Not all the energies of "literary" innovation resided in journalistic efforts to celebrate the present moment, but many of them did, and it is important to recognize the cultural depth and breadth beneath and around the surface signs. Perhaps the cultural anxiety about present time intensified gradually throughout the seventeenth century, or perhaps by fits and starts, but by the 1690s, the world of print had joined the world of conversation, gossip, and rumor in a singular devotion to issues of the moment, and the directions of publishing in the nineties represent a milestone in the developing concern with contemporaneity. The pragmatic social and ethical concerns of the reign of William and Mary, manifested in phenomena like the Societies for the Reformation of Manners and in public reports of even the most trivial behavioral aberrations, are one sign of the cultural mania for news.[6] But there are many other signs as well. The publications of the 1690s and just after suggest how fully the concerns of the moment had absorbed the world of print and show how the world of print interacted with the oral culture, especially in London where pamphlets, periodicals, and informal talk fed each other in an ever-intensifying attention to the latest news or pseudo-news.

I I

HISTORIES of English journalism seriously begin with the 1690s, for the sharp increase in the number of periodicals published in London and the proliferation of news pamphlets and news sheets that eventuate in the founding of a London daily in 1702 suggest that the cultural moment for journalism had just then come.[7] The term "journalism" apparently did not enter the language until 1833,[8] but according to the OED the word "journalist" came into use as early as 1693 to describe those who wrote about daily doings for the public press. In their etymology, "journalist" and "journalism" suggest a range of preoccupations with contemporaneity—with the daily and the ordinary—that marked the nineties and the following decades. The French word jour is, of course, the root from which "journalist" and "journalism" spring, and "journal" and "journey" have their derivation there as well. In its original meaning, a "journey" was a day's travel (although it quickly became extended to cover travels that could be measured by a specific number of days), and "journal," both in its sense as a public account of daily events and as a private account of personal details in daily life, emphasized in its origins the centrality for the recording and receiving consciousness of immediate moments in time.[9] The term "journal" and its derivatives separated themselves from the sense of order and predictable repetition that a word like "diurnal" has continued to carry, so that "journalism" in the sense that it is popularly used today carries (much like the term "novel") accurate suggestions about what was happening in the culture at a very deep level.[10] By the 1690s, the culture became so obsessed with the potential significance to human consciousness of any single moment that an immediate written record needed to be created, and the preoccupations with news and novelty in fact coalesced in the popular consciousness much as Dunton suggests.

Journalism was beginning to "rise" elsewhere too, but it became culturally significant more slowly and tentatively, and nowhere else does there seem to be, so early, the obsession with contemporaneity that characterizes English culture at the beginning of the eighteenth century. The English were notorious among Europeans both for their attraction to novelty and their devotion to news. A French traveler to England concludes that the "melancholy temper of the English has rendered them, in all ages, exceeding fond of every thing which appears to be out of the

English passion for news distinctive

common order,"[11] and the English fondness for wide-ranging gossip, masquerading as news of foreign affairs, was regarded as beyond debate, although Englishmen regularly took umbrage at that "common Imputation cast upon *Englishmen* by Forreigners."[12] "The writings most in fashion at the present period," claims a Swiss visitor to England in 1727, "are pamphlets for and against the government, on politics and different subjects of interest relating to England and her allies. Almost every day some of these works appear and are eagerly sought after, for politics in this country seem to interest everyone."[13] The Frenchman Pierre Jean Grosley, visiting London in 1765, found the English "infatuated with politics" and "passionate for news," and seems puzzled that "news-papers are regularly filed, kept from year to year, and are referred to in public and in private, like the records of law in Westminster-hall."[14] Another sort of traveler, Lemuel Gulliver, notices similar habits in Laputa and implies they mirror English fads. "But, what I chiefly admired, and thought altogether unaccountable," he says of the impractical mathematicians, "was the strong Disposition I observed in them towards News and Politicks; perpetually enquiring into publick Affairs, giving their Judgments in Matters of State; and passionately disputing every Inch of a Party Opinion."[15] Years before, a proud and equally troubled native, Richard Baxter, had lamented that "[a]ll men are affected most with things that seem new and strange to them." He linked taste for novelty with a lust for news and argued that this "English" characteristic was in fact universal: "If nature were not much for Novelty, the publishing of *News-books* would not have been so gainful a Trade so long."[16]

The creation of such a public consciousness in England was probably not engineered so much as just permitted, although the new brand of party politician and information manipulator like Robert Walpole obviously perceived advantages to be gained from heightened public consciousness of public events and attitudes loosened from their traditional moorings. The cultural institution that had the most to do with encouraging the new consciousness has been studied in literary history only in a peripheral way. That institution is the coffeehouse, often treasured for its benign and lovable (if somewhat obtuse) denizens who value good conversation, or praised for its attempts to raise the cultural level of cits and tradesmen, or gently teased for the foibles of sotted squires or sparks gone to embers. But a larger cultural contribution resides in the structural tendency of the institution to bridge levels of discourse (with at least as much influence from below as above) and to blur the distinction between oral and written discourse.[17]

The conversation of the coffeehouse, while sometimes perhaps as "improving" and high-minded as its literary admirers would have us believe and sometimes as irrelevant and banal as satires on it suggest,[18] often was determined not by abstract or "universal" human concerns but by events of the day—or rather, by what public gossipmongers defined as "events" of the day. Timeliness was the crucial element in the conversation; talking to the moment was as crucial to the coffeehouse consciousness (and to daily life in London) as writing to the moment became to the novel. Reports, rumors, and stories from the street vied with printed "news" and speculations—from the regular periodicals and the daily variety of occasional publications—as subjects of conversation. It may have been amusing to hear the mixture of information, misinformation, speculation, and opinion that resulted, and apparently the joy of participating was widely prized. Not many major decisions about government or trade (or anything else) resulted from these conversations (although journalists and spies for various groups regularly listened in, used them as sounding boards, and probably planted additional "information"), but the illusion of involvement in matters of moment and of "knowing" the state of London and the world seems to have appealed mightily to Londoners of many classes and stripes. "What attracts enormously in these coffee-houses," writes the visitor Saussure in 1726, "are the gazettes and other public papers. All Englishmen are great newsmongers. Workmen habitually begin the day by going to coffee-rooms in order to read the latest news. I have often seen shoeblacks and other persons of that class club together to purchase a farthing paper. Nothing is more entertaining than hearing men of this class discussing politics and topics of interest concerning royalty. You often see an Englishman taking a treaty of peace more to heart than he does his own affairs" (FV, p. 162).

Even allowing for the bemused chauvinism of a visitor anxious to regale the folks at home, the picture confirms the view from English observers. The virtuosi and coffeehouse politicians widely portrayed in plays and other texts were essentially the "Athenians" with an itch for news and novelty that Dunton described, and their significance lies not in what they actually knew, said, or accomplished, but in the expectations they set for eighteenth-century conduct and consciousness. As early as 1667, a London broadside (News from the Coffe-House [sic]) satirized the already-accepted expectations:

> You that delight in Wit and Mirth
> And long to hear such News
> As comes from all Parts of the Earth. . .
> Go hear it at a Coffe House
> It cannot but be true.
>
> There's nothing done in all the World,
> From Monarch to the Mouse

> But every Day or Night 'tis hurld
> Into the *Coffe-house.*

> So great a *Vniversitie,*
> I think there ne're was any;
> In which you may a Schoolar be
> For spending of a Penny.[19]

Seven decades later, the expectations and jokes were still the same; a 1733 satire invites its readers to

> See yon spruce busy *Man,* he asks you hasty,
> What News from *Coffee-Club,* or who just past ye?[20]

No doubt real news did sometimes get passed on in such company, for real doers as well as imaginary ones frequented coffeehouses, often with their judgment fully intact, but a "Coffee-house Tale" was synonymous with unreliability, the love of stories for their own sake, and ultimately with triviality.[21]

In the mixture of journalism and conversation, print record and loose talk, fiction and fact, informed opinion and baseless speculation, the oral and written cultures dramatically meet and interact in the coffeehouse milieu, reflecting changes in the larger world and demonstrating not only how quickly booksellers had learned to exploit the daily possibilities of print but also how "talk" and current opinion joined and enlarged the cycle of "now" consciousness. The sense of what was appropriate, timely, and "in" spread outward from London. The effect was not so much in the provincial proliferation of coffeehouses themselves as in the acceptance of London values and conversation as normative. For many in villages and in the countryside, the sense of the city and its alluring fashions of busyness and knowledge of the world set expectations that profoundly affected the sense of what was worth talking about, thinking about, and reading about. And if such a cycle of communication and such a mixture of human modes characterized daily London life and set a pattern elsewhere for those who aspired to live a fashionable modern life, they also led to an important conditioning of the reading public and those who wrote for it. As the reading public for journalism, didactic works, biography and travel, history, and literature in the late seventeenth century became the reading public for the novel a generation later, the sense of urgency about present time and current concerns was deeply built into the public consciousness. The private reading of novels in a sense displaced the taste for public discussion.[22] The early novelists shared the public taste for contemporaneity and novelty and quickly discovered how to blend it into a substantial and complex web of narrative and discursive prose, creating in effect a portable coffeehouse of elongated conversation in print.[23] For Henry Fielding, the world became a stagecoach in which a narrator could nudge and twist hearers, for Sterne a private library where readers were present with the author as he wrote. But the effect is finally just as evident in the expository "dear Reader" world of Defoe or the epistolary totality of shared circumstance in Richardson or Burney.

I I I

THE rapid rise of journalism at the turn of the century shows what the public was thinking and talking about and underscores the increasingly successful attempts to exploit that interest for profit. The failed journals even more than the few successful ones suggest the perceived need for up-to-date information and news and the willingness of booksellers and writers to turn that need into cash. No one knows how many readers periodicals had or how the readership of periodicals overlapped.[24] But the broad effect is plain. Readers steeped themselves in events and issues, talking all the time, debating vigorously. And parties and factions fueled the fires of controversy, hiring pens to perform all kinds of tasks—some traditional, some not—in many forms and contexts.

Important as they were, periodicals are not the characteristic outlet for journalism of the time nor do they chart the directions of the culture as fully as do the multitude of separate pamphlets and single sheets that call attention to events of the time one by one. Periodicals had the virtue of predictability and continuity; they tended to "follow" stories and present consistent views. But their virtues as broad, continuing, interpretive narratives limited their appeal and their usefulness in giving fresh perspective and in uncovering new material. Although convenient for publishers anxious for a constant readership and reliable income, comfortable for readers who could know what to expect, and useful to political or church leaders eager to infuse or enforce a particular point of view, regular periodicals (whether weeklies, twice- or thrice- weeklies, or dailies) had severe limits, largely involving their ability to surprise an expectant reader or attract an unlikely one. The journalistic habits of the time— with new items appearing every day, sometimes cloaking themselves familiarly and sometimes in devious disguises—were calculated to keep the public off balance. The mixture of predictable periodical publications, frequent but irregular examples of standard para-literary subspecies (such as the confessions of condemned criminals), and one-of-a-kind surprises published anonymously provided both excitement and uncertainty. It was the journalistic enterprise as a whole that helped to create— and then enlarged and extended—the culture of now. To study journals and newspapers in isolation from the scores of pamphlets, broadsheets, and other occasional vehicles of contemporaneity is to miss the broad effect produced by the heightened consciousness of moments that came, receded, and were replaced by one new moment after another in a ceaseless attempt to penetrate, interpret, and hold the sense of present moment.

The immediate aim of the writers, publishers, and promoters of controversy was not always so high-minded as my terms may suggest. Often they were driven by party zeal, sectarian commitments, or financial greed rather than a desire for clarity or understanding of contemporary events, and many controversies involved pseudo-events and pseudo-issues, news manufactured by booksellers who, in effect, got a writer to light a fire and then hired other writers to keep it lit before hiring still more writers (or the same ones in a different function) to spread it or transfer it elsewhere and (finally) extinguish it. A pamphlet taking a particular position or offering a certain interpretation often was followed by answers, replies, rejoinders, defenses, and various shades of attack and sympathetic response, sometimes all written by the same writer or by others within the same stable. A clever promoter could keep a good pseudo-controversy in the public press for days or even weeks, boosting sales and raising the heat of interest in contemporaneity sometimes altogether without political, social, or philosophical commitments or assumptions and with only cash, a sense of power, or amusement in view. But sometimes also with deeper cultural aims.

Whether or not there was a real event or actual circumstances behind a particular discussion, controversy, or pamphlet war—whether real persons, places, and things were the basis for a prose that purported to air ideas and ultimately move them toward some significant resolution, whether the basis was entirely fictional, or whether facts were embroidered toward fiction—the stress on contemporaneity accelerated and intensified the public sense that the present times were all that mattered. Accounts of public drunkenness, sabbath breaking, thievery, and murder in the 1690s, for example, provided a heightened sense of disorder and moral decay in times that were boisterous but hardly desperate, but they also dramatized how fully the contemporary moment had absorbed the attention and dominated the imagination of preachers, moralists, philosophers, politicians, writers, readers, and talkers in the now urban-centered kingdom.

"The times" get repeated attention and serious excoriation in printed item after printed item in the late seventeenth century, and sermons and informal conversations echo and reecho the theme of corruption and deterioration. Rising urban crowding, nervous memories of the Fire and Plague, international uncertainties, and a tense sense of contrast with the tight controls during Puritan rule all played a part in the tone of near desperation that characterizes almost every assessment of the state of public conduct in London, and those in the countryside devoutly believed that depraved behavior was moving their way from the city. Much of what observers saw or thought they saw was exaggerated, and the tone was often grimmer than it needed to be, but the social contract was severely stretched, and those alive at the end of the seventeenth century believed "the times" to be even worse than they were, often predicting imminent disaster and prophesying "last days" and a coming millennium. "The *days* wherein we live," writes Defoe's former schoolmate Timothy Cruso in 1695, "are extremely *Evil;* but yet we have a sad and doleful Prospect of the *next Age* becoming *worse,* if God do not by some effectual means stop the wicked Course of the *Rising Generation.* We see . . . Crowds and Swarms of *young ones* continually *posting down* to Hell, and *bringing up* . . . Hell in the midst of us. . . ."[25] In accounts of those times—accounts that alternated between precise details of a particular episode and generalizations about the meaning of events for interpreting the directions of English culture—one can see both the importance accorded to authentic human experiences and the desire to interpret by accumulation. Many pamphlets, booklets, and single sheets told a particular story and provided explicit or implicit interpretation, usually along moral or religious lines. Huge collections of such stories and anecdotes were organized by subject or theme, but (before discussing them in the next chapter) I want to look at shorter works that illustrate the age's interest in present events and suggest their narrative possibilities.

I V

WORKS that detail a single event or series of related ones had been fairly common early in the seventeenth century. In titles such as *A Wonderfull and most Lamentable Declaration of the great hurt done, and mighty losse sustained by Fire . . .[,] Winde, Thunder, Lightning, Haile, and Raine* and *The Wonders of this windie winter* (both 1613), one can see the interests of those who wrote about the contemporary scene. Every event, no matter how small or apparently isolated, was seen as part of some larger plan. The woodcut at the front of *Wonders of this windie winter* suggests the recurrent theme; there God (or an angel) is breathing toward Earth, while in the ensuing wind, people and ships tumble helplessly about in the sea. No event is independent; nothing just happens.

A similar thematic emphasis continues in much of the material published about contemporary events throughout the late seventeenth century and into the eighteenth, especially when a dramatic natural occurrence focuses attention on human limits in the face of wind, earthquake, or fire. The prodigious storm of November 1703, for example, inspired a number of detailed accounts of destruction and the frustration of human efforts. There was virtual unanimity in regarding the event as a divine visitation upon England, although the grounds for divine anger were located variously, depending upon the assumptions, affiliations, and biases of the individual writer. Defoe's account, *The Storm, Or, A Collection Of the most Remarkable Casualties And Disasters Which happen'd in the Late Dreadful Tempest, Both by Sea and Land* (1704)—one of the best of his early blends of narrative interest and thematic coherence—is a detailed and comprehensive treatment (285 pages long), and it may be the best. But there were many other notable accounts, including *The Terrible Stormy Wind and Tempest . . . Consider'd, Improv'd, and Collected, to be had In Everlasting Remembrance* (1705); *A Wonderful History of All the Storms, Hurricanes, Earthquakes &c. That have happen'd in England for above 500 years past* (1704); and *An Exact Relation Of the Late Dreadful Tempest: or, a Faithful Account Of the Most Remarkable Disasters which hapned on that occasion . . . Faithfully collected by an Ingenious Hand, to preserve the Memory of so Terrible a Judgment* (1704). "So remarkable and signal a Judgment of God on this Nation," the last pamphlet argues, "no History either forreign or domestick, can parallel"; it claimed the storm destroyed more than had the Great Fire (p. 24). "To transmit," it argues in another passage, "a distinct and true Account of that unheard of and fatal Accident, and to observe an exact Decorum in each particular . . . will not be unacceptable to the Reader; since a matter of this important Consequence must and will stand as a Monument of the Anger of Heaven, justly pour'd down upon this Kingdom to all posterity" (p. 3). Accounts like these emphasize, with key words in their titles as well as by repetitions in the text, their factuality and particularity ("Exact Relation," "Faithful Account"), and details are in fact very important to their effect, but the emphasis still falls, as it did a century earlier, on meanings assigned to the storm. Those meanings remain traditional in their reliance on religious and moral assumptions about how human events are, and should be, controlled and in their insistence that such events can be "read" as God's judgment on human behavior and events. "Readings" often differed, of course, the storm being regarded alternatively as God's displeasure with Queen Anne or with those who frustrated her plans, but regardless of disagreements in application, interpreters agreed that dramatic events had deep meanings. One popular interpretation of the storm, especially among Dissenters, was as a judgment on playgoers (the Collier controversy still churned on), and when *Macbeth* was produced just after the storm, apparently to mock providential interpreters, many prophesied disasters even more dire.[26]

And so it went. Every event offered lively possibilities, and every context had multiple referents. Sometimes the emphasis in such accounts stayed on the details of the event and left readers on their own to draw conclusions. *A True and Perfect Narrative of the Great and Dreadful Damages Susteyned in Several Parts of England by the Late Extraordinary Snouus* (1674) describes on its title page snow "covering the Tops of . . . Houses" and people burning "all their Goods to keep them warm," but avoids blaming the event on any particular evil practice. More judgmental is an account of rains and floods in 1683, *A Strange and Wonderful Account of . . . the late Dreadful Thunder, Lightening, And Terrible Land-Floods . . . Giving an Exact Relation of the Men, Cattle, Houses, &c that have been Thunderstruck*, although blame is cast rather broadly and generally.

It is tempting for modern readers to see in such accounts increasing evidence of insincerity and erosion of belief in divine control and intervention, a temptation that snares more literary historians than intellectual or cultural historians. The climate of religious belief is different in 1703 from that in 1613, but if the nation is more secular in 1703 (as it surely is), those who continue to be believers are neither less sincere nor notably less certain. Accelerated secularism and diminished religious faith are facts of life in the eighteenth century, but the change is one of degree, and the degree was not yet radical. The Restoration of the monarchy, the Plague of 1665, the Great Fire of 1666, the Glorious Revolution of 1688, the storm of 1703, the Peace of Utrecht, and every major military and political event throughout the seventeenth century and well into the eighteenth inspired pamphlets and in many cases long books that argued religious interpretations of events. The difference between seventeenth- and eighteenth-century accounts involves the fact that earlier writers readily assume that their audience will already believe that *some* sort of religious and moral meaning is true and relevant, whereas later accounts have to be prepared to argue in a context of less certainty about ultimate causes. The change in rhetoric is indeed an index of contexts beginning to change, but most interpreters continue to be supported by the same philosophical and theological assumptions, while being aware that their task of persuasion becomes every day more difficult because of cultural slippage.[27]

But journalism did change dramatically during the seventeenth century, reflecting broadened curiosity more than abandoned commitments. If readers continued to be fascinated with accounts of storms and shipwrecks, they developed an interest as well in lesser events and more private and personal ones. Everyday and domestic events began to appear more and more frequently in print, both in periodicals and in separate titles. Even at the beginning of the century, pamphlets sometimes described murders, acts of treason, and other acts of individual behavior that seemed to threaten the public peace or the social fabric. *A true relation of a most desperate murder committed upon the body of Sir John Tindall* appeared in 1617; in 1605, *A True relation of Gods vvonderfull mercies, in preseruing one aliue, which hanged fiue dayes, who was falsely accused.* By the 1670s individual accounts of murders appeared routinely almost every week, no doubt reflecting increased crime (especially in London) but also demonstrating heightened interest in a more individualized definition of current events. In late 1677, for example, was published an extensive collection of stories, *A true relation of all the bloody murders that have been committed in and about the citie and suburbs of London, since the 4th of this instant June.* The range expanded to include accounts of robberies, household quarrels, discoveries of witchcraft, fires, and all sorts of out-of-the-ordinary events occurring to ordinary people in ordinary circumstances. Literally hundreds of these "true accounts" appeared, some claiming to tell of larger patterns and plots. Here are simple titles from a single year, 1679:

A True Account of The Horrid Murther Committed upon . . . The Late Archbishop of Saint Andrews;

A true Account of . . . strange and prodigious Apparitions;

A True Narrative of the Horrid Hellish Popish Plot;

A True Narrative and Discovery of several very Remarkable Passages Relating to the Horrid Popish Plot;

A True Narrative of that Grand Jesvite Father Andrews;

A True Relation of a Devilish Attempt to Fire the Town of Barnet;

A True Narrative Of the Late Design of the Papists to Charge Their Horrid Plot Upon the Protestants;

A Full Narrative, or, a Discovery of the Priests and Jesuites.

Many "events" in titles like these were tied to political concerns, rumored occurrences, and deep suspicions. The "Popish Plot" was responsible for hundreds of titles that promised the "exact relation" of this or the "true narrative" of that. The term "narrative," in fact, although occasionally used on title pages earlier, became a title catchword in the late seventies to signal events related to Catholic Europe's intrusive interest in English affairs. Although the terms "narrative," "relation," "account," and "news" strictly speaking only indicate that contemporary events are to be the center of attention, such code terms came to imply a connection with intrigue of some larger, ongoing sort, an implication of human conspiracy nearly as useful as "Providential" explanations to make sense of random, apparently isolated events.

One of the most popular short narratives of the 1690s is *The Second Spira* (1693) which, according to the publisher, sold more than 30,000 copies in six weeks, an astonishing figure.[28] Its contents, publication history, and public reception are in several ways at once indicative of developing cultural interests. *The Second Spira* is a deathbed account of "An Atheist, Who Had Apostatized from the Christian Religion, and dyed in Despair at *Westminster, Decemb.* 8. 1692"; it contains "an Account of his Sickness, Convictions, Discourses with Friends and Ministers; and of his dreadful Expressions and Blasphemies when he left the world."[29] Precisely who this "Atheist" is remains mysterious throughout, and the popularity of *The Second Spira* owes something to the contemporary notoriety surrounding the supposed deathbed repentance of the Earl of Rochester in 1680, as well as to the public memory of the Spira alluded to in the title, one Francis Spira, a sixteenth-century Italian convert to Protestantism who recanted under persecution and died an agonizing death. Spira's own deathbed details had been recounted by John Bunyan in *Grace Abounding*, which reached a seventh edition in 1692. Deathbed accounts were in fact extremely popular at the time, and they remained so for more than a half century, a taste to which eighteenth-century novels repeatedly pay homage, sometimes by squeezing every possible tear out of parting scenes, sometimes (as in *Tom Jones* and *Tristram Shandy*) by showing how different tones can be achieved out of such materials.[30] The widespread belief that truth will out in the final moments before death may help account for the widespread circulation of "last words" and "dying speeches"—a small but important subgenre of the late seventeenth and early eighteenth century that often merged with, or became embedded in, criminal biographies and funeral sermons—although a counter belief that deathbed sentiments and last-minute conversions were untrustworthy also sponsored a number of publications that helped keep alive the hot theological and ethical issue.[31]

The appeal of *The Second Spira*, though, cannot be accounted for solely by the contexts of curiosity about deathbed situations. It rises above most contemporary accounts in its vivid and dramatic detail, and it insists that its interest depends crucially on the factuality and immediacy of the events it describes. The author claims that "this *Treatise* may be a means to startle some that are *Atheistically Inclin'd;* and perhaps reclaim others, who by seeing this, may conclude it their Interest, *Rather to be a thoughtful Reader of such an History, than to be such an History themselves*" (fols. [A6v]–B1), and one need not doubt that explicit aim to see that artful narration plays a key role in the effects achieved in its fifty-six compelling pages. The "Preface" claims, with some justice, "That whereas in *dreadful surprizing Relations,* the *Bookseller, Author,* or both together, do usually clog the Matter of Fact with long and tedious Observations, impertinent Reflections & such like *Stuff,* only to make the Volume swell; here he will find no needless or trifling Digressions, but *unmixt Relation,* barely and *purely* deliver'd, so that the Reader all the while he reads, will be upon his Subject, and not perplex'd with an Expectation of it" (fols. [A6–A6v]). The power of the narrative seems to derive from the commanding personality of the dying atheist, who presents his torments articulately. " 'God is become my Enemy,' " he exclaims near the moment of death,

> "and there is none so strong as he to deliver me out of his Hand; he consigns me over to his Eternal Wrath and Vengeance, and there is none that is able to Redeem me. Was there another God as Mighty as he who would Patronize my Cause, or was I above, or Independent of God, then I could Act and Dispose of my self as I pleased, then would my Horrors cease, and the Expectation and Designs of my Formidable Enemy be frustrate; but this cannot be, for I——" Here his Voice failed him again, and he began to struggle and gasp for a little Breath, which having recovered, with a Groan so Dreadful and Loud, as if it had not been Humane, he Cried out, *"Oh the insufferable Pangs of Hell and Damnation!"* and so he Died, Death setling the Visage of his Face in such a Form, as if the Body, tho' Dead, was *sensible of the Extremity of Torments.* (p. 55)

One of the ironies of the compelling effect achieved here is that the entire pamphlet represents a fraud—that is, an invented fiction masquerading as fact—perpetrated on the public, a fraud that the publisher, John Dunton, claimed had been sprung on him as well. Dunton claimed that the manuscript was delivered to his bookshop by a "Reverend J.S." who had witnessed the final sickness and who had played Burnet to the atheist's Rochester.[32] Later, Dunton claims to have "discovered" that J.S. was none other than his colleague, the Athenian mathematician Richard Sault, and his account of how he was deceived seems almost plausible. The early editions, published when Dunton was apparently not suspicious that the manuscript had been planted, contain the standard claim that the episode can be verified, and Dunton offers himself as the witness: "if any one doubts the Truth of any Particulars in the *following Relation,* if they repair to Mr. *Dunton* at the *Raven* in the *Poultry,* they will receive full Satisfaction" (fol. [A5v]), apparently by getting to see the manuscript.[33] By the third edition, "The Methodizer's Apology" had been added, offering details of how "J.S. a minister of the *Church* of *England*" had rechecked the anonymous Methodizer's editing of the original manuscript and claiming to "discover . . . to the World the Substance of every Particular that he knows of in relation to this Narrative" (title page). But regardless of where fact left off and fiction began or who provided the narrative voice and direction, *The Second Spira* is a successful impersonation in which detailed narrative, vivid characterization, and contemporary relevance are combined with an interest in didacticism, religious commitment, and curiosity about afterlife and the supernatural. It fits the category of *"dreadful surprizing Relations"* that its Preface cites, and although better written than the average short narrative of its time, it typifies anecdotes available to readers a generation before the novel emerged. It had immediacy, urgency, and a raw subjectivity that was almost embarrassing, and it claimed to detail matters of verifiable fact while making questionable claims of authenticity.

"God," the supposed second Spira asserts midway through his "Confession," ". . . *has chosen me out as an example to you all, and as a Warning to the lazy indifferent Christian"* (pp. 35–36), and the example stood (through many editions) even when credibility disintegrated, replicating the fate of many exemplary and evitational narratives of its time and, in a sense, predicting the effect hoped for by early novelists who were self-conscious about inventing "false" stories. *"Religion . . . is no fictitious Imposture"* (p. 35), the dying man insists, and, even if there is irony in the confession itself being an imposture, the text remains a monument to the power of narrations to transcend referents and embody intention beyond the integrity of their central consciousness. Readers, writers, and arbiters of taste remained nervous about factitiousness for more than a century, and into the nineteenth century novelists remained defensive about their invented worlds, even while always insisting that factuality was less important than the uses a story was put to.

The reception of *The Second Spira*—and Dunton's own ambivalences toward it, at once repenting he had printed it and regarding it as one of his major successes—suggest how divided the public was about issues of history and example. *The Second Spira* became both an example of fraud and an excuse to bring forward accounts that traded on its popularity and notoriety. *Spira's Despair Revived* (1694), for example, was published just after the questions of authenticity surfaced; it decried *The Second Spira*'s deviousness and insisted that "There needs no *Pious* Fraud, nor *officious Lies* to help *Religion,* and uphold the Truth"—claiming that real events make the point just as well and asserting that its own events are based on fact: "Every age, and every quarter hath some *Monument* or another set up, with this kind of Inscription, *Look upon me, and learn to fear God.* . . . There are Pillars of Salt set up every where for our remembrance" (fol. A5v). *Spira's Despair Revived* admits a certain self-consciousness about its title, clearly chosen to capitalize on public knowledge of the earlier fraud: " 'Tis common to put a Title to *Treatises,* and not to perform what is promised thereby," the author says defensively. He goes on to claim that the end justifies his means, much as writers of exemplary, parabolic, or allegorical fiction had done for years—Bunyan's defense in *Pilgrim's Progress* and Defoe's in *Robinson Crusoe* were typical—and would do more systematically later. According to its title page, *Spira's Despair Revived* was published by Richard Baldwin, a close friend of Dunton, although whether Dunton himself had a role in the project remains unknown, and it would be hard to know whether its story is based on fact.[34]

V

TIMELINESS was essential for most of the separate journalistic publications. Accounts were rushed into print within days, or even hours, of a dramatic event. When available, personal confessions of horrible conduct were preferred by publishers to simple accounts of the events, apparently because such statements seemed to finesse the issue of authenticity while often providing vivid, immediate, and convincing detail. A *Narrative of the Extraordinary Penitence of Rob. Maynard, Who was Condemnd For the Murder of John Stockton, Late Victualler in Grub-street* (1696), for example, includes both an account of "Several Conferences Held with him in Newgate" and "a Copy of the *Papers* which he left to be Published after his Death" (title page); and A *Full and True Relation of the Examination and Confession of W. Barwick and E. Mangall, of two Horrid Murders* (1690) typically glories in the discovery, after an initial uncertainty or cover-up, of the real facts, as does a single sheet, *Concealed Murther Reveil'd* (sic), of 1699.[35] The sense of filling in the details, helping to write the full history of the times and ultimately of reality itself, is prominent in most of these titles, however hurried on by sensationalism or commercial greed. Behind the formerly-concealed-but-now-revealed motif is a powerful sense that chunks of reality are apt to get by without being recorded, and the journalistic writers seem to see themselves as sleuths whose duty it is to capture it all for print. Swift thought it was silly to regard oneself as the universe's amanuensis, but for many contemporaries it was not just a living and a comprehensive record of the times that was at stake but also a view of reality. In the Puritan view, nothing could be known without a full account of events: that was where meaning lay.

Other events less momentous than political treason and less horrendous than murder were swept into the public record as well. Physical ailments and curses were detailed (A *Narrative Of the Late Extraordinary Cure Wrought in an Instant upon Mrs. Eliz. Savage . . . With an Appendix, attempting to prove, That Miracles are not ceas'd* [1694]), local instances of

1690—1710 period

detected witchcraft described (*A True Narrative of the Sufferings and Relief of a Young Girle . . . Strangely Molested By Evil Spirits and their Instruments* [1698]), or news brought in from remoter places (*A True Narrative of the Murders, Cruelties and Oppressions, Perpetrated on the Protestants in Ireland* [1690]). Sometimes collections of miscellaneous events were pulled together to provide annals of a particular year, as in *God's Marvellous Wonders in England: Containing divers strange and wonderful Relations that have happened since the beginning of June, this present Year 1694,* a work that includes accounts of murders discovered, destructive hailstorms, the surprising sprouting of corn in barren fields, a "Shower of Wheat that fell in Wiltshire," and the appearance of a whale in the River Humber. Sometimes the record reads like the *Daily Mail* or the *National Enquirer,* but serious assumptions support its desire to be all-encompassing.

Many short narratives of the 1690–1710 period come from, or purport to come from, documents such as diaries, packets of letters, or notes taken by someone present at the occurrence or at an eyewitness account of it.[36] Other narratives claim to derive from court documents and proceedings.[37] Full, or at least detailed, many such accounts were, but their truth is sometimes a matter of doubt, regardless of the claims of their titles. The important thing is that they assert factuality, for whether they were literally and completely true, based upon facts but liberally embroidered, or made up out of whole cloth, the narratives achieved much of their appeal through their claim to represent what the present-day world was like, what kinds of amazement and surprise and horror were available to those whose lives were uneventful, drab, and apparently trivial, increasingly buried in the routine impersonality of modern life.

Eight-page

Between 1700 and 1710, a large number of eight-page pamphlets focused on contemporary life with a vengeance. Most were half-sheet octavos or half-sheet duodecimos, designed (like chapbooks) to sell cheap. Some are dated and some are not (the ones that are, are mostly from 1705–09), but most recount events of recent date—often startling or at least surprising ones—and all are anecdotal in the new journalistic spirit. Many are told in a frolicsome and spirited way, but some offer pathos, poignancy, or even tragedy. What these episodic pamphlets have in common is that they commit to print "surprising" and "wonderful" tales of contemporary life that in another age would have found room, at least passingly, in oral traditions transmitted within families or villages or groups of workers. Such stories had sometimes found their way into print as *exempla* in moral works, but in earlier ages few would have been preserved beyond their immediate geographical area or contemporary moment. Scattered instances of such pamphlets exist on the Continent,[38] but the printing of large numbers of them is a new phenomenon, marking a cultural desire for access to narrative that is neither moral nor political in thrust but that regards the recording of the present as obligatory.

The "plot" of most of these short narratives is entirely given away in the lengthy title, and the writing is usually indifferent, but the tone is sometimes experimental and the subject matter daring. Thus, *An Alma-nack-Husband: or, a Wife a Month: Being A very Comical and Pleasant Relation of a Merchants Son near the Monument, who Married a Wife every Month, for a Year together* . . . (1708) takes a detached view of polygamy and the confusion of progeny that ensues. The "Almanack-Husband" gets all his wives pregnant, "and being discovered, gave them all an Invitation to a Tavern, where they were exceeding Merry," and the tone (if not the syntax) is maintained in "A commical *Dialogue* which pass'd between him and his Wives, and after parted very lovingly" (title page). Only the cautionary words at the end violate the spirit: "but I would have the Reader not to mind a Libertine's Advice, for nothing but Destruction attends such lewd Debauchees" (p. 8). A plain example of after-the-fact and disingenuous moralizing, such a brittle postscript is, however, less common than is sometimes thought. The moralizing tendency native to the period usually results in works that are wholeheartedly didactic, and the quick moral gloss that is antithetical to the spirit of the whole here is as rare as a total lack of any moral or religious sentiment. Most comic narratives involve man-woman relationships and domestic deception, and their plots resemble those of stage plays. The emphasis on factuality and currency is heavy; many offer ways to verify the facts. *The Comical Bargain: or, Trick upon Trick. Being A Pleasant and True Relation of one Thomas Bocks, a Baker's Prentice, near Milk-Street, that* . . . *courted an Eminent Doctor's Daughter near King-Street in Bloomsbury* (1707), a story of two sharpers who deserve each other, contains this "authentication" on the title page: "*If any one Question the Truth of this Relation,* let them En[quire] for the New-married Couple at the Sign of the Dog and Cat in Bread-street, London." More common than comic stories are ones that purport to be serious or tragic, describing occurrences that are violent and brutal. Typical are such titles as *The Cruel Son, or, the Unhappy Mother. Being a Dismal Relation of one Mr. Palmer and Three Ruffins, who Barbarously Murder'd his own Mother and her Maid* . . . *November the 7th, 1707. by Cutting their Throats from Ear to Ear, in a Cruel and Unnatural manner; and afterwards setting the House on Fire* (1707); *The Cruel Mother. Being a strange and unheard-of Account of one Mrs. Elizabeth Cole* . . . *that threw her own Child into the Thames* (1708); and *Wonder upon Wonders, or, the London Histories* (1710), in which several stories are collected.[39]

"Reader," begins the narration proper of a 1707 eight-pager called *The*

Horrors of Jealousie, or, The Fatal Mistake, "I here present you with a very amazing and dreadful Relation." Adjectives like "amazing," "dreadful," "terrible," and "horrible" are common on title pages and in the texts themselves, as is the repeated insistence on the immediacy and literal truth of the accounts. They are "true relations," "exact accounts," and "faithful narratives," and events are located and dated precisely. For most stories, a basis in fact is likely, and the suggestion of larger human patterns—whether they involve the certainty of remorse and punishment or the tendencies of a sizable minority of human beings toward behavior that ends in robbery, rape, murder, and incest—is secondary to the emphasis on accurate recording of particulars. But it would be foolish to separate these narratives too rigidly from fictional ones or to discount what they tell us about contemporary taste for narrative because of their insistence on truth. Novels written a little later insist just as strongly on the factual basis of their events, and early novels repeatedly verify their claims by citing documents or referring readers outside the text to verifiable persons, places, and events.

What readers found in such narratives as the eight-pagers is similar to what they sought in the longer narratives of "real" life written by Defoe and his successors; and if the style and artistic structure of narratives like these does not seem to offer a model for potential novels—any more than the brief moments used here to capture some surprising aspect of life in eight pages resemble the resonant length and complexity of Defoe's narratives—their subject matter and focus does suggest what interested readers in the generations before they had novels to read. It is not that the eight-pagers are proto-novels or novels in miniature. But like other journalistic phenomena of the turn of the century, they suggest both what was on the minds of large numbers of people in the culture and how the ground was prepared for print strategies that became characteristic of the novel.

V I

INTEREST in contemporaneity takes many other journalistic and quasi-journalistic forms, some narrative and some not. Some involve incidents and disputes that gained national attention and controversies that remained at the center of public attention for weeks, months, or years; some involve forgettable incidents that flared for a moment in the public consciousness and died. Famous anniversaries of public events often inspire remembrances and reviews, or, more often, meditations upon a danger averted or a mercy received. Sermons preached on November 5 (Guy Fawkes

Day) or November 4 (William's "birthday") were published regularly, and cumulatively they represent a rather full historical review of the dangers (or supposed dangers) of popery.[40] In fact, public meditations—usually delivered first as sermons and then published, but sometimes simply issued in print—on a number of anniversaries regularly became political reminders and social reviews, with each extreme of opinion having its favorite day. May 29, the day Charles II returned to London in 1660 and his declared "birthday," came to be celebrated as a day of thanksgiving for the Restoration of the monarchy (it was also known as Oak-Apple Day and some of the Mayday customs were transferred to it), and January 30 was the anniversary fast for the martyrdom of Charles I. September 2 became the anniversary fast day for the "Dreadful Fire," and later March 8 was celebrated for the accession of Queen Anne and August 8 for that of George I, who also had January 20 and October 20 set aside to commemorate the Protestant succession. Traditional fast days, saints days, and other holidays, such as Lammas, Midsummers Day, Lady Day, and All Saints Day, often served also as occasions for appropriate reviews of events and signs. Such "anniversaries" provided convenient reminders of patterns, thus calling attention to cycles and long-range trends as well as the latest events and examples, and suggesting how the culture reconciled event with larger meaning, the momentary with the lasting, the journalistic with the diurnal.

Journalistic materials were often "occasional" in a different way, their extensive broils deriving less from an event than an issue that became focused by some statement or event. One such issue at the turn of the century involves the role of wives and, more generally, the "place" of women in society. The controversy developed from a sermon preached in a Dorsetshire village in 1699 but soon had everyone's attention in London. It was John Sprint who preached the original sermon, on May 11, at Sherbourn, and in the published version he expresses bewilderment that he had occasioned such a stir. His "Discourse," he says, "was designed only for the Pulpit, not for the Press; but it hath so fallen out, that the Doctrine therein contained is so unhappily represented to the world by some ill-natur'd Females, that I am necessitated to offer it to a Publick View . . . yet I hope I shall . . . convinc[e] the world that I am not such an impudent Villain as my waspish Accusers have reported me to be."[41] Sprint was not so lucky as he hoped, however, perhaps because he seldom missed a chance to patronize women. "Be it known unto thee Reader," he says in an effort at self-defense, ". . . that I have not met with one Woman among all my Accusers whose Husband is able to give her the Character of a dutiful and obedient Wife" (p. [2]).

Sprint is opinionated, insecure, and altogether lacking in self-consciousness. Even in the plainly male world of seventeenth- and eighteenth-century writings, there is little to compare with his aggressive characterization of women as inferior. *"It is a Duty incumbent on all Married Women,"* he states as "the Foundation of my Discourse," *"to be extraordinary careful to content and please their Husbands"* (p. 3), and he doubts that women have the ability to understand what he is saying— "Because Women are of weaker Capacities to learn than Men, and therefore when they have a hard and difficult Lesson, and but weak Abilities to learn it, they had need of more Help and Assistance," he says early on (p. 4). At the conclusion he ends abruptly for their benefit: "I must forbear enlargement," he writes, "least, that, by overlading the memories of the Women, I should cause them to forget their Duty which has been set before them" (p. 16). In fact, Sprint allows women no character at all: *"A good Wife. . . should be like a Mirrour which hath no Image of its own, but receives its Stamp and Image from the Face that looks into it: So should a good Wife endeavour to frame her outward Deportment, and her inward Affections according to her Husband's"* (p. 7).

Sprint was often answered in subsequent months, and sometimes his views were supported in attacks on his critics, although I have found no one who actually defended him. One of the earliest, most reasonable, and best responses to Sprint was *The Female Advocate; or, A Plea for the just Liberty of the Tender Sex, and particularly of Married Women. Being Reflections on a late Rude and Disingenuous Discourse* (1700), signed by "Eugenia." It is a witty, intelligent proto-feminist piece—rational, fair, and a little sad in correcting Sprint's substance and tone. "[W]hen I had follow'd him to the end of the Chapter," the author begins ruefully, "I could not but wonder to find a Sex attack'd from the Pulpit with more confident Impudence than ever they were on the Stage, tho with far less Wit and Ingenuity" (p. 1). Several other titles kept the issue alive. *The Pleasures of a Single Life, or the miseries of Matrimony* (1701), although it claims to be "Occasionally Writ Upon the many Divorces lately Granted by Parliament," begins a new chapter of the Sprint controversy by offering a long and bitter misogynist poem in which a married man bewails his loss of the single state:

> Tho' I once happy in a single Life,
> Yet Shipwrack'd all upon that Rock a Wife,
> By Gold and Beauties Pow'rful Charms betray'd,
> To the dull drudgry of a Marriage-Bed;
> That Paradice for Fools, a Sport for Boys,
> Tiresome its Chains, and brutal are its Joys. (p. 3)

It is answered by a fairly good poem called *Wedlock a Paradice; or, a Defence of Woman's Liberty against Man's Tyranny* (1701), and another title of the same year attacks Sprint in a poetic dialogue (*The Ladies Defence: or, The Bride-Woman's Counsellor Answer'd*). And chapters went on.

No one may have been enlightened by such occasional controversies, and perhaps no idea or cause was often advanced, but the fact that Sprint was still being reprinted a decade later[42] suggests not only that he had more sympathetic allies than would declare themselves in print but also that any issue that could be made to seem occasional, contemporary, and modern could be kept alive for quite a while, regardless of the arguments mustered in its support. The issues in the Sprint controversy, like those in many similar print debates, represented deep feelings in the culture, and the "event" that occasioned the articulation was, in a sense, simply a cultural vehicle for widespread conversation, in sermons, pamphlets, periodicals, coffeehouses, and private homes. The reading public was hungry for attention to its own time and receptive to almost anything that focused attention on the present moment. The world of print repeatedly tapped into veins flowing with sources of contemporary energy, and by the 1690s it had developed techniques and skills—once a lively contemporary event or issue had been identified—to capture a wide spectrum of public attention and keep readers interested over a substantial period of time. The pamphlet wars on political, economic, and some social issues are well known, but other events and issues are just as important journalistically, and they suggest not just the state of hackdom but varieties of cultural desire that underlay reading.

Another episode that gained rapt attention in London and that gathered up a variety of cultural loose ends also grew out of a provincial sermon. John Mason, rector at Water-Stratford in Buckinghamshire, was a talented and beloved preacher, and his famous sermon *The Midnight Cry* (first preached in 1691) achieved its extraordinary fame because it claimed special knowledge of an imminent moment, prophesying the "Second Coming" of Christ at a specific moment in 1694. Mason had a local reputation as a sincere and pious man, and his writings had achieved a small attention, but *The Midnight Cry*, which he preached in several places, vaulted him into the national spotlight. Mason ultimately began to claim that "*Water-Stratford* was the very Spot of Ground where [Christ's] Standard was to be set up," and that "Those who would repair thither, might find a safe Retreat, but all other parts of the Nation would *infallibly* be expos'd to Fire and Sword."[43] Local observers ultimately claimed that "*on the sixteenth day of [April], the Lord Jesus Christ did appear in this House to his Servant my Brother Mason in his glorious Person,*"[44] and there was frenzied celebration of the upcoming event, now expected within a few months. But Mason died, and like many another local headline event, the episode receded.[45] Half a century later, Mason's work was still being reprinted—recommended by Isaac Watts[46]—although his more general religious observations and reflections were by then prized over his alarmist didacticism.

Such local sensations occurred from time to time in the highly charged religious atmosphere and providential debates of the seventeenth century, and the Mason episode is not especially important in itself. But it illustrates the age's insatiable curiosity about out-of-the-ordinary events in contemporary life, its addiction to "news" even in matters of piety, and its eagerness for a sense that normal probabilities could sometimes be violated. More important, it demonstrates the power of London and the press to take a remote local incident and make it a matter of national concern, giving it currency with coffeehouse habitués and people on London streets. The developing flair of booksellers and pamphleteers to retail every bit of new quasi-news every day furthered the cultural impression that the present was the only place, that the only meaningful moment was now.

All sorts of episodes, events, and conditions of contemporary life became the subject of journalistic attention in the late years of the seventeenth century and the early years of the eighteenth. Sometimes bits of general knowledge or subjects of public rumor were sharpened into apparent news items or elevated to attention through allegory or some other indirect means. Walpole's lengthy affair with Molly Skerrett, for example, repeatedly surfaces—or gets journalistic attention just below the surface—in the mid-1730s, and countless other subjects of conversation and rumor are "preserved" in the public press.[47] Many of these chapters of contemporary life are in themselves fascinating for a sense of exactly how readers (and gossips) of the age regarded public and private events, but here it is enough to note how frequent, detailed, immediate, and popular such accounts tended to be and what their existence tells us about the taste and direction of the public mind. It is no wonder that serious poetry in these years more and more came to involve itself with current events and a sense of contemporaneity, that all literature intensified its commitments to public events and occasional strategies, and that serious prose fiction soon found the life of the moment to be its central subject and method.

In a variety of events that inspired short journalistic narratives in the final years of the seventeenth century and the early years of the eighteenth, we can readily see audience tastes expanding and growing even more voracious, as well as intensifying toward matters of the moment. In sheer quantity, the number of "news" accounts increases sharply during the 1680s and then even more dramatically near the turn of the century.[48] Part of the reason may reside in the tendency of journalistic inter-

est to beget journalistic interest: the widespread desire for news clearly
had developed during the Civil Wars, when average Englishmen and
Englishwomen felt they had much personally at stake in every public
event. By the 1690s, with subject matter rapidly expanding, an audience
of eavesdroppers was in effect creating itself. When the Licensing Act
was finally relaxed for good in 1695—after several temporary lapses earlier—the amount of publication increased generally.

But the major reason for expanded journalistic subject matter involves
a discernible shift in taste toward a greater interest in private life, the
personal, and the subjective. There is increasing emphasis on the personal feelings of those involved in significant occurrences, and quite a
number of short narratives (like A *True and Perfective Narrative of the
. . . Snovvs*) seem almost to be interested in narrative for its own sake.
Few of those narratives lack moral or religious application of some kind,
and in most of them the application seems natural and genuine enough,
but an interest in other effects is obvious as well. Many intend primarily
to amaze or amuse, and many others blend delight and instruction attrac-
tively. Cumulatively these narratives suggest a nearly infinite variety in
human events and feelings, and in the way they blend contemporaneity,
subjectivity, concentration on detail, emphasis on the unusual that happens even to the most ordinary of mortals, and sponsoring interest in the
patterns of human events, we can see a number of novelistic features not
comfortably present in romance or other earlier narratives.

V I I

SOME of the early English novelists—most notably Defoe—cut their
teeth in print journalism, learning narrative and expository craft by
interpreting what was happening almost at the moment of action. For
others, like Richardson, the routines of their daily lives meant that journalistic accounts of the times were more immediate to them than *belles
lettres*, and their notion of the present was shaped by the way their journalistic contemporaries saw and phrased it. Still others, like Haywood
and Henry Fielding, although less personally involved in popular print
culture during their formative years, ultimately discovered just how steeped
they were in journalistic assumptions and found themselves later in their
careers shifting back and forth between fictional narratives of a certain
magnitude, scope, and literary pretension and journalistic treatments of
the everyday.[49] For Burney, devotion to a personal and private account
of everyday events amounts to almost the same thing as journalism, and
the sense of immediacy and of minutiae in her fiction depends upon ways

of thinking, perceiving, and articulating that she developed for her diaries, a record of daily life that depended on a crucial sense of immediacy and the values of contemporaneity.

For almost all the early novelists, individual segments of what they wrote when they wrote novels might easily be mistaken for the stuff of everyday popular print, and both the matters they wrote about and the way they wrote about them owed much to the journalistic context of the previous half century. Distasteful as it may be to traditional literary history, the relationship between ephemera and serious literature in mid-century was a very close one, not always clear even to the writers who were producing one or the other, and writers moved back and forth in their commitments and accomplishments in a very confusing way. A literature of the everyday cannot make very persuasive claims to be high-born and elitist, and despite Henry Fielding's attempts to establish a classical heritage, the novel has seldom had much luck in dissociating itself from origins in a broad popular consciousness and allegiances that are broad rather than narrow, leveling rather than hierarchical.

More important, however, than any apprenticeship individual writers got or direct influence that they felt was the context of expectation that they inherited, participated in, and ultimately enhanced. A significant aspect of that contextual inheritance involved the belief that contemporary events demanded attention and interpretation, and the cultural consciousness of contemporaneity meant that the narrative intention and definitions that they developed had a fertile ground. Telling the story of what life is like now and helping to explain how it got that way—the literary job that novelists defined for themselves—could hardly have come about without such a friendly everyday context, and an important aspect of what the novel came to do is a palpable result of the journalistic agenda. Other aspects of popular consciousness also conditioned novelists, the readers of all kinds of print material, and the preoccupations of the culture more generally, so that journalism is not *the* explanation of where the novel comes from or why it developed when it did. But the consciousness that made the present moment the center of human attention and led to the directions of modern journalism helped prepare the cultural context for novelists' preoccupations, too, and crucial dimensions of the modern novel seem unimaginable without the peculiar combination of "News, and new Things" that obsessed English culture at the turn of the eighteenth century, dominated most of the directions of the print culture, and re-fused, for just one brief moment before the novel took over as the dominant form of modern discourse, the written and oral worlds, the sign of one world dying and another new born.

CHAPTER EIGHT

"Strange, but True":
Fact, Certainty, and the
Desire for Wonder

■

THOSE who saw themselves as guardians of the literary heritage distrusted the new journalism from the start, and much of their suspicion
carried over to the novel. The "Athenian Itch," they thought, signified
superficiality, rootlessness, and restlessness, and the "News, and new
Things" that dominated publishing practices reflected inferior intellectual habits and merely trendy social behavior. But two kinds of questions—about the source of the taste and the seriousness of its implications—
provoked continuing disagreement, a disagreement that suggests why the
novel emerged when it did and why it took a particular shape. Both
questions, even though neither was resolved decisively or even precisely
formulated, have implications for the novel's relationship to readers and
to fundamental desires in the culture, and both affect the kind of conclusions we can draw now about texts and contexts. The question of cause—
do writers bear the responsibility for creating taste, or do desires of readers in effect create texts?—goes to the heart of a theoretical problem in
literary and cultural history,[1] and although the question involves many
literary species, early novels pointed the issue crucially because they strove
to represent, in collusion with increased literacy and consciousness of a
wider range of reader needs, the literary tradition to the broader culture.
The question of implication, equally unresolved even among those most
worried about "deteriorating" taste, focuses in a different way the issue of
how texts and life interact, making effectiveness of language the crucial
test. Both questions lead, in their very lack of focus, to a version of

journalism that represents readers and writers caught in an epistemological squeeze. Uncertain about the relation of language to knowledge, that
journalism addresses superficial needs through the rhetorical flash of
unexpected—"strange and surprising"—"fact."

The rhetoric of desire constructed by Athenian projectors like Dunton, while more directly responsive to consumer wishes than that of most
other forms of print, was typical of the popular press in its willingness to
address curiosities of any kind, sometimes risking authority and credibility to do so. Reading in practice thus came to have some unpleasant
associations that reading in theory avoided; and readers—presumably the
best-meaning of mortals in their ambition to realize their human potential—were quickly castigated for debasing traditional taste. When it comes
to credit for literary history, readers seldom figure, but when it comes to
blame, taste and desire (rather than pens and publishers) often become
culprits, and the story of the novel, like the story of early journalism,
often is mistold because of too precise a division of labor based on literary
predispositions and class prejudice.[2] The suspicion of ordinary readers
and the distrust of the ordinariness of the novel were almost the same
thing. Both involved a snobbish rejection of popular culture and a belief
that nothing serious and sustaining could come from trendiness and the
tastes of the many. Newness is worth nothing when it comes from the
nouveau riche, the newly literate, or the newly recognized.[3]

The association, in the public mind, of news and newsmongering with
London ways also did not help the novel with thoughtful observers. The
novel's preoccupation with contemporaneity was often seen as inappropriate curiosity or downright impiety—an attempt to pluck fruit from the
forbidden tree—or as a radical questioning of moral and political authority. Or it was regarded as just another passing fad among young urban
émigrés, an example of fashion in those not deep enough to have serious
intellectual interests. This contempt for those who seemed in their urban
desires to be rejecting the traditions of the culture—regarding them as
too silly to be troubled about and (at the same time) calling them deeply
subversive rebels who threatened assumptions, institutions, and continuity—characterizes the age and its texts generally, and the uncertainty
about what kind of threat novelty posed is an essential part of what has
regularly been called "neoclassical," "Augustan," or "eighteenth-century." Swift, for example, was never sure (even after he had sorted out
the loyalties of Athenian desire)[4] whether the likes of Dunton and Wotton were devils or mere gnats, and he treated them as both. And Pope's
debate with "Arbuthnot" about how to treat Lord Hervey (as yapping
annoyance or deadly infection) similarly externalizes an issue he remained
unsure about.

Much of the journalistic romance with the present—like its opposite,

the conservative hearkening after a past already receded—had little substance in itself and was adequately represented by Pope's image of ephem-
erae that covered the rails of Soho until they blew away of their own
levity. It pleased old guardians to think that the materials of popular
print would quickly be gone with the wind. But however imperfectly the
materials of popular print represented cultural desire, they did represent
it. Desire was not, however, just a matter of trendiness and novelty.
Journalism was finally more than a matter of passing events and the present time, and the epistemological claims of the novel derive in part from
larger circles of desire that drove journalism. The larger contexts of desire
involved a sense that a merely factual response to the itch for knowledge
was not enough. Among things to be known were, quite beyond the
detailed and the passing, matters that stretched the mind's possibilities—
discoveries of geography, history, science, and the secrets of the human
mind itself—and although the popular press did not probe such matters
in their full complexity, it did deal with them repeatedly, with a close
eye on what readers wanted. If journalism in its most obvious forms was
contemporaneous and timely, centered on individual action and event,
it also sought to place present concerns and attitudes in some larger perspective.

The rise of journalism relates to two converging cultural movements
that, directly or indirectly, it introduces to the novel. One is the empiricism that had, for a century, been changing the grounds of authority in
the whole Western world through its claims that meaning derived only
from the observation of data. The second involves the validation of individuals, not necessarily trained individuals, as observers and interpreters.
It manifested itself everywhere; it is the essence of Protestantism. In the
convergence of these two movements is the core of modern literature
and of modernism as idea, way of life, and lens for examining a vast,
intractable universe.[5] Crucial to this world—and to the world of perception that informs both journalism and the novel—is a wholly new mode
of interpreting fact and event. In its pure form, of course, empiricism
insisted on observation of data under rigidly controlled conditions, but
heightened interest in all kinds of observation was a natural result of its
practice as the culture more generally became aware of its assumptions.
And although the doctrine that everyone could be his or her own priest
originated as a credo about received texts, it was quickly applied to the
Book of Creation as well. Observation of the natural world became a
duty for all, not just for scientists or priests.[6] Interpreting the natural
world came to mean interpreting not just the phenomena of nature—
plants and animals, earthquakes and tempests, the sun and the stars—
but human events as well.

Once unleashed, the power of the individual to interpret was impossible to control, and (as interpretations of events like the storm of 1703 or the Great Fire of 1666 exemplified) the impulse to "read" all events intensely became very strong. As readings were increasingly paraded for public view, self-appointed "priests" turned up everywhere. Preachers, scientists, and journalists combined to make priests of us all: readers of texts of any verbal or non-verbal kind. In times of great anxiety or when a special event dramatically captured the public attention (whether a natural event like a flood or a human one like the accession of a new monarch), different interpretations competed for acceptance. But the public print record is only the edge of the issue, for once the idea of universal interpretation was established in the culture, examples readily multiplied in daily life. The need to read even the most minute events in the lives of the most ordinary people became central to the culture. The old sacramental world available to priests and specially designated decoders (but only to others through them) was translated to a dynamic world with emblems spatial and temporal that anyone with determination and patience could read. The democraticization of empiricism meant that texts were constantly evolving and crying out to be read; "readers" did not even have to be literate. Reading in its literal sense became necessary because "reading"—in the sense of construing everything one observed—had already become basic to the culture. Milton and Bunyan, Watts and Blake in different ways all saw to the heart of English Protestantism in insisting that the only enemy to light was the suppression of the free trade of ideas. The vigorous, often contradictory, and sometimes bewildering array of printed "readings" sprang from the energy of the culture's desire to know.

In this chapter, I want to explore the widening circle of interpretive possibilities and suggest how it related to the other acquisitive pressures in the culture. To do this, I will examine three little known and poorly understood traditions of popular print, all of them richly illustrative of fundamental needs at a particular cultural moment late in the seventeenth century. I will first look at a strategy developed by scientists and theologians for "ordinary" people, suggesting how the practice of "Occasional Meditation" reflects the delicate poise that print sought to find between rational interpretation and creative imagination. Then I will look at a journalistic direction that had little to do with contemporaneity and writing to the moment, a phenomenon that tried to be journalism's reach for larger perspectives in place and time. Finally, I will examine the displacement of this phenomenon into a theological defense that renewed attention to contemporary detail and to a preoccupation with the meaning of events in time.

I

IN the world that spawned journalism, knowledge was important, but knowing—the personal experience of discovery—was everything. Mere facts, though being known to know them was crucial to anyone's social reputation, were only the most direct route to secrets of nature, for in the wake of scientific advancement and the growing emphasis on observation and experience, the world seemed there to be read, and the discovery, accumulation, and recording of miscellaneous facts could point to larger patterns of understanding. The recording of everyday observations and events came to seem essential as a means to knowing the nature of things; the record became, in fact, a kind of rival to life itself. Human aspiration thus involved the desire to possess—dangerously—the fruits of the Tree of Knowledge and something very like the Book of Life itself. But recording events was, theoretically, only of instrumental importance: preserving the moments, deeds, and observations of humankind— what Swift called parodically the outer "husk" and "shell" of things that an empiricist used to discover the "essence" of the kernel—ultimately meant that the record was there to be read, reread, and studied. The importance of having the full record was that it could then be interpreted—studied and reviewed until pattern, principle, or order became clear—but the means became for some an end in itself. The ultimate Protestants (although they were systematically distrusted and excluded from carrying matters to the extremes that Protestantism by its nature implied) actually thought that subjective views—what individuals could themselves observe, experience, and interpret—could lead to ultimate truth, that the light of the individual consciousness brought results superior to those of any controlled, communal, or handed-down method, and that the individual judgment was finally the only route to understanding. If some of Protestantism's nominal adherents were frightened of its radical manifestations and pulled timidly back to authoritarian orthodoxies, its radical prophets chased the inherent subjectivism almost to the solipsistic extremes that their critics said they did. Dissent, with nearly as many forms and sects as its internal logic demanded, carried out the implications most fully and deeply. It is no accident that journalism and the novel—as well as the adventurous spirit and preoccupation with the epiphanic moment of discovery that sponsored both—got their impetus primarily from Protestantism in general and Dissent in particular.

Even when individual writers (or observers) eschewed putting an interpretation on the events they recounted, reporting on the known, the seen, or the experienced came to seem important in itself. In the plethora of circumstantial detail in the early novel, the textual outcome of such habits is manifest. The early novel's circumstantiality, "realistic" though it may be, is not so much a device to establish factuality and credibility as it is an outcome of the habit of observing and reporting. The transference of detail to manifest fictions may create verisimilitude, for it appropriates to fiction a strategy of recording reality, the world of brute and unignorable fact. But the impetus for it involves ways of thinking and experiencing rather than a rhetoric calculated to convince doubters. Novelists repeatedly assured readers that the substance of their story was real and historical and that their account was faithful—a reporting of actuality—but "recording" circumstances is less an attempt to back up claims of authenticity than an extension of habits formed when they recounted matters they themselves had experienced. Those habits were created by diaries that proliferated in Protestant England, Scotland, and America in the seventeenth century and that thus became useful in producing expectations novelists could take advantage of. The traditions of autobiography, biography, and memoirs developed from habits of observation and recording that diaries made familiar,[7] but the practice of observation in daily life is the basis of knowing on which desire is built. The promulgation of that practice is the aim of a specific, little known tradition that derives directly from the premises of empiricism and individuation cum subjectivity.

The tradition of Occasional Meditation enjoyed enormous popularity in the second half of the seventeenth century among varied practitioners, not all of them Puritans. It had a clear effect on diarists, who often appended meditations or interrupted their narratives to insert them. Diarists learned to "meditate" on earthly objects by imitating the printed meditations of figures like Robert Boyle, Edward Bury, and John Flavell, who encouraged readers to observe all the details of everyday life and preserve their thoughts on everything.[8] Bury, for example, himself meditated on such objects as snails, toads, apples, falling leaves, and "a Tuft of green Grass." But more important, and more complex, is the way these observational habits came to apply to event as well as object and became an influence on narrative as well as discursive writing. That influence did not develop in a strictly literary way; rather, it involved practices of everyday life common to farmers, artisans, tradesmen, and servants as well as to scientists and theologians.

The beauty of Occasional Meditations was that everyone could do them, with little guidance and no talent beyond the ability to observe and free associate. A little familiarity with the most frequent biblical metaphors and the herding and hunting metaphors that gave them human resonance could be a help in leading to the most obvious spiritual meanings in everyday objects and events, but only a desire to know was really necessary. Even illiterates could create oral meditations on chance objects they might encounter, although the ability to write down one's lucubrations had obvious advantages for preservation, re-use, and sharing. The advice to record one's meditations on the spot and at the moment—or to compose them while recollecting in tranquility—was, like the encouragement to record the full range of daily experiences in a diary, part of a larger program of articulating the universe and summing it up, making the world into a series of interlocking subjective texts. The literate felt enjoined to become scribes, to do their part in making the universe known both to themselves and others who might benefit from the lead. Readers of the world are elevated to unprecedented power; every reader becomes, in effect, his or her own writer.[9]

The practice of Occasional Meditation helped to create a class of writers the likes of which had never yet been seen in the world, and it is no wonder that traditional humanists, with their sense of writers as privileged figures who performed priestly functions, felt threatened by the democratization of the writing process and by the interpretive implications of Protestantism more generally. Traditional writers understandably distrusted such Here Comes Everybody textuality. For all his joking about being "born for nothing but to write" and being doomed to letters by some ancestral sin, Pope took his singled-out talent seriously. His career is a record of his resentment of interlopers, and Swift's anger similarly bursts through his wit about hacks being the amanuenses of the universe, his parodic representation certifying his belief in the specialness of the writing function gone awry. The "deluge" of print seemed a legitimate concern to serious writers. Londoners who daily saw the bookstalls in St. Paul's Churchyard or on London Bridge might be forgiven for thinking that the channels of information had been clogged to overflowing. But beyond the world of public print itself, meditators (and diarists) represented hordes of still others who took up the pen but who had not gone public with their results. Having so many writers—people who knew what the writing process was like and who, more important, shared the sense that the nature of the world and its events could be understood by observation and interpretation—meant a new kind of reading public, one with verbal habits and expectations that novelists soon would learn to exploit.[10]

I I　*Occasional Meditation*

AS a good scientist should, Robert Boyle set out in 1665 to describe this new category of writing. He decided to call it Meletetics.[11] Unlike earlier practitioners who had neglected to formulate rules for Occasional

Meditation, he stresses method as a means of providing discipline and regulation, but he does not seek *"Uniformity in the style."*[12] The "method" he advocates is in fact quite casual, involving none of the controlled procedures of Scientific Method, and what Boyle seems to mean by method simply involves an insistence on close observation—a close reading—of even the smallest and most trivial things encountered in daily life. It is method in the same sense that New Criticism is method, and for many of the same reasons. Boyle thinks that the discipline of making meditations leads to rigorous habits of analysis and strengthens the mind itself. "[T]he custom," Boyle argues, "of making Occasional Meditations . . . accustomes a man to an attentive observation of the Objects wherewith he is conversant" (p. 28), allowing him "to make Reflections upon the things he takes notice of, and so, by exercising, improves his reasoning Faculty" (p. 31). He advocates aggressive observation and interpretation, insisting that events but especially *things* encountered in even the most ordinary life are clues to basic truths in the universe. In plowing a field, rowing a boat, picking a flower, or walking along a street, even ordinary men and women could gain not only pleasure and inspiration but knowledge, just as scientific observers could, except that the process was easier. What observers would learn was not, however, subject to the same limitations as the "truth" of science, any more than it was subject to the tests of Scientific Method. "We need not in this case, as in most others," Boyle writes, "make an uneasie Preparation to entertain our Instructors; for our Instructions are suddenly, and as it were out of an Ambuscade, shot into our Mind, from things whence we never expected them, so that we receive the advantage of learning good Lessons, without the trouble of going to School for them" (pp. 15–16).

The "discovery" in meditation was circumscribed only by the observer's own limits of seeing or interpreting. Imagination—finding analogies with other objects in the universe or thinking of how what one experienced was a metaphor for something else—was the determining factor in what one could derive from meditation, but the "scientific" claims of the procedure, its pompous name, and the fact that it was championed by a great scientist gave it not only currency but a certain epistemological status. Boyle called it a "way of Thinking" (p. 1); whatever he actually believed about its epistemological potential, he saw it as a popular extension of scientific outlook, a procedure that allowed ordinary individuals in everyday life to do what scientists did more grandly, engage fully in the experience of knowing.

The idea of Occasional Meditation is based on assumptions—scientific and religious—that "the VVorld is the great Book, not so much of Nature, as of the God of Nature . . . crowded with instructive Lessons, if we had but the Skill, and would take the Pains, to extract and pick them out: The Creatures are the true Aegyptian Hieroglyphicks, that under the rude forms of Birds, and Beasts, &c. conceal the mysterious secrets of Knowledge, and of Piety" (p. 47). "The whole world," wrote George Swinnock in advising how to "get honey and sweetness by occasional meditation, out of the carcass of every creature," "is a great *vast library*, and every creature in it a several *Book*, wherein he that *runs may read.* . . . Every object is as a *Bell*, which if but turned, makes a report of the great Gods honour and renown."[13] "The book of the creature stands open to us," Edward Bury went on to insist in 1677 in his collection of meditations, "and God may be read in every line of it."[14] Boyle elsewhere described (sounding a lot like the speaker of *A Tale of a Tub*) the world as displaying the "stenography of God's omniscient hand."[15]

The emphasis of the tradition was repeatedly on what could be learned from even the smallest object of contemplation or from the most minute detail. "[T]hough the Thing itself, which sets a mans thoughts a-work," Boyle argues, "may be but Mean in Other regards, yet that which the Reflector pitches upon to consider, may be of another Nature. . . . [T]hough the Glo-worm . . . be but a small and contemptible Insect, yet the Light which shines in his Tail, and which makes the chief Theme of the Meditation, is a noble and heavenly Quality" (*Occasional Reflections*, fol. [a6]). "A devout Occasional Meditation," he concludes, "from how low a Theme soever it takes its Rise, being like *Jacob's* Ladder, whereof though *the foot lean'd on the Earth, the top reach'd up to Heaven*" (p. 80).[16] Thus, the meditator authored a book of his own, a kind of rival to the Book of Nature on which his representations were based. Those who make Occasional Meditations, Boyle said, "may have the Satisfaction of making almost the whole World a great *Conclave Mnemonicum*, and a well furnished *Promptuary*" (fol. b2). And the knowledge thus secured might be extensive: "I would not confine Occasional Meditations to Divinity it self . . . but am ready to allow mens thoughts to expatiate much further, and to make of the Objects they contemplate not onely a Theological and a Moral, but also a Political, an Oeconomical, or even a Physical use" (p. 24).

While not claiming that the pursuit of Occasional Meditations would produce significant discoveries of the magnitude of those by scientists in formal experiments, Boyle suggests that a better understanding of the world—a personal knowing—results almost automatically from the practice of meditation. He emphasizes that making meditations leads to habits, discipline, and a frame of mind crucial to knowing, regardless of the quality of individual reflections. Throughout his writing, he is critical of Aristotle not so much for what he had said or done as because of the authoritarian symbol he had become, and although Boyle avoids attacking traditional religious authorities—the commentators, the Church Fathers, or the Bible itself—it is plain that he thinks that virtually all knowledge of the world can and should be derived from personal experience. In taking the position he does, Boyle speaks for countless contemporaries of a similar "modern" stamp. Anxious to discredit traditional authority, distrustful of received opinion, open to new "truth" of almost any kind but still "devout" in a traditional sense, reverent (and sometimes even awestruck) about the universe, and concerned not to find modernity and especially science in conflict with personal religious belief and commitment, he sets out to be a model for contemporary thinkers, a "Christian virtuoso." For Boyle, the "way of thinking" in Meletetics leads to habits and methods conducive to discovery, and if new information does not result from the close, devotional observation of a flower, a butterfly, or an act of farming or fishing, better character, attitudes, perspective, and even wisdom do. Knowing becomes both process and accomplishment, method and value.

From a very different set of philosophical assumptions—rational rather than associative, authoritarian rather than empirical, communal rather than individual—Swift might well find it ludicrous that a broomstick could reveal the nature of man or that an individual reader of such physical "texts" was any kind of interpreter at all, but Boyle celebrates such individual capacity even in the meanest of observers. For all his celebrity as a scientist and scientific interpreter, he emphasizes his likeness to the generality of individual readers and chooses not to segregate his talents from theirs or make discriminations about principles or modes of interpretation. He writes as spokesman for the new science rather than as a practitioner, someone who champions its possibilities rather than one who carries along its accumulating body of knowledge. When he celebrates himself in The Christian Virtuoso (1690–91), it is as a member of that great ill-defined body of amateurs who want to help the world reveal itself to the observing senses. He chooses to define himself simply as one of the virtuosi rather than as an intellectual leader or expert in the growingly professional scientific world. There is, in Boyle's stance, vanity and even arrogance, his contemporary critics saw plainly; no matter how Boyle pretended to be just another butterfly-watcher or meditator on country walks, he betrayed pride in his accomplishments and the fact that he dared assume such a role. His was the pride of a humble face; he thanked God that he could be like other men.

But he was deeply committed to the universal priesthood of observers and interpreters. Boyle saw in his Meletetics a means of supporting a culture for science, if not a furthering of scientific observation itself. If he did not expect common readers to find new laws of thermodynamics or isolate new phyla of plants or animals, he did expect them to develop a sense of humility—of awe and wonder—in the face of a rich and bountiful universe, and he saw Meletetics as a way of furthering that attitude and extending the culture of science. Empowering the senses, the individual observer, and the subjective interpreter involved a deliberate decision to make the forwarding of science and pious everyday religious practice seem one and the same thing, and Boyle spent much of his intellectual capital to establish a Christian scientific community, not only insisting that scientific evidence and religious belief were not in conflict but "proving" that their aims were harmonious and their principles mutually supportive.

Boyle is emphatic about how easy it is to make meditations for oneself and is anxious to provide a do-it-yourself guide.[17] His own meditations—more than three-hundred pages of them—are mostly based on common occurrences, illustrating his point that even the simplest of things or events can become the stimulus or occasion for reflection and devotion.[18] He meditates on "His Horse stumbling in a very fair way," "Upon the Sight of a Wind-mill standing still," "Upon the want of Sleep," "Upon my Spaniel's fetching me my Glove," and "Upon Fishing with a counterfeit Fly," showing how easy it is to extend the range of meditation beyond natural objects. Sometimes his subjects are dictated by moments in his own life and career as an experimental scientist: "Upon his distilling Spirit of Roses in a Limbick," "Upon comparing the Clock and his watch," "Looking through a Prismatical or Triangular Glass," or "Upon the Magnetical Needle of a Sun-Dyal." But even the more "scientific" of the meditations use simple language and draw upon simple observation rather than a knowledge of sophisticated principles or laws. No one (except perhaps Boyle himself)[19] ever imagined his style to be distinguished or even very organized—he often rambles along about whatever interests him, and sometimes the sentences seem to unfold or re-entangle in a way that surprises the author himself—but as an encouragement to would-be meditators, his practice is exemplary. He stresses simplicity: "Nor would I have any man be discourag'd from this way of thinking, that cannot express so much wit or eloquence in Occasional Meditations, as perhaps he may aspire to. . . . [M]uch subtilty of wit is not to be expected, or at least exacted, in this kind of composures, where we commonly make use of things rather out of haste than choice, as frequently being but the first thoughts we meet with, not the best we have" (p. 26).

"[T]he difficulty," Boyle emphasizes, "of Occasional Meditations, need not be estimated by that which we find when we first addict our selves to the making of them; for practice will by degrees so much lessen that difficulty, that after a while we shall find, that Occasional thoughts will need but small invitation to frequent those minds where they meet with a kind entertainment" (p. 27). Boyle regards himself as teacher and guide as much in his role as meditator and religious writer as in his laboratory and scientific writings. His emphasis is on how "the custom of making Occasional Meditations . . . conduces to the exercise and improvement of divers of the faculties of the mind" (p. 28). And his followers repeatedly insist that people in all occupations—but especially those who encounter nature daily by tilling the soil or navigating the high seas—learn to create meditations as a way of at once furthering their piety and extending their intellectual reach.

Whichever is the primary desired result of meditation—whether pious feelings or a more searching grasp of the universe—the assumption behind the form is that the physical world of thing and event will bare its secrets to the sincere and thoughtful observer, whether expert or amateur, priest or lay, scientist or plowman. But if the tradition presumes that data is decipherable and the world knowable, the grounds of understanding are seldom addressed, nor are ways of deciding between legitimate and illegitimate interpretations sorted out. The ebullient optimism of Boyle about the human mind stands for the tradition: Protestant confidence in the individual to discover and decide for him- or herself sponsors the whole notion that when the universe surrenders the meaning of its texts, the reader shall decide exactly what those meanings are.

Boyle's blissful vagueness about how to discriminate among possible interpretations does not look, to a modern observer, very scientific.[20] Boyle is no help at all in sorting out false leads or providing tests for judgment, and others who give advice on "spiritualizing" events, experiences, and locations are even less concerned to show that meditations are subject to some higher test of truth. John Flavell, for example, offers examples that stretch the art to Swiftian absurdity; he encourages the preservation of individual efforts that, in effect, recreate the universe textually in daily life. Although seventeenth-century science aspired to precision of method and yearned for grounds to judge between interpretations, its most immediate and arguably its most lasting contribution to the culture involved its openness, enthusiasm, and sense of possibility—the refusal to accept received opinion or honor old authority—not its ability to discriminate and establish why one reading was right and another wrong. That was a major part of what Swift had against it. His attack on the projectors in Book III of *Gulliver's Travels* is a logical extension of his attack on Boyle in *A Meditation upon a Broom-Stick*: not only did modern science have no clear program of usefulness and no plan for sorting between practical and impractical methods, but it offered no authoritative conclusions and depended simply on the subjective application of individual observation and experience.

The broomstick meditation goes to the heart of the matter, attacking both the absurdities of the emerging literary "kind" and the philosophical assumptions upon which it was based. Principal among these is the prescription, which Swift usually associates with Dissenters but which he here sees embodied in Boyle, that a simple observer can move to cosmic conclusions on the basis of a chance sighting and undisciplined figurations. Swift correctly saw that this assumption licensed all kinds of interpretations and that, once allowed, there was no stopping the sharing of such a priestly function. If grand conclusions could be supported by individual experience and the subjective observation of any thing or event, who knew what might result—heretical ideas in religion and politics, irresponsible readings of natural and human events, grand journalistic claims about the everyday and ordinary, even novels, with their extraordinary claims for subjectivity.[21]

The ability to regard a rock, a tree, a cloud, a comet, or a whale in the Humber as a meaningful event may be puzzling to a twentieth-century reader steeped in a body of scientific thought that has gradually hardened interpretation and emphasized the rejection of theses. But the same sense of open possibility that led to the founding of the Royal Society and that generated experiment after experiment—many of them unproductive and some as silly and ill-conceived as Swift suggested—offers status to Occasional Meditations and to religious and political readings of tempests and omens.[22] Boyle's contemporaries—and Clarendon's and Defoe's—accepted the sense of intellectual and political conflict that went with the belief that all things and events carried inside them signs and secrets of nature and divine will. Not that they liked the ensuing uncertainties or the sometimes violent conflicts their assumptions engendered. But they lived with—thrived on—the fact that an event might inspire wildly different interpretations of its meaning and totally antithethical analyses of political, economic, social, or religious causes. A storm could mean that the Whigs were wrong or the Tories, that sabbath breaking had to stop or reformers of manners had gone too far, that the stage was corrupt or the theater of politics debased. But few doubted that interpreting matters this way was appropriate, however much they might disagree about a particular construal. And the fact that there were no reliable rules for deciding (beyond the judgment of the individual interpreters) derives from the sense, represented by Boyle, that opening up meaning was more productive than shutting it down. Such thinking leads to—and justifies—the subjective interpretation of events that the novel exploits, and the popular proliferation of the idea of reading the universe as text instills in the culture a need for texts that offer similar ambiguous possibilities while themselves remaining stable. Without an openness to subjective authority and a willingness to tolerate (even encourage) radically divergent "readings" as equally true, the culture could hardly have been ready for any kind of narrative or discourse that encouraged readers to find themselves and their own resonant potential in texts. It is no wonder that Boyle and the novelists scared the Augustans and made them worry about the implications of modernism even when they made fun of its silliness.

I I I

MELETETICS was designed to comprehend the ordinary as well as to order the disorderly in everyday life, and it sought to extend the realm of fact and the mode of realism into areas characterized by uncertainty or mind-neutral familiarity. "Real" science had, of course, just as much interest in the unfamiliar and extraordinary, and much of its program involved explaining what seemed to the untrained eye or unlearned mind inexplicable. Among ordinary readers, science made much of its impact by demystifying phenomena that had a history of astonishing observers. But there was a seventeenth-century backlash against demystification, too, and there developed a counter tradition of just celebrating—not trying to explain—the strange, the surprising, the awesome, and the wonderful. This tradition, never systematically explained as a piece of cultural history, was a popular counter to the many forms of explanatory journalism and offers a very different sense of audience needs in the years just before the novel's emergence.

Explaining was not the only print mode for dealing with the uncertain or the unknown. Anti-explanatory modes existed as well, bent on retaining a sense of mystery and reverence for the unknown. One tradition of printed materials became especially important and held sway over the popular imagination in England from the last quarter of the seventeenth century until the novel emerged as a cultural force. It in effect links the empirical thinking that finds its way into the novel with its opposite, the desire to retain a sense of awe and mystery and find, even in everyday life, something strange and surprising. This tradition has been noted but not placed in intellectual history, and it is crucial for understanding the cultural resistance to science as well as for contextualizing one of the novel's most curious representations.[23]

The novel revels not only in discovery but also in resistance to knowledge and the baring of secrets. Awe and wonder are central to the novel just as surely as subjectivity and social realism, and for reasons that grow out of the same sponsoring culture. Episodes like the finding of the solitary footprint in *The Strange and Surprizing Adventures of Robinson Crusoe* and the "incest" scene with Mrs. Waters in *The History of Tom Jones: A Foundling* remind readers of shortcomings of observation and the limits of human knowledge even in a world in which explanations are daily rolling back the darkness. Here are uncertainty, terror, unsolved mysteries of the universe, a purging fear of what might be. They relentlessly underscore human limits, shroud meanings in mystery, and evoke awe in the face of the unknown, treasuring areas in which the universe fails to surrender its secrets. If the novel emerges at a time when science seemed triumphant, it testifies also to a context that mixed ready acceptance with stern resistance, and its own features involve an odd combination of rational orderliness and murky uncertainty.

The tradition of Wonder—the literally hundreds of books, pamphlets, and verses that traded on anti-explanatory desires—at first glance may seem, like the novel's own odd engagement with the strange and surprising, an anachronism. The phenomenon seems out of place in a world and time desperately concerned to penetrate the mysteries of the universe and find the patterns that explain and justify the seeming oddities in the observable world. But if the new science made the defeat of magic and superstition ultimately inevitable, it also heightened the taste for wonder and made people cherish whatever record they could find that confirmed uncertainty and mystery. Ultimately it is the relentless attempt to understand the universe that explains the popularity of these strange books—books that retail oddities, curiosities, and rarities of nature, things and events that seem incredible and at odds with rational understanding of an orderly world. The writers and booksellers responsible for the books of Wonder were guided by expediency rather than any formal principle, so that the species is ill-defined even at its peak of popularity. But the tradition had a sizable audience, having found a raw edge of cultural curiosity. Title pages emphasize how astonishing the contents are. The word "wonder" appears so often as to constitute a catchword for readers. Wonder becomes in fact a code word in all sorts of writings that engage uncertainty and revel in the mysterious.

Bunyan, like many another observer who professed that his heart was in another world, nevertheless celebrated this one for its mystery and challenge. "O World of Wonders!" he has Christian exclaim about what he sees (*Pilgrim's Progress*, p. 100, Penguin ed.). Similarly, Robinson Crusoe is struck by the wonderful quality of what happens to him: he describes his deliverance as "a chain of Wonders," and looks back over his story as "a scene of wonders" or "a life of wonders."[24] To describe wonders in journalistic accounts or fictional narratives was to give the public something it expected, the verbal equivalent of what was sought in public exhibitions, museums,[25] and travel. Obadiah Walker, writing in 1673, lists as one of the "Advantages of Travel" for young people, "To *satisfy* their minds with the actual beholding such rarities, wonders, and curiosities, as are heard or read of."[26] The taste for "wonder" in life reproduced itself in texts; the worlds of print and exhibition reinforced one another. The textual celebration of wonders of all kinds—unusual human events, mind-boggling freaks of nature, unexplained variations on patterns in the natural world such as tempests and earthquakes—fanned the desire to see the exhibited wonders in London and at fairs: a wild boy raised by bears, creatures that were thought to be half-human and half-something else, savages brought from the new world, "siamese" twins, and other bits of the carnivalesque.[27] Elias Ashmole's desire to collect odd phenomena from far-away places (and his founding of a museum to house his collection and to make "rarities" available to the general public) was not an unusual taste in his time; his interests and his museum stand for a deep cultural desire tied closely to patterns of belief and epistemological need. "Wonders" were sought after whether they involved contemporary examples or accounts from ancient times.

The literature of Wonder often involved collections of stories and accounts gleaned from old sources and made popularly available at a relatively low price. The many Wonders collections of the bookseller Nathaniel Crouch are, for example, almost all gatherings of material that could have been put together by any diligent reader with access to two or three good private libraries.[28] No great learning would have been necessary to find the many accounts of freaks of nature like monstrous births, ancient accomplishments like the construction of pyramids, famous omens like the biblical dream of Joseph, dark human practices such as those of witchcraft and magic, or spectacular events such as conflagrations and regicides. Standard books of history held the basic materials, and they could be supplemented with tales and speculations passed along orally or in contemporary journalistic accounts.

In the early years of the tradition, Crouch was the primary purveyor of such materials, which he usually gathered under the name of "Robert Burton," and the name or initials of Burton seem to have growingly signaled to the public the precise kind of book being presented.[29] Crouch was not the first, however, to exploit such materials. His awareness of commercial possibility was stimulated by the publication, in 1678, of Nathaniel Wanley's *The Wonders of the Little World: Or, a General History of Man.*[30] This folio volume of more than 650 pages includes "many thousands of Examples" to show "what MAN hath been from the *First Ages of the World to these Times.* In respect to his *Body, Senses, Passions,*

Affections: His *Virtues* and *Perfections,* his *Vices* and *Defects,* his *Quality,* *Vocation* and *Profession;* and many other particulars not reducible to any of the former Heads" (title page). The topics covered are wondrously various. All sorts of spectacles, miracles, *lusus naturae,* and bits of information and misinformation about different human societies are included in a not-quite-random but also not-quite-organized way, in chapters like these:

Of Pygmeys and Dwarfs, and men much below the common height (Book I, chap. 23);   *Dwarfs*

Of Natural Antipathies in some Men, to Flowers, Fruits, Flesh, Physick, and divers other things (I, 9);

Of such Persons as have changed their Sex (I, 33);   *Sex Change*

Of the dead Bodies of some great Persons, which not without difficulty found their Graves; and of others not permitted to rest there (I, 37);

Of the Imagination or Phantasie, and the force of it in some persons, when depraved by melancholy or otherwise (II, 1);   *Madness*

Of such as have been seised with an extraordinary Joy, and what hath followed thereupon (II, 12);

Of such as have despised Riches, and of the laudable Poverty of some Illustrious Persons (III, 49).

One of Crouch's volumes, *Unparalleld Varieties: Or, the Matchless Actions and Passions of Mankind. Displayed in near Four Hundred Notable Instances and Examples* (1683), is largely pilfered from Wanley,[31] and Crouch's other books also borrow heavily, although usually not so single-mindedly. Each of Crouch's volumes focuses on some awe-inspiring topic, anthologizing accounts that show human habits, give instances of some kind of occurrence, or illustrate a theme, but the volumes all share a concern to surprise and amaze at any cost. "Strange and wonderful," one volume begins typically, "have been the Miraculous Productions of Nature in all Ages, or rather of the God of Nature and Divine Providence. . . . I shall now proceed to give an Account of the most surprizing Signs and Wonders which I find recorded in History."[32]

Crouch's most distinctive Wonder volumes (usually pocket-size, duodecimo, cheaply printed volumes of about two-hundred pages) have title pages that read like this:

—*Memorable Accidents, and Unheard of Transactions, containing An Account of several Strange Events: As the Deposing of Tyrants, Lamentable Shipwrecks, Dismal Misfortunes . . . Perilous Adventures . . . and Select Historical Events* (1693);

—*The Extraordinary Adventures and Discoveries of several Famous men. With the Strange Events, and Signal Mutations and Changes in the Fortunes of many Illustrious Places and Persons in all Ages* (1683);

—*Wonderful Prodigies of Judgment and Mercy: Discovered in Above Three*

Hundred Memorable Histories, Containing . . . Dreadful Judgments upon
Atheists, Perjured Wretches, Blasphemers, Swearers, Cursers, and Scoffers.
. . . The Miserable Ends of divers Magicians, Witches, Conjurers, &c. with
several strange Apparitions. . . . The Wicked Lives, and Woful Deaths of
Wretched Popes, Apostates, and Desperate Persecutors. . . . Fearful Judg-
ments upon Cruel Tyrants, Murderers, &c. with the Wonderful Discovery of
Murders. . . . Admirable Deliverances from Imminent Dangers and Deplor-
able Distresses at Sea and Land (1682);

—The General History of Earthquakes [:] Being An Account of the most
Remarkable and tremendous Earthquakes . . . in divers Parts of the World,
from the Creation to this time. . . . (1694);[33]

—The Kingdom of Darkness: or the History of Daemons, Specters, Witches,
Apparitions, Possessions, Disturbances, and other wonderful and Supernatural
Delusions, Mischievous Feats, and Malicious Impostures of the Devil. Con-
taining near Fourscore memorable Relations . . . Collected from Authentick
Records, Real Attestations, Credible Evidences, and asserted by Authors of
Undoubted Verity (1688);

—The Strange and Prodigious Religions, Customs, and Manners, of
Sundry Nations. Containing . . . Their ridiculous Rites and Ceremonies
in the Worship of their several Deities . . . All intermingled with pleasant
Relations of the fantastical Rites both of the Ancients and Moderns in the
Celebration of their Marriages, and Solemnization of their Funerals, &c.
(1683).

Crouch's books of Wonder are conventionally religious, vaguely historical, and aimed at readers with an amateur curiosity about comparative anthropology, much as are contemporary books of travel. Long sections
are narrative in mode, and the stories they present—whether familiar
ones from biblical and classical sources or new ones gleaned from contemporary books or periodicals or from oral tradition—are capably, if not
compellingly, told.[34] They offer enough detail to create a vivid impression of incidents. Wonderful Prodigies, for example, relates the story of
seven men in a boat who run out of provisions and are "forced by cruel
necessity to cast Lots amongst themselves, to see whose Flesh and Bloud
should satisfie the hunger and thirst of the rest" (p. 184). Once the victim is chosen and killed, all but one of the survivors (a relative of the
victim, who throws himself overboard rather than participate) set upon
the dead man, "of whose Carcass (I tremble to relate it) each of them
was so desirous of a piece, that it could scarcely be divided quick enough;
They fell to the flesh with eager Teeth, and sucked out the blood into
their thirsty Stomachs . . ." (p. 185). A few pages later, another story
of survival at sea depends for its suspense on the cannibalism episode.
The situation is similar, and one of the men in a boat

made this sorrowful Motion, that they should cast Lots which of them should die first, to satisfie the ravenous Hunger of the rest; after many a sad debate, they came to a result, the Lot is cast, and one of the Company is taken, but where is the Executioner to be found to act this Office upon a poor innocent? It is Death now to them to think who shall act this bloody part in the Tragedy; But before they fell upon this involuntary Execution, they once more went into their Prayer, and while they were calling upon God, he answered them, for there leapt a mighty Fish into the Boat. . . . (p. 207)

Once the fish is eaten the pattern occurs again, and God sends a bird. After a third bout with lots and indecision, they spot a ship just as the victim is about to be cashiered.

But in the structure, narration, and local style of these books, there is seldom anything even as artful or self-conscious as this. It is in their conception and their reading of public taste that their appeal lies. To a modern reader, they seem just odd, reading rather like a compilation of Ripley's "Believe It or Not" or an endless version of "That's Incredible." Their aim to amaze and astonish readers with their account of "Unparalleld Varieties" in the world is repeatedly emphasized by the kind of illustration that appears opposite the title page, usually an engraving picturing a beast, or building, or custom, or human attire visibly different from that of their English equivalents.

Crouch, like Wanley before him, sometimes worries about his credibility. "[I]f some of these Examples which I have set down may seem utterly incredible," Wanley had written in *Wonders of the Little World,* "or at best but improbable, let it be remembered that I am not the Inventor, but Reciter; not the Framer, but only the Collector of them" (fol. a1v). Crouch claims that his stories are taken from sources "of undoubted Authority and Credit" (*Wonderful Prodigies,* title page), and says that "if the Perusal of these Stupendious Examples produce . . . a real Belief in the Reader, the Publisher will think himself sufficiently recompenced for his Labour and Pains" (*Extraordinary Adventures,* fol. a2v). He invokes the Horatian formula of instruction and delight and emphasizes the practical effects of his work. About his *General History of Earthquakes,* for example, he says:

the collecting and publishing the terrible Relations of Earthquakes, needs no Apology, and may I hope be influential upon the minds of men, who appear affected with the dismal accounts that have been lately given of these terrible Visitations of God. I have been the more incouraged to proceed in Printing these small Manuals by the acceptance that others of this nature have already met with, which, I find, has occasioned many, (especially young people), to lay aside those vain and idle Songs and Romances wherewith they were formerly Conversant and to divert their vacant hours with reading the real Transactions, Revolutions, and Accidents . . . recorded by Authors of the greatest Veracity, to have happened in divers Ages and Countreys. (fols. A2–A2v)

Crouch's books imply, consciously or not, the uniqueness of individual experience. It is not just that the events he chooses are surprising and wonderful and often one of a kind, but also that his net effect is to isolate the particularity of situation and stress how circumstances alter cases. As in books of travel, the very fact of the accounts tends to undercut the old assumption (still largely current in Crouch's time—or for that matter in Pope's or Johnson's) that people in all ages are pretty much alike, and Crouch sometimes seems close to understanding the thrust of his work. "The Surprizing Adventures and Events that daily assail Mankind," he writes in one piece, nearly making the point but then sliding off it, "are so Numerous and Extraordinary, that nothing seems more inseparable to our Mortal state, than constant and continual Vicissitudes, Changes and Alterations; But since we find in History, that some more Remarkable Accidents have happened to some Places and Persons than to others, it must needs be very delightful among such a multitude of Instances, to give an Account of the most Considerable Relations I have met with. . . ." (*Extraordinary Adventures*, p. 1). On another occasion, he is more precise and reflective:

Amongst the many millions of Faces which have been, and are to be seen in the World there are not any two of 'em that are exactly, and in all points alike: and tho there may be some similitude in Voices, and in the Deportment and Behaviour, yet there is something in every one that is peculiar, and a certain Air that serves to difference and distinguish one man from another; so there is no less variety in the Wits, Minds, and Inclinations of men. From whence proceeds, not only the alteration and variety of the Customs and Manners of Nations, and particular Persons, but the several sorts of Idolatrous Worship and Paganism, that have been in the World, and the many Sects and Schisms that have started up. . . .

(*Strange and Prodigious Religions*, p. 1).

Still ahead are many years, and thousands and thousands of pages, in which human nature is universalized; but in the books of Wonder—although they are not aimed at an audience sophisticated in philosophical thinking—seeds of dissent are popularly planted. And their power may lie in the fact that they are not argued strongly or spelled out fully but rather are left implicit in the nature of the books themselves.

After Crouch, no one publisher picks up the literature of Wonder as his own, although Dunton once more sniffs cultural desire and capitalizes on the market.[35] Crouch's books continued to be issued and sold well into the eighteenth century, and many, many new titles followed in his wake, both collections more or less like his and shorter accounts of individual rarities. Crouch's successors, in fact, tended to use the word "wonder" in their titles more often than he did, in that regard following Wanley's model and bearing testimony to the market that Wanley and Crouch had identified.[36] Scores of titles trade on the word and what it stood for, and a variety of causes are served by the claims of strangeness and rarity. Two broadside ballads of 1710, for example, use the idea that modern wonders are everywhere to argue political positions, *The Age of Wonders* attacking the ministry, and *Wonders upon Wonders. In Answer to the Age of Wonders* supporting it, both claiming the old tune of Chevy Chase.[37] The term "Wonder" soon becomes in fact a catchword in many works that are actually quite different; it is as if the power of the term, like that of other words such as "marvellous," "prodigious," and "miraculous," had— in gaining its luster and currency—lost its distinctive sense of magic. The word outlived the things it stood for, and in titles like *The Wonderful Wonder of Wonders: or the Hole-History of the Life and Actions of Mr. Breech, The Eighth Wonder of the World* and *The Blunderful Blunder of Blunders* (both 1722) we can read a kind of silly epitaph for the tradition—or at least an indication that observers were wearying of Wonders.[38]

But at the height of the Wonders craze, all kinds of writers and texts took advantage of the interest. Everyday journalistic events could be invested with mysterious significance or have their "strange and surprizing" aspects emphasized. Contemporary Wonders were sometimes gathered into collections like *The SIGNS of the Times: or, VVonderful Signs of Wonderful times. Being A Faithful Collection and Impartial Relation of several SIGNS and WONDERS, call'd properly PRODIGIES* (1681), all of its contents involving events of the year 1680.[39] Texts often centered on a single event,[40] and sometimes Wonders stories were imbedded in other collections, as when Dunton includes in one of his periodicals "A strange and surprizing Account . . . Of Mrs. Emma Topliss, who was bury'd alive, and deliver'd of two Children in her Coffin,"[41] or when Thomas Welde recounts the story, turned to theological uses, of a woman who "brought forth not one . . . but (which was more strange to amazement) thirty monstrous births or thereabouts, at once; some of them bigger, some lesser, some of one shape, some of another; few of any perfect shape, none at all of them (as far as I could ever learn) of human shape."[42]

Many texts between 1680 and 1720 participate in the tradition of

Wonder, whether or not they use the term itself as a lure. Other terms that express the rarity of what is to be described—"awful," "astonishing," "strange," and "surprizing"—often tumble over each other in the titles and in the accounts themselves, but such words are yoked with terms that certify actuality and truth. "News" is one term that tries to anchor the accounts in reality (the Wonders books really are journalism), and "True" is another.[43] Accounts are often said to be "strange but true," the basic formula of the tradition indicative of the motives behind it.[44]

What all these books seem to have been designed to do involves the cultural need—an expanding and intensifying cultural need—to find phenomena and events that eluded ready rational explanation. There had long been, of course, a tradition in both written and oral materials of certifying the unusual and bizarre as actual—unnatural natural histories, stories of miracles, tales of customs and exotic phenomena in faraway places, accounts of apparitions, witches, and extraterrestrials. But the mind's thirst for things out of the common way that did not fit conventional definitions of everyday reality seems to have heightened considerably in the late years of the seventeenth century as science increasingly regularized the common sense of what was to be expected and as phenomena long worshiped, feared, or held in awe—comets, lightning, earthquakes—more and more came to be explained as part of some larger system.[45] Science seemed on the way to explaining everything—so some of its proponents hoped and so many of its enemies feared—and the "wonder" that had thrilled centuries of observers seemed to many in danger of extinction. Looked at in terms of dominant ideas, books of Wonder may seem anachronistic, but they are a significant sign of the times—a mark of the desire in readers of all classes and sophistications to find something that challenged their conventional sense of order and ordinariness.

"We are almost to a Man," wrote the London Journal on September 24, 1725,

> mightily delighted with extraordinary occurrences and marvellous events; in the Relation of which we cannot help discovering a sensible Pleasure, though at the same time we are positively sure, or at least have all the Reason in the World to believe that they are entirely groundless, false and fictitious. It is owing to this strange love of Novelty in some, and the Desire of others to indulge them in this romantick Taste, that our common Books of Travels and Voyages are stuffed with such monstrous and incredible Narrations. People love to read and hear of Things which they never read or heard of before.[46]

In fact, books of travel are closely related to books of Wonder. The Journal observer understood the tastes of his contemporaries and the practices of fellow journalists very well, making this further point about those who cooperated to produce the journalism with which I have been concerned in this chapter and the previous one. When there is no news to report, he observes,

> How often do we see them driven to the last shift, by having Recourse to Prodigies and Omens? They are forced to alarm our Apprehensions with Accounts of terrible unheard-of Monsters in one County, and most surprising Apparitions in another; Earthquakes, Volcano's, Hurricans, and Inundations, Rivers flowing with Blood, and Mill-stones swimming against Tyde, floating Islands, and Castles in the Air are frequent Articles in our Modern Diaries and other papers of Intelligence.

It is a good description of a publishing world in which up-to-the-moment accounts of daily humdrum events co-existed with books that involved prodigies, miracles, and strange and surprising events and phenomena of all kinds, and where one, paradoxically, led to the other. That was the world of popular journalistic reading materials in which the novel developed. Novelists did not compose their art simply by putting together features from the various literary and para-literary kinds that they inherited, but they wrote for readers who cut their literary teeth—in part—on the sorts of writings that I have described here. *[1790's]*

I V   *Providence Books*

CLOSELY related to the books of Wonder, in fact sometimes overlapping with them, are materials in another tradition that was extremely popular in the waning years of the seventeenth century when Christianity perceived itself to be under severe attack from "Atheists"—that is, deists, freethinkers, some scientists and philosophers, and untraditional thinkers of many kinds. This tradition of Providence books often contained the same kinds of stories as did Wonder books, except that in Providence books they were recast and pointed to demonstrate continuing divine control over the world. If Wonder books sought merely to prompt awe or astonishment with their accounts of the strange and surprising, Providence books drew specific thematic conclusions and tried to persuade readers that God was still (as in biblical times) directly involved in human events. Comets and earthquakes became warnings and judgments, wonderful rescues at sea became divine deliverances, and all kinds of unusual, unexplained events became tinged with meanings that illustrated God's continuing intervention. Often, Providence books labored to invest an event with a particular lesson—that God disapproved of a particular government policy, for example, or that He was offended by debased theatrical practices—but the global strategy of Providence books (and the rationale that enlarged them into a major textual tradition at the end of the seventeenth century) was to illustrate God's continuing influence in human history. Rather than an absentee ruler or clockmaker who wound his machine and watched it go, God was, providentialists argued, an interventionist. By reading events that way, they believed that they proved both God's existence and His power, thus assuring the continuing relevance of a Christian history.

Providence books and Wonder books overlap considerably in their interests, and although the two traditions comfortably exist side by side, near the end of the century Providence books begin to outdistance their rivals in number and popularity. Providence books took on a special poignancy then as part of the concerted political effort to gather all available "evidence" to use against "deists" and "atheists." What had been random and scattered providential accounts, mostly endeavors to interpret a particular occasion in some judgmental way, now turned into systematic collections marshaled as explicit polemics.[47] "[T]o Record Providences," wrote William Turner in 1697 in his introductory remarks to one of the largest and best collections of providential anecdotes, *"seems to be one of the best Methods that can be pursued, against the abounding Atheism of this Age."*[48]

The potential effectiveness of a comprehensive collection like Turner's had been imagined much earlier, and Matthew Poole had evidently begun to collect, by about 1658, stories that might be included.[49] Several later anthologists, including Turner, claim to have made use of Poole's unpublished manuscript, and they gathered materials as well from ancient texts, contemporary journalism, and stories passed on orally. Many were simply wonders providentialized. In 1684, Increase Mather published in Boston a Poole-inspired collection of mostly American providential narratives (*An Essay for the Recording of Illustrious Providences*) and called for a continuing effort to keep track of such events. Injunctions to record and promulgate such stories were heard with increasing intensity across the waters too. Such preservations of narrative were, after all, consonant with the motives behind the diaristic impulse and the philosophy behind Meletetics. Christian apologists, in fact, sometimes insisted that the only way that a full record of providence could be provided was through the individual preservation of stories based on one's own observation—a stenographic record of the world rather like that imagined by Swift's Tale-teller. "Reader," wrote John Flavell in 1678, "thou only art able to compile the History of Providence for thy self, because the *memorials* that furnish it, are only in thine own hands."[50]

The call to preserve and gather such materials was echoed many times around the turn of the century. John Dunton, who published Turner's collection in folio, several times announced his plan to gather such stories as part of a larger intention to compile totalizing records of modernity. To an elaborate volume of 1695 intended both to announce and puff the forthcoming *Compleat History*, Dunton added an afterword in which he pleaded with readers to contribute their own providential stories, properly documented, of course, and personally delivered. "[W]e desire the ingenious Reader . . . to send us *accounts* of as many of them as fall under his *own proper Experience and Knowledge*, directed to *John Dunton*, at the *Raven* in *Jewen-street*. . . . But always remember, that what you send be circumstantiated with the *Name of the County, Town, and Place* . . . and of the particular persons concern'd . . . for we shall not take notice of any thing that is *trifling* or *uncertain*."[51] In the next decade Dunton issued similar calls for providential material to fill *The Post-Angel* and *The Christian's Gazette*, in both of which he devoted sections to a "history of Providence."[52] Similarly, Josiah Woodward envisioned universal preservation of providential stories, enjoining readers to "record the *special* Mercies of God in some Book for that purpose." He emphasized, as well as their public impact, the experimental value they offered the recorder: "For, by Reading Them over as you sit in your House, and in rehearsing them to your Relations and Friends in your Discourse, you will have a fresh Taste of God's Goodness."[53]

Beyond "compleat" records like those of Turner or the continuing narratives in Dunton's periodicals, specialized thematic collections sprang up everywhere—recording mercies, judgments, or sea deliverances, for example—and many separate titles interpreted some single event such as a storm, a special healing, or a political occurrence. *God's Wonders in the Great Deep* (3rd ed., 1710), for example, collected "several Wonderful and Amazing Relations . . . of Persons at Sea who have met with strange and unexpected Deliverances" (title page),[54] and there were countless extensions of the old "God's Revenge" tradition updated to include evidence that God was very much interested in unmasking and punishing sinners of all sorts, not just murderers and adulterers but swearers and drunkards and sabbath breakers as well.[55] *Gods Judgment against Murderers* (1712) concentrates primarily on "a Cruel and Barbarous Murther" on a recent Thursday night but adds an account of "The Dreadful Fate of a Young Gentleman who Murder'd his own Mother, and the Terrible End he came to" (title page); and *Eight Dreadful Examples of Gods immediat Judgement on wicked Persons for several sorts of Notorious Sins* (1710) includes the story of a cruel tax gatherer who wrongfully took away a "poor Womans Cows" and "for blaspheming God . . . was turned into a

Dog" (title page). Sometimes accounts are full and long, as in *God's Protecting Providence . . . Evidenced In the Remarkable Deliverance of Robert Barrow . . . From the cruel Devouring Jaws of the Inhumane Canibals of Florida* (1700),[56] a narrative of eighty-nine pages; sometimes the story and moral are compressed to the length of a broadside, as in *A Warning for all Lewd Livers: By the Example of a Disobedient CHILD, who riotously wasted and consumed his Father and Mother's Goods, and also his own, amongst vile Strumpets, and other lewd Livers, and died most miserably on a Dunghil* (1700?). Many of the events involve anger, rebellion, and violence— always punished in some appropriate providential way[57]—and sudden deliverances from illness or infirmity frequently (especially in the 1660s and 1670s) involve marvels so similar to those in books of Wonder that questions of justice or providential intervention may seem almost moot, the condition or event itself gaining the primary attention, as in *God's Strange and terrible Judgment in Oxford-shire: Being a true Relation How a Woman at Atherbury, Having used divers horrid Wishes and Imprecations, was suddenly Burn'd to Ashes all on one side of her Body, when there was no Fire near her; the other part of her remaining untouch'd, and not so much as Sindg'd* (1677). Similarly in *The Miraculous Recovery of a Dumb Man at Lambeth* (1676), the focus is on the fact that the man is suddenly struck dumb and remains so for four years and four months, and his "wonderful Restauration . . . by the immediate hand of God" (title page) seems, if not an afterthought, somewhat anti-climactic.[58]

Even in their most clumsy instances, however, Providence books are reminders of the cultural desire to thematize narratives, to make some interpretive sense of what are otherwise only wonderful random events. The tradition of Providence books offers one paradigm for how events may be used in support of some thesis or moral; whether or not they imitated such practices when they came to write ideological and ideational narratives with plainly pointed morals, individual novelists were drawing on desire, habit, and cultural precedent. Novels almost never, no matter what they may say about subordinating the fable to the moral, lose track of the story in support of an idea, but their task as writers of pointed, idea-centered narratives is, from the first, beset by issues of how stories and ideas, examples and theses, can be made to interact in a new and compelling way. If Wonder books fall off one side of this balance, Providence books tend to fall off the other, and when they do not, they come very close to creating (for a moment at least) the kind of effect that novels go on to make into an art.

Many Providence books center on some major public event, sometimes a political occasion or action like the Restoration or the settlement of the succession, sometimes unusual manifestations of nature like storms or earthquakes,[59] sometimes an occurrence like the London Fire or the Plague that could not be surely assigned to human agency or intention but that had enormous cultural impact. Public events were especially subject to providential readings because they involved shared experience and nearly everyone seemed to believe that they must mean something beyond the obvious. In a famous sermon of 1727—*The Religious Improvement of publick Events*, preached on the occasion of the death of George I and the succession of George II—Isaac Watts insists that "If we overlook the Hand of the Almighty in the Events of human Life, we lose much of the spiritual profit of awful and afflictive Providences, and much of the sweetness of temporal Mercies. Such a sinful neglect will also lead us by degrees to a woful omission of our daily Duties, and bring us into great danger of degeneracy and backsliding, into a carnal and worldly frame of Spirit" (p. 13). Such lofty goals did not, of course, prevent those who disagreed (Jacobites, for example, in the case of Watts's sermon) from finding an interpretation self-serving and ludicrous, and long debates attended some famous providential readings. Many of the interpretations in Providence books were of course controversial, some of them wildly so, and there were clearly risks in arguing (contra "atheism") that an event was providential and then getting embroiled in debates with other believers about the precise significance. Few were above party or sectarian strife in their interpretations, however high-minded they might be about the dangers of atheism and the need to preserve the idea that human events were interpretable and that history had meaning.[60] But if Anglicans often battled Dissenters and Whigs Tories over details of providential intervention in the pages of Providence books, there was still a strong cultural bias—a bias the Providence books exploited and furthered—that God was still active in human affairs, however doctors might disagree about when, where, and why.

But there was also a philosophical justification for reading public events as against private ones and for drawing judgmental conclusions about parties or nations. As Abraham Campion argues in a 1694 sermon, "God may reward or punish a single person . . . in another world: But Nations are temporal bodies, and must therefore be dealt with after a temporal manner. . . . Nations can only be rewarded or punish'd where there are Nations, and therefore only in this temporal life."[61] Battles about interpretation were often bloody, with every group accusing every other group of trying to monopolize providential interpretations, and sometimes the common enemy—"atheism"—was temporarily forgotten as the heat increased.[62] And the basic position—that all events had meaning, and that God was involved in reward or punishment at all moments—was easy enough to caricature, as Pope for example did in his *God's Revenge*

Against Punning. Shewing the miserable Fates of Persons addicted to this Crying Sin, in Court and Town (1716): "A *Devonshire* Man of Wit, for only saying, in a jesting manner, I *get Up-Pun* a *Horse,* instantly fell down, and broke his Snuff-box and Neck, and lost the Horse" (p. 2).

The significance of Providence books as an index to audience tastes and reader needs lies in the way their basic narrativity is turned to thematic ends. Most, but not all, of the narratives they offer are short and almost anecdotal, and each subgroup is held together by a common theme and aim. Many of them combine discursive with narrative prose, and although not always artfully written, they are usually pointed. Often they combine a ruthless concentration on a main point with a richness of circumstantial detail, a spillover perhaps from contemporary journalism, or from scientific investigation, or from habits of diary keeping. Many of the stories in the Providence books were repeated again and again in book after book, becoming in effect a kind of minor narrative corpus that was, in a sense, a substitute for the disappearing oral tradition. The "art" in Providence books is not impressive enough to suggest that writers were working out complex problems of how to present narrative, and almost none of the narratives are long enough to pose the structural problems that novelists confront. But if there is a basic human need for narrativity, Providence books addressed that need at the end of the seventeenth century with something of a flourish, and they demonstrate the taste of the time for narratives that have a thematic thrust, that offer a sense of cosmic order beyond the vicissitudes of human circumstance, and that taunt readers to pursue the implications of all human events. Like other didactic works in their time, they reached thousands of readers and placed vast amounts of information (and misinformation) at the public disposal, conditioning a public hungry for facts and narratives and moral uplift to a literature that brought together, and focused, materials from printed and oral, old and new sources.

V

PROVIDENCE books are primarily works of a didactic rather than journalistic kind, and their thematic thrust, ideological bias, and urgent tone is more akin to the works that I will discuss in the next three chapters than to the journalistic materials I have been considering in this and the previous chapter. But Providence books do *use* contemporary events in ways related to several journalistic subspecies, and their overlap with the materials and aims of Wonder books illustrates the uncertainty of borders in popular reading materials. This kind of uncertainty about margins angered traditional literary figures when it carried over to species like the novel that made literary claims. Readers who went to Wonder books to be astonished by the splendor and mystery of the universe might well find themselves quickly enmeshed in controversies about cause and implication: even in "pure" entertainment, there is seldom a totally free lunch. And just as there are thematic, ideational, ideological, theological, philosophical, and political agendas in Providence books and some Wonder books, there are similar edges of desire and persuasion in other journalistic texts. Readers often were surprised around the borders of popular kinds they knew and depended on, for writers learned to use the ambiguities of generic overlap and exploit the claims that title pages made. And readers (consciously or not) are complicitous by their participation in the generic pretense, which they explicitly join at the moment they pass the title page and begin to discover where it was—and where it was not—honest in promising what lay beyond.

In the journalistic materials I have been examining, the commitment to fact and relevance often slides uneasily into aims more consciously thematic and didactic. Materials that try to present themselves as ideologically neutral repeatedly find that ideas impinge—that cultural agendas or some more personal motive find their way into texts whatever the generic or individual commitment starts out to be. Some texts—those in the Providence tradition, for example—consciously study how to thematize and adapt to their own ends materials considered to be philosophically and politically neutral. Neutral or recalcitrant materials are important to novels, too, given the way novels swallow and contain all kinds of discourses and subnarratives, and one thing early novelists had to learn to do was harness, under some thematic, ideological, or other comprehensive rubric, a host of odd and unrelated materials into something long and coherent. Their task was far more complicated than simply thematizing and subordinating, but the presence of models that abused borders and fudged on aims prepared readers for certain rhetorical habits and structures, "educating" them for novelistic wares. And observation of the process at work in the culture may have educated writers, too, to what was possible.

Still, novelists were far more conscious and directed in their writing than the writers of most of the popular materials I have been examining, and I now turn to texts where the rhetoric is more conscious and explicit, where aims and commitments are usually explicit, and where arm twisting and other coercion are most openly engaged. For if novels are influenced in their subject matter and stance by the popular taste of the public they first tried to please and engage, they are also provided some assumptions of mode and tone by the widespread acceptance of certain attitudes and aims. Writers might well look to particular texts for examples and models of what could be done or what would go down with a particular audience. But equally important are larger contextual matters that may involve less conscious artistic choices, matters where what readers desire or believe they desire determines what it seems possible to do in any new species that presents itself.

CHAPTER NINE

Didacticism:
The Biases of Presentism and
the Question of Pleasure

■

RELIGIOUS in subject matter, didactic in intent. That description fits most published writings and an astonishing amount of private discourse in the late seventeenth and early eighteenth centuries in England—so fully so as almost to constitute a definition of taste, desire, and habit. The difficulty this focus has caused for modern readers is hard to calculate and almost impossible to exaggerate. The trouble is that readers of our time are not comfortable with such content, such aims, or the tones that support them, and literary historians and critics seem to spend their time wishing—or pretending—that texts were otherwise. All "period" literature—that is, any text that is firmly anchored in some historical present—sooner or later becomes problematic for subsequent readers with different knowledge and different needs, but modern and post-modern contexts of reading present special difficulties for certain traditional modes of writing. Post-Romantic biases have a powerful tendency to resist entire modes that derive from uncongenial assumptions. Eighteenth-century texts, having fared badly with nineteenth-century readers because of their supposed ease and complacency, have now come to grief from something almost opposite: their tendency not to be satisfied and self-sufficient but instead to pursue readers and pry into their private commitments. Even in times when there was a modest resurgence of interest in satire, rhetoric, and the literature of public affairs, eighteenth-century works, when appreciated at all, were often praised for beauties not their own.

Central to almost all the distrust, the misunderstanding, and even the misconceived praise is the present difficulty of being fair about explicit didacticism. What is a general problem for belletristic texts is close to an issue of unreadability for "popular" materials aimed at the widest segment of the reading public: guides for daily conduct, for example, or treatises arguing a religious interpretation of current events. On the surface, novels might seem immune to the problem: they are, after all, "modern" in many of their affinities, and critics and common readers alike continue to defend them when poems, plays, and essays fall unceremoniously out of fashion. But ultimately novels may be the most problematic of all "literary" texts for the present-day reader because of their closeness to popular literature and their responsiveness to historic tastes. That closeness has been less noticed than it ought to be—and less systematically studied—because of a pervasive modern resistance to their insistent didacticism. Coping with "para-literary" materials from which novels take many of their crucial cues is not easy, and (paradoxically) it has gotten more difficult as literary study has become more sophisticated and as theoretical problems have been more historicized.

One reason that popular reading materials antecedent to the novel have not been studied more fully is that most of them seem to a modern sensibility inherently wrongheaded, narrow, ineffectively focused, and boring. A second reason is that these materials are most closely related to features of the novel that we care least about today, features that make us uncomfortable—that we apologize for, dismiss, or downright ignore. Why should we care about, readers now may well wonder, the origins of moralistic, lapel-gripping techniques that we temperamentally resist and wish did not exist? But however alien to moderns such tones and aims may be, the didacticism of the early novel is central to the conception of the species. Its origins are so tied up with needs of contemporary readers and its early history is so dependent on the didactic assumptions in popular non-narrative forms that to miss—or excuse—its characteristic didacticism is to misappreciate its features and misdefine its nature. Understanding its rationale and function is not only important for the reading of novels like Defoe's or Burney's or Godwin's but also for coming to terms with later novels like those of Camus or Lawrence or Hemingway where didacticism, though considerably more disguised, is equally important to formal conception and dynamic intention. Given the contexts of readership and authorship that I have been describing, it is not surprising that many of the everyday didactic materials enjoyed by early eighteenth-century readers—books and pamphlets that even in these anti-canonical times are still usually considered "background" and "subliterary"—have rhetorical features similar to those in novels. Didactic materials of no literary pretension may, in fact, help us to a fuller understanding

[handwritten marginalia: "modern reader's dismissing, great, detest, moralistic, wanting, 18TC readers liked it more, persuasion, coercion, ideology, control"]

of aspects of early novels that modern readers have trouble with, for characteristics shared across generic and even "literary" lines show us important aspects of a cultural psyche that felt the need to influence behavior at any psychological cost.[1]

The controversial word *enjoyed* in the previous paragraph is where the trouble starts. It is not obvious to modern readers that anyone could ever have taken pleasure in having "oughtness" addressed so directly. For all the honorific allusions to Chaucer's classic line about his clerk—"And gladly wolde he lerne and gladly teche"—little genuine respect has accrued to the idea of basic cultural teaching or learning through texts, and there is no present sense that readers who learn the world through books do so gladly. For modern readers, to be pursued by a writer who has a palpable design upon us is to drop the book and run, hence the rise of the term "didactic" as evaluative rather than descriptive. But historical evidence suggests that many real eighteenth-century readers seem actually to have enjoyed the tones and intentions of the texts their culture characteristically produced, even though to take such a pleasure in being told what to do—sometimes even in being harangued or harassed to do it—bears no relationship to any idea of pleasure that we in our time honor. When didactic issues are approached at all in present-day criticism or theory, authorial designs are treated as at best a nuisance, at worst a fake. The values found in such writings are assumed to be displaced ones, with readers surreptitiously finding morsels of forbidden fruit among tables laden with dull didactic gruel. If such a description were accurate, then eighteenth-century texts would be almost universally the most perverse of all written materials, utter failures as communication, seriously problematic as art. Whatever one thinks of such principles as a general strategy for reading, applied to a whole mode (didacticism) and a whole cultural epoch (the English eighteenth century), the refusal to honor face value at all has the effect of dismissing as irrelevant a full quarter of the English literary tradition.[2]

The historical and cultural issues reflect a deeper set of questions largely finessed by philosophers of history. Does the human psyche change from age to age and culture to culture? Has "human nature" changed historically, or does it stay constant, a universal against which changing texts can be measured? Such questions have serious implications for didacticism. What if readers in Defoe's time or Pope's actually *liked* the didactic? What if it was not only a matter of what they expected of texts—part of their sense of what all communication was about—but a way of satisfying their deepest human needs? Suppose that human nature is not one continuous consciousness with small cultural variables but rather a pernicious invention, only a presumed "universal" that lays a veneer on human differences that are basic, extreme, and subject to major local and temporal variables.[3] To challenge the easy assumptions of criticism and most history here is to raise major cognitive and ontological questions, and they will have to be addressed beyond the laboratories of experimental psychologists where there is no significant temporal dimension. No historicism has much point unless the possibility of variation is at least entertained. The alternative to asking about historical variation is to project an absolute from observation of ourselves—what most forms of reader response criticism in fact do—and to construct a universal history on presentist biases. It is a cliché that eighteenth-century England in its rationalist assumptions tended to see other cultures in its own terms, as projected extensions of itself that demonstrated the universality of human nature. But our own bias, because its assumptions are less readily recognized, may be worse. Present-day prejudice against the didactic mode suggests that there is no solipsism worse than our solipsism—our very enlightenment being the source of blindness—and that presentist principles have limited the entire act of historical imagination.

I

THE modern resistances to eighteenth-century didacticism are of several kinds and spring from various causes. Most involve our disbelief and distrust: disbelief in systems of value and dogma that then prevailed, in the rhetorical power of writing to do what it professes, in the whole process of history and change; distrust of piety, moral earnestness, simplicity, directness, confidence, and the zealous tones of intrusion. The basis of the problem thus seems to be primarily in modern times, where presentist principles prevail, rather than in the eighteenth-century—and in readers, who are ignorant or miseducated, rather than in texts. Even if the central problem is elsewhere, the texts themselves need to be examined because the special didactic features offer clues about didacticism's historic standing. Even if modern prejudices prevail and readers are incorrigible, the beginnings of the novelistic enterprise, the early history of its development, and the nature of the species can be clarified by a recognition of just how basic the cultural devotion to didacticism was at the dawn of the modern era.

Six features of didactic texts seem important in clarifying at once didacticism's cultural significance and the modern resistance it has generated. The first of these involves a powerful sense of good and evil, leading to plain, binary, and dogmatic distinctions and choices. The easy and overly simplistic values—reflections of a Manichaean world view—

that we often find in these texts suggest our own historic position along a good/bad continuum—how far we are theologically and ideologically, as well as temporally, from the days of William III, Robert Walpole, and the Wesleys. Much of the difference involves perspective on historical process. To the writers of Defoe and Swift's generation (or even Milton and Bunyan's), the world seemed fuller every day of shades of gray, far less absolute in its distinctions than earlier ages had been. Clean choices between good and evil, for worshipers of the past as well as for its critics, always reside in remote times or places far away. Still, the sense of a clear distinction between good and evil in most human choices *was* firmer and more secure than ours. The insistence on clear choice in the late seventeenth century was in fact a result of the fear of shades of gray. Contemporary disputes—whether about national and international matters, party strife, or matters of contemporary manners, morals, and faith—divided people rather too neatly by later standards of compromise, coalition, and confusion of loyalties. At a time when politics throughout Europe tended to split along Protestant and Catholic lines, when anyone suspected of unorthodox views about God and man was assumed to be a godless deist, and when notions about observance of the sabbath or public swearing were considered an appropriate basis for public policy, it is no wonder that matters of faith and conduct divided people quickly and surely.

Our vast distance from the traditional Western view that human life was a manifestation of divine purpose and history a record of the conflict between angelic and satanic forces means that older ages are all, by comparison, Manichaean.[4] The "modernism" of early novels is thus somewhat deceptive; the early novelists were still close to a world view that subordinated everything—including those everyday things reflected in novels—to struggles that transcended time and place, and the novel today still pays homage to transcendental views of human life and emblematic ways of thinking. Even with the radical changes that removed separatists from England and moved England itself away from the medieval and toward the modern, assumptions about human destiny in the early years of the novel were still quite old-fashioned. It is easy to allow the poles of religious and secular outlooks to obscure the long and uneven historical process that changed human assumptions over a period of several centuries. If the contemporaries of Dryden and Behn, Haywood and Richardson were a long way from the views of Spenser and Hooker, Donne and Hall, they were also far from those of Shelley and Godwin, Darwin and Dickens—perhaps farther by absolute measures. For while they had begun to move away from a sense that life on earth was only a chapter of trials on the road to eternity, they were still far from a sense that an individual life lacked higher purpose and cosmic meaning.

Between the medieval sense of total otherworldliness and modern secularism are centuries of emotional struggle and intellectual agony, and in our time we are too apt to leap to drastic conclusions when we spot minimal departures from the old norm—whether because we are biased toward progress and change, because we are too anxious to find earlier generations too much like ourselves, because we would like to move England more centrally into an Enlightenment that only brushed its edges, or because we simply do not fathom the complex processes by which a culture changes unevenly (and often slowly) in its emotional and ideational commitments. Views of history are attracted to quantum assumptions, even against all cultural evidence; "ages" are neater if they turn like pages and leave no traces.[5] Those who lived in Swift's time or Richardson's still had old philosophical reasons—as well as new political ones—to regard all choice in terms of good and evil, although few did so quite as neatly as did Benjamin Keach in *War with the Devil*, John Bunyan in *The Life and Death of Mr. Badman*, or Henry Sacheverell in his war with Dissent. For modern readers to accept the view that readers shared at the end of the seventeenth century (one that looks simplistic to us, but which looked complex in the world out of which it developed) is to make an enormous leap of the historical imagination.

Increasing shades of gray notwithstanding, writers from Milton to Johnson still thought that choices reflected polar commitments, and in early novels human decisions, while complex by the standards of epic or heroic romance, finally retain a good / evil clarity that parallels the clean choices of popular didacticism. The language of early novels, like the language of treatises and tracts, often reflects confidence in absolutes and projects alternatives with clear positive and negative consequences. There are few Forests of Error, Bowers of Bliss, or Vanity Fairs here, and seldom are simple equivalents asserted between the ordinary world and a Platonic or allegorical world that transcends time and makes automatic meaning: novels resist allegory or representation as a simple mode. But there are countless garden scenes, satanic and angelic figures, and places with names like Paradise Hall, Millenium Hall, and the Island of Despair, where symbolic actions just below the level of allegory suggest ideas and values that depend on an old system whose authority is still nervously recognized.[6] Squire Allworthy is not infallible in such a world, nor are moral values absolute even when country confronts city or innocence sophistication, just as in popular treatises like *The Whole Duty of Man* the promises and fears of heaven and hell sponsor behavioral choices without being allegorized or dramatized on every page. The everyday world of the novel reflects individual complexities against a backdrop of nominal absolutes; it pledges allegiance to old names and old values but represents their manifestations and complex outcomes in modern life. The world of absolutes is distanced but still remembered—and honored more than casually.

Confidence that there are binary differences between choices characterizes the eighteenth-century world of didacticism in ways that often make the shades of gray disappear in the face of actual decisions. The attraction to absolutes apparent in names of places and people in novels parallels the frequent appeals to authority in practical didactic guides. The confidence derives not from the theological certainty of earlier ages but from a belief, bolstered by philosophers like Shaftesbury and "natural theologians" like Richard Fiddes, that human beings have within them innate ability to tell the difference between right and wrong—and a widespread conviction still that the health of human society, as well as the success of individuals, depends on individual determination to choose aright. Anxiety about whether right and wrong do actually exist in a world where circumstances seem to alter cases becomes, in eighteenth-century didacticism, a rigid insistence that right is right and wrong is wrong, and in novels—those laboratories in which individual cases are examined—both the anxiety and the rigidity are a part of their contemporary appeal.

belief that it affected readers in that way — very straightforward

I I

A *SECOND* troublesome characteristic of eighteenth-century didacticism has to do with its directness and its faith in language to affect the behavior of readers in rational and predictable ways. Didactic texts sometimes use elaborate strategies of indirection, it is true, and didacticism sometimes loses confidence in the power of language to persuade and the ability of readers to respond to traditional forms of rhetoric.[7] But the method is fundamentally plain and the rhetoric straightforward: look-them-in-the-eye advice from a sitting-straight-in-the-saddle posture was the preferred mode of moralists. Still anchored in a tradition of plain speaking that was supposed to reflect sincerity of character, honesty of commitment, and clarity of values, didactic rhetoric prized the trust it placed in readers to choose rationally when choices were explained clearly. It claimed the high and direct road as its own.

The rhetoric of examples tended to follow the same clarity of presentation and purity of choice. Samuel Johnson's famous worries about mixed examples, in part a reaction to the convoluted method of *Tom Jones*, reflect the traditional didactic commitment to offer examples that were either exemplary or cautionary without too much confusing complication. The saints and villains who people popular didactic materials ordinarily illustrate clean choices. Most writers (though not the Fielding of *Tom Jones*, hence the objections of Johnson) were willing to risk seeming too simple; they preferred being simplistic to being misapplied.

Almost by definition, novelists provide a richer sense of context for human choices than do treatises and tracts, and they portray human decisions as characterized by more complex motives and values. Still, there are vestiges of simplicity that tend to embarrass modern readers who prefer to dig and sort for themselves. Richardson's footnotes chastizing readers who miss the point about Lovelace, Fielding's naming of Blifil to suggest the contemporary pronunciation of devil, Burney's portrayal of would-be seducers as serpentine guides—these and their opposite characterizations of angelic purity or people (even though the world is dominated by uncertain graynesses and ethical plaids) suggest how the novel clings to a rhetoric of directness and clarity of value. If novels seldom fall into intense directives that become, in John Dennis or James Janeway, simple verbal harassment, they still contain a generous sprinkling of passages, sometimes put into the mouth of a character and sometimes offered through the author's own persona, in which simple, direct, and plain statements of value are openly set apart from any pretense of storytelling or objectivity. In novelists like Henry Fielding or Sterne, careful ironies almost—but not quite—disguise the fact that the essay mode alternates with the narrative mode, but in most eighteenth-century novelists—Defoe and Haywood, Smollett and Lennox, Godwin and Inchbald—direct comment with plainly stated conclusions is almost as frequent as any forward motion of the novel's story.

There were, of course, much more varied tones in both precepts and examples than any contrast between eighteenth-century and modern is likely to suggest, and the world of rhetoric was not a static one between 1650 and 1800. Those who allowed for perversity in human nature (and its tendency to react to any kind of advice or direction by becoming rebellious and balky) certainly had their say increasingly as the eighteenth century wore on.[8] The shades of irony in eighteenth-century prose— almost all of them delicately discovered in the service of a distinct didactic function—still have never been matched. If we forgive ironists for designs that were just as palpable and plain as those of other didacticists, it is because we can find in them a certain art that modern critical methods allow us to appreciate. We experience Swift and Fielding because we can temporarily forget, or at least suspend for ourselves, the didactic commitments and concerns in their designs: we forgive their trespasses in honor of our sympathy for artistic (but not necessarily philosophical) biases we share. But finding in any art the kinds of things that interest us is not the best way to penetrate to the center of what another aesthetic aimed to do: it only shows that any aesthetic finds among its many means some that will meet the tests of other arts, other times. Appreciating Swift in full cognizance of his reactionary attitudes is crucial to understanding eighteenth-century didacticism and literary art more generally, but so is appreciating Richard Allestree and Isaac Watts, both of whom were more widely read in their own time. Seeing one side of the didactic impulse can readily lead—as it has with both Swift and Fielding—to misestimates of what they were up to and what they represented. But common to all tonal varieties of didacticism, straightforward and ironic, is a faith in language to mean clearly and to affect attitude, behavior, and social balance. Our own doubts about language lead to major problems of trust.

III

A THIRD characteristic of eighteenth-century didacticism is its heightened tone and urgent sense of intensity. It is hard to imagine documents more fevered than those from eighteenth-century pens, and for us the intensity is one reason the medicine is hard to swallow. Seldom is there impersonal detachment or cool disengagement from larger issues; no human act or gesture seems immune from judgment or implication, and every personal decision is made to seem crucially connected to behavior patterns, belief systems, and social outcomes. Questions about how individuals use their time (even spare moments) or about what musings they allow in their private thoughts seem as important as life decisions about marriage or career because the level of rhetorical engagement is just as intense. Exhortation and pleading, promises and threats, coaxing and harassment, breathless anxiety and heavy-handed insistence—all these strategies and tones are part of the urgent message that a reader's life and afterlife may well depend upon a writer's success in being heard. The imperative mood, the second-person constructions, the exclamation points, and the unrestrained interjections all presume that didactic success comes from the spontaneous overflow of righteous indignation and moral concern.

The urgency of eighteenth-century didacticism seems genuinely to derive from deep concerns about behavioral trends and the health of the social fabric, but as soon as writings are separated from their referential contexts, the question is less one of sincerity or authenticity than of credibility. Passing centuries are never kind to a rhetoric of urgency. After the fact, no one believes dire warnings of doom or shrill prophecy; overexcited tones create distrust. Historically, warnings of impending disaster always seem to later readers exaggerated, not only because most prophecies turn out to be wrong but because, even when they are right, subsequent ages do not feel the force of failure the way contemporaries do. Excitement runs down, and the record of excitement always seems a bubble and a cheat. Jaded by cries of wolf, overheated prose, and rampant quackery, modern readers may well be excused for thinking that hyper-urgent tones are signs of dishonesty or self-delusion.

And the intensity was too much for some readers in the eighteenth century as well—because they were in rebellion against authority and advice, because they constitutionally disliked jeremiads, because they distrusted the social analysis, because they disbelieved in the values being promulgated, or because they wanted, in their reading materials, more space of their own. But the surprising thing is that, relatively speaking, so few readers seem to have responded with the claustrophobic sense we take to be "normal." Perhaps it was that reading itself was so new for so many, or that reading materials were relatively scarce, or that new urbanites, recently dislodged from their villages and detached newly from family closeness, needed connection to the point of wishing to be (morally speaking) publicly pawed. Whatever the cause, the tones of urgency prevailed while calmer and cooler didactic materials made a lesser impact. A look at the treatises that were constantly reprinted shows why intensity replicated itself in new tracts: the titles that go into scores of editions are not necessarily the ones that are imaginative, well written, and almost "literary." Often-printed titles are quite primitive in their hortatory nagging and their devotion to fevered intimacy.

The historic popularity of didactic materials is legendary and a continuing source of embarrassment to historians, especially those who find circulation figures to be a certification of misguided bad taste rather than evidence of cultural character. The fact that moral treatises and theological discourses continued to be by far the most frequently printed materials until after the end of the eighteenth century tells us something about the values of the culture, whether or not readers devoured such materials with as much gusto as buyers bought them. The publication numbers we have are not very precise, of course: figures on press runs are relatively scarce, "editions" mean different things for different kinds of publications, and sales "statistics" represent guesses rather than actual facts. Then, too, caution needs to be exercised in translating any sort of circulation figure into reading habits: some materials were cheaply printed and distributed in bulk to those presumed in need of them, and more handsome and expensive texts were probably also bought and distributed as philanthropic gifts by those who thus purchased their own piety wholesale.[9] Still, once we discount the evidence generously and allow for vast slippages between texts printed and texts read, we are left with a startling record of success for texts undistinguished by verbal or formal artistry or by any apparent attractions beyond their drab and repetitious precepts.

By modern standards, it would be comic to speak of even the most tenacious didactic texts as "classics," yet judged by their enduring popularity at least a score of didactic texts outdistanced all "literary" classics by wide margins. Endurance, in fact, meant something quite substantial for many of the titles that continued to be reprinted at frequent intervals for more than a century. Lewis Bayly's *The Practise of Pietie*, for example, first published about 1610, had reached a "59th" edition by 1734, and *The Whole Duty of Man*[10] (1658) had appeared in at least thirty-eight editions by 1700 and over a hundred more by 1800.[11] More skilled pieces of writing with similar purposes often did not fare as well. Defoe's *The Family Instructor*, for example, although very popular when compared with novels, never attained the status of Bayly or *The Whole Duty*. The first volume (1715) of *The Family Instructor* reached, by 1787, a "16th" edition; it was reprinted more often than any Defoe novel except *Robinson Crusoe*.[12] But Defoe, although a "name" in didacticist publishing circles, never quite challenged the older and simpler leaders.

How can we explain the popularity of Bayly, *The Whole Duty*, and other perennials like Arthur Dent's *The Plaine Mans Path-way to Heauen* (1601)?[13] In what did their appeal consist? Why did readers continue to read, or at least buy, these titles instead of newer or more artful texts? Was their satisfaction merely a matter of feeling good about buying or reading something they had been told would do them some good? an attempt to appease parents, neighbors, friends? a wish to impress clergymen, counselors, and teachers? a conventional form of fire insurance for eternity? Each of these reasons may account for some of the popularity of materials that clearly, by 1800, did not correspond very accurately to the most "advanced" contemporary thinking about religion or morality. But there were other satisfactions too: pleasure in hearing familiar formulas and phrases, for example, and the common feeling—one that Western religion, Catholic and Protestant, has always counted on heavily and counts on still—that reading, hearing, or repeating proper statements of contrition and aspiration produced a kind of atonement for one's own shortcomings. The pleasures of repetition and the comforts of familiarity are seldom given their due in sophisticated literary theory,[14] even though we know how important they are for oral audiences (well beyond their function as a mnemonic device for tellers) and for children who love to hear anything—rhyme, phrasing, story line—that they can recognize from a previous telling.

The fact that a single translation of the Bible dominated the English verbal memory from the early seventeenth century until the middle twentieth is suggestive. Half a dozen good translations co-existed and competed in the late sixteenth century, but then for literally hundreds of years the cadences of the King James Version—cadences that even the most secular readers have found familiar until the last two generations—totally took over, representing a stability of language and suggesting a stability of faith and practice that, when it ended, was widely missed in the everyday lives of all sorts of people, literate or not, devout or detached. Only with the deterioration of the cultural memory of biblical texts did a "Revised Standard" version become possible, even though the linguistic and theological means for such a revision existed for a century. Quality may have been a factor in the King James Version's original edge over the competition, but to regard centuries of familiarity as due altogether to innate superiority over versions unread is to overrate taste and underrate habit. We also underrate vicarious apology. Without a formal procedure for confessional and atonement, Protestantism found that the private reading of works like *The Practise of Pietie* and *The Whole Duty of Man* would perform a purgative function when believers found themselves alone or among alien unbelievers, just as public testimony and oral confession to the assembled saints performed that function in the meetings of many Protestant sects.

I V

A *FOURTH* characteristic of didacticism is the tendency to address readers directly and personally, almost as if a printed text—for all its public and anonymous qualities—could be a private communication between friends.[15] Didactic texts are not, of course, really very intimate, no more so than most printed documents and in some ways much less so, but writers at the end of the seventeenth century, painfully aware that they were writing for people they did not personally know, tried to make their writing seem customized for particular readers or categories of readers. Unable to call readers by name, writers regularly address them by kind, as if doing so created a private relationship that would result in knowledge and friendship. Writers are in fact very self-conscious about "talking" to someone they do not know personally and to whom they have no right of access. The print world in the late seventeenth century replicates, in a series of devices resulting from technological possibility as well as from mass-publication necessity, forms of address among strangers. Texts are regularly "introduced" by someone other than the author, often someone with a specific constituency who can presume to address a certain group of readers—members of a parish, for example, or those of a particular social group or political persuasion—and give a seal of approval to author and text. The several prefatory "words," epistles, dedications, testimonies, or other introductory essays that in fact stand between reader and text pretend instead to be connecters, things that bring together writer and reader in a more personal way. Their aim—to deal with the distance of print and randomness of readership—led to a host of devices designed to make a reader feel a part of some larger community of sharers. When a book bursts into the world without a proper introduction, the author addresses the unknown reader warily. "Courteous Reader . . ." or "Gentle Reader . . .", such unintroduced texts begin, and then they proceed to negotiate a temporary friendship.[16]

Seventeenth- and eighteenth-century writers—especially writers of didactic materials but writers of many other kinds as well—regularly address kinds of readers they expect to sample their work but not necessarily be sympathetic to it. Sometimes the address is simply to a "dear Reader," but more often readers are grouped into "curious" or "learned" readers or "Christian" or "judicious" or "ignorant" ones. Whether such strategies made readers feel warm and welcome may be questionable, but writers then regarded such addresses as necessary, dictated by the impersonality of print and unknowns in the marketplace process. And whether or not individual readers were thus lured into a sense of belonging, these strategies create an atmosphere—intrusive and unattractive to most modern readers—of directness, a feeling that the author is right there with us, intruding as we read, observing and sorting us. The modern convention that readers own their space in a text—and that their privacy is inviolable—was no convention at the time the novel emerged, and didactic texts, like early novels, regularly produce a sense of watchfulness and nervous overseeing.

The direct address to readers is part of the larger project I discussed in Chapter Six in which print uses oral strategies, or synthetic substitutes for oral strategies, to try to recreate an earlier and, supposedly, more intimate world. The novel itself is full of such devices—from Defoe's equivocal but personal prefatory addresses and Richardson's one-on-one footnotes to Henry Fielding's pretense that he is in a stagecoach telling us his story and Sterne's that he is writing his novel in the presence of readers gathered around his desk. All writings of the time, not just didactic addresses to the young and vulnerable, were affected by the perceived problem of lost orality and audience distance, and the "solution" was not, strictly speaking, an invention of the didactic tradition. But the problem of how to affect readers who were perceived to need special attention— of how to make individual readers feel singled out from a crowd when *[handwritten marginal notes: "Closer to orality", "intruding authors", "(modern reader a whore)"]*

they looked at a cold, mechanical, completed page of depersonalized print—was an especially serious one for the zealous didacticist, and the strategies employed in didacticism tended to infect other kinds and modes, sometimes parodically as when writers like Henry Fielding claim their work is "Necessary to be had in all Families,"[17] sometimes because even among those who wish to dissociate themselves from a proselytizing spirit there is nervous kinship with those who seem to sail in the same leaky vessel.

Didactic texts are subjectively charged fields at the turn of the eighteenth century. They are not neutral spaces where writer and reader meet to share the text and compromise their differences; they are authorial possessions where readers are welcome as guests, or (better) as subjects to be governed. As Fielding insisted (certifying a treaty already made and honored for decades), writers needed to see themselves as keepers of a public ordinary, not hosts of an eleemosynary feast; but, however accommodating they might be to consumers, they retained authority and had proprietary rights. They had to seem democratic, tentative, open to disagreement, and solicitous of subjective variation, although in fact authors remained in authority, trying to sound benevolent and gracious while retaining despotic control of the text. Like other writers, didacticists fought hard the tendency of the reading process to be lonely and impersonal. They were unwilling to surrender to the phenomenology that later writers assumed to be necessary to the nature of written texts. Still close enough to oral modes to regard them as the norm, they worked out ruses to disguise the phenomenology of a process that starts with one person writing and ends with one-by-one reading. They created the pretense that here was a communal fund, socially arrived at, from which readers could draw as they individually chose to do.

Modern readers do not expect an intruding author behind their backs or at their elbows. Reading for us may be a highly personal act even as it is a solitary one, separating us from some larger group involvement, but what makes it personal is the choice of a particular text that is already determined and programmed in a particular, defined, and knowable way: it is not personalized by the author's reaching out to us, and attempts to pretend otherwise seem to us pretentious and cute. Writers in the eighteenth century repeatedly refused to settle for the givens of mass print and the fact of an audience out of the range of their observation and— once the text is released—out of their control. They tried for intimacies of relationship or some pretense of them. The narrator's facetious conversation with us for eighteen books in *Tom Jones* and Sterne's direct address to readers whom he even sends off on errands are more dramatic but in some ways less complex that the strategies of Smollett, Defoe,

Richardson, or Burney. Smollett emulates the oral telling of long narratives; most of his novels are like rambling, indulgent anecdotes gathered
to be told privately to guffawing cronies. Defoe's heroes and heroines
intimately confess private behavior before a heaven on whom falls the
burden of forgiveness and redemption, and as readers we intrude on a
private, semi-reflective journal; but side by side with the serious confessional, and sometimes mixed with it, is jocular vainglory, a kind of oral
boasting about how the rules were circumvented and the system conquered, so that we half eavesdrop on something beyond us and half hear
a garrulous friend we partly envy and partly disapprove. Richardson creates letters that seem to be aimed at a single reader, but the privacy is
easily violated if the intended audience shares or if a would-be reader
intrudes. His sense of a closed circle of friends with similar values is richly
communal in an old nostalgic mode. Burney's mixture of the politely
formal and intimately personal moves a long way toward a modern neutral field of undifferentiated readers, but there is about her almost-straight
prose an invitation to distrust and invade, as if readers can sort themselves out by how complexly they hear the delicate tones. Burney's ironies work like Maxwell's demon—they sort readers just as Henry Fielding's
do but more subtly. Indelicate readers have a place to go in Fielding, not
in Burney.

Defoe's mode is in one sense the most modern and in another the least
so. It is the most modern because it is the easiest for a solitary reader to
tune in on without personal threat: the appeal for reader involvement is
general and involves no commitment to the narrator. But is is also the
least modern for it implies that the text is not complete, or the narrator
redeemed, until the reader has completed the act of reading, justified the
confession, heard the full revelation, and made a judgment.[18] Richardson's strategy is, in a way, the most ingenious, for the medium turns the
tables on readers and makes them invaders of privacy rather than the
invaded. In a variety of ways the epistolary mode that insinuates itself
into most literary forms in the seventeenth and eighteenth centuries—
in the form of verse epistles, epistles dedicatory, letters of advice, packets
of mail broken open and exposed to public view, and weekly periodicals
that take the shape of letters or that include letters from readers, as well
as epistolary novels—is a clever way of addressing the phenomenology of
reading in an age that refused to accept the fact that writing, and then
the printing press, had forever altered the way that people reach out to
each other.[19]

V

A *FIFTH* characteristic involves basic assumptions about what writing is for. Despite the pretense that the Horatian dictum to instruct and delight is a contest between equals, the sense of life as a struggle rather than a celebration and of writing as a means rather than an end in itself was very powerful in England from the time of the Civil War until at least the middle of the eighteenth century. Despite the frequently invoked parallels with Roman culture and Roman literary ideals, English writers regularly saw their public function in more utilitarian terms than a strict reading of Roman literary theory would support, and the Horatian ideal usually meant an attempt to make instruction palatable, as delightful as possible within the understood—but seldom directly stated—assumption that instruction was the only appropriate end. Such an assumption is not very surprising among devout and zealous Christians and devoted moralists, and later generations have accepted that Dissenters and others who shared their Puritan vision might well have operated from such principles. Harder to accept, though, is the equal truth that those who vigorously attacked the humorless rigidity of such aims—or who parodied them outrageously—also shared a conviction that not to persuade others was to lose one's own persuasion. Politics, economics, and social prejudice just as surely as religious zealotry led to the anxious sense of crisis that sponsored powerful feelings and inflated rhetoric, and in such a cultural context didacticism could hardly help being the central mode. When delight loses its equal place in the twin aims of Horatianism, the result is the exaggerated importance of the didactic mode that I have been describing in this chapter. There is, of course, in writing of all kinds (not just in novels) plenty of delight to be found, but when delight is, in theory, either means or by-product rather than an end in itself, the mode requires different receptors from those that moderns possess.

It is easy to exaggerate the tilt toward instruction in those times because the bias in ours is so strong toward delight. But there was imbalance then, virtually the mirror image of ours; even in poems and plays where literary and aesthetic concerns were greatest and practical effects least insistent, instruction was always the majority partner. And in prose works of any kind—vernacular prose then still having a firm reputation as utilitari. and functional—the imbalance was extreme. It is, in fact, hard to ii gine that age developing a form of prose fiction that was not straig tforwardly and emphatically didactic, almost illustrative in its emphasis on ideas and their everyday implications. The earliest examples of the new prose fiction were not so extreme as the apologues that sprang up later as an alternative,[20] but the novel from the first was idea-centered and socially and morally conscious to a very great degree, far more so than either the old or the new versions of romance. The extended discussion then—in prefaces, reviews, critical treatises, and private letters—of the relationship between fable and moral in fiction tells, of course, only the intentional part of the story, but as far as it goes it provides a reliable guide to contemporary rhetorical theory and to cultural desire. The connection, structural as well as theoretical and associational, between the didactic aspects of prose fiction and the broader didacticism of the whole print marketplace is plain to anyone reading the full didactic context, but few scholars—and almost no general readers—now know that context.

Life for the typical reader was, if short, still difficult moment by moment, and the moment was almost always the epicenter of conscious attention. *Ars longa?* Little comfort. When writing took long views, it was of little use. What I have described as imbalance in prose fiction was, however, in the didactic treatises themselves not even an issue; delight in such para-literature had a place only as lure or palliative, something to make the instruction work. Even so, the craft that went into the conception of packaging merits attention because of the way it captured both the preoccupations and central tones of the age. Our modern suspicion of instructive intention allows us to isolate with ease even the slightest traces of didactic rhetoric and to see its cultural origins. But we may be too quick in our judgments of its effects—then or now—on readers, and we are certainly wrong to regard the culture's pervasive taste for instruction as simply misguided. Flaws, limits, and insecurities there surely were in the hundred years of revolutions, aborted revolutions, diverted successions, and human and intellectual migrations that came in the wake of parliamentary reform, regicide, and Puritan cleansing. But the appropriate response to such a phenomenon, when it affects a whole culture for more than a century, would seem to require analysis and understanding more than dismissal as a colossal historical mistake.

V I

A *SIXTH* characteristic involves the tones of authority and the air of certainty in didactic writings. Many eighteenth-century readers—like twentieth-century ones—were alienated or embarrassed by one form or another of didactic insistence. Every reader of that time, in fact, probably considered all but one particular group of authors (those who fit the reader's own social, religious, and political profile) to be excessively arrogant and dogmatic, and the divisions formed along party or sectarian lines stamped writers of any other persuasion unacceptable—as moralists, as Christians, as patriots, and as human beings. Debating the dogmatics of doubt or questioning the zeal of the zealous has never been a very satisfying venture, and the fact of the arrogance and dogmatism itself, as well as the fact that every gesture was suspected by partisans of a different stripe, tells us two crucial things about the age: that issues discussed in didactic materials were perceived to involve a crisis at the center of the culture, and that the partisans were all wracked by doubts of their own.

Looking beneath the surface and finding its contradictory substructure is what our century will bequeath to posterity as our most characteristic contribution to textual analysis.[21] It is an important corrective to views of history that have been too trusting, too charitable toward human intention, and too impressed by conscious monuments that human beings have erected to establish their particular version of history. As an alternative to heroic history, it offers an attractive sense of how complex results can be in the wake of uncertain motivations, and the record it unearths of verbal strata offers a rich gloss on historic markers that pretend, in their stark factuality and precisions of place, to be the whole story. Subsurface analysis does have its limits (as I have argued in suggesting why modernity has had so much trouble generally with didacticist rhetoric), for it sometimes licenses us to overlook the obvious, which may be just as true as the devious and complex. But a distrust of surfaces can bare ambivalences, doubts, and difficulties that authorities, markers, and texts consciously try to hide. The uncertainties behind the bold claims in didactic texts are often hard to be sure of, one by one, but the brash dogmaticism of the species in general is instructive in its very refusal to admit the possibility of doubt. The stolid determination not to move an inch, the air of protesting too much one's certitude and absolute virtue, and the all-encompassing, filling-up-every-space-and-time preoccupation with making the whole world stand at attention to salute one's own rigid values suggest a powerful unwillingness to tolerate difference, a fear that the Other is so strong that to allow it to exist at all may mean the extirpation of oneself. The fact that anxiety about "evil" centers explicitly on young people implies not only the deep caring about the future that the moralists themselves allege, but also a deep distrust of the prevailing tendency of things to change, to threaten received values, and to destroy those who support received values. Didacticism ultimately means more than that conservatives genuinely wanted to influence individual behavior, affect the shape of society, and arrest change; but it also helps to know what they thought they were doing, what they cared about, what they were anxious about, where their discomforts lay.

Whether or not their fear was justified, most moralists did see cultural deterioration as imminent. They thought their evidence was empirical, and observers of the harsh realities of everyday life repeatedly cited physical violence, crimes of property, street gangs, public drunkenness and disorderliness, and loose sexual behavior as indicators that the social fabric had broken down and moral standards had been lost. Whether behavior, especially behavior among the young, was worse than in other ages is debatable. What is not, however, is that many observers *thought* that individual behavior was deteriorating and that moral standards were dropping. Methods of social analysis were not sophisticated, and perhaps no "objective" way of evaluating the historical situation is any more possible now than it was then. But the question is why moralists felt the desperation they did and why the moralistic rhetoric they developed became at once so popular, so shrill, and so self-righteous.[22]

Urbanness itself is part of the answer. The urban life was alien to most older observers; it represented a threat to familiar habits and ways of life that earlier generations had assumed to be normative. Unfamiliarity itself—unfamiliar places, jobs, social structures, human interactions, economic opportunities, temptations—represents uncertainty and fear; the mere fact of change was a threat to things held dear. But there is also something deeper, some sponsoring fear that legitimates the extreme criticisms of minor acts of behavior—swearing, sabbath breaking, card playing, novel reading—that were repeatedly blown out of all proportion by moralists in book after book.

Some larger clue to the extent and basis of the fear may be gathered by reading the Augustan satirists as partners in the cultural guardianship. Superficially, the satirists—robust, worldly, often contemptuous of religiosity, self-righteousness, and intense solemnity—appear to have little in common with either the tone of popular didacticism or the vision that sponsors it, but they share the same urgent fear that something valuable (they are often not sure what) is being lost in the brave new world. Tradition is the most common name for it in belletristic texts, but other terms describe it equally well: family coherence, community values, cultural loyalty, shared ethical standards, human dignity, heritage, honor, integrity, continuity. It may be wise ultimately not to choose among these terms. All of them meant, to the persons who defended them then, much the same thing: a loss of familiarity most often expressed as the waning prestige of religion. Fading religious values may have been only a metaphor for a lost sense of balance or for a lost explanation of human history, and perhaps it does not matter much what we call either the loss or the fear. But it is important that we take seriously the feelings themselves and allow dignity to the structure of belief that sponsored them, however we feel about the beliefs themselves. It is significant that the world of didacticism took the shapes it did, insisting that Christian belief and ethical practice were inextricably tied together and putting politics a distant third as a consideration. Ideology then did not parse itself as we have later come to think.

Especially in the last decade of the seventeenth century—in the backlash from the Restoration and the aftermath of the Glorious Revolution—the Williamite "reformation of manners" licensed a broad cultural analysis of decline and invited novelty as a means of reinvigorating old values. Deterioration of the familiar and the revered became then the justification for a boldness and intensity never before seen in a time of peace and cultural stability, and even as controversies swirled and binary party strife emerged triumphant, rhetoric hardened and narrowed to concentrate on specific cultural lapses and personal vices. The constant talk was of loss—of ideals, standards, ethics, values, fiber, character, honor, belief, all the words that "old-fashioned" comfortably fits in front of—but whatever the particulars of perceived loss, anger about the present and anxiety about the future was what came through in the unswerving dogmatism. Such singularity of vision and tone, however narrow-minded or insecure the analysis behind it, produced in readers fast or furious loyalties and antipathies, overcoming to some extent the initial problems of impersonal print unsurely directed to audiences writers could not be certain about. Intensity was a form of identity, even though its origin was in anxiety and insecurity.

The fact that literature then was openly and aggressively public and occasional helps to account for the rhetorical urgency, and the fact that the reading public included many untraditional readers accounts for more. Writing for readers one did not know personally meant that one's premises and aims had to be plainly in view (or, as an alternative, totally hidden) and that in-group subtleties reserved for friends were often suppressed or even temporarily abandoned. By the late seventeenth century, people of any sort might well pick up books that weren't intended for them, and authors had to consider that fact in an age that had not yet sorted through the specialist possibilities that would ultimately prevail in an age of undifferentiated literacy. Swift, for example, although he pretends in A Tale of a Tub only to be irritated by the problem, addresses it head-on. One reason critics have such trouble sorting out the Tale's stance is that the address to readers keeps shifting, paragraph by paragraph and sentence by sentence. The Tale's rhetorical focus is, in fact, on the very problem of co-opting curious readers who, so to speak, wander into the text from the street.

V I I

THE problem for a modern sensibility is not just that we recoil from writing that seems to have a palpable design upon us, but that didacticists of the generations of Dryden and Shadwell, Pope and Cibber—whether writing treatises, essays, plays, poems, or novels—actively sought to let readers know their palpable designs: it was part of the process of living through a radical historical change in the writer-reader relationship, in going from a language of familiarity among friends to a language designed to communicate with strangers. Their own self-consciousness and explicit admission of their concerns did not mean that they refused strategies of indirection. Books are full of verbal ironies, misleading title pages, allusive names that summon false expectations, and convoluted structures that correct and recorrect directions. But these features did mean that readers and writers alike understood that any published document had a definable public purpose beyond the self-expression of the author. Some didactic writings are, of course, better than others—some because they are more subtle and oblique, others because they find ways to turn the potential intensity of agreed-upon aims into emotional *tours de force*— and the same discernment that can distinguish a Faulkner from a Margaret Mitchell, an Austen from a Gene Stratton Porter, or a Richardson from a Charles Gildon, can also distinguish William Law, Richard Baxter, and Isaac Watts from the scores of wordmongers and sermonizers that littered every bookstall in London week after dreary week. Some didactic works are simply clumsy, inept, or crude, and distinctions of quality are ultimately as important in didacticism as anywhere else to both readers and critics; but it seems important—in making these distinctions at all— to resist a broad brush of dislike and appreciate the potential of qualities we tend to suspect or detest.

The continuity between popular didactic materials and novels (the reason that early eighteenth-century readers could move so easily to novels from their experience with other reading materials available to them in the years just before the novel emerged) has much to do with the practical needs of people caught in the culture—urban, moment-centered, subjective, private, literate—I have described in Chapters Three through Six. People (especially young people) in new circumstances— loosened from the security of family, the familiarity of their community, and traditional sources of stories and lore—needed desperately to feel grounded, to gain basic information about how their new world worked and what was expected of them. What were the codes and rules? What behavior was appropriate? Who could one trust? What were the implications of deviation and ignorance? Conditions in which new knowing was not just desirable but fundamentally necessary meant a climate of special receptivity to teaching. Tonal subtleties were less important, and the pragmatic and moral could mix freely. In such a context there were satisfactions, perhaps even deep pleasures, in being the addressee of direct advice. In practical matters of life and death, profit and loss, physical and emotional health, and social adjustment to changing circumstances, receptivity to guidance from those who knew the world's ways made everyday good sense to many readers. The sheer amount of such advice provided in popular print—in periodicals like *The Athenian Mercury* or *The Spectator*, in journalistic narratives of contemporary life, and in dedicated treatises and tracts—argues a voracious public appetite for being told what to do. Traditional moralists took advantage of this receptivity to retain some of the most conservative strains of moral and social advice and lace them with various versions of modern fright, so that the methods, tones, and interests of older religious and moral didacticism prevailed into many areas of everyday life.

It is hard now—it was hard then—to separate old didacticism from new, to tell the zealous, intrusive tones of concern for religious salvation and moral well-being from the eager desire to make things easier in the workaday world. The old and new sat side by side in the same paragraph, often in the same sentence or phrase, and ordinarily there is no sorting out the moral and religious concerns from the pragmatic: the attitude is all "ought" and "must." Didacticism meant telling readers how it was, what they needed to know to survive in this world and the next, and although one might be able, analytically, to slice away the old warnings and heavy-handed, nose-guiding directiveness from flat how-to-do-it practicality, didactic treatises of the time almost never made an effort at distinction, merging instructions for cooking or taking shorthand or keeping accounts with directions for living the devout and holy life. The traditions of shrillness and heavy-handed guidance in traditional moral theology, while often objectionable to the young and the mobile as reminders of the closed world they had left behind, retained the virtue of familiarity in the midst of new information about a strange new world.

Didacticists had no desire to distinguish between old needs and new, and didacticism in its broad aspects continued to fulfill traditional expectations and offer a familiar psychological sense of order and an aesthetic sense of closure at the same moment that it fed the acute hunger for self-improvement and ministered to a perceived need to address a deep sense of personal inadequacy. Such needs may well have been created by a theology and eschatology that described earthly life as a testing ground for something higher, later, and more refined. But whatever the histori-

cal reason, the needs were there—prominent, conscious, and intense—
for readers who saw their literacy as an extension and heightening of
their general human obligations. Didacticism moved quickly into the
breach, seizing the opportunities offered by the excitement of a new world
of challenges and uncertainty, modifying itself a bit as it did so but never
losing its zeal to improve the plight of degraded human souls adrift in
dangerous seas. "Literature," even literature like the novel that makes
special representational claims on ordinariness, often tries to act above
the needs and wants involved in such writing, anxious to separate itself
from mere journalistic description. But for all its eagerness to stake its
reputation on intrinsic merits, literature—no matter how "polite" and
formal—often finds its words, its structures, and its desires in instrumen-
talities of the commonest sort.

VIII

BEYOND sly winks and smug smiles, we have no methodology for reading the bread-and-butter popular works of eighteenth-century England.
The texts that social historians use calmly and perhaps too literally are
embarrassments to literary chroniclers and thorns in the flesh for critics
and theorists. Their power to annoy and disturb, a crucial part of their
original phenomenology, usually translates simply to lack of control and
failure, and the result is that we have written for ourselves a context for
the novel that represents a gross distortion of the one readers lived in
when there began to be significant numbers of novels to read. This distortion exists whether one takes the "historical" view of Augustan satirists or the presentist (or neoclassical) one that novels, like people, are
pretty much ever the same. In offering a revisionary view of the context,
I want to suggest not only what pre-novelistic reading materials looked
like but why in their characteristic concerns and tones novelists find
helpful clues to deep cultural desires. Not all didactic, religious, and
ethical materials were alike, however, and in the next two chapters I
want to sort out the directions of publishing most relevant to the novel's
emergence, and to describe how the concerns and methods of didacticism came to affect the novel formally, structurally, ideologically, and
phenomenologically.

CHAPTER TEN

Didactic Para-Literature

Directions of Didacticism:
The Guide Tradition

■

DIDACTIC writings in the early eighteenth century were everywhere but they were not everywhere the same. Because there is no scholarly map to their bewildering variety (let alone a typology or a historical guide to their development), what I can say here about exactly how didacticism helped prepare the way for the novel is only tentative. My sketch of the didactic landscape is no detailed guide; I aim merely to suggest the emphases of materials that have most to do with the directions of novels a little later. I have read mostly in the years between 1660 and 1720—the years when what became an audience for the novel was refining its tastes and defining the expectations for popular reading—and thus I can offer little sense of how various types and subtypes changed over time. The full historical typology that literary history needs could show us how forms interrelate and suggest how "literary" species like the the georgic, the formal verse satire, the epistle, and the dialogue interact with "popular" pamphlets and books. Even without a good map, however, we can get an idea of how cultural desire set pens to work and see why "literature"—especially the novel—is so dependent on a dynamics that it prefers to feel superior to.[1]

I

THOSE who study the religious and moral "backgrounds" of literature usually begin with sermons; the reasons are formal and habitual rather than contextual and historical. Of all didactic forms, sermons are closest to traditional literary forms. Behind them are recognizable conventions and habits of mind, and in them is careful if undistinguished writing. Because literary figures of the time were often clergymen some of whose sermons are extant, the link between "literature" and para-literature often seems easiest here, and a casual observer is apt to regard sermons, because of their sheer number and easy accessibility, as the most significant terrain on the didactic landscape. Everyone, even the most rigid formalist, can figure out what to do with sermons, for habits were established and largely based on the traditions of classical rhetoric.

Sermons are not, however, typical of the didactic forms of the time, nor were they (usually) very creatively written. A few sermon writers, it is true, achieved remarkable success, and some of those have, on the basis of their sermons, become fairly well known as literary figures in their own right—Lancelot Andrews, for example, in an earlier time, and John Tillotson and Jonathan Edwards near the time when novels need to be reckoned with. What is surprising is that writers of demonstrable talent—Swift, for example, or Donne, or Sterne—wrote sermons of such arresting mediocrity, and among the tens of thousands of texts by lesser lights there are few undetected gems and none one would wish longer.[2] Unless there was some external reason for popularity, they seldom caught on with the public. Tillotson's sermons are an exception; collections of them were reprinted fairly often from 1671 to the middle of the next century. Much of their popularity had to do with plain merit in a homiletical wasteland, but some of the popularity had to do, too, with Tillotson's place in what was still, in his time, a relatively small and personal nation for people in the public eye. His position as Archbishop of Canterbury made him a visible figure, and his reputation as a preacher and religious leader found him readers he otherwise would not have had. Many lesser sermon writers who had significant symbolic places—Robert South and Isaac Barrow are good, dull examples—apparently found their relative popularity in a similar way, and most of the collections of sermons that achieved even modest popularity gained the attention they did because of the reputation or cultural standing—either personally or by office—of the author. The man, rather than the writing, was crucial to the reputation of sermons.[3]

Other circumstances determined popularity and commercial value as well. Beloved local priests often had their favorite sermons (or their most famous ones, or ones delivered before a notable personage) printed so that admirers had a memento or so that their modest reputation could be perpetuated. Prefaces often claimed that some group had demanded that a certain sermon be printed, and sometimes it may have been true. To have ventured as they did, booksellers must have been encouraged by prospective buyers with special interests, although the convention was abused and preachers planted wares for their own vain ends. Being "beloved" was quite an important avocation among clergymen in country parishes, and the printing of isolated sermons was an inexpensive mark of affection. Literary talent, theological acumen, skill at biblical exegesis, preaching ability, and pious intention counted for very little.

Even more frequently, sermons owed their currency to a special occasion. Sermons on events, public or private, that inspired the journalism I have described in Chapters Seven and Eight made their way into print with depressing regularity, and those in a regular series—the Pinner's Hall lectures, for example, or the Boyle lectures—were printed because of the prestige of the series or the preacher, or because the audience for the event constituted a market for a salable souvenir. Sermons on special days—commemorations and anniversaries, for example—had a strong record of publication, even though most of them say predictable things in a predictable way. Increasingly also, funeral sermons were printed, often with a life of the deceased added. Early on, such sermons were printed only if the deceased was famous or infamous, but as the lives of ordinary people—saints or sinners—increasingly commanded public attention, more and more funeral sermons were printed, often with appendices recounting details of fame or infamy, the circumstances of early piety or religious conversion, details of remarkable experiences or aspects of character, testimonials of friends and associates, or last words of the deceased. And, increasingly, a narrative of the life was inserted in the sermon or appended to the printed version, sometimes even expanded to full book length.[4]

But the taste for sermons, such as it was, faded early in the eighteenth century. Sermons were sometimes revised into other forms of discourse, but as sermons they had lost their market share long before the novel became popular. Abraham Adams, a clergyman whose heart lies in an earlier age and whose awareness of the world is outdated as well, naively believes that the public yearns for his sermons, and his old ways collide with market reality when, on the road to London, he meets a bookseller who recognizes an anachronism when he sees one.

"Sermons [the bookseller tells Adams] are mere Drugs. The Trade is so vastly stocked with them, that really unless they come out with the Name of *Whitfield* or *Westley*, or some other such great Man, as a Bishop, or those sort of People, I don't care to touch, unless now it was a Sermon preached on the '30th of January,' or we could say in the Title Page, published at the *earnest request* of the Congregation, or the Inhabitants; but truly for a dry Piece of Sermons, I had rather be excused. . . ."[5]

Precisely when sermons fell out of favor with booksellers is hard to say, but sales (and ultimately popular tastes) seem to have been responsible.[6] Perhaps our inherited sense of earlier popularity is inflated, but their diminished importance derives from shifts within the didactic context rather than from a steep decline of religiosity or a swelling of a secular spirit. Earlier sermons had represented a specialized taste at best. Why they had not been a more genuinely popular form of art invites speculation, especially because some of the best minds and best-educated figures of every generation since the time of Henry VIII had entered the pulpit, and "preaching the Word" was a proud English tradition. Perhaps they remained too narrowly conventional and formulaic. Perhaps theological issues in a time when religion itself was beleaguered came to be too arcane for most preachers and the shift to ethical issues did not suit the tradition. Perhaps their peculiar mix of the written and the oral kept talents from reaching the crucial edge. Or it may be that not enough people—hearers or preachers, readers or writers—took sermons seriously enough, or that weekly familiarity bred content with the merely satisfactory. Whatever the reason, except for a few men and a few occasions, little of artistic merit or intellectual impact came from sermons between the days of Lancelot Andrews and the mid-eighteenth century when Methodism gave old forms new improvisational life. But the fact that sermons were moribund does not mean that nothing good came from the clergy or that all religious discourse was in decline. Sermons sometimes became transformed to something more vital, and divines whose homiletic prose is slow, uninspired, and expectable found vital voices (and substantial audiences) in other forms.

I I

MANY forms of didactic discourse prospered:

—theological treatises which, although usually addressed to other clergymen, theologians, or philosophers, often argued points of practical divinity and moral obligation as well as creed;
   —biblical commentaries, sometimes on individual passages or even single verses, sometimes on larger units or the entire Bible;
   —meditations of both the traditional and occasional kinds;
   —devotional manuals for family prayers and closet duties;
   —interpretive, usually cautionary, discussions of current events;
   —catechisms, sometimes formal, sometimes improvised;

—retellings of old stories (Bible stories, bits of classical lore, fables, and traditional tales) with a pointed moral;

—collections of anecdotes about mercies, judgments, and other "interpositions" of providence;

—spiritual biographies and recountings of significant moments in the life of a particular individual;

—diatribes against current manners and morals;

—exhortations to good conduct and a daily walking with God.

Emphases vary widely, as do quality, length, and format, but the several kinds share a hortatory spirit, intense zeal, and intrusive concern for regulated behavior. They differ in their views of what proper conduct consists in, some of them adamant in their attacks on swearing, drinking, gaming, sabbath breaking, and even the playing of traditional country games or the telling of old stories, while others tolerate old ways and loutish behavior and train their guns on serious debauchery. But they agree in a basic worry about contemporary tendencies to ignore higher principles and indulge individual appetites. And they share a view that the times have become luxurious, indulgent, and precarious for anyone trying to lead a life of righteousness.

This large body of "popular" material, written from various religious, political, and social perspectives, critically examines contemporary life in much the same spirit as do belletristic works like *Absolom and Achitophel, The Rape of the Lock, Gulliver's Travels, The Beggar's Opera, The Dunciad* and *Moral Essays,* the essays of Addison and Steele, or the plays of Etherege, Congreve, Vanbrugh, Lillo, and Fielding. The quality of criticism in popular tracts seldom matches that of Swift or Johnson, but the concerns and attitudes are surprisingly similar. Contemporary behavior, however evaluated, fails to measure up, and modern life gets more censure than pity. The ethos that sometimes troubles modern readers in literary works is often, in these miscellaneous didactic materials, extended, intensified, and rendered shrill and harsh. Most of these texts are not themselves very entertaining, and many make no attempt to "delight" or to court posterity, but together they show the extent of contemporary concern and suggest the rhetorical climate from which the novel emerged.

By far the most popular of the identifiable "kinds" in all the didactic para-literature of the time—and the closest in spirit to the novel—is the Guide. Guides address all sorts of situations and circumstances; some are provided for particular occupations and conditions of life, others intended for certain age groups, still others written to direct conduct relative to a particular problem, occurrence, or event. Many Guides offer practical instruction in manual arts, the procedures of a particular craft, or the demands of a certain discipline. The social history of eighteenth-century London is, in fact, well preserved in the treatises on cookery, conversation, ciphering, writing letters, dancing, playing games, keeping a household, and performing the duties of a trade, for most of them plainly state social expectation while implying which aberrations are the most popular. The proliferation of such treatises argues the existence of many youths who felt themselves cut adrift from the traditional systems of advice that had treasured the passing on of family habits and secrets from generation to generation. Here is graphic evidence that new practical needs were arising in a culture beset by previously unforeseen problems and populated by people who lacked the resources of traditional lore and crafts that had been passed from generation to generation. Print culture took over functions that the oral culture could no longer handle, becoming a vehicle for social change as well as a measure of it.

Among these practical Guides were some few whose devotion to the know-how of a particular craft or procedure is total and uninterrupted, sponsored by little or no religious or ethical intention.[7] They are didactic only in a literal and technical sense: they offer instruction, mechanical guidance, and practical information that tries to seem ethically neutral in the way that *The Joy of Cooking* or Drs. Spock and Ruth have done more recently. Such practical Guides are not ideologically innocent, but they try to seem so. Most didactic materials were informed by a strong, obvious moral zeal and a desire to influence conduct directly. Even those that address questions of a morally neutral art, craft, or activity often begin or conclude (if they are not infused throughout) with moral advice that is more than an afterthought. *The Whole Duty of a Woman: Or, an infallible Guide to the Fair Sex* (1737), for example, focuses its 694 pages primarily on how to choose, prepare, and serve food, but the first quarter of the book is concerned with such topics as "Of Religion," "Of Meekness," and "The Duty of Virgins."[8] Most didactic treatises in fact subordinate information to the hortatory guidance which is the central thrust of the work. Richard Steele's *The Trades-man's Calling* (1684), for example, or Defoe's two-volume *The Complete English Tradesman* (1726–27), provide broad advice about the human aspects of being a tradesman, and, although they contain facts and "professional" advice, their focus is more ethical than pragmatic.

Steele's title page defines his treatise as "A Discourse concerning the Nature, Necessity, Choice, &c. of a *Calling* in General: And Directions for the right Managing of the *Tradesman's Calling* in Particular." His "present *Endeavour*," says Steele, is "only to guide the honest-minded Tradesman in the right way to Heaven" (fol. A2); his first four chapters explain in detail the nature of a calling and distinguish one's "spiritual calling" from the "temporal calling," which involves secular employment and the way to make a livelihood. Later, Steele offers more specific advice on topics like "Prudence or Discretion," "Diligence," "Justice," "Truth or Veracity," "Contentedness," and "Religiousness, or true Piety and God-liness," providing examples and investigating cases that illustrate partic-ular conflicts.

Defoe's volumes two generations later show how much more compli-cated the concerns of a London tradesman had become. In his aim to be "complete," Defoe provides 921 pages of detailed advice, including dis-cussions of such matters as "Engrossing" and "Underselling" and adding elaborate tables of information about manufactures and available min-erals. But for all its factuality and practicality, Defoe's advice is seldom value-free, and a major part of his concern is to guide tradesmen ethically so that they will lead respectable lives and trade as a "profession" will improve its reputation. Defoe was capable of equivocal reasoning about practical / ethical matters, and not all of his contemporaries would have approved his resolutions of moral issues, but a major aim here is to influ-ence tradesmen morally and religiously as well as in economic and prac-tical matters. His guide is more "secular" in spirit than Steele's—and the 1720s are generally less religious than the 1680s—but the difference is subtle, and both these Guides for trade are deeply and pervasively didac-tic. Together they suggest how Guides and other didactic literature of the late seventeenth and early eighteenth century were changing and yet were basically staying the same.

In his introductory remarks to The Husbandmans Calling (1665), Steele emphasizes that much of his advice is transferable from one calling to another—"applicable to every good Christian"—but, he adds, "it were to be wished, that the like particular Tracts were written about other Callings" (fol. [a8]).[9] Guides for many "callings"—soldiers, seamen, hus-bandmen, weavers, tavernkeepers, servants, schoolmasters—were in fact printed, and the competition was fierce for the attention of some groups. By 1705 nearly a dozen titles, by at least seven different authors, sought to guide those in a single occupation—seamen—in their proper spiritual duties, and many of these Guides had gone into several editions.[10] Some professional didacticists, most of them clergymen who adapted sermons to practical prose and everyday occasions, developed a subspecialty in Guide writing for the various callings. Josiah Woodward, for example, wrote for both soldiers and sailors, and John Flavell for sailors and hus-bandmen. The typical Guide was packaged for easy carrying; it was usu-ally a small volume about 3 inches by 5, but many were thick—two to three hundred pages long. They often contained, after long, anxious exhortations to virtue and celebrations of the calling itself, suggestions

for prayers and daily devotions; and many were written in highly metaphorical styles, the metaphors being suggested by the nature of the specific calling. Many show themselves steeped in the new theory of
Occasional Meditation popularized by Boyle. In, for example, *The Soldier's Monitor, being Serious Advice to Soldiers, to Behave themselves with a
just Regard to Religion and true Manhood* (1705), Woodward directs soldiers to

> accustom your mind to consider spiritually and religiously the ordinary Acci-
> dents that fall out in the Course of your Life, which will be particularly useful
> to you in your way of Life, because you have not such Advantage of *publick
> Sermons* as some others enjoy, and because your *Military Profession*, taking it
> in a spiritual Sense, is the very Business of a Christian. . . . It will therefore
> be easie, and even natural to you, when you accustom your self to think of
> spiritual Things, to improve the ordinary Passages of a Soldier's Life to the
> Advantage of your *Spiritual Warfare*. (pp. 33–34),

*The Husband-man's Manual: Directing Him how to Improve The Several
Actions of His Calling . . . To the Glory of God* (probably by Edward
Welchman, 1694) offers many Boyle-like practical meditations; and it
includes inspirational infusions (which it calls "ejaculations") at the end
of most meditations, as if readers were expected to habituate meditative
practice so naturally as to make their articulations spontaneous overflow-
ings of metaphor. These ejaculations, says the author, "I would have you
put up to God, in the midst of your Employment" (Dedication, 1706 ed.,
fol. A2v), and he includes headings on Plowing, Sowing, Weeding,
Reaping, Winnowing, "Setting forth of Tythe," and "Going home from
Work." The meditations are typically plain and homespun. Here, for
example, is the way he begins to meditate on Mowing: "In this Meadow
here, how doth the Grass stand before me, some Old and withering,
some Young and blooming mixt together! Both must fall from the same
Stroke of my Scythe. . . ." (1706, p. 13).[11] The Guides for callings were
reprinted again and again. *The Soldier's Monitor* had reached a seventh
edition by 1776; *The Seaman's Monitor* a seventh edition by 1767 and a
seventeenth by 1806; *The Husband-man's Manual* had reached a tenth
edition by 1747 and a twenty-third by 1811.[12]

Sometimes sermons preached on some occasion to representatives of
a particular calling were printed as an extension of the Guide tradition.
Philip Stubbs's *God's Dominion over the Seas* was, for example, originally
a "Sermon Preached at Long-Reach . . . on board Her Majesty's Capital
Ship The Royal Sovereign," and besides exhortations to piety it includes
arguments for God's continuing providential control, "His Soveraignty

over the *great Waters,"* (p. 18).[13] Guides for particular callings (Richard Lucas's *The Duty of Servants* [3rd ed., 1710], for example) may sometimes have been designed to be read to those for whom they were directed, for they contain advice to superiors as well, but the evidence that Guides achieved a mass distribution suggests that they were circulated directly to menial laborers and probably read by many of them with little difficulty. Thomas Negus's *The Publick-House-keeper's Monitor: Being a Serious Admonition to the Masters and Mistresses of Those, commonly called Publick-Houses, Of what Kind or Denomination soever* (3rd ed., 1730), for example, seems to have been intended to be distributed wholesale to anyone connected with innkeeping; it was priced in 1769 (in a new, unnumbered edition) at "2½d. or 15s., a hundred" (title page), down from 3d. in 1730. Often even the most practical guidance was laced with admonitions about moral implications, and emphasis was placed on the kinds of impressions one made, the lower classes especially being advised to create the proper appearance under the assumption that appearance and reality would ultimately, if not always at first, merge. Here, for example, are two sets of directions from a late seventeenth-century treatise by John Shirley, *The Accomplished Ladies Rich Closet of Rarities: or the Ingenious Gentlewoman and Servant-Maids Delightfull Companion. Containing many Excellent Things for the Accomplishment of the Female Sex, after the exactest Manner and Method . . . To Which is added a Second Part, Containing Directions for the Guidance of a Young Gentlewoman as to her Behaviour and seemly Deportment* (1687):

> When you are at Church, let not your Eyes by any means wander, nor your Body move in an unseemly gesture; but in all things so behave your self, that you may be an example to others. If at any time you are exposed to Melancholy or discontent, pray to God to remove it; if to mirth, let it be harmless and innocent, avoiding leud sights, or hearing songs that may tend to corruption and debauchery. . . . (p. 184)

> . . . observe that you walk not carelessly or lightly, shouldering as it were your companions, nor strutting or jutting in a proud manner. Keep (in your walk) your Head steady, your Countenance not too much elevated, nor too much dejected. Keep your Arms likewise steady, and throw them not about as if you were flying. Let your Feet rather incline a little more inward than outward, least you be censured [as] Splay-footed, for by the motion of the Body the thoughts of the Mind may be discovered; as whether the party be of loose or proud behaviour, or humble and complacient. . . . Keep your Eyes, as we may call it, within compass; that is, let them not be too much fixed upon idle and vain objects, nor drawn away by unseemly sights: Roll them not about in a careless or lacivious [sic] manner; nor stare Men in the face as if you were looking Babies in their Eyes. (pp. 201–02)

I I I

HELPFUL as such advice may have been to some readers, Guides more often assumed a higher level of sophistication, describing problems and situations likely to confront a generality of readers. Most Guides were in fact addressed not to readers in particular occupational groups but to broad categories of readers thought to be in need of knowledge of the world and advice about how to live appropriately within it. Some guides show a distinct sectarian bias, and attitudes toward controversial pastimes such as playgoing, attending masquerades, and gambling vary considerably, depending on the economic and social as well as religious stance of the author. Readers could sort out rather quickly those Guides with which their own assumptions were most compatible. Certain sections—those on card playing, dancing, and how to spend sabbaths, for example—could usually be counted on to flag extreme positions, and most Guides had chapter titles and tables of contents that allowed readers a fast scan. But most Guides sought to cross lines—social, religious, and economic—and appeal to readers of all sorts. The name of a particular bookseller might tip knowing readers that a book was authored by someone of a certain religious background (Thomas Parkhurst, for example, was considered a Presbyterian bookseller), but every bookseller wanted best-sellers with wide appeal. A well-known Guide could carry a bookseller for years, despite a relatively low unit price. The most famous Guides far exceeded books of "entertainment" in status and popularity.[14]

Staples like *The Practise of Pietie* or *The Whole Duty of Man* were issued over the years by many different publishers, and the practice of congering[15] enabled several booksellers to share the profits from successful new books without opening texts to free enterprise or rampant piracy. Still, printers and editors played fast and loose with the texts; copyright laws were designed to protect the property of booksellers, not to serve authors or guarantee the integrity of texts. Honoring authorial intentions and preserving textual "purity" were not high priorities in the age generally, but even in these relaxed contexts of textual ownership the fluidity of texts of Guides stand out. They were not "letters." Popular didactic materials seemed to most readers and booksellers to belong in the public domain in an ethical sense, whatever legal restrictions might technically apply, and some of the most popular Guides appeared anonymously or under some disguise.[16] *The Whole Duty of Man*, for example, never bore the name of its author (and we still do not know for sure if Richard Allestree wrote it), and a host of works capitalized on its popularity by advertising themselves as "by the author of the Whole Duty of Man." Some likely were, some were not. Loose ownership of texts often meant that new editions added or subtracted at will, sometimes to update a Guide by addressing a new issue, sometimes to modify a particular text to the biases of a new editor or printer.

When the history of the Guide tradition is written, it will have to be by someone patient enough to collate texts carefully and sort among titles that vary and overlap wildly. Books that appear under the same title often differ considerably from edition to edition, and books with different titles sometimes have identical contents. And long passages—even whole sections—of one book are sometimes appropriated for another without malice, often without awareness of any oddness. An effective passage may appear in several places, and treatises sometimes take on new, trendier titles. Plagiarism really was, in Guide books, the sincerest form of flattery, and often—because it invoked familiarity—the most effective tool of rhetoric. To trace the mazey texts of this tradition would be to look in an altogether new way at social history; until that task is performed we will remain uncertain about crucial aspects of everyday conduct and changing behavioral attitudes.

I V

I USE the term "Guide" to describe this branch of didacticism because direction as a metaphor appears so frequently in the titles and is worked out so fully in the texts proper. The Christian's Daily Devotion (1704), for example, promises in its title to give "Directions How to Walk with God all the Day long," and many titles literalize the metaphor as a statement of the relationship between life on earth and life after death, as in The Plain Man's Guide to Heaven (by Richard Lucas, 1692), or The Christian Directed In His Race to Heaven (1700).[17] The old metaphor of life as a pilgrimage is not far from the surface in such books, and often the text is so metaphoric as to impinge on, or cross, the borders of allegory. Pilgrim's Progress (1678; Part II, 1684) is, among many other things, a Guide in a quite literal sense, and it existed in a historical context in which its central metaphor informed many titles that had a similar purpose. Benjamin Keach, a Baptist with a vivid sense of biblical metaphor and an ear for biblical echoes, repeatedly pursued both the pilgrimage metaphor (in The Travels of True Godliness, from the Beginning of the World, to this Present Day; In an apt and pleasant Allegory [1683; 9th ed., corr. 1726] and The Progress of Sin; or the Travels of Ungodliness [1684; 4th ed., corr. 1724]) and the closely related metaphor of Christian warfare (in War with the Devil [4th impression, 1676]).[18] Similar, although much more rambling and imperial in its ambitions, is *The Pilgrims Guide From the Cradle to his Death-bed: with His Glorious Passage from thence to the New-Jerusalem. Represented to the Life In a Delightful new Allegory, Wherein the Christian Traveller Is more fully and plainly Directed than yet he hath been by any in the Right and Nearest way to the Celestial Paradice,* published by John Dunton in 1684 and ascribed to his late father.[19] "[Y]ou may see (throughout the whole Allegory)," Dunton explains in his usual way of underscoring things his contemporaries quietly assumed,

> how that this present transitory Life is called a *Pilgrimage*, a *Travel* and a way, because it continually plieth to an end; For as they which are carried in *Coaches*, or sail in *Ships* do finish their *Voyage*, tho they sit still and sleep, even so every one of us, *albeit* we be still busied about other matters, and perceive not how the *course* of our *Life passeth away*, being sometimes at *Rest*, sometimes *at work*, sometimes *Idle*, and sometimes in *sports* and *recreations*, yet our life alwaies wasteth, and we in posting speed with *winged hast* [sic] towards our last end. (fol. A_{4v})

Earlier in the century, the pilgrimage metaphor lay behind nearly every work of practical divinity, and the language of Guides was resonant with seas, highways, travels, progresses, and walks. Two of the most popular early Guides—Arthur Dent's *The Plaine Mans Path-way to Heauen* (1601) and Lewis Bayly's *The Practise of Pietie Directing a Christian how to walke* (about 1610; the 2nd edition is dated 1612)[20]—suggest in their titles how basic the metaphor was for writers and readers, and both offer a vivid sense of space that needs to be negotiated through proper direction. Dent describes the world as "a sea of glasse . . . a gulfe of griefe . . . a vale of misery . . . a river of teares . . . a wildernesse of Wolves," and adds a dozen more metaphors of difficulty and torment. Other titles suggest just as plainly the sense of the world that leads to a spatial narrative like *Pilgrim's Progress*:

Timothies Taske: or A Christian Sea-card, guiding through the coastes (by Robert Mandevill, 1619);

The Way To The Celestiall Paradise (by Robert Whittell, 1620);

Some Generall Directions for a Comfortable Walking With God (by Robert Bolton, 1625);[21]

The Christians Daily VValk in holy Secvritie and Peace (by Henry Scudder, 6th ed., 1635; first published about 1625);

The Sovles Progresse To the Celestiall Canaan, or Heavenly Jervsalem (by John Welles, 1639);

Circumspect Walking: Describing the seuerall Rules, as so many seuerall Steps in the way of Wisedome (by Thomas Taylor, 1631).

As time wore on, the pilgrimage metaphor waned as a vivid expression of the travails of human life, not only because the sacramental view of the universe was breaking down but also because readers of Guides were increasingly urbanized and distanced from a sense that confrontations with nature—the sorts of difficulties readily allegorized by pilgrimage— were the central challenges to modern life. Increasingly, terms like "Guide" and "Directions" move away from their powerful figural past. But the metaphor still is visible in title after title, from the Restoration well into the eighteenth century:

Christian Directions, Shewing How to walk with God All the Day long (by Thomas Gouge, 1661);[22]

The Young Man's Guide, Through the Wilderness of this World to the Heavenly Canaan. Shewing him how to carry him self Christian-like in the whole course of his Life (by Thomas Gouge, 1670);

The Way of Good Men for Wise-Men To Walk in (by Charles Morton, 1681);

A Help to Holy Walking, or, A Guide to Glory. Containing Directions how to Worship God, and to Walk with him in the whole Course of our Lives. (by Edward Bury, 1675);

A Guide To Eternal Glory: or, Brief Directions to all Christians (by Thomas Wilcox, 1685; first published in 1676, under several titles this Guide had reached a 40th edition by 1732);

The Christian Race (by Richard Lucas, 1692);

The Pious Soul's Daily Exercise: or, a Guide to Eternal Glory . . . [for] the True Christian in his Passage through this Vale of Tears to the Heavenly Canaan (by G. Liddell, 6th ed., 1700);

The Heavenly Foot-man: or, A Description of the Man that gets to Heaven . . . With the Way he Runs in, the Marks he Goes by: Also some Directions, how to Run, so as to Obtain (by John Bunyan, 1698);

A Sure Guide to Heaven (1702);

The Christian's Way to Heaven (2nd ed., 1703).

The prose of the Guides tries to revivify the metaphor as they speak of life as a journey and thus define their writerly tasks as consisting of proper directions. "We are," says Nathanael Wyles in 1699, "all of us but Pilgrims and Travellers here."[23] Adds Matthew Henry in 1714: "The Practice of Religion, is often, in Scripture, spoken of as a *Way*; and our walking in that *Way*. . . . The School-men commonly call Christians in this World *Viatores, Travellers*; when they come to Heaven they are *Comprehensores*; They have then *attained*, are at Home; Here they are in their *Journey*, there at their *Journey's* End. . . ."[24] Richard Baxter describes his task, in his *Christian Directory* (1673), as to provide *"plain Directions"* and to "Guide [readers] safely in their *Walk with God*, to Life Eternal" (p.

2), and Thomas Gouge, in *Christian Directions* (1661), describes his intention as to "draw up some practical Directions for your better Guidance in the way to Heaven" (1664 ed., fol. A2). Adds Timothy Cruso in his *God the Guide of Youth* (1695): "This is the proper work of a Guide, to *direct* the Ignorant Traveller in a strange Land, and unknown Countrey. Such is our Case during the *time of our Sojourning* here in this World; and it is the work of the *only wise God*, to *guide our feet, and direct our steps*" (pp. 12–13).

By the end of the seventeenth century, the metaphor had far less force as natural description of life's travels or travails (the two words had once been one, and Guide writers traditionally made much of the implications), but didacticists enforced the metaphor of guidance and direction as something the written word could provide. The verbal guidance of books began to replace the sense that exemplary personal guidance—of parents, pastors, or patriarchs—was necessary to proper conduct. By the beginning of the eighteenth century, the metaphor of the book as guide— a verbal map to space and time—had become fully established, words in print having replaced human leadership as the model for appropriate walking with God. It is sometimes hard to be sure in individual titles (such as John Rawlet's *The Christian Monitor, Containing an Earnest Exhortation to an Holy Life. With some Directions in order thereto,* 1686) whether authors and readers are still aware of the old spatial implications, but even in language that had become dead to the history of the metaphor, the sense of pulling, pushing, or drawing readers along remains powerful.

Like many other guides, *The Christian Monitor* was often reprinted (the 1701 edition is labeled the 27th) well into the eighteenth century in a cheap and portable form. Its 1728 version was a typical *vade mecum* in 24°, about 2½ inches by 4¼ inches in size and 144 pages in length, and it probably sold for even less than the price of the first edition, 3d. Neither elegant nor eloquent, it still has a lively style and maintains an intense tone and relentless concern with keeping the reader's attention on ethical issues. Sometimes, it is dramatic and vivid, as when describing "the sad Effects of Whoredom, which is commonly followed with Poverty and Disgrace, and many times with a filthy loathsome Disease, which makes Men rot above Ground" (p. 44, 1728 ed.), but most of its effect derives from its fervent, never-looking-to-the-right-or-left manner rather than from especially well presented examples or artful narrative.

Most of the Guides are directed specifically at young people in the formative stages of life, when they are still under their parents' guidance and jurisdiction. Most have lengthy sections on the crucial choices of life and give detailed advice about choosing careers and marriage partners. Their discussion of routine daily matters and of traditional ethical concerns is aimed at those who lack experience in making decisions for themselves. Guides were plentiful and evidently popular: there were hundreds of titles, hundreds of thousands of volumes, and they circulated through all social strata. They were easy enough to read, cheap enough to buy, and portable enough to be convenient companions for anyone who wanted a physical artifact of piety or a verbal prompter to virtue.[25]

V

MANY Guides for Youth grow out of documents originally given to a particular person (often a son or daughter) about to reach a certain age or embark on an independent course of life. The best known of these, the Marquis of Halifax's *The Lady's New-Years Gift: or, Advice to a Daughter* (1688), is not typical; it is too elegant, too self-consciously "literary," too anxious to extend into new times older aristocratic ideals.[26] But "lesser" writings, not so retentive about traditional languages and old social values, also transcend their occasions and reach for a broader social range. *A Grand-Father's Advice* (by Philip Taverner, 1681) claims on its title page to be "Directed in special to his Children" and the dedication mentions three grandchildren by name. But the title page adds: "And published for Common Good." Such a claim of particularity with general application is typical, and title pages often make both origin and aim clear, as in *The Young Gentleman's New-Year's Gift: or, Advice to a Nephew . . . Together with Some Maxims of general Use in the Conduct of his Life* (1729), or *Advice To an Only Child: or, Excellent Council to all Young Persons* (by Oliver Heywood, 1693). Whatever their origins, most Guides for Youth are directed to sons, daughters, or young people generally of whatever class or social background, and they try for a definition of issues and level of discourse that readers of any capacity or station could appreciate.[27]

Halifax and some few others aim, however, more narrowly for traditional readers, and in these more belletristic essays one can still see remnants of the old courtesy books. Literary history has traditionally felt more comfortable with the likes of Halifax, who addresses the young with detached (though somewhat patronizing) humor.[28] His graceful style and cutting wit stand apart from the standard popular Guides, and his concerns would be irrelevant to servant girls. The attitudes in his *Advice to a Daughter* (in later editions this subtitle was usually used as title) betray at every turn its aristocratic assumptions, from patriarchal expectations about female roles to gentle tolerance of treasured men-will-be-men vices.

Still, Halifax tries to generalize the bulk of his advice. He does best on issues such as those of age and habit, where problems transcend social and cultural lines, but he never gets past the gender biases set by his limited intention and by his even more limited attitudes:

> . . . let every seven years make some alteration in you towards the [Graver] side, and not be like the Girls of Fifty, who resolve to be always Young, what ever Time with his Iron Teeth hath determined to the contrary; unnatural things carry a deformity in them [never to be] Disguised; the Liveliness of Youth in a riper Age, looketh like [an old] patch upon [a new] Gown; so that a Gay Matron, a chearful old Fool may be reasonably put into the List of the Tamer kind of Monsters. There is a certain Creature call'd a Grave Hobby-Horse, a kind of she [Numps], that pretendeth to be pulled to a Play, and must needs go to Bartholomew Fair . . . ; such an old Butterfly is of all Creatures the most ridiculous. . . . (pp. 114–15)[29]

Such a passage suggests how close Halifax sometimes comes in Advice to a Daughter to the kind of character writing for which he was to become famous, and although Guides rely primarily on straight discursive and hortatory prose, they often incorporate brief narratives as examples or manage in some other way to present a resonant and sophisticated sense of what it is like to be a full human being—usually by dramatizing the complications of social and contextual choice. But those treatises (like Halifax's) that seem most "literary" and urbane were not necessarily more effective, and few of them were as popular as straightforward, buttonholing examples of fevered fret. Less artful hortatory prose—the kind of writing that may strike us as nagging and shrill—seems more attuned to readers' expectations and desires. Even the best of the Guides designed for readers with better pedigrees seem to succeed, like their more leveling counterparts, because of their driving energy, frank engagement with contemporary issues, and vigorous style rather than because they reflect wider reading and awareness of the older traditions of courtesy books and guides for princes and courtiers. The paler Guides may be easier to read today because they offend less our literary sensibilities or our wish for a more disengaged tone. But their calmer voice and lessened sense of urgency may well have made them less effective than their cruder counterparts, just as polite literature had more trouble than popular literature in interesting a public weary—or ignorant—of the old ways and anxious for a little novelty and a lot of vigor.

Among Guides for selected audiences, the best is William Darrell's A Gentleman Instructed in the Conduct of a Virtuous and Happy Life. Written for the Instruction of a Young Nobleman (1704), to which "A Word to the

Ladies" was appended in the fifth (1713) and later editions.[30] Darrell casts his treatise as a dialogue between "Neander" and "Eusebius," and he anticipates some of the strategies of dialogue that William Law used effectively later, but his greatest strengths lie in the energy of his style and his vivid focus on contemporary mores. His vigorous condemnation of those who brag about sexual conquests suggests how awareness of contemporary behavior and stern righteousness interact:

> . . . can Fancy frame any thing more disingenuous, more diabolical, than first to wheedle a Lady out of her Innocence, and than [sic] to prostitute her Honour to the wanton Caprice of a Club of Reprobates, who will not fail to discover her shame at the next Rendezvous, and to multiply their own Crimes by lampooning hers. . . . I know in the next World God will call to a most severe Account these Christian *Canibals* that welter in Blood, and (like famish'd Wolves) worry their own Species. But I would have the Wisdom of the Nation make some Provision against such brutal, such inhumane Attempts. Why shall a High-way-man hang for taking my Purse, and a Rake go unpunish'd, who invades my Honour? Why shall a Rape upon a Woman's Body be revenged with a Haulter, and violence upon her Fame be rewarded with Applause?[31]

In *The Ladies Calling* (1673) and *The Gentlemans Calling* (1660)—both probably by Richard Allestree—there is a more even sense of structural control and a firmer sense of an authorial self at peace with himself and totally at ease with his rigorous moral and religious commitment, and those two guides written for Everyreader were reprinted frequently. According to Wing, *Gentlemans Calling* had reached an eighteenth edition by 1696 and *Ladies Calling* an eighth by 1700.[32] It would be too simple to say that treatises addressed to the lowest common denominator were always the best. But those who felt themselves a part of the older social, cultural, and literary traditions—those with university educations or a traditional reading program and a classical sense of rhetoric and eloquence—did increasingly find themselves ill-equipped to deal with modern audiences. The animosity that Pope, for example, expresses so frequently toward the expanded audiences of print has a counterpart in the "para-literary" didactic treatises as well. The world of writing was changing radically on all levels, and new strategies provided by new writers had begun to move into a vacuum that developed when tradition began to lose its hold on audiences.[33]

In the titles I have mentioned, one can readily see the awareness of female readers, and by the turn of the century the addresses to young women were almost equal in quantity to those to young men. But Guide writers were not sexual levelers, and, as the Darrell passage above suggests, Guides tended to be protective about women, often patronizing their feelings and needs, sometimes tossing a chivalrous cloak over dangers to their virtue so that the pens of men could waft them across the puddles of unrighteousness. Sometimes Guides in effect cordoned off women from the rougher and more "real" world of problems and human confrontations reserved for men. Most of the accepted conclusions of social history about the sexism of the age, not just traditional and aristocratic but modern and democratic, are confirmed in popular didactic writing. Women in Guides are often advised that their imaginations can become overheated if they read romances (the source of Swift's joke about maids of honor in Lilliput), or they are warned to guard against a wandering fancy while employed at the needle, while men may grapple with the choice of a calling and the ethics of everyday commerce and political intrigue. Still, it is important to see the growth of interest in women's "improvement" by the late seventeenth century (whatever its origins or biases) and to note the developing assumption that women readers are responsible for themselves. The expanded ethical interest in women is part of the deepening concern for individual choices that, moralists knew well, had serious impact on a culture changing as fast as theirs was.

V I

CLOSELY related to Guides for Youth are Guides for Families, sometimes designed for parents, sometimes divided into sections for different family members, and sometimes apparently intended for joint use, perhaps during family prayers.[34] Many such Guides consist of, or contain, sets of catechetical questions obviously meant to be used by parents and older children for the drilling of the young. William Burkitt's Family Instruction: or, Principles of Religion Necessary to be known by Family Governors, And needful to be Taught their Children and Servants (1704) is such a Guide, and, as its title suggests, its thrust is doctrinal rather than ethical. Similar is the anonymous A Short and Plain Account of Religion, for the Instruction of Families, by being often read in them (2nd ed., 1703). Whether "family religion"—morning and evening prayers, catechetical exercises, and communal readings from the Bible or a "godly book"—was actually deteriorating is uncertain. What evidence we have, most of it based on the impressions of those who were nostalgic for more pious times, suggests that traditional religious practices were increasingly neglected, especially among mobile and urban families. Certainly increasing was the likelihood of late adolescents leaving rural families to become apprentices or otherwise seek their fortune in the city, where they lived alone or with someone from different traditions and patterns of life. Significant changes in national and social patterns meant serious alterations in the routines of daily life, and observers were full of concern that "family religion"—which they saw as not only the symbol but also the fountainhead of personal ethical conduct—was in danger. "One of the greatest causes of that Irreligion and Wickedness that so much abounds amongst us," according to the anonymous *Family-Religion: or, the Exercise of Prayer and Devotion in Private Families* (2nd ed., 1690), "is the neglect of Prayer, and all Worship of God in private Families" (p. 1). The new breed of apostates, the treatise goes on, "give themselves up to a worldly and sinful, and meer brutish course of Life, living as Beasts that only eat and sleep together, and making no other use of their Houses, but as Stables and Styes to feed and lye in. . . ." (p. 2).

Family-Religion is still, however, a fairly traditional Guide for Families, offering a short hortatory introduction and a collection of prayers for various uses. But in the next decade and a half, when the Williamite concerns about a reformation of manners had their most powerful impact, worry about the decay of family religion became heated.[35] Sermons were preached and published (*A Church in the House. A Sermon Concerning Family-Religon* [1704], for example), and exhortations repeatedly issued:

—*The True Interest of Families*, by James Kirkwood, 1690;

—*An Earnest Call to Family-Catechising* (1693);

—*A Discourse of Family-Worship* (by George Hamond, 1694);

—*An Earnest Exhortation to House-Keepers, To set up the Worship of God in their Families* (by Robert Nelson, 2nd ed., 1702);

—*Advice to Parents; or, Rules For the Education of Children* (by John Mortimer, 1704);

—*Family-Devotion: or, A Plain Exhortation to Morning and Evening Prayer in Families* (by Edmund Gibson, 1705; by 1750 it had reached an 18th edition);

—*The Necessary Duty of Family-Prayer and the Deplorable Condition of Prayerless Families Consider'd* (by Josiah Woodward, 2nd ed., 1704; 11th ed., 1768).

Typical of their advice is Gibson's direction: ". . . the only sure way to keep up daily Devotion, is, for every Family to fix and appoint for that end, the two most convenient parts of the day, namely, Morning and Evening. For except the times of doing it be fixt and certain, the Duty will either be wholly neglected and forgotten, or at best, there will be many Pretences to omit it" (p. 12). Didacticists kept up pressure of this sort for a long time,[36] and Guides addressed to issues about roles, duties, and habits—defining the duties of different stations and exhorting families to maintain their religious function in the communities—stay popular throughout the century. Later, though, there was less concern with "family religion" as such, perhaps because the push of the early eighteenth century had some effect, more likely because it was seen as a lost cause, as families became fragmented geographically and as daily routines became more complicated even for individuals in families that pursued traditional habits and remained intact.

Daniel Defoe's three *Family Instructor* volumes (1715, 1718, and 1727) are now the most famous of the Guides for Families. They were often reprinted well into the nineteenth century, and despite their length and complexity were always popular. Perhaps they do suggest Defoe's growing interest in narrative fiction (the reason they are remembered now when similar titles lie covered with dust), for they show a mind intrigued by dialogue and story line in the service of social ideas and cultural analysis. But Defoe is not the only writer to become fascinated by examples. It is misleading to describe, as some Richardson critics do, a writer's interest in the "lives" of characters as betraying a secret commitment to "art" instead of to "teaching," "morality," or "religion," and no easy switch explains the rising contemporary interest in narrative, but examples do come to enrich texts, often in complex and mysterious ways. Richard Baxter's *The Poor Man's Family Book* (1674) includes dialogue rather like Defoe's, and so does Darrell's *A Gentleman Instructed*. The character creation, the dialogue, the mini-scenes, and the attempt to balance ethical instruction with pleasure suggest a climate growingly hospitable to new modes of persuasion and a widening circle of narrative and dramatic interest among traditional didacticists.

It is easy to be simplistic about "changing intentions" betrayed by such features and find them predictive of growing interest in stories "for their own sake." But such an explanation, sometimes offered to rescue novelists from the shadows of didacticism, does not begin to suggest how complex Guides themselves sometimes could be within their own narrow aims, nor does it provide an adequate idea of how forms and aims interact across formal, generic, and audience lines. The inclusion of lengthy examples and segments that are narrative in manner and fictitious in origin does broaden the contexts of reciprocity, and ultimately these passages may make it easier for readers to accept full-length fictional narratives. But they are not experiments toward independent narrative; they exist, just as do early novels, within a governing ideological intention that subordinates fable—however interesting—to moral. It is not that there is an evolution toward independence on the part of narrative that had begun as ethical illustration, but rather an increasing anxiety that moral efficacy had to be engineered in ways that used every possible vehicle. Such updated didacticism reflects the desires of both readers and writers to find something beyond precept and discourse, something that acknowledged and challenged the full complexity and resonance of modern life. Stories "for their own sake" purely—however entertainingly told and however gripping in their basic narrative power—did not exist in Guide books or even in most early novels. It was a long time before novels got far enough from their roots to tell stories "for their own sake"— although the sake they told them for might be ever so complex in its aims.

Some Guides for Families are defensive and embarrassingly intimate. *Parents Groans over their Wicked Children* (by Edward Lawrence, 1681), for example, seems designed to justify the author's failures with his own offspring and concludes that having wicked children "is a greater calamity than to be without Children . . . a greater misery than to have diseased, or deformed children . . . is more grievous than the death of children" (pp. 33–34). Some analyze and systematize the duties in various relationships and circumstances, and all emphasize the crucial role of parents because of the malleability of the young. "It has been always reckoned by the best and wisest men," says *The True Interest of Families*, "a thing absolutely necessary towards a Reformation in the World, to begin with the Instruction and right Education of Children; those of elder Years being ordinarily so rooted and hardned in their sinful habits, that, for the most part, there's very little can be done to reform them, and make them better (p. 1). Clement Ellis in *The Duty of Parents, and Masters of Families* (1734) adds that the

> *early* educating of children in Goodness, prevents the Devil and all his wicked Instruments; and the Seeds of Virtue and Goodness get good Rooting in the Heart, before he can have Opportunity to sow his Tares; so that the good Corn grows strong, and will not so easily be choaked with them. We have by this *early* Care well altered the Nature of the Soil, prepared a good and honest Heart, wherein good Things henceforward will even naturally grow, but other Things are not so agreeable now to it, and will not easily take Root in it. We give them thus the Start of the Devil, the World, and the Flesh, and prevent a great many Troubles and Difficulties. . . . (p. 53)

The attention to families represents social nostalgia as much as ethical need, but it is no less sincere for being largely irrelevant to urban émigrés.

VII

IT was not only educational theorists like Locke, "reformers" like Defoe, or proto-feminists like Astell who insisted that women's education was being sadly neglected or that women were an under-utilized human resource. Voices deploring the poor education of women were everywhere; even reactionary social critics and Tory satirists were, for their own reasons, bitterly critical of what society expected of women and of the waste of female talents.[37] The most insistent words came from Dissenters who felt strongest about access to the Bible for all and who therefore emphasized the necessity of reading, but many joined in the chorus. "Nothing is more neglected than the Education of Daughters," begins *The Education of Young Gentlewomen*, the 1699 Englishing of Fénelon. The 1713 "Ladies' Supplement" to Darrell's *A Gentleman Instructed*, after lamenting the conduct of women, assigns the cause: "ill Education: This is the fatal Source of their Misery, the true Origin of all their Failings. Young Ladies are brought up as if God created 'em meerly for a Seraglio, and that their only Business was to charm a brutish *Sultan:* One would think they had no Souls, there is such a care taken of their Bodies" (p. xxxiii). "You may season Work with Reading," he adds, "for though Women should not pretend to commence Doctors, yet I would not have 'em forswear Knowledge, nor make a vow of Stupidity" (pp. lxvi–lxvii).

Not pretend to commence Doctors . . . nor make a Vow of Stupidity. Darrell's careful position, ridiculing those who want to keep women barefoot and pregnant but also unwilling to break cleanly with traditional gender roles, is typical of the time and represents the culture's ambivalence in insisting that everyone must read but then circumscribing what new readers, women more than men, dared read. But some Guides did go farther. An early one, William Ramesey's *Gentlemans Companion* (1672), takes quite a strong stand, though its point of view is decidedly male: "I am not of their Opinion who think a Woman wise enough, if she can keep herself out of the Rain, and can distinguish between her Husbands Hat and his Cloak; concluding it never a good World since they could either Write or Reade. For *Women have souls* as well as we, and differ nothing from us but in the odd Instruments of Generation" (p. 9). The rationale for the education of women is usually the pragmatic one articulated by the anonymous *An Essay on Modern Education* (1747):

> Since thus equal is the Power of Woman, and so principal is her Concern in the Instruction of Youth, ought we not to shew an equal Regard to their Education? Ought we to think it sufficient to teach them to read in their Mother-Tongue only, and not instruct them in the thorough Knowledge of what will be of highest Service both to themselves and Children? . . . [T]hat they should be even better versed in the Knowledge of human Nature, and the Affections of the Mind, than Men, I believe is obvious to all, since they must of Necessity have the Management of the tenderest Ages. . . . (p. 41)

Insistence on the importance of female education is not, of course, the same as advocating equality or even equity, and the utilitarian cast of the religious argument is apt to put off modern readers. But, modern assumptions aside, the rhetoric is often patronizing and the logic demeaning. The authors were, almost without exception, men who meant to be patriarchs, and their attitudes, though perhaps sincerely "religious," were frequently self-serving. Still, the insistence itself is stronger than historians have usually said, and the quality and range of the education recommended for women is somewhat surprising. Included are, to be sure, assumptions about arts and crafts associated with motherhood and traditional gender roles, and there is strong emphasis on nurturing and "soft" human qualities. But much of the advice, especially among Dissenters, those with "Puritan" social attitudes, and (later) Methodists, transcends the needle, cosmetic affectations, and social graces. It involves reading (often in several languages), knowledge of history and geography, and (usually) mathematics.[38] Practice was often far below expressed ideals, and the ideals themselves are seldom if ever egalitarian. But the concern for women's education in these years is deeper and more detailed than older historians—the ones still inexplicably used by literary historians who should know better—recognized.[39] And that concern seems to have permeated all segments of the society well before Locke. Comments like the 1747 one I have quoted above are often seen as reflections of Locke, and sometimes they may be, but Locke was in fact uttering mostly commonplaces of educational "theory" (if one may so dignify the doctrines and assumptions in Guide books). Locke was as often imitator as imitated. And the practical Guides may have been, cumulatively at least, more influential than Locke. Intellectuals, especially academic intellectuals, like to think that other intellectuals hold and disperse the power, but in early eighteenth-century England popular thinking was sometimes as advanced ethically as that of philosophers and self-appointed social analysts—sometimes more so. Those who brought the Smithfield Muses to the ear of kings often transmitted ideas as well as taste.

By the second decade of the eighteenth century, women seem to be disproportionately the addressees in Guides for Youth—just as they come to be in novels—probably the result of a strong cultural sense of their excessive vulnerability. But if the exaggerated attention is, in intention, demeaning, in effect it provides a place, however simplistic and inadequate, for the lives of women—a place in writing.[40] Almost universally Guides assume that young women lead lives full of decisions and that they can and do read. One might imagine a popular literature designed for reading aloud to illiterates, but few didactic works—of any kind, for any audience—were so aimed. It is, in fact, amazing how seldom the question of literacy comes up as an issue except in works designed to instruct parents on the rearing of infants, where didacticists insist that all children must be taught to read at the earliest possible moment. Otherwise, the need for everyone to read is, from the mid-seventeenth century on, simply assumed.

The most common warning in Guides for Youth involves, in fact, the question of what will be read. Didacticists worry incessantly about the corruptibility of the young by bad books that turn their heads or overheat their imaginations. Worries about "novels, romances, and plays"—the phrase occurs so often as to be for all practical purposes a single term—are everywhere in didactic materials. Young women are regarded as especially subject to the influence of evil books or of "ill Company" (*The Ladies Calling*, 2nd pt., p. 7), and on the subject of choosing a mate the advice to women is typically more detailed and more cautionary, as if women have more to fear from their own desires. But much of the content of Guides for young women is similar to that in Guides for young men, and, in Guides addressed to both sexes, most admonitions apply equally. Translating the cultural protectiveness usually reserved for women to youth generally, Guide writers see all young people as needing all the help they can get. As *The Ladies Calling* puts it, seeming to worry about men as much as women: "youth is for the most part flexible, and easily warps into a crookedness. . . ." (2nd pt., p. 7).

Flexibility, crookedness, warping. Moralists could defend the hostility of such terms as justified by fear—fear of evil's potential to destroy innocence, not their own fear of change and being supplanted. Both views—theirs from the brink of presumed cultural crisis, ours from the perspective of generational changes absorbed in the process of history—need to be honored to get a proper sense of paradox in a culture about to represent itself in novels. Having frailty bear the name of man as well as woman—making all youth marginal instead of just femaleness, translating marginality into questions of age instead of gender—is a basic move in the culture and has an important, if at first indirect and ambiguous, effect on the species that was to become the main cultural vehicle. In earlier generations, before the Revolution, women had had a "place" in English society, the place that Halifax wanted them to reclaim, but now they do not know their place. They do not recognize it, understand it, or accept it. Sometimes the age expressed, as in Sprint and his followers, powerful anger that women dared try to carve out some new place of their own, and even in the most sympathetic and inclusive texts there is resistance to any place at all. Women in the Restoration have no sense of place, and lost place seemed to threaten identity altogether. Like Clarissa, whose mythic power derives more from the cultural crisis she

embodies than from any of the roles she consciously assumes, women in
the middle of the eighteenth century both find and lose themselves in
cramped spaces of oppression. As their traditional place in family, estate,
and culture becomes uncertain and they move into a tantalizingly promising world of apparent choice, they lose their inherited roles, relationships, estates, and identities in society and make a place in novels instead.

But even that new paper place, while a triumph of its kind, involves
a frustration, an ambiguity, and something of a delusion. For even when
women are central in early novels, they are central objects. When they
appear to be subjects, even when their subjectivity is featured as in *Clarissa,*
they turn out to be objects in disguise. Even their own authorship, when
it happens, brings only illusory authority, for women writers imperson-
ating men often hide in male anonymity or slip behind the coats of a Dr.
Burney or a Dr. Johnson. Or, like Manley, Barker, Aubin, or early Haywood, they present themselves in the male stereotypes of hapless whores
and pedestaled virgins. When men impersonate women there is often a
certain trying on of role, an experimentation with a possible identity, a
personation tried but not a road taken, a powerful "as if." Women writers, on the other hand, are more in a conscious position of cross-dressing,
knowing that they can project a role for a moment but not take on a real
identity.[41] None dare call the place women occupy in novels dominant,

but women quickly begin to dominate the writing as well as the reading
of novels.[42] From the first, novels project what is to be expected of women
in daily habits, in reading, and in values. That place had been outlined
in Guides and other didactic kinds before it was presumed, then extended
in novels.

It is not that Guides—for Youth, for Families, for Women—are especially "progressive."[43] Certainly they are not radical, and in one sense
they are bastions of the status quo or worse, for the place they offer
women is at best a place in the mind. But they articulate a culture that
is shifting, finding that women cannot be patronized back to the needle,
learning that literacy offers a power to knit fate in a new, more effective
and almost open way. The place in the cultural landscape that novels
share with Guides involves the recognition of changing roles—both of
individuals and of classes of individuals—and an announcement that
models for change involve the new vehicle of popular reading. It is a new
world in which—for better and worse—ideas, principles, and assumptions become more prominent and necessary to be sorted out, for the old
world of personal human interactions among people who know each other
is being replaced. Gone are not only the warmth and intimacy of that
world but the fuzziness and ambiguity that go with differences being
smoothed over by love, friendship, and personal sacrifice.

V I I I

IF the "place" of women in popular didactic materials suggests a larger cultural change that becomes reflected more obviously in novels, the place of the Guide in the didactic landscape similarly indicates cultural redefinition. The very fact of Guides suggests structural changes that make novels possible in the culture. In the old oral culture, written sets of instructions did of course exist. They functioned as extensions of advice provided by fathers, mothers, and other figures of authority and respect, but there was little need for spelling things out in detail and none for a wider, more generalized address to the public at large. People passed on crafts and lore, information moved from person to person. The context that led to the extensive production of Guides involves lost personal contact and radically changed institutions and situations. Whatever the triumphs they ultimately achieved, Guides begin in desperation and despair. They are a poor substitute for human exemplars and teachers, and the displacement of parental guidance to the impersonality of the public press makes for a vastly different set of human relationships in a radically different world. It is easy to get nostalgic about earlier times and old values—and plenty of people in Richardson's time and Austen's did it—but it was that very change that made novels not only possible but in some basic sense necessary.

CHAPTER ELEVEN

Didacticism:
The Contexts of Concern

■

AS both the most popular and most typical species of didactic literature, the Guide reflects social and behavioral issues most on the minds
of readers and writers just before the novel became the characteristic
expression of the cultural consciousness. Whatever their religious or social
cast, Guides nearly always attended to certain issues. Among those on
which there was continual emphasis are four that influence the directions
of the novel:

—warnings about idleness as a threat to both individual self-realiza-
tion and the integrity of the social fabric;

—concern about the ethical dangers in contemporary patterns of leisure, recreation, and play;

—celebrations of the power of paradigm and example, gathered into a
program to convert the magnetism of human guidance into effective rhetorical ways—through narrative, words, and print—of saving human beings
from their worst impulses; and

—insistence that continual self-examination gave individuals a means
of emotional and social, as well as spiritual, fulfillment.

All four issues bear crucially on the way novels shape themselves in
the early eighteenth century. In part, their relevance is thematic: all the
prohibitions and anxieties imposed from an adult world of lost opportunity and encroaching nothingness relate, though often ludicrously, to
concerns youths themselves feel at points of choice. Ideas, especially
cautionary ideas, find special relevance to shape and meaning when peo-

ple try to work out the way the story of their lives is going to go. Novelists, identifying experientally with youth and trying to present issues from
their perspective,[1] have in mind the same concerns and often display
them essayistically, monologically, or dialogically, but they also find
alternate ways to address them, to embody them in narrative choices and
outcomes. As Guidance, from the older perspectives of those who have
had their opportunity at patterning themselves and are now agents of the
print metaphor of Direction, there is little basically wrong with what
Guides have to offer, but the sense of life and choice is bloodless even
while being too intense. The idea of living life over again without the
accrued errata—the formula Dunton had tried to use to structure his
autobiography in *Life and Errors*[2]—is too obvious, too fantastic, too painful, and too irrelevant to be of much use to anyone else. It lacks the
virtue of displacement, the vitality of metaphor, and the sense of design
that projects a world ahead.

Reviewing life from the perspective of lessons learned that now have
to be passed on cautionarily is quite different. Advice from generation to
generation takes on, in published form, a crudeness and rigidity that had
been disguised by the personal intimacy of conversation between fathers
and sons or mothers and daughters, and even in the halfway house of a
Dunton fictional autiobiography the mode is still advisory more than
"what if." But when novelists explore this issue somewhat differently,
offering the opportunity to create life as text rather than being a paradigm by which to revise old errors, something quite transforming emerges
from the odd contexts of anxiety and concern. The same four issues
determine what novelists, in their transformation, cannot do as well as
what they must.

I

ON the hazards of idleness, there is powerful agreement from the time
of the Puritan Commonwealth until late into the eighteenth century.
Whether one regards the cultural anxiety about idleness as an aspect of
Puritan consciousness, the Protestant ethic, urban economics, rising worries
about education and personal fulfillment, or revulsion against aristocratic
customs and rural pace, the net result is that writers of all religious,
social, and political persuasions agree that, as *The Ladies Library* (1714)
puts it, "Idleness is not only the Road to all *Sin*, but is a *damnable Sin*
itself, quite opposite to the great Ends of the Creator, both in our *Creation* and *Redemption*" (I, 7). "There is hardly a Sin that can be charg'd
with so many tragical Effects as *Idleness*" (I, 9), the same volume says in

another place. *The Gentlemans Companion* (1672) calls idleness "the Nurse of all manner of Vice," nothing being more pernitious to the Soul than Idleness" (p. 121), and Archbishop Tillotson says that "*Idleness* is the bane and ruin of Children; it is the unbending of their Spirits, the *Rust* of their Faculties, and as it were the laying of their Minds *fallow*. . . ."[3] Sometimes the fruits of idleness are dramatized at length:

> What a Misfortune is it to some younger Persons, that partly by the negligence of their Friends, and partly by their own sluggish temper, they doze and dream away their precious time. They contract a habit of Laziness and Dulness while they are Children, which they can scarce shake off all the days of their Life. They are left to loyter Abroad, and to linger at Home, till their Body is all heaviness, and their very Soul is a Lump; till they are stupified into Drones or Sots, to feed on others Labour, and devour what is not their own.[4]

The Guides' "advice" on idleness ordinarily involves simple exhortation to children to keep body and mind busy at all times and to parents to be sure that their sons and daughters have no time in which to get into trouble. But some particular ways of wasting time are specified as loathsome and dangerous. Especially worrisome is what Burkitt calls "a sinful Excess of Sleep"[5] and Baxter says is "a swinish love of sleep."[6] Some didacticists speculate about why sleep seems so dangerous; according to *Advice to a Son* (1716), "Sleep is the Image of Death, its Picture and Resemblance: Sleep is but a breathing Death, and Death a breathless Sleep. . . . [I]t is the Dream of Death not the Sleep we are afraid of" (p. 68). And some (Baxter, for instance) get interested in the nature, function, and dangers of dreams, but the concern about excessive sleep is usually phrased in pragmatic terms. The catechetical *Whole Duty of a Christian* poses the question, "To what Sins does Excess in Sleeping betray us?" and answers, "To the wast of our Time; and to the filling our Bodies with Diseases; and dulling the Faculties of the Soul; it moreover Crosses the End of our Creation, which was to serve God in an Active Obedience" (3rd ed., 1711, p. 44). *The Gentlemans Companion* puts it more pompously: "Too much sleep hurts the sensitive faculties, renders the Body stegnotick, Hebitates the Head, and infartiates the Brain with many fumes. . . . Long and tedious sleeps ingender many emplastick humours apt to septifie in the Veins, and Brain especially. It also Resolves, Refrigerates, and stupifies the Nerves, dulls the Spirits and Senses, causes defluxions and Rheumes, and extinguisheth natural heat" (p. 119).

Often whole chapters of Guides, mostly just hortatory but sometimes with specific directions or examples, are devoted to idleness, and it is not unusual to find extensive philosophical discussion of the importance of time or even a separate treatise appended to a more general Guide, as *A Discourse About the Right Way of Improving our Time* (1690) is appended to James Kirkwood's *The True Interest of Families*.

At the base of the worry is a deep cultural fear of passivity (perhaps why anxieties about idleness, femininity, and reading converge), together with a sense that vacuums in activity (of either mind or body) tend to be colonized by dangerous desires and impulses. The idea of activity as a hedge against death is close to the surface in many passages urging the stewardship of time. The horrors of idleness are often painted to resemble a proximity to nothingness, and the novel, beyond thematic and discursive engagements with the issue, reaps the energy of the concern at great narrative length in a time, place, and circumstance when mortality was an issue every day, especially for those who migrated to the city where life expectancy was particularly short.

I I

THE ethics of using time are closely related to concerns about recreation and play. "*I wish to redeem all time from idle words and frivolous discourses; to avoid [when] I can the hearing of such pratlings; to shun all light, and frothy, and amourous Books,*" says Herbert Palmer in *Memorials of Godliness and Christianity*,[7] and his desire typifies the counsel against idle talking and idle reading as recreational pastimes. Any visiting with friends and neighbors that goes beyond the polite exchange of pleasantries and basic information is frowned upon by most didacticists, especially when such talk or gossip involves children or youth, though some Guides allow casual conversation, storytelling, visiting, and recreational reading in certain circumstances, especially on sabbaths, feast days, and market days.

Anxiety was widespread about the proper activities for the sabbath, that privileged time that sometimes seemed to contradict the culture's devotion to activity, productivity, and the absolute value of time. There was little agreement about how sabbaths ought to be used, but the subject—since sabbaths *did* have to be used and controlled—interested everyone. Dissenters were often more rigid about sabbath observance than Anglicans, but not always so, and except during the Reformation of Manners vigilance, the general direction from mid-seventeenth century to mid-eighteenth century was toward the gradual relaxation of tight rules. Social expectations about leisure more generally, not just about sabbath observance, loosened steadily from the 1660s on, and the Williamite crackdown on public and private "manners"—with its campaigns not only against sexual indulgence and drunkenness but also against swearing and gaming—gathered up and focused the simmering resentment toward Restoration rebellion and defiant self-assertion. Long before the 1690s when pressure for reform became public policy, didacticists railed against licentious conduct of all kinds, often landing on sabbath observance as an index of slipping standards. Rawlet's *Christian Monitor* (1686) typifies the more conservative Guides; "when you come from Church," Rawlet advises, "spend not the remainder of the day in sports and idleness, much less in drinking and gaming, as too many do: but if you have a Family, let some time be spent with them, in praying, in reading God's Word, and some good Book; and let Children and Servants be instructed in their Catechism" (p. 38).

But frequently there is recognition that recreational pleasures as well as religious devotion and pure rest are desirable for sabbath observance and that recreation and play are desirable spiritually as well as emotionally and physically. "[I]t is not only lawful, but sometimes very convenient and necessary," says *A Discourse About the Right Way of Improving our Time*, "when virtuous and excellent persons meet together, that they recreate and divert themselves a little by chearfulness and innocent mirth, that thereby their minds may be made more fit for serious and sacred things. Such is the state and condition of man, while in the body, that his Soul cannot be always employed about those things which are of a Divine and Spiritual Nature."[8] According to Theophilus Dorrington, in *The Regulations of Play Propos'd and Recommended* (1706), "when the just Use of Recreation and Pleasure promotes our Work and Duty, it does promote our Reward and future Happiness too" (p. 24). " 'Tis as necessary as natural," adds *The Ladies Library* (1714), "to unbend our Thoughts, when they are too much stretch'd by our Cares" (I, 59), but it adds a caution: "to turn our whole Lives into a *Holy-Day*, is ridiculous and absurd, destroying Pleasure instead of promoting it" (p. 60). "All *Recreations* are design'd to relieve, and not to soften the Mind," the same volume says a little later; "they are no longer lawful than they answer that Design" (p. 64). "Be careful," advises *The Poor Man's Help and Young Man's Guide* (which reached a 24th edition by 1741) "that your Recreations be short and diverting, such as may fit you for Business, rather than rob you of your Time" (1694 ed., p. 21 [misnumbered 19]). "To be lawful," according to *The Ladies Library*, recreations "must be such as have no Sin in them; by which Dancing and Gaming . . . are in great Danger of being excluded: They are placed on the very Margin of Virtue, and the least stumble flings one into the Precipice of Vice" (I, 64). *The Gentlemans Companion* is more worldlywise and permissive, arguing that activities like gaming and wine drinking should not be prohibited just because some people abuse them, although it rates chess and tennis as preferable (pp. 125–127). *The Young Gentleman's New-Year's Gift* (1729), on the other hand, although critical of Dissenters, condemns gambling, even losing its syntax as the heat rises: "I would . . . have you contemn and slight all sedentary, lazy Games, play'd with Cards, Dice, or Chess, &c. especially for Money; an indolent, lazy Life, Lying, Cheating, Swearing and Drinking, Poverty, Quarrels and Murders; Vices, so gross, so offensive, and so odious, so naturally attend them, that more or less, they are inseparable. The best Way to abstain from this abominable Vice is never to begin to learn . . ." (p. 28).

Toward the middle of the century, Isaac Watts reflects calmly on recreational possibilities: ". . . I have often earnestly wished," he writes in *A Discourse on the Education of Children and Youth*, "that instead of all these Games there were some more profitable Sports invented for a long Evening, for a dull Hour, or a rainy [s]eason . . . if some ingenious Mind, which is well skilled in mathematical Learning and in Games, would but take Pains to contrive some such Diversions, there might be a much better Account given of the Hours of Leisure and Remission of Business by Persons of both Sexes, and of all Ages, than can be at present, for want of such useful and improving Recreations."[9]

For most, reading is the preferred recreation, although cautionary sentiments abound about the choice of books. "[O]f the *Diversions of Life*," *The Gentleman's Library* says in 1715, "there is none so proper to fill up its empty spaces as the *reading* of useful and entertaining *Authors*, and employing our Dead unactive Hours in *Improvements* by *Study*, and *Pursuits of Knowledge* . . . [yet] our *Studies* should be kept within the Compass of *Use* and *Utility*; . . . there are *Impertinent Studies*, as well as *Impertinent Men*; . . . it is not reading *much*, or *hastily* which turns to account, but the Choice of our Authors, and care to digest them. . . ." (fol. a1v). *The Young Gentleman and Lady Instructed* (1747) borrows the phrasing of this passage but moves to a more general point: "of all the diversions of life, there is none so proper to fill up its empty spaces, as the reading of useful and entertaining books. Reading is to the mind, what exercise is to the body" (II, 115, pilfered [as is much more in the volume] from *The Gentleman's Library*, p. 193). "Your vacant and spare hours," agrees the Marquis of Argyll in *Instructions to a Son* (1661), "you cannot better afford to any thing then [sic] to Books; nay, there is a necessity of making such leisure time, if the multiplicity of business press to[o] fast upon you" (p. 100). *The Ladies Library* is, however, fairly typical in warning readers (especially women readers) to choose their books carefully and avoid "the gallant Writers": "The Poyson . . . is conceal'd as much as possible, and 'tis insensibly that they would lead the Heart to Love: Let them therefore be avoided with Care; . . . the Danger of reading soft and wanton Writings, which warn and corrupt the Imagination, is so great that one cannot be too careful" (I, 25).

Anxieties about lost time ultimately derive from the powerful sense of limit—and the effort to stretch it—that Protestants emphasized as part of the individual experience of human life. Although orthodox Christianity had traditionally talked about the "brief span" of human life and interpreted individual duty in terms of making the most of one's early opportunities, the Calvinistic stress on individual stewardship made the husbanding of time a far weightier matter, in which idleness meant not only the chance for temptation to find wider passages to the soul but also that time itself, seen in quite material terms, became lessened and lost. "Improving" one's time meant not only refusing to lose time in idleness or irrelevant pastimes (the word "pastime" raised powerful aversions in many Protestants because it implied a devaluation of time itself) but also a proper investment in it. Time was, like money or property, to be used for added profit. The parable of the talents (Matthew 25: 14–30), with its emphasis on using what one had so as to gain more, was widely cited. Although capitalism was thus grounded in theology,[10] the thrust was to alert individuals that they were subject to audit—their own, their neighbor's, or God's—at any time. The terms are material: stewardship involves possession; ownership needs capital gains. The Protestant concept of grace is a material notion (through such language has implications beyond economics), but the sense of lost opportunity ("*Thou* wicked and slothful servant . . .") becomes a powerful motive not only for work itself but for clever investment of time that would make other time more valuable.

What the novel inherits from this context of concern is not only the need to discuss such matters, although the frequency with which such topics arise in conversation or in the essayistic parts of novels dramatically suggests the continuity of function for readers between Guide books and novels. More important, the odd place of novels in the didactic context—they taught, but their teachings were distrusted—meant that they were a peculiarly poignant and confused illustration of time use. Novels tried to engage the issue by insisting that time spent reading fiction made the rest of life more efficient as well as more efficacious.

The redemption of time through reading thus became one of the paradoxes at the center of the Protestant dilemma. Reading, though necessary to proper religious observance and virtually necessary to salvation, could equally well lead to flagrant abuses, and the novel as a species quickly highlights the issue. The potential of novels to guide was seen by many moralists—not just rationalized by novelists eager to justify themselves—as a powerful force for good. But what could guide could also misguide, sometimes with the best of intentions, and again the problem of sending words out into the cold world where unknown and alien readers might make of them something quite unintended became crucial.[11] Given the cultural worries about youth and the dynamics of human choice, guiding and misguiding became the central ethical issues for adults, and by midcentury novels were the most influential texts involved in the issue. The novel thus opened up issues of intention, direction, and exemplarity in a way that didactic treatises only hinted at. Exemplarity, positive and negative, offered the terms in which most of the debate about results was cast—a matter I shall discuss shortly—but questions about the power of language determined, for texts, how guidance and examples obtained. Novels not only emerge from the context of such concerns and dramatize their relevance to the everyday practical world but, given their own desire to teach, take on certain representational functions as a result. Thus, for example, the tendency of novels to describe young people as always busy and restless, almost hyperactive, results as much from the necessity of absolving themselves from charges of promoting lost time as it does from formal conventions or necessities of individual plots.

Pamela's and Clarissa's dedication to recording themselves, besides providing a convenient justification of text, offers a model for the use of time. However insignificant in themselves, or however isolated or limited in social circumstances people might be, avenues of activity were open: writing was a form of activity and interaction, work that produced results. Idleness was inexcusable, even unthinkable, regardless of situation or circumstance. Similarly, the frenetic activity of Robinson Crusoe on his island and the restless motion of Moll Flanders in London streets, even though they involve wayward actions that are culpable, are errors in the right direction: to act is better than to be idle, and correcting the direction of activity is seen to be easier than stimulating youth from laziness, complacency, and stasis. Even the unceasing search for adventures of Smollett's heroes, the uncontrolled sexual energy of *Tom Jones*, and the intellectual, social, and physical curiosities of Evelina, Roxana, and Fanny Hill demonstrate a *kind* of exemplarity, activity that, however much in need of directional correction, is preferable to passivity or stasis. Idleness was something the novel could not afford to represent.

III

EVEN when they presented protagonists who were less than exemplary, novels had at their center a concept of imitation and evitation developed in popular didactic treatises and projected into the popular imagination by repeated emphasis and argument. Guide literature constantly sought to establish the importance of example as the crucial influence on human conduct and elevated it to a principle of human behavior, often giving an account of human motivation as sophisticated as in more learned and theoretical contemporary treatises. The doctrine of teaching by example is of course an old one; in one form or another it has dominated much modern psychological theory as well as older philosophical descriptions of human behavior. One is almost as likely now to hear about "role models," human paradigms, and the search for symbolic figures as a reader in the late seventeenth century was to find discussions of ethical models and insistence on the rhetorical necessity of living an exemplary life. But the discussions of example in Guide books then had a double purpose—to suggest the significance of human examples in real life, and to dramatize how written materials could, in effect, substitute for human examples.

Didacticists repeatedly cite ancient authority as well as common sense in support of their arguments about the power of example. "It is an Ancient Saying," according to one collector of "lives," "That *Examples prevail more upon Men than Precepts.* The truth of which our constant Experience too sadly verifies; for how many (Young Persons especially) are in this last and worst Age of the World debauch'd and ruin'd by the Examples of their Companions and others. . . . And as evil, so good Examples also, have a great Influence upon the Lives of Men."[12] "Example has strange Attractives," adds Darrell in *The Gentleman Instructed* (1704); "the Way to Virtue by Precepts (as the Philosopher notes) is long, but by Example short and easie" (fol. A6v). "The duty of Parents," writes George Swinnock in *The Christian-Mans Calling . . . Second Part* (1663), "is *to set a good pattern before their children.* It's the saying of *Lumbard, The instruction of words is not so powerful as the exhortation of works.* Do thou live exactly, as thou desirest thy children should do; take heed lest thou set them an ill copy. Its ordinary for children to follow their fathers though it be to the *unquenchable fire.* . . . Children will observe their fathers courses and carriage, and sooner follow their poysonous patterns, then [sic] their pious precepts."[13]

Example is said to have an especially powerful attraction for the young, and discussions of the power of example are usually directed toward parents and guardians. "Children have a wonderful Proneness to imitate," writes Edward Cobden in *The Religious Education of Children* (1754), "Upon which Account it should be your Care to admit them to the Sight of as much Good and as little Bad as possible. . . . Your Sins will soon become theirs, and therefore doubly yours. . . . The Contagion of Immorality is very apt to spread, especially in youthful Blood, and you should keep them from vicious Company as you would do from those who are infested with the Pestilence" (pp. 18–19). Such advice quickly became specific directions for companions and servants, and the widespread fear of ignorant, pagan, or corrupt nurses bursts out frequently. Parents, says *The Ladies Library* (1714), "must . . . take Care that their *Children*, as far as is possible, have no bad Examples to converse with, either among their Servants, or their own Companions. . . . There is Contagion in Example, and nothing does more slily insinuate it self and gain upon us, than a living and familiar Pattern" (II, 245). "The Ignorance of Children," adds Fénelon's *Instructions for the Education of a Daughter* (Hickes adaptation, 1707), "in whose Brain nothing is yet imprinted, and who have not as yet attained any Habits, renders them pliable, and inclinable to Imitate whatever they see; wherefore it is a thing of the highest Consequence not to lay before them any other than the best Patterns. You must not suffer any to come near them, but such whose Examples are useful, and proper to follow. . . ." (p.29). "Chuse good Company for your Children," adds *The True Interest of Families* (1690); ". . . otherwise, neither your Admonitions nor Examples will signifie much: Their ordinary Company, if naughty, will pull down faster than you are able to build: Corrupt Nature is easily drawn away by the Example and Allurements of sinners; This is like going down hill, which is easie, considering Mens natural bent and inclination" (1692 ed., pp. 38–39).

Henry Fielding may exaggerate contemporary thought when he describes the power of example as "irresistible" (*Joseph Andrews*, I, i), but he does not exaggerate much. The repeated metaphors of disease, contagion, and infection to describe the effects of bad examples suggest the mysterious power that writers fear as well as exploit, and although no one claims that the force of virtue is quite automatic, the language does often drift toward the mystical. As Edward Cobden says in a 1740 sermon entitled "Of Good Examples," "one brave Pattern set before our Eyes . . . insensibly attracts, and strangely leads us on, before we are aware, and wins us, with a gentle Violence, almost against our Wills."[14] Defoe creates a character in the first *Family Instructor* volume (1715) who is so impressed by exemplarity that he asks his sister for an example in the form of a narrative of her life: "I wish," he says, "you would give me the short History, that I may judge how to regulate my Conduct by yours" (p. 430). The language of pattern or model, suggestive about implication and outcomes, regularly drifts into a language of raw force that can bypass or even subjugate individual will. Metaphors of magnetism and repulsion just as surely as those of infection suggest prevailing doubts about the ability of human will to control behavior, an assumption that empowered words and stories even as it denigrated intentionality.

The confidence in the power of human example readily leads to the recitation of dramatic examples in the Guide books themselves and in collections of stories and anecdotes on various subjects and themes. Anxiety about how to make such examples seem alive and alluring amounts to deep concern about the limits of any verbal medium and uncertainty about how to harness the power that growing literacy and the rapid expansion of print had brought into being. Almost every didacticist, no matter how insistently hortatory, *says* that examples are more powerful than precepts.[15] "Examples are always more powerful," according to Samuel Say, "and more affecting to us than mere Precepts; and especially the Examples of those who were of the same Age with our selves," and he advises readers to "often read over the Histories of those young Ones recorded in holy Scriptures, who were . . . remarkable for their Piety."[16] "Set before them," Cobden advises parents about their children, "the Examples of those early Converts to Piety . . . *Samuel* . . . *Timothy* . . . *John*. . . . And while you recommend to them the Patterns of others, above all Things, forget not to show them a good One of your own."[17] Less famous and more recent examples are, in fact, recommended for use in books as well as in life. "The setting before youth the infamous or honourable characters of their contemporaries," says *The Young Gentleman and Lady Instructed* (1747), "is a good method to incline them to any particular virtue, or give them an aversion to any particular vice; and, by hearing the ill report it brings upon others, youth is often frighted from vicious inclinations" (I, 146).

Some writers emphasize positive example, some negative. Most agree that attraction and repulsion are reciprocal and equivalent properties, although many worry that impressionable minds may seize on models without sufficient discrimination about whether they are properly emulable. Mixed examples thus become worrisome to Samuel Johnson, and his rather intemperate attack on fiction in *Rambler* 4 derives from his distrust of any examples but those of pure virtue. Others, whatever they say about the power of example, place much more emphasis in their own writing on precept, perhaps because they are not sure how to make examples sufficiently attractive or cautionary, perhaps because their old habits are mainly preceptual; and on balance Guides contain much more discourse (most of it in the imperative mood) than narrative or portraiture. Still, the stress upon the potential of example as a moral force is almost ubiquitous in didactic literature generally in the two or three generations just before the novel emerges, and the claims are sometimes extraordinary: "[M]ay the lively and indelible Idea's of such noble Examples," says *An Essay of Particular Advice to the Young Gentry* (1711), "remain imprest upon [young people's] Minds, so as to provoke a just

Emulation, and inspire them with a mighty Courage and Resolution for the like Excellent Practices, whatever Obstacles they meet with. . . ." (p. 101). And some didacticists stress how lucky we are to have had others to go before us and make mistakes so that we don't have to: "Let us be *thankful* to God, "writes George Wade in 1721, "that He has been pleased to order, that *others* should be a *Warning* and *Example* to Us, rather than *We* so to Them: Let *Gratitude* excite us to fresh Endeavours of Obedience; and let us seriously reflect, what a Favour it has been to us, to be *Spectators*, or rather *Hearers*, only of that *Tragedy*, in which, to our Sorrow, we might have been made the *Principal Actors*."[18] As Samuel Clarke insisted, "Good examples are for imitation, bad for evitation."[19] The final lines of a poem ("The Author's Speaking Picture") that John Dunton prefaced to his autobiography might well stand as a motto for the attitudes toward the use of example in Guide books:

> *Dissected thus, I stand a Living Martyr grown.*
> *Come Read my Errors, and Reform your own.*

In novels, example becomes considerably more complex because of the issue of factitiousness, but the fundamental premise that verbal portraits have exemplary or cautionary effects on readers derives directly from the didactic tradition.

I V

A *FOURTH* almost universal topic in Guide books involves the practice of self-examination. Lacking the powers of tradition inherent in both clergy and ritual in Catholicism, Protestants had from the start put heavy emphasis on personal responsibility and the need for individuals to chart their own spiritual course. In its early history, the Anglican Church had minimized its alliances with Protestantism and emphasized its historic continuity with Catholic traditions, but the religious and political movements that led to the Commonwealth made a lasting impact so that, despite narrow post-Restoration laws and policies, the Church continued to move increasingly away from Catholic practice and onto a more and more independent course. At the turn of the eighteenth century, there were of course major ways in which Anglicans differed from Dissenters, and on some subjects the gulf was wide, but on issues like the need for self-examination, the continuing influence of Puritan individualism was clear. It is through "Serious Self-examination," writes William Burkitt, listing it as one of the "Closet-Devotions" or "Secret Duties" incumbent upon Christians" (*Family Instruction*, p. 43), that "we make a daily enquiry into the State of our Souls, and thereby arrive at a well-grounded K[n]owledge of the safety of our State and Condition, by comparing the Frame of our Hearts and the Course of our Lives with the Holy Rule of God's Commandements . . ." (*Poor Man's Help, and Young Man's Guide* [2nd ed., 1694], p. 43). Over and over the chorus recurs: "Bring your self to a deep Self-*Examination* concerning your past life," writes Woodward.[20] "[S]ee that they accustom themselves to Self-Examination," *The True Interest of Families* advises parents about their children, "that they spend a few moments every night . . . in calling themselves to an account. . . ." (1692 ed., p. 30). "*Call thy self to an Account at evening,*" advises *The Christian-Mans Calling* (3rd pt., 1665); "Take a review of thy carriage the whole day. . . ." (p. 523).

The close link between reading and its application to introspective analysis is emphasized repeatedly. Just after the advice on reading I quoted above (p. 279), *The Gentleman's Library* (1715) adds: "[W]e should read our *Lives* as well as *Books*, take a Survey of our *Actions*, and make an Inspection into the *Division* of our *Time*" (fols. a1v–a2). "And now, Reader, whoever thou art," writes John Mason in 1745 in *Self-Knowledge. A Treatise, shewing the Nature and Benefit of that Important Science, and The Way to attain it,*

> whatever be thy Character, Station, or Distinction in Life, if thou art afraid to look into thine Heart, and has no Inclination to Self-Acquaintance, read no further; lay aside this Book; for thou will find nothing here that will flatter thy Self-Esteem; but perhaps something that may abate it. But if thou art desirous to cultivate this important Kind of Knowledge, and to live no longer a Stranger to thyself, proceed; and keep thy Eye open to thine own Image, with whatever unexpected Deformity it may present itself to thee. . . . (p. 13)

Something of the importance placed on self-examination is implied by *The Royal Diary: or, King William's Interiour Portraiture* (1703), which purports to be taken from papers found after the king's death and which claims that he always engaged in formal self-examination before receiving the sacraments.

The tradition of self-examination had also been, of course, an honored one in Catholic thought and practice from the early history of Christianity, but Protestantism (and especially Calvinism) gave it special emphasis and formalized it into written procedures because of its insistence on discovering the divine plan for individual lives. In a theology that stressed individual election for salvation and that concerned itself with the epistemology of discovering the divine plan for individuals, hav-

Conv. narrative

ing a formal procedure to keep track of one's pattern of life was crucial, and Guide writers concurred with seventeenth-century theologians that individuals should undertake self-examination daily. Such a procedure involved taking stock of one's spiritual condition by reviewing moral triumphs and failures and by recording all the details of one's daily fortunes. Few believers held a simple view that early rewards and punishments were indexes to eternal salvation or damnation—certainly fewer than naive modern commentators have claimed—but it was widely held that those who examined their own lives carefully would be able to discover, in patterns of outcome, God's pleasure and displeasure with their acts. Such a notion is easy to caricature, and there were crude minds in those times as well as ours whose understanding of the idea was parodic. Perhaps some actually did believe that earthly successes and failures simply meant election or damnation. But the practice of self-examination (when properly conducted) guaranteed that the process of evaluation was subtle and subject to minute scrutiny; it had to involve a detailed "reading" of moments and the positing of patterns they might represent. In its extension into diary keeping, the practice took on dimensions that profoundly affected the form and articulation of introspection in the novel.

The culture took the injunctions to self-examination very seriously indeed. We can only speculate about what those private sessions in closets were really like—were they more like Pamela's or Clarissa's, Johnson's or Boswell's?—but because wider literacy made possible extensive record-keeping about private lives, the injunction to examine the self became an injunction to record the self and to trace daily all the vicissitudes of an individual's life. Theoretically, such a record was an account of the soul's progress (or regress), but in fact those who kept diaries kept track of nearly everything, a normal consequence of the belief that led to self-examination in the first place, for until one had a total sense of one's life—all its details, all its relationships, all its possible patterns—one could not be sure what was important and what was not. And so the diaries—and the resulting spiritual autobiographies and biographies that were privately distributed and later increasingly published for the good of others—often included matters that hardly look "spiritual" to a modern reader. Boswell is one predictable effect of the practice, Jay Gatsby another.

Whether the Puritan predilection for self-examination was ultimately responsible for the distinctively English version of individualism and subjectivity, and whether self-examination led in the early eighteenth century to the ethical emphasis in so-called Broad Church Anglicanism which in turn brought about the Methodist reformation, are questions that intellectual historians will ultimately have to re-answer when the popular

materials I have been discussing have been read more thoroughly in relation to the new social history now being written. But we do know that
the practice of self-examination dictated the practice of diary keeping
and the habits of mind that went with it, and ultimately (through the
formal removes of spiritual autobiography and spiritual biography) the
novel became the beneficiary of the emotional landscape, daily habits,
and written formulas. For all its circumstantiality and subjectivity, the
novel owes much to the deep assumptions of Puritanism and their daily
manifestations, and one might argue whether it is Defoe or Dunton,
Boyle or Bunyan, who offers the most sympathetic link. But ultimately
it would be silly to choose: all the insistence to record and analyze, however illogical or eccentric its manifestations, is part of the enabling context for writers as well as readers of the novel.[21]

The novel's response to the four issues I have isolated was not conscious or calculated but it was direct and pointed. The novel did not
emerge simply because of the anxieties, but those anxieties produced a
climate receptive to a certain kind of texts with particular features. The
convergence of these features into a particular kind of text is what the
novel, in part, is. Other kinds of writing (spiritual autobiographies, for
example, or Providence books) addressed one or more of the issues and
sometimes all four more or less at once, but only novels used the cultural
anxieties to full creative advantage, presenting themselves as exemplary
instances of self-examination that turned their readers' leisure to account
by becoming practical (and moral) guides for life. Their direct engagement with the reader, patterned on the engagement of Guides which
similarly began from a concern with the choices made by youths, enabled
them to claim an affective relationship that fulfilled readers' needs exactly
where Guides worried most about their vulnerability. In insisting that
they were redeeming leisure, transforming idleness into practical guidance, both recommending and illustrating self-examination, and (especially) materializing examples within a rhetoric of attraction, novels set
themselves to answer directly the charges made most often against "idle
fictions" and "wanton tales." Not all the claims made by novels were, of
course, true, and perhaps novels never worked so totally counter to the
anxieties as they claimed. But they found their rationale against the worries and claims of Guides, and some features may be traced directly to
received didactic opinion about how youths act and readers think.

V

THE second of Defoe's *Family Instructor* volumes (1718) carries this
description as part of its "subtitle": "with A great Variety of Cases relat-

ing to setting Ill Examples to Children and Servants." Early in the volume, two of Defoe's "characters" discuss how such "cases" are "useful":

> Citizen: . . . it is my own Case exactly . . . so I must acknowledge it has made your Relation exceeding pleasant to me.
>
> Friend: I am very sorry, that what is my Affliction should be your Diversion; I am sure it has been a very unpleasant Circumstance to me.
>
> Citizen: You mistake me very much, it has not been pleasant to hear that you have been under such a severe Affliction; but it was a great Pleasure to me, to find a dear Friend in a Case, from which I was so likely to receive Instruction, Comfort, and Advice in my own, which is almost the same in every Circumstance, and in which I have been so much at a loss how to behave. (p.39)

Defoe's articulation of the Friend's resentment at having his "Circumstance" considered an example is characteristic of his ability to transform principles into human reactions and has something to do both with his method in· *The Family Instructor* volumes and in the novels he began writing the year after he wrote the above lines. Ultimately even more important, though, both for Defoe personally and for the novel more generally, is the whole theoretical base that Defoe acknowledges here and then explains—the interest in "cases."

Whatever its social, intellectual, and formal roots, the novel only becomes distinct from its didactic contexts when it gets down to cases, recording particulars and telling an individual's story. But even the ability to find and represent those cases owes much to both the didactic and journalistic context and even more to the theological and philosophical assumptions that give those contexts their working power. The complexities of modern life, in which specific circumstances may well complicate simple issues of right and wrong, are notoriously difficult to reconcile with absolute principles, and much of the resonance of the novel comes from its rich layering and turning of these issues so that their full psychological and cultural (as well as ethical) dimensions are clear. The reconciliation of particular instances to abstract principles had, of course, always been an issue in serious intellectual history, but in the century before the novel a rising concern with how to understand individuation and how to adjudicate the governance of law and rule on particular cases became a significant matter of cultural concern. Casuistry, long an honored discipline in theology and philosophy, began its journey into the popular ken as a way of interpreting the ordinary and the everyday, a journey that has since seen case theory develop in law, case study become the central method in business schools, and "cases" become the main way that medicine uses to study how individual illnesses may or may not relate to "medical science."[22]

A large body of Protestant "casuistical" literature—ethical wrestlings with individual "cases of conscience"—had developed by the late seventeenth century, inheriting from medieval theology a concern to extend Christian tradition to its full interpretive range and adding a distinctive Protestant emphasis. In the hands of learned practitioners, older casuistry had sometimes become reasoning for its own sake (turning "casuistical" into a pejorative term for specious, overly clever argumentation), but later English Protestants tried to resurrect the art and purify its name, wishing to apply biblical injunctions sensibly to modern conditions. In Elizabethan and Jacobean times, English casuistry developed a respectable body of case materials,[23] but it was at the end of the Puritan Interregnum that casuistry took a turn that allies it with the cultural consciousness out of which the novel develops.

The traditional purpose of casuistry was to examine how moral and ethical generalities apply to specific circumstances. When, in the mid-seventeenth century, it begins to apply its method to highly particular circumstances and specific situations within a context of changing assumptions about human nature, it becomes a version of the developing "individualism" upon which novels are dependent. Casuistry's relationship to Guides is imprecise; both are manifestations of the intense cultural concern with behavioral decisions, and both are most often pointed toward the young. But if Guides are primarily hortatory, intended to provide direction for a generality of circumstances, casuistical treatises wrestle with issues, focusing not on general rules or patterns of guidance but the ethical shading of a particular instance. The growing dependence of ethical theory upon a case-study method represents a crucial chapter in cultural change and helps explain innovations in the new literature that grows out of that change.[24]

In their polemical study of casuistry, Jonsen and Toulmin regard the period from the end of the sixteenth century to the mid-seventeenth as the golden age of English casuistry. They may be right if one uses classical casuistry as the measure. Figures like William Perkins, William Ames, Jeremy Taylor, and Robert Sanderson then produced major theoretical works which, although distinctively English, followed the philosophical lines of traditional casuistry. But the distinctive power of English casuistry seems to me to begin as just the moment when Jonsen and Toulmin see it ending,[25] when it moves into the weekly pulpit and ultimately into journalism, becoming a phenomenon that affects popular thought and practice. The full potential of casuistry's interest in individual difference is realized only when issues of circumstantiality join with new beliefs about individual temperament. The power of casuistry as a cultural force

dates from the Interregnum when England had to confront what individuation had made of tradition and authority.

The distinctively English modern casuistical tradition derives from the
"Morning Exercise" sermons preached at St. Giles in the Fields, just outside London, beginning about 1655.[26] The first extensive collection of
these sermons was published in 1659 or 1660; its editor was, ironically,
one Thomas Case, a clergyman whose own turbulent case relative to
state policy was complicated by changing norms in the Interregnum itself
and then in the Restoration.[27] The earliest sermons in the series remain
more concerned with principles than with particulars, and there is a certain nervousness about becoming too "situational" or "relative." As the
first sermon in Case's collection says, the value of the developing method
lies primarily in juxtaposition and comparison: "the Hearer or Reader,
may, as in a *Map* or *Table*, (sometimes of one sort, sometimes of another),
behold *divine truths* standing one by another in their *Method* and *Connex-
ion*; mutually casting *light* and *lustre* upon each other" (p. 16). But Restoration politics soon produced very tough "cases" for the devout who
would not conform, and the morning exercise sermons and casuistry more
generally took a swift turn toward resolving issues between faiths and
(more particularly) between Church and State. In 1661, the prominent
divine Samuel Annesley brought together the first collection of Morning
Exercise sermons from St. Giles Cripplegate, twenty-eight of them in all,
preached by a variety of divines, not all of whom would be "separated"
(as Annesley himself was) in 1662; Tillotson, for example, was in the
volume, and so were some lesser lights who conformed under the Act of
Uniformity.[28] Annesley, who became the father-in-law of both Samuel
Wesley (the father of John and Charles) and John Dunton, and who
thus was a kind of forefather of the "case" journalism I described in Chapter One, was pastor of St. Giles Cripplegate until the Bartholomew Day
separation; he led the congregation in which Defoe was reared by God-
fearing parents.

The practice in the morning exercises was to bring together the views
of various respected divines ("that *in the multitude of Spirituall Counsellors*
your souls may have *safety*" [fol A3]), and the 1661 volume already shows
distinct signs of moving in a "modern" casuistical direction. The sermon
by Benjamin Needler, for example, "How may beloved Lusts be discovered and Mortified," is concerned with the particularities of time and
circumstance, if not exactly an argument that each individual is altogether distinct from every other. "Men have," says Needler (in an extension of the idea of *peccatum in deliciis*),

particular *temperaments* and *constitutions* of body, and therefore they have
their particular sins sutable to their *temperaments* and *constitutions*. . . . There

are distinct and peculiar periods of times, *distinct and peculiar ages,* that encline to *peculiar sins;* for instance, *childhood* enclines to *lenity* and *inconstancy,*
youth to *wantonness* and *prodigality,* *manhood* to *pride* and *stateliness, old age* to
frowardnesse. . . . Men have distinct and *particular callings,* that encline them
to *particular sins:* For instance, a Souldiers employment puts him upon *rapine*
and *violence.* . . . Men have distinct and *particular wayes of breeding* and *education,* and upon that account have their *particular sins.* (pp. 47–49)

Such emphases suggest a distinct shift toward individualized psychology, and three later volumes in the series, also edited by Annesley, show
intensified interest in situationality, moving case study toward the popu-
larization that made it staple fare in 1690s periodicals.[29] The extension
of casuistry into the weekly popular press may have, in a strict theological
sense, reduced casuistry almost to a one-by-one consideration of issues—
an "abuse" from a purist perspective—but it was in such abuse that the
significance for the culture, and for the novel, lay. The key name in this
moment of popular culture become intellectual history is, once again,
that of John Dunton. It was his *Athenian Mercury* that set the tone and
created the scope for the extraordinary popularity of cases of conscience
that the public press explored from the nineties on, and it was his idea
(the "Thought I'll not exchange for Fifty Guineas") that initiated readers
into a contributory role in the journalistic venture, for he invited them
to send in their "cases"—that is, accounts of their particular ethical
dilemmas and those of their friends and acquaintances.[30] Dunton's journalistic mixing of these cases with accounts of "wonders" and providential events and with brief lives of saints and sinners who had recently
passed on suggests—accurately—the common intellectual heritage of
various subspecies that the novel brings cogently together.[31]

The cognizance that circumstances alter cases spread well beyond theoretical discussions among theologians and even beyond the popular air-
ings of audience-participation journalism. The didactic tradition—and
educational theory more generally—had already begun to absorb many
of the subjectivist principles implicit in casuistry. Guide books, for example,
recognized that individual needs and circumstances had to be regarded
in putting into practice the ethical advice they offered. More and more,
Guides for Parents and Families emphasize how important it is to discover the particular constitutions and dispositions of children as they
grow and develop. As early as 1663, *The Christian-Man's Calling* was
tentatively advising parents to regard particularities in choosing a child's
calling:

I think it not a miss [sic] . . . in the choyce of a Calling to have some respect
to thy childs disposition; none are so excellent at any Art or Science as they

that delight most in it. All creatures thrive best when they are in their own elements, because there they delight most. It is therefore commended for an ingenious policy of the *Athenians,* that before they placed out their children to any setled course of life, they brought them into a room furnished for that end with all sorts of tools or instruments for callings, and narrowly observing with what there they were most delighted, bred them up accordingly. Thy piety must help thee to chuse a fit Master, and thy prudence to chuse a fit calling. . . .[32]

Over the next two or three generations, such advice became less tentative and more commonplace, and John Locke simply reflects his contemporaries in many of his thoughts concerning education in particular circumstances. In a sermon "Of the Education of Children," Tillotson is insistent: "Endeavour, as well as you can, to discover the particular *Temper* and *Disposition* of Children, that you may suit and apply your selves to it, and by striking in with Nature may steer and govern them in the sweetest and easiest way" (1701 sermons, p. 621). Another educational theorist, Francis Brokesby, writes similarly in 1701: ". . . it is requisite to observe the Capacities of Learners that hence we may know what kind of Learning, and afterwards what sort of Calling, each person is fitted for, that hence we may suit their studies to their *genius.*"[33] A little later, Isaac Watts summarizes what he plainly takes to be received opinion: "Let the teacher always accommodate himself to the genius, temper and capacity of his disciples, and practise various methods of prudence to allure, persuade and assist every one of them in their pursuit of knowledge."[34]

The individuation of motive and experience posed serious threats to traditional literary programs. Swift's parodic version of the subjectivity that such views imply may be extreme, even paranoid, but it is essentially accurate in its assessment of the challenge to authoritarian and universalist positions. The novel's program of recording the world case by case, trying to tell all the possible stories from all the possible points of view, is a lot like regarding writers as amanuenses of the universe: the metaphor makes claims that are not much in excess of those by Dunton, Boyle, Defoe, or Richardson. What the novel does, however, by making up new, possible stories instead of just recording ones already lived, is to give the individual case an imaginative and cumulative reach rather than an analytical one. From a need to record the world and represent it as it has been, the novel gets down to cases in a fashion that extends the sense of subjectivity into a dimension of futurity by taking novelty seriously enough to consider what might be as well as what is. Casuistry helped to open psychological possibility and make it morally and theologically respectable. The novel needed approval of the moral guardians and the screeners of fundamental cultural anxieties to gain access to the popular readership that would allow it to be the culture's representation of its new self.

V I

DIDACTICISM took many forms between 1660 and 1720; a full review of them would need to describe in detail the changing climate of ideas recorded by the writers and also to survey the many subspecies in which writers contracted with audiences. The response of readers was no doubt even more varied than writers were able to calculate, but expectations set up by the entire magnetic field in didacticism conditioned not only what happened within the didactic kinds but beyond them. Besides showing us what kinds of subjects and issues interested readers, these popular, everyday, "para-literary" materials suggest the climate of print into which writers, as well as readers, of novels were born. "Traditional" literature was part of that climate, too, of course; most of the early novelists were at least moderately well read in the classics and the "polite" literature still being written in traditional categories, and at first the aspiration of many of them was really to be men of letters, not founders or practitioners of a new species. Defoe meant to be a poet and only turned his pen to other uses for bread or politics. He expected, and probably would have preferred, to be known for *Jure Divino* and *More Reformation*, rather than *Robinson Crusoe* and *Roxana*. Henry Fielding aspired to poetry but chose the role of playwright; he turned to journalism, and the "comic epic in prose" only when his higher literary intentions had been thwarted. Smollett, like Samuel Johnson, aspired to a life of letters through the theater, and he tilted toward novels (although keeping up a variety of projects in letters) more because of the developing tastes for lengthy narrative than because of any inherent personal preference. Rowe was a poet and, more than anyone but Lady Mary Pierrepont (later Wortley Montagu), capable of creating the new category of woman of letters; her turn to fiction seems to have been dictated by her strong moral agenda and a desire to reach a broad readership. Burney was a woman of taste whose reputation was more likely to depend on her sage criticism and private papers than on invented stories; her novels probably represent a desire for approval from friends more than any career desires of her own. Others—Sarah Fielding, Samuel Richardson, Charlotte Lennox—though perhaps less impressively educated in traditional terms, could also have taken any

Novelists - generally
traditionally
learned

Readers— no

number of writing directions and found the approval of friends or public success more important than any special career aims. [35]

Most journalists and hacks—the class from which novelists chiefly came—were educated at least as well as those who made reputations as poets. Neither formal education nor breadth of reading constituted the dividing line between poets and novelists or between those who were belletristic writers and those who lived by their professional pens in semi-exile from literary circles. Despite modern snobbishness (based in earlier snobbishness) about the low birth and inferior educations of those who wrote novels or pursued new literary directions generally, it would be hard to sustain divisions between traditional and innovative directions by looking at where writers went to school or what they read. In fact, a good classical education was ordinarily necessary to a hack who sought employment in a bookseller's stable such as that of Curll (because of the nature of the tasks to be performed), whereas a "polite" writer could do without. It would be hard to predict who would do what from the early lives of, say, Pope, Gildon, Brown, Defoe, Oldmixon, Prior, Tickell, Thomson, Johnson, or Henry Fielding. Predicting the writing career of any woman was, in early century, more difficult still, for unless one had the birth of Lady Mary or fell into the destitution of Manley or Haywood the chances of any life of writing were slim. [36] Few novelists, men or women, seemed altogether respectable to most observers, but the gradations among them involved their "moral import" more than anything else. The biggest difficulty for women novelists was that their subjects and themes were more narrowly circumscribed than were those of men, and their personal lives—or rather, their personal reputations, especially their sexual reputations—mattered more.

But because many of the readers of novels were less well read, because the whole notion of what constituted a reading public was changing, because also changing was the idea of what "literature" itself had to be, and because novelists as writers in an emerging species were consciously seeking ways of finding and engaging an audience for their work, the so-called subliterary "background" was more than a cultural context and potential "source" of subject matter and technique. It was also an index to taste, a source of competition, a practice field, and an incubator for fledgling notions. Most early novelists learned their craft as didacticists by writing in one or more of the approved subkinds. Defoe wrote Guides (for Families, Tradesmen, Gentlemen), Providence books, travel books, many varieties of political and economic propaganda. Richardson as a printer was responsible for many religious and moral treatises, and his attempt to write a practical guide to letter writing quite literally "led" to his becoming a novelist. Henry Fielding, besides being a journalist and playwright, was also a collector and recorder of providences and author of a variety of political, social, religious, and moral essays in many didactic subkinds. Manley was a political journalist and controversialist who studied scandal, rumor, and gossip and learned to make the half-fiction of narrative from polemical essays. Haywood was an essayist and social critic who (like Manley) edited a periodical of her own, Smollett a historian and journalist, Sterne a homilist and political allegorist. Often novelists wrote in the didactic mode for money, sometimes because they needed it badly and had no other means and sometimes out of abiding belief in causes they espoused, but always they wrote for a potential effect, trying to change their world as well as record, explain, and make a living in it. Readers were not abstractions to them, and the act of reading was not an armchair experience. Reading might be done in private, but its consequences were public, active, implicative. Novels were, to most novelists, just one more species in which to work their skills and promote their ethical and social ideas—a bit looser and less defined than most of the standard didactic subkinds but otherwise not, at first, much better, worse, or even different.

There is nothing simple about the way the popular didactic context helps to create a readership or writership for the novel. Literary history— the actual history of how species emerge and texts become—is seldom simple. The simplicities that arise from traditional literary history—in which texts father (or mother, but usually father) other texts and all the procreation stays within the extended family—do not reflect the rough-and-tumble world of people reading to live as well as to skim a few leisure pleasures off the top. I have described so fully here one aspect of the popular context in order to suggest the complex interplay of ideas, motives, assumptions, cultural needs, and individual desires that is reflected in the stories and other directives written or said by large numbers of people who perceive themselves to be driven (or attracted) by similar forces. I have hoped to give a sense of how lusts and taboos, fears and enthusiasms intermix across social lines and categories of writing. Novels are not the same as Guides—in some senses they are worlds away—but the areas of overlap are large, surprisingly large if we begin from assumptions of kind derived from the subsequent history of "imaginative" versus "didactic" modes. Novelists, though not always consciously, covet the territory didacticists have claimed and (like politicians in search of a constituency) adapt their interests and desires to the apparent needs of an audience which the print world had developed and continued to define as well as manipulate. Desire in the novel is partly that of writers who have their own agenda, partly that of readers who may call it fantasy or pursuit of pleasure—or (just as dangerous) practical need or restless aspiration.

V I I

OF all the features of late seventeenth-century journalistic and didactic materials, the most striking (and most basic) is their utter fragmentation. These materials are typically brief, composed for short attention spans, and characterized by quick, pointed, get-right-at-it attitudes. When such materials are expanded, strung together, or recast into some larger "whole," the result is additive, episodic, and often lumpy. Seldom is there a systematic building and releasing of expectation or a climactic structuring of event or idea, and closure is likely only to mean that new topics are no longer being introduced and that what is to be said about old topics has been exhausted. There is no more sense of related parts designed for symmetry and relationship than there is a sense of an ending. Even where a clear temporal skeleton or thematic singlemindedness exists, the text shows little concern about "unity" or "organicism" or other structural features the aesthetician or literary historian is apt to ask after. It is not that authors are careless, artless, or innocent of a sense of structure, but that their conception of form is utilitarian and their commitments are to the practical and the momentary, to providing information and stimulating behavior rather than to giving pleasure in the reading process itself. The immediate needs of readers—or rather, the writers' notions of them—dominate formal decisions, and in spite of claims that a larger vision inspires the writing, no holistic sense dominates individual pieces.

When didactic materials become books rather than tracts or pamphlets, they divide quickly into chapters or parts that can be tackled one at a time, without continuity or any obvious commitment to the longer work. And when journalistic accounts are lengthened, it is almost always by gathering together several accounts under some single head: events from a particular period of time, for example, or categorical instances of behavior or event—accounts of murders, or sabbath breakings, or tempests, or plagues. Seldom is there is a sense of larger commitment (at least as far as literary or bookmaking matters go) to longer ranges, bigger things, or more comprehensive forms. It seems in their nature. And yet . . .

Journalistic materials may seem to be almost by definition short and fragmentary. As renderings of moments of experience and as quick reads intended to fill fleeting intervals for readers, they are ready candidates for the fallacy of imitative form, and seldom are their moments explicitly subsumed in some larger sense of time or space. Contemporaries of Dunton or Defoe were hardly puzzled by the choppy and episodic quality of their (and their fellow journalists') engagements with the new and

momentary. More surprising to them were the restless attempts to accu-
mulate and tie together matters whose likenesses were hardly apparent if
in fact they existed at all; and when readers complain of anything in such
works, it is about their ambition or length or complexity rather than
about matters of local style or consistency. The struggle to add up by
adding on is frequent, most visibly in quick hackwork where art does not
complicate nor craft corrupt. In the single volume *Athenianism* (1710),
for example, Dunton prints, among more than a dozen other things, the
following miscellany of materials:

—"The Mathematic Funeral" (Project IV);

—"*Dunton's* Shadow: *Or the Character of a* Summer Friend" (Proj. V);

—"*Parnassus Hoa! Or a Frolick in Verse: Being Poems on none but* merry,
odd, barren and trifling Subjects" (Proj. VII);

—"*The* Weeping Elegy; *or* Tears *to the Memory of* . . . Samuel Treacher,
Lace-man, who dy'd . . . of the Small Pox . . . Intermix'd with an Essay
upon lawful Murder . . . as practis'd by the Country Doctors,"* (Proj. II, 2nd
ser.);

—"Double Hell; *or an Essay on Despair*" (Proj. III, 2nd ser.);

—"*The* He-Strumpets: *A Satyr on the* Sodomite-Club" (Proj. IV, 2nd
ser.);

—"The New Creation; or Dunton's *Thoughts in a Fit of Sickness, upon
those Words,* Arise ye Dead" (Proj. V, 2nd ser.);

—"Judas:—*Or, the secret Narrative of Four Dissenting Parsons* . . . *who
were lately silenc'd by their Congregations for Whoredom*" (Proj. XI, 2nd
ser.);

—"Family Duty: *Or, a modest Essay upon* Due Benevolence; *shewing*
. . . *the chast and lawful Use of the Marriage-Bed*"—*Intermix'd with several*
Nice Cases *relating to* Conjugal Venery" (Proj. XV, 2nd ser.);

—"The Marry'd Widower; *or* Dunton *in Mourning for the Death of his
living Wife, and New Life of his dead Friend, a* Paradox" (Proj. XVI, 2nd
ser.).

These "chapters" tumble one after the other. The key word is *"Intermix'd,"* and the result is a miscellaneous quality that seems lunatic; the
only thing that binds such items is the desire to seem original, up-to-
date, and curious, a wish to be all things to all people and cover everything. The intermixing is more egregious than anything Defoe ever did
or Swift ever parodied; it is close to the cultural fringe, a journalistic
extreme. But it represents the desire to record reality, fragmented moment
by fragmented moment, and to surprise readers with novel ideas, subjects, structures, attitudes, and styles—to mix the ordinary and familiar
with the strange and surprising so as to domesticate the puzzling and
complex. Longer books, just by being longer, were trying to make grander claims.

Behind such a book as *Athenianism* is a half-conscious desire to find relationship, to connect, to overwhelm random possibilities and some-how get hold of some larger sense of form, pattern, plan, order, or con-tinuity in the midst of an engagement with the here and now.[37] In such odd attempts—ineffective as most of them were—one can see a primi-tive, unself-conscious version of an emerging stage in epistemology. Long gone are the easy correspondences and analogies; there is no simple con-fidence in oneness or cosmic purpose, and efforts to invoke spiritual truth through meditation on earthly habits or things suggest longings in a world where information has grown too complex for any individual mind. But the desire to connect the passing and the minute with some grand scheme—to see the lasting in the momentary—had not diminished; it had just taken new forms. From a concentration on objects, as in traditional med-itative practice or in the new Meletetics and physico-theology, there had begun to be a concentration on moments, epiphanies, "spots of time," which could emblematize some longer unit of time or be a key to seeing a larger sequence. Increasingly, anxiety about the interrelationship of discrete spaces came to be anxiety about the interrelationship of discrete moments, and one of its manifestations was a concern to define person-ality and find the nature of the self by seeking evidence of continuity between moments of consciousness and memory.[38]

If journalism by the nature of its cultural and intellectual commitment seems to lead to short, limited, and discrete fragments of narration that go nowhere and diminish one's sense of connection to longer and larger patterns, the historical direction was, hesitantly, toward an accumulated and tabulated understanding. The tendency of Wonder books and Prov-idence anthologies to gather narrations, anecdotes, and examples of a certain type under methodized headings suggests how didacticism, old-fashioned and backward-looking though it is in its intentions, gave to the journalistic tendency a direction that moves toward the novel. Between the desire to capture the fleeting moment and the hope to harness such temporal energies and direct them to some grander thematic goal lay enormous cultural and artistic possibility, for however fragmented the journalistic may tend to be, in combination with other tendencies it leads directly to novels like *Robinson Crusoe*, *Tristram Shandy*, and *Evel-ina*, and ultimately toward *The Pickwick Papers*, *Middlemarch*, *The Sound and the Fury*, and *Hiroshima, Mon Amour*.

The fragmentation of didactic materials is rather different. Most didactic treatises are organized locally, and the units of organization are very small. Typical Guides of two-hundred pages have twelve to fifteen chapters, and it is not uncommon to have even more chapters of very short length, sometimes of only two or three pages each, or even of a single paragraph. Didactic anthologies of stories, anecdotes, and sayings are normally divided into chapters too (usually by theme or subject matter), and although chapters can be lengthy, each small narrative or discursive unit—an anecdote of a paragraph or two, or even a single pithy sentence—is normally a subdivision set off by a subhead or another mark of discreteness. The "resting places" for readers (as Henry Fielding calls chapter breaks) are thus frequent, and even the longest books are easy to approach in small, digestible chunks. The organization and visual format in fact encourage piecemeal reading, and—even though common themes run through chapters, sections, and sometimes a whole book—any sense of a larger wholeness is accretive rather than organic or even developmental. The materials look like what they are: quickly accessible, topical reference guides, or quick fixes of information and advice.

In view of didacticism's avowed aim to minister to the whole man or whole woman and work toward integration of character and personality, the emphasis on parts, subsets, and short takes seems ironic. Except for the conceptual reach in titles that promise long views and wholeness, most didactic treatises made little effort to use a form or method that shadowed forth the holism they professed. The claim in *The Whole Duty of Man*, for example, is not that it offers complete advice but that its precepts derive from a unified ethical conception that leads to an integrated life. And other titles—Law's, for example, or Dent's[39]—profess a concern with the wholeness of life they sought to foster. But regardless of aim, conception, mode, form, or method, Guides seldom achieve a sense of completion or closure; the attention is always focused on this act or that problem. Implicit in the idea of didacticism is a notion that reach will always exceed grasp, that all the words in the world will never bring human performance into perfect line with ethical aspirations, and a sense of failure, fragmentation, or incompleteness seems built into each aspiring work. Only in works that cast their didactic aims within some frame that by definition allows satisfaction—allegories like *Pilgrim's Progress*, spiritual autobiographies like *Grace Abounding*, histories like Clarendon's *History of the Rebellion*, or novels like *Tom Jones*—is there a sense of closure, resolution, and finality.[40] There words do become flesh in the sense that they are given a chance to work out their destiny in some defined—and limited—set of human circumstances. There, a defined temporal unit and a focused series of events provide not only shape and pace but a sense of satisfaction and completion. In the best of them one can see a successful blending of discursive and narrative techniques striving toward a cogent aesthetic of its own.

That is not to say that autobiographies, memoirs, pilgrim allegories, histories, travel books, and thematic anthologies of anecdotes are protonovels or imperfect, "draft" stages of a form destined for narrative success.

But discursive, expository, and didactic modes did mingle promiscuously in species controlled by temporal designs, often producing forms that did not neatly fit old generic categories but actualized the potential of temporality to transcend itself. The bookstalls were full of books that mixed temporal and spiritual commitments uncertainly—now depending on topicality, now on sequence, as occasion or opportunity dictated. Stories were methodized; precepts were transformed to events and causes. The mixing of discursive and narrative modes, like intentions to at once instruct and delight, sometimes led to formal achievement and aesthetic satisfaction, but appreciating such works depends on understanding how competing aims achieved creative balance. To describe works we find readable today as triumphs of narrative over didactic impulses—or as victories of art over moral expectations—is not only to miss the historical point but the aesthetic one. What was brewing in the seventeenth century, as variations on Horatianism were explored in different proportions, was a powerful modern elixir with both ideological and aesthetic power. Most of the works involved in the experiment achieve imperfect (and highly volatile) versions of the mix, but it is their existence—and their restless striving for new combinations—rather than their achievements as proto-novels or near-novels that marks them as important. They are part of the context that makes the novel possible, but they do not lead to it in a simple, mechanical, and straightforward way.

If the structural tendency of didactic literature is toward fragmentation rather than wholeness, it does not matter much within the framework of aims that inspires didacticism. Didactic books are by definition helps, adjuncts, guides to something larger and more important. Just as a Guide such as *The Whole Duty of Man* may still be appropriately called a *vade mecum,* so even the specialized ones are also designed as carry-alongs, sets of directions, helps, supplements to human life; they do not propose to substitute for it, and their representational claims are limited. They do not present an alternative world, as works of imaginative literature often do, and they offer nothing self-sufficient or holistic. To attain completion or even closure, they must not only be read—like poems or novels—but lived out in some explicit way. The text is not completed by the act of reading.

But however involved the heritage of the novel may be with didacticism, novels do present alternative worlds, even if those worlds are more closely related than those in earlier forms of fiction to the actual world. And if writings in the journalistic mode and the didactic mode show some of the things that readers needed, they do not show them all. Crucial to what the novel is able to do are two accomplishments that have no analogue, no source, barely even the hint of a beginning in the texts

I have considered so far. Both the subjectivity and the outreach of the novel relate to quite different tendencies. Before there were novels, these tendencies are visible in writings of a quite different character. In the final three chapters, I examine some of the contemporary forms of writing that purport to present whole worlds, that reach toward some larger sense of connection and movement, and that show the contemporary mind becoming more analytical, more introspective, and yet more intensely aware of a sense of place in time. The personal literature—diaries, autobiographies, biographies—that became both increasingly popular and increasingly accepted as a genuine literary mode reflects a culture becoming ever more intensive and interior, perhaps the logical extension of urban landscapes. And the literature of perspective—books of travel, memoirs, histories—reflects a culture striving to discover how a new subjectivity "fits" and becomes intersubjectivity, how people and cultures interrelate in a world in which there is no single "human nature" but a multiplicity of individual persons in particular situations and cultural traditions and circumstances, with natures each of their own.

Three forms of writing that unlike (didacticism and journalism) purport to present whole worlds not fragmented

CHAPTER TWELVE

The Self and the World: Private Histories

Personal Writings — diaries, biographies, autobiographies

PERSONAL writings were in the seventeenth century private writings, and they were legion. They came to exist because many Englishmen and Englishwomen, not just a few religious extremists, believed that their eternal salvation was closely linked to the events of their everyday lives—that "reading" one's life analytically could provide awareness of one's spiritual status. The recording and analysis of these events, in minute and painstaking detail, became a sacred duty and a common Protestant practice, and diary keeping (although primarily insisted upon by Puritan theorists) became a national habit practiced by a large percentage of those who were literate. But by the early eighteenth century, this intimate and precise world of privacy began to shift into the public realm. Exactly why personal writings began to be mined, refined, and sent abroad into the world of print is a complex story involving fundamental cultural changes. Those changes are also crucial to the emergence of the novel as a species that invaded privacy yet seemed to preserve a cloak of decency by keeping human secrets in private places and times. The novel did not "descend" from the seventeenth-century diary, but the diary (and the spiritual autobiography and biography that grew out of it) did provide a model that defined shape, scope, and epistemology. The changing ideologies that created the diary, then transformed it into a respectable form—ideas of selfhood, personality, subjectivity, propriety, and the way to verbalize the personal and unspeakable—made it possible for the novel to emerge by creating a cultural climate receptive to issues of privacy.

The novel addressed these issues in two ways: by exploring the interpretive mind bent on sorting human experience, and by seeking a didactic content for readers willing to look into their hearts and read.[1]

I

DIARIES proliferated in England and Scotland in the early seventeenth century and a little later in America. How many of them existed we have no way of knowing, but, judged by the great number that have survived, they must have been very common, perhaps almost universal among those who were both devout and literate, whatever their religious persuasion. The nature of their contents and the ways they were kept suggest that, in their early history, there was no effort to save diaries and some pressure to destroy them so as to preserve privacy as secrecy or to keep quasi-sacred documents out of unauthorized hands. "Saints" kept diaries for their own benefit—to have a precise record of behavior that would help reveal the state of their soul and to provide a basis for review of life patterns. Diaries were an archive of data and implication intended for the diarist alone, and at first little thought was given to finding a way to transmit their value to others.

In the Protestant culture that then prevailed, the impulse to keep diaries was powerful. The need to record the self extensively and analytically comes from Puritan—especially Calvinist—theory, but, like so many other religious or quasi-religious habits, diary keeping did not follow strict ideological lines; the pious personal behaviour of sectarians did not vary much from that of Anglicans. Puritanism was a cultural revolution before settling for goals in Church and State polity. The righteous spirit and strict personal accounting that already dominated the Anglican communion before the midcentury political crisis—dictating among other things a slant to the Thirty-Nine Articles that makes it a straight Calvinist document[2]—shows up in a host of daily ways in England, and the changing social practices I described in Chapters Three through Six came about because a great many people began to rebel against what they saw to be pagan ways, not because a few wild radicals broke up country fairs with axes and clubs. By midcentury, Puritan religiosity had permeated the culture so widely in so many everyday ways that, except in some strains of aristocratic culture, it was hard to say what was "Puritan" and what was not in everyday practice, despite bitter debates about matters of doctrine, ritual, and authority. The Puritans won English culture long before they won—then lost—the political revolution; and the widespread infiltrations of Puritan principles in the culture were never expunged, even after the Restoration, despite ruthless political repressions.

The perceived need to keep a record of one's daily life—a need closely related to the belief in self-examination that I discussed in Chapter Eleven—was apparently very intense. Exhortations are ubiquitous, and the desired review was often put in ledger-like terms. "[C]all your selves every Night to a strict Account," says Josiah Woodward, "for the Actions of the past Day: ask your selves what you have been doing? What Company you have kept? What Temptations you have met with? What Sins you have committed? What Corruptions you have subdu'd? What experiences you had of God's Goodness, and how you entertain'd them? What use you have made of his Dealing with your self or others? In a Word, What Progress you have made Heaven-wards?"[3] John Norris agrees, calling the practice a *"Nightly Review"* (p. 11):

> [A]t night when you go to Bed . . . you would do well to take a Review of the day past, and particularly examine how you have spent it, not only that if you have done well you may glorifie God; and if ill, may humble your selves before him, and make your Peace with him before you commit your selves to sleep; but also that by this Exercise you may know what progress you make in Piety, what the State of your Souls [sic] is, and how accounts stand between you and God; and may also learn to spend every day the better, as you will find your selves induced to do, by the very prospect of that returning Account which you are to render of it to your selves at Night.[4]

Standard Guide books like *The Gentleman's Library* (1715) simply take the practice for granted and only explain its uses: "as *Books* are Profitable, and *Reading* an Improvement, so much more will the *Reading* of our own Lives, a *Survey* of our Actions, and an Inspection into the Division of our *Time*, be an Advantage, as it certainly is a Duty" (p. 194).

The illiterate could engage in oral self-examination without having to record their deeds (and no doubt they did); but the injunction to record—make a permanent, scannable, daily account—extended the process so that it might include periodic reviews and attempts to chart one's progress, discover patterns of life that could reveal providential meanings, or indicate the divine plan for an individual life. Texts recommending daily accounts kept over a long period and reviewed regularly were often animated and insistent. Protestant suspicions of oral tradition gave a certain urgency to the admonition to record. Distrust of memory is a frequent theme in didactic literature of the time; the writers of Guides did not believe (as modern students of literacy do) that memory among the illiterate is superior or that oral tradition offers a reliable account of events or a sufficient record for an ethical and spiritual evaluation to be based on. The practice of public confessional at gatherings of the "saints"—quite common among certain sects—is related to the "confessional" habits that developed in private diaries, but public confessional represents a later step (different in implication) in the sharing of intimacy—the historical process of allowing the private, personal, and intimate to have public utterance. The authority Protestantism assigns the written word as a record of divine will and human destiny is intimately related to the injunction to record one's life and not just live it (a value that Henry Fielding comically addresses when he suggests that Colley Cibber had lived his life only in order to write about it), and so is the Protestant sense—clear in Boyle's Meletetics and in the revised modern versions of Occasional Meditation generally—that the physical world and events in it can be read clearly, accurately, and usefully for their spiritual implications, cosmic as well as personal.

But whatever the philosophical basis for diary keeping and the relationship between oral tradition and recorded text, the larger context of increasing reliance on written records must also be kept in mind. The late seventeenth century marks the start of modern dependence on data. Compared to us, Restoration London may seem tentative in its commitments to having everything recorded, yet the strong bias we have toward excessive information for its own sake was just then becoming established toward records that could be examined, reviewed, meditated upon, obsessed about, but above all trusted. Just as tradesmen's accounts could be inspected and the journalistic record of contemporary events assessed and summed into a running history, so could records of an individual life if the individual could be persuaded to preserve it moment by moment. Ultimately it is in the writing down of information rather than the reliance on transmittal through conversation and community memory that the connection of spiritual accounts to financial accounts consists. It is not that a trade mentality leads to spiritual and ethical review—or vice versa, as interpreters of Ben Franklin and Jay Gatsby have often implied—but that prevailing opinion had come to distrust an oral tradition that was associated with primitive, country, and pagan ways, and that a new era of trust in records—that is, a world of archival information—had begun. Diary keeping was an assertion of modernity, or rather, of the uses of modernity for the preservation of traditional religious values.

Although diary keeping as a widespread phenomenon was quite new and distinctively English, the practice did not spring out of nothing, and, whether or not they were needed, there were models. Early English diaries resembled the *Confessions* of St. Augustine, even if writers did not have him consciously in mind, because the Puritans shared with Augustine a strong sense of personal responsibility, a firm belief in a divine master plan for each individual human life, and a vivid awareness of the human capacity to change quickly and without warning. These assumptions, though somewhat contradictory among themselves, led to both brooding and introspection. The anxiety felt by Puritans about election and the state of grace may be, at base, quite different from the torment of Augustine about the inadequacies of his commitment and performance, but the result was similar in terms of self-examination, recall of events so that interpretable patterns could emerge, and an analysis of both motive and event. Early diary keepers shared with Augustine a profound sense of individual responsibility, and they both had a fierce sense (one we are now likely to associate with Calvin and label as "Puritan") of causality in a rational world where the exercise of individual will leads to a series of consequences—personal and social, cosmic as well as particular—because the plan for an individual life cannot be separated from the Larger Plan.

Precisely how one is to regard the route from Augustinian Christianity to Protestantism and Puritanism is a question of lively interest to literary scholars,[5] but ultimately the issue will have to be decided by theologians, Church historians, and theorists of intellectual history. Similarities of consciousness are striking enough to remark, as are equally important connections between the Puritans and St. Bonaventure. But model and paradigm may not be the right words to describe the *Confessions* relative to English practice, even if the habits of mind and written records are similar. The habits of mind lead in each case to introspective processes that result in circumstantiality, accumulation of detail, ruthless self-criticism, and a shape involving episodic daily units; and the presence of St. Augustine on the literary landscape is useful to modern readers because they are more likely to be familiar with—and to respect—his personal and introspective writing than the obscure early diaries of England and America. The Augustinian mode of confessional is similar enough in intention and direction—because similar in motivation—to Puritan diary keeping to justify and clarify historic practice. That similarity is philosophically closer than the early English novel's parallels to the later confessional mode of Rousseau, which represents a later and decidedly more "secular" stage of personal narration, one that has an impact on the English novel only through French fiction of the later eighteenth century, *after* the Richardsonian version of private writing had already made its impact on the French novel.

The typical diary recorded almost everything in a diarist's day. In a world thought to be sacramental, hieroglyphic, and often cryptic, finding the meaning of God's mysterious ways was not easy, and any detail could provide a clue to pattern. Often diarists stop to take stock, looking back over previous entries and noting their impressions of direction and possible meaning. It is true that their introspectiveness is limited by the focus of their curiosity—directed toward God's plan and pattern rather than their own—and issues of will, intention, and self-direction are addressed only as manifestations of some larger force so that their idea of self-examination is thus vastly different from ours. Still, their devout version of introspection, although inspired by otherworldly motives and injunctions, can lead to some sharp human and personal insights, and (even when its analysis is clumsy) it offers a comprehensive record of the self as experiencer and observer. Science and theology had both blessed the process; diaries recorded what the culture valued, the attempt to make facts instrumental to larger quests for meaning. But it was the novel that transformed the closely scrutinized detail and the subjective process into something more than a spiritual convenience.

I I

DETAILS are the coin of novelistic fiction, and diaries—while they are not a "source" (in the conventional sense) for the novel's commitment to detail—are the most personal and poignant written record of the culture's growing dependence on factual precision, and they are probably the most direct conduit through which circumstantial features flow into the novel. The culture's preoccupation with detail is part of early modernism's commitment to systematization, quantification, and the accumulation of data for analysis. It is probably right to stress not some cause-effect relationship between science and Protestantism but rather their common heritage in a rapidly changing culture. As Hill says, "both science and protestantism sprang from the shift by which urban and industrial values replaced those appropriate to a mainly agrarian society."[6] The culture's rising dependence on information can be measured in a variety of ways, and the scientific revolution is one reminder of the growing importance of precision and detail. But there are other reminders, too—the rise of economics as an intellectual interest, the growing international complications of commerce, the beginnings of industrialism—and the implications for literature of this cultural shift are major.

If one compares Prior's social poems with Waller's or Lovelace's, Pope's satires with Donne's or Dryden's, Gay's outdoor world with Herrick's or Traherne's, or Thomson's long poems with Spenser's or Milton's, the changes in representational commitment are readily apparent. Not only does literature come to represent an urban and commercial world that

has replaced the rural and agrarian one as the focus of both discourse and
imagination, but the language of description also dilates into endless
exemplifying, amplifying, and explaining by observation: the streaks of
the tulip are not only numbered but reproduced in great detail, and the
world of pavements and buildings is inventoried, catalogued, and appraised
item by item. But it is the novel that creates a formal space for such a
proliferation of detail. The novel needs, depends upon, and devours detail,
while other species only tolerate it or adjust themselves to take account
of its possibilities in features they already have.[7]

Whatever ultimately lies beneath the diary's devotion to detail, the
motivation of individual diarists to discover the grander patterns of the
world provides the most direct impact on the writing of novels. It is not
that diarists provide a formal model for novelists or that the world of
detail is somehow transferred from diaries (representing an attempt to
record fact) to novels (an attempt to recreate in fiction a plausible and
recognizable reality). Rather, the sense that the details of the world can
be observed fully enough that the ordering pattern behind them can be
discovered and described—a sense shared by Newtonians, Linnaeans,
physico-theologians, Protestant meditationists, and diarists—becomes
methodized for individuals who are habituated to setting down the details
of their lives. Ultimately it is the way of perceiving the world that is
important, and the diaristic tradition is both the pervasive record of the
culture's valuing of detailed data and the most popular and personal vehicle for the discipline of observation, recording, and discovery.

But it is not the source of the idea. The diary's importance to the
novel as a conduit has more to do with habituating readers to the process
and with forming, conforming, and furthering habits of mind for both
readers and writers than it does with providing either an intellectual
source or a formal model. No novelist needed to read diaries in order to
discover that circumstantial detail was important to contemporary epistemology or to see how it could be employed toward credibility and persuasion. But novelists lived intellectually and emotionally in the context
in which the diaristic impulse flourished and, whether or not they themselves kept diaries, shared the assumptions and habits of mind that
demanded diaries and enabled novels. In a novelist like Defoe, analysis
of the details of a hero's life often takes an openly diaristic form, and in
Defoe's first novel diaristic analysis is set in overt juxtaposition with later
summary reflection on the same events as an exercise in interpretation.
In a novelist like Sterne, the diaristic influence is comically distanced
and turned to satiric purposes right at the beginning: the circumstantial
account of Tristram's conception not only fails to decode the meaning of
his life but actually impedes knowledge by implying that the heap of facts

presented means much more than it does. Only a thoughtfuul calculation by the reader—a calculation Tristram himself refuses to make in his zeal to give details—reveals that Tristram's extreme circumstantiality is seriously misplaced, leaving the text reeling in uncertainty about basic matters of paternity, heroic lineage, and identity.[8] But even Sterne's ultimate rejection of the assumptions built into a circumstantial method testifies, in the way he asserts the rejection, to the novel's very dependence on the method, whether or not it succeeds philosophically in actually revealing truth. Tristram's story may be read as a demonstration that the method leads to a failed life and that such methodizing is futile. Certainly, it is a critique of epistemological and cultural assumptions in Sterne's time. But Sterne's telling, inverted though it is, shows what the novel as a species makes of circumstantiality and how, in fact, it depends upon it for its assumptions and methods. Without the impulse to record, sort out, and conclude, there is no novel as we know it.

The absence of detail in older fiction is nearly as striking as its ubiquitous and necessary presence in novels. The novel has no corner on circumstantial detail, of course. Other narratives and journalistic accounts—even didactic treatises and anthologies—from the later seventeenth century on depend increasingly on circumstantiality and the recounting of fact, and pamphlets and treatises thrived on the feeling that they could glut the eye and overwhelm the mind with sheer bulk data. Even plays and poems (Shadwell's *Virtuoso*, for example, or Gay's *Trivia*) felt the cultural urge to circumstantiality; it had become the way of the world, as Swift's Tale-teller notes regretfully when he has to pass up giving a detailed account of what had interrupted his writing process. It "would be," he notes ruefully, "very seasonable, and much in the *Modern* way, to inform the *gentle Reader*" of all the details, and "would also be of great Assistance towards extending this Preface into the Size now in Vogue" (Preface, p. 54), but he begs off because of circumstances beyond his control. Yet seldom do "modern" writers as typical as the Tale-teller pass up the opportunity to tell all, whatever their claims about brevity and sensitivity to readers' tedium. They may claim, like the satiric biographer of Thomas Burnett, that "It may seem strange to trouble the Reader with such minute Trifles,"[9] but they know it is *not* strange to practiced readers, and they go on to provide all the minutiae. " 'Twould be too tedious," writes John Dunton about one of his journeys in the *Life and Errors*, "to give the Reader the *Particulars* of the Voyage, which would swell to a *Folio* of Sea-Affairs" (p. 117), but (like Crusoe and the Lemuel Gulliver who mimics Crusoe's circumstantial style at the start and finish of each of his voyages) he provides enough information to stupefy an Inquisitor, and his self-consciousness about reader expectations is representative. In fact, writers of all kinds of narratives and discourses regularly risk that "tediousness"—the swellings are everywhere—and novelists are their legitimate heirs.

As the species emerging just as detailed circumstantiality was triumphing in the culture (and as a species that was, from the start, adaptive and eclectic), the novel becomes especially detail-conscious. It becomes the form with detail built into its fabric and rationale, as diaries had been in earlier generations, when the culture's fascination with detail was nascent. Novelists repeatedly apologize for their length and circumstantiality, pleading the tangled nature of reality or their desire to be credible and fair, and they often claim to pass over huge treasures of information to save the reader trouble.[10] "I shall not trouble the reader with . . ." is in fact one of the most frequent phrases in the early novel, actually a *topos* that testifies to expectations of excessive detail. The phrase is rampant in Defoe and his contemporaries, still frequent at midcentury. It is both a short cut and a lie; it becomes an excuse for not giving more detail as well as a way of implying that less detail is given than actually is. Its presence indexes the self-consciousness of novelists, and an analysis of its uses show just how big the mounds of detail pile up to be. But self-conscious at they are, writers like Ned Ward and Dunton, Swift and Gilbert Burnet, Richardson and Burney usually do take the trouble to provide the details anyway, however much they protest about their restraint. Like Crusoe when he finds the hidden money in the shipwreck, on second thought they usually decide that, however useless it may seem at the moment, the coin may come in handy in the long run, so they collect it and keep moving.

I I I

HOWEVER it came about and whatever the importance of the content of individual diaries, the diarist movement meant that, suddenly, there were in England tens of thousands of "authors" of texts, some of the texts just fragments, letters, notes, or anecdotes it is true, but still written texts, there to be reviewed and reread. These authors had, of course, only limited authorial status; they had no public recognition and, in the beginning, no readers except themselves. And they probably did not, in the beginning, think of themselves as authors, even if they recognized their "sacred" function as amanuensis and worried about the question of their authority as observer, recorder, and subject. Still, they were all proprietors (and, in a way, heroes) of texts, and they had experienced the joy and frustration of articulation, selection of material, perspective.

Literary history has not taken into account the effects upon readership of this large class of authors or quasi-authors, people who brought to their reading of works with strong diaristic and autobiographical strategies (works like *Moll Flanders, Clarissa, and Evelina*) a certain formal familiarity and intense personal recognition.

Whether or not novelists consciously imitated the structures of auto-biography, their shared knowledge of habits of mind and formal expectations conditioned the way they told their stories and made the truth claims of their fiction structurally more plausible. And for readers, whether or not consciously counted on or even taken into account, their own writing experience made them better prepared formally and more richly expectant than popular reading publics are usually said to be. The prevailing preoccupation with turning life into an examined record thus had a profound early effect on the shape of early novels, not only influencing narrative and expository features but also creating a kind of centripetal mode that drew readers toward the center of public texts just as they were pulled to the center of their own.

For someone like Defoe who grew up in a literate atmosphere of Dissent, the awareness of recorded experience, habits of self-examination, and repeated readings of life experiences in quest of meaningful patterns clearly affected the way he organized things when he came to write lives, factual and fictional. For Richardson, the sense of familiarity with diaristic analysis is equally strong, and the habitual self-recording of his characters in letters seems conceptually dependent on a world in which diary keeping and self-presentation were assumed. Formally, the epistolary mode masks somewhat the essentially autobiographical strategy that Richardson depends on, but his writing-to-the-moment originates in the diaristic impulse, taking it to obsessive lengths. The fact that, after *Pamela I*, Richardson increasingly moves away from the perspective of a single character and toward conflict among multiple consciousnesses, suggests at once the ultimate autobiographical (and diaristic) origins of his art and his growing recognition that multiple I-perspectives can deepen psychological analysis, complicate plot, and create formal resonance. But however sophisticated Richardson's manipulation of perspective becomes and however he moves (in his editing and answering of critics) in the direction of omniscience, his art is still basically first-person narrative, and it depends upon the sense that a human observer is the best source of detail on him- or herself as the observed, whether or not we trust the self-evaluation. And *Evelina,* half a century after Defoe, shows that Burney clearly learned her insights into point of view as much from her own experience with reading and writing letters and from keeping a journal as from the practice of novelistic forbears.[11] Others who work variations on first-person conventions—Smollett, Sterne, Sarah Fielding, and a host of anonymous writers of fictional memoirs—also seem personally conversant with the familiar world of personal letters and private accounts, and they plainly expect concomitant familiarity from readers.

By midcentury, however, readers and writers alike were conditioned by the then-developed conventions of the novelistic tradition, and it is difficult to be sure whether writers who began their careers then developed the habit from colleagues or from broader contexts. But the patterns they follow come ultimately from private, personal narrative. Conventional literary history, having dwelt upon issues of conscious intention, imitation of examples, and the setting of expectations in authorial terms, has tended toward milestone theory, giving credit for a "first" of something here and the invention of something there—the "here" and "there" being located within the mind of an author. In the terms I have chosen for articulating literary history, it is less easy to trace "influence" and the creative innovations of individuals but easier to specify contexts dominated by the developing awarenesses of readers and audiences. A readership of "authors" clearly knew the conventions and habits of autobiographical narrative; it also understood the epistemology that had created such a rich but covert heritage for contemporary narrative. The availability and variety of autobiographical texts expanded possibility for writers eager to understand the reading context, just as the sense of community intensified among private diarists and autobiographers who increasingly knew how large their numbers really were. It is no wonder that novelists often found it prudent to pretend that their narratives were actual histories of real people telling their own stories so that their texts seemed to join a larger community of texts and authors.

I V

THE movement from diary to autobiography—from a private document intended only for one's own self-scrutiny to something circulated to others for their possible spiritual enhancement and edification—did not come quickly, but by the early eighteenth century there was both a formal change and a deeper cultural change in attitude that had enabled the formal change. Formally, what happened was that moralists had decided that the "lives" of others could provide useful examples for contemporaries struggling with an increasingly complex, increasingly urban, increasingly encroaching reality. To some extent English Protestantism had always licensed the publication of lives, although it had no hagiographic tradition to match the saints' lives that Roman Catholicism had fostered in such forms as *The Golden Legend*. But until the late seventeenth century, the lives published were (as in the Catholic tradition) those of extraordinary people, usually those celebrated for their saintly virtue and Herculean heroism, and the exceptions involved mighty heroes gone wrong, those who found appropriate space in cautionary collections like the *Mirror for Magistrates*. The roster of Protestant saints and heroes was, however, painfully short. Spiritual standards were very high, perhaps unreasonably so because of wide suspicion that Catholicism had debased the standard for public heroes and altogether fictionalized the claims for saints. Besides, Protestant ideals, despite the emphasis on private experience, expected Gargantuan accomplishment in human events. Beyond biblical models (who got the most "biographical" attention in Protestant religious literature until late in the seventeenth century), only figures as prominent as Luther and Elizabeth and Cromwell seemed proper subjects. Beyond the high ethical expectations applied to potential heroes, partisan politics also limited choices. Milton's quest for an adequate epic hero may be paradigmatic of Protestantism's plight, but less "literary" writings show even more plainly the intellectual history of the change that leads to different standards in biography and (ultimately) in novels.

As the seventeenth century wore on, a broader variety of spiritual biographies began to appear in England, detailing the lives of pious clergymen or lay followers whose ethical conduct, if not necessarily their worldly accomplishments, seemed of special merit. These were usually third-person accounts that drew on diaries or other private documents. The shape of the life was ordinarily imposed by some editor, and the person whose life was published was nearly always someone already dead. Sometimes such a life was published in a short individual volume, usually just after the person's death and often as an adjunct to the funeral sermon, but there were also attempts to collect lives so as to create a broad sense that Protestantism, and modernity more generally, also had heroes. At least one major compiler of such collections, Samuel Clarke (minister of St. Bennet Fink in London), consciously sought to build up a contemporary Protestant martyrology, a roster of "saints" whose lives individually would provide guidance and inspiration and cumulatively would offer a sense of modern possibility and human power. Throughout his career, Clarke wrote biographies of many of the mighty—Alexander the Great, Hannibal, Julius Caesar, William the Conqueror, and Queen Elizabeth, for example—but he became increasingly interested in lives of the less famous, and gradually his collections became more inclusive. In 1651, he appended "The Lives of sundry Modern Divines" to *A Generall Martyrologie*; in 1660, he published a separate collection of the lives of twenty-two English clergymen; and in 1662, he broadened his interest to include lay figures (A Collection of the Lives of Ten Eminent Divines, Famous in their Generations . . . and of some other Eminent Christians). His final biographical collection, The Lives of Sundry Eminent Persons in this Later Age (1683), included sections on divines, members of the nobility, and women. Clarke was no leveler, but his collections reflect changing cultural needs. He spoke for many in wishing to develop a bank of biographical data. "I have been encouraged," he wrote in 1683, "to make this Collection, and now to Publish it, finding that my former Labours in this kind, have been accepted with the Saints . . . ; they have been Printed four times in a few years space, and yet never less than a Thousand at a time. I am now in the Eighty third year of my Life, and therefore am never like to do more in this kind: but hope that God will raise up some more able person to carry on this so useful a work. . . ." (fols. Al–Alv).

Materials for contemporary biographies nearly always came from the diaries and private papers of the biographees, although oral anecdotes and the memories of companions were also popular sources. The line between biography and autobiography—always hard to draw in spite of the obvious mechanical distinction—was especially difficult in a time when individuals seldom published their autobiographies but nearly always kept documentary evidence easily convertible to biography or—if they chose themselves to edit, organize, and sum up—formal autobiography. Around 1700, a conceptual change allowed both more biographical materials and a greater variety of them to be published. Portions of private documents began to turn up regularly in anthologies of anecdotes and thematic collections such as William Turner's A Compleat History of the Most Remarkable Providences (1697), and people began to recast their diaries into "spiritual autobiographies," for their own use or for private circulation among friends or members of their congregation, giving their own sense of shape to their lives as lived so far. And a few—a very few— spiritual autobiographies (such as Bunyan's Grace Abounding, 1666) had begun to be published, sometimes even when the subject was still alive if (as in Bunyan's case) there were compelling practical reasons.

Converging events and conditions produced the change: the Restoration itself (with its move to marginalize radical Protestants), the increasing desperation of moralists, threats to Christian belief generally, a changing sense of how examples could be useful even when they involved mixed behavior and less than clear models for imitation or evitation, rising urbanism and a fragmentation of old communities. And it may well be that, as cliché has long had it, the populace grew impatient for heroes of any sort, less able to conceive the grandeur that had surrounded, in the collective mind at least, the ideals of yore. Perhaps, too, changes in the social status of the reading public began to create a different sense of what models were relevant or adequate. But whatever the immediate social forces, the cultural consciousness changed, making "prominence" possible in a new way. Attitudes began to soften about the uses of privacy and about the propriety of making personal history public if it could conceivably have edifying effects. For this different sense, the familiarity with diaristic expectation and the concomitant emphasis on human fallibility has to bear some responsibility. Revelations that would have caused profound embarrassment—even shame—a generation earlier began to find their way into print, slowly at first and always with a clear moral pointed, but inexorably they annexed some areas of personal behavior into the public domain of print. The shock threshold lowered noticeably in the late seventeenth century. Even the mighty had their warts increasingly exposed.

The easiest comprehensive way to account for such changes is to invoke another famous rise—that of secularism—and to say that saints and heroes were increasingly secularized and humanized. Secular assumptions were indeed gaining momentum every day and modifying even the most conservative and traditional social and cultural structures. But however inevitable and comprehensive such a force may have been, other more immediate factors were involved, too, and it may be more helpful to notice the way didactic theorists adjusted to changing contexts. Very important, for example, is the changing emphasis in the psychology of reach and grasp. The disillusionment with absolutes that surfaces in mid-century novels, probably in reaction to William Law and George Whitefield and the tenets of holiness and Methodism, has a modest earlier incarnation in the generations immediately following Puritan rule, and one can see in much of the didactic rhetoric—in biographies, in moralized anecdotes, and in the more preceptual Guides—increased emphasis on the acceptance of human limitations in ethical achievement and escalated exhortation to be undiscouraged by backslidings and fallings short. It would be simplistic, cynical, and unfair to regard the acceptance of flaws and fallibility as simply an excuse to sensationalize narrative and hortatory writings, but it is true that the raised threshold of acceptability for accounts of sin or ethical slippage provided an enlarged scope of human activity, an enlivened tone, and (sometimes) an unrestrained dwelling upon peccatory particulars.

The mining of private documents for anecdotes and records of human responses to events clearly fits the spirit of authors and printers who sought illustrations everywhere when they detailed the world's wonders or gathered evidence for providential intervention. Someone like John Aubrey sought his illustrations largely in older texts that had the blessings of antiquity, but Providence books, Wonder books, and the periodical columns devoted to similar ends sought contemporary information wherever they could get it and were heavily dependent on private papers and anecdotes.

Publishers who felt no guilt about borrowing or stealing from other published works plainly had no compunction about seeking private stories as well. John Dunton's advertisement in *The Post-Angel* (1701) for short biographies and Providential anecdotes is not much of an extension of his request in 1693 that readers of *The Athenian Mercury* send in their "cases" for his casuistical comment. The earlier "cases" had emphasized issues, not events, but the inherent interest of casuistry in circumstantiality meant attention to life particulars that were inevitably personal, anecdotal, and narrative in direction. The stories Dunton sought from readers for his later projects thus were more openly contributions—they did not need answers or even annotations—but they involved similar instances of experience and observation. When, for example, he began *The Post-Angel* in January 1701, he announced that most of his material, especially for the sections on "Remarkable Providences" and "Eminent Lives," would come from the submissions of readers: "'[T]is desir'd,'" he wrote in his Preface to the first number, "that all *serious Christians* would send what they find remarkable every Month" (fol. B1v), and within six months he was including in every number an advertisement for material: "The Ingenious are desired to send such *Remarkable Providences, Eminent-Lives, Nice Questions, Occurrences, and News-Books*, and such other Pieces, in Verse or Prose, as may properly be inserted in the Post-Angel for [the next month] (I quote from the August issue, [II, 66], but all issues had similar statements). At first, Dunton (always ambitious to provide a full record of everything) hoped to describe the life of everyone who had died during the past month. "'[T]will be very useful,'" he argues, "to give some Account of the *Lives* (as well as of the Deaths) of eminent Persons; for to describe the Lives of Good-men, will invite us to follow their Holy Examples, that we may die in the like Triumphant manner; and to relate the Lives of bad men *(for I'll omit no Life, whether good or bad, that has been remarkable)* will teach us how to avoid their Snares and Temptations. . . . I design *a compleat History of modern Lives*. . . ."[12] In his desire to print a total record of modern life—he did mean to be the kind of amanuensis to the universe that Swift made fun of in *A Tale of a Tub*—Dunton wanted to recruit everyone into the effort:

> For should every Man write an exact Narrative of the various Experiences and Circumstances of his Life, comprehending as well his Vices as Vertues, and have them with simplicity related, how useful would this prove to the

publick, tho' it would much increase the number of Books, but this so impartial an Account may rather be wisht for than expected, since Men have ever
preferred their own private Reputation before the real good of themselves or
others.[13]

Actually, Dunton (like other journalists, printers, and editors) had
long used private documents available to him, perhaps with the author's
permission, perhaps not. Not only had he combed his father's papers for
publishable religious and moral treatises (or for hints and beginnings of
things he might himself write), but parts of his first wife's diary had appeared
in Turner's *Compleat History*, along with quite a few other accounts that
must have come from private sources, diaries perhaps, or possibly sometimes by word of mouth. And the private documents of his wife also
appeared in other things he published; the *Life and Errors*, for example,
is full of her letters, notes, and pieces of her diary.[14] Other people who
had dealings with Dunton, especially women he sought or who sought
him, also ran high probabilities of finding their private words, written or
oral, permanently and publicly preserved. To be connected to Dunton
was to risk a life more public than one might intend. Although he claimed
to be scrupulous about following authorial wishes,[15] Dunton evidently
thought the public had the right to know all about everything and, as
publisher and author, helped himself to documents he came upon by
whatever means. Some of his publications in the 1690s are simply pas-
tiches of other people's words, often personal and highly private words,
strung together and edited by Dunton's own heavy and visible hand.[16]
Dunton was always a conscious reader of public tastes and trends, and
his practices exaggerate those of his contemporaries only in the number,
frequency, and audacity of his private borrowings and exposures. He may
have been extreme, even in that age, as a blatant anthologist of whatever
came into his hands, but he was very much of his age in wanting to
contribute to a public record that essentially preserved, event by event
and jot by jot, everything that happened in his time. History was not
summary, or distillation, or illustration, but total preservation, and the
retention of details—whether in diaries or in Dunton, in trade ledgers or
the *Transactions of the Royal Society*, in meditations or personal letters—
may be essential to the spirit of a time that provided a friendly and populous context for the omnivorous novel. The tendency of the novel toward
representation that quantitatively imitated life had an extreme prophet
in Dunton.

The excerpting of private writings, often in funeral sermons and related
forms, amounted to much the same thing as the use of discrete anecdotes
in anthologies and periodical or occasional publications. The brief (eight-

page) life appended to the funeral sermon for Samuel Pomfret (*Watch and Remember*, 1722), for example, suggests how materials from a diary and from oral anecdotes may contribute to a short narrative,[17] and *An Account of the Life and Death of Mrs. Elizabeth Bury* (1720) more lengthily and elaborately shows how private documents may be used to shape a "life" that has become independent of its funeral occasion and taken on an ethical and literary form of its own. There, a twenty-four-page funeral sermon is only a tenth of the volume, reversing the usual proportions; and the life itself, although written by the clergyman-husband, largely summarizes her collected diaries and then prints passages from them (*"Fragments, which will rather serve as a Specimen, than give any full Account of her Life . . ."* [fol. A2v]).

Somewhat different are the autobiographies that amount to self-edited and compressed versions of diaries. Quite a number of such documents evidently circulated within particular congregations or among friends of the person, whose life was thus reshaped into a pattern for private imitation or evitation. It is hard to say how widespread such practice became or how broad its effect may have been on the habits of diarists and the expectations of readers, but in the countless extant manuscripts of edited and summarized diaries we have a fair indication that private circulation of personal autobiographical materials—whether just to families and close friends or within the larger family of congregation or local community—played a significant role in the rise of autobiography long before autobiographies were published in any significant number. Clarendon, for example, carefully prepared a long manuscript on his life that he seems to have regarded both as an *apologia* and a family document. Some of it, the more public part, was incorporated in the *History of the Rebellion,* thirty years after Clarendon's death, and the rest, a substantial volume in its own right, was ultimately approved for publication by his great-grandson; it appeared in 1759, eighty-five years after his death, freely edited so that it patched together different manuscripts written at different times. Quite a number of seventeenth- and early eighteenth-century autobiographical manuscripts, in fact, found their way into print long after their subject's death, most of them probably prompted by family pride rather than by principled dedication to art, truth, or the good of posterity. But the fact that autobiographies came to be published with reasonable frequency suggests that thousands—perhaps tens of thousands—of similar manuscripts were prepared for private uses (familial or congregational) and that their resting place became a parish library (where quite a few unprinted early lives still repose), a family archive (who knows how many manuscripts may still exist there?), an attic, a cabinet, or a trashcan. The tendency to edit one's own diary into a patterned narrative account—

although not necessarily for other eyes—appears to have become very powerful by the days of Ben Franklin and James Boswell. It is not surprising given the constant advice that all diary keepers repeatedly review their record in search of meaning and pattern.

But published autobiography was quite rare in the seventeenth century and remained so well into the eighteenth. By far the most famous instance was Bunyan's *Grace Abounding* (1666), which remained for three quarters of a century a nearly unique example of its kind—because of its compelling prose, intense spirituality, and quality of observation, of course, but also because it was singular in being prepared explicitly by the author for publication during his own lifetime. Bunyan had an explicit reason to publish: imprisoned in Bedford Jail, he was cut off from communication with his congregation, and he sent forth, in print, his testimony of God's grace because he could not witness orally and personally. Brief, intense, rhetorically powerful, and not very detailed, Bunyan's account is untypical of autobiographies digested from diaries and intended for private use; it is neither circumstantial nor analytical. Neither is *Grace Abounding* an I-was-born narrative for a stranger or new acquaintance but rather the continuation of a kind of preaching conversation with his flock. Although it features the same homely language and earthy use of metaphor as *Pilgrim's Progress*, it contains far less narrative as such. *Pilgrim's Progress* tells the life story of an individual (although a composite one) in full and engaging detail (and thus derives more obviously from the tradition of personal diaries), whereas only the story of Bunyan's conversion holds much narrative interest in *Grace Abounding*. Still, *Grace Abounding* drew readers far beyond Bunyan's congregation, reaching a seventh edition by 1688,[18] and if it did not inspire direct imitators, it did demonstrate that living autobiography was possible.

Of the lesser spiritual autobiographies that appeared in the wake of *Grace Abounding,* most were printed in an effort to buoy the spirits of a particular group of believers, usually an especially beleaguered group. Most were published shortly after the death of the subject, and most were prepared by the autobiographer—just in case—for possible publication. The autobiography of Lodowicke Muggleton (*The Acts of Witnesses,* 1699), for example, was published just a year after Muggleton's death, plainly as an inspiration and comfort to his unorganized but devoted followers. Its self-conscious biblical cadences, modeled on the phrasings of the King James Version, tell Muggleton's story as if he were an extension of the apostolic succession. It seems only a stylized curiosity now, and even in its own time it must have had little impact beyond an immediate group of followers, but it illustrates the growing importance, to Protestantism, of having a temporary record that could be circulated and then become a kind of mythology. Similarly aimed at selective audiences were George Fox's *Journal* (revised posthumously by a committee and published in 1694, three years after Fox's death) and Isaac Penington's polemical manuscript, "A true and faithful relation, in brief, concerning myself, in reference to my spiritual travails," a manuscript that was later drawn on in published accounts of Penington's stormy life.[19] Both detail their lives and hard times as Quakers in an alien world, Fox in an engaging and modest personal style, Penington in the lively but embattled manner of a dedicated controversialist. Fox's *Journal* bears some evidence of authorial reworking, summarizing, and editing, but the published work represents primarily the desire of successors to promulgate, or perhaps exploit, Fox's memory by drawing on private materials probably not intended for the public eye. Muggleton and Penington, on the other hand, prepared their "lives" with posterity in mind, although neither seems to have considered the possibility of letting his papers become public before death. Richard Baxter, long an Anglican clergyman and only a reluctant Nonconformist when driven to that position in 1662, was more reticent still, turning over to a friend at his death in 1691 a great quantity of personal papers that were edited into *Reliquiae Baxterianae* in 1696. Far more than just autobiography (although it is that, too, and an under-appreciated one), *Reliquiae Baxterianae* is a virtual compendium of seventeenth-century ideas, blurring even more than most personal accounts the lines dividing autobiography, memoir, and cultural history.[20]

By the second decade of the eighteenth century, the number of published autobiographies began a dramatic and then steady increase. In 1714, for example, *The History of the Life of Thomas Ellwood* appeared, primarily Ellwood's own account of his early life written with an eye to eventual publication, but supplemented with a third-person account of his later life and death. "*Gather up the Fragments that remain,*" the editor justifies,

> *that nothing be lost,* John 6. 12. Was the direction of our *Saviour* to his Disciples, after he had fed the Multitude. Which may well and usefully be applied, to the Collecting and Preserving the Accounts of the *Lives* of Good Men. . . . And this preserving, by *Publication,* is the rather to be done, when themselves do leave behind them, in Writing, an *Account* of their *Lives,* and of the *signal Mercies of God* to them therein. . . .[21]

The same year produced *The Life Of the Reverend Mr. Geo. Trosse . . . Written by Himself, and Publish'd according to his Order,* actually only a record of the rebellious youth of Trosse, who later became a devout and revered clergyman. Trosse fully details his errors, although being careful to moralize everything extensively, but one can see among his surviving friends a certain anxiety about the efficacy of such autobiography, for a year later another publisher brought forward a second *Life of . . . Trosse*, this one containing only a 29-page abridgement of his own narrative, supplemented by more than 150 pages (written by Isaac Gilling) on his later, pious years.[22] Also published in 1715 were the lives of William Edmundson (*A Journal of the Life, Travels, Sufferings and Labour of Love in the Work of the Ministry*, with editions printed in both London and Dublin) and Thomas Halyburton (*Memoirs of the Life*),[23] the first the story of a Quaker elder who had prepared his life (334 pages worth)[24] for later publication, the latter that of a professor of divinity at St. Andrews who had digested much of his diary into standard autobiographical form but had not finished the job. "The first three Periods of his [Halyburton's] Life," the editor explains, "were all found after his Death in a Manuscript, written with his own Hand as they are printed; but all we could have of the fourth . . . is only some Gleanings from imperfect short Hints of Things in his Diary, which he had never digested nor enlarged, which is certainly a very considerable Loss. . . ." (fol. ¶4).

The number of *published* autobiographies of any stripe was still very small until the middle of the eighteenth century, and most of the ones that did appear were those of famous or beloved religious leaders.[25] Only occasionally and for special polemical or political reasons were lay lives or the lives of women brought forward. In 1711, for example, a substantial autobiographical manuscript by Thomas Beard was published along with his funeral sermon (Joseph Porter, *The Holy Seed*) because his early death at seventeen and his moving account of his own piety amidst failing health were thought to provide an inspiring counterexample to the youthful *"bad Examples . . . we see Daily"* which *"Corrupt and Debauch"*[26] (fol. A2v). Beard's account was evidently not, however, written for public consumption. The editor explains of the published account that "It is not indeed all; yet all I can well Collect; It being Wrote in Characters, and for his own Private use; with Secret References" (fol. A4). Similarly, the much earlier autobiography of Jane Turner (*Choice Experiences of The kind dealings of God*, 1653), although neither very detailed nor personal in its account, excuses its presumption to publish by claiming to expose indifferent and corrupt Church practices. Even with so clear a political agenda, the publisher feels obliged to explain, repeatedly, why a woman's life was being brought forward. As the wife of a frequently absent sea captain, Turner had a lot of time, she says, and writing for the public about her self-examination and about experiences in the Church seemed to her less wasteful than other alternatives. And, as if to justify the volume further, there are three explanatory prefaces by men.[27] By the death of Elizabeth Bury in 1720, however, lives needed no particular justification.

Grace Abounding remains, however, the primary example before the mid-eighteenth century of what might be done in spiritual autobiography by someone yet alive. Probably an increasing number of hopeful autobiographers of various kinds prepared their private papers for posterity's possible uses, but few such manuscripts found their way into print, even after the author's death.[28] The awareness of autobiography as a retrospective, digested form of diary rose considerably in England during the later years of the seventeenth century and early years of the eighteenth, but the primary form of personal writing remained the daily journal, where the flotsam and jetsam of everyday detail was seldom sorted or put into large perspective but where the raw materials were presented as data available for later review and a larger understanding of meaning and pattern. However undigested and disordered such materials might be, they are prime examples of "writing to the moment," and they bear the mark of immediacy, freshness, and ingenuousness that the novel comes to prize heavily. The two main stages of self-examination—the immediate recording of the self and the retrospective task of discovering patterns of meaning—are in fact both instructive to the novelistic process of making meaning from the interstices of events and attempts to understand them.

CHAPTER THIRTEEN

The Self Observed: Private Vices, Public Benefits

■

THE lives to be found in diaries and in the published autobiographies I have described so far offered the perspective and perhaps all the formal models that a Manley, a Defoe, or a Haywood might find useful to write biographies and novels in the first quarter of the eighteenth century. Suddenly in 1740 the landscape of lives looked quite different, however, when Henry Fielding approached the writing of prose fiction. The fictional and non-fictional—novels and accounts of real lives—had begun to interact, to teach each other how to extend the potential of narrative. It was not just that Richardson had vastly extended Defoe's accomplishment in the novel itself—by expanding its emotional range and sharpening its formal focus—but that other kinds of lives had entered the public consciousness and were available as models, good or bad, of what could be done in print. All the works that Fielding notices parodically in *Shamela* are ones that in fact helped prepare his own art. Cibber's "autobiography," for example, represents a major movement in personal narrative after Bunyan. Although an identifiable offspring of the tradition of spiritual autobiography, *An Apology for the Life of Mr. Colley Cibber, Comedian* is many other things as well;[1] its appearance and reception in 1740 indicates that major changes had taken place in the public sensibility and that public peeks into the personal and intimate were viable in ways not possible a few years earlier.

When it appeared, the *Apology* seemed very odd to many contemporaries, although the public received it graciously if not exactly enthusiastically. The *Apology* is not pure autobiography, although it does tell the story of Cibber's life pretty fully and achieves a fairly intimate, if never actually self-analytical, portrait of the subject. Besides being auto-biography, the *Apology* is also a history of Cibber's own time, especially of those events involving the theater—the best and most complete account there is. It is more than a memoir, too, for the emphasis is not on exter-nal events at the expense of personal detail or an interest in subjectivity. Cibber represents a viable merger between private and public history, the story both of personal life and of larger events. Such a merger did not, of course, take place in a vacuum, and because that merger has large implications for the cultural sensibility and for the novel in particular, I want to drop back from the *Apology* to two historical strands that in-form it.

I

"ONCE upon a time . . ." and "I was born . . ." are worlds apart con-ceptually. These are the stories respectively of make-believe and make-do, and their narrative structures contrast the probabilities of "let's pre-tend" and "isn't it pretty to think so?" with those of "that's the way it was" and "this is how we became the way we are." The first story, although often vivid, concrete, and believable, paints human life in a generic way and usually at its highest reaches of imagination, while the second gives us back our mundane selves as we might have been in a different body. "I was born" is our story in some particular identity; in a once-upon-a-time world, identity is neither fixed nor certain, and narrative is not necessarily history or made of materials of the temporal world at all.

But in the modern romances that English culture was beginning to grow away from during the years I have been speaking of, that gulf appears to be bridged, at least superficially. Very often a main narrative of "once upon a time" is interrupted by narratives that purport to be the life stories of people the main characters meet: "Your story, if you please," the pro-tagonist often invites, and sometimes the response begins as if it were to be an "I was born" story—except that these mini-histories turn out not to be accounts of a temporal world at all, but rather of romances as well, usually melancholy tales set in an exotic never-never-land. Never mind that they begin with temporal particulars and appear at first to be staking, like novels, a claim to a world in time. Never mind that sometimes they copy the verbal formulas of another world and begin literally with "I was born"—as if they were going to cope with the actual world of birth, death, and probability. As a group, these stories are not very impressive, and they do not stand out as distinctive in the fabric of romance because the same laws operate within the interpolated tales as within the main narrative. Even though they may literally begin with "I was born" and tell the story of an individual life from a first-person perspective, they are subjective only in the most superficial sense, and like oral narratives (which they imitate and from which they spring) they do not raise questions of reliability or believability: they exist as part of a world in which the question of credibility has already been answered in a special, privileged sense.[2] They are by definition fictions that owe no homage to the ordinary world of cause and effect. Even though they pretend to represent real history, they remain part of the special imagined world of romance.

Sometimes in novels, such romantic tales are interpolated as well. When they are, they do not seem at home, and a great deal of modern critical energy has gone into attempting to justify the presence in novels of such digressions—"excrescences," Ian Watt has called them, and at least a hundred critics have answered, explained, or justified.[3] In novels, interpolations are of several kinds,[4] but the most frequent one carries over from romance the strategy of having a newly met character tell his or her own story in that same romantic style sponsored by the same romantic assumptions. The difference is that these tales are patently not at home in the novel's world, and they stand out sharply. The same tale that would readily fade into the borders of a surrounding romance seems foreign in a novel because the surrounding context subjects it to a different kind of question. We ask troubling questions about Mr. Wilson in *Joseph Andrews* and the Man of the Hill in *Tom Jones;* those characters come from a different world of time, space, and probability, and do not really belong in the rough-and-tumble fallen world of everyday which the novel reflects. And (like interpolated tales by newly met strangers in romances) in spite of their beginning with "I was born," these tales do not deal in subjectivity or introspection very deeply: "I was born" is a misleading introduction (because of its apparent temporal claim) and the mere phrase itself, like its counterpart "once upon a time," is not an infallible indicator of what world we are in. But when "I was born" really does represent its implied fallen world of labor and pain, it can stand for the whole range of possibility in one of those narrative worlds, a range that the novel came to realize when it decided to tell, in its full subjectivity and temporality, the story of an "I."

In the novel as a species, the potential of "I was born" is realized in a way quite different from romance. The potential is not reaped all at once, perhaps not fully in any one work or even in the works of any one novelist, although partisans of some individual novelists would have us believe that only that one novelist—James, for example, or Lawrence, or Flaubert, or Tolstoi, or Joyce—saw what was possible. Not all novels, even in the early history of the species, are literally "I was born" first-person novels, but many are: all of Defoe's, several of Smollett's, both of Sterne's, and in essence all of Richardson's, although his use of letters complicates (or at least confuses) the issue. First-person telling is not, of course, necessary to the individualism and intense subjectivity that characterize the novel. But it provides the simplest access to that inner world of thought, feeling, and process, and for the early novelists the first-person angle, usually extended to its logical beginning of "I was born" (or, with Sterne, even further), seemed the most "natural" way to explore the nature of a self. Birth and the implications of beginnings are one element, with emphasis falling more heavily on environment than on ancestry (for the novel believes in visible influence more than abstract cause), but the other element—the I—is finally the most crucial, for, whatever the beginnings and whatever the paths that are traversed thereafter, the specific, developed, individualized identity of the teller becomes the subject of the book. In romance and in oral literature generally, the teller is never as important as the tale. Narrative is more focused and ultimately more important in romance; in novels, the story is only one of several important elements, and often character, analyzed through a central consciousness or through some other individuating strategy, is at least as important as the plot.

As a number of historical observers (and, more recently, literary theorists) have stressed, it is no accident that the fortunes of the novel and autobiography meet so frequently in their emerging and developmental years. No single consciousness fashioned the emergence and early history of either species, and so the problem of sorting out their interrelationship is not a matter of reconstructing artistry or conscious direction in the same way that one might reconstruct the process of creation for an individual text. But retrospectively we are in a position to see, as contemporaries did not, what the two species have in common, how they differ, and (if we consider the surrounding contexts of each) why each exerted on the other, during the eighteenth century, a kind of pressure that influenced form, direction, and development. The novel and autobiography are, as Patricia Meyer Spacks says, "the two developing genres that flourished during the century," and it is no wonder that, given their common concerns, they interacted in ways that indicate their "shared assumptions, shared techniques, and shared demands on the reader."[5]

The novel's pressures on autobiography are easy to see almost as soon as the novel becomes identifiable as a new species, and in such autobiographies as those of Rousseau and Boswell consciousness of literary possibility leads to formal features that have more to do with rhetoric than revelation, much as the decision to go public had made autobiography a form with certain expectable features instead of the phenomenon it had been when there were only the daily accretions of a personal diary and no known audience. But here I want to confine the discussion to the pressures in the opposite direction, from autobiography to novel, and confine still further my discussion to two issues, the first a formal one, the second a question of enabling contexts and reader expectations. Formally, autobiography's pressure on the novel involves mainly the opportunity to focus and restrict scope: in its reflection of the fortunes and misfortunes of a single human life (however interrelated with other human beings, the whole world, and the otherworldly), autobiography has a built-in beginning and end. And, in its emergence out of diaries that involved injunctions to read details and try to decipher patterns, its early examples provide a paradigm for finding shape, direction, and meaning in an individual life. As early as 1678 (just a dozen years after describing his own life), Bunyan identified the paradigm sufficiently to construct a composite life with many novelistic features, the foremost of which is a form for the understanding of an individual's life in the full resonance of its potential meaning. In Defoe, the understanding of form is quite similar, and, although the possibilities of form become far more complex by the end of the eighteenth century, the basic pattern remains much the same. Most eighteenth-century novels center on the life of an individual and become essentially the telling of that person's story. Novels take the idea of "I was born" to the full logic of its human, temporal meaning within the eighteenth-century ideational context, going back to the ramifications of beginnings and then showing what the person was born to. Then they detail the workings out of that pattern in full circumstantial variation, throughout the person's life. The short titles we use for eighteenth-century novels suggest the point dramatically; most of them are people's names—*Robinson Crusoe*, *Clarissa*, *Tom Jones*, *Betsy Thoughtless*, *Tristram Shandy*, *Evelina*—and the titles are faithful to the books' emphasis on the unfurling of that person's life story, for novelists regularly set themselves the task of telling the story, usually at least in part from the inside, of one person's life.[6]

Sometimes novels select only part of that person's story and confine themselves to a shorter time period than the full duration of the life—as *Clarissa*, for example, confines itself to a single year of its heroine's crisis—but seldom do early novels expand their interests beyond the scope of that titular individual. Other individuals may appear and affect the hero's or heroine's life, but they seldom compete for central attention, nor do settings or relationships or themes compete for central focus. We are asked to attend primarily to the history and fortunes and identity of one person; the few exceptions—*Humphry Clinker* (whose title clearly operates against expectations that are already well set), apologues like *Rasselas,* and Gothic romances like *The Castle of Otranto*—are calculated to work from the expectation that novels will trace a single life, and they at once test and confirm the rule. Early on, there were abortive attempts to steer the novel toward a different path—back to romance, for example, or into philosophical tales[7]—but not until almost the end of the eighteenth century does the novel expand its horizons beyond the single individual to consider relationships, or sponsoring ideas, or settings, or symbols as central. Again, the titles show it: *A Simple Story, The Mysteries of Udolpho, Mount Henneth, Elinor and Marianne* (the original title of *Sense and Sensibility*), *The Watsons, Pride and Prejudice, Things As They Are,*[8] *Mansfield Park, Kenilworth, The Heart of Midlothian.*[9]

Throughout almost all of the eighteenth century, it is as if readers meet a stranger / novelist for the first time and say, as does Parson Adams to Mr. Wilson, "Your story, if you please." The English novelists one by one oblige by telling as much as they can, as much as they know, far more than a Mr. Wilson or an interpolated tale-teller in a romance could possibly articulate, and they tell it in a framework of sympathetic and realistic narrative. Sometimes a reader may be made to think, as in *Moll Flanders* or *Clarissa,* there but for the grace of God go I. But just as often it is (as in *Tom Jones* or *Evelina*), there with a little good luck go I, and whether the force is exemplary or cautionary, the question of being in the protagonist's place is a real one. We may still not understand exactly how sympathy, or empathy, or identity work in art, but the eighteenth-century novel makes it possible—and necessary—to raise such issues because the protagonists are enough like us in social, economic, and psychological possibilities that all of us—whether members of the aristocracy, or gentility, or the intelligentsia, or people of trade, or the working class—can imagine facing those contexts and circumstances. Whatever our social loyalties, the novel reminds us—often in its plot, as in *Roxana, Joseph Andrews,* or *Evelina,* and always in its arrangement with readers—that distinctions, destinies, and heritages are fragile and subject to radical change, with or without intent.

I I

BEYOND form, the novel reaps from autobiography a capacity for introspection, self-awareness, and subjectivity—or rather, it reaps this capacity from the cultural context in much the same way and at much the same time that formal autobiography does. The pervasive daily formal self-examination and the diary keeping it led to represent the first crucial stage in the cultural process that enabled both autobiography and the novel to flourish, but two other stages were also crucial. One involves a willingness to go public with the fruits of subjectivity, a step that (as we have seen) was partially taken by 1700—when autobiographers like Bunyan, Muggleton, Penington, Fox, and Baxter had consciously made all or part of their lives available to others, when printers and editors had—by forcible taking—helped themselves to private documents, and when individual members of some sects unburdened themselves to fellow saints in public confessions. The second stage involves the dislodging of self-analysis and self-disclosure from the utilitarian theological ends that had originally sponsored it.

Neither of these stages was entirely complete when Cibber published his *Apology* in 1740 (and in fact the publishing and reading of novels may have been instrumental in bringing each stage to closure), but by Cibber's time each stage was well along. Cibber had little shame in revealing himself, even if it meant exposing his foolishness, to anyone willing to listen. "But why make my Follies publick?" he asks himself rhetorically early in the *Apology*; and he answers, "Why not?" (p. 2). He openly admits to motives quite different from those that had sponsored religious self-examination. He is, he alleges, anxious to see himself, to watch himself at work and play in what he imagines (mistakenly, but significantly) to be a dispassionate and objective observation, and to reveal to readers what they might not themselves have observed from his public roles. There are still traces of the Puritan diaristic spirit in the *Apology*—preoccupation with circumstantial detail, for example, and a plain didactic desire to affect the thinking of his contemporaries—but Cibber is also straightforward in admitting his desire to set the record straight, to set down his version of the doings of his age, to revise his contemporaries' estimates of himself, and even openly to give himself personal pleasure in publication. For observers like Pope and Henry Fielding, that made Cibber an exhibitionist, an egomaniac, and a fool, but novelists in fact had to face, for similar reasons, similar charges from the beginning, and their only defense ultimately was that the selves they exhibited, and celebrated, were not fully their own.[10]

Never mind that Cibber was not an especially perceptive viewer of himself. Never mind that his secularized efforts at self-examination are both less inclusive and less incisive than countless older-fashioned religious efforts so that his readers, from the first, have seemed to glean more about him than he himself could understand. Never mind that his is a limited self-portrait done by an artist better at playing the selves of others than at finding, or creating, a self for himself. The point (and it was not a negligible point in 1740, as the outraged reactions of Pope and Fielding both suggest) is that he was willing to put himself on the line, literally— that he would, in print, record himself as he understood himself to be: no holds barred, no secrets willfully kept, no perceived flaws unmentioned. It was an extraordinarily daring act, historically, but its time had come. Even Pope, his literary and political nemesis who liked to portray himself as an exact opposite, was in the process of doing almost the same thing (though for very different ends) in the cumulative autobiographical portrait of the *Moral Essays* and the *Imitations of Horace*. For if Pope created a persona in his later poems that was a selective, carefully chiseled, and laboriously crafted self, Cibber only sallied forth as he thought he was, imperfections intact and plainly in view. If Pope created in his poems a life for himself that was, in effect, a substitute for his incomplete and inadequate life outside the poems, Cibber did nearly seem, as Fieldiing said, to have lived his life merely to give himself something to print. In one case, art was a substitute for life, an imitation, revision, and improvement; in the other, it sought to *be* nearly life itself in the intimacy of its record, a writing to the moment that subsumed and almost absorbed the moment itself, and the range from one to the other comes close to suggesting the changing sensibility that enabled a literary species like the novel to emerge. In both Cibber and Pope, the artifact consumed the self, a process the novel made safer by inventing a self that was only a fiction.

I I I

BETWEEN *Grace Abounding* and the *Apology*, the contexts of autobiography had shifted radically. For the *Apology* even to be conceivable, some major changes in sensibility had to occur. One reason that the *Apology* was such a shock to readers in 1740 was that *Grace Abounding* continued to be, at least officially, the model of expectation. No autobiographies between 1666 and 1740 seriously engaged the public imagination (although several of them—Baxter's, Fox's, and Muggleton's, especially—have historical and literary value), and relatively few full-length autobiographies were published. But the publisher and writer John Dunton once more provides crucial perspective on the shifting terrain. In his autobiographical musings scattered through several published titles, he relentlessly tried, without much success, to inflict a good deal of his personal life on the public, attempting to market himself and his personal problems in an indiscriminately detailed account, published by himself, of his amatory and financial adventures.

The life of Dunton, as life, was not a finished work of art. Although he was one of the most active and prolific booksellers and publishers at the end of the seventeenth century, and although he pioneered several schemes and projects that became the staple goods and accepted procedures of his profession, his career was never an economic success, and his attempts to record his life in print can hardly be regarded as triumphant. Still, his contribution—halting and sometimes silly as it was—is culturally significant in the way it charts a change in tastes and assumptions. Several of Dunton's publications—especially his forays into autobiography—predict (often in crude ways) what happened more subtly in the works of others a little later. His refusal to bow to standard procedures and his inability to understand restraints of custom and good taste was his license, and his way of revealing his private life both illustrates a social possibility and creates a public precedent.

His most sustained autobiographical effort was *The Life and Errors of John Dunton*, a volume of more than 530 pages that dropped onto the scene in 1705. Dunton unaccountably thought that the public would relish a full record of himself, and later (regretting he had been so generous to an uncaring world) he blamed the poor sales on the fact that he was not politically powerful. His books sell better when they go forth anonymously, he notes.[11] It does not seem to have occurred to him that the personal and private subject matter he had chosen might be a factor, that people might simply not care about the fortunes and fate of John Dunton, or that the reading public was not yet ravenous for individual subjectivity and private lives. A year after publication Dunton complained that it "han't bore the Charge of Paper and Print,"[12] a measure both of Dunton's high hopes and the public's indifference.

And yet Dunton was onto something. The *Life and Errors* gave both less and more than the title page promised. Dunton does not get around to recounting all the years of his life, but he is full of information about his contemporaries, including brief characters of a variety of booksellers, clergymen, and writers. The book's chief readership since his own time has been, in fact, among historians searching for details about someone else or about the bookselling trade, for Dunton is a retentive and full, if erratic, historian. But helpful as it is as a social document about a variety of groups and professions, its chief interest ultimately is as a document in the history of taste.

Some of the *Life and Errors* is exceedingly intimate, although it is seldom confessional or salacious. Dunton gives no bedroom details and offers few whispers about highly personal secrets, but he gives the impression (like Cibber a generation later) that he is holding nothing back as too personal or private. He talks with apparent openness about his courtships and, later, about his marital difficulties; all is, he implies, open to view. His pretense is that nothing is too private to tell, but he makes no attempt (and this may be his crucial artistic mistake) to give the impression that the reader is eavesdropping or being let into a secret that no one else knows. He views the world of print as a public arena—taking the bookshop as synecdoche for the whole phenomenology of books—and does not come to terms with the basic solitariness of reading: at least he fails to exploit it. One of the central hitches in almost all his books involves his failure to distinguish between written and oral discourse.

Dunton portrays himself as a religious man, just as concerned as are diarists and the subjects of spiritual biography about his own salvation and the implications of his conduct, and he goes out of his way to label, and count, his mistakes. The "Errors" of his title is both characteristic and revealing; he thinks like a printer and maker of books, and his life is to him a text riddled with misprints—but corrigible if only the public will justify another edition. The narrative of the life itself alternates with sections labeled "The Idea of a New Life," which the title page advertises as "Wherein is Shewn How he'd Think, Speak, and Act, might he Live over his Days again."[13] Later, in referring to the whole volume, Dunton sometimes called it the *Idea of a New Life,* and, although there is often reason to think him confused, there is no reason to find him insincere. But the emphasis of the *Life and Errors* bears little relationship to *Grace Abounding* or other spiritual autobiographies and biographies, even though the spirit of his self-analysis does derive from the same ultimate impulse. Regardless of Dunton's interest in matters spiritual, and irrespective of its sometimes religious self-examination and introspection, the *Life and Errors* is a secular work in its main thrust. It may be the first full-scale autobiography in English that is *not* almost totally a spiritual autobiography, and the mere fact of its existence, let alone publication, signals an alteration in the cultural consciousness. Dunton correctly read the changing social context, but he was born thirty years too soon.

Even before the *Life and Errors,* Dunton had established himself as the first English writer to be, openly, his own favorite subject. In *The Dublin Scuffle* (1699), for example, he offers vivid personal details within a lengthy account of a business venture in Ireland. In a scheme to bolster his bookselling trade, Dunton had made arrangements to ship tons of books to Dublin and sell them at auction, but (predictably, although not to Dunton) he encountered resistance from his Dublin competitors. Part of the scuffle involves a sometimes heated feud between Dunton and Patrick Campbell, a Dublin bookseller, but almost equally important in the book's 400-plus pages[14] is the alleged sexual pursuit of Dunton by "Dorinda," a

autobio
didactic thrust

"Citizen's wife," who, according to Dunton, tried to set up an assignation with him. The pages of *The Dublin Scuffle* contain letters written by the wife, Dunton's chastising (and supposedly cooling) answers to her, and narrative accounts of their non-encounters, as well as a 141-page account of how he *did* spend his time in Ireland and a 42-page review of it by "an Honourable Lady." It is not that the would-be liaison is very interesting or that Dunton describes it well, but the ludicrous burst of such personal matters into print brings together autobiography, contemporary detail, didactic thrust, and journalistic pursuit of matters of public curiosity in a peculiar and altogether new way. The personal detail of *The Dublin Scuffle* is, in a sense, merely one personal step beyond the casuistical wrestlings of *The Athenian Mercury* and its imitators where cases of conscience and human conduct were reviewed in almost equally vivid ways, although in less detail and more impersonally.

As is often the case with Dunton titles, *The Dublin Scuffle* defies generic categorization, coming closest perhaps to journalistic accounts of contemporary life but pointing (unconsciously) toward the kind of autobiography one finds much later in the century—and also toward novelistic subjectivity and flirtation with the taboos of privacy. How Dunton copes with the advances of the Dublin wife, how he fears the eyes of her husband (ominously named "Argus" by Dunton), and how he tries to turn the episode into a cautionary tale is an exemplary—although clumsy—circumstantial account of individual tribulations and trials presented for the joint purpose of reader entertainment and edification. Dunton may not have lived an interesting enough life to turn it into a public autobiography, and he lacked the talent to sustain a narrative of any kind, even about the most compelling events. But he was hot on the trail of modern narrative discourse, and the novelties he published at the turn of the century are, jointly and severally, hints of what novels can be, once authors are more self-conscious and clear about their complex purposes, once readers are adequately prepared for a new kind of formal expectation, and once techniques, strategies, and features can be refined into something substantial and not merely odd.

I V

Dunton—a candidate for Geraldo but 350 years too soon

DUNTON'S most extensive flirtation with the public baring of the private involves his two marriages. In the *Life and Errors,* he describes his courtship of Elizabeth Annesley and sometimes writes movingly about her early death, although his own tolerance for nostalgia exceeds that of most readers. More significant (and ultimately more pathetic), though, is his description in print of his unsuccessful second marriage, and it is the financial rather than emotional turmoil that is the substance of the accounts Dunton offered the world in a variety of publications scattered over nearly thirty years. Five months after the death of his first wife (who becomes "Iris" in his narrative account), he remarries, and his new wife (whom he calls "Valeria") proves to be trouble from the start, largely because her shrewd mother suspects that Dunton, in precarious financial circumstances, needs her modest financial resources. From his repeated public defenses of remarrying so soon[15] to his pleas for attention, both emotional and economic, from his new wife and mother-in-law, Dunton produces a detailed, almost month-by-month, account of his personal affairs in print. Dunton offered everything from pamphlets of a few pages to long, rambling books in which his autobiography figures prominently, from *An Essay, Proving, We Shall Know Our Friends in Heaven. Writ by a disconsolate widower, on the death of his wife* (1698), *The Case of John Dunton . . . with respect to his mother-in-law* (1700), and *The Case Is Alter'd: or, Dunton's Re-marriage To the same WIFE* (1701), to *The Life and Errors of John Dunton, Mordecai's Dying Groans from the Fleet-Prison: or, the Case and Sufferings of Mr. John Dunton* (1717), and *Mr. John Dunton's Dying Groans from the Fleet-Prison: or the National Complaint, That the Author . . . has gone Twelve Years Unrewarded* (1725).

Many of Dunton's other publications contain autobiographical passages or references, as well as bizarre reveries and lucubrations that tend to trace the history of Dunton's own curious and sometimes wandering consciousness. He writes about "The Marry'd Widower; or Dunton *in Mourning for the Death of his living Wife, and new Life of his dead Friend, a Paradox*"; "Dunton:—Or, the Projector of the *Rhiming Frolick*: Being a merry Character of himself, the meanest of all the Poetick Tribe"; *The Night-Walker: or, evening rambles in search after lewd women;* and *Stinking Fish: or, a foolish poem, attempted by John the hermit.* And he promises others on such topics as "The Funeral of Mankind: A *Paradox, proving we are all dead and bury'd,*" "The Double Life: Or, *a new Project to redeem the Time, by living over to Morrow before it comes,*" "Non Entity: Or, *a grave Essay upon Nothing,*" and "The Spiritual Hedgehog, *a Project (or Thought) wholly new and surprising.*"[16] Even in his sad last years when he languishes in poverty, loneliness, and neglect, he continues to present his own desperate self—in need of patronage, reward, or any attention at all—to a public that had never taken his life or errors very seriously.

The distinction between fiction and fact is often hard to mark in Dunton. His own lack of certainty about such matters, together with his eccentric and often zany (but also sometimes canny) sense of what subject matter can be addressed and how, leads to the central source of his historical interest. Dunton is often not very clear about the demarcation between himself and the rest of the world, and he often refuses to honor the established sense of what could be printed and how it should be organized. Dunton's hold on sanity was always precarious, and late in his career he regularly lost touch with reality, becoming a pathetic figure whose early accomplishments as a political polemicist were unrewarded and forgotten, except by Dunton himself who repeatedly reminded readers of his situation in pamphlet after pamphlet.[17] His uncertainties of border between self and other, reality and fantasy, narrative and meditation, fiction and fact early on produced exuberant works that, while not thoroughly under control and certainly not "finished" artistically, represent sheddings of tradition that almost signaled creative breakthroughs. Far and away the most theoretically interesting single work of Dunton's is his three-volume A Voyage Round the World (1691), a kind of allegorical autobiography that in many ways anticipates the theme and method of the Life and Errors.

A Voyage Round the World—with its roots in spiritual autobiography, travel literature, didactic tracts, contemporary journalism, and the printing of novelty and gimmickry—suggests the eclectic heritages of the novel and gives some broad hints of the direction modern narrative will take. In its use of developments in print technology, mixing of narrative and expository strands, inclusivity of other quasi-related documents, didactic insistency, and playful refusal to move the story forward while savoring its own obsessive reflexivity, Voyage is technically way ahead of its time. But the Voyage is not an artistic success. It has entirely too much of Dunton's flair for novelty and restlessness and too little care to push a story line forward, resolve narrative or compositional difficulties, or realize a character in a full enough way to generate identification or anything beyond superficial curiosity about what comes next. And, like so many of Dunton's other novelties, it was not a commercial success. Dunton had first tried to retail this project in a periodical called A Ramble Round the World (1689), but gave up after a few issues,[18] then expanded his failed short narrative into three volumes two years later, promising (in a Shandean way) to add more volumes in which he would present matters pledged-but-undelivered in the first three. But the public did not clamor for more, and the original volumes were never reprinted until an enterprising publisher reissued a version of them as a curiosity in 1762 shortly after the first appearance of Tristram Shandy.[19]

But if the Voyage is more novel and (in its way) creative, the Life and Errors points more steadily to the autobiographical tradition that had begun to set the subjective context for the novel. The Life and Errors gathers many of Dunton's characteristic concerns and summarizes much of his life and career. In its innovation, Athenian curiosity, and contemporary concerns, as well as its secularization of autobiography, Dunton's distinct talents, as well as his aberrations, are plain to see. And besides the inreach toward the psyche and consciousness of Dunton himself, there is significant outreach to the world beyond Dunton the recorder and observer. The *Life and Errors* is hardly a typical early-century work; it does not seem quite at home in its 1705 context, and its interests and strategies are, whatever else they may be, well ahead of their time. But among the restless strivings to catch his public's eye, Dunton creates identifiable features that point to sensibilities a full generation away and that suggest tastes any new literature will have to satisfy. Beyond the careening subjectivity, revisionary structure, and experimental crisscrossing between the secular and religious consciousness is a larger reach for the public realm, a kind of prediction of the merger of the inreach of autobiography and the outreach of memoir brought off later by Cibber and by novelists. In retrospect, what Dunton was doing makes historical sense relative to the shifting configurations of printed materials and the changing of literary forms; but in its own unpropitious time—and in the hands of a writer who, for all his self-preoccupations, never knew exactly what he was up to—it all looked like madness.[20]

But to return to Colley Cibber.

CHAPTER FOURTEEN

The Self in the World: History, Biography, and Travel Books

CIBBER'S ambition to write history, his definition of what contemporary history consists in, and his sense of how to do it from a personal perspective point to another cultural change that shaped the novel. Crucial to the novel as a new species is not only the inscape of autobiography but the outreach of history. When Henry Fielding says that his "new Species" is a comic version of epic, the primary claim he is making—within his culture's understanding of epic theory[1]—is not formal but historical: his aim is to represent his own age and culture and to capture its spirit. All Fielding's novels reflect this desire, but *Tom Jones* validates the historical claim, defining the ethos of its age, and the same case could be made for at least one novel by most early English novelists, both those who look outward toward society and those who look inward toward the heart. Characteristic of the species from the first was the desire to define something essential in the historical moment, a need to record the crucial interactions of its time and represent the cultural consciousness. *Clarissa* and her problems are just as much a story of the midcentury culture as Tom and his. Manley, Defoe, Haywood, Sarah Fielding, Lennox, Sarah Scott, Sterne, Mackenzie, Horace Walpole, and Burney all present situations and issues characteristic of their time, representing cultural values as clearly as Austen and Sir Walter Scott a little later.[2] Even novels that set out to be minor in scope and limited in ambition—like *Fanny Hill* or *Millenium Hall* or *The Man of Feeling*—end up trying to define a cultural ethos. Setting out to write about the warp and woof of ordinary life in a particular time—and writing for readers who are just then experiencing choices that have to be made within culture-bound limits—leads naturally to narratives involving culturally characteristic situations and a discourse that contextualizes them.

But despite the aim at outreach and scope that a term like "epic" suggests, eighteenth-century novels are a long way from being epics in a formal sense. They accrue too many miscellaneous new features from popular species, and they develop a distinctive new personality and tone. The term "history," which many novelists use to describe what they write, is more accurate, and it is more suggestive about audience expectations— what readers needed and what they might reasonably expect to find in a culture going the way theirs was. But "history" was still only part of it. Cibber's *Apology* is not far in the *nature* of its accomplishments from what the midcentury novelists were able to do. For it takes advantage of the traditions of both autobiograpty and history, pursuing both the inscape and the outreach—the intensity and the scope—that his culture had just made available, to create a special kind of book.

I

HISTORIOGRAPHY was undergoing significant changes just as the novel began to emerge as a historical form, and the popularity of histories may have helped lead, at least indirectly, to the popularity of novels. Individual histories had done well in the early seventeenth century (Raleigh's and Daniel's were among the most popular), but there was no great rush to write history and little inclination to discuss the historicity of contemporary affairs. As a vague concept, "history" generated great respect, and all sorts of intellectual activities paid homage to the past without necessarily recognizing that other times and places had different rationales or perspectives. As a locus of values or a touchstone for firm standards, the past attracted admiration and offered models, but history remained more of a useful myth than an actual basis for comparative analysis or even an object of genuine curiosity. Without a sense of cultural or historical difference, other times and places do not readily stand for any "other," and as a measure of the English present, history offered little but quaintness and a sense of the strange, the exotic, or the unknown.

The Civil Wars represented, for many, the need to grapple with the past in new and deeper ways, for suddenly a present offered itself as outgrowth and implication rather than as a strange abyss, and the chance to found a "new" culture in a new world similarly offered the challenge to define identity by considering alternative possibilities. Still, the challenge was slow to be taken up, and it wasn't until a rather different intellectual context developed—in which on the one hand there was a strong antiquarian interest and on the other a genuine sense of cultural difference—that the present and the familiar had to be evaluated in comparative terms. Once the idea of replanting the old world in the new had begun to fizzle, and once the implications of differential culture had begun to sink in, the basis for a genuine historicity came to exist, and outcomes in the present could seem dependent on a dynamic and implication-producing past. The existence of institutions like the Ashmolean Museum or even the popular London freak shows were everyday material reminders that a new age of assumptions had arrived.

One manifestation of the new spirit, in spite of its largely conservative analysis, was Clarendon's *History of the Rebellion*, a relentlessly analytical account of the seventeenth century as a developmental phenomenon, though Clarendon's view took time to become the dominant sense of what history was.[3] A case could be made that it was the Civil Wars themselves, more than Clarendon's own consciousness, that changed the sense of history in English culture (even though the effect was not immediate), for it had become increasingly hard to believe that all times and places were fundamentally alike, even harder not to feel the implications of a past as intrusive as that one. The popular press thrived for a half century on the issues of civil disputes; the Wars made history seem relentless, the past relevant to every moment of the present. But it was Clarendon who refused to let the issues go away once they had begun to fade in popular memory. His timing in dredging up the resonant recent past when the present was occupying center stage in the cultural consciousness, his insistent analysis that made a continuous narrative of past and present, and his willingness to mix personal narration with cultural analysis meant that historiography became at once more complex and more immediate. It remained for Hume to *articulate* the philosophical implications of the developing modern sense of history and to insist on secular rationales, but Clarendon had already exemplified many of the insistent forces. History was alive, it was about difference; it told you who you were by telling you where you had been, and it was becoming popular to read and popular to write.

After Clarendon, intensifying self-consciousness about method and style meant that readers expected a new sophistication and literary care and that writers who cared about language, as well as about human affairs, could anticipate a receptive audience.[4] Many of those we now regard as primarily literary figures took at least a brief turn at writing history— Defoe, Swift, Arbuthnot, Addison, Goldsmith, and Smollett, among others. And, even more important, increasing numbers of hack writers, intellectuals, antiquarians, and others concerned to clarify present events came to view themselves chiefly as historians and cultural critics—Old-mixon, Strype, Lediard, Echard, Hume, Bolingbroke, Kennett, Warbur-ton, and (later) Gibbon, Burke, Godwin, and Sir Walter Scott—not to mention those who (like Calamy, Dunton, Boyer, Oldys, Gildon, Neal, and Burnet) tried history of a more limited and particular kind. Many would call most of this writing journalism, and it often was (in the sense that the present was its driving force), but it established a firm cultural sense of the past as different and implicative. Too, the reading of history gained greatly in popularity, so that many readers, quite possibly includ-ing readers beyond those in social classes expected to read history, began to develop an increasingly complex sense of how history was to be writ-ten and read. Early novels, especially in the middle decades of the eigh-teenth century, regularly adopted the word "history" to describe themselves, often incorporating it formally in their titles, as in *The History of Tom Jones; Clarissa. Or the History of a Young Lady;* and *Evelina, or the History of a Young Lady's Entrance into the World.*[5]

Novels are not really "histories," of course, or rather they are only partly histories and that in a special and limited sense. Even if they share the desire to define a particular cultural moment, novels and histories differ in other aims and methods. Conceptually, the writing of history had an impact on the context in which novels began to be written and read, and as an enabling force on the scope of novels it would be hard to overestimate its importance. But it is surprising how little direct influ-ence the writing of history seems to have had on the writing of specific novels, decidedly less than more personal and private forms of writing. The novel is not, as is sometimes said, only interested in individuals, subjectivity, privacy, and the inner self; its distinctive character involves the way it holds the individual will in tension with social and interactive values. That is why both "panoramic" novels and "novels of character" (or novels of the self) can be said, accurately, to be "characteristic" of the species. The novelistic attempt to incorporate a larger social and cultural view—a more comprehensive context for individual lives, a per-spective in both time and place—owes something to history writers and much more to friendly contexts that made readers feel as if they wanted, or needed, both chronicles of daily life and a sense of how hours and days and local places fit into larger patterns. But it remained for later ages, largely through Continental cultures, for the panoramic possibilities of the novel to emerge fully, and what we see at first in the eighteenth century in England is a restless striving for outreach, with some tentative success inspired by hesitant models. The claims to history are, until the early nineteenth century, more impressive than any large understanding of temporal process, and social implication remains similarly underdeveloped, despite Henry Fielding and Burney, until Austen. *Tristram Shandy*, with its anxieties about the past, lineage, and time, and with its frustrated inability to locate individuals appropriately in full intersubjectivity, is the paradigm of the eighteenth-century novel, both in its reach and in its limits of reach.

Histories, because of their ambitions, might well provide potential formal models for long narrative works of a fictional kind, and one might expect to find strategies in the novel that are adapted from history writing. Many readers of novels—and most writers of them—read history regularly and in detail, so that some narrative expectations probably were set by the conventions and habits of historical writing. Leo Braudy's suggestive account of the relationship between history and fiction points to some parallels out of commonalities of aim,[6] and detailed analysis of techniques and style in individual writers might suggest other narrative carryovers, but the importance of history to the novel seems mainly to consist in projecting broadened objectives. History, as written and read in the early eighteenth century, fostered a sense that some grander perspective on events ought to emerge from any account of event and sequence, and suggested that such perspective was desirable even on contemporary events or matters of immediate or passing interest.

I I

HISTORIES like Burnet's and Oldmixon's—and like Dunton's and Cibber's, insofar as their autobiographies were accounts of the times as well as of themselves—perhaps had the greatest indirect influence on the directions of the novel, if only because they legitimized the subjective structuring of history as a way of seeing a certain historically definable culture. Despite all the attempts to make it otherwise, history writing became increasingly involved with subjectivity during the early eighteenth century. Clarendon, with his inability to separate the grand intentions of his huge history from autobiography, was the paradigm.[7] And if the subjectivity of histories contributed to a more lively interest in interpretation and debate about current policy (as writers tried to answer or modify Clarendon, Burnet, and Oldmixon), it also meant that one of the most stable and revered of prose species opened itself to generic "confusion." The respectability of history as a branch of traditional letters (something the novel tried to turn to its own uses in adapting it for titles and, even more questionably, for its truth claims) was in fact damaged, at least temporarily, as its borders—traditionally heavily guarded against memoirs, personal anecdotes, journalistic gossip, and *histoire scanda-leuse*—became difficult to maintain. Ultimately (and this does not always happen at times of generic breakdown) history's loss was less significant than gains made by personal writing, perhaps because social and cultural factors dictated that subjectivity would take new ground in all the tradi-tional areas of discourse; but the novel took significant advantage of the border disputes, especially those involving both private and public his-tory.

Fielding's attempt to associate the novel with epic is based on inher-ited ideas of history, but confidence in the inheritance is less justified once subjectivity and party bias come to take the role they do in early eighteenth-century interpretation.[8] Novels could only take advantage of enlarged possibility because, by the 1740s, history had already given up ground to—as well as having enlarged and entangled its alliances with—more personal forms of writing. The memoir—that notoriously indistinct and imperialistic but very popular species that emerged in the seven-teenth century, flowered in the eighteenth, and went prodigally to seed by the late nineteenth—represents the general direction of cultural inter-ests and the growing uncertainties about formal boundaries. It started from the self but then tried to encompass the world, space first, then time. Its struggle to escape the solipsistic predicament prefigures (and clarifies) the novel's, though memoirs by definition always finally reen-compass the world in a single consciousness, while novels fictively escape it by (at least in theory) keeping multiple consciousnesses—the author's, the narrator's, the various characters', the readers'—in unresolved ten-sion. But the novel, as a species not yet really identified and openly in search of both content and form, took more immediate and definitive advantage of the context. Some novels and proto-novels called them-selves "Memoirs" (Defoe's *Memoirs of a Cavalier* [1720], for example, or Cleland's *Memoirs of a Woman of Pleasure* [1749], or the anonymous *Memoirs of an Oxford Scholar* [1756]), but many more might have and, without giving anything away about their individual concerns, capital-ized on the contextual confusion and possibility. "Life and Adventures" titles came very close to being "Memoirs" substitutes (although perhaps not making quite such strong claims to factuality), and "Life and Opin-ions" or "Lucubrations" claims on title pages are almost the same thing.[9] The novel, in its various phraseological claims in titles, regularly stakes out its desire to yoke an individual life to some larger perspective, and "memoir," if the novel's heroes actually were in places of national signif-icance or had the status of place or position, might well be the appro-priate metaphor for what the novel tries. "Memoir" suggests the novel's hopes and some of its methods, but the term as yet had no specialized

status and simply indicated a mixture of autobiographical and observational elements; to think of it as appropriate, we have to remember its
problematic generic status and not impose later, more rigid notions of its
implications.[10]

One other feature of history is worth notice in thinking of features of
the new fiction: its tendency to organize narrative along thematic or
ideological lines. History, when it gets beyond the barest chronicle (or
perhaps even before), has always meant interpretation, rather than simply a transcription, a point recent historiography legitimately insists on.
The choice of which events to include, even in a pure "record," puts
interpretation on history of even the most "factual," "objective," or "tab-
ular" kind. Long before the invasions of subjectivity that dominated
eighteenth-century history writing, history had borne, as one of its standard features, the tendency to see events relative to some thesis, or at
least along a particular set of ideational lines. In the West, this tendency
usually meant a teleological or Providential history, the popular manifestations of which I described in Chapter Eight. Critics of the novel—and
readers of history—are apt to resist the implications of this tendency,
even deny that it is there, but both species take some of their distinctive
strengths from it. It is true, of course, that in its more rigid, simplistic,
or political forms, the tendency to thematize events is not only unpalat-
able but subversive of larger rhetorical aims (part of the difficulty in any
didactic species), but it is also true that one of the novel's differences
from earlier fiction involves its open and intense engagement with ideas
and its willingness to go beyond storytelling and easy philosophical
assumption to argue some larger sense of the order beyond the variety of
human events. It presents—or develops or argues—cosmologies and
philosophies, whereas the romance had simply reflected or assumed them;
that is one more way that the novel reflects the movement into the
modern world of change and heightened uncertainty about all kinds of
traditional wisdom.[11] This tendency, especially noticeable in early novels, probably is not imitated from histories. More likely, history and the
novel both derive their tendency from human desires held in common
within a particular cultural context.

But the novel does owe history a direct debt. The novel, as a variety
of fiction with no tradition behind it and plenty of suspicion about its
newness, strangeness, and the lack of verifiability of its truth claims,
could hardly have made its assault on cultural interpretation so broadly
without the precedent of a more established and respectable species. And
the novel would not have succeeded so well without the fading of borders. It is hard to imagine the novel taking so much ground in cultural
interpretation without a developing uncertainty about what history was,

where it stopped, what the limits of fact might be. For all its revisionist tendencies and broadening scope, history as a species had begun to lose its distinctive sense of itself and its mission, leaving ample room for rival claimants to cultural interpretation.

The historiography of the seventeenth and eighteenth century is just now being written, and broader readings of social power may show that history anticipated the novel more than I have suggested. Because novelists consciously and repeatedly associate fiction with works of history, however, the connection is at least contextual and generic, whether or not individual texts are involved. Claims of novelists about this connection may be exaggerated, based on their need for respectability and the desire to achieve status through heritage or formal association with established literary species, but the claim itself has substantive reaches; even if it is rhetorically pumped up, it is not spurious or misleading. The presence of a substantial body of history in the reading contexts prior to the emergence of the novel and the fact that the writing of history changed as much as it did just about the time of the novel's emergence have important implications for the novel's capabilities of outreach. Whatever it does for novels formally and ideationally, the tradition of history writing provides a precedent for incorporating cultural meaning into narrative; and, for readers, histories provided experience in seeing cultural meaning presented in symbolic events.

I I I

JUST as history and autobiography become entangled in the early eighteenth century—with memoirs as their metaphor—so history and biography are closely related both structurally and temporally. For many critics now—and for many readers then—the two often seem in fact indistinguishable. For one thing, history at the end of the seventeenth century was still regarded by many observers as the story of heroes and great men, with an occasional great woman. For another, the rising kinds of biography, which tended to portray less heroic figures, still tended to emphasize their subjects' relationships to historical context, often making them in some sense representative of, if not responsible for, their times. Exemplary or not, history was "lives."[12] And just as novels have broad relationships to histories without directly adapting many technical features, so the novel develops in a context conscious of the growing popularity and increasing importance of biography without being as imitative of its formal features as it is of those more openly subjective forms that involved writing self-consciously about one's self.

Biography, because of its "objective" stance, made a point of *seeming* less subjective than autobiography, but it could not stay aloof from the rising tide of subjectivity. The desire to discover the springs of behavior quickly became a tendency to probe the consciousness and the psyche of a subject. As the century wore on, biographers became obsessed with a desire to uncover desire and interpret motive (and not just provide instances for imitation or evitation), and the portraits became increasingly detailed and complex. By the late eighteenth century, biography had (in examples like Boswell) become something like its modern analytical counterpart. It might still be too awestruck or too judgmental by our standards, but already it was chronicling movements of the mind, offering deep explanations of behavior, and piling up facts, facts, facts. The same force— interest in explaining individual behavior and thought—led to the proliferation of published autobiographies and brought a surge of biographies as well. As early as midcentury, according to John Butt, "the public's appetite for biography" had become "insatiable."[13]

But early in the century, progress in the conception of biography was scarcely visible. Bonamy Dobrée, rehearsing the development of biography to midcentury, finds only Roger North's *Lives of the Norths* (1742–44) worth more than a sentence of comment.[14] A case might be made that the development of biography owes more to the novel than does the novel to biography, for the popularity of fictional narrative clearly spurred biographers to more lively styles and perhaps to a control of narrative structure. The critical tendency of the past twenty years to regard biographies in novelistic terms, while sometimes illuminating both species, means primarily that novelistic terminology has come to seem useful for discussing non-fictional narrative forms, not that the *Life of Savage* is a proto-novel or the *Life of Johnson* a documentary one.[15] In any case, direct influences of biographies on individual novels are difficult to specify, and suspected debts are possible at best. Many novelists did read biographies and some wrote them, and they may have at first imitated, either consciously or unconsciously, some local or structural features. But if apprenticeship or slavish copying got some novels off to a sound structural start, novels do not seem to have converted much of importance. Except for the habits-of-mind argument I have made for autobiography, biography has little influence on the form or shape of the novel beyond general contextual support.[16] No single biography seems essential to the emergence and early development of the novel as a species, and biography as a species, while providing avuncular emotional support and the book equivalent of friendly letters of introduction, is more a symptom of cultural change than architect or guide.

Still, the changing conception of appropriate subjects for biography had an early impact on contexts, and the tendency of biography to adapt autobiographical documents of various kinds provided an enabling, perhaps exemplary, context for novelists. Like autobiographies, many biographies early in the century were essentially "spiritual." The biographies before Johnson that literary historians tend to look at—Ruffhead's Pope, for example, or Middleton's Cicero—represent little advance over seventeenth-century practice, while the spiritual biographies (seldom noticed by literary historians and largely unread by modern readers) at least suggest the enlarged sense of subject matter, the broadened audiences for biography, and the rising taste for homely detail. Most spiritual biographies are short and try to get very quickly to the center of life; missing is the suspense, continuing drama, and quest for a center that characterizes the best autobiography. Usually spiritual biographies are utilitarian, pointed, and fairly brief (as I indicated above in discussing their relation to autobiography), and their rationale lies in the power of example, positive or negative. The several anthologies by Samuel Clarke—*A Collection of the Lives of Ten Eminent Divines,* for example—typify the seventeenth-century tendency to glorify clergymen and to try to lure young men toward the Church or to spiritual leadership in dissenting flocks. Clarke is sure published lives are important; "There are," he says, drawing on Sibbes, "four wayes . . . of teaching, Rule, Reason, Similitudes, and Examples . . . [but] . . . onely Examples conform us in a sweet alluring manner . . ." (fol. A2v). In addition to the rhetorical power sought in such examples, the idea of preserving the story of the life grows increasingly important, although "story" is something of a metaphor since many of the biographies contain as much expository and hortatory prose on various religious topics as account of the hero. Spiritual biographies demonstrate that there can be chronology, chronicle, and comprehensiveness without real narrative.

These texts grew in size, as well as frequency of publication, as the eighteenth century wore on, and spiritual biography began consciously to compete with more traditional hero worship. William Hamilton complains in 1703 that

> The *World* is daily more and more over-stock'd with . . . [the lives of famous people in public life] which, as commonly Written, have a *Fatal Influence* upon our *Minds,* and prove very Pernicious to *Religion.* They give a dangerous Turn to our *Thoughts,* and Infect the *Soul* with wrong *Notions* of Things. The little Regard that's had to *Justice* and *Piety,* in the Characters of Princes and Warriours; And the Praises that are given to all their *Successful Actions,* however *Violent* and *Bloody . . .* Inflame those *Passions* in us, which our *Religion* requires us to *Subdue.* A wild *Ambition* Fires the Mind, and drives it furiously on, in pursuit of *Mistaken Honour. . . .* (*Life of Bonnell,* pp. i–ii)

Hamilton's answer is a pious life of 272 pages, to which is added the 31-page funeral sermon for his subject.[17] Few spiritual biographies go into as lengthy detail as Hamilton—more typical is the 98-page life of Lieutenant Illidge by Matthew Henry (1710)—but most of them (like Hamilton) use any autobiographical and private documents they can find to provide detail and give a personal sense of character. It is not unusual to find, as one does on the title page of Joseph Boyse's *Some Remarkable Passages in the Holy Life and Death of . . . Edmund Trench* (1693), a claim that the details are "Most of them drawn out of his own DIARY." Similarly, Henry advertises that *A Short Account of the Life of Lieutenant Illidge* is "Chiefly drawn out of his own PAPERS" (title page), and he argues the necessity of relying on autobiographical perspective:

> But as to . . . the most hidden, and yet most excellent Part of Man, the Thoughts, the Designs, the various Workings of the Heart, and the secret and solemn Transactions between God and it; here a man is best able to draw his own Picture, which this good Man had done for his own Use, in the Manuscripts he hath left behind him, that he might know (but not with any Design to make known to others) what manner of Man he was. (pp. iv–v)

Often, too, the accounts contain evidence that the subject read and reread his or her own diaristic account. *A Narrative of the Holy Life, and Happy Death of . . . John Angier* (by Oliver Heywood, 1683), for example, offers in the midst of its narrative "some observables gathered out of his own Diary, under his own hand" (p. 82), including a prayer with the inserted note. "*Written with my own hand,* April 6, 1625" and "*Perused with comfort,* May 1, 1655" (p. 84).

Sometimes the transition from "I was born" to "He was born" seems artificial, awkward, or forced. It was not uncommon to mix biographical and autobiographical segments or documents in the same volume. In *The Life and Death of Mr. Vavasor Powell* (1671), for example, the first long narrative is an autobiographical account of Powell's conversion and ministry, and it is followed by a "confession of faith" and several cuttings from his diary and other papers; then begins on p. 106[18] a third-person narrative of "Some remarkable Passages in the Life and Ministry," followed by accounts of his last words, transcriptions of his conversations, third-person accounts of his imprisonment, and poems written about him.

The power of example is a constant theme in these lives. Biographies of heroes and saints may well be the logical outcome of the preference of didacticists for example over precept, but, even as the range of lives broadens and complicates, the rationale continues to be articulated in similar, although somewhat expanded, terms. "[T]here is," says a 1672 spiritual biography, "a sweet power and holy efficacy in good examples to draw men to good" (*The Life and Death of Mr. Tho. Wilson*, fol. A3). "I shall heartily desire," another testimonial to that same life summarizes, "his . . . pious examplary life, may still live in your lives, in which he dead yet speaketh" (by "Master Bright," included in *Life*, p. 66). "I wish it were in my Power," a somewhat later biographer (J. Gillane, 1714) writes of John Sage, "to Write a Compleat History of his Life, and thereby to draw such an exact Picture of him, that the Reader might have no more to do, but only carefully to imitate so fair an Example."[19] Henry Fielding's parodic claim that example has an "irresistible" power to command virtue is not a challenge to the efficacy of example but does suggest that by 1742 many no longer believed that pure and unmixed examples of virtue would convince, let alone edify. Johnson's argument for unmixed examples was a consciously reactionary position, promulgated in the teeth of complexities espoused not only in novels but in biographies, and if moralists and rhetoricians often longed for purer forms and simpler times, booksellers and authors with all kinds of intentions moved with the shifting tide.

Between the Restoration and *Joseph Andrews*, emphasis on the negative power of example grows, and Fielding himself, among many others, seems convinced of the power of repelling examples even when questioning magnetic ones. His view of crime and punishment as a magistrate is an extension of that widely shared view; " 'You are not to be hanged, Sir,' " he once approvingly quoted a fellow magistrate as having told a convicted horse thief, " 'for stealing a horse, but you are to be hanged that horses may not be stolen.' "[20] Some cautionary lives had long been available, of course, as the alternative to hagiography, but inverted "mirrors" for magistrates and others tended to be as pure in their way as were those of saints: it was imitation *or* evitation, and more mixed lives were scarce until biography and the novel, more or less in unison in the early to mid-eighteenth century, began to sacrifice some of their rhetorical purity for mimetic accuracy.

By 1740, spiritual biographies, influenced by the eclectic inclusiveness of autobiographies, tended to include some of the bad with the good, putting an increasing burden on the reader to sort and decide. The editors and writers often remained ethically committed, of course, to narrow sectarian or social aims and noted editorially errors and patterns to be shunned, but they tended to admit mistakes into even the most exemplary lives and, sometimes, ethical beauties into even the most cautionary ones. The easy simplicities of heroes and villains, saints and sinners, had been seriously eroded, even in lives intended for the least educated or least literate of believers, and the growing awareness of how important it was to present a whole, balanced, credible account led to more variety within individual biographies as well as among them. William Ayre prefaces his two-volume *Memoirs of the Life and Writings of Alexander Pope, Esq;* (1745) with an account of difficulty that argues full awareness of the plight of the "modern" biographer: ". . . here lies the Difficulty, so few are true to their Subject, for Partiality either of Love or Hate, has caused many . . . to magnify or multiply the good or bad Actions of those whose Lives they write" (I, v). Ayre also provides a solid (and typical midcentury) defense of the growing democratizing tendency of both biography and spiritual biography:

> The Lives of private Men, though they afford not Examples which may fill the Mind with Ideas of Greatness and Power, like those of Princes and Generals, yet are they such as are more open to common Imitation; there are few within whose Compass those Actions are, that is, there are, comparatively speaking, few Princes or Generals, but the Actions of a private Man are as Counsel to all; if good eligible, if bad detestable, and to be avoided: For this Reason most wise Men have delighted in faithful *Biography.* (I, v)

Spiritual biographers (and other writers of lives, too) were, by midcentury, having it two or even three ways—recounting mixed conduct that sometimes required almost a Maxwell's Demon to sort, while still often insisting without irony that models drew (almost "irresistibly") readers to follow their patterns, or to repel them from detestable conduct. Not all biographies were equally mixed, of course, nor were cultural and ethical observers in full agreement. Exemplary lives were still sometimes presented in an unmixed or nearly pure fashion, and some moralists, like Johnson, still worried that the presentation of less than ideal behavior in fact justified and promoted bad conduct, whatever the text's intention. But from the late seventeenth century to the mid-eighteenth, biography (and spiritual biography) moved to present a broader range of heroes, villains, and ordinary people of mixed conduct, and it tended to present each of them more fully, more complexly, less purely as a pattern for either imitation or evitation. That range of portrayal was part of the context in which the novel emerged. Even if biography had little describable influence on individual novels or novelists, or structually on the form, it is hard to see how narratives of lives as complicated as those presented in the novel could have emerged without such a fecund context, for readers had to come to expect both a focus and a fullness in life stories, and writers needed some sense of the possibilities of range, scope, and audience interest, even if they had better formal models elsewhere and seem not to have studied biographies as either sources or analogues.

Biography, then, does not lead to novels in the conventional sense that its structures and features are transformed into novelistic ones, but its status as a respectable literary and didactic species, providing significant, accepted reading material to a wide (and widening) range of readers, means that it runs a certain interference for the novel, opening up the context in ways that novelists soon learn to take full advantage of. There is more to note than the invention or adaptation of formal features, for the reading public was readied quite beyond any individual's conscious intentions. Like novelists since, novelists then were conditioned, both consciously and unconsciously, by the market, by what readers know and want and expect. Novelists are readers of culture in ways beyond just making their heroes embody the values of their times or in making their stories "epical." A good novelist, like a canny bookseller, reads audiences as readily as history and tradition; the novel reaches into the past for nourishment or support only in order to reach toward a future in which its readers' expectations and desires are located.

I V

TRAVEL literature provides a similar kind of macrocontext, and some of the novels' outreach to larger issues—especially those involving far-off places, anthropological data, sea lore, and the accrual of knowledge through the physical experience of movement through space—was eased by the broad cultural consciousness of travel books of many kinds. As with books of history, the particularity of models seems not to be the major issue, although for earlier generations of historians committed to "sources and analogues" there was a determined effort to find originals among factual (or pseudo-factual) travel accounts because so much eighteenth-century fiction used a travel format. Some individual books perhaps provided, for some individual novels, structural hints and rhetorical help, as well as gold (and lead) mines of information. But travel literature now seems less a "source" than it once did, and the detailed studies of sources and analogues, such as the ones Arthur W. Secord did on Defoe, now seem literal-minded and heavy-footed, tied to notions that fiction's relation to fact meant a kind of mechanical derivativeness. Source hunters then sought a license for particulars rather than a licensing of taste or desire.[21]

The literature of travel was, however, a powerful enabling presence for the novel, perhaps nudging it in particular directions involving cultural and historical differentiation. It is hard to imagine readers responding to any Defoe or Smollett novel, or to some sections in almost any other novelist, without awareness of vast numbers of factual or quasi-factual predecessors. The context provided expectations, even demands. The impact of travel literature on readers—and therefore on expectations of writing about most contemporary places and subjects—was enormous, but I will be brief about it here because Percy Adams's extended account makes so fully the case for its importance.[22] Everyone knows the lengthy story of England's growing interest in foreign (especially exotic) cultures, and there is no need to rehearse the history of audience fascination with even the most mundane and boring narratives of exploration and adventure. Adams offers, too, a rich sense of the variety and ubiquity of published materials and a just account of formal features, together with a history of the development of the several kinds of books that are generally grouped under the broad heading of "travel literature." Rather than summarizing the learning crowded into Adams's pages, I will simply add a few footnotes and offer a view, from the perspective of my interest in pre-novelistic reading contexts more generally, of how travel books fit the larger context in which the novel comes to exist.

Like many other species that depend on extensivity, travel books (while they may not provide a lineage for formal features) help to suggest the range of cultural interests that the novel had to engage. Some small expository structures transform themselves more or less bodily into novels (in *Robinson Crusoe*, for example, the geography, flora and fauna, and customs of the natives come in for a paragraph of explanatory background, just as they do in Dampier and Woodes Rogers), but here, as in other formal features, the novel is eclectic rather than directly imitative, taking a feature of convenience when it is available in a pre-fabricated form but neither taking its identity from the "source" nor surrendering much of its own character in absorbing one more small structure into its own cumulative one. Later novels tend to disguise such visible marks of heritage by absorbing information more quickly, digesting it more easily into the narrative flow, and diffusing its effect, as in, for example, Hemingway or Dinesen. The texture is more uniform, the style less various in later novels as writers work to simplify the multiple directions and functions of the novel or (the same thing) to subordinate all features to a more coherent, more consuming, less digressive narrative interest. But the same kinds of "facts"—about foreign rituals, strange plants and beasts, the comparativity of human judgments and habits—are just as surely, if less parenthetically, introduced. The heritage from travel books is less visible in more recent novelists, and the generic influence might not be discoverable at all without the obtrusive lumpishness in early novels. So much of the curiosity about how others live and in what physical contexts seems "natural" to modernity—because the idea of cultural clash and adjustment has become such a part of modern consciousness—that no one reading LeGuin or Theroux is apt to think of voyagers or marauders as predecessors. Yet neither the curiosity nor the ease of absorption would be there had the novel emerged from a different context or in a different, less accretive, and less imperialistic way. But that is also to imagine a different species than the novel is.

The most concrete single mark of travel books on the novel seems to be on title pages, and the fact that so mechanical—and relatively substanceless—a feature is so prominent is in itself suggestive. The setting of reader expectations is not, of course, negligible, and the early novelists were almost as shameless in their attempt to borrow readers as they were, in their allusion to epic and history, to achieve prestige by association. The first novelists openly tried to capitalize on the contemporary popularity of travel books by suggesting the similarity of their wares. Formally, those promises are seldom kept, but very often the topics of interest to readers of travel books—information about societies that are very different and often far away, for example—are in fact engaged. The sense of being in an expanding world—and not one where things are much the same everywhere—becomes crucial to travel books as soon as explorers discover that the world is various and not just full of parodic Europeans. Few eighteenth-century novels stay in one place; even the ones, like *Clarissa, Tom Jones,* or *Humphry Clinker,* that are set wholly in Britain emphasize cultural comparisons between different regions or social groups that minister to similar curiosities.

The vehicle for the comparison in novels is often a journey or series of journeys by the main character, who thus has to interact with people with different customs and assumptions; emblematic perhaps is the French sequence in Book Seven of *Tristram Shandy,* which (despite its odd tonal as well as digressive quality) is there to put English ways into a larger perspective. The journey is usually, however, a structure of convenience—movement through space means learning—rather than a feature formally adopted from travel books, and precise location is usually less important than the fact that there *are* different locations and that people in different places actually differ from one another. The menu of *Tom Jones* and most novels may be human nature, but there are several courses, and the implication is that no single view of human nature will serve— that cultures alter people, people alter circumstances, and circumstances alter cases. Both old and new romances had traipsed all over the world without any significant effect on how people thought, acted, or felt, and with little difference in whom one met, but the novel is a product of serious cultural thinking about comparative societies and the multiple natures in human nature. Again (as with so many novelistic characteristics and features), the point seems to involve not an issue of formal influence or even a case where ideas are borrowed or stolen, so much as it does the novel's ability to exploit a fact of historical change. Travel literature, because it chronicles the developing awareness of cultural coloration and the deterioration of belief in universal truths, helps us clarify the novel's assumptions, and for early novelists travel books were—as soon as they plainly espoused comparative rather than absolute standards of value—useful as a starting point. If title pages claiming an alliance with travel books are often misleading in their particulars, they do accurately point to psychological assumptions and the loci of cultural value. Such journeys often carry mythic overtones of one kind or another (most of which predate the popular travel books), but, except for the idea of travel itself as a structural device, the novel's journeys owe little to movement through space in travel books.

Cashing in on cultural curiosity does not lead necessarily to a seeking after formal features; the formal similarity between novels and travel books consists mostly in their both being loosely constructed, capable of almost infinite expansion, and susceptible of a great variety of directions and paces. But just as important are formal differences. Travel books almost never have, or need, a sense of closure, for example. Journeys in most travel books just end, they do not culminate in much of anything, nor do they bring to fruition some theme or series of themes set up earlier in the book, though they usually get the narrator home for a while. It is, of course, true that some of the better travel books consciously present some theme or concern which allows resolution and closure, and it may be that individual novelists got hints from such performances, but there is little reason to think of travel books as a species having provided such features for the novel.[23] Like other books that fed single desires before novels saw the way to satisfy multiple ones at once, travel books offer clues about direction, provide a feature here and there, and offer novelists general encouragement, but mostly they just provide readers of novels with the comfortable feeling that they have been here—or somewhere very like it—before.

V

FEW things about novels are as simple as they try to seem. Not only do they share, at their best, complexities available to all verbal constructs and forms, but they have almost always—perhaps by definition, certainly by tradition—achieved elaborate contextuality as well: they make and they refer. But more too: even in their making, even beyond their desire to refer, they grow out of historical moments more than do most other referential new creations, for in the nature of the novel—in its very definition—there is a new extension from a temporal world, a flowering out of things as they are. Novels sometimes achieve as elaborate, elegant, resonant, and intense verbal textures as lyric poems, and when they do, their size and varied tonalities offer intricacies almost peerless in the verbal universe. Novels investigate, analyze, and construe human behavior in ways sometimes so sophisticated that they rival the "science" of social and behavioral science without quite as often slipping into morasses of data in forgettable or unforgivable prose. And their outreach to meaning and implication through everything from the details of everyday to the world of intellection, pattern, and perspective often rivals, at least in the minds of its most dedicated readers, the reaches of academic discourse about history and the nature of culture.

Novels do not always attain these reaches, of course; to describe the novel becoming is only to describe potential, and not many novels in any age rise to the full possibility of the species. But almost always novels strive mightily, and they self-consciously consider their proper aspiration. Novels sometimes claim to tell a simple story, point a simple lesson, or provide a simple escape, and readers who know better sometimes fall unaccountably for these disingenuous claims; but the simplicity will not hold, even when great clarity of vision or intensity of passion makes it seem as if it will. And questions involving the history of the novel slip quickly beyond simplicity, too, not only because novels from the first grappled for complexities like those in later novels, but also because questions of origin leap so quickly beyond the formal ones that old literary history and traditional criticism have learned to deal with. Formal patterns are only part of the issue in a new literary species. Equally important, although more difficult to specify, are territorial issues involving what ground the species may dare to explore—and much of what I have tried to suggest in this chapter about the novel's outreach involves models of daring.

The world that enabled the novel to emerge—or insisted that it did— was a world that, so to speak, did not know about modern forms, but it knew what it liked. It is the task of the modern literary critic / theoretician / historian to read and chart those likes and the patterns they make, or so it has seemed to me in the assumptions that have governed the research and writing of this book. Although my immediate interest is in novels and novelists, I have tried to raise questions about them (and about what they were doing in beginning so worthy a craft) in a context of broader human issues of place and time. The novel does not exist for the novel's sake, but human culture is for human culture's sake, and the rest is implication and detail. In part, that is what literature helps us to see—richly, resonantly, complexly—about our lives and the lives of others in other ages, and the novel has been for the last two hundred and fifty years the species that has done it best in the most cultures for the most readers.

Notes

∎

PREFACE

1. Nancy Armstrong, *Desire and Domestic Fiction: A Political History of the Novel* (New York, 1987); John Bender, *Imagining the Penitentiary: Fiction and the Architecture of Mind in Eighteenth-Century England* (Chicago, 1987); Terry Castle, *Masquerade and Civilization: The Carnivalesque in Eighteenth-Century English Culture and Fiction* (Stanford, Calif., 1986); Cathy N. Davidson, *Revolution and the Word: The Rise of the Novel in America* (New York, 1986); and Michael McKeon, *The Origins of the English Novel, 1600–1740* (Baltimore, 1987).
2. "The Loneliness of the Long-Distance Reader," *Genre*, 10 (1977), 455–84. See also "The Insistent I," *Novel*, 13 (1979), 19–37; "Biography and the Novel," *Modern Language Studies*, 9 (1979), 68–84; "The World as Stage and Closet," in *British Threatre and Other Arts, 1660–1800*, ed. Shirley Strum Kenny (Washington, D.C., 1984), pp. 271–87; " 'The Young, the Ignorant and the Idle': Some Notes on Readers and the Beginnings of the English Novel," in *Anticipation of the Enlightenment in England, France, and Germany*, ed. Alan Kors and Paul J. Korshin (Philadelphia, 1987), pp. 259–82; "Fielding and the Modern Reader: The Problem of Temporal Translation," in *Fielding in His Time and Ours*, by J. Paul Hunter and Martin C. Battestin (Los Angeles, 1987), pp. 1–28; "*Gulliver's Travels* and the Novelistic Tradition," in *The Genres of Gulliver's Travels*, ed. Frederik N. Smith (Newark, Del., 1990), pp. 56–74; and "The Novel and the Contexts of Discourse," in *Theory and Tradition in Eighteenth-Century Studies*, ed. Richard B. Schwartz (Carbondale, IL, 1990), pp. 118–39. All of these essays are reprinted in a forthcoming collection to be published by Cambridge University Press.
3. Ian Watt, *The Rise of the Novel* (Berkeley, 1957).

CHAPTER ONE

1. Two studies that use the term "novel" to describe earlier fiction give, in spite of what I regard as imprecise terminology, sensible accounts of the narratives they are concerned with. In *The Novel Before the Novel* (Chicago, 1977), Arthur Heiserman provides good analysis of some ancient Greek narratives that have many novelistic features; and in *Novel and Society in Elizabethan*

England (Totowa, N.J., 1985), David Margolies provides a fair account of Elizabethan "novels" without making extreme formal or contextual claims for them.

2. "[T]he term 'origins' is generally inapplicable to literary forms. . . . [F]orms cut across the most sharply defined historical and national boundaries, affirming the existence of creative processes mysteriously linked together regardless of their sequence in time," *The Rise of Romance* (New York, 1971), p. vii. Vinaver also says that "whatever [form] has been, in some sort it still is," p. vii.

3. Robert Scholes and Robert Kellogg, *The Nature of Narrative* (New York, 1966), p. 8. Frye's most important claims for romance are in *The Secular Scripture: A Study of the Structure of Romance* (Cambridge, Mass., 1976), but he also discusses the relationship between the novel and romance in *The Anatomy of Criticism* (Princeton, N.J., 1957).

4. The most powerful case for elements of romance in Fielding is made by Henry Knight Miller, *Henry Fielding's "Tom Jones" and the Romance Tradition* (Victoria, B.C., 1976, English Literary Studies Monograph No. 6). See also Sheridan Baker, "Henry Fielding's Comic Romances," *Papers of the Michigan Academy of Science, Arts, and Letters*, 45 (1960), 411–19.

5. See, for example, Mieke Bal, *Narratology: Introduction to the Theory of Narrative*, trans. Christine van Boheemen (Toronto, 1985); Gerard Genette, *Narrative Discourse Revisited*, trans. Jane E. Lewin (Ithaca, N.Y., 1988); and Ross Chambers, *Story and Situation: Narrative Seduction and the Power of Fiction* (Minneapolis, 1984, Theory and History of Literature, Vol. 12).

6. It was originally called *The Athenian Gazette* but renamed for legal reasons; the collected edition was called *The Athenian Oracle*. See Gilbert D. McEwen, *The Oracle of the Coffee House* (San Marino, Calif., 1972), pp. 8–9.

7. The range of questions included by Dunton is discussed by Mabel Phillips in an unpublished Yale dissertation (1925). Dunton apparently did reject some questions as frivolous or obscene, and later, in *Athenae Redivivae: or the new Athenian Oracle* (1704), he sometimes replied testily to questions he found offensive, as in the following exchange:

    "*Q. Whether a Badger has ev'ry Year a New Arse-hole?*
    A. What Reason has the Querist to trouble us with this Impertinence?*"

8. *The Athenian Gazette*, No. 1 (March 17, 1690); *The Athenian Mercury*, No. 3 (March 31, 1690).

9. For example, *The London Mercury* (later called *The Lacedemonian Mercury*), and the "Little Review" section of Defoe's *Review*. See Stephen Parks, *John Dunton and the English Book Trade* (New York, 1976), esp. pp. 84–104.

10. Parks, pp. 89–90.

11. It is possible, but unlikely, that Swift intended the Ode as an elaborate spoof. At the time, he expressed extraordinary pride in the poem and its appearance, and its mode and tone are similar to his other poems of those years. The possibility that it might be a spoof seems enhanced by the date of publication, but that Swift could have known enough about publication plans to control the date is unlikely. Swift's later addiction to April 1 hoaxes is thus probably just a nice little irony—or possibly a complex outcome of his own early gulling.

12. The historical Dunton bears a lot of the features of the Tale-teller, and if the figure is a composite (as seems most likely), Dunton was almost certainly one of the models. Certainly, he is a more significant presence in the *Tale* than he has usually been recognized to be.

13. For the details of this publication, see Chapter Seven.

14. *Maggots: or, Poems on Several Subjects, Never before Handled. By a Schollar* (1685). It is a volume of 172 pages, with elaborate notes.

15. See the 1729 *Dunciad* I, 59–60 and 126, and notes.

16. *Athenae Redivivae* (1704), fol. A2.

17. See *The Life and Errors of John Dunton* (1705), p. 256.

18. See John Robert Moore, *Daniel Defoe: Citizen of the Modern World* (Chicago, 1958), p. 232, and Parks, pp. 83–84.

19. Contemporary satirists and parodists had quite a bit of fun with Dunton's pretensions. In *The New Athenian Comedy* (1693; probably by Elkanah Settle), for example, a Duntonesque character named Joachim Dash brags that "we are (take us together) the whole *Bodlaean* of Learning, Universall, as you well observe, being the very Crest of our Scutcheon. Or what wou'd our undertaking signify else?" (Act III, p. 21). The most amusing touch in *The New Athenian Com-*

edy is to bring on stage characters of the sort who send their questions to Dunton. Dorothy Tickletext, for example, is an Islington milkmaid who comes for consultation because she can't hold her water.

20. See McEwen, and especially G. A. Starr, *Defoe and Casuistry* (Princeton, 1971). I discuss the larger casuistry tradition, of which Dunton's *Athenian Mercury* was a manifestation, in Chapter Eight.

21. The phrase is ubiquitous in Dunton. *The Athenian Library* (1725) was advertised on its title page as "a universal entertainment for the lovers of novelty."

22. *Athenianism* (1710) was dedicated to the "Lovers of Novelty."

23. See Robert Wilde, *Poems on Several Occasions* (1683), p. 83. Dunton quotes the couplet in, among many other places, *The Athenian Library* (1725).

24. Title pages were generally the responsibility of printers rather than authors. See Rodney M. Baine, "The Evidence from Defoe's Title Pages," *Studies in Bibliography*, 25 (1972), 185–91.

25. This commonality is further discussed in Chapter Six.

26. *The Young Students Library*, 1692. A lengthy poem at the bottom of the emblem emphasizes the anonymity of the Athenians: "Behind ye scenes sit might we, / nor are we known nor will we be. . . ."

27. McEwen, p. 27.

28. *Life and Errors*, fol. [A5].

29. See pp. 104–5.

30. For how long the "general embargo on novel-reading" hung on (well into the nineteenth century), see Kathleen Tillotson, *Novels of the Eighteen-Forties* (London, 1961; first published, 1954), pp. 15–16.

31. William Park, "Fielding *and* Richardson," *PMLA*, 81 (1967), 381–88.

   Fielding's responses to the older Pope are especially problematic; they range from simple fawning and youthful imitation to serious disagreement about literary strategies and aims. See C. J. Rawson, *Henry Fielding and the Augustan Ideal under Stress* (London, 1972), esp. pp. 158ff, and my discussion in *Occasional Form* (Baltimore, 1975), pp. 22–46. I now suspect that Tom Thumb's demise in *The Tragedy of Tragedies* (he is eaten by a cow) alludes cruelly to a well-known episode in Pope's childhood when he was attacked by a cow.

32. See "Fielding *and* Richardson," and "What Was New about the 'New Species of Writing'?" *Studies in the Novel*, 2 (1970), 112–30.

33. *An Essay on the New Species of Writing founded by Mr. Fielding* (1751), p. [i]. Ioan Williams conveniently reprints much of the essay in *Novel and Romance 1700–1800: A Documentary Record* (New York, 1970), pp. 150–59.

34. *Rambler*, 4 (31 March 1750) in *The Rambler*, ed. W. J. Bate and Albrecht B. Strauss, Yale Edition of the Works of Samuel Johnson (New Haven, Conn., 1969), III, 19.

35. Clara Reeve, *The Progress of Romance, through Time, Countries and Manners* (2 vols., London, 1785), I, 111.

36. Because its main claims involve familiarity and wide, often indiscriminate, use, the term "novel" is not without problems, even as a working label, for in addition to the core of connotations that suggest how the novel is distinctive among forms of prose fiction, it has also accrued some other meanings that are less precise and less useful. For some, it encompasses all prose fiction— or even all narrative—in all times and places. Under such a definition, Heliodorus and Thomas Nashe are novelists, and *The English Rogue*, *The Castle of Otranto*, and *The Free-Lance Pallbearers*—perhaps even *Gulliver's Travels* and *Troilus and Criseyde* and Boswell's *Life of Johnson*—are novels. For others, the term is a little less inclusive but gathers in all prose fiction once the novel entered the scene, as if the romance suddenly ceased to exist and no other modes of fiction could compete with the novel's reign, a position that is close enough to accurate to be quite dangerous. And if some use the term too broadly for my taste, others are too restrictive, reserving it for some narrower subspecies and awarding it (for this narrower use is a valuative term) only to those books that pass a particular geographical, temporal, or political test or to those that belong to a particular school. For them, the Jamesian novel, or the panoramic novel on the model of Tolstoi, or the proletarian novel, or some other honored subset, is the only novel there is.

However one uses the term (or any other term in the imprecise business of literary classifi-
cation) there are difficulties or uncertainties about borders, and the problems of overlap, vesti-
giality, and encroachment become difficult ones, especially complicating the discussion of particular
texts. Whether or not traditional poetic genres suffer from identity problems at their edges, the
novel (as a new form seeking a distinct identity) certainly does. Even in books one feels entirely
comfortable calling novels according to a careful definition, there are often elements from competing species—strong elements of romance in *Tom Jones*, for example, or of satire in *Humphry
Clinker* or *Tristram Shandy* or *The Cry*, or of the picaresque in *Moll Flanders*. Such invasions of
the novel's "purity," however, should not threaten the basic definition or our fundamental
understanding that something very specific began to be generated as a distinct pattern at a
certain cultural moment in the early eighteenth century.

37. Continental narratives often share "romantic" and "moralistic" features; the tradition does not
break, in France or Italy, nearly so clearly as it does in England, perhaps a result of Protestant
cultural features that forced, in England, a sharper break. See my discussion of Protestant legi-
timation of moralistic epistemology in Chapter Eight.

38. Michael McKeon makes as strong a case as can be made for the historic continuity between
romance and novel in England—*The Origins of the English Novel 1600–1740* (Baltimore, 1987),
especially pp. 273–314. See also Lennard J. Davis, *Factual Fictions: The Origins of the English
Novel* (New York, 1983).

39. Heiserman, p. 221, n. 2.

40. The line-drawing question is, of course, a vexed one, and in a writer like Eliza Haywood one
can see the old and new frankly at odds in the same narrative. Most of the features in early
Haywood books (of the 1720s) seem to ally them firmly with romance—the plots are stock, the
language formalized, the names conventional, the settings exotic, the fantasies aimed more at
escape than aspiration—but there are "novelistic" features too. Events take place in the present,
ideologies bear a close relation to contemporary situations and concerns, the problems facing
the characters resemble the life choices of contemporary women, and sometimes the circumstantial detail and psychological curiosity are extended in ways that seem consciously modern
(or at least not consciously old-fashioned). This seems to me unsurprising in a transitional time,
not just because borders are still being formed and new compounds are often unstable, but
because authors in a time of change are often caught up unknowingly in new tastes and new
movements even while expressing their conscious loyalties to something old, known, and stable.
It is especially unamazing that "marginal" writers and editors—women, hacks, menippean gath-
erers—frequently present to the world works that seem neither this nor that; but even the most
determined and self-conscious of writers who belong to confident, well-defined groups (Henry
Fielding is a good example among novelists, Pope among poets) seem often to be drawn temperamentally in one direction while declaiming in another.

41. *Incognita: or, Love and Duty Reconcil'd. A Novel* (London, 1692), "The Preface to the Reader,"
fols. [A5v–A6].

42. Burney, in the Preface to *Evelina* (1778), briefly anticipates Reeve's distinctions and counts
herself firmly among the novelists. There was, however, substantial agreement about characteristics of the "new species" by the 1750s; it was the term "novel" that remained cloudy: "history"
was a preferred term. For another view, see Homer Obed Brown, "Of the Title to Things Real:
Conflicting Stories," *ELH*, 55 (1988), 917–54, especially pp. 938–48.

43. Howard D. Weinbrot's cautionary words about the use of the term "Augustan," although very
useful in reminding us just how ironic it is for most English Augustans, does not persuade me
that the term does not accurately—in large part because of its irony—describe both a group and
a cultural moment. See *Augustus Caesar in "Augustan" England* (Princeton, N.J., 1978); but
also see Howard Erskine-Hill, *The Augustan Idea in English Literature* (London, 1983); Claude
Rawson, " 'Neo-classic' and 'Augustan,' " in *Order from Confusion Sprung* (London, 1985),
pp. 235–58; and Margaret Doody, *The Daring Muse: Augustan Poetry Reconsidered* (Cambridge,
1985).

44. Novelty was, of course, a significant part of the answer—in fact, the soul of it—but it is a mark
of the power of the tradition and the reluctance of the culture that the response was so guarded,
so careful to couch itself in traditional terms that would seem unthreatening. There were, of

course, blatancies of the sort illustrated by Dunton and catalogued by Pope, but Henry Fielding's attempt to provide a pedigree for a new species is a better emblem of the way a permanent pattern of change got established. It is no wonder that the term "novel" did not quickly establish itself, in spite of its deep accuracy.

45. French, for example, encompasses both romance and novel in its term *roman*, and although the best literary historians in France have long acknowledged that quite a break occurs in French prose fiction at about the same time as in English, the distinction seems to most observers less sharp there, in part perhaps because of the history of terms.

46. See Philip Stewart, *Imitation and Illusion in the French Memoir-Novel, 1700–1750* (New Haven, Conn., 1969), and English Showalter, Jr., *The Evolution of the French Novel 1641–1782* (Princeton, N.J., 1972).

CHAPTER   TWO

1. The most powerful challenge to older definitions of novelistic features has come through the "discovery" of Mikhail Bakhtin, whose "Discourse in the Novel," written more than a half century ago, has liberated many critics from thinking about novels in purely formal terms. His discussion of "heteroglossia" is especially helpful in making competing discourses (or "voices") in the novel seem a legitimate feature rather than a blot (*The Dialogic Imagination: Four Essays by M. M. Bakhtin*, ed. Michael Holquist [Austin, Tex., 1981], pp. 259–422. Old, organic definitions of the novel, somewhat modified by the concept of "formal realism" of Ian Watt (*The Rise of the Novel* [London, 1957]), remain, however, operative in most criticism of the novel.

2. However facetious he may be about Homeric precedent, Fielding set the polar terms of tradition and novelty in claiming classical precedent and, at the same time, insisting that he was founding a new species. See the "Preface" to *Joseph Andrews* (ed. Martin Battestin [Middletown, Conn., 1967], pp. 3–11) and the so-called "intercalary" chapters of *Tom Jones*—that is, the first chapters of each book.

3. Fielding's discussion of the marvelous (*Tom Jones*, VIII, i, 395–407) needs to be read in the context of his effort to distinguish his new kind of fiction from older romance and other narrative kinds. Ultimately he praises the "marvellous" and approves the restrained, judicious use of it in works of the kind he is writing. The fullest discussion of the issue is in Mitchell Kalpakgian, *The Marvellous in Fielding's Novels* (Washington, D.C., 1981), but the discussions by Robert V. Wess ("The Probable and the Marvelous in *Tom Jones*," *Modern Philology*, 68 [1970], 32–45) and Battestin (note to the opening lines of *Tom Jones*, VIII, i, 395–96) are more pointed.

4. See *Rise*, pp. 260–89.

5. Novel criticism no longer dominates so thoroughly the conception of narrative, but the new narratology has not yet been assimilated into historical, or even theoretical, accounts of the novel. Resistance to "theory" by traditional students of the English novel is in part responsible, but equally important is narratology's tendency—in its quest for basic principles in narrative—not to distinguish among narrative modes and thus in effect to blur borders between the novel and other species of narrative.

6. The title of Defoe's first novel—*The Life and Strange Surprizing Adventures of Robinson Crusoe*—consciously works from expectations in the context of popular reading. "Strange and surprising" was a catch phrase common on the title pages of both fictional and non-fictional narratives, evidently intended to attract readers interested in unusual but actual (or presumed to be actual) events.

7. While I do not trust the terms of Northrop Frye's theory that the novel is a "displacement" of romance, he is right to emphasize the similarity of the two species in responding to certain basic human needs.

8. Daniel Defoe, *Moll Flanders*, ed. G. A. Starr (London, 1971), p. 154.

9. Charlotte Brontë, *Jane Eyre*, ed. Jane Jack and Margaret Smith (Oxford, 1969; reprinted with corrections, 1975), pp. 452–53; Thomas Pynchon, *The Crying of Lot 49* (New York, 1986), esp. pp. 179–82.

10. Martin Battestin has suggested that a childhood incident may have led to Fielding's literary

preoccupation with incest; in any case the issue finds intense expression in the false suspense that informs key moments in *Joseph Andrews* and *Tom Jones* ("Henry Fielding, Sarah Fielding, and 'the dreadful Sin of Incest,' " *Novel*, 132 [1979], 6–18). The pervasiveness of incest as a theme in eighteenth-century fiction has not yet been put into a full cultural perspective. Until recently only "literary" incest—comparisons between Tom Jones and Oedipus, for example— has gotten much attention, but now the focus has begun to shift to cultural anxieties that may be responsible for the novelistic obsession. See, e.g., Ellen Pollak's essay, "*Moll Flanders*, Incest, and the Structure of Exchange," in *The Eighteenth Century: Theory and Interpretation*, 30 (1989), 3–21.

11. The study of "minor" female novelists is largely responsible for present revisionist thinking that has widened the canon and begun to open up definitions. The broad implications of recent study have not yet been summed up, but some hint of the changed contours are evident in Jane Spencer, *The Rise of the Woman Novelist* (Oxford, 1986).

12. For many years it was the critical convention to ignore, in all but the most mechanical ways, the obvious similarities between autobiography and the early novel, but now the subject commands rapt if not always very exact attention. The best detailed account is that of Patricia Meyer Spacks, *Imagining a Self* (Cambridge, Mass., 1976).

13. See especially *The Cry* (3 vols., London, 1754), which Fielding apparently wrote in collaboration with Jane Collier. The quotation is from I, 14.

14. Ian Watt provides a good analysis of character names and related matters in "The Naming of Characters in Defoe, Richardson, and Fielding," *Review of English Studies*, 25 (1949), 322–38. But see also Carol Kay, *Political Constructions: Defoe, Richardson, Sterne in Relation to Hobbes, Hume, and Burke* (Ithaca, N.Y., 1988), pp. 12–14.

15. Implying that *Robinson Crusoe* attracted poor and ill-educated readers, Gildon wrote that "there is not an old Woman that can go the Price of it, but that buys [the] Life and Adventures"—*The Life and Strange Surprizing Adventures of Mr. D——DeF—— of London, Hosier* (London, 1719), reprinted in *Robinson Crusoe Examin'd and Criticis'd*, ed. Paul Dottin (London and Paris, 1923), pp. 71–72.

16. *Rambler* 4, in Yale Edition, III, 21.

17. I have treated this matter in more detail in "The Loneliness of the Long-Distance Reader," *Genre*, 10 (1977), 455–84, and "The World as Stage and Closet," in *British Theatre and Other Arts, 1660–1800*, ed. Shirley Strum Kenny (Washington, D.C., 1984), pp. 271–87.

18. See Mark Girouard, *Life in the English Country House* (New Haven, Conn., 1978).

19. See Scholes and Kellogg, *The Nature of Narrative*, p. 264; and Walter J. Ong, *Orality and Literacy* (London, 1982).

20. One of the most interesting early experiments in this regard is *The Cry* (1754; probably written by Sarah Fielding and Jane Collier jointly), in which characters plead their case before a tribunal figure, Una, and a chorus (or anti-chorus) of contemporary figures (the "cry") responds as putative readers would.

21. John Preston, *The Created Self* (London, 1970), p. 117.

22. For a more detailed discussion of the "whole-as-observed-part" tradition, see my "Response as Reformation: *Tristram Shandy* and the Art of Interruption," *Novel*, 4 (1971), 132–46.

23. *The Adventures of Peregrine Pickle*, ed. James L. Clifford (London, 1964), chapter LXXXVIII, p. 538.

24. Although, as Margaret Anne Doody and Florian Stuber point out, most abridgers do diminish the plot as well. See "*Clarissa* Censored," *Modern Language Studies*, 18 (1988), 74–88.

25. Dedication to *East of Eden*.

CHAPTER THREE

1. *MacFlecknoe*, l. 101.

2. On some of the cultural implications of the move from an oral to a written culture, see Walter J. Ong, *Rhetoric, Romance, and Technology* (Ithaca, N.Y., 1971), and William Nelson, "From 'Listen, Lordings' to 'Dear Reader,' " *University of Toronto Quarterly*, 46 (1976–77), 110–23.

3. *The Rise of the Novel* (Berkeley, 1957), p. 25.

4. Preface to the first volume of the *Penny Magazine* (1832), as quoted by Richard D. Altick, *The English Common Reader: A Social History of the Mass Reading Public 1800–1900* (Chicago, 1957), p. 49.

5. On the problems of determining historical literacy and other historical demographic information, and on modern statistical methods for dealing with these problems, see the Introduction to E. A. Wrigley and R. S. Schofield, *The Population History of England, 1541–1871: A Reconstruction* (Cambridge, Mass., 1981), pp. 1–12. I am greatly indebted to this comprehensive study for much of the information in this chapter. For a far-reaching review of the contribution of Wrigley and Schofield, by several hands, see "*The Population History of England 1541–1871:* A Review Symposium," *Social History*, 8 (1983), 139–68.

6. Altick reports that "Efforts to locate the statement in Burke's own writings or speeches have been fruitless," p. 49n.

7. *Reflections on the Revolution in France.* See Altick, p. 69. Altick offers a wealth of statistics on printing and publication data, and his account of reading habits is a lively one, but his assumptions about the reading public in the eighteenth century must be treated with caution because of the different kinds of data about literacy that have become available since his book was published.

8. See Lawrence Stone, "Literacy and Education in England 1640–1900," *Past and Present*, 42 (1969), 69–139. For more conservative figures backed up by a wealth of detail, see R. A. Houston, *Scottish Literacy and the Scottish Identity: Illiteracy and Society in Scotland and Northern England 1600–1800* (Cambridge, 1985). On the complex mix of cultural factors that led to enhanced literacy, see Thomas Laqueur, "The Cultural Origins of Popular Literacy in England 1500–1850," *Oxford Review of Education*, 2 (1976), 255–75.

9. See Kenneth Lockridge, *Literacy in Colonial New England* (New York, 1974); Lawrence Cremin, "Reading, Writing and Literacy," *Review of Education*, 1 (1975), 517–21; and David D. Hall, "The World of Print and Collective Mentality in Seventeenth-Century New England," in *New Directions in American Intellectual History*, ed. John Higham and Paul K. Conkin (Baltimore, 1979), pp. 166–80.

10. The only serious competitor is Sweden, where the ability to read and the ability to write were not necessarily correlated in the same way; see Egil Johansson, "The History of Literacy in Sweden," in *Literacy and Social Development in the West: A Reader*, ed. H. J. Graff (Cambridge, 1981), pp. 151–82.

11. Stone, "Literacy and Education. . . ," p. 121.

12. Early and frequent deaths among the young and literate in London probably meant that more individuals learned to read each year even when the percentage remained constant. Mortality rates were lower in segments of the population less likely to be literate; London mortality rates hit the young, ambitious, migratory population the hardest. In that sense, reading and dying were highly correlated (though obviously not causally); newly arrived or newly literate Londoners just about evenly replaced the dying during much of the eighteenth century.

13. There is substantial disagreement about what happens to literacy rates after 1775; Stone ("Literacy and Education") thinks literacy again begins to rise, but most demographers find evidence of a decline in the wake of increasing industrialization, long work hours, and decreasing incentives to read. See especially R. S. Schofield, "Dimensions of Illiteracy, 1750–1850," *Explorations in Economic History*, 10 (1973), 437–54.

14. On issues of genre identity and genre breakdown, see Rosalie Colie, *The Resources of Kind: Genre-Theory in the Renaissance* (Berkeley, 1973) and Michael McKeon, *The Origins of the English Novel 1600–1740*, pp. 25–64. One of the most important differences between McKeon's approach to the novel's origins and my own involves his emphasis on intellectual history and his reliance on traditional literary conceptions of texts.

15. Ellen Pollak, phrasing her argument in terms that are *contra* Stone, takes an even stronger position on the deterioration of the status of women, and she seems, using some older historical studies (Alice Clark, *Working Life of Women in the Seventeenth Century* [London, 1919], for example), to totalize the regress to include education and literacy. For an informed corrective to older impressionistic social history (which had been based on nineteenth-century notions of

the eighteenth century and nostalgic ideas about earlier ages), see Margaret J. M. Ezell, *The Patriarch's Wife: Literary Evidence and the History of the Family* (Chapel Hill, N.C., 1987).

16. Lawrence Stone, *The Family, Sex and Marriage in England 1500–1800* (London, 1977), p. 348. "They were as ignorant as their grandmothers," Stone goes on about eighteenth-century women, drawing uncritically on Lady Louisa's observations, "but now devoted themselves to parties, visits, cards, and the theatre—pursuits that characterized a far more leisure-oriented and pleasure-loving society."

17. Stone quotes, on p. 322, Lady Louisa Stuart on another issue on which she is plainly wrong, believing that in the first decade of the eighteenth century, "for a young lady to interfere or claim a right of choice [about a marriage partner] was almost thought . . . a species of indelicacy." By the late seventeenth century, women—although repeatedly advised to consult parents and other elders—were presumed to have powerful wills of their own and expected to exercise personal rights in the family; not even the most conservative treatises assumed that parents had the right to inflict their own will on daughters. Clarissa's position, that she has the right of refusal of anyone but may also allow the family to exercise veto power, is pretty close to standard doctrine by 1700. Richardson's social and moral assumptions, as many have pointed out, are unfailingly conservative and usually two or three generations old; he could clearly count on his readers to find Clarissa's position reasonable, even generous. It was her family that was being unreasonable by contemporary standards; his text wouldn't make much sense otherwise. Had Lady Louisa been right on such matters, reader expectations for *Clarissa* would have been considerably different. For detailed discussion of how the conduct books advised women on marriage choices, see Chapter Ten.

18. On the satirists as social commentators, see Felicity Nussbaum, *The Brink of All We Hate: English Satires on Women 1660–1750* (Lexington, Ky., 1984).

19. Margaret Spufford and David Cressy are two students of literacy who do especially well coordinating quantitative and anecdotal evidence in the construction of a new social and cultural history. See Spufford, *Small Books and Pleasant Histories: Popular Fiction and Its Readership in Seventeenth-Century England* (Athens, Ga., 1981), and Cressy, *Literacy and the Social Order: Reading and Writing in Tudor and Stuart England* (Cambridge, 1980).

20. Cressy, p. 176.

21. All the evidence turned up by new demographic studies and the back projections they make counters such a position; see, for example, Cressy's summary chart (p. 177) which suggests that male and female literacy improved at similar rates in virtually all decades until the mid-nineteenth century.

22. See "The Measurement of Literacy in Pre-industrial England," in *Literacy in Traditional Societies*, ed. Jack Goody (Cambridge, 1968), pp. 311–25. "The actual level of literacy that is measured," says Schofield, "is relatively unimportant compared with the suitability of that level as a comparative measure" (p. 318).

23. Schofield, "Measurement. . . ," p. 321. For a cogent challenge to such working assumptions, see Jo Ann Hoeppner Moran, "Literacy and Education in Northern England, 1350–1550: A Methodological Enquiry," *Northern History*, 17 (1981), 1–23. Moran argues in another place that book ownership, which can be partially measured by wills, needs to be considered as important evidence of reading ability—*The Growth of English Schooling 1340–1548: Learning, Literacy, and Laicization in Pre-Reformation York Diocese* (Princeton, N.J., 1985), pp. 152–62.

24. Moran (*Growth of English Schooling*) is good on this issue, although her data are from early periods when relatively few women were literate and hard evidence is scarce. Women in the aristocracy were, for example, almost three times as likely to bequeath books to offspring than were their male counterparts (p. 152n). See Joel T. Rosenthal, "Aristocratic Cultural Patronage and Book Bequests, 1350–1550," *Bulletin of the John Rylands University Library*, 64 (1982), 522–48, and Susan Groag Bell, "Medieval Women Book Owners: Arbiters of Lay Piety and Ambassadors of Culture," *Signs*, 7 (1982), 742–68. See also Spufford, *Small Books and Pleasant Histories*, pp. 19–44, esp. pp. 34–37, and Spufford, "First Steps in Literacy: The Reading and Writing Experiences of the Humblest Seventeenth-Century Spiritual Autobiographer," *Social History*, 4 (1979), 407–35.

25. Such as, for example, John Sprint. See Chapter Seven, pp. 189–91.

26. See Johansson, "The History of Literacy in Sweden," esp. pp. 55–60.

27. See Susan Groag Bell, "Medieval Women Book Owners" (see n. 24, above), and Natalie Zemon Davis, *Society and Culture in Early Modern France* (Stanford, 1979), esp. pp. 72–82.

28. Robert Darnton, among others, has called for such a comprehensive look at just what readers' habits are in different cultures at different times. See "What Is the History of Books?" *Daedalus,* (1982), 65–83.

29. Now we tend to contrast the "passivity" of television watchers with readers, but in the early eighteenth century reading was often regarded as passive and, if used only for amusement or recreation, idle. See Chapter Eleven.

30. See Wayne Booth, " 'The Way I Loved George Eliot:' Friendship with Books as a Neglected Critical Metaphor," *Kenyon Review,* n.s. 2 (1980), 4–27. Metaphors of companionship and recovered community are frequent in discussions of books in the early eighteenth century. Isaac Watts, for example, in *The Art of Reading* (1721) says that "the *Art of Letters* does, as it were, revive all the past Ages of Men, and set them at once upon the Stage; and brings all the Nations from afar, and gives them, as it were, a general Interview: so that the most distant Nations, and distant Ages of Mankind may converse together, and grow into Acquaintance" (p. 154). And in *A Practical Treatise upon Christian Perfection* (1726), William Law says that "READING, when it is an Exercise of the Mind upon wise and pious Subjects, is, next to *Prayer,* the best Improvement of our Hearts. . . . We commonly say, that a Man is known by his *Companions,* but it is certain, that a Man is much more known by the Books that he converses with. These *Closet-companions* with whom we chuse to be alone and in private, are never-failing Proofs of the State and Disposition of our Hearts" (p. 351).

31. The critical tendency to underrate practical motivations, discussed in the next chapter and (from a different perspective) in Chapter Ten, is in part due to snobbishness and a pervasive academic sense that aesthetics ought to be "above" mere human needs, but in part it derives from inadequate knowledge about what happens historically when cultural institutions shift from oral to written information systems, discussed in Chapter Six.

32. See Wrigley and Schofield, *Population History,* esp. pp. 332ff. and their table of life expectancy in Appendix 3. A person born in 1701, for example, had a life expectancy of 37.11 years; in 1731, of only 27.88 (p. 529). Dorothy George's chapter on "Life and Death in London," though it now needs to be modified by subsequent research, is still one of the most vivid accounts of what daily expectancy was like—*London Life in the Eighteenth Century* (London, 1925).

33. The growth of literacy was much slower throughout Catholic Europe and apparently throughout the other parts of the world that interacted with Britain or Europe. There is almost universal agreement among literacy scholars that Protestant emphasis on access to the Bible through individual reading led to radically different growth rates in literacy universally.

34. See his *Essay on Charity and Charity Schools* (London, 1723).

35. "A Discourse on the Education of Children and Youth" (written in the 1740s and published posthumously in *Improvement of the Mind, Second Part* [1782]), II, 137, 139. For a good discussion of the theoretical aspects of the eighteenth-century pressures to literacy, see David Bartine, *Early English Reading Theory: Origins of Current Debates* (Columbia, S.C., 1989).

36. See Keith Thomas, *Religion and the Decline of Magic: Studies in Popular Beliefs in Sixteenth- and Seventeenth-Century England* (London, 1971), and my discussion in Chapter Six.

37. See Laqueur, "Cultural Origins," Schofield, "Dimensions," and David Cressy, "Literacy in Pre-industrial England," *Societas,* 4 (1974), 229–40.

38. Henry Fielding is often said to be caught in such a conflict of cultural values, illustrated by his vacillation—in his life and in his novels—between the country and the city.

39. *The Introduction to the True Understanding of the Whole Arte of Expedition in Teaching to Write,* fol. Bv, as quoted by Cressy, *Literacy and the Social Order,* p. 26.

40. See Jack Goody and Ian Watt, "The Consequences of Literacy," in *Literacy in Traditional Societies,* ed. Jack Goody (Cambridge, 1968), pp. 27–68, and Thomas W. Laqueur, "Toward a Cultural Ecology of Literacy in England, 1660–1850," in *Literacy in Historical Perspective,* ed. Daniel P. Resnick (Washington, 1983), pp. 43–57.

41. The increasing importance of English nationalism is now being studied in a variety of ways; Howard Weinbrot, for example, is now at work on a study of the self-conscious construction of

an English literary history in the eighteenth century. For a broad view of the subject, see Gerald
Newman, *The Rise of English Nationalism: A Cultural History 1740–1830* (New York, 1987).
42. But see David D. Hall, in his Afterword to *Worlds of Wonder, Days of Judgment: Popular Belief
in Early New England* (New York, 1989), for a cautionary note about applying too broadly the
conclusions of Keith Thomas on these matters.
43. On varieties of available reading materials in Britain, see Marjorie Plant, *The English Book Trade*
(London, 3rd ed., 1974), chapter 2; Jeremy Black, *The English Press in the Eighteenth Century*
(Philadelphia, 1987); and John Feather, "British Publishing in the Eighteenth Century: A Pre-
liminary Subject Analysis," *The Library*, ser. 6, vol. 8, no. 1 (March 1986), 32–46, *The Provincial Book Trade in Eighteenth-Century England* (Cambridge, 1985), and *A History of British
Publishing* (London, 1988). On the situation in France, see Robert Darnton, "Reading, Writing,
and Publishing," in Darnton's *The Literary Underground of the Old Regime* (Cambridge, Mass.,
1982), pp. 167–208; for Germany, see Albert Ward, *Book Production, Fiction, and the German
Reading Public 1740–1800* (Oxford, 1974). On the varieties of fiction available in England from
seventeenth-century writers, see Paul Salzman, *English Prose Fiction 1558–1700: A Critical History* (Oxford, 1985).

CHAPTER   FOUR

1. In her fine study of the early novel in America, Cathy N. Davidson suggests the power of readers
and their needs in helping to formulate literary directions—*Revolution and the Word: The Rise of
the Novel in America* (New York, 1986), pp. 55–79. See also the collection of essays she has
edited, *Reading in America: Literature and Social History* (Baltimore, 1989). On the ideologies of
writers and their effects on readers, see W. A. Speck, *Society and Literature in England 1700–60*
(Dublin, 1983).
2. I use the term "Guide," explained in Chapter Ten, to describe the many varieties of conduct
books and didactic treatises designed to direct readers through the practical and ethical difficulties of ordinary life.
3. For extended discussions of didacticism generally, see Chapters Nine through Eleven; for cases
of conscience in particular, see Chapter Eleven, pp. 288–94.
4. "The fable," Defoe wrote in "Robinson Crusoe's Preface" to *Serious Reflections during the Life and
Surprising Adventures of Robinson Crusoe* (1720), "is always made for the moral, not the moral
for the fable"—*The Works of Daniel Defoe*, ed. G. H. Maynadier (16 vols, New York, 1903),
III, p. ix.
5. Very persuasive on the effects of novels in readers' lives is Wayne Booth, *The Company We
Keep: An Ethics of Fiction* (Berkeley, 1989), esp. pp. 226–63. It is surprising how often writers
speak self-consciously about the practical needs of readers and how confident they are that young
readers especially will find their wares necessary. In Francis Kirkman's *Don Bellianis* (3 parts,
1664?), for example, the narrator addresses the reader this way: "I my self have been so great a
Lover of Books of this Nature, that I have long since read them all; and therefore shall give thee
some Account of my experience, that may be both Pleasant and Profitable to thee. At first, I
tell thee be thou of what Age, or Sex soever, it is convenient for thee to read these sorts of
Historyes, if thou art Young, begin now, or else when thou comest to be Old and hast any
leisure; and if one of these Books chances into thy hand, thou wilt be so pleased with it, that
read them thou must, and be in danger to be laughed at by those of the younger sort, who
having already read them, and being past that Knowledge, Laugh at thy Ignorance," fol. [A4].
6. Although *Amelia* sold very well at first, obviously taking much of its initial thrust from the
public memory of the author's earlier work. The first printing of *Amelia* (5,000 copies) sold in
less than a week, but within months Fielding was claiming (correctly) that the work was neglected.
7. A "typical" woman of the time is more difficult to define. Many women migrated to London
because of—in one sense or another—opportunities there, and many young women strongly
desired to change their lots, but seeking one's fortune or finding a new venue in which to seek
a career was not, for any woman, a real possibility. There were women who ran printing busi-
nesses and others who made livings as writers competing in the developing commercial world of

popular print, but there was no one in a position to attempt to respond to, and control, popular taste in the way Dunton tried to do. Many women writers, of course, developed substantial reputations, and young women migrating to London might have consideredd a number of figures as models or exemplars of what was available to them intellectually or professionally, but every woman's writing career was, for all practical purposes, the only instance of its kind. In different ways, one might consider the writing career—in poems, plays, fictions, and many varieties of practical prose—of Aphra Behn or the self-conscious programs of social reform of Mary Astell as comparable, but neither had the position or pretension to try a broad program to read audiences as Dunton more or less consciously attempted to do. Both lived, though, very interesting lives that are illustrative of the kinds of daily problems faced by those whose ambitions and personal needs depended on a favorable reception by a habitual culture hostile to many of their values but growingly anxious about the grounds of its values. See Angeline Goreau, *Reconstructing Aphra: A Social Biography of Aphra Behn* (New York, 1980), and Ruth Perry, *The Celebrated Mary Astell: An Early English Feminist* (Chicago, 1986). For a sensitive attempt to sort out the different interests of female and male writers, see Ann Messenger, *His and Hers: Essays in Restoration and Eighteenth-Century Literature* (Lexington, Ky., 1986).

8. I do not wish to slight the achievements of the "city" writers of a century earlier—Thomas Nashe, Stephen Gosson, Thomas Lodge, Thomas Dekker, and other who chronicled London's underworld and the seamier sides of ordinary life. Their inventiveness and vigor remains underappreciated in literary history, but their accomplishments did not have the impact on a wide audience that the later hacks had, in part because the printing establishment was much more developed by the early eighteenth century and in part because later, and wider, readership was far more conscious of—and interested in—Londonness as cultural center. For an informed discussion of some aspects of popular writing in that age, see Sandra Clark, *The Elizabethan Pamphleteers: Popular Moralistic Pamphlets 1580–1640* (Rutherford, N.J., 1983).

9. "[W]e see," according to a "Lady's Answer" to Dunton in 1700, "the defects of what we are thoroughly acquainted with, but we are pleasingly deluded with great Expectations from every thing that's New"—*Art of Living Incognito*, p. 58.

10. Dunton's anxiety about the spiritual import of novelty is illustrated again in a curiously contorted passage in 1710: ". . . such as are curious to know more than's reveal'd, are [sic] a sort of Madness, that *to be cur'd of the Athenian Itch, go to the Devil for Brimstone.* One wou'd think indeed one cou'd not be too curious, nor delicate, in searching after Novelties; but Men *overrefine* sometimes with thinking too nicely, and then the *Thought* (or *Project*) degenerates into a Subtilty which stretches into what we call *Vain Curiosity.* . . . But Athenianism (or a *Search after Novelties*) may be so refin'd as to become a Duty"—"Dedication" to *Athenianism*, p. v. Part of this passage is also printed in *The Christian's Gazette* of 1709, p. ii.

11. Travelers who visit England repeatedly comment on the English love of trendiness; for some of the reactions, see Chapter Seven, pp. 172–74. As early as 1650, Francis Hawkins comments on "that English itch of running after fashions," describing it as "a vanity so peculiar unto us, that we are become the scorne of the severall Nations, whence wee borrow them"—*New Additions unto Youths Behaviour*, 1652 edition. The additions are dated 1650.

12. See Chapter Seven.

13. See Chapter Five, pp. 131–35, for a discussion of one important aspect of religious thought, Methodism, and its relation to the novel. On Hill's description of the relationship between science and Puritanism, see Chapter Eight, p. 197.

C H A P T E R   F I V E

1. E. A. Wrigley has mounted a powerful argument, backed by a solid statistical model, that by the end of the seventeenth century London asserted an influence over the rest of the nation unmatched in any other nation. He concludes that "one adult in six . . . had had direct experience of London life," and believes that this contact "acted as a powerful solvent of the customs, prejudices and modes of action of traditional, rural England"—"A Simple Model of London's

Importance in Changing English Society and Economy 1650–1750," *Past and Present*, 37 (1967), 50. His statistical model shows London more important to England than Paris to France. Wrigley is also persuasive on the high migration rates of young people to London.

2. Detailed anatomizing of London began early in the eighteenth century, and modern scholarship has produced a wealth of information on historic London and its rapid growth in size and importance during the seventeenth century. Early accounts include John Strype, *A Survey of the Cities of London and Westminster* (1720), and William Maitland, *The History and Survey of London* (1739); the most broadly informative modern account of eighteenth-century London is in *The History of London* series published by Secker & Warburg: George Rude, *Hanoverian London 1714–1808* (London, 1971). Also see Roger Finlay, *Population and Metropolis: The Demography of London, 1580–1650*, and, for a readable account of the seventeenth-century transition, Harold Priestley, *London: The Years of Change* (London, 1966).

3. By the 1750s, London had come to figure crucially in almost all novels, its centrality having a lot to do with curiosity about city ways and with country readers' longings to be there—or at least to be in-the-know about modern life. The importance of the London scenes in *Clarissa* (1747–48) and the London section of *Tom Jones* (1749) is well known. But it may be less obvious how often, and how quickly, most novels find a way to get their hero or herione there. *Betsy Thoughtless* (1751), for example, finds a reason to move the action there by the middle of its second chapter, and *Evelina* (1778) almost throughout performs for readers the function of describing London sights and ways, often quite self-consciously and sometimes with elaborate plotting against its heroine's apparent best interests. London is usually suggested to be both wondrous and a den of iniquity: in both cases it has to be dealt with for readers of all kinds. Even novels like *Tristram Shandy* (1759–67) that try to maintain their location in the country use London for important symbolic reasons—in Tristram's case to explain why he is born the way he is—and scenes in London are often held out as the locus of action and anticipation. Some index of how central London is to midcentury novels is provided by *Millenium Hall* (1762), which takes place far from London in the West Country. The rural paradisal location is crucial to the effects of the book in offering a utopian experience, and it takes exactly five words to distance its location from the city and establish its status as other. "Though, when I left London," the novel begins—and it never returns.

4. One of Defoe's favorite themes, one he explores quite fully in *A Tour through the Whole Island of Great Britain* (1724–26), involves the interdependence of London and the country. Defoe seldom misses an opportunity to talk about the matter. In *A Journal of the Plague Year* (1722), for example, he has a Londoner fleeing into the country explain to the townsmen of Epping how dependent they are on London's consumption of goods: "[H]e told them, 'That London was the Place by which they, that is, the Townsmen of Epping and all the Country round them, subsisted; to whom they sold the produce of their Lands, and out of whom they made their Rent of their Farms. . . .' "—Oxford English Novels Edition, ed. Louis Landa (London, 1969), p. 142.

5. I have used the Wrigley and Schofield back projections for England and rounded off their figures (*The Population History of England, 1541–1871: A Reconstruction* [Cambridge, Mass., 1981], pp. 528–29). The London numbers here are the ones that have been agreed upon for some time by most demographers (except for Dorothy George, who estimates the 1700 population at 674,350). Gregory King's late seventeenth-century estimates are, in one way or another, central to all modern calculations; their reliability is sensibly discussed by D. V. Glass, "Gregory King's Estimate of the Population of England and Wales, 1695," *Population Studies*, 3 (1949–50), 338–74.

6. *A Journal of the Plague Year* offers anecodotal evidence, presumably from the memory of H. F., that illustrates what demographers have now concluded:

> It must not be forgot here, that the City and Suburbs were prodigiously full of People, at the time of this Visitation, I mean, at the time that it began; for tho' I have liv'd to see a further Encrease, and mighty Throngs of People settling in *London*, more than ever, yet we had always a Notion, that the Numbers of People, which the Wars being over, the Armies disbanded, and the Royal Family and the Monarchy being restor'd, had flock'd to *London*, to settle into Business; or to depend upon, and attend the Court for Rewards of Services,

Preferments, *and the like*, was such, that the Town was computed to have in it above a hundred thousand people more than ever it held before; nay, some took upon them to say, it had twice as many. . . . (p. 18)

7. Behn was probably about twenty-four when she went to London; her husband died within two years. Facts are very scarce about her early years in London. See Angeline Goreau, *Reconstructing Aphra* (New York, 1980), pp. 78–87.
8. See Carole Fabricant, *Swift's Landscape* (Baltimore, 1982).
9. For an ingenious (though obviously highly speculative) account of Manley—put together as an "autobiographical" account from passages in her fictional works—see Fidelis Morgan, *A Woman of No Character: An Autobiography of Mrs. Manley* (London, 1987).
10. For those few women of letters for whom making a living by their writing was not an issue, the pattern could be quite different. Elizabeth Singer Rowe, although perhaps best known now for her 1728 novel, *Friendship in Death*, developed her main literary reputation as a poet, and her virtuous life (often held up in contrast to the more dubious lives and careers of Behn, Manley, and Haywood) seems to have been lived privately—for some years in London with her husband, the rest of the time quietly in Somerset. Although she had many friends, she seems not to have been part of any community of writers, and her years in London involved convenience for her husband more than her own choice. Similarly, the poet Katherine Philips (over and over called, rather patronizingly, the "matchless Orinda") had lived in the mid-seventeenth century a private life free from both the competition and community of other writers. She divided her time between London (she was born there) and Somerset, and she gathered around herself a circle of friends, but London life had little to do with her writing. Lady Mary Pierrepont (later Wortley Montagu), because of her social standing, her sophisticated views, and her freedom of mobility, was in a sense a paradigm of what a woman of letters freed from economic necessity might become, but until much later others did not or could not follow her lead.
11. Play titles begin to signal the change, too, not just those like *The London Cuckolds* (1681) and *The City-Heiress* (1682) that named urbanness itself as their subject but also many others that called attention in their titles to specific city locations and contemporary urban activities.
12. Except in plays, however, the popular attention to street life and urban brawl had little impact on "serious" literature. David Margolies provides useful contextual information on the "low-life" fiction of the late sixteenth century—*Novel and Society in Elizabethan England* (Totowa, N.J., 1985).
13. Such satiric works as *MacFlecknoe* and many of the *Poems on Affairs of State* were set prominently in London, perhaps following the lead of drama; it was apparently more acceptable to provide contemporary and local settings to poems intended primarily to circulate within a privileged group. But most "literary" works were still set, until the turn of the century, artificially in some remote location.
14. Still valuable for its vivid sense of everyday life is Dorothy George, *London Life in the Eighteenth Century* (London, 1925). A handy summary of information is offered in Richard B. Schwartz, *Daily Life in Johnson's London* (Madison, Wis., 1983), and Jack Lindsey has provided a readable account of social life—*The Monster City: Defoe's London, 1688–1730* (London, 1978). Ralph Houlbrooke has put together a very useful collection of passages from diaries which describes daily family life, both in London and the country—*English Family Life, 1576–1716* (Oxford, 1988). See also D. V. Glass, "Socio-Economic Status and Occupations in the City of London at the End of the Seventeenth Century," in *Studies in London History*, eds. A. E. J. Hollaender and William Kellaway (London, 1969), pp. 373–89.´
15. There is as yet nothing on England quite like Fernand Braudel's *The Structures of Everyday Life: The Limits of the Possible*, trans. Sân Reynolds (New York, 1979), volume 1 in his *Civilization and Capitalism 15th–18th Century*. For a brilliant theorizing of cultural desire through the analysis of everyday pursuits, see Michel de Certeau, *The Practice of Everyday Life*, trans. Steven Rendall (Berkeley, 1984).
16. But see Chapter Eleven for a discussion of the dangers of reading and warnings against the wasting of time.
17. The smell of London was said to be noticeable miles before travelers arrived there; see Herbert

Butterfield, "England in the 18th Century," in *A History of the Methodist Church in Great Britain*, eds. Rupert Davies and Gordon Rupp (London, 1965), Vol. I, pp. 1–33. Jessica Munns records the intriguing suggestion (which she attributes to Susan Krantz) that the association of excrement and sexuality is a specifically masculine phobia, an observation that might help to focus on the generic preoccupation with scatology in male Augustan satire rather than on the individual psyches of writers such as Swift. See "Barton and Behn's *The Rover*: or, The Text Transpos'd," *Restoration and Eighteenth-Century Theatre Research*, ser. 2, vol. 8, no. 2 (1988), p. 22n.

18. Blake's late-century poem of experience, "London," explores that prevailing sense, insisting that the "chartered" quality of life there means limits and oppression rather than urbanness meaning liberty.

19. On satire's habit of presenting things as jumbled, messy, filled with a variety of things, see Kernan, *The Plot of Satire* (New Haven, Conn., 1965), pp. 66–80. Kernan calls it the "mob tendency" of satire and sees it as generically related to such other tendencies as rising and falling, magnifying and diminishing.

20. See *Amusements Serious and Comical, Calculated for the Meridian of London* (1700), pp. 132–55.

21. On reciprocities between satire and the novel, see Ronald Paulson, *Satire and the Novel in Eighteenth-Century England* (New Haven, Conn., 1967).

22. The relationship between literature and urban experience has received a lot of attention in studies of nineteenth- and twentieth-century literature, especially during the past decade. See David R. Weimer, *The City as Metaphor* (New York, 1966); John H. Raleigh, "The Novel and the City: England and America in the Nineteenth Century," *Victorian Studies*, 11 (1968), 291–328; B. I. Coleman, ed., *The Idea of the City in Nineteenth-Century Britain* (London, 1973); H. J. Dyos and Michael Wolff, eds., *The Victorian City: Images and Realities* (2 vols., London, 1973); Burton Pike, *The Image of the City in Modern Literature* (Princeton, N.J., 1981); Michael C. Jaye and Ann Chalmers Watts, eds., *Literature and the Urban Experience: Essays on the City and Literature* (New Brunswick, N.J., 1981); William B. Thesing, *The London Muse: Victorian Poetic Responses to the City* (Athens, Ga., 1982); and John H. Johnston, *The Poet and the City: A Study in Urban Perspectives* (Athens, Ga., 1984). The last title contains some material on the eighteenth century, but urbanness has gotten relatively little attention, far less than it deserves, in relation to eighteenth-century texts. One very suggestive account, however, is Max Byrd, *London Transformed: Images of the City in the Eighteenth Century* (New Haven, Conn., 1978).

23. The urbanizing tendency did, however, involve smaller cities and towns as well; P. J. Corfield points out that "By the end of the eighteenth century over two and a half million people, or about 30 per cent of the country's population, lived in towns of 2,500 inhabitants or more"— *The Impact of English Towns 1700–1800* (Oxford, 1982), p. 2. On the ideology of traditional contrasts between country and city, see Raymond Williams, *The Country and the City* (London, 1973).

24. See *Mountain Gloom and Mountain Glory: The Development of the Aesthetics of the Infinite* (Ithaca, N.Y., 1959).

25. In "London" (1738), Johnson described the dangers of walking in the park this way:

> Prepare for death, if here at night you roam,
> And sign your will before you sup from home. (ll. 224–25)

26. I have discussed the phenomenology of reading novels more fully in "The Loneliness of the Long-Distance Reader," *Genre*, 10 (1977), 455–84.

27. Terry Castle and John Bender, when their classic studies of the directions of early English fiction are put together, come close to confronting the central irony in the reading experience insisted on by most eighteenth-century novels. Castle emphasizes the "unbounded license, lacking any spatial or sociological restriction" (p. 27) that the carnivalesque introduced into life and fiction in the culture, and Bender suggests, among other things, how the novel embodies structures of constriction and re-formation. The desire to encompass liberating structures of behavior while insisting on disciplined responses that remain within frames of imagination and solitude seems to me central to what early novels want and do, and these conflicting—but balancing—desires are reflected both in the urban reading habits for which novels were designed and in didactic representations of a self struggling with life choices that had to be worked out within the con-

fines of ordinary expectation. See Castle, *Masquerade and Civilization: The Carnivalesque in Eighteenth-Century Culture and Fiction* (Stanford, Calif., 1986), and Bender, *Imagining the Penitentiary: Fiction and the Architecture of Mind in Eighteenth-Century England* (Chicago, 1987), especially chapter 1 in each book.

28. On the tendency to look back to a rural and communal past with nostalgia, see Chapter Six.

29. David Riesman's formulation of the cultural psychology of this phenomenon is now widely applied to urban cultures generally, but it has not been discussed fully enough in relation to developing urban cultures or explored sufficiently relative to the expectations and desires of those who migrate from simpler rural communities. See *The Lonely Crowd* (New Haven, Conn., 1950).

30. See Roy Porter, *English Society in the Eighteenth Century* (Harmondsworth, Middlesex, 1982), p. 34.

31. See George, *London Life*, p. 32. Her long and powerful account of the effects of gin drinking (pp. 27–42), though discounted by some later commentators, is the classic indictment. George details contemporary estimates of lost life and reduced births ascribed to gin consumption.

32. For a different view of Methodism's political role, see the famous discussion by Elie Halévy, *The Birth of Methodism in England*, trans. and ed. Bernard Semmel (Chicago, 1971). There are many accounts of the political and social implications of early Methodism, but little has been said about how the structure of its ideas relate to other cultural phenomena, another ripe subject for New Historicist analysis.

33. For a good discussion of Law, see John Sitter, *Literary Loneliness in Mid-Eighteenth-Century England* (Ithaca, N.Y., 1982), pp. 50–73.

34. I take the main implication of Castle's cultural examination of masquerade to reside in the temporariness of the relief from behavioral implication. The novel as a cultural phenomenon performs a similar function—it addresses solitariness, offers a sociality based on disguise and imagination, and has limited duration—but its "otherness" from everyday reality is crucially limited: its probabilities, unlike those of the masquerade, are the same as in ordinary life, and the subjective consciousness is only freed from its individual identity for purposes of sympathetic exploration, not for a licensed escape into fantasy, exoticism, or implicationlessness. The limits of the novel's engagement with phenomena like the masquerade have much to do with its commitments to representation of everyday desires and to didactic effects beyond the act of reading.

35. See Samuel Pickering, *The Moral Tradition in English Fiction 1785–1850* (Hanover, N.H., 1976).

36. See George Parker, "The Allegory of *Robinson Crusoe,*" *History*, 10 (1925), 11–25. Michael Seidel provides a more plausible—and more important—explanation of representational parallels based on political events in "Crusoe in Exile," *PMLA*, 96 (1981), 363–74. See also my discussion in *The Reluctant Pilgrim* (Baltimore, 1966), pp. 204–05.

37. For Dunton's account of Welby, see *The Christian's Gazette* (1709; not to be confused with a Dunton publication of 1713 with the same title), pp. 59–65. Dunton claims that Welby lived "invisible" in Grub Street for forty-four years.

38. For elaboration of the differences between the visions of Defoe and Swift—and of the novel, on the one hand, and Augustanism on the other—see "*Gulliver's Travels* and the Novelistic Tradition," in *The Genres of Gulliver's Travels*, ed. Frederik N. Smith (Newark, Del., 1990), pp. 54–74. For a provocative discussion of alternative models of society as reflected in methods of incarceration, see Kai Erikson, *Wayward Puritans: A Study in the Sociology of Deviance* (New York, 1966). Erikson's study has been too much neglected in the wake of Foucault's *Discipline and Punish.*

39. *The Life and Strange Surprizing Adventures of Robinson Crusoe, of York, Mariner*, ed. J. Donald Crowley (London, 1972; Oxford English Novels series), p. 35.

CHAPTER   SIX

1. W. Jackson Bate, *The Burden of the Past and the English Poet* (Cambridge, Mass., 1970), and Harold Bloom, *The Anxiety of Influence* (London, 1973).

2. Scholars have long known that Dunton used his "sources" quite liberally, even by the standards of his time. Unacknowledged borrowings of long passages—even in autobiographical documents (see C. N. Greenough, "John Dunton's Letters from New England," *Publications of the Colonial Society of Massachusetts* XIV [1912], 213–57, and "John Dunton Again," *Publications of the Colonial Society of Massachusetts* XXI [1919], 232–51)—is rampant in Dunton. But what Dunton seems to have done with his father's papers is the reverse of plagiarism. Some of the volumes he published under his father's name do seem to have been based on materials his father left behind at his death (see, for example, *Dunton's Remains: or, the Dying Pastour's Last Legacy to his Friends and Parishioners* [1684]). But others, *An Hue and Cry after Conscience: or the Pilgrim's Progress by Candle-light* (1685), for example, sound a lot like the irrepressible younger Dunton, and he seems almost to admit, in "The Epistle to the Reader" of *Heavenly Pastime* (1685), that he has begun to trade on his father's reputation: "Thy courteous and ready reception of . . . three well known and delightful Treatises . . . hath encouraged me now a *fourth* time to present thee with another very useful Piece, bearing my Father *Dunton's* Name" (fol. A2). *Heavenly Pastime* is incredibly uneven in tone and focus and includes several passages of verse that are similar to young Dunton's efforts at rhyme.

3. *A Journal of the Plague Year* reverses the process, telling a "historical" story and making it "relevant" to a present crisis, but there too the confusion between past and present is useful to Defoe as a device to distance his journalistic strategies. Paul K. Alkon thoroughly airs the issue of Defoe's anachronisms in *Defoe and Fictional Time* (Athens, Ga., 1979).

4. Jean Redpath, the Scottish folk singer, points out that folk songs about leaving home and family are always upbeat and celebratory, while those about returning, even when they are ostensibly jubilant, are normally thoughtful, subdued, and melancholy in tone. "The Prairie Home Companion" (April 12, 1986), on National Public Radio.

5. It is, of course, always hard to know how to read good-old-days nostalgia (which is often simply a matter of faulty memory among those growing older), but the theme of lost culture and lost communality at the end of the seventeenth century often has a poignant ring that sometimes seems to indicate both strong feeling and considered thought. For example, the mock nostalgia of the Preface to *Mundus Muliebris: or The Ladies Dressing-Room Unlock'd And her Toilette Spread* (by Mary Evelyn, 1690) quickly slides into real nostalgia as the gentle satire on fashion uses the past as a measure, citing ballads and dances, old habits, and cruder material things: "In those happy days . . . Things of Use were Natural, Plain, and Wholesome, nothing was superfluous, nothing necessary wanting." It then goes on to note "how the World is alter'd among us" (fols. A3v, A4).

6. Katharine M. Briggs, perhaps the best known student of fairy materials and the most prominent anthologizer of British fairy tales, simply says that "Modern England is more sparsely provided with Fairy Tales than the rest of Europe. Literary references show that we were once rich in them" (*British Folktales* [London, 1977], p. 19). In another place, she says that "the thread is spun thinner, but it is not broken" (*The Fairies in English Tradition and Literature* [Chicago, 1967], p. 153), but she admits that the tradition almost disappears in the eighteenth century. Other scholars offer a harsher picture of the relationship between fairy tales and English culture. Richard M. Dorson, in a foreword to a collection of tales edited by Briggs and Ruth L. Tongue, says that "The fact had become painfully evident, by the close of Victoria's reign, that the treasure trove of fairy tales unearthed for nearly every European country . . . were not to be found in England" (*Folktales of England* [Chicago, 1965], p. vi). "Why," he asks, "had a blight struck merry England?" See also the preface to E. S. Hartland, *English Fairy and Other Folk-Tales* (London, 1890), which notes that fairy tales seemed to be totally missing from Wales and almost nonexistent in England and lowland Scotland.

Folklorists classify "fairy tales" as *märchen;* the common English name for them tends to blur the kind of tale they represent with fairy lore more generally. Vladimir Propp, faced similarly with a terminological problem, gave them a name in Russian which is usually translated "wonder-tales," a term that more accurately expresses their relationship to folk worlds of belief and response.

7. See Hartland, pp. x–xx, esp. pp. xv–xvi. Some confirmation of the thesis that religious repression was responsible for the demise of fairies—if not necessarily of fairy tales—appears within

the folk tradition itself. There are many stories, in different cultures and languages, about fairies being driven from a particular locality by church bells. See Katharine M. Briggs, *The Vanishing People: A Study of Traditional Fairy Beliefs* (London, 1978), pp. 49–51. Chaucer's Wyf of Bath similarly claims that ecclesiastics drove off the fairies.

Briggs herself, although often making disparaging incidental remarks about Puritanism, seems to put primary blame for the decline of fairy lore and of oral tradition more generally on the Industrial Revolution: "There can be no culture without a leisure. . . . Among the English poor in the time of the Industrial Revolution there was no holiday, the machines claimed men through winter and summer. In countless homes the chain of tradition was broken and could not be mended"—*The Fairies in English Tradition and Literature*, p. 178.

8. The resurrection of interest in such stories in the nineteenth century is well known, although the conscious role of writers in "contributing" to "folk" traditions may not be widely enough appreciated. The familiar story of "Goldilocks and the Three Bears," for example, was penned by Robert Southey. For an interesting attack on those who repressed fairy tales in favor of more realistic stories, see Charles Lamb's letter to Samuel Taylor Coleridge, October 23, 1802. For Wordsworth on fairy tales, see Book V of *The Prelude*.

The best comprehensive account of the growing religious distrust of folk tradition is still that of Keith Thomas, *Religion and the Decline of Magic* (London, 1971). Thomas notes that "Protestantism . . . presented itself as a deliberate attempt to take the magic elements out of religion" (Peregrine ed. [1978], p. 87), and his detailing of how widely the broom swept is very persuasive. Robert W. Malcolmson emphasizes similar attitudes in the 1730s and after: "Evangelical sentiment was almost always at odds with the traditions of popular diversion. It was forward-looking, morally 'reformist,' profoundly concerned with sin and salvation and the need for social and self-discipline, interested more in the individual's private life than in the affairs of the community . . . suspicious of worldly pleasures . . . and contemptuous of much of the culture of earlier generations"—*Popular Recreations in English Society 1700–1850* (Cambridge, 1973), pp. 100–01.

Christopher Hill is especially good on the assumptions and daily milieu of the old world. "Most men and women in seventeenth-century Britain," he says, "still lived in a world of magic, in which God and the devil intervened daily, a world of witches, fairies and charms"—*The World Turned Upside Down* (Harmondsworth, Middlesex, 1975; first published, 1972), p. 87.

On other aspects of daily life in the countryside and in villages, see W. G. Hoskins, *Provincial England* (London, 1965); Robert W. Malcolmson, *Life and Labour in England 1700–1780* (London, 1981); Margaret Spufford, *The Great Reclothing of Rural England: Petty Chapmen and Their Wares in the Seventeenth Century* (London, 1984) and *Contrasting Communities: English Villagers in the Sixteenth and Seventeenth Centuries* (Cambridge, 1974); and Peter Laslett, ed., *Household and Family in Past Time* (Cambridge, 1972).

9. *The Young Gentleman and Lady Instructed* (2 vols., 1747). The same book, however, goes on to warn that "there is nothing more ridiculous, than an old trifling story-teller" (I, 250), and earlier in the volume there are severe warnings about the bad influence of stories told by servants (p. 100). For an interesting contemporary account of storytelling, see *The Modern Story-Teller* (Dublin, 2 vols., 1753).

10. The tendency in any case to locate all difficulties in the "rise of the middle class" is anachronistic, for whatever social changes had taken place in England by the time the novel became a cultural factor, no "middle" class was yet sufficiently developed to deserve the name.

Many other accounts, besides Ian Watt's famous one in *The Rise of the Novel*, link the novel with the "middle class." See, for example, Helen Sard Hughes, "The Middle-Class Reader and the English Novel," *Journal of English and Germanic Philology*, 25 (1926), 362–78. Most accounts, however, mean by the middle class simply those who were somewhere between the aristocracy and servants, although sometimes the term incorporates all those below the aristocracy so that servants are included as well.

Peter Earle's argument that Defoe's "middle station" in the early eighteenth century becomes in effect a middle class involves very good social analysis of Defoe's England and valuably suggests a process that was under way, but does not demonstrate that the kind of bourgeoisie that developed out of the Industrial Revolution was in place by the time there were novels to read

(*The Making of the English Middle Class: Business, Society, and Family Life, 1660–1730* [Berkeley, 1989]).

11. *The Parable of the Top-Knots*, p. 3. The title was pseudonymously published by Dunton (under the imprint of "R. Newcome") but whether he wrote it himself is uncertain.

12. Especially in *Some Thoughts concerning Education* and to a lesser extent in the *Essay Concerning Human Understanding*, Locke repeatedly expresses his distrust of servants, describing, for example, "the Examples of the Servants" as "the most dangerous of all" (*Some Thoughts concerning Education* [1693; ed. James L. Axtell, Cambridge, 1968], p. 187). Geoffrey Summerfield has a good discussion of Locke's concerns in *Fantasy and Reason: Children's Literature in the Eighteenth Century* (Athens, Ga., 1984), pp. 1–22.

13. As well as attempts to discourage or destroy the oral tradition, there were also attempts to modify old practices by putting new wine in old bottles. One such scheme is recommended by James Talbott in *The Christian School-Master* (1707): "After each Meal, the Elder Boys, and those that have the best Memory, may be Required . . . to Repeat, in the Hearing of their Fellows, some Story out of the Holy Scriptures, or some Parable of our Saviour's upon *Sundays* and *Holidays*; and on other Days some Fable of *Esop*, with the *Moral* belonging to it; which may equally Contribute to the Entertainment and Instruction of the Hearers" (91).

14. "The Seven and Twentieth Account of the Progress" of the Societies for the Reformation of Manners, appended to the annual sermon preached in 1722 by William Butler, announced the following figures for prosecution of offenders for that year:

Lewd and Disorderly Practices	1,197
Keeping of Bawdy and Disorderly Houses	15
Exercising their Trades . . . on the Lord's-Day	709
Prophane Swearing and Cursing	161
Drunkenness	13
Sodomitical Practices	4

The account calculates that 77,469 persons had been prosecuted by the societies in and near London over the previous thirty-one years.

15. According to M. G. Jones, 32 parishes in London and Westminster had set up 54 schools by 1704, and by 1729 there were 132 schools there with 5,000 pupils. Throughout the nation, by 1729 there were 1,419 schools with more than 22,000 pupils (*The Charity School Movement* [Cambridge, 1938], p. 57). Richard Altick notes the difficulty of trusting the statistics usually given out; see *The English Common Reader: A Social History of the Mass Reading Public 1800–1900* (Chicago, 1957), p. 34. The "religious societies" movement—comprehending the SPCK and SPG—dates from 1678. See D. E. Jenkins, Introduction to reprint of Josiah Woodward, *An Account of the Religious Societies* (Liverpool, 1935), pp. 5–19.

16. I don't, of course, mean to imply that Shakespeare's violent yoking of these worlds was automatic or engineered simply, but he could draw on folk belief and fluid world views among classes far more readily than Pope, who needed to reach rather esoterically and self-consciously to produce an "Ariel" and an elaborate supporting cast of sylphs and gnomes—and had to regard the spirit world as "machinery." C. L. Barber's classic study, *Shakespeare's Festive Comedy: A Study of Dramatic Form and Its Relation to Social Custom* (Princeton, N.J., 1959), remains the most persuasive account of the relationship between literature and popular belief in Elizabethan times.

17. The changing idea of "literature" deepened the chasm too, as literature became more exclusively a class property—partly in response to challenges of the new literacy and partly because criticism was becoming, in England for the first time, a serious pursuit that saw one of its tasks as the identification and development of a serious native tradition.

18. The complaint of Briggs about "the Puritan bigotry which confounded the fairies with the witches" (*The Anatomy of Puck* [London, 1959], p. 27) may at first seem rather comic, but a common fear of the unknown or not understood seems to be behind both the repression of the oral tradition and the burning of witches. Briggs is right that "the condemnation of the churches lumped together all magical practices, and even much folk medicine, under the heading of

witchcraft" (*Pale Hecate's Team* [London, 1962], p. 2), and an index of the fear may be seen in the fact that as many as 4,400 witches were burned in Scotland alone, the last in 1709.

19. Tickell's attempt to move fairies—with all their history and mythology—into the urban (or at least suburban) world of Kensington indicates his awareness of the difficulty of drawing upon the old heritage, and may suggest why it was that such poems as this never gained much currency in their time or a place in the tradition. Tickell draws consciously on what he perceived to be contemporary nostalgia:

> The landskip now so sweet we well may praise:
> But far far sweeter in its ancient days,
> Far sweeter was it . . . (ll. 39–41)

20. *The Morphology of Folklore*, published in Russian in 1928, was first translated into English in 1958.

21. Propp's own "formalism" became a subject of substantial debate. Propp insisted on his historicist interests, and his rejoinder to Claude Lévi-Strauss (who had "accused" him of formalism) deserves to be better known. See Vladimir Propp, *Theory and History of Folklore*, a collection of essays and excerpts trans. Ariadna Y. Martin and Richard P. Martin and ed. Anatoly Liberman (Minneapolis, 1984), pp. 67–81.

22. Iona and Peter Opie, for example, say that "there seems to have been no motive for telling them [fairy tales] other than for wonder and for entertainment"—*The Classic Fairy Tales* (London, 1974), p. 18.

23. *The Uses of Enchantment: The Meaning and Importance of Fairy Tales* (New York, 1976), p. 24. As Bettelheim acknowledges, most early interpretive work on fairy tales (in spite of Freud's own interest in them) was done by Jungians. See, for example, Erich Neumann, *Amor and Psyche* (New York, 1956), and Marie Louise von Franz, *Interpretation of Fairy Tales* (New York, 1970).

24. "Tell me that *bad* story about . . .", one of my own children used to ask unself-consciously when requesting her favorite bedtime story. The element of forbiddenness and mystery seems important to children's needs, but whether such an element is "universal" or more important in civilized and "safe" environments remains to be decided.

25. See, for example, Roger Sale, *Fairy Tales and After* (Cambridge, Mass., 1978), for a sensible account of effects. For excellent accounts of the relationship between fairy tales and their cultural contexts, see Robert Darnton, "Peasants Tell Tales: The Meaning of Mother Goose," in Darnton's *The Great Cat Massacre and Other Episodes in French Cultural History* (New York, 1984), pp. 9–72, and Ruth B. Bottigheimer, "Silenced Women in the Grimms' Tales: The Fit Between Fairy Tales and Society in Their Historical Context," in *Fairy Tales and Society: Illusion, Allusion, and Paradigm*, ed. Ruth B. Bottigheimer (Philadelphia, 1986), pp. 115–31.

26. Géza Róheim says that ". . . we can not only apply the standard technique of dream interpretation in analyzing a fairy tale but actually can think of tales and myths as having arisen from a dream, which a person dreamed and then told to others, who retold it again, perhaps elaborated in accord with their own dreams"—"Fairy Tales and Dreams," in *Psychoanalytic Study of the Child*, 8 (New York, 1953), 394.

27. For an account that puts more emphasis on similarities between the species, see John Buchan, *The Novel and the Fairy Tale* (London, 1931, English Association Pamphlet No. 79).

28. *The Nature of Narrative* (New York, 1966), p. 241. Their answer is that "stories appeal primarily because they offer a simulacrum of life which enables an audience to participate in events without being involved in the consequences which events in the actual world inevitably carry with them," p. 241.

29. For a thoughtful discussion of how the "ends achieved by fiction and drama are not fundamentally different from those of a great deal of gossip and everyday narrative," see D. W. Harding, "Psychological Processes in the Reading of Fiction," in *Aesthetics in the Modern World*, ed. Harold Osborne (New York, 1968), p. 306.

Puritan objections to plays and to fairy tales are almost identical, but the objections to novels, though equally strong, are rather different, perhaps making it easier for writers and readers to rationalize anxieties about fantasy and "lying." However false to fact novels may be, they do not involve role transferral or the fleshly acting out of roles in public, and their devotion to wish-fulfillment—because it was phrased in terms of the ordinary and everyday—was more difficult to characterize as fantasy. Harding says that "what is sometimes called wish-fulfilment in novels and plays can . . . more plausibly be described as wish-formulation or the definition of desires" (p. 313).

30. See Marshall McLuhan, *The Gutenberg Galaxy* (Toronto, 1962); Walter J. Ong, *Rhetoric, Romance and Technology: Studies in the Interaction of Expression and Culture* (Ithaca, N.Y., 1971) and *Interfaces of the Word: Studies in the Evolution of Consciousness and Culture* (Ithaca, N.Y., 1977); Elizabeth Eisenstein, *The Printing Press as an Agent of Change: Communication and Cultural Transformation in Early Modern Europe* (2 vols., New York, 1979); Alvin B. Kernan, *Printing Technology, Letters, and Samuel Johnson* (Princeton, N.J., 1987); Henri-Jean Martin, *The Coming of the Book: The Impact of Printing 1450–1800*, trans. David Gerard, ed. Geoffrey Nowell-Smith and David Wootton (London, 1984; first published in French, 1958); Roger Chartier, *The Cultural Uses of Print in Early Modern France*, trans. Lydia G. Cochrane (Princeton, N.J., 1987); and Albert Ward, *Book Production, Fiction, and the German Reading Public 1740–1800* (Oxford, 1974).

31. The titles of devotional treatises often are emphatic about the metaphor. See, for example, *Enter into Thy Closet* (by Edward Wetenhall, 1676).

32. I have discussed the implications of solitary reading more fully in "The Loneliness of the Long-Distance Reader," *Genre*, 10 (1977), 455–84, and "The World as Stage and Closet," in *British Theatre and Other Arts, 1660–1800*, ed. Shirley Strum Kenny (Washington, D.C., 1984), pp. 271–87.

33. Flavell's *Husbandry Spiritualized* (1669), for example, has eight separate prefatory items (including an Epistle Dedicatory, "To the Christian Reader," "The Epistle to the Intelligent Countrey Reader," "The Author to the Reader," a "Proem," and poems addressed to the author by three different writers) before the text proper.

34. For some other implications of this prefatory phenomenon, see Chapter Nine, pp. 236–37.

35. The following passage containing two anecdotes is from a very popular volume intended to demonstrate divine intervention in human affairs (William Turner, *A Compleat History Of the Most Remarkable Providences* [1697], p. 43); it suggests how easy the transition could be from oral to written anecdote. It also demonstrates how interest in magic and the unknown was displaced into the treasuring of other kinds of unexplained happenings, and gives some sense of how books tried to replicate a small-town atmosphere (even though both anecdotes take place in London) in which everyone knows each other.

> *Philip Up-John* (the Son of a Reverend Divine) being about 11 Years of Age, whilst he lived with Dr. *Annesley* in *Spittle-yard*, in the Year 1686. being alone, reading the Bible, he thought he heard a Voice, *Bidding him prepare for Death, for he should die in a short time.* Upon which this Boy being surprized, he came down Stairs, and acquainted the Family with it: Two or three days after he heard this Voice, he went to one Mr. *Mallerye*, a Joyner, who work'd to the Family, and seeing him making a Coffin, he told Mr. *Mallerye, he should die shortly,* and desired he would make for him such a Coffin as that was; which passage Mr. *Mallerye* acquainted the Family with the same Day, and though then in perfect *health, in a few days after fell sick, of which sickness he died.* This remarkable Passage I received from a Person who was at Dr. *Annesley's* House when this hapned.

> Mrs. *Elizabeth Dunton,* as she was walking through *Moor-Fields* (to see her Reverend Father Dr. *Annesley,* who then lay dangerously ill) she fancied she heard a Voice saying to her, *You need not be so much concerned for your Father, for as near as he is to death, you shall go before him.* This made a great Impression upon her Mind, and in a few Days after she fell Sick, and her Recovery is much doubted. This happened about the latter end of *October,* 1696. [She died in May 1697]

36. Carol Fabricant's insistence—in *Swift's Landscape* (Baltimore, 1982)—that Swift and Pope are often thoughtlessly lumped together and that they frequently support quite different values is well taken, but they do share some crucial notions about contemporary writing that lead them

to very similar programs for "literature." If anything, Swift was the more retrogressive in his attitudes toward the new prose fiction, and even if the vehemence and rigidity of his rejection stem from deep personal ambivalence (as I believe they do), the effect of his position helped divide the world of writers more neatly than was necessary. For all his contributions to letters, his attitudes toward contemporary writing did major damage to individuals and perhaps to directions, even though those he fought most vigorously did ultimately prevail.

CHAPTER SEVEN

1. The quotation is from a couplet by Robert Wilde:

> We are all tainted with the *Athenian* Itch,
> News, and new Things do the whole World bewitch
> —*Poems on Several Occasions* (1683), p. 83.

Dunton several times uses the line as an epigraph for his books.

2. For an extended argument that the novel derives directly from journalism, see Lennard J. Davis, *Factual Fictions: The Origins of the English Novel* (New York, 1983). The issue of origins seems to me far more complex than Davis suggests; a number of cultural forces converge to make the novel possible, and a great variety of literary and para-literary forms provide crucial paradigms for the novel. For a good critique of Davis, see Michael McKeon, "The Origins of the English Novel," *Modern Philology*, 82 (1984), 76–86.

3. Superb work on the oral tradition and on the difference between oral and written modes has appeared in recent years, although literary history has yet to absorb its conclusions. For a good characterization of the tendencies of oral literature, see John Miles Foley, *Oral-Formulaic Theory and Research: An Introduction and Annotated Bibliography* (New York and London, 1985). For ongoing discussion of the literary implications of oral literature for literary theory and history, see the journal that Foley founded in 1986, *Oral Tradition*.

4. The old view that the novel began in Elizabethan times, or perhaps even in classical Greece, has largely disappeared in the wake of increasingly precise definitions of how the novel differs from other types of fiction, but in the past few years, narratology (despite numerous virtues and accomplishments) has tended to lose track again of distinctions, historical and otherwise, among different kinds of narrative.

5. Recent social history has had so far too little effect on eighteenth-century studies, and the impact of popular culture—on the novel, let alone canonical forms—has been largely unexamined. For a promising direction, see Pat Rogers, *Literature and Popular Culture in Eighteenth-Century England* (Brighton, Sussex, and Totowa, N.J., 1985). Ronald Paulson's provocative *Popular and Polite Art in the Age of Hogarth and Fielding* (Notre Dame, Ind., 1979) stands almost alone among earlier studies, although C. J. Rawson's *Gulliver and the Gentle Reader: Studies in Swift and Our Time* (London, 1973) is brilliantly suggestive about the popular origins of Swift's creative energy.

6. The moral fervor of reform during the reign of William and Mary was heavily dependent on public accounts, awareness, and outrage. Whether vice flourished more successfully or even more openly then is questionable, but the proliferation of accounts convinced the public that "the times" were especially desperate, and newspapers and pamphlets became the most significant weapon in the reformation-of-manners craze.

The question of when and why the preoccupation with contemporaneity became so obsessive in England is vexed and complex. The proliferation of printed materials at the time of the Civil Wars suggests that some combination of ideology and concern for personal safety must have been involved. Certainly the growing presence of pamphlets about contemporary events in the 1640s and 1650s helped to create the taste that printers tried in wider ways to satisfy near the end of the century.

7. "Periodical" publication, defined broadly enough, dates from antiquity, and something vaguely resembling newspapers may be traced back at least as far as 1620 in England. For detailed

information on the early history of newspapers, see Joseph Frank, *The Beginnings of the English Newspaper, 1620–1660* (Cambridge, Mass., 1961); R. M. Wiles, *Freshest Advices: Early Provincial Newspapers in England* (Columbus, Ohio, 1965); G. A. Cranfield, *The Development of the Provincial Newspaper 1700–1760* (Oxford, 1962); and J. A. Downie, *Robert Harley and the Press: Propaganda and Public Opinion in the Age of Swift and Defoe* (Cambridge, 1979).

8. C. T. Onions, et al., *The Oxford Dictionary of English Etymology* (Oxford, 1966), p. 498.

9. The intellectual justification for this practice was articulated by Boyle in his account of Occasional Meditation (see Chapter Eight, pp. 201–8); the most immediate implications for writing involved diaries and spiritual autobiographies (see Chapter Twelve).

10. For a provocative account of a complex set of historical interrelationships, see the entry under "Diana" in Eric Partridge, *Origins: A Short Etymological Dictionary of Modern English* (New York, 1983).

11. Pierre Jean Grosley, *A Tour to London; or, New Observations on England, and its Inhabitants*, trans. Thomas Nugent (2 vols., London, 1772), I, 239.

12. Nathaniel Crouch, *England's Monarchs* (London, 1685), fol. A2.

13. César de Saussure. *A Foreign View of England in the Reigns of George I & George II: The Letters of Monsieur César de Saussure to His Family*, ed. and trans. Madame van Muyden (London, 1902), pp. 178–79; further references to this work, cited as *FV*, will be included in the text.

14. Grosley, *A Tour to London*, II, 75.

15. Jonathan Swift, *Gulliver's Travels, The Prose Works of Jonathan Swift*, ed. Herbert Davis (14 vols., Oxford, 1939–68), 11, 148.

16. Richard Baxter, *A Christian Directory; or, A Summ of Practical Theologie, and Cases of Conscience* (London, 1673), p. 36. Baxter, anticipating Dunton's etiology and analysis, goes on to quote the biblical passage about the Athenians who "spent their time in nothing else, but to tell or hear some new thing" (Acts 17).

17. For all the critical determination to define and separate genres and kinds in the eighteenth century, there is a remarkable tendency, in practice, to blur and merge, a tendency that has been insufficiently discussed, especially in relation to oral traditions.

18. In a letter of October 29, 1726, Saussure reported that "Some coffee-houses are a resort for learned scholars and for wits; others are the resort of dandies or of politicians, or again of professional newsmongers; and many others are temples of Venus" (*FV*, p. 164). He seems to be reflecting prevalent clichés and oversimplifications, which are still honored. Although the leading coffeehouses no doubt did attract distinctive audiences, contemporary treatments of the phenomenon suggest that all or most were characterized nearly equally by newsmongering and a love of gossip about current topics. The classic treatment of the coffeehouse phenomenon is still Robert J. Allen's *The Clubs of Augustan London* (Cambridge, Mass., 1933), although it badly needs updating. For details of individual houses, see Bryant Lillywhite, *London Coffee Houses: A Reference Book of Coffee Houses of the Seventeenth, Eighteenth, and Nineteenth Centuries* (London, 1963).

19. *News from the Coffe-house* (London, 1667). I quote from the first, sixth, and tenth stanzas.

20. *News. A Burlesque Poem* (London, 1733), p. 6. "And here I'll stop," the poem ends, "lest I'm with *News* confounded," p. 12.

21. See, for example, the way Sir Roger L'Estrange uses the term in *Citt and Bumpkin* (1680; reprinted Los Angeles, 1965), p. 32.

22. The importance of women in the reading public for novels has much to do with this displacement. Women were largely excluded from, or at least underrepresented in, coffeehouses, and thus were denied access to the most direct means of hearing and sharing news. But if I am right that the novel became a kind of substitute for news and gossip, the importance of novels to female readers and soon to female writers suggests the way women came quickly to relate to the deep cultural phenomenon.

On the evidence for female literacy and readership of novels, see "The Young, the Ignorant, and the Idle," in *Anticipations of the Enlightenment in England, France, and Germany*, ed. Paul J. Korshin and Alan C. Kors (Philadelphia, 1987), pp. 259–81, and Chapter Three, pp. 69–75.

23. On gossip and the novel, see Homer Obed Brown, "The Errant Letter and the Whispering Gallery," *Genre*, 10 (Winter 1977), 573–99, and Patricia Meyer Spacks, *Gossip* (New York,

1985). The illusion of companionship that both Fielding and Sterne try to further relates to the tendency of the novel to associate itself with gossip and with oral discourse more generally.

24. Estimates of how many people read a single copy of a periodical available in coffeehouses vary widely, for no one has yet found a way of measuring that kind of "circulation." G. A. Cranfield says that "it was always accepted that a paper's influence was out of all proportion to the size of its actual sales, each copy being read by twenty or more people" (*Development of the Provincial Newspaper*, p. v). Richard Altick, who despite his concentration on nineteenth-century habits often has valuable things to say about the eighteenth century, may exaggerate when he claims that "the number of coffee-drinkers who pored over a single copy of . . . [a periodical] ran into many scores" (*The English Common Reader: A Social History of the Mass Reading Public 1800–1900* [Chicago, 1957], p. 47.

25. *God the Guide of Youth*, pp. 5–6.

26. See, for example, Arthur Bedford, *Serious Reflections On the Scandalous Abuse and Effects of the Stage* (Bristol, 1705), especially the Preface in which Bedford defends his having preached the sermon in the first place and says that he only publishes it because it was so badly misrepresented. "Some have been offended because I was too particular in describing the Judgments of God, which have lately befallen this Nation, and imputed the same to the Abominations of the Play-house. I think the Reasons which I offered were sufficient for such a Conjecture; and therefore if People will not take Warning by such Alarms, they are guilty of the greater Provocation; and indeed, if such Judgments will not reclaim us, God may justly suffer us to go on without Correction for the future, and fill up the Number of our Iniquities until Vengeance come upon us to the uttermost" (fol. [A3v]). He insists that he was only one of many who believed that the theater was responsible for the great storm. When a General Fast was proclaimed as a result of the storm, he says, "it is very remarkable that most of our Right Reverend Bishops and the Clergy in the City of London did on that day declaim against the Corruptions of the Stage, and look'd on the same as the just Cause of that dreadful Judgment" (fol. [A4]).

"Are we not . . . loudly called upon to lay aside this prophane Diversion, by the late dreadful Storm?" asked the anonymous author of *A Representation of the Impiety & Immorality of the English Stage*, 3rd ed. (1704; reprinted Los Angeles, 1947), p. 4. Other events inspired similar interpretations. John Barnard, for example, interpreted a contemporary earthquake in New England as displeasure with sabbath breaking. A sermon preached in Colchester on the "providential" victories of the Duke of Marlborough created such a fuss that its author claimed he was invited to the local coffeehouse to hear himself parodied and scoffed at, an indication of how wide a net was cast by providentiality and how controversial even patriotic interpretations could become. See Josiah Woodward (?), *Some Thoughts Concerning the Stage in a Letter to a Lady* (1704; reprinted Los Angeles, 1947), p. 12; John Barnard, "Earthquakes Under the Divine Government," *Two Discourses Address'd to Young Persons* (Boston, 1727), pp. 71–99; and the Preface to William Smithies, Jr., *The Coffee-House Preachers* (London, 1706), esp. fols. [A4v]–B1.

Similar charges were also made earlier. In H. Jessey's *The Lords Loud Call to England: Being a True Relation of some Late, Various and Wonderful Judgments, or Handy-works of God, by Earthquake, Lightening, Whirlewind, great multitudes of Toads and Elves; and also the striking of divers persons with Sudden Death . . .* (1660), there are several stories of actors in plays at Oxford who played the part of Puritans and then died.

27. I discuss Providence books and their rationale more fully in Chapter Eight, pp. 217–23.

28. See Dunton, *Life and Errors*, p. 157.

29. Title page. Except as otherwise indicated, all quotations are from the first edition. At least five more editions came out by the end of 1693. By 1719 a "30th" edition, with substantial additions, was published.

30. Both the humorous account of the death of Captain Blifil in *Tom Jones* (II, ix, 110–15) and the "grave" black-page comedy of Yorick's demise in *Tristram Shandy* (I, xii, 30–38) seem to owe their *tour-de-force* quality to popular pieties in deathbed narratives.

31. The justification for such accounts is usually put in terms of the human inability to falsify character at such a moment. According to Allured Clarke, "the characters of men have always been formed from their behaviour at the time of their death, when it is justly presumed every

disguise is laid aside. . . ."—*An Essay Towards the Character of Her late Majesty Caroline* (1738), p. 26.

32. For the details of the deception, see Stephen Parks, *John Dunton and the English Book Trade* (New York, 1976), pp. 57–59; for Dunton's own account and for his "recantation" of publications like *The Second Spira*, see the *Life and Errors*, pp. 218–23.

33. Parks, p. 58, recounts how doubters took up Dunton on the offer.

34. There were other spinoffs that claimed to be authentic; for example, *A True Second SPIRA: or, A Soul plung'd in his Case* (1697); *Spira Respirans: Or, The Way to the Kingdom of Heaven by the Gates of Hell; In an Extraordinary Example* (1695); and *The Third Spira* (1724). Dunton, as well as others, capitalized on the spuriousness of *The Second Spira* for years. As late as 1719, Dunton was himself still collecting new stories under the old title, and he had printed *A Conference Betwixt a Modern Atheist, and his Friend [.] By the Methodizer of the Second Spira* in 1693.

35. *Concealed Murther Reveil'd.* [sic] *Being a Strange Discovery of a most Horrid and Barbarous Murther . . . By Mary Anderson . . . On the Body of Hannah Jones an Infant of 8 Weeks Old . . . As also How it was Conceal'd 3 Years, and not Discovered till Monday last . . .* (London, 1699).

36. See, for example, these two brief, single-page items from 1706: *A Full and True Account of the Examination and Condemnation of Handsome Fielding This 6th of December 1706. For Having Two Wives . . . For which he was found Guilty,* and *A faithful Account of the Examination of Robert Feilding, Esq.; before the Rt. Hon. the Ld. Chief Justice Holt, and his Commitment to Newgate.*

37. An example is the thirty-eight-page folio transcript of *The Tryal of Spencer Cowper. Esq.; John Marson, Ellis Stevens, and William Rogers, Gent. Upon an Indictment for the Murther of Mrs. Sarah Stout, a Quaker . . . July 18, 1699. Of Which they were acquitted.* Faithful full-transcript accounts of law trials were frequently printed as well.

38. David Paisey tells me that there are instances in Germany, for example.

39. Some of the eight-pagers included straight didactic and hortatory material as well; a few were practical guides to vocations or crafts. Most eight-pagers were similar in intent, narrative structure, and quality of printing to chapbooks, which were generally twenty-four pages in length but smaller in page format.

Additional titles of eight-pagers include:

A Full and True Account of Benjamin Child, a Quaker; A Notorious Cheat and Imposter (1708);

A Scourge for Oppressors, and such as Wrong the Poor: Being a True and Faithful Account of God's Divine Judgment, Shewn upon one James Adams of Milton near Cambridge (1708);

The Guilford Ghost. Being an Account of the Strange and Amazing Apparition or Ghost of Mr. Christopher Slaughterford; with the manner of his wonderful Appearance [to named people in named places and times] *in a sad and astonishing manner in several dreadful and frightful Shapes. . . . With other amazing Particulars* (1709);

The Norfolk Wonder, or, The Maiden's Trance: Being a Strange and True Relation, of one Sarah Baker of Elsom in Norfolk, of Sixteen Years of Age; who on the 2d of this Instant May . . . fell into a Trance, and lay as Dead for Three Days and Nights (1708);

A true history of the base and unnatural murther of a man by his own son near Uppingham (date cut off from B.L. copy);

Here is a full and true Relation of one Mr. Rich. Langly, a Glazier, Living over-against the Sign of the Golden-wheat-Sheaf in Ratcliff-Highway, London, that lay in a Trance. . . . (n.d.);

The Constant, but Unhappy Lovers. Being a full and true Relation of one Madam Butler . . . a great Heriss at Hackney Boarding-School . . . forced to Marry . . . against her Will . . . and [who was] *found dead in the Morning, with a Copy of Verses lying by her on a Table, written in her own Blood* (1709);

Strange and Wonderful News. Being a True, tho' Sad Relation of Six Sea-Men . . . who sold Themselves to the Devil And were Invisibly Carry'd away (1700?); and

A full and True Relation Of the strange and wonderful Apparitions, Which were seen in the Clouds, upon Tuesday Evening at Seven of the Clock, till three of the Clock on Wednesday Morning, being the 6th and 7th of March 1715/16. . . . (1716).

40. Anniversaries of special events involving a monarch often were conflated with birthdays so that a single day could be set apart for celebration.

41. *The Bride-Woman's Counselor,* p. [2]. The published sermon is undated; it must have been issued

in 1699 or 1700 because *The Female Advocate* (see below) is clearly answering a printed version of the sermon.

42. Sprint was included in collections, such as *Conjugal Duty: Set forth in a Collection of Ingenious and Delightful Wedding-Sermons* at least until 1732.

43. Henry Maurice, *An Impartial Account of John Mason of Water-Stratford, and his Sentiments* (1695), p. 4.

44. Testimony of Margaret Holms, quoted in Maurice, p. 6.

45. Many accounts of the episode were printed, including *A Letter from A Gentleman in Buckinghamshire near Water-Stratford . . . giving an Account of the . . . Behaviour of Mr. Mason . . . With the Hymns they usually sing* (1694); *The Trial and Condemnation of the Two False Witnesses Unto the Late Midnight-Cry* (1694); *Some Remarkable Passages in the Life and Death of Mr. John Mason* (1694); and *The Angels Oath . . . A Prophecy from Mr. Mason's People at Water-Stratford* (1694).

46. See *Select Remains of the Reverend John Mason . . . Recommended by the Rev. I. Watts* (2nd ed., 1742).

47. On the Walpole-Skerrett relationship, see, for example, *The Secret History of an Old Shoe. Inscribed To the Most Wondrous-wonderful of all Wonderful Men and Lovers* (1734). Although only a shilling pamphlet, it shows an awareness of the whole tradition of secret histories and *chroniques scandaleuses* and thus provides an instance of a kind of merger of that more lengthy narrative tradition with the shorter instances of the journalism of the moment. "I am not unaware," writes its author,

> of the great Dis-advantage, under which this little History will appear in the World, and of the Objections made to *Secret History* in general: First, because the *Materials* of which it is composed being necessarily of a *private Nature*, its veracity, which is the real Beauty of History, cannot be depended on, and consequently it exhibits to us nothing but a Heap of *Fabulous Scandal*; and secondly, because, even supposing the Facts undeniably true, supported by the strongest Evidence, it is neither *Christian-like* nor *Man-like* to rake into, and expose the *Errors* of our Neighbors, and Fellow-creatures. (p. 5)

Other accounts include *The Rival Wives. Or, the* GREETING *of Clarissa to Skirra In the Elysian Shades* (1738). There were also slightly oblique sermons like Joseph Trapp's *The Royal Sin: or, Adultery Rebuk'd in a Great King* (1738), and there was a revival of interest in older works that were reprinted in 1738 such as John Dunton's *The Hazard of a Death-Bed Repentence, further argued . . . to which is added, Conjugal Perjury, or an essay upon whoredom; address'd to the husbands of quality that keep misses* (originally published in 1708). Another version reprinted the same year by an enterprising bookseller was titled *The Danger of Living in a Known Sin, and the Hazard of a Death-Bed Repentance.*

48. On the issue of whether the increased number is related to licensing, see the extended discussion in J. A. Downie, *Robert Harley and the Press* (Cambridge, 1979).

49. Even early on, when her fictions were often rather exotic in plot and style, Haywood recognized the appeal of the immediate. "For the Reader's better Understanding," she wrote in the Preface to *The Secret History of Queen Zarah* (1705), "we ought not to chuse too Ancient Accidents, nor unknown Heroes, which are fought for in a Barbarous Countrey, and too far distant in Time, for we care little for what was done a Thousand Years ago among the *Tartars* or *Ayssines*" (reprinted in Ioan Williams, *Novel and Romance 1700–1800: A Documentary Record* [New York, 1970], p. 34).

CHAPTER   EIGHT

1. The classic study of desire in fiction is René Girard, *Desire, Deceit, and the Novel: Self and Other in Literary Structure*, trans. Yvonne Freccero (Baltimore, 1966); more recent and more closely related to issues at stake here is Linda S. Kauffman, *Discourses of Desire: Gender, Genre, and Epistolary Fictions* (Ithaca, N.Y., 1986), although both these accounts, like most studies of desire, are based more in psychoanalytic theory and less in cultural study than are my own

concerns. For an account of the novel that regards cultural desire as causal, see Nancy Armstrong, *Desire and Domestic Fiction: A Political History of the Novel* (New York, 1987). See also the forthcoming study by Patricia Meyer Spacks, *Desire and Truth: Functions of Plot in Eighteenth-Century England* (Chicago, 1990). The issue of exactly how desire—even assuming that one can define it as a cultural phenomenon—influences the writing process has not been adequately theorized, but Armstrong seems to me to be on the right track in seeing "ordinary" and "popular" reading materials as the crucial link. Booksellers and hack writers are in a better position to read at least some aspects of desire—and more motivated to be successful—than are writers with "higher" concerns, though there are, of course, serious pitfalls in trying to separate the reading of desire from the creation of it.

2. Some of the confusion about female readership in this period seems deeply based in discomfort about femininity, "passivity," and responsibility. There is a fascinating parallel between historic responses to readers as "causal" factors in the perceived deterioration of literary taste and women as "provokers" of rapes, and it is probably no accident that reading publics that have been said to lower taste have almost always been assumed to consist heavily of female and other "new" readers. No one has historically been the least curious about what readers "do" for writing unless it is something bad; then they become culprits, in the same way that women become culprits if they are raped. Causes always seem to be located in some active / male principle unless a disaster has been spotted; then passivity or "luring" becomes causal. A good feminist theorist may be able to work out the phenomenological implications of attacks on readers in times of rising female literacy, and perhaps Marxists may be able to work out the role of readers from other unimpowered classes in this blame-casting analysis.

3. Pope's patronizing of Arabella Fermor in the dedication to *The Rape of the Lock* may involve just personal dislike, rather than dismissal of her because of her *arriviste* social attitudes. But his treatment of readers in the *Dunciads*, implied especially in the way he constructs the explanatory footnotes, suggests firmly his distrust of the broad sweep of "Smithfield" tastes which seem, at least by the 1743 *Dunciad*, to include a strong dimension of dissent (Moorfields) as well as involving the poor, the politically misguided, and the artistically inferior. Charles Gildon, in *The Life and Strange Surprizing Adventures of D—— DeF—— of London, Hosier* (1719), also makes disparaging remarks about "new" readers, implying that the audience for Defoe and the new fiction consists only of those who have just arrived in respectability and suggesting that they bring no dignity to the works they help create.

4. His enthusiasm for the Athenian Society dates from 1692, when he submitted his Ode in praise of it to the "Society"; by 1696, possibly long before, he had changed his mind.

5. The collision of these two movements has occasioned vigorous debate about the development of science in England and about causes and effects more generally. The crucial issues are isolated in a spirited exchanged between Christopher Hill and A. M. Kearney, in essays with identical titles, "Puritanism, Capitalism, and the Scientific Revolution." Both are included in Charles Webster, ed., *The Intellectual Revolution of the Seventeenth Century* (London & Boston, 1974), pp. 218–53. See also further contributions in that volume by Hill, Kearney, and Theodore K. Roff, pp. 254–85. For other important interpretations of the issue, see Stephen Toulmin, *Foresight and Understanding* (London, 1961), and John Morgan, "Puritanism and Science: A Reinterpretation," *The Historical Journal*, 22 (1979), 535–60.

6. I'm not sure intellectual historians put enough emphasis on the inclusive tendencies of scientists in the seventeenth century, tendencies that admitted virtuosi and encouraged a general amateurism in scientific theses. The subsequent exclusivity of scientific discrimination is often read back into earlier science, a problem for interpreting the toleration of such figures as Boyle and Newton.

7. In Chapter Twelve I suggest how the practice of diary keeping affects both the writing and reading of novels.

8. See Robert Boyle, *Occasional Reflections upon several Svbiects. Whereto is premis'd* [sic] *A Discourse About such kind of Thoughts* (1665); Edward Bury, *The Husbandmans Companion: Containing One Hundred Occasional Meditations Reflections and Ejaculations, Especially Suited to Men of that Employment. Directing them how they may be Heavenly-minded while about their ordinary Calling* (1677); John Flavell, *A New Compass for Seamen* (1664; often reprinted as *Navigation Spiritual-*

ized) and *Husbandry Spiritualized: or, the Heavenly Use of Earthly Things* (1669); and William Gearing, *The Mount of Holy Meditation: or a Treatise Shewing the nature and kinds of Meditation* (1662).

9. "My desire," wrote Bury of his purpose in *The Husbandmans Companion*, "is that thou maist take out this lesson, prove an artist, and set up for thy self. . . . No ship that sails either to the East or West *Indies* brings home richer lading than meditation doth, if rightly steered; This is the chewing of the cud, that turns all to nourishment, the true Philosophers stone that turns all to gold" (fols. a3v–a4).

10. For the implications of writers as readers, see Chapter Twelve, pp. 311–13.

11. The name derives from μελετᾶν, to meditate. Boyle thinks of Bishop Hall as his model and appears to credit Hall with inventing this kind of meditation.

   Prolix as it is, Boyle's prefatory "Discourse" to his *Occasional Reflections*, in which he defines his subject and promulgates a method, may have originally been intended to be longer. The meditations proper begin on p. 161 of the volume, while the "Discourse" goes through p. 80 and there are no pp. 81–160. I would guess that space was left by the printer for prefatory materials and that Boyle found himself writing a less long theoretical justification than he had at first intended, perhaps a hint that he had more reservations about his large epistemological claims than he may have admitted to himself. Boyle might simply have been pressed for time, but (as readers of Boyle know only too well) he never seemed at a loss for words and usually elaborated everything more lengthily than was required. On the other hand, the printer, knowing Boyle, could have left room for 160 pages instead of the planned 80.

12. *Occasional Reflections*, "An Introductory Preface," fol. [A8v]). The preoccupation with Method as a means of mental discipline and as a structural device for writing is well known and extends to all levels of discourse. In *A New Family-Book; or The True Interest of Families* (1693, a 3rd edition of *True Interest*), James Kirkwood gives this "advice to parents" about how to help children with their prayers, meditations, and self-examination: "It will be convenient, in order to their doing this to good purpose, to be directed to a method, that so their thoughts may not wander and be unfixed" (p. 81). See also Thomas White, *A Method and Instructions for the Art of Divine Meditation. with Instances of the severall Kindes of Solemne Meditation* (1655). On the implications of the preoccupation with Method, see Walter J. Ong, *Ramus: Method, and the Decay of Dialogue* (Cambridge, Mass., 1958); Nelly Bruyère, *Méthode et Dialectique dans l'Oeuvre de la Ramée* (Paris, 1984); and Philippe Desan, *Naissance de la méthode: Machiavel, La Ramée, Bodin, Montaigne, Descartes* (Paris, 1987).

   For accounts of traditional patterns of meditation, see Louis Martz's classic study, *The Poetry of Meditation* (New Haven, Conn., 1954); H. R. McAdoo, *The Structure of Caroline Moral Theology* (London, 1949); Frank Livingstone Huntley, *Bishop Joseph Hall and Protestant Meditation in Seventeenth-Century England* (Binghamton, N.Y., 1981); and Isabel G. MacCaffrey's important essay, "The Meditation Paradigm," *ELH*, 32 (1965), 388–407.

13. *The Christian Mans Calling, Third Part, Directing a Christian to perform his duty* (London, 1665), p. 451. Although the title page of this volume (catalogued in the British Library as 3751. de. 1) claims to contain all of Swinnock's *Works* (including parts I and II of CMC), it actually contains only part III of CMC; hereafter I refer to this title as CMC III.

14. *The Husbandmans Companion*, fol. [A4].

15. "Of the Usefulness of Natural Philosophy," Part I, Essay 5, in *Works* (6 vols., London, 1744), I, 462.

16. Bury uses the same metaphor: "we may of these earthly materials frame to our selves a *Jacobs ladder* to ascend to heaven; for all those visibles will mount us up to beholde invisibles, and give us a *Pisqah* sight of the heavenly *Canaan*" (*The Husbandmans Companion*, fol. [A3v]).

17. Boyle designed his treatise largely as a guide for others, and he goes out of his way to encourage all readers to make their own meditations, and other meditationists are similarly anxious to encourage the craft." "[L]abour to *spiritualize earthly things,*" advises Swinnock; "this is one of the most excellent and enriching arts in Christianity; Though these *occasional* thoughts resemble *lightning* . . . yet such *light gains, with quick returnes, make an heavy purse. He that hath learned this mystery, is the true *Chymist*, he leaves the *dregs* and *lees* of things, and extracts the *substance* and *quintessence*"—CMC III, p. 372. Dunton uses the language of the meditationists when he

describes what modern Athenian virtuosi do: "When a *Virtuoso* thus seriously reflects on the *Visible World*, (and upon what's Curious in it) he does as 'twere *spiritualize Earthly Things:* He can here make *New Discoveries*, as well as raise his mind from Earth to Heaven. . . . In a Word . . . [this process] is a Divine Improvement of *all the Wonders under the Sun"—The Christian's Gazette* (1709), p. viii.

How many believers followed such advice is anyone's guess, but spiritual biographies of the period, which I will discuss below in Chapters Twelve and Fourteen, often contain samples and testify to longer private documents. In William Hamilton's *The Life and Character of James Bonnell* (1703), e.g., the hero is said to have "left behind him many Volumes of Meditations & Prayers," p. vi.

18. ". . . there is scarce any thing that may not prove the subject of an Occasional Meditation," p. 28. Swinnock agrees: "No sight, no sound but may afford matter for meditation"—CMC III, p. 383. And so does Bury: "there is nothing in *rerum natura*, but may be a fit object for occasional meditations," fol. [a5].

Boyle was so anxious that individuals cultivate meditation as a habit that he often falls into the language of addiction, as when he says that "they that would compleat the good Fortune of these Papers, may do it more effectually, by Addicting themselves, (as considerable Persons have been of late induc'd to do) to Write Occasional Reflections," fol. b3. Another example is quoted on pp. 205–6.

19. In his "Introductory Preface" to *Occasional Reflections* (as elsewhere), Boyle praises the "moderns" for their writing as well as for strides in observation and knowledge; see, for example, fols. [a5v]–[a6]. Boyle sometimes seems to take personal credit for advances in writing, and he seems to crave a reputation as a writer and stylist even more than as a scientist or thinker. "I see no great Reason to *confine* my self to the Magisterial Dictates of either Antient or Scholastick Writers," he writes somewhat arrogantly in the "Introductory Preface." "For, living in this Age, and in This part of the World, where we are not like to have those for Readers that dy'd before we were born, I see not why one may not judge of *Decorum* by the Examples and Practices of those Authors of our own Times and Countries," fol. [a5]. Boyle's praise of modern style and his desire to help create an accessible discourse for a large audience is a crucial part of his larger intellectual aim to popularize science and generalize the culture of scientific thought.

20. Although Boyle had little to say about tests of evidence, he did place a lot of emphasis on the power of experience to help one decide. In *The Christian Virtuoso*, he says that "the knowledge . . . [that the virtuoso] has of the Various, and sometimes very Wonderful, Operations of some Natural things, especially when they are skilfully improv'd, and dexterously apply'd by Art . . . will qualify him to distinguish, between things that are only *strange* and *surprizing*, and those that are truly *miraculous*," p. 83.

21. Quite beyond Boyle's status as a scientist, Swift might have had good reasons to dislike Boyle and suspect his literary and ideological commitments. Boyle regularly championed the moderns as writers (as well as as scientists), his distrust of traditional authority extending well beyond his scientific skepticism, and his position as a loyal Anglican was nevertheless marked by some strong religious opinions that allied him closely with the emphases of Dissent. Boyle had refused to take orders because he did no feel he had been "called," and he repeatedly lamented his lack of a personal "conversion" experience, a matter that for him devalued his religious authority.

For Boyle's own extended account of his skepticism about scientific evidence, see *The Sceptical Chymist* (1661) in which it becomes clear that Boyle has, intellectually, no faith in any kind of authority, ancient or modern, though he repeatedly claims elsewhere his total trust in divine revelation and the Scriptures. "I can yet so little discover what to acquiesce in," he concludes, "that perchance the Enquiries of others have scarce been more unsatisfactory to me, than my own have been to my self," p. 436.

22. Boyle's kind of meditation flourished at least through the 1680s, perhaps well into the eighteenth century. As late as 1734, Isaac Watts published meditations on such subjects as "A Hornet's Nest destroy'd," but he suggests they were written when he was young. See *Reliquiae Juveniles: Miscelaneous Thoughts in Prose and Verse, on Natural, Moral, and Divine Subjects; Written chiefly in Younger Years* (1734).

23. The best account of Wonders material is that of David D. Hall, *Worlds of Wonder, Days of Judgment: Popular Religious Belief in Early New England* (New York, 1989), esp. pp. 71–116,

although he misses the way the tradition compensates for scientific advancement. There is no adequate account of the tradition of Wonder in England.

24. See *Robinson Crusoe*, p. 212; *Serious Reflections during the Life and Surprising Adventures of Robinson Crusoe*, p. 1 and fol. A4v in first edition of 1726, pp. 3 and xi in the edition of G. H. Maynadier (New York, 1903). A 1759 abridgment of *Crusoe* was entitled *The Wonderful Life, And most Surprizing Adventures of Robinson Crusoe*. The original title page of *Colonel Jacque* describes the hero as living a "Life of Wonders."

25. The first public museum (the Ashmolean in Oxford) was opened in 1683.

26. *Of Education, Especially of Young Gentlemen* (Oxford, 1673), p. 193.

27. *The Wonder Of all the Wonders, That ever the World wonder'd at* (1722) purports to be an advertisement for a carnival magician, John Emanuel Schoitz, who performs in Smithfield. Presumably this elaborate quarto inspired *The Wonderful Wonder of Wonders*. On the taste for "strange sights" and the ways it was satisfied, see Richard Altick, *The Shows of London* (Cambridge, Mass., 1978), especially pp. 5–49 and 87–98.

28. Such practice was of course common in all kinds of writings, and occasionally writers show themselves to be self-conscious about it. The Preface of *The Gentleman's Library* (1715), for example, confesses: "That the *Reader* may not be surpriz'd to meet with frequent Passages, which his *Recollection* tells him he has elsewhere found, I think it behoves [sic] me to avoid the Odious Imputation of a *Plagiary*, and confess my *Work* more a *Collection* than a *Composition*," fol. [a11v].

29. It may be that, in claiming the authorship or blessing of R.B., Crouch was (consciously or unconsciously) invoking the authority of Robert Boyle or at least inviting readers to make that confusion, although he could not of course use Boyle's usual, proper signature, R.B., F.R.S.

30. Wanley dedicated the volume to Sir Harbottle Grimston, a prominent judge who had been speaker of the House of Commons in the Convention Parliament at the Restoration. James Sutherland (*English Literature of the Late Seventeenth Century*, p. 242) mentions Wanley and Crouch, suggests the importance of the tradition, and points to its connection with some of Dunton's journalistic projects; he is one of the few literary historians to see the significance of such materials.

31. A handwritten note by Francis Douce in the Bodleian copy calls attention to the debt.

32. *Surprizing Miracles of Nature and Art* (1708). This title was actually a new ("4th") edition of the 1678 volume, *Miracles of Art and Nature*.

33. Two different editions for this year, 1694, are in the British Library. This title was apparently first printed in 1692. Crouch seems to have issued multiple editions of many titles, varying the illustrations (on which he placed much emphasis in his title pages) but making few textual changes. The date I have given for each Crouch title is for the copy I examined; in some cases (*Earthquakes*, for example) the "first" edition may have been a year or two earlier: Wing's record of editions for this kind of cheap and popular volume is not very complete.

34. Crouch sometimes claims that his volumes are an alternative to romances. He says, for example, that *Memorable Accidents* "containeth Adventures as rare as any that are to be found in Romances; here you are entertain'd with Shipwracks, overthrown Fortunes, Revolutions of Kingdoms, and the surprizing Effects of the Commotions of all the Passions," fol. A3v. But he asserts the superiority of "true History": "How great soever the Diversion and Pleasure be that we find in Reading Romances, nevertheless true History hath all the advantage over it that Truth hath over a Fable. . . . [T]he reading . . . [of history] produceth more certain Effects," fol. A3.

35. Dunton's collection of narratives about executed criminals is somewhat strangely titled *The Wonders of Free-Grace: or, a Compleat History of all the Remarkable Penitents that have been Executed at Tyburn, and Elsewhere, for these last Thirty Years* (1690), and he is the London publisher of Cotton Mather's *The Wonders of the Invisible World* (1693).

36. Some use the Crouch and Wanley material liberally. For example, a 566-page volume of 1704, *The History of Man; or, the Wonders of Humane Nature . . . with Examples Antient and Modern, Alphabetically digested under their Proper Heads*, uses so much of Wanley's material, though arranging it somewhat differently, that the British Library catalogues it under Wanley.

37. A number of people refer to the end of the seventeenth century and the beginning of the eighteenth as the "Age of Wonders." See, for example, Timothy Rogers, *Practical Discourses on Sickness & Recovery* (1691), p. 273.

38. Both these strange titles have been at one time or another attributed to Swift. Not that parodies

marked the end of the craze nor even circumscribed its uses. As late as 1726, one of the accounts of the notorious Mary Tofts was titled *The Wonder of Wonders: or, A True and Perfect Narrative of a Woman near Guildford in Surrey, who was Delivered lately of Seventeen Rabbets, and Three Legs of a Tabby Cat, &c.* (Ipswich, 1726). Pamphlets regularly refer to Tofts as "the Surrey Wonder." For a fascinating account of how the Tofts episode led to a lengthy debate about the power of the imagination, see Dennis Todd, "Three Characters in Hogarth's *Cunicularii*—and Some Implications," *Eighteenth-Century Studies,* 16 (1982), 24–46. Quite a few different pamphlets, broadsides, and broadsheets used the "Wonder of Wonders" title for all different kinds of events (in 1682, 1694, and 1700, for example); evidently the doubling upped the stakes of wonderness, and the pseudo-Swiftian pamphlets of 1722 only raise the claims a little more outrageously.

39. Another collection of events in 1680 was titled *Wonderful Signs of Strange Times . . . Being Strange Signs and Wonders that have lately Happened* (1681). Collections of the Wonders of a particular year were quite common. See, for example, *The Wonders of the Year 1716* (Dublin, 1716), or *God's Marvellous Wonders In England: Containing divers strange and wonderful* RELATIONS *that have happened since the beginning of June, this present year 1694.*

40. See, for example, *A Brief Narrative of A Strange and Wonderful Old Woman that hath A Pair of Horns Growing upon her Head. Giving a true Account how they have several times after their being shed, grown again* (1676); *A New Wonder: or, A strange and True Account from Shrewsbury of a Dreadful Storm, which happened on the 4th of May last* (1681); and *A Strange and Wonderful Account of the Great Mischiefs, Sustained by the late Dreadful Thunder, Lightening, and Terrible Land-Floods . . . Giving an Exact Relation of the Men, Cattle, Houses, &c that have been Thunder-struck* (1683). The first of these pamphlets is prefaced by a verse (said in a handwritten note in the British Library copy to be by Mary Davies) that reads this way:

> You that love Wonders to behold
> Here you may of a Wonder read.
> The strangest that was ever seen or told
> A Woman with Horns upon her Head.

The second is altogether in verse (ballads and broadsheets participated in the Wonder tradition as well), and calls attention from the very beginning to its concentration on Wonders:

> It is well known for some years past,
> strange wonders we have often seen;
> A Wonder very lately past,
> more strange in England hath not been.

41. See *The Christians Gazette,* 2nd ed., corrected and enlarged (London, n.d. [1713]), pp. 16–19.

42. *A Short Story Of the Rise, Reign, and Ruin of the Antinomians, Familists, and Libertines That Infected the Churches of New-England,* 1692, fol. [B3v]. This pamphlet was first published in 1644 but reprinted as an example of "God's strange Remarkable Judgments" (title page).

43. As in *Strange and Wonderful News . . . or, A Full and True* RELATION *. . .* (by John Cother, 1678), or *A Strange and Wonderful (Yet True) RELATION Of the Cursed and Hellish Design of Abraham Mason, a Pretended Quaker, to give himself to the Devil* (1700?). There are many "Strange News" titles from various local areas, including *Strange News From Oxfordshire: Being A true and faithful ACCOUNT of a Wonderful and Dreadful Earthquake* (1683); *Strange and Wonderfull News from Cornwall* (1687); *Strange and Wonderful News from Exeter* (1690); *Strange and Wonderful News from Ireland* (1697); *Strange and wonderful News from Chipping Norton* (n.d.); and *Strange and Terrible News from Sea. Or: A True Relation of a Most Wonderful Violent Tempest* (1678).

44. For example, *A Strange, but true Relation Of the Discovery of a most horrid and bloudy Murder* (1678). The formula is common in the narratives themselves, too. Dunton, for example, says in *A Voyage Round the World,* "But now I'll tell you a *strange story,* and a true one" (I, 132). Sandra Clark notes an earlier pattern, before 1620, of titles that combine truth claims with a stress on wonder: "Alongside 'true' and 'just' stand 'wonderful,' 'rare,' 'dreadful' and 'unnatural' "—*The Elizabethan Pamphleteers: Popular Moralistic Pamphlets, 1580–1640* (Rutherford, N.J., 1983), p. 90. The context that Clark investigates is different in thrust, however, for printed materials then are full of all kinds of curiosities—unnatural natural histories, miracles, strange

sights, etc. The wonder is then the norm, and "news" is emergent; as Clark appropriately concludes about the directions then, "The tendency towards informing is constantly counteracted
by that towards amazing, warning, and teaching by example," p. 90.

45. A cheap eight-page pamphlet of about 1710, *The Age of Wonders*, focuses on the "Fiery Apparition [sic] that was seen in the Air . . . May the 11th 1710," then goes on review other comets
from 1664, 1665, 1680, and 1682, noting that great events often followed their appearance.
But the pamphlet does not interpret the comets or argue a political or theological significance,
settling instead for emphasizing how "Strange and wonderful have been the Miraculous Productions of Nature in all Ages."

46. This kind of observation about contemporary taste was common. Thomas Phelps, for example,
in dedicating a narrative account of himself to Samuel Pepys in 1685, lists among his motives a
desire to satisfy "the curiosity of my Country-men, who delight in Novel and strange Stories"—
A True Account of the Captivity of Thomas Phelps, fol. [A3v].

47. I have discussed this historical development in some detail in *The Reluctant Pilgrim* (Baltimore,
1966), pp. 51–75.

48. *A Compleat History Of the Most Remarkable Providences, both of Judgment and Mercy, Which have
Hapned in this PRESENT AGE* (1697), fol. [b1v]. John Flavell's motivation two decades earlier
had been similar—"to assert the *Being* and *Efficacy* of Providence against the *Atheism* of the
times"—but he seems to have felt the need less urgently and is less on the defensive than writers
of the 1690s who perceive atheism as a formidable antagonist. The difference between the 1670s
and 1690s is similar to the differences expressed in Milton's and Pope's theodicean aims: to
"justify" the ways of God to man seemed in 1667 sufficient, but by Pope's time it seemed necessary to "vindicate" them.

   Turner's *Compleat History* contains almost six hundred folio pages and recounts perhaps five
thousand stories, some involving historic events from antiquity that had affected the subsequent
course of the world, others describing ordinary folk and the quite trivial events of everyday,
William Foxly's "14-day sleep" (4th pagination, p. 17), for example, or "The M.P. who never
entered the Parliament-House without a Bible in his pocket" (2nd pagination, p. 83). Turner's
stories came from everywhere—biblical and classical sources, histories, contemporary publications, and oral accounts (I quote an example in Chapter Six, note 35.)

49. The Poole project and the Turner manuscript are, in a sense, a thematic updating of the effort
Francis Bacon envisioned much earlier when he called for a systematic recording of all known
wonders.

50. *Divine Conduct: or, the Mysterie of Providence*, fol. B2v.

51. "A Further Specimen of the History of *Remarkable Providences*: with Proposals . . . For Printing
the said WORK By Way of SUBSCRIPTION," in William Turner, *An Essay upon the Works of Creation and Providence: being an Introductory Discourse to the History of Remarkable Providences, Now
preparing for the Press* (1695), p. [169].

52. See *The Post-Angel* (1701), fol. B1v, for a typical call for his reader to send him appropriate
providential accounts: " 'tis desir'd that all *serious Christians* would send what they find remarkable every Month." In the 1713 *Christians Gazette*, he suggests that he has already made arrangements for a sufficient number of stories: "the *serious Reflections* will be always mine, but as to the
Remarkable Providences, I shall stand indebted for 'em to several *Eminent Persons*, with whom I
have settled a Monthly Corespondence . . . and I don't fear but I shall receive such well attested
Relations from *diverse Parts of the Three Kingdoms*," p. 1.

53. Woodward's injunction was directed particularly to seamen. See *The Seaman's Monitor* (1705):
"[T]hese *Demonstrations of God's Being*, and of his gracious and *special Care* of Man ought to be
recorded in some *Publick Register*" (p. 44). John Ryther, also writing to seamen, advised similarly: "Register your Preservations, and Deliverances, you will find much, yea very much benefit
in such a Course"—*A Plat for Mariners; or, The Seamen's Preacher* (1675), pp. 97–98.

54. Similar stories are collected in *Mr. James Janeway's Legacy to his Friends: Containing Twenty Seven
Famous Instances of Gods Providences in and about Sea-Dangers and Deliverances; with the Names
of Several that were Eye-witnesses to many of them* (1675). Other collections include *Prince-Pro-
tecting Providences: or, a Collection of some Historical . . . Personages, (Born for Great Actions)
[who] have had Miraculous Preservations* (by John Gibbon, 1682), and *A Memorial of God's last*

Twenty nine Years Wonders in England (1689). Also common were lengthy accounts of a single event with a series of analogues appended. See, for example, John Barnard, *Ashton's Memorial: Or, An Authentick Account of The Strange Adventures and Signal Deliverances of Mr. Philip Ashton; who, After he had made his Escape from the Pirates, liv'd alone on a desolate Island* . . . (1726), which extends to eighty-eight pages and has appended to it a shorter account (thirteen pages) of another man, Nicholas Merritt, who also escaped from pirates, and a sermon on "God's Ability to save his People out of all their Dangers" (another forty-six pages).

55. See, for example, *Gods Judgment Upon Drunkards, Swearers, And Sabbath-breakers* (1659). John Reynolds's *The Triumphs of Gods Revenge against the Crying and Execrable Sin of Wilful and Premeditated Murther,* probably first published in 1622 and reprinted fairly often throughout the seventeenth century, became very popular as a reprint (sometimes with added material) at the turn of the century (I quote the title page from a 1704 edition), and it had many imitators. *God's Revenge Against the Crying and Execrable Sin of Adultery* was reprinted throughout the eighteenth century.

56. Published first in Philadelphia a year earlier.

57. Sometimes such accounts are not only in the service of a providential thesis but also self-justifying to the author. See, for example, Thomas Astry's *A True Relation of A Young Man . . . who was struck Dumb for the space of Twenty Four Hours, Because he would not believe what was said unto him* (1671), in which the episode involves the rebellion of Astry's own son. The fourteen-page tract was published in London "for the author" (title page).

58. One of the signators who "attest the truth of this . . . Narration" is Elias Ashmole.

59. See, for example, *A Discourse of Earthquakes; as they are Supernatural and Premonitory Signs to a Nation; with a respect to what hath occurred in this Year 1692* (by Robert Fleming, 1693); *God Almighty's Providence Both in the Sending and Dissolving Great Snows and Frosts; and The Improvement we ought to make of it* (a sermon from 1684 that was still being reprinted in 1740; I read the 1740 version); and Jonathan Owen, *Englands Warning By Late Frowning Providences: especially the Immediate hand of God upon the Straits-Fleet* (1694).

60. Samuel Wesley (in his early years himself on the fringes of Dissent, and later the father of John and Charles) took a rather arch-Anglican position in a debate with a fellow churchman, Samuel Palmer, on this issue, and one of his accusatory comments sums up pretty well the complaints each side makes of the other: "he [Palmer] asks, 'Why the Dissenters mayn't *admire Providence?*' I know no Reason why they may not do it as much as they please. . . . Let 'em *admire Providence,* but then let 'em not *monopolize* it to their own Party, and insist on their *Old Whimsies,* that they are the *only People of God*"—*A Defence of a Letter Concerning the Education of Dissenters* (1704), p. 53. For another example of the feuding between Anglicans and Dissenters about providential interpretations, see *The Oracles of the Dissenters: containing Forty Five Relations Of Pretended Judgments, Prodigies, and Apparitions, In Behalf of the Non-Conformists* (1707), first published in 1662 as *Mirabilis Annus Secundus.*

61. Abraham Campion, *A Sermon concerning National Providence* (Oxford, 1694), p. 30.

62. There was, of course, an old and honored tradition of using providential interpretations to justify political positions or decisions, and when I emphasize the late-century attempt to unite all Christians against "atheism" through the collection of providences, I am not suggesting that the old motives disappeared or that anyone expected that disagreements among believers would cease.

CHAPTER   NINE

1. I have discussed, from a somewhat different perspective, the problem modern readers have with didacticism in "Fielding and the Modern Reader: The Problem of Temporal Translation," in J. Paul Hunter and Martin Battestin, *Fielding in His Time and Ours* (Los Angeles, 1987), pp. 1–28.

2. Still, the principles behind these easy conclusions can be helpful, when assumed tentatively and applied sensibly, in opening up texts to the discovery of new complexities. My objections to sweeping conclusions about the total irrelevance of intentionality are quite different from the

objections of intentionalists who refuse to admit any effects beyond those consciously created. The reasons for the general distrust of deconstructionist procedures has unfortunately come to seem political even more than ideological. In spite of their claims, most older historicisms had powerful political loyalties and remain genuinely uncomfortable with pluralism—even more uncomfortable than most dyed-in-the-wool theorists are. Deconstructionists would, however, probably be quite uncomfortable with the kind of expropriation of their position that I here suggest, for in accepting the validity of their questioning procedures I am not accepting their linguistic principles, and in deconstructionism, as in many powerful theories, there is often an all-or-nothing, buy-my-principles-or-leave-me-alone attitude that refuses to honor pluralism or tolerate any competing assumption or practice. And non-believers often buy the absolutes too. Very instructive is the review by David Marshall of Philip Stewart's *Half-Told Tales: Dilemmas of Meaning in Three French Novels* (Chapel Hill, N.C., 1987), in which Marshall agonizes over the fact that Stewart uses Paul de Man without adopting a full deconstructionist approach (*Eighteenth-Century Fiction*, 1 [1989], 335–38). Marshall is plainly uncomfortable with his own assumptions here, and backs away from the implications in a final paragraph but leaves the objection intact.

3. See Julian Jaynes, *The Origin of Consciousness in the Breakdown of the Bicameral Mind* (Boston, 1976). Jaynes's thesis, while unpersuasive in its specifics, raises deep, troubling questions about the nature of historical differences in consciousness and about how evidence of changes in human feeling can be evaluated.

4. For an excellent discussion of the shift in moral rhetoric once belief is gone, see Alasdair MacIntyre, *After Virtue* (Notre Dame, Ind., 1981), esp. pp. 210–26, although I think he overrates the influence of thinkers like Hume and undervalues the broader intellectual context illustrated in materials of popular print.

5. Foucault's historical observations, however astute they are one by one, suffer from the stony refusal to consider why epochal changes occur or even admit that they do; Foucault really does seem to believe in abyss theory. See, for example, *Discipline and Punish*, trans. Alan Sheridan (New York, 1979; originally published as *Surveiller et Punir*, Paris, 1975), and *Madness and Civilization*, trans. Richard Howard (New York, 1965; originally published as *Histoire de la Folie*, Paris, 1961). The extensive criticism of Foucault by Jurgen Habermas and historicisms of most disciplinary kinds finally comes down to distrust of a position that is, however eager to deal with historic particulars, uncomfortable with any notion of orderly historical change dictated by analyzable factors. See Allan Megill, "The Reception of Foucault by Historians," *Journal of the History of Ideas*, 48 (1987), 117–41.

6. See Paul de Man's important essay, "The Rhetoric of Temporality," in *Interpretation: Theory and Practice*, ed. Charles S. Singleton (Baltimore, 1969), pp. 173–209.

7. I have dealt extensively with these matters in " 'Peace' and the Augustans: Some Implications of Didactic Method and Literary Form," in *Studies in Change and Revolution*, ed. Paul J. Korshin, (London, 1972), pp. 161–89.

8. "There lurks in the Heart of Man," argues a treatise of 1745, "so strong a Principle of Revolt against all Advice or Instruction, that there is not, perhaps, a surer Way of giving his conduct a wrong Byass, than by attempting . . . to guide and set him right" (*Directions to Mankind in General*; the title page claims that the author is a "Dr. Fitzpatrick"). Such sentiments, while not often expressed so explicitly as here, underlie much of the ironic rhetoric of the period.

9. Many religious and moral treatises list, on their title pages, prices both for individual copies and by the hundred.

10. The original title was *The Practice of Christian Graces, or, The Whole Duty of Man Laid Down in a Plain and Familiar Way for the use of All, but especially the Meanest Reader.* Subsequent editions most always used *The Whole Duty of Man* as the principal title, and the phrase caught on so fully that many other didactic works used variations on it.

11. According to present (1989) Eighteenth-Century Short Title Catalogue (ESTC) listings, at least 109 versions were printed between 1701 and 1800. *The Whole Duty of Man* is traditionally ascribed to Richard Allestree. The question of edition numbers is a vexed one, for booksellers sometimes inflated the stock of a title by pretending it had appeared in more editions than it really had, and sometimes the number of previous editions was simply miscounted or unknown.

An edition advertised as the "15th" often turns out to be more like a 10th or 12th, but sometimes editions are under-counted too. Edition claims are thus seldom exactly right in number, but the claims themselves usually do indicate roughly how popular a title actually has been over the years. ESTC listings often show several different editions claiming the same number as well as suggesting that numerical gaps may exist.

12. *Moll Flanders*, for example, seems to have been reprinted more or less in its entirety about nine times by 1800, according to present ESTC records; there were also two severe abridgements and seven chapbook editions that amounted to brief plot summaries.

13. Dent had reached a 20th edition by 1629 and a 41st by 1831. Dent and Bayly were not, however, as frequently printed in the eighteenth century as they had been in the seventeenth, probably because new titles with more situational and updated advice were increasingly available. William Law's *A Serious Call to a Devout and Holy Life* (1728), for example, reached a 10th edition by 1771.

14. An exception is J. Hillis Miller, *Fiction and Repetition* (Cambridge, Mass., 1982). Folklorists, students of oral theory, and to some extent narratologists put a higher premium on the power of repetition than do most other literary theorists.

15. I have discussed this characteristic of didacticism rather differently in "Fielding and the Modern Reader."

16. Other, more general implications of prefatory strategies are discussed in Chapter Six, pp. 158–59.

17. *Shamela*, title page. Early editions of *The Whole Duty of Man* often claimed on the title page that it was "Necessary for all Families."

18. Modern reader response critics who claim that texts are not complete until read seldom are willing to support the implications of their observation—which would seem to require response rather than simply receiving.

19. On the implications of this strategy, see Janet Gurkin Altman, *Epistolarity: Approaches to a Form* (Columbus, Ohio, 1982); Robert Adams Day, *Told in Letters* (Ann Arbor, Mich., 1966); Homer Obed Brown, "The Errant Letter and the Whispering Gallery," *Genre* 10 (1977), 573–99; and Roy Roussel, "Reflections on the Letter: The Reconciliation of Distance and Presence in *Pamela*," *ELH*, 41 (1974), 375–99.

20. The best discussion of apologues is still that of Sheldon Sacks, *Fiction and the Shape of Belief* (Berkeley, 1964), though I think Sacks expresses the relationship between apologues and other forms of fiction somewhat too rigidly. In most cases there is no clear line between novels and apologues: many eighteenth-century novels have obvious affinities with apologues, and nineteenth-century novels only disguise their connection a little more subtly.

21. Terry Castle's brilliant cultural analysis in *Masquerade and Civilization* exemplifies both the problem and its often happy results. She seems always to assume that the answer to cultural questions lies beyond their own articulation and thus sometimes passes by conscious and perceptive analyses of what is going on in areas of cultural desire. But because she makes that assumption, she finds in unconscious needs some extraordinary "deep" structures of desire.

22. Morroe Berger's account of how the parallel rise of the novel and social science suggest the underlying structures of cultural change confirms, from a different perspective, the point I am making here. Berger may be too simplistic in his account of parallels, but his cultural analysis is fundamentally sound. See *Real and Imagined Worlds: The Novel and Social Science* (Cambridge, Mass., 1977).

CHAPTER   TEN

1. Except for studies of the older courtesy books (which emphasize aristocratic and genteel codes rather than the rules and rhetoric intended for broader audiences), there has been until quite recently little interest in these materials. Now, however, some studies of particulars have been completed and more extensive ones are under way. See, for example, Ellen Pollak, *The Poetics of Sexual Myth: Gender and Ideology in the Verse of Swift and Pope* (Chicago, 1985); Nancy Armstrong, *Desire and Domestic Fiction: A Political History of the Novel* (New York, 1987); Rita Goldberg, *Sex and Enlightenment: Women in Richardson and Diderot* (Cambridge, 1981); and

Sylvia Kasey Marks, *Sir Charles Grandison: The Compleat Conduct Book* (Lewisburg, Pa., 1986), which has a useful, if sketchy, bibliography. William Beatty Warner is at work on a comprehensive study that is likely to be very sophisticated in its implications for the novel.

2. What needs study is the ideology of sermons, a ripe topic for the New Historicism.

3. James Sutherland (*English Literature of the Late Seventeenth Century*, p. 305) speaks of the "keen contemporary interest" in sermons, but he exaggerates their popularity. There may be two reasons: (1) the number of published sermons was still, in the late seventeenth century, large compared to later times that seem more normative to us; (2) the keenness of interest was mostly evinced when a special occasion or topic of current interest was involved. Popularity waned not far into the reign of Charles II, and by the beginning of the eighteenth century sermons were a drug on the market unless offered by some celebrity.

4. In *The Post-Angel* (1701), John Dunton announces his desire to collect all the funeral sermons then being preached so that he can publish a full set of contemporary lives. Later I discuss spiritual biography (in Chapter Fourteen) as an outgrowth of diaries and spiritual autobiographies (Chapter Twelve).

5. *Joseph Andrews*, I, xvii, 79–80.

6. Until the fruits of the ESTC project are analyzed, such questions cannot be certainly answered, for much of the printing of sermons was decentralized and library holdings of sermons (never highly prized, even when rare book prices skyrocketed) are unevenly scattered.

7. A typical example is *The Accomplish'd Lady's Delight, in Preserving, Physick, Beautifying, Cookery, and Gardening* (10th ed. "Inlarged," 1719), 177 pages of details about practical daily matters. Such Guides were fairly uncommon until the early eighteenth century, although some were provided for aristocratic women (*The Ladies Cabinet Enlarged and Opened* [4th ed., 1667], for example), or for particular occupations (for example, *The Young Clerk's Companion or, a Manual For His Dayly Practice* [1664], a tiny volume—2 by 4 inches—but with 262 packed pages). In the eighteenth century there were more (*The Young Clerks Assistant; or Penmanship made easy, Instructive and Entertaining* (1733?), for example, or *The New Horse-Houghing Husbandry: or, an Essay on the Principles of Tillage and Vegetation* (by Jethro Tull, 1731), and by midcentury such Guides were quite common—because knowledge had become increasingly specialized, because urban isolation from the oral past continued to intensify, and because novels had begun to take over some of the more general functions of guidance. For examples of later practical Guides, see *The Gentleman's Companion, and Tradesman's Delight* (1735); *The London Tradesman. Being a Compendious View of All the Trades, Professions, Arts* (by R. Campbell, 1747); or *The Husbandman's Jewel, Directing How to Improve Land . . . Brew Ale and Beer . . . order Bees and Silkworms; Destroy Vermin* (c. 1750).

8. This was a much-enlarged version of *The Whole Duty of a Woman: Or a Guide to the Female Sex. From the Age of Sixteen to Sixty. Written by a Lady* (3rd ed., 1701), which, in its 184 pages, had similarly begun with ethical counsel, then turned to daily practical concerns. Later, *Whole Duty* was published under the title *The Lady's Companion*. Similar in pattern is Thomas Lye, *The Child's Delight* (1671), an instructional manual for reading, pronunciation, and grammar, but also saturated with religious and moral instruction. Another pattern is illustrated by William Mather's *Young Man's Companion* (8th ed., 1710), in which detailed directions are given for making wine and beer. "The Poor that has no Beer," Mather says, "may boil Water with Treacle, and work it with Yeast; or stir a little Treacle into every Cup of Water, you drink it, which is both pleasant and wholesome; and taken often upon an empty Stomach, cures Coughs and Shortness of Breath." But then Mather quickly adds, to moralize his song: "the Drinking of Strong-Drink to Excess, is the Nurse of Impiety; the Original of most Diseases, and Vices; the Seed Plot of Diseases; the Subversion of the *Senses;* the Canker of the Understanding; the Corruption of Manners; the Shame of Life; the Harbinger of Hell; the Grave of Honour; the Pest of the Body, a Rape upon the Soul; the Plague of Cities; the Ruin of Kingdoms, &c.," p. 188. Mather's book was, in its first edition, entitled *A very useful Manual, or the young Mans Companion* (1681). By 1761 it had reached a 21st edition.

9. Its full title is *The Husbandmans Calling: Shewing the Excellencies, Temptations, Graces, Duties, &c. of the Christian Husbandman* (1665). Steele says his Guide is "the Substance of xii. Sermons Preached to a Country Congregation" (title page).

10. See, for example, John Flavell, *A New Compass for Seamen . . . Directing them to Stear their true*

course to Heaven (1664, often reprinted as *Navigation Spiritualized*) and *The Sea-mans Companion* (six sermons adapted to Guide format, 1676); John Ryther, *A Plat for Mariners; or, The Seaman's Preacher* (1672) and *Token for Mariners and Sea-Dangers and Deliverances Improved* (1674), included in Mr. *James Janeways Legacy to his Friends* (1675, pp. 89–133); William Balmford, *The Seaman's Spiritual Companion: or, Navigation spirituallized. Being a New Compass for Seamen . . . Directing every Christian how to stear the Course of his life, through all Storms and Tempests* (1678); Philip Stubbs, *The Religious Seaman* (1696) and *God's Dominion over the Seas, and The Seaman's Duty,* consider'd (1701; 5th ed. in 1706); George Stanhope, *The Seaman's Obligation to Gratitude and a Good Life* (1699); Cotton Mather, *The Religious Marriner. A Brief Discourse Tending to Direct the Course of Sea-men* (1700); and Josiah Woodward, *The Seaman's Monitor: wherein particular Advice is given to Sea-faring Men* (1705).

11. Swift's *A Meditation upon a Broom-Stick* seems a lot closer in particulars to this meditation than to anything in Boyle.

12. Other examples of Guides for individual callings include *Religio Militis: or, The Moral Duty of a Soldier* (1690); *The Soldiers Manual, or Directions, Prayers and Ejaculations for such as lead a military life* (1694); John Flavell, *Husbandry Spiritualized: or, The Heavenly Use of Earthly Things* (1669); Edward Bury, *The Husbandmans Companion* (1677); Richard Mayo, *A Present for Servants, From their Ministers, Masters, or Other Friends, Especially in Country Parishes* (1693); *Instructions for Apprentices and Servants* (1699); John Collinges, *The Weavers Pocket-book: or, Weaving Spiritualized* (1675); James Talbott, *The Christian School-Master: or, the Duty of those who are Employ'd in the Publick Instruction of Children* (1707); and *The Public-Housekeeper's Monitor: Being a Serious Admonition to the Masters and Mistresses Of those commonly called Public Houses* ("new" ed., 1769; the ESTC records no first edition).

All the Guides emphasize "spiritualizing" the individual calling by learning to do meditations on the normal activities and sights involved in that calling. "There is," says Steele in *Tradesman's Calling*, "scarce any thing which you trade in, but a Religious Heart may learn something of God out of it. And this (surely) is one end of *Similes* and *Comparisons*, so frequent in the *Bible*, not only that God may come down by them to us, but that we may by them ascend to him; he hath translated the world into the *Scripture*, that we may think of the *Scripture* in the World. This is the safest and richest *Chymistry*, whereby you may extract the purest spirits out of the grossest Bodies" (pp. 204–05). In *Husbandmans Calling*, Steele says that "The matter herein is but ordinary Practical Divinity applied to the condition and calling of the Husbandman" (fol. [A7v]), but goes on to say that, "Though it accost onely the Husbandman, yet the matter thereof for the most part is applicable to every good Christian" (fol. [a8]). Adds Joseph Caryl in an essay introducing Flavell's *Husbandry Spiritualized*, " 'Tis a great part of our holiness to be spiritually minded . . . when we are conversing with the clods of the earth. . . ." (1669 ed., fol. ˙v).

13. Stubbs, in fact, made something of a minor career of guiding seamen; he earlier authored *The Religious Seaman, Fitted with Proper Devotions On all Occasions* (1696, a 98-page Guide) and later published another sermon, *The Sea-Assize; or, Sea-faring Persons to be judged according to their Works,* 1709.

In the fifth edition of *God's Dominion*, Stubbs added "Some Devotions proper for Seamen," giving his pamphlet more of the normal appearance of a Guide. Stubbs became the first chaplain of Greenwich Hospital, according to the Dictionary of National Biography because of his demonstrated interest in the welfare of seamen.

14. In his *Life and Errors*, Dunton tells an anecdote about a friend who recommended that he court Sarah Doolittle so that he would be allowed to print "her *Fathers Copies* for nothing, and his *Book* on the *Sacrament*, you know, has sold to the Twentieth *edition*, which would have bin an Estate for a *Bookseller*," p. 74.

15. For a lucid explanation of this popular cooperative process, see Stephen Parks, *John Dunton and the English Book Trade* (New York, 1976), pp. 205–210.

16. William Darrell, who was a Jesuit, was apparently never publicly identified as the author of a very popular text, *The Gentleman Instructed.*

17. I have not examined a copy of this title.

18. The full title is *War with the Devil: or the Young Mans Conflict with the Powers of Darkness . . . Discovering the Corruption and Vanity of Youth . . . Worthy the Perusal of all, but chiefly intended*

for the Instruction of the Younger sort. It had reached a 19th impression by 1728.

19. Whether Dunton's father in fact left a manuscript upon which this Guide was based is open to question, for the published volume is a typical Dunton production encompassing everything that seems to have been lying around on his mind or in his shop at the time. Appended, for example, are fifty numbered treatises on such subjects as "The Doleful End of Swaggering World-lings," "The Most Ingenious Art of Printing Spiritualiz'd," "Charms and Knots," and "The Careful Seaman's Guide," and then assorted paragraphs on witches, fairies, phantasms, goblins, and ghosts, but *The Pilgrims Guide* proper runs to 141 pages before the appendices begin and the generic identity fades. See Chapter Six for a discussion of the problems of attribution in the books Dunton publishes as his father's.

20. I have used the 3rd edition copy in the British Library. *The Practise of Pietie* in its early editions was more than 1,000 pages long, the 3rd edition containing 1,031 pages; by 1719, Bayly's book had reached a 53rd edition; Dent had reached a 25th by 1640.

21. Wing lists a 1624 edition; I used the 1625 copy in the British Library.

22. I used the 1664 edition in the British Library.

23. Nathanael Wyles, *All Men must die* (1699), p. 20.

24. Matthew Henry, *The Pleasantness of a Religious Life . . . Recommended to the Consideration of All: Particularly of Young People* (1714), p. 102.

25. Many Guides make clear by their titles who they conceive their audience to be:

The Young-Man's Monitor: Shewing The Great Happiness of Early Piety: and The Dreadful Consequence of Indulging Youthful Lusts (by Josiah Woodward, 1706; often reprinted, it had reached a 9th edition by 1720, a 19th by 1821);

Advice to the Young: or, the Reasonableness and Advantages of an Early Conversion to God (by Joseph Stennett the Elder, 1695);

The Young Man's Duty. A Discourse Shewing The Necessity of Seeking the Lord betimes . . . Designed especially for Young Persons before they are debauched by evil Company, and evil Habits (by Richard Kidder, 1671; it had reached a 6th edition by 1690);

The Poor Man's Help, and Young Man's Guide (by William Burkitt; 2nd ed., 1694 [apparently first published in 1693]; it reached a 10th edition in 1712, a 24th in 1741, and a 36th in 1787);

The Christian Scholar: in Rules and Directions for Children and Youth Sent to English Schools (by Samuel Brewster the Elder, 1700);

The Pleasantness of a Religious Life, Open'd and Prov'd; and Recommended to the Consideration of All; Particularly of Young People (by Matthew Henry, 1714);

The Young Mans Monitor. or A modest Offer toward the Pious, and Vertuous Composure of Life from Youth to Riper Years (by Samuel Crossman, 1664; usually entitled, in subsequent editions, *The Young Man's Calling: or the Whole Duty of Youth,* it had reached a 7th edition by 1713);

An Exhortation to Youth to prepare for Judgment (by John Shower, 1681; 5th ed., 1699);

Youths Behaviour (said to be translated from the French by Francis Hawkins at the age of ten, 4th ed., 1646);

The Second Part of Youths Behaviour, or Decency in Conversation Amongst Women: Containing Excellent Directions for the Education of young Ladies, Gentlewomen, and other Persons, and Rules of Advice how . . . to deport themselves, and . . . govern the Affairs of a Family (by Robert Codrington, 1664);

Of Education, Especially of Young Gentlemen (by Obadiah Walker, Oxford, 1673; 6th ed., 1699);

The Gentile Sinner, or, England's Brave Gentleman: Characterized In a Letter to a Friend (by Edward Synge[?], 1660);

A New-years-Gift Composed of Prayers and Meditations (2nd ed., 1681; 4th ed. by 1685);

The Illustrious History of Women, or, A Compendium of the many Virtues that Adorn the Fair Sex (by John Shirley, 1686);

Instructions for Children: or, the Child's and Youth's Delight (by Benjamin Keach, 9th ed., c. 1710; first published about 1664, it was reprinted many times under variant titles, reaching at least a 15th edition by 1723);

A Looking-Glass for Children. Being a Narrative of God's gracious Dealings with some Little Children (by H.P., 1673);

A New-Years Gift for Youth (by Samuel Peck, 1687);

The Christian Education of Children (a translation from the French of Alexandre Louis Varet, 1678);

Youths Mirour, or Lookinglass (1660?);

The Christian-Man's Calling: or, A Treatise of Making Religion ones Business (by George Swinnock, three parts, 1662, 1663, and 1665);

A Memento to Young and Old: or, The Young Man's Remembrancer, and The Old Man's Monitor (by John Maynard, 1669);

The Young Man's Instructer, And the Old Man's Remembrancer (by Thomas Doolittle, 1673).

The Young-Man's Guide in his Journey to Heaven, or Travelling Spiritualized (about 1718); I have not seen this title, which is advertised in *The Young Man's Monitor.*

Youth's Interest (by Robert Bragge, 1706);

The Devout Christian's Companion. or, a Compleat Manual of Devotions (1707); sometimes, in subsequent editions, entitled *The Devout Christian's Best Companion in the Closet;*

The Young Man's Remembrancer, and Youth's Best Choice (by Matthew Mead, 3rd ed., 1701);

The Child's Delight (by Thomas Lye, 1671);

The Instructor: or, Young Man's Best Companion (by George Fisher, 5th ed., 1740).

Published lists of "appropriate" books for the young were also quite common. See, for example, *The Young Christian's Library: or, a Collection Of Good and Useful Books Proper to be given to Young Persons* (1710); *Education of Children and Young Students in all its Branches, With a Short Catalogue of the Best Books* (2nd ed., 1752); and an 88-page postscript to the 1699 English translation of Fénelon, *The Education of Young Gentlewomen.*

26. The prevalence of "New Year's Gift" titles suggests the frequent practice of giving books, especially books of advice, when the beginning of a new year signaled the need to review the past and plan the future. The emphasis on beginning anew—and revising or blotting out the past—was a powerful one in didactic tracts; when Dunton entitles alternating sections of his autobiography "The Idea of a New Life" and tries to suggest how he would revise his life if he had it to live again, he is expressing the tacit assumption of spiritual autobiography, a species that takes its cue from the Guide subspecies of the didactic tradition.

27. Many Guides claim to have originated in some particular and practical set of circumstances. Crossman's *The Young Mans Monitor* (1664) claimed that it "was first sent as a more private Letter to the Children, and Servants of some Friends, for their encouragement and direction in the good waies of God. . . ." (fol. A3v).

28. Ellen Pollak's admirable attempt to rethink Pope and Swift on women mistakenly considers Halifax's treatise to be typical of its time. Its biases are, however (as one might expect), decidedly aristocratic; Halifax looks back to an older tradition of courtesy books, whereas the new Guides that became popular after the Restoration were aimed at a wide range of social classes and often at Anglicans and Dissenters at the same time. Their attitudes are far more "progressive" and less patronizing than those of the genial but rigid Halifax. Pollak mistakenly sees "Puritan" tracts as heralding a more conservative attitude toward women; Halifax is the throwback, Puritan guides the new direction.

29. I have corrected, in brackets, serious misprints in the first edition by comparing it with subsequent editions. The first edition is full of typographical errors—did the printer work from an unclear hand draft? did Halifax not take the publication seriously?—and even later "corrected" editions retain egregious errors. Halifax, for whatever reason, seems to have paid very little mind to how his advice was presented.

30. Darrell, a Jesuit, was not identified on the title page. The 1713 edition also adds a second part for gentlemen. Hickes wrote a prefatory recommendation for the 4th and 5th edition.

Here are some representative titles of Guides for selected audiences:

Instructions to a Son (by Archibald Campbell, Marquis of Argyll, 1661; of political as well as didactic significance);

Instructions for the Education of a Daughter (1707, a translation and adaptation by George Hickes of Fénelon's *Traité de l'education des filles* [1687]). An earlier English edition of Fénelon was published in 1699, *The Education of Young Gentlewomen Written Originally in the French . . . And improved For a Lady of Quality;* this edition is often overlooked, the Hickes adaptation of 1707 usually being said to be the first English translation. The 1699 volume is close enough to the Hickes version to suggest that it may have been an earlier draft by Hickes. Or possibly Hickes simply used it in preparing his later adaptation.

The Ladies Library ("Written by a Lady. Published by Mr. [i.e., Sir Richard] Steele," 3 vols., 1714);

The Gentleman's Library, containing Rules of Conduct in all Parts of Life, Written by a Gentleman (1715);

The Gentlemans Companion: or, A Character of True Nobility, and Gentility (by William Ramesey, 1672);

Advice to a Son. or Directions for your better Conduct, Through the various and most important encounters of this Life (by Francis Osborne, 5th ed., 1656);

A Rational Cathechism: or, An instructive Conference between a Father and a Son (1687);

A Gentleman's Religion: with the Grounds and Reasons of It (by Edward Synge, 1693);

A Directory for the Female Sex: being a Father's Advice to his Daughter (a broadside, in couplets, 1684);

The Excellent Daughter . . . With Proper Lessons of the Duty of Daughters (1708);

Advice to a Son, Directing him How to demean himself in the Most Important Passages of Life (4th ed., 1716); and

Advice to a Son in the University (1708).

31. Darrell, *A Gentleman Instructed* (1704), pp. 118–19.

32. The fact that the Guide for men appeared first (by more than a decade) typifies didactic practice in the Restoration, but new editions of the women's Guide were almost as frequent by the turn of the century.

33. I have discussed this matter more fully in " 'Peace' and the Augustans: Some Implications of Didactic Method and Literary Form," in *Studies in Change and Revolution*, ed. Paul J. Korshin (Menston, Yorkshire, 1972), pp. 161–89.

34. Shared religious reading, usually from the Bible or from approved didactic and devotional treatises, was a commonly recommended practice during family prayers, which traditionally took place both in the morning and evening. Reading aloud was prized not only for its communal implications but as an opportunity to allow children to practice the art of reading in front of their elders. I have found occasional references to the benefits that might accrue to illiterate family members or servants, but such mentions are surprisingly scarce from the Restoration on, suggesting that the literacy battle was by then regarded by Protestant moralists as largely won.

35. These Guides spill over into Anne's reign but begin to subside into other issues by 1710.

36. See, for example, Edward Cobden's sermon on "Family Religion," preached "before the King, at St. James's Dec. 11, 1743," included in *Discourses and Essays in Prose and Verse* (1757), pp. 357–69.

37. Catherine Gallagher has asked the hard question about conservatives and reform, noting that Tories often sponsor more genuinely daring independence of principles than their more liberal-sounding opponents. See "Political Crimes and Fictional Alibis: The Trials of Delariviere Manley," forthcoming in *Eighteenth-Century Studies*. See also a fine corrective study by Margaret J. M. Ezell, *The Patriarch's Wife: Literary Evidence and the History of the Family* (Chapel Hill, N.C., 1987), and Felicity A. Nussbaum, *The Brink of All We Hate: English Satires on Women, 1660–1750* (Lexington, Ky., 1984).

38. According to *The Ladies Library* (1714), "young Ladies should . . . read the Greek and Roman Histories in the best Translations. . . . Neither should they be ignorant of the History of Britain, which furnishes them with many Examples of brave Actions, hardly exceeded by any thing in Antiquity. Among their own Sex too, they will in both meet with illustrious Patterns of Virtue, which will make the Stronger Impressions on their Minds. The *Histories* of other Nations, Accounts of Voyages and Travels, the Lives of Heroes and Philosophers, will be both a pleasant and instructive Entertainment. The reading the best Authors on these Subjects, will enlarge and elevate their Souls, and give them a Contempt for the common Amusements of the Sex. Let them in their reading avoid Vanity and Affectation; but let them not have so mean an Opinion of themselves as to think they are incapable of improving by it; nor of Books, as to think they are incapable of improving them" (I, 20–21).

39. My point is not that educational conditions for women were good or that the culture was

sensitive to their needs, but that the sense that women were *more* neglected than in previous ages seems, on the evidence of behavioral treatises, wrong. Concern was rising, perhaps because changing economic conditions and changing legal status meant that women were more than previously under threat. Lawrence Stone's puzzling view of women's social regression has been surprisingly influential.

40. Nancy Armstrong's thesis in *Desire and Domestic Fiction* seems to me largely right, though I think she dates the effect much too late. Armstrong is very good on the ideology of conduct books.

41. On these crossings of role, see Nancy K. Miller, *The Heroine's Text: Readings in the French and English Novel 1722–1782* (New York, 1980); Ruth Perry, *Women, Letters and the Novel* (New York, 1980); Anne Robinson Taylor, *Male Novelists and Their Female Voices: Literary Masquerades* (Troy, N.Y., 1981); and a forthcoming study by Kristina M. Straub on role shifts as illustrated in the theater.

42. Jane Spencer's *The Rise of the Woman Novelist: From Aphra Behn to Jane Austen* (Oxford, 1986) is a good step in suggesting how this took place.

43. For another view, see Armstrong, *Desire and Domestic Fiction.*

CHAPTER   ELEVEN

1. There are heavy ironies in the way novelists tend to identify with the problems and perspectives of the young. Many of the early novelists were themselves middle-aged or older when they wrote their first novels. Defoe was fifty-nine when he wrote *Robinson Crusoe,* Richardson fifty-one when he wrote *Pamela,* Sterne forty-six when he wrote *Tristram Shandy.* Poets and dramatists are a different story.

2. Dunton alternates the narrative of his life with corresponding sections of "an Idea of a New Life; Wherein is Shewn How he'd Think, Speak, and Act, might he Live over his Days again" (title page). "The Burthen of my *New Idea,*" Dunton says, "is no less than the Business of the *Christian Life.* If there's any thing *peculiar* in it, perhaps it may meet with a Reader, here and there, whose Circumstances are *a Kin to mine,* and upon that Score 'twill be capable of doing him the better Service. The Life which I here UN-LIVE, has been an Amusement to me *Forty Years;* had I been so happy as to turn the Tables much sooner, my Satisfaction had been greater: And if any have been so unfortunate as to Copy after my REAL LIFE, I here take the Opportunity to tell 'em, that I solemnly disown the Original; however in the Room of it, I here substitute a *New Method of Living,* for 'em" (fol. A3v).

3. Sermon 51 in *The Works of the Most Reverend Dr. John Tillotson* (3rd ed., 1701), p. 611.

4. *The Christian Scholar* (3rd ed., 1704), pp. 41–42.

5. William Burkitt, *The Poor Man's Help and Young Man's Guide* (2nd ed., 1694), p. 16. This title was apparently first published in 1693 but Wing lists no first edition.

6. *A Christian Directory* (1673), p. 289.

7. P. 16. I quote from the 10th edition, corrected and enlarged, 1670; the book was originally published about 1644.

8. In James Kirkwood, *The True Interest of Families* (2nd ed., 1692), pp. 178–79.

9. Included in *The Improvement of the Mind: Second Part* (1782), II, 175. The "Discourse" was apparently written not long before Watts died in 1748.

10. The classic Max Weber formulation (in *Die protestantische Ethik und der Geist des Kapitalismus*) of the relationship between Protestantism and capitalism, though often challenged and amended, remains substantially intact.

11. For a provocative account of the potential dangers of reading novels, see Lennard J. Davis, *Resisting Novels: Ideology and Fiction* (New York, 1987).

12. "To the Reader," in *Remarks upon the Lives of several Excellent Young Persons of both Sexes,* appended to the "7th ed. corr." of Crossman's *Young Man's Calling; or the Whole Duty of Youth* (1713), a retitled and shortened version of *The Young Mans Monitor. Remarks,* possibly written by the bookseller Nathaniel Crouch, was appended to *Young Man's Calling* at least as early as

the unnumbered 1678 edition, but I have quoted from the later text because in 1678 the passsge has an entire line of text omitted.

13. Pp. 19v–20. (The volume early on is numbered only on right-hand pages.)

14. In *Discourses and Essays in Prose and Verse* (1757), p. 417. The sermon was originally preached "before the King."

15. Jonathan Lamb's analysis of the relationship between precept and example is suggestive about how the two conceptually interact even when there is illusion of choice—"Exemplarity and Excess in Fielding's Fiction," *Eighteenth-Century Fiction*, 1 (1989), 187–207.

16. *A Sermon Chiefly Address'd to Young People* (1737), p. 10.

17. *The Religious Education of Children* (1754), p. 19.

18. *The Providence of God in the Plagues of Mankind. A Sermon . . . Occasion'd by the Pestilential Distemper in France* (1721), p. 17.

19. *A Collection of the Lives of Ten Eminent Divines* (1662), fol. A2v.

20. Josiah Woodward, *Pastoral-Advice to a Young Person In order to his being Confirmed* (1702), p. 40.

21. I discuss the way diaries, spiritual autobiographies, and spiritual biographies contribute to this process in Chapters Twelve through Fourteen.

22. On the importance to narrative of case study in other disciplines, see Kathryn Montgomery Hunter, *The Patient as Text: The Narrative Structure of Medical Knowledge* (Princeton, N.J., forthcoming), and Lawrence Rothfield's forthcoming *Vital Signs*.

23. On early Protestant forms of casuistry, see E. Rose, *Cases of Conscience: Alternatives Open to Recusants and Puritans Under Elizabeth and James I* (Cambridge, 1975), and Camille Wells Slights, *The Casuistical Tradition in Shakespeare, Donne, Herbert, and Milton* (Princeton, N.J., 1981).

24. George Starr, *Defoe and Casuistry* (Princeton, N.J., 1971) richly details the implications of the tradition of Defoe and suggests the individualing tendency which casuistry provides for fiction. What I have tried to do here is historicize Starr's argument relative to the didactic tradition of the late seventeenth century and offer a new account of the significance of the "Morning Exercise" sermons. See also Starr's important essay, "From Casuistry to Fiction: The Importance of the Athenian Mercury," *Journal of the History of Ideas*, 27 (1967), 17–32.

25. See Albert Jonsen and Stephen Toulmin, *The Abuse of Casuistry* (Berkeley, 1988), p. 162.

26. There is no adequate modern scholarly account of these materials, but a small book intended as a devotional guide (Edward Leroy Long, Jr., *Conscience and Compromise: An Approach to Protestant Casuistry* (Philadelphia, 1954), offers a sensible account of the process and its aims.

27. *The Morning-Exercise Methodized; Or certain chief Heads and Points of the Christian Religion Opened and Improved in divers Sermons, by several Ministers of the City of London. In the Monthly Course of the Morning Exercise at Giles in the Fields.* The volume is dated 1660, but one British Library copy has the date November 9, 1659, penned in above the printed date. In 1655, Case had published a briefer forerunner, *The Morning Exercise, or Some Short Notes taken out of the Morning-Sermons.*

28. Annesley's 1661 volume was entitled *The Morning-Exercise at Cripplegate: or, Several Cases of Conscience Practically Resolved, by sundry Ministers.* For a lucid account of what happened under the Act, see N. H. Keeble, *The Literary Culture of Nonconformity in Later Seventeenth-Century England* (Athens, Ga., 1987), pp. 25–33.

29. Annesley's later volumes were published in 1674, 1683, and 1690, the last published by Dunton. Other casuistical collections also appeared, but the most important casuistical work intellectually was written by Richard Baxter, who included some substantial discussion of the process and its implications in *A Christian Directory*, which he subtitled "A Summ of Practical Theologie, and Cases of Conscience." Baxter has an amazingly modern sense of individuality. "I must speak to many *Cases*," he writes early on, "because I speak to *Families* where all are not in the same condition, and the same persons are not still the same" (p. 2). For an amusing response to the new form of casuistry, see Sir Roger L'Estrange, *The Casuist Uncas'd, in a Dialogue Betwixt Richard and Baxter, With a Moderator Between Them, For Quietnesse Sake* (2nd ed., 1680).

30. See Gilbert D. McEwen, *The Oracle of the Coffee House* (San Marino, Calif., 1972); Stephen Parks, *John Dunton and the English Book Trade* (New York, 1976); and especially Starr, *Defoe and Casuistry*.

31. See the discussion in Chapters Eight and Fourteen.
32. Swinnock, *Christian-Mans Calling II*, p. 25.
33. *Of Education, With respect to Grammar Schools and the Universities*, p. 30.
34. "A Discourse on the Education of Children and Youth" in *Works* (1753), V, 324.
35. The whole issue of literary careers is a vexed one in the early eighteenth century. It was especially so for women writers who seldom had patrons and who seldom felt free to write commercially under their own name. But in an age of rising commercial expectations, it was also vexed for men who chose to rely on public taste rather than patronage. Sterne and Richardson were special cases—Sterne an exhibitionist and aspiring celebrity more than a novelist or man of letters, Richardson a man of type, of business, and of a certain kind of conversation. Neither tried to mold a "career" in the usual sense, as did, for example, in different ways Defoe and Pope, Smollett and Johnson.

    The early women novelists were all special cases. Their collective case was different because of severely different social expectations. They pursued livings and lives more than careers because the latter were not really open to them. Lady Mary Pierrepont had the status, as well as the constitution and talent, to become a woman of letters, but there was no such category and few who could have followed her if they had chosen to do so. Women who wrote prose fiction were, like playwrights, a different breed, from different circumstances, Elizabeth Singer Rowe being the only exception. Aphra Behn aspired to a literary career but of that budding sort that— because it differed from the old amateur programs associated with patronage—is usually called "professional." Whether, had circumstances differed, she might have chosen a route more like Lady Mary is difficult to say. Class, gender, and economic status conspired to dictate the shape of her "career" as it did those of the next generation who saw in the life of a "professional" writer a way to make a bare living and achieve some small attention from contemporaries. Behn remained, like Defoe, most proud of being a poet, but the living she eked out came from writing plays that mostly conformed to male formulas and fiction that usually (but not always) looked backward toward the ideals and manners of high-life romance rather than toward present-centered stories of the ordinary and everyday.

    Delariviere Manley, whose narratives a generation later were more plainly novelistic even though often factual and satirical, had a life even more obviously controlled by circumstance— in Jane Spencer's words, "driven by political setbacks and by the scandal that surrounded her personal life" (p. 62)—and like her male contemporaries (Gildon, Ward, Defoe), she made a living by transcribing and transforming the materials of everyday life (see Fidelis Morgan, *A Woman of No Character: An Autobiography of Mrs. Manley* [London, 1987]). Like Behn (and Catherine Trotter, and most male "professional" writers), Manley began as a dramatist, and her thematic interests—in love, political intrigue, and sexual politics—helped define both the parameters of women's writing (as Spencer has argued) and the territory of the novel. Eliza Haywood, also a dramatist as well as a writer of fiction, seems actually to have begun with prose fiction, then turned to drama (inverting the usual pattern), but her career too was determined by necessity. An "abandoned woman" without resources, she carved out, between acting and writing, a real career that became a type from which, or against which, other women novelists could measure themselves. Others whose fiction is roughly contemporaneous to Haywood's— Davys, Barker, Hearne, Aubin—were usually motivated by necessity, too, but already in this generation one can see some conscious choice about how to present oneself morally, artistically, and sexually, and what kind of appeal to make.

    "Career" is too fancy a term to describe what most writers of fiction carved out for themselves, and money was an important motivator for female and male writers—but by the mid-twenties some pattern that could almost be called a logic had developed among those writers whose primary outlet was fictional narrative. What we call the "careers" of the better-known male novelists of a generation later is not much more conscious or patterned, and even the "careers" of "men of letters" are not much more rationally or programatically put together. But that is another—and larger—story that urgently needs to be told.
36. Still, the lot of a professional woman writer of fiction was, even at the beginning of the century, as good as any professional lot for women. Being a woman writer, if one was in the tradition of Aubin or Barker rather than that of Behn or Manley, was not much worse than being any single

woman without independent resources. By the time of Burney, women novelists often had rather respectable livings as well as reputations.

37. On the ordering tendency in the eighteenth century, see Martin Battestin, *The Providence of Wit* (Oxford, 1974). But there were counter tendencies as well; see *The New Eighteenth Century: Theory, Politics, English Literature*, ed. Felicity Nussbaum and Laura Brown (New York, 1987), and *Rhetorics of Order / Ordering Rhetorics in English Neoclassical Literature*, ed. J. Douglas Canfield and J. Paul Hunter (Newark, Del., 1989).

38. On contemporary debates about the nature of the self, see Christopher Fox, *Locke and the Scriblerians: Identity and Consciousness in Early Eighteenth-Century Britain* (Berkeley, 1988), and John O. Lyons, *The Invention of the Self* (Carbondale, Ill., 1978).

39. In *A Serious Call to a Devout and Holy Life* and *The Plaine Mans Path-way to Heauen*.

40. Even novels, even the most ritualistic and well-made ones, show a tendency to go for sequels and repent or withdraw the closure (*Robinson Crusoe, Pamela, David Simple*). The frequency of self-allusion (both Fieldings, Sterne) and the tendency to move a character from one novel into another one (Pamela into *Shamela* and *Joseph Andrews*; Yorick from *Tristram Shandy* into *A Sentimental Journey*) betray the desire not to end.

CHAPTER   TWELVE

1. I have described more fully the shape of diaries and autobiographies in *The Reluctant Pilgrim* (Baltimore, 1966), and the process by which private writings become public in "The Insistent 'I,' " *Novel*, 13 (1979), 19–37. See also G. A. Starr, *Defoe and Spiritual Autobiography* (Princeton, N.J., 1965); Paul Delany, *British Autobiography in the Seventeenth Century* (London, 1969); Daniel B. Shea, Jr., *Spiritual Autobiography in Early America* (Princeton, N.J., 1968); Patricia Meyer Spacks, *Imagining a Self* (Cambridge, Mass., 1976); and Steven E. Kagle, *American Diary Literature 1620–1799* (Boston, 1979). On the implications for the history of fiction of the autobiographical directions of narrative, see H. Porter Abbott, *Diary Fiction* (Ithaca, N.Y., 1984), and especially Erich Kahler, *The Inward Turn of Narrative* (Princeton, N.J., 1973). For an excellent study of women's autobiographies, see Felicity Nussbaum, *The Autobiographical Subject: Gender and Ideology in Eighteenth-Century England* (Baltimore, 1989).

2. On the impact of Puritanism within the Church, see Patrick Collinson, *Godly People: Essays on English Protestantism and Puritanism* (London, 1983).

3. *The Christian's Daily Devotion; with Directions how To Walk with God all the Day Long* (London, 1708; first published, 1704), p. 18.

4. *Spiritual Counsel: or The Father's Advice to his children* (1694), pp. 10–11.

5. See, for example, Donald Greene's provocative essay, "Augustinianism and Empiricism: A Note on Eighteenth-Century English Intellectual History," *Eighteenth-Century Studies*, 1, (1967), 33–68.

6. "Puritanism, Capitalism and the Scientific Revolution," in Charles Webster, ed., *The Intellectual Revolution of the Seventeenth Century*, p. 244.

7. Ralph Cohen puts the emphasis somewhat differently in his brilliant analysis of the rationale and properties of literary forms in "The Augustan Mode in English Poetry," *Eighteenth-Century Studies*, 1 (1967), 3–32.

8. Sterne criticism has been reluctant to grapple with the fact that Tristram was born eight months— rather than the nine he asserts—after the infamous night on which Elizabeth Shandy interrupts Walter with her unseasonable question about the clock. A *Notes and Queries* reader of 1895 pointed out the "error" but editors have regularly, until very recently, passed over the discrepancy in silence, and critics have been equally hesitant to interpret the serious misdirection with which Sterne chooses to begin Tristram's story. I have discussed the implications of Sterne's circumstantiality and truth claims in "Clocks, Calendars, and Names: The Troubles of Tristram and the Aesthetics of Uncertainty," in *Rhetorics of Order / Ordering Rhetorics*, pp. 173–98.

9. George Sewell, *A True Account of the Life and Writings of Thomas Burnett* (2nd ed., 1715), p. 7.

10. Sterne's strategy is to admit freely that his reader wants *everything*, making clear the expectation that all will be provided. He often pretends that it is against his nature (or better judgment) to

provide details, but he does it anyway. It is, he says (I, iv, 5), "from a backwardness in my nature to disappoint any one soul living, that I have been so very particular already." Later (VII, v, 584), he claims, as an excuse for providing excessive detail, that "it would be injustice to the reader, not to give him a minute account of that romantic transaction."

11. See Kristina Straub, *Divided Fictions: Fanny Burney and Feminine Strategy* (Lexington, Ky., 1987); Margaret Anne Doody, *Frances Burney: The Life in the Works* (New Brunswick, N.J., 1988), and Spacks, *Imagining a Self*, pp. 158–192.

12. Preface to January issue, *The Post-Angel*, 1701, fols. B2–B2v.

13. *The Informer's Doom*, 1683, fol. A2v.

14. The funeral sermon for Elizabeth Dunton, preached by Timothy Rogers (*The Character of a Good Woman*, 1697), also draws heavily on the diary. Rogers says that she had "kept a *Diary for near Twenty Years*, and made a great many *Reflections*, both on the *State of her own Soul*, and on other *Things* [and] judged by the Bulk, would have made a very considerable *Folio*. But she was so far from *Vain-Glory*, or *Affectation* of being talkt of after *Death*, that she desired that all those *large Papers* might be burnt *though* even much of what she writ was in a *Short-hand* of her own Invention" (fol. e5).

15. In the "Dedication" to *Athenianism* (1710), Dunton insisted that "in all this great Variety of Books I never printed another Man's Copy without his Leave, or ONCE stole his *Thought* or *Project* . . . ," p. x.

16. Besides the materials procured from his readers for such periodicals as *The Athenian Mercury* and *The Post-Angel*, Dunton sometimes used private letters and documents. See, for example, *The Dublin Scuffle* (1699) and *The Art of Living Incognito* (1700), and (for examples of anthologizing carried to extreme proportions) *The Young-Students-Library* (1692) and *The Compleat Library: or News for the Ingenious* (1692).

17. *Watch and Remember*, by Thomas Reynolds (1722). Reynolds apparently follows a diary that had been written in a private shorthand. A few months later (still in 1722) a much-enlarged version appeared, entitled simply *A Funeral Sermon For . . . Mr. Samuel Pomfret*, 112 pages in all, more than half of it a life.

18. *Pilgrim's Progress*, published twelve years later, reached a "14th" edition by 1695.

19. J. G. Bevan, *Memoirs of the Life of Isaac Penington* (1807). Sutherland refers to another title, *A Brief Account of my Soul's Travels towards the Holy Land*, which I have not been able to trace.

20. See my discussion in Chapter Fourteen (pp. 00–00) of what "memoirs" meant at this time.

21. Fol. a2. A 2nd edition appeared the same year.

22. In 1713, just after Trosse's death, another memorial had appeared in the form of a ten-page poem, *An Essay to the Pious Memory Of that Late Reverend Divine, Mr. George Trosse*, by J. Mortimer.

23. I used the 2nd edition, Edinburgh, 1715; I have not been able to determine when the first edition appeared. A London edition appeared in 1718, "With a Large Recommendatory Epistle by I. Watts."

24. In the Dublin edition.

25. There are a few scattered examples, most of them short; they appear not to have achieved much recognition except among local readers who knew the deceased.

James Sutherland, whose compact account of late seventeenth-century autobiography is better than most monographs on the subject, is a little misleading about the authorship and availability of autobiographies. He says that the "literature of inward experience is comparatively uncommon in men and women of the Anglican communities" but "springs without inhibition from the various sectarians"—*English Literature of the Late Seventeenth Century*, p. 259. Few Anglican autobiographies were indeed published, but even the sects seldom published autobiographies until after the turn of the century.

26. Matthew Henry, "To the Reader," fol. A2v. The title page calls Beard's manuscript "a Review of his Own LIFE." A 3rd edition, with additions, was published in 1715.

27. Like many other published autobiographies, Turner's seems to have polemical motives as well as inspirational ones. Turner gives credit to "some who were then called Puritans" (p. 12) for opening her eyes to the limits of her traditional religious upbringing.

28. For example, Nehemiah Lyde at the age of eighty, in 1731, published a life of his father for the

benefit of his descendants (*A Narrative of the Life of Mr. Richard Lyde*). "[A]s others have left their last Legacies in Writing to their Children," he writes, ". . . so I of [sic] mine" (fol. A3).

CHAPTER   THIRTEEN

1. Elsewhere I have discussed the *Apology* as a crucial document in the displacement of literary energy from drama to novel and from communal audiences to solitary and private ones. See "The World as Stage and Closet," in *British Theatre and Other Arts, 1660–1800*, ed. Shirley Strum Kenny (Washington, D.C., 1984), pp. 271–87.

2. On the traditional reliability of narrators in oral tales, see Robert Scholes and Robert Kellogg, *The Nature of Narrative* (New York, 1966), pp. 51ff.

3. See Ian Watt, *The Rise of the Novel* (London, 1957), p. 268. The answerers are much too numerous to mention. Howard Weinbrot conveniently summarizes many of them in "Chastity and Interpolation: Two Aspects of *Joseph Andrews*," *Journal of English and Germanic Philology*, 69 (1970), 26n. See also Jeffrey Plank, "The Narrative Form of *Joseph Andrews*," *Papers on Language and Literature*, 24 (1988), 142–58.

4. I have discussed some of the varieties in *Occasional Form* (Baltimore, 1975), pp. 151–61.

5. *Imagining a Self*, (Cambridge, Mass., 1976), pp. 4, 301.

6. One variation, though it proves the point, uses an epithet for the titular protagonist—*The Female Quixote, The Unlucky Citizen, The Man of Feeling, The Fortunate Mistress*. Haywood's titles are interesting as an index to experimentation with focus and audience expectation. Her first novelistic success had a thematic title (*Love in Excess*, 1719), and although some of her early fictions used names or epithets (*Idalia*, 1723; *The British Recluse*, 1722; *Cleomelia; or The Generous Mistress*, 1727), the titles then are as likely to indicate setting or situation as to define a protagonist. There are *Memoirs of a Certain Island* (1725) and *The Fatal Secret* (1724) as well as *Philadore and Placentia* (1727). But later in her career she regularly used the names that had by then become standard title-page indicators of a fictional life or "history": *The Fortunate Foundlings* (1744), *The History of Miss Betsy Thoughtless* (1751), *The History of Jemmy and Jenny Jessamy* (1753). Even *Life's Progress through the Passions: or, the Adventures of Natura* (1748) represents only a slight variation, indicating as it does the illustration of process in an individual life.

7. See Frederick M. Keener, *The Chain of Becoming* (New York, 1983).

8. *Caleb Williams* was first issued as *Things As They Are; or, The Adventures of Caleb Williams* (1794). Gary Kelly has commented extensively on the significance of the original title and Godwin's decision, in 1831, to change it to *Caleb Williams—The English Jacobin Novel 1780– 1805* (Oxford, 1976), pp. 179–208. Godwin seems to be answering Robert Bage's *Man As He Is* (1782), and Bage, in turn, is rejoining in the title of his last novel, *Hermsprong: or, Man As He Is Not* (1796).

9. I have dealt with the issue of titles and shapes more fully in "Biography and the Novel," *Modern Language Studies*, 9 (1979), 68–84. For an excellent account of novelistic shifts at the end of the century based on a different kind of question, see Patricia Meyer Spacks, *Desire and Truth* (Chicago, 1990).

10. The question of why Pope and Fielding attack Cibber so vigorously is an interesting one, and the full answer must involve something beyond political differences and personal animus. Cibber's version of the self plainly threatens Pope's belief that subjectivity should be repressed (although Pope found himself wrestling this issue quite openly, if uncomfortably, in the autobiographical poetry of his later years), and Fielding also seems disturbed by Cibber's exhibitionistic posturing as well as his power-displaying representations of himself. A good study of this issue could, I think, suggest the several dimensions of ideology—and the several directions— that were up for grabs as midcentury approached.

11. *Dunton's Whipping-Post: or, a Satyr upon Every Body* (1706), pp. 1–2.

12. *Dunton's Whipping-Post*, p. 1. There were evidently a substantial number of unsold copies of the first edition, and there was not a second until John Bowyer Nichols issued an abbreviated and bowdlerized one more than a hundred years later.

13. Paging is wildly off in the pages just before the beginning of "Idea of a New Life"; there are two sets of pages labeled 353–68.

14. The last page is actually numbered 544, but pagination is badly mishandled throughout; large blocks of numbers are omitted near the end.

15. See, for example, the fifth letter, *"Being a Defence of Speedy Marrying after* the Death of a Good Wife," in *The Art of Living Incognito,* 1700, pp. 60–63. "[M]y Marrying again *(five Months after wy* [sic] *Wife dyed),* " he explains there, "was no slight to her Memory: SLIGHT! no . . . 'twas to fulfill her DYING REQUEST; 'twas the desire of my *Dear her self,* that after her Death I'd speedily Marry again (such regard had she to my future happiness) and I cou'd not deny such a Wife any thing, especially her *last Request on her Death-Bed . . ,"* p. 62.

16. Dunton promises these titles in his "Dedication" to *Athenianism.*

17. See, for example, *The Neck Adventure; or the Case and Sufferings of Mr. John Dunton* (appended to *King George for Ever,* 1715); *The Manifesto of K. John the Second* (1715); *Royal Gratitude; (Or King George's Promise never to forget his Obligation . . .)* (1716); *Dunton's Recantation* (1716); *Mordecai's Memorial* (1716); and the aforementioned *Mordecai's dying groans* (1717), and *Mr. John Dunton's Dying Groans* (1725).

18. Only numbers 1 and 2 survive, and there may have been no more.

19. *The Life, Travels, and Adventures, of Christopher Wagstaff, Gentleman, Grandfather to Tristram Shandy . . . The whole being intended as a full and final answer to every thing that has been, or shall be, written in the out-of-the-way way.*

20. I have discussed Dunton and the public / private issue more fully as a basis for seeing the relationship between autobiography and the novel in "The Insistent 'I,' " *Novel,* 13 (1979).

C H A P T E R   F O U R T E E N

1. Pope's views, largely derived from Bossu, on the epic as a reflection of a particular culture and time represent standard assumptions of the time. See his "A General View of the Epic Poem," included in Vol. IX of the Twickenham Edition of Pope, ed. Maynard Mack (London, 1967), pp. 3–24.

2. The classic study of the relationship between the epic and the novel—E. M. W. Tillyard's *The Epic Strain in the English Novel* (London, 1958)—is flawed by its too general definition of epic, uncertain knowledge of historical contexts, and broad range, going from Defoe to Joyce in less than two hundred pages. Thomas E. Maresca's *Epic to Novel* (Columbus, Ohio, 1974) is more theoretically sophisticated and benefits from a strong historical sense, but often gets lost in byways so that the central issues are not fully and clearly delineated. Fielding's pretentious (but ambiguous) claims have been the lightning rod for most passing discussions; they are not the best point of departure for a serious consideration of complex generic issues. We still need a good study of seventeenth- and eighteenth-century notions of epic relative to the generic ferment that led to the novel.

3. The best account of Clarendon's context and aims is Martine Watson Brownley, *Clarendon and the Rhetoric of Historical Form* (Philadelphia, 1985). On earlier directions of historiography, see F. S. Fussner, *The Historical Revolution: English Historical Writing and Thought, 1580–1640* (London, 1962), who describes a "revolution" wrought by antiquarianism; F. J. Levy, *Tudor Historical Thought* (San Marino, Calif., 1967); Joseph M. Levine, "Ancients, Moderns, and History: The Continuity of English Historical Writing in the Later Seventeenth Century," in Paul J. Korshin, ed., *Studies in Change and Revolution* (Menston, Yorkshire, 1972), pp. 43–75; and Achsah Guibbory, *The Map of Time* (Urbana, Ill., 1986).

Historiographers differ about the date of the significant change in ideas of history, though there is general agreement that it occurred between the middle of the seventeenth century and the middle of the eighteenth. Scholes and Kellogg, reflecting historiography of the 1960s, assume an early date: "Historiography in the West may be said to have remained static at Thycydides' level until Hobbes's famous translation of the *Peloponnesian War* in the seventeenth century, at which point the new empiricism was able to begin providing the kind of scientific concepts and data which were necessary to continue the separation of fiction from history in historical narrative," *The Nature of Narrative* (New York, 1966), p. 61. The case for a considerably later date, usually built on David Hume, would make the essential historiographical change parallel with the emergence of the novel. The shift in focus of a work like *Bishop Burnet's History of His Own Time* (1724–34)—subjective, contemporary in focus, party-ridden, obsessed with individual responsibility, secular in outlook, modern in its biases—seems to me more definitive than what might be regarded as earlier and "deeper" structural changes.

4. Hayden White, who dates this process a little later, provides a brilliant analysis of its working power in *Metahistory: The Historical Imagination in Nineteenth-Century Europe* (Baltimore, 1973).

5. For *Evelina*, I quote the title of the 3rd edition. The term "history" in a title does not, of course, always indicate a novel, for the term was used widely and carelessly for whatever purposes booksellers chose; its claim was to some kind of truth, and that claim could be useful for all sorts of narratives. But the increasing use of the label for fictions of contemporary life begins to suggest conscious efforts at both labeling and definition, a desire to distinguish them from other kinds of available texts. Richardson's "Advertisement" to Volume I of the 2nd edition of *Clarissa*, for example, asserts that it is "not to be considered as a *mere Amusement*, as a *light Novel*, or *transitory Romance*; but as a *History* of LIFE and MANNERS . . .* intended to inculcate the HIGHEST and *most IMPORTANT Doctrines*" (quoted by Benjamin Boyce in his "Introduction" to *Prefaces to Fiction* [Los Angeles, 1952, Augustan Reprint Society Publication No. 32], p. viii). The definition implied here, it is important to notice, involves didacticism (both moral and practical) as well as representation of the cultural moment.

Labeling is not, of course, the only indicator of what kind of consensus there was about definition. McKeon seems to me right that a considerable agreement was developing about the nature of the new species, especially by the end of the 1740s when *Clarissa* and *Tom Jones* had rather fully charted the extremes of internal and external direction. For a vigorous criticism of this view of definition, see Homer O. Brown's review of McKeon in *ELH*, 55 (1988), 917–54.

6. See his *Narrative Form in History and Fiction: Hume[,] Fielding and Gibbon* (Princeton, N.J., 1970).

7. See C. H. Firth for an account of how the separate manuscripts merged, then again were indi- viduated, "Clarendon's 'History of the Rebellion,' " *English Historical Review*, 19 (1904), 26–54, 246–62, and 464–83.

8. The relationship between poetry and party politics at the turn of the century (the context for Pope's ideas and practice) has been insufficiently discussed. For a suggestive account, see Pat Rogers, *The Augustan Vision* (London, 1974), and a fine Emory University dissertation by Arthur Shelden Williams, *Politics and the Social Battleground of English Augustan Verse, 1688–1744* (1979).

9. In the *Dictionary*, Samuel Johnson defines memoir as (1) An account of transactions familiarly written; (2) Hint; notice; account of any thing.

10. The term was used so generally that few bother to define it. Johnson's very general definition is typical; it had not yet become a technical term of any use. In his "Alphabetical Table, explain- ing the Words and Terms of all Sciences, Arts, and Learning, most frequently used," for example, Francis Hawkins does not include the term "Memoirs" (*Youth's Behavior* (1672), fols. G2v–[I2]).

11. This is one reason there has been so much argument about the role of providence in novels. The classic statements emphasizing providentiality are by Aubrey L. Williams, "Interpositions of Providence and the Designs of Fielding's Novels," *South Atlantic Quarterly*, 70 (1971), 265– 86, and Martin Battestin, *The Providence of Wit* (Oxford, 1974), especially pp. 141–63; the classic arguments against by Melvyn New, " 'The Grease of God': The Form of Eighteenth- Century English Fiction," *PMLA*, 91 (1976), 235–44, and Claude Rawson, "Order and Misrule: Eighteenth-Century Literature in the 1970's," *ELH*, 42 (1975), 471–505. See also Leopold Damrosch, Jr., *God's Plot and Man's Stories* (Chicago, 1985).

12. The argument that lives are the most effective kind of didactic tool is repeated again and again. Typical is the comment of William Hamilton: "*Lives* are usually Read with greater Pleasure and Application, than any other kind of *Writing*; and it must be own'd, that when rightly chosen, they give us the most useful views of *Humane Nature*. . . . [T]he World is chiefly fond of know- ing their *Story*, who have Acted the most Embroyl'd and Busie Parts of *Life*"—*The Life and Character of James Bonnell* (1703), p. i. Often the implicit enemy in the defense of lives is fiction, but lives are preferred consistently to other kinds of factual writing as well.

In the 1701 *Post-Angel*, Dunton announces that he will include a biography section each month, "that I may gratifie the curious Palate of the Nicer Reader, who is for New Lives, (as well as for *new Expresses* [sic], *new Fashions*, and *new Projects*)," fol. B2v.

13. *Biography in the Hands of Walton, Johnson, and Boswell* (Los Angeles, 1966), p. 19. Butt makes almost the same statement later in a volume edited and completed by Geoffrey Carnall, *The Mid-Eighteenth Century* (Vol. 8 in the Oxford History of English Literature, Oxford, 1979), p. 43.

14. *English Literature in the Early Eighteenth Century 1700–1740* (Vol. 7 in the Oxford History of English Literature, Oxford, 1959), pp. 340–43. "Biography in this period is almost non-existent," he says (p. 340).

15. For treatments of Boswell's *Life of Johnson* in novelistic terms, see David L. Passler, *Time, Form, and Style in Boswell's Life of Johnson* (New Haven, Conn., 1971), and William R. Siebenschuh, *Fictional Techniques and Factual Works* (Athens, Ga., 1983), pp. 53–104.

16. For a good argument that the "outward form of the novel is essentially biographical," see George Lukacs, *The Theory of the Novel*, trans. Anna Bostock (Cambridge, Mass., 1971; first published, 1920), p. 77. I have discussed the relationship of biography and the novel in more detail in "Biography and the Novel," *Modern Language Studies*, 9 (1979), 68–84.

17. Hamilton says that "another kind of LIVES" (that is, the kind he writes) of the pious "who have been Great in Religion and Goodness" would prove "an Antidote to the Poyson of those other Histories" (p. 3).

18. Actually somewhat later in the volume than the page number would suggest, for the pages are badly misnumbered.

19. *The Life of the Reverend and Learned Mr. John Sage*, p. 1. Typical is the 252-page volume *An Account of the Life and Death of Mrs. Elizabeth Bury . . . Chiefly Collected out of her Own Diary. Together with Her Funeral Sermon . . . and Her Elegy by the Reverend Mr. J. Watts* (1720; 2nd and 3rd editions were published a year later). Her husband, Samuel, composed the life; he says he had to leave out nine parts in ten of the diary to keep the volume manageable. "Her LIFE, I am well assured," he writes, "has been of great Service to many, and would hope these few Memorials of it may be useful to more. And that such as have not been duly influenced by the Precepts of Religion, may be somewhat induced by such an *Exemplar* to the Practice of it" (fol. A3).

20. *The Journal of a Voyage to Lisbon*, ed. Harold E. Pagliaro (New York, 1963), p. 36.

21. See, for example, Arthur Wellesley Secord, *Studies in the Narrative Method of Defoe* (Vol. 9 in the University of Illinois Studies in Language and Literature, Urbana, Ill., 1924).

22. See Percy G. Adams, *Travel Literature and the Evolution of the Novel* (Lexington, Ky., 1983).

23. It is of course true that novels, especially early on, often resist closure in a similar way. The tendency to offer sequels—another voyage or another adventure—may be something that novels take from travel books by analogy, but the tendency first to welcome closure and then to resist it—to make a logical ending and then pull back if one can sense another idea or more sales coming on—seems to be characteristic of all print narratives, and its roots may not be formal.

Index

■

Eclectic heritages of the novel
Spiritual auto B
travel lit
didactic tracts
Journalism
printing of novels

auto B
Bunyan's Grace Abounding
Cibbers Apology (1740) — secularized self examination

Boswell   } infl. by
Rousseau } lit.